W9-APQ-918

Municipal Management Series

The Practice of Local Government Planning

International City Management Association

The International City Management Association is the professional and educational organization for chief appointed management executives in local government. The purposes of ICMA are to strengthen the quality of urban government through professional management and to develop and disseminate new approaches to management through training programs, information services, and publications.

Managers, carrying a wide range of titles, serve cities, towns, counties, and councils of governments in all parts of the United States and Canada. These managers serve at the direction of elected councils and governing boards. ICMA serves these managers and local governments through many programs that aim at improving the manager's professional competence and strengthening the quality of all local governments.

The International City Management Association was founded in 1914; adopted its City Management Code of Ethics in 1924; and established its Institute for Training in Municipal Administration in 1934. The Institute, in turn, provided the basis for the Municipal Management Series, generally termed the "ICMA Green Books." ICMA's interests and activities include public management education; standards of ethics for members; *The Municipal Year Book* and other data services; urban research; and newsletters, a monthly magazine, *Public Management,* and other publications. ICMA's efforts for the improvement of local government management—as represented by this book—are offered for all local governments and educational institutions.

Municipal Management Series

The Practice of Local Government Planning

Editors

Published in cooperation
with the American
Planning Association

Frank S. So
American Planning
Association

By the
International
City
Management
Association

Israel Stollman
American Planning
Association

Frank Beal
Illinois Institute of
Natural Resources

David S. Arnold
International City
Management Association

Municipal Management Series

David S. Arnold Editor

The Practice of Local Government Planning

Community Health Services

Developing the Municipal Organization

Effective Supervisory Practices

Local Government Personnel Administration

Local Government Police Management

Management Policies in Local Government Finance

Managing Fire Services

Managing Human Services

Managing the Modern City

Managing Municipal Leisure Services

Policy Analysis in Local Government

Public Relations in Local Government

Small Cities Management Training Program

Urban Public Works Administration

Library of Congress Cataloging in Publication Data

Main entry under title:
The Practice of local government planning.

  (Municipal management series)
  Bibliography: p.
  Includes index.
  1. City planning—United States. I. So, Frank S.
II. Series.
HT167.P7   352'.96'0973   79-21380
ISBN 0-87326-020-1 (v. 1)

Printed in the United States of America.

Foreword

Of all the Green Books in the International City Management Association's Municipal Management Series, the successive editions of the volume devoted to planning in local government have probably achieved the widest recognition and had the greatest professional impact.

As the late Dennis O'Harrow noted in his preface to the immediately preceding (1968) edition of this book, "The first edition [published in 1941] of *Local Planning Administration* was a god-send, undoubtedly the most influential planning book in the United States during the first half of the twentieth century." The first edition was prepared under the direction of Ladislas Segoe. Under the same title, it was published in a second edition in 1948 to reflect the changed post–World War II environment. This work was carried out by one man, Howard K. Menhinick. The third edition, the work of editor Mary McLean and a dozen authors, appeared in 1959.

The fourth edition, guided by a committee with Dennis O'Harrow as chairman, edited by William I. Goodman and Eric C. Freund, and using the talents of almost two dozen authors, appeared in 1968 under a new title, *Principles and Practice of Urban Planning*. This book gave substantial recognition to contemporary management with coverage of quantitative methods, policy analysis, and organization and management of the planning agency. This 1968 edition has served literally tens of thousands of local government practitioners within local government

planning agencies and aspiring practitioners in colleges and universities across the nation. In addition to recording this gratifying acceptance, it is also a pleasure to note that this edition was honored by the American Institute of Planners' Merit Award in 1969 and was cited as the best single volume source of urban planning.

As all who work in local government management are aware, times have changed—and perhaps more so during the later 1960s and on through the 1970s than during any other recent decades in national and international history. Dennis O'Harrow's words in his preface to the last edition have proved prescient: "If I were to be asked, I would predict that the next edition, too, would have to be substantially if not completely rewritten."

The changing economic, social, and legislative environments of the last decade are too familiar to need repetition here: suffice it to say that the volume now in your hands represents not only the sustained efforts of the four editors and two associations listed on the title page, twenty-eight individual chapter authors, and numerous advisers and consultants, but also fully reflects those changing times.

Indeed, when we at the International City Management Association first discussed this project with our colleagues at the American Society of Planning Officials (now consolidated with the American Institute of Planners as the American Planning Association) it became clear that no single volume could, as in the past, encompass the entire field of urban planning in its managerial context. It was therefore decided to produce a two volume successor to *Principles and Practice of Urban Planning* under the general title of *The Practice of Public Planning*. The present volume, *The Practice of Local Government Planning*, represents the joint efforts of our two associations to address the core area of urban planning. The second volume, *The Practice of State and Regional Planning*, will appear in due course under the aegis of the American Planning Association but as a full member of the Municipal Management Series and as an essential companion to the present text.

Having set this volume in its past (and future) context, it will now be helpful to make three general points about its content which are applicable to all books in ICMA's Municipal Management Series.

First, every effort has been made in the planning, editing, and writing of *The Practice of Local Government Planning* to emphasize the managerial perspective, whether it be that of urban planners, city managers, other department heads, elected officials, involved citizens and community groups, or those involved in teaching, research, or study at colleges and universities. Points that are relevant to decision making are emphasized throughout, and policy issues are addressed and explored.

Second, the authors of individual chapters have been selected on the basis of their expertise in particular subject areas and their ability to communicate their expertise to specialists and nonspecialists alike. They have also been given appropriate latitude to discuss their subjects and to express their own policy preferences in terms, and by examples, that they deem appropriate. A lively blend of individual perspectives has emerged;

the end result is a text that, like those of the other Green Books, offers authoritative coverage.

Third, this book, like its companions, will be used by the Institute for Training in Municipal Administration as an integral part of its program. The Institute offers in-service training specifically designed for local government administrators whose jobs are to plan, direct, and coordinate the work of others. The Institute, sponsored by ICMA since 1934, has prepared a training course to accompany this book.

The Practice of Local Government Planning is a collective endeavor, and it is a pleasure to thank the many organizations and individuals who have given so much time and effort to this book.

Our thanks go first to the editors of the book: Frank S. So, Deputy Executive Director, American Planning Association; Israel Stollman, Executive Director, American Planning Association; Frank Beal, Director, Illinois Institute of Natural Resources; and David S. Arnold, Director, Publications Center, International City Management Association. Their work was particularly vital during project planning, manuscript review, and substantive editing.

Next we are grateful to the chapter authors for their fine efforts and for their willingness to work with the editors in revisions and chapter reviews. Then we want to acknowledge the support of the American Society of Planning Officials (now the American Planning Association) in editorial work, documentation, preparation of the bibliography, and many other aspects of developing the book. Our thanks go also to Louis B. Schlivek for preparing the Planning Portfolio, which includes his text and his photographs, and to the Regional Plan Association, New York, for cooperating with ICMA in this effort.

Many planning agency directors and staff, city managers, university teachers, consultants, and other persons helped in planning the content of this book and in reviewing chapter drafts in various stages of preparation. These persons, listed alphabetically, are as follows: J. Richard Aronson, Professor of Economics, Lehigh University; Michael B. Barker, Administrator, Department of Practice and Design, American Institute of Architects; Clark S. Binkley, Assistant Professor of Forestry, Yale University; Norman C. Boehm, Associate Professor, Institute of Government Service, Graduate School of Management, Brigham Young University; Richard S. Bolan, Professor and Chairman, Community Organization/Social Planning, Graduate School of Social Work, Boston College; John Eckenroad, Village Manager, Northfield, Illinois; Jon Elam, City Manager, Lucan, Minnesota; Andrew F. Euston, Jr., Principal Urban Design Officer, U.S. Department of Housing and Urban Development; John F. Fischbach, City Manager, Robbinsdale, Minnesota; Gerald G. Fox, City Manager, Wichita Falls, Texas; Bernard J. Frieden, Professor, Department of Urban Studies and Planning, Massachusetts Institute of Technology; Thomas J. Graves, Senior Associate, Cultural Resources; Dale F. Helsel, City Manager, Middletown, Ohio; James F. Hudson, Vice President, Urban Systems Research and Engineering, Cambridge, Massachusetts; John B. Legler, Professor of Banking and Finance, University of Georgia; Robert H. Maxey, Planning Director, Northeast Georgia Area Planning and Development Commission, Athens; Ernest E. Melvin, Director, Institute of Community and Area Development, University of Georgia; Arthur A. Mendonsa, City Manager, Savannah, Georgia; Robert Morris, Kirstein Professor of Social Planning, Brandeis University; Ronald

Neislar, Athens–Clarke County Planning Commission, Athens, Georgia; Mary Nenno, Associate Director, National Association of Housing and Redevelopment Officials; Howard A. Schretter, Assistant Professor of Geography, University of Georgia; Eli Schwartz, Professor of Economics and Finance, Lehigh University; David C. Slater, Vice President, Hammer, Siler, George Associates; Burton Sparer, Governmental Program Planning Associate, Institute of Government, University of Georgia; Roger A. Storey, City Manager, Arcata, California; and R. Douglas Taylor, Executive Director, Western Piedmont Council of Governments, Hickory, North Carolina.

The Practice of Local Government Planning is a visually-oriented book with over 110 figures and 51 sidebars. Herbert Slobin and Frank S. So developed the ideas for most of the illustrations and sidebars, and Mr. Slobin prepared the figures in final form. David S. Arnold assisted in illustration and sidebar planning and wrote the captions.

The Municipal Management Series is the responsibility of David S. Arnold, Director, Publications Center, ICMA. Richard R. Herbert, Senior Editor, worked with the editors in the planning and early developmental stages of the book. Emily Evershed handled final editing of the manuscript and prepared the Index. Ellen W. Faran and Cheryl L. Crowell, Editorial Associates, coordinated editorial schedules and assisted in the development of illustrations and sidebars.

Mark E. Keane
Executive Director

International City
Management Association

Washington, D.C.

Contents

Figures

Tables

Introduction

The city has to echo life. If our life is rough and tumble, so is the city. I have always felt that ugliness with vitality is tolerable.

I. M. Pei

Our national flower is the concrete cloverleaf.

Lewis Mumford

Time can heal even new towns.

Ada Louise Huxtable

There are no right decisions, but decisions have to be taken.

William Rogers

Surely, more than almost any other field, planning is subjected to epigrams and aphorisms. Like most generalizations, however, they oversimplify. One of the purposes of *The Practice of Local Government Planning* is to get behind such generalizations and look at the setting and processes of planning as well as the methods. Perhaps the most important underlying theme in this book is the transition to professionalism, a change of kind as well as degree. This transition is evident in the bringing together of physical, social, and economic planning to an unprecedented extent; the increase in policy formulation and management roles of planning agencies; and the depth and diversity of subjects within the purview of planning.

When Ladislas Segoe and his associates produced the first edition of *Local Planning Administration* in 1941, the book summarized the existing state of knowledge in the local planning field. This was possible because the planning field was relatively in its infancy (for example, the American Institute of Planners had under 200 members). During the last forty years the planning field has expanded considerably (the American Planning Association now has over 20,000 members), has become complex, and is now divided into many areas of specialization. Clearly, then, this fifth edition must have a different objective: it is to provide a comprehensive introduction to the field for the planning student, the planner without extensive formal education in planning, and the urban administrator who is trained in another field yet must understand the scope of planning in local government.

This slightly different objective has editorial implications. Thus, while we realize that analytical techniques are becoming increasingly sophisticated, we choose to emphasize the principles of planning practice rather than its techniques. We do this because we believe there is a need to "develop and emphasize the fundamental *principles* upon which the professional tasks are based rather than rule-of-thumb procedures."[1] Moreover, as the planning field has developed and matured there is a growing awareness that cookbook approaches to planning problems do not work. Along with other professions, planning today no longer has a brash overconfidence in many traditional planning solutions. Many planners have changed from true believers to agnostics.

This is a healthy development in planning because, as one author has stated the matter:

The first criterion of a professional person is, then, an ability to operate in concrete situations with full sensitivity to their novelty, because reference is made steadily to the basic principles that imply and include the potential variations. . . .

The second criterion of a profession lies in its use of technical means. But the technical means of a profession, whatever their specific nature, are servants not masters. They are used to free, not to fetter thinking and action.[2]

We want to quickly reassure users of previous editions, however, that this effort does not deal in abstract planning theory. Rather, it still deals with *substance* of local government planning. But this substantive focus is characterized by a greater attention to issues rather than techniques. Thus the chapter on zoning presents the basic concepts, elements, and techniques of this planning tool but also stresses public policy issues relating to equity, exclusion, and the balance between the local community and the region. Or the chapter on economic development describes the economic studies commonly used and the current efforts at promoting economic development yet raises fundamental questions about how many economists focus on the region and not the city and, therefore, hinder analysis and subsequent intelligent policymaking.

The reader and student will also discover that this edition reflects its times in that there is far more emphasis on the mature city, whether it is stable or declining. In the previous texts there was the explicit assumption that most cities were growing. There usually was but a single chapter on renewal. In the present edition the last six chapters on social, economic, and housing planning are oriented toward the mature city. Moreover, other chapters focus on how planning differs in the mature city. For example, the urban transportation chapter emphasizes the fact that major expressway systems have either been completed or have been stopped. Today's planner concentrates on how to use the existing system more efficiently within the amenity requirements of the city, the community, and the neighborhood. In the chapter on recreation, for example, the emphasis is not on acquiring new open space but rather on planning for more extensive urban-oriented recreation experiences.

The editors feel obligated to persons considering or just entering the planning field to discuss the values of the planner (Chapter 1) so that such "newcomers" have some idea of the kind of "mental baggage" that planners carry. This is the first time material of this kind has appeared in an International City Management Association planning text.

Community growth, and the inevitable changes associated with growth, are no longer accepted without challenge. "Bigger and better" is no longer best for every community, and the correlative "We must grow or we'll shrink" no longer has the consensus it once had. Stability is held by many as a value. Reflecting this and other developments, about one-third of *The Practice of Local Government Planning* covers subjects that were not covered at all or were given only cursory attention in the four predecessor editions.

Perhaps the best way to provide some of the flavor is to briefly summarize some of these developments. In addition to judgment and experience, planning now demands a high order of disciplined thinking, whether this is reflected in a sophisticated budgeting system, forecasting models, systems analysis, or cost–benefit studies. The planner is not likely to be a demographer or other data professional, but he or she must understand and use a variety of approaches that were scarcely touched until the 1970s.

Changes are shown also in business and industrial development, where growth is no longer uncritically regarded as a blessing. Although initial decisions on location and expansion are made in the private sector, the planning agency can react more quickly and has more tools for negotiating with developers and other interests. In addition to zoning, the planner is concerned with industrial processes; the trade-off between the central business district and the outlying shopping center; and the effects on housing, traffic, and schools.

Even the schools, a group to which many planners were formerly indifferent, are planned much more thoroughly with respect to location, services, and facilities. The imaginative reuse of obsolete school buildings shows that "less is more" in some circumstances.

The processes of changing, and of aging gracefully, are the unstated themes of this book's Part Five, "Social and Economic Development." Although our large central cities have been subjected to extraordinary stress during the past generation, it now seems that a modus vivendi is attainable. One of the major reasons has been the range of federal government programs, especially the Community Development Block Grant program and its predecessors. Another reason is the increasing ability of the local planning agency to work with a panoply of public and private agencies and interests.

But this is only part of the picture. All cities and other local governments are involved in (or at least concerned about) the social elements that permeate the planning process and planning decisions, the many varieties of citizen participation, the city as an economic system (and how this system fits into the larger regional and national systems), and the ramifications of planning for all housing, not just publicly assisted housing.

The table of contents outlines the extensive coverage of this book, but a word is in order about several other elements. The twenty-one chapters contain more than 110 figures—photographs, charts, line drawings, and all-text figures—that clarify text discussions and amplify and interpret coverage. In addition, 51 sidebars, in effect verbal illustrations, provide background, explanation, and, through direct quotes, other points of view. The bibliography is selective and short, emphasizing general works that are the next logical references for students and practitioners. We have included only a few local planning agency studies and reports in the bibliography because such documents are not available in most libraries. The Index is comprehensive and explicit; it is a useful source for details of coverage.

As an editorial decision, major elements of metropolitan planning, state planning, and intergovernmental relations have been omitted. These and correlative subjects will be covered in the companion volume, *The Practice of State and Regional Planning,* which is now in process.

Finally we want to thank the many planning practitioners and teachers, city managers, and other persons who reviewed chapter drafts and helped us in other ways in the preparation of this book. These persons are individually acknowledged in the Foreword.

1   Harvey S. Perloff, "Education of City Planners: Past, Present and Future," *Journal of the American Institute of Planners* 22 (Fall 1956): 203.

2   Seward Hiltner, "Planning as a Profession," *Journal of the American Institute of Planners* 23 (Fall 1957): 163–64.

Part one:
The context of
local planning

1 The values of the city planner

Are the professions accomplishing the opposite of their central goals? Contemporary criticism often says yes. Doctors cause illness. Teachers keep children from learning. Lawyers break laws. Ministers lead people to Hell. Planners produce unexpected disasters.

Professional people often contribute to this adverse reaction by evolving a remote and elevated status for the professions. The aura of knowingness, the command of mysterious forces, the privilege of the expert, the hard and narrow path of access to professional standing—these have built illusions of professional infallibility, of problems invariably solved if professional advice is sought and followed.

Once the consumers of professional advice discover its limitations they discover also the need to be active participants in how the advice is developed and used. The aloof professional is replaced by the accountable professional. The passive consumer is replaced by the consumer who affects professional decisions. Some of the professional's attention turns from case-by-case advice to showing you how to be your own professional. The self-help movement in medicine illustrates these new partnerships of professionals and consumers in our society.

As a new profession, not quite a hundred years old in its modern American existence, planning scarcely had time to build the walls of illusion around its exclusive professional competence before the siege came. Now the beleaguerment of the professions is leveling those walls. The expansion of malpractice responsibility, commercial advertising of professional services, competitive bidding for services, and citizen review of professional standards are leading us to the unwalled profession.

As long as the professions stick to their central aim society will continue to want and need them. That central aim is to muster the best knowledge, skill, and imagination in solving complex problems and in making the solutions work. The active client sets the priorities among problems, judges whether the best effort has been used, and in addition judges whether the solution is effective, whether its cost is too high, and whether the solution gets in the way of other good things.

Clemenceau's saying, that war is too important to be entrusted to generals, was turned about by General de Gaulle when he said that politics is too serious a matter to be left to the politicians. It is a saying that can be applied to any profession.

To get effective results, however, it is important also not to leave the professionals out. Here, the aim of planners is like the aim of other professionals: to put the meaning of our experience into ideas and to test our ideas in experience, solving problems as we go.

In the paragraphs that follow are comments on the values of a planning profession that some say does not exist. Samuel Johnson once replied to an elaborate argument that proved that matter did not exist. He kicked a large stone with great might and said, "I refute it thus." The planning profession has also been kicked with great might.

Planning values

A theme runs through these views of the values held by planners and the issues affecting the conduct of planning. It is a theme well put by the lawyer Paul Freund: "When you perceive a truth, look for the balancing truth." Many debates in planning, as in other fields, pose choices as either–or. Is planning scientific or is it not scientific? Can we forecast the future or is it unknowable? Both parts of each debate may be true and thus are balancing truths.

The place of values in the work of planners is itself debated in these terms.

Do, or should, planners work objectively, keeping their own preferences out of their advice, serving their employers as neutral technicians? Yes, of course. Who elected them to work for their own program?

Do, or should, planners express their own vision in their work? Give priority to matters that they think are important? Fight for whatever they think best? Yes, of course. Why hire an independent-minded professional if a faithful taker of orders is what is wanted?

Planners in practice strike a balance between these competing principles, a balance that differs with the personality, temperament, and convictions of the planner. Although the balance will differ with the client's or community's rapport with the planner, it is hazardous to let the balance tip to one extreme or the other.

Figure 1–1   Marking the boundary for an early Roman city (circa 25 B.C.). A plow, guided by a Roman priest and drawn by a white cow and a white bull, symbolized the solemn religious ceremony for the location of the city wall.

If it tips toward the neutral technician, it is self-deceiving. As a whole person the technician cannot be empty of views, values, and biases. Even the collection of facts requires choosing questions to ask, choosing methods of getting answers, and making judgments about their validity. Different values will yield different choices. The technician's biases may be subtle, quiet, and hidden, but they are there. A neutral technician is a passive professional.

Tip the balance toward a professional who is actively promoting the planner's values and you risk an idiosyncratic program, one that is not responsive to the community. That responsiveness, an explicit acknowledgment of the planner's values, leadership, and fairness in presenting contrary evidence, contributes to making these opposing tendencies complementary rather than conflicting.

How do the values of planners sort out? Which are deemed by planners to be more important than others? The following discussion shows that many planning values are in competition with each other and with values of the broader community as well. This is not a report of a consensus among planners. It expresses views that are based not on a scientific poll but on years of knowing many planners and many plans, and listening to many planning debates.

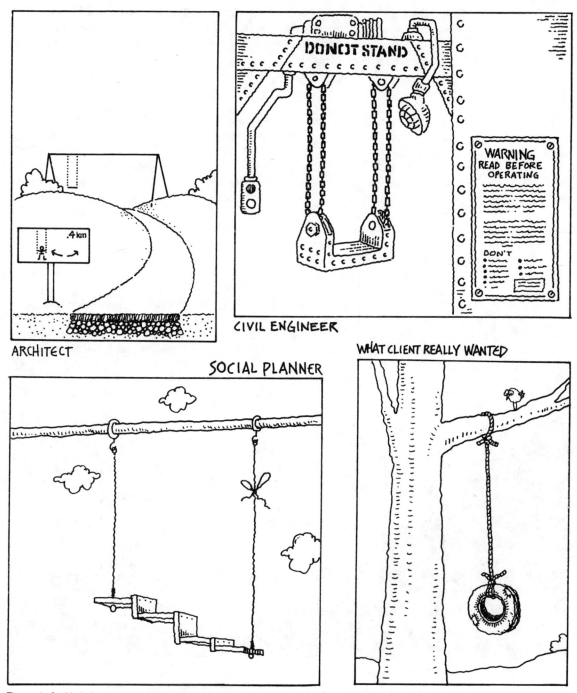

ARCHITECT

CIVIL ENGINEER

SOCIAL PLANNER

WHAT CLIENT REALLY WANTED

Figure 1–2 Variations on the design of a swing.

The planner's techniques in balancing competing values are not special to the planner, whether they are old-fashioned horse-trading or new fashioned cost–benefit trade-offs. Planning brings to these techniques a concern for long-run consequences and side effects and an interest in devising solutions that consider the costs and benefits to people outside the immediate circle of participants in making a decision.

The planner's values are not special to the planner. They are widely held and generally shared. Everyone favors health, happiness, prosperity, and justice. Planners used to advertise the objective of a city plan as that of making the community a better place to work, live, and play in. What is now special to the planner is an inclination toward those public values that are fragile and hard to maintain in competition with values that are sturdier because they command more predictable acceptance.

Health

Health, for example, strongly and universally valued, is a composite of subsidiary values. Planners favor the more fragile among them. There is no lack of appreciation for serving the needs of the person afflicted with physical illness, but planners look more to environmental health, to preventive programs, to clean air and clean water, to surroundings and services that nurture self-development, and to the integration of handicapped people so that they can live a full life in the large society. Even with respect to individual physical illness, the planner turns to the more fragile values: access to services by the poor, control of priorities and costs, equity of service.

Conservation of resources

The conservation of resources is a value that has been gaining adherents, but it is a value that remains fragile. The conservationist/planners are concerned with long-range consequences which handicap them when their values are juxtaposed with immediate values. Norbert Wiener illustrated the point when he ad-

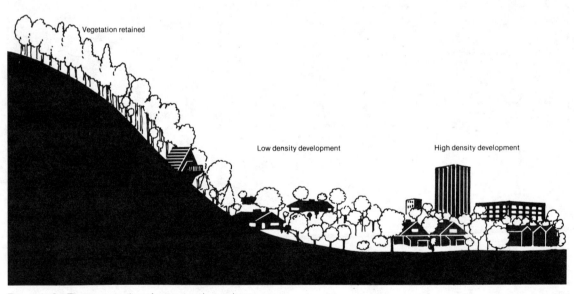

Figure 1–3   The conservation of resources is a value . . . that remains fragile.

dressed a planning conference in the following words: ''No firm can underwrite the growth of a redwood forest. [If it is] to be grown by anybody, it can scarcely be by an organization of less respected prominence than the State or perhaps the Church.''

The fragilities that a planner's biases lead that planner to worry about include topsoil, good agricultural land, and the wildlife of a swamp. Conservation objectives may be strengthened with the public by stressing present-day enjoyments. Once sacrificed to expediency, however, these objectives are not recoverable in the long, long, long range.

Efficiency

Efficiency is a popular value. All of us want to see it, especially in those who serve us. Although the work of planners probably is done as efficiently as the work of other professionals, the special significance of efficiency for planners is not in the efficiency with which plans *are produced* but in the efficiencies that plans *can produce*. The solutions that appeal to planners, for example, are those that produce multiple services from one investment: using school facilities after hours, for example, for recreational and community activities, or buying land in excess of that needed for a highway right-of-way to use for other public purposes. Such solutions are often resisted by administrators of specific functions who value the competing efficiency of concentrating every resource on the one function.

Efficiency leads planners to oppose urban sprawl, which results in overbuilt sewer, water, and transportation facilities that provide too much, too soon to unserved land. Efficiency is the value that evokes an intelligent stinginess in capital improvements programming.

Beauty

Beauty is a value that shares eternal life with its companion, truth. The life they share, however, is often poverty-stricken. Planners, dealing with public expressions of beauty, cope with two elements in trying to alleviate that poverty.

One is that public beauty must satisfy public taste. While common denominators need not be low, and a high common denominator is a reasonable aspiration, some lasting delights in our environment require hospitality toward, or at least tolerance of, heretic and prickly designs that have only a small audience. We can choose our delights in music or poetry, but the environment is communal. The wide diversity among high cultures and pop cultures, and their basis in our emotional rather than rational needs, make it difficult to strike this communal balance.

The second element is the long-lasting quality, visibility, and psychological uplift (or oppression) of urban design. Although a community obviously can live with sterile and ugly environments, it will cherish—and use—developments, large and small, that fulfill the complex demands of living, looking, and using.

Equity

Social equity is profoundly influenced by public plans and the way they are carried out. Can low paid people live close to their jobs? Are they cut out of jobs by business location decisions? Is police protection as good in a poor neighborhood as in a better off one? Is the school giving a poor child a full enough chance to become a not-so-poor adult? Are homes available on a fair basis?

Our recent progress toward greater equity has been particularly remarkable in the realm of principle. Legislation, judicial findings, and public attitudes now buttress the general value of equity. Many policy issues involving equity have moved into the area of application—how to allocate resources for more equitable results. Such allocations are political decisions, case by case, but decisions strongly influenced by planning analysis and recommendations.

A neutral planning stance on equity issues ignores the windfall and wipeout effects not only of land use decisions but also of capital expenditures and service programs. It is a paradox that those who most strongly hold to the value of individualism are often the most skilled in exploiting the organized structure and resources of government, law, and finance. Those who must make it on their own—owing to poverty, physical handicap, geographic location, lack of education, lack of employment opportunities, or discrimination—often are the least skilled in exploiting government, law, and finance. Fairness in the planning process requires that steps be built in to redress this imbalance.

Pluralism and individuality

To assert that planners value pluralism and individuality seems to run counter to much contrary evidence. Haven't our planners produced the American suburb of conforming sameness? The urban renewal project that replaces small scale diversity with super-block rigidity? The expressway that slices up an old neighborhood? The zoning ordinance that isolates every land use in its own unmixed district?

Planners have indeed contributed to each of these majority visions of what urban development everywhere should be like. To a large extent they have done so in response to the strength of these majorities and their rooted values. And to some extent they have done so because, as citizens, many planners may share these values. The foundation of zoning regulations was built upon majority views of the need to protect and separate residential areas from business and industry. The design of new subdivisions was based on a view of the urban neighborhood as a village transplanted into the city.

Figure 1–4 "The planner is a leader . . . urging progress with quiet but unrelenting persistence."

Yet planners have also concerned themselves with satisfying plural tastes and meeting minority needs. Planners worked to get public support for mass transit during its long decline; adopted the planned unit development to remove the imposed uniformities of a zoning ordinance; promoted rehabilitation and conservation instead of wholesale clearance; favored scattering public housing in existing neighborhoods; and did much to push environmental concerns into the status of a majority value.

Like other values, individuality cannot be asserted absolutely. Its importance —as well as the need to balance plural values against values held in common—

is expressed in the comment by Jean Renoir, "You see, in this world there is one awful thing, and that is that everyone has his reasons." Our plans should accommodate more of those reasons. But if we cannot arrange for the city of all virtues, we can arrange for each city to be true to its own individuality: "It's the best place in the world to live in if that's the kind of place you like."

Democratic participation and democratic responsibility

Democratic participation means participation in making public decisions as well as in electing officials. No other local government activity generates more citizen participation than does planning. The planning agency is responsible for holding more public hearings, conducting more attitude and opinion surveys, arranging more neighborhood meetings, and appointing more citizen advisory committees—in addition to giving official duties to unpaid citizens on planning commissions and boards and publicizing the alternative decisions being considered.

Planners are concerned with the quality of participation and the substantive degree of understanding with which it is accepted. Genuine participation has to begin before ideas are crystallized—long before a hearing is held on unchangeable proposals with contracts about to be let. It must proceed without the condescension of technician-knows-best, the selective packaging of facts that will sell best, or glib replies to problems that may trip up the project.

The most effective participation will not produce automatic decisions. The elected officials have the democratic responsibility of resolving the "tough ones" in which some participants gain and some lose, of balancing a neighborhood interest against a citywide interest or a citywide interest against a regional interest. Public policy disputes often show heavier support of a facility in someone else's backyard: a nuclear plant but not in my city, an expressway but not in my neighborhood, a halfway house but not on my street. Resolving these conflicts is a political responsibility. With genuine and widespread participation, better decisions should be made (although they may not please all participants).

Rational management

Planning is an integral element of good management. Management needs to anticipate events; it is weak if it merely responds to them. The tempo and complexity of change have rapidly established administrative and management planning as a distinct executive responsibility. The public planner was there even earlier as part of the management team. A central value of both the administrative planner and the public planner is the progressive displacement of "seat-of-the-pants" judgments with reasoned judgments. The evolution of planning methods has stressed the validity and pertinence of information, the logic of analysis, the worth of evaluating the consequences of alternative decisions, and the effectiveness of standards and policies in achieving goals.

This evolution has been greatly assisted by computer technology—a situation which gives the impression at times that decision makers also will be replaced by machines. Although the models and the computer games should help us understand what happens and why, should help us deal with complex relationships, and should improve our guesses about the limits of action and the opportunities for solution, it is neither likely nor rational for us to hope for or to fear a conspiracy that will completely replace wisdom with knowledge. Planning solutions, like scientific hypotheses, can be methodically tested, but it takes a certain amount of inspiration—not just a formula—to come up with either one.

A rational balance does not require a choice between inordinate faith in computer products and a return to intuitive decisions. Our appreciation of the limitations of computers and mathematical models can make these models more, rather than less, helpful. If we know the assumptions and guesses and "fudge factors" that helped put the model together, we also know the points at which professional and political judgments must enter if we are to make use of what the model tells us. A small drinking story may illustrate this point. President Franklin D. Roosevelt is said to have mixed his martinis by pouring gin into a graduated beaker and holding the beaker up to eye level to see that the prescribed amount came exactly to the line. Then he would pour the right proportion of vermouth into the beaker and hold it up again to see that it came exactly to the line, avoiding what scientists call parallax error. He then stirred. But before serving he upended the gin bottle over the beaker and vigorously sloshed in a lot more. The most rational rationality is leavened with emotion.

Planning issues

A few general planning issues are reviewed here that are discussed perennially; there is no intent to settle them once and for all. They illustrate the balancing of opposing tendencies to reach a conclusion that may be proper in one case but may not be in another.

The far-off goal and the immediate decision

Plans are made to reach some goal which is generally years away. The usefulness of a plan, however, is in helping to make decisions today. The press of problems needing answers today will not be lightened by the posting of a sign that says, "Plans being prepared." And competing demands will not subside by our adding to the sign, "Quiet, please, long-range goals being formulated." But our decisions will not improve much if the emphasis is reversed and the sign says, "We don't know where we're going, but we've got to move fast."

Two steps that are important in themselves will also reduce the conflict between making plans and making decisions. One is to ensure against "stop-and-go" planning. An intensive planning effort is funded, reports are produced, some recommendations are carried out. Then the job is considered done, the planning budget is cut, and the staff assigned to general planning is reduced. The volume of day-to-day decisions, however, does not get smaller. It takes more of the staff's time, while the quality of staff advice on day-to-day issues grows poorer as the general plans that this staff must consult grow rapidly obsolescent. When the advice has become poor enough, there may be a decision to fund another attempt at planning. How much more effective it would be to eliminate the peaks and valleys in favor of an ongoing, serious level of general planning, and to strive for a successful balance with decision making.

The second step is to develop all the connections that Meyerson's famous paper called *the middle-range bridge:*[1] the activities that connect long-range plans with short-range implementation. Planning is part of management, and management is part of planning. Plans must be translated into programs and budgets, and the effects of carrying out plans must be checked to measure success and find the surprises.

If such measures succeed, there will still be a balancing problem to keep the planners from skimping on help with immediate decisions and to keep the decision makers from skimping on support of long-range planning.

Incrementalism – ad hocism – and comprehensive planning

One response to the difficulties of comprehensive planning has been the prescription of incrementalism. Incrementalism involves concluding that long-range and comprehensive planning is not only too difficult but is inherently bad; that problems are harder to solve when you group them together and are easier

Alternative futures for decision making   We are not going to find technological fixes to any of the problems in our culture that matter. . . . These are social problems, but we keep on looking for technological fixes. . . .

If you look at the evidence from the last ten years there has not been a significant increase in standards of living in the United States. What has been happening . . . is a transfer towards those families that now have two wage earners instead of one.

We are not going to get a major rise again in the standard of living. We are going to have to learn to manage stability, not growth. . . .

Rapid growth [is] no longer necessarily in the interest of those who are getting it any more than decline was in the interest of those experiencing that. With rapid increases in marginal costs, rapid growth may be the best way to wreck your city. . . .

Management means the dealing with incomplete, uncertain information and making the best decision that one can. It means that one of the key priorities is preserving enough social cohesion that people will go along with decisions that are not ideal, but merely optimal. It means that one works with imperfect people. And one recognizes that decision making is not a tidy, decent, clean-cut process, but a messy, untidy, unsatisfactory, and gutsy process.

Source: Excerpted from Robert Theobald, "Strategies for the Future," speech reprinted in *Public Management,* January 1979, pp. 15, 16.

to solve when you take them one at a time; that solutions are best negotiated with the few people who have a direct interest, not with the many whose interests have a remote connection to the problem in hand; that genuine reform is accomplished in "small bites," not in "whole swallows"; and that small increments of change can be better fitted to the real needs of people than can the tyranny of a grand design.

Some of the weaknesses documented in examples of comprehensive planning encourage the promises of incrementalism. Many long-range proposals have been put forward in the form of an "end state," a condition to be reached in, perhaps, thirty years, in which all the problems are solved, all the resources are allocated, and all the books are balanced. Cheerful people encounter no lot that is vacant, no building that is crumbling, no stream that is dirty. No doubt the planners responsible for these misleading visions did not intend to mislead. They understood the projected plans as generalized forecasts of the consequences of following alternative policies. But forecasts oversimplify the future, as myth oversimplifies the past, and forecasts can also mislead. Planners may mislead more intentionally by fearing to forecast the persistence of problems. Overpromising is so easy when the delivery date is so far off.

Long-range plans also tend to design solutions that are too uniform for the diversity of cases that will come up. The attraction of ad hoc solutions is in tailoring each one to fit the problem, in making each solution a spontaneous invention that is uninhibited in its improvised answers. Ad hocism is attractive also in getting rid of the burden of worrying about tomorrow. Today's solutions may become tomorrow's problems, and another layer of ad hoc solutions may multiply the problems further for the day after.

Incrementalism is a truth about how things get done but not necessarily a truth about how the right things get done. The "right things," when we deal with complex events, will always be elusive, but are more approachable comprehensively. The environmental impact approach to evaluating proposals took hold because incremental solutions satisfied a narrow interest in the short run but not the broader environmental interests in the long run. The extension of impact analysis to social and economic issues returns us to one of the original central concepts of comprehensive planning: the plan was intended as the basic reference in evaluating all of the impacts of a particular proposal. In the 1920s this sort of impact analysis was named *mandatory referral,* but that phrase is now obsolete. If the contemporary version of impact analysis should yield again to incrementalism, mandatory referral would be invented once again to restore the balance with comprehensive planning.

That balance may be incremental in the implementation of plans, but not in their preparation. The qualification of the comprehensive planner, if that planner is to be the best incrementalist, is to know what it is, in the long run, that must be accomplished bit by bit.

Public decisions and private decisions

Our cities operate in a mixed political economy. Public dollars and private dollars mix in the development of a project. Public policies and private policies mix

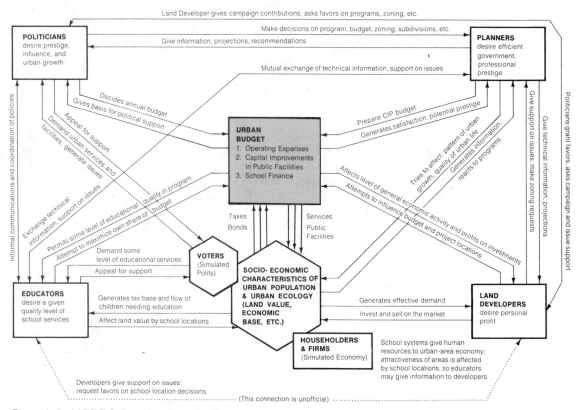

Figure 1–5   M.E.T.R.O. functional interactions in planning and policy.
This visual representation of a gaming model is a hybrid of operational
gaming and computer simulation models. It was developed in 1966
by the Tri-County Regional Planning Commission,
Lansing, Michigan. It illustrates the complex interactions
of a local land development system.

in determining that project's design and operation. Public policies help determine private profits. Private policies help determine the success of public programs.

The mix of dollars and policies is often settled by negotiation. A suburb and a developer will hammer out agreement on the size of a development, its density, housing types, kind of shopping area, payment for the sewer, land for a school, length of time it will take to develop. An older city wants to create jobs and will offer incentives for business development with special zoning permissions, tax allowances, new services at city expense, or public acquisition of land with a writedown of costs.

Benefits do flow both ways—to the public and to the developer, but with so much money at stake clear precautions must be established, to keep public and private interests from blurring to the public detriment and to lessen the opportunities for corruption.

Precautions include the adoption of standards and guidelines to set limits on the negotiator's discretion and to prescribe the tests to be met by acceptable development agreements. Approvals should not be recorded as bare conclusions but should be accompanied in the public record by statements of the findings that justify the approvals. The proceedings and record of negotiations should be public, although the early and tentative stages may involve business confidences to be protected. Development opportunities that are created by public action should be open to competitive offers, including competition based on design quality or on meeting special housing needs.

In balancing the public and private responsibilities for development, there have been, at times, extravagant gifts of publicly created value to private entrepreneurs in the name of entrepreneurial rights. But a heavy burden of requirements, imposed on the developer in the name of public interest regulation, has also accumulated. Developers add up the demands for installed utilities, land for schools and recreation, fair housing, low income housing, design standards, art, performance bonds, and assurances of development to a fixed schedule, and then protest that translated into costs the requirements will stop the development.

These debates are not effectively resolved by the exchange of slogans on behalf of free enterprise and the public interest. Active community development does need the partnership of both public and private sectors; some public investments and incentives to private development are justified, and a public concern for the marketability of that development is needed. The balance will be better struck if all the computations of costs and benefits and markets are explicitly and publicly examined, case by case.

Who is the client?

The quick answer to the question of who is the client is that the planner's client is whoever pays the planner's salary. The professional does owe diligent service to the client-employer. Ethical performance requires that a planner not serve at the same time two employers who may have conflicting interests.

One peculiarity in identifying the planner's client is that the planner may often have *one* employer with conflicting interests. For example, in one city a planner may be recruited, interviewed, and recommended for appointment by a committee of a planning commission. The planner is appointed by the mayor or city manager and then confirmed by the city council. Subsequently, this planner reports, let us say, to the city manager providing studies and advice on many aspects of the manager's business. The planner also advises the planning commission on its decisions and the city council on its legislation.

Where their interests or views differ, whose does the planner serve among these multiple bosses? One refuge is in the standards of the profession. The same thorough and dispassionate analysis will be presented to all participants; the same careful analysis of alternative possible decisions will be made for all. Hazards, opportunities, and possible compromises in resolving issues are conscientiously disclosed.

This model of the conscientious professional answers the problem only partially. The decision makers want more than the facts and analysis. They want a recommendation. If the statement made earlier about the impossibility of being completely neutral as a planner is true, then even the analysis alone contains a gentle steering toward a particular recommendation. Make it explicit, the decision maker asks, and give your justifications.

Planners serve the public interest primarily (say ethical codes) and must fit the client-employer's interest to the public interest or else not serve that client. This guide is needed most when the public interest is hardest to identify. It is needed most, then, when its guidance is least clear.

The public interest is an amalgam of many specific interests. These include serving the interests of democratic majorities; improving the conditions of the weak, poor, or handicapped; protecting resources in the long run; economizing in the use of public funds; living up to our laws; protecting health and safety; preserving human rights—in short, doing all the things that pursue our abiding values. Even the ability to pursue private interests is part of the public interest, in light of our high value of government as servant of the individual.

Figure 1–6 "The planner is dedicated. . . . He has seen the light."

We cannot codify a consensus on a permanent balance among these competing parts of the public interest, nor a permanent balance between the public interest and the right to pursue private interests. A planner, then, has the professional responsibility of achieving such a balance personally and using it as a personal guide.

Some planners have found a durable imbalance in the public interest, especially as public decisions affect the poor and minority groups. Some have become advocate planners, advocating the special interests of those groups that do not normally command articulate, knowledgeable, skillful, and aggressive representation. Advocate planners have cited precedents for the advocacy of a special interest by pointing to planners who have "advocated" for builders and developers, for example, or for transportation interests.

In a common phrase, planners are sensitive to the needs of a client, to the needs of an elected official, or to the needs of a special interest as advocate planners or special purpose planners. The common allegiance that unites planners is a sensitivity also to the needs of publics beyond the immediate client. As a planner in the job of finding a balanced public interest to serve, you are your own client.

Localism and interdependence

The problems of metropolitan areas are not fragmented, but the governments are. The neatness of metropolitan government was once looked to for solutions and has been adopted in a few places, but most people are looking to solutions that make local government a little more complex. Metropolitan councils of governments (COGs) have been set up as a new but modest layer to work for coordination of plans and programs. States have been setting up regions within the state and taking a more active role in some local decisions with effects beyond local boundaries. Highly urbanized counties have sought a new identity as local urban governments.

The councils of governments have tried to achieve coordination primarily through elected officials representing autonomous units. The states have acted, especially on environmental issues, when state governments have found that localities have not acted in setting environmental goals or in working toward them. Counties have acted in serving the clusters of cities within their boundaries by initiating or stepping up many urban services.

These efforts all seek more centralization or coordination on a metropolitan basis. At the same time, there has been greater interest in decentralizing some of the decisions within large central cities—giving neighborhood councils at least the power to review and advise.

This interplay of governments often illustrates the point that administrators wish to coordinate all of the units that are below theirs in size or authority but do not wish to be coordinated by units that are above theirs.

Planners work at each of these levels and balance a loyalty to localism and the need for decisions closest to the problem with a loyalty to coordination and decisions that span all parts of the problem. The advocate planner is redefined for this purpose as the advocate for a level of governmental decision.

Coordinative and functional planning

Comprehensive planning does not comprehend all the planning that must be done. Each function of government carries out its own specialized and detailed planning: health planning, transportation planning, school planning. These types of planning will be studied by the general planning agency in their interrelationships, for their secondary effects, and for their relative priorities. The specialized departments study and plan for their functions—as they should—as though nothing else mattered.

Better planning is done when there is sound, mutual respect between the people responsible for these two kinds of planning. The general planner, as the one working with all the departments, has the heavier burden of making the relationships go well by seeking to understand the needs and reasoning of the various departments and by providing useful services to them.

Planning objectives and constitutional ends

Planners are often painted in the colors of frustration—as having marvelous plans but facing insuperable obstacles. The search for more effective tools to implement the plans, therefore, continues.

It is often better to let plans for the immediate future be frustrated than to risk the frustration of the relatively few ends that we have embedded in the Constitution. Due process, removal of discrimination, freedom of belief, and individual privacy are constitutional ends that may impede or defeat a plan. A proper balance, then, calls for a better plan, not a more potent implementation.

The constraints and opportunities of planning

Adherence to planning, as to religion, requires continuing persuasion. Its work is abstracted from daily experience and its rewards will not come until the day after tomorrow.

It takes much time to find out which measures work well and which do not. Urban renewal programs, for example, were adopted as a novel solution to city rebuilding. Novel solutions can bring novel problems as they are implemented —some of them anticipated and some not. The problems of urban renewal included difficulties with adequate relocation of displaced families, and the need to relocate small businesses, as well as finding good new uses for cleared land, fitting isolated projects into plans for the entire city, and moving from wholesale clearance to selective clearance with more rehabilitation. The administration of urban renewal changed over a period of years as experiments around the country provided information on these difficulties. The reputation of urban renewal, however, still largely ignores its successes and, more particularly, its successful evolution.

Other experiments were conducted in spite of the predictions by planners of some built-in failure. Public housing was built in dense, tall buildings because of a political reluctance to allow subsidized housing to approximate normal housing. Expressways were built to consolidate the concentration of activity at the heart of a metropolis and had the effect of accelerating decentralization.

The urban renewal example illustrates an impatience with long-extended learning experiences. The other examples illustrate an unreadiness to follow advice without the benefit of long-extended learning. But both reactions share a political response to solutions that promise too much. The selling of planning often includes the overselling of specific programs. When the program does not solve everything, it appears that it will solve nothing.

Modesty in the claims for planning may achieve more appreciation of the benefits of planning. The immodest claim leads to profound disappointments and to oscillation between expectations that are too high and those that are too low. There need be no modesty, however, in acknowledging the present accomplishments of a process that can marshal the best information available and deal with gaps and uncertainties constructively; that is responsive to officialdom and also to citizens' opinion; that learns from precedents in other communities but also applies research to invent new precedents that better fit a particular community; that studies future needs to better manage the present and studies the present to better care for the future.

Paul Valéry said that "the future, like everything else, isn't what it used to be." Planning is our only effort to shape its surprises.

1   Martin Meyerson, "Building the Middle-Range Bridge for Comprehensive Planning," *Journal of* *the American Institute of Planners* 22 (Spring 1956): 58–64.

Historical development of American city planning

City planning in the American colonies may have had its beginnings in the seventeenth century fortress–villages, which were often surrounded by land farmed on a communal basis. Early colonial settlements that were preplanned with regard to their physical form commonly used a grid street system laid out on a scale appropriate to the number of inhabitants. This chapter begins by tracing American city planning from those early colonial times through the nineteenth century and then focuses on subsequent developments grouped into four periods: 1900 to 1920; 1920 to 1940; 1940 to 1960; and 1960 to the mid-1970s. Decennial census figures are presented as guideposts, and highlights are given in sociology, economics, and technology to support historical generalizations about planning. In addition to tracing the history of planning in America, the chapter shows how, during the twentieth century, planning evolved from a citizen based, reform-oriented movement to a profession that is currently at the heart of urban development processes.

Before 1900

In 1800, sixteen years after the ratification of the Treaty of Paris, which officially ended the Revolutionary War, only New York City and Philadelphia among American cities had more than 25,000 inhabitants. At that time a mere 6 percent of the 5 million residents of the new nation were "urban" dwellers by census count. This first year of the new century was also the first year of occupation of Washington, D.C., a vast new city on the Potomac planned by Major Pierre Charles L'Enfant, a French volunteer who had served on General Washington's staff. The preplanning of the capital city of the new nation concluded a 200 year period of planned community development during the colonial era. Intended to mark the success of the Revolution, this event also marked the end of that town planning tradition, because of the success of the Revolution it commemorated.

The colonial tradition

Preplanned community development had been the norm for the establishment of European colonial settlements in the New World since the Law of the Indies had fixed the form of Spanish municipalities in the Americas in the late 1500s.

New Haven, Connecticut, established in the 1630s, which was one of the earliest of the preplanned colonial towns, was laid out as a grid of nine square blocks. The grid pattern was also used in Philadelphia (1682), Detroit (1700), New Orleans (1718), and Savannah (1733). In Williamsburg (1699) a geometric variation was used having a main avenue with two secondary streets paralleling it and a mall intersecting the main axis, all provided to attain visual and symbolic linkages between the College of William and Mary, the colonial capitol, and the governor's palace.

During the latter half of the seventeenth century and most of the eighteenth century these colonial cities were quite small in population and accommodated few specialized land use activities in the modern sense. Industry as we know it was unknown, as was the commercial area. Virtually all production and commerce were conducted as elements of residential life.

These early settlements consisted of residences, streets, open public spaces, and a few specialized structures such as churches, government buildings, and warehouses. Even the largest of the American colonial cities was quite low in density of development, consisting of one and two story structures with large areas of gardens and arbors interspersed between the structures. At the time of the American Revolution New York City, the largest American city, had only 33,000 people, while the village–cities of the frontier were mere hamlets.

American colonial town planning traditions were predicated upon a European concept of the powers of municipal government derived from the development of the free town and the charter city during the Middle Ages. Such communities were municipal corporations of considerable authority commonly capable of owning and disposing of all vacant land in the city, of holding monopolies on certain aspects of trade, and of approving or disapproving physical changes to the city. They were generally authorized to play a heavy role in guiding and directing the physical form of the community as well as its social and economic policies.

As a result of the American Revolution and the subsequent adoption of the Constitution, however, American cities became creatures of their respective states. Almost all local authority belonged to state governments, with counties acting as agents of the states and with cities and towns (usually designated as municipal corporations) functioning under city charters or legislative enactments that gave them only certain designated powers. These powers were few, were strictly controlled by the states, and were concerned primarily with the maintenance of order and the provision of basic services. Cities had no clear authority to control, let alone direct, the development of private property, an authority the states then failed to exercise.

A new trend

The Ordinance of 1785, which established a system of rectangular survey coordinates for virtually all of the country west of the Appalachians, opened the American West to rapid settlement and resulted in rampant land speculation for private gain. Thus a century of cheap land was inaugurated. The same year saw the opening of the first American turnpike, which ran to the west of Alexandria, Virginia. Such a development pointed the way to future improvements in overland transportation, which would ease migration to the vast, sparsely settled western lands.

The late eighteenth century witnessed the evolution of an agrarian ethic of intense antiurban bias predicated on the belief that a life rooted in agriculture is the most humanly valuable way of life, and founded on the principles of nonrestrictive and minimal government.[1] This agrarian philosophy—eagerly adopted by American intellectuals and rapidly internalized in political theory—in combination with the decline of municipal government and vast land speculation, sounded the death knell of the American colonial town planning tradition.

The first order of business for the new country, upon attainment of independence, was the establishment of a capital for the new federal government. In 1790 Congress designated Philadelphia as the temporary seat of the government until 1800, when a new capital city was to be ready for occupancy on the Potomac. Three commissioners were appointed to arrive at a plan for the new capital. These men, with President Washington, commissioned Pierre Charles L'Enfant to design the new city. L'Enfant was a Frenchman in the grand monarchial tradition, Washington was an aristocrat, and Alexander Hamilton, then Secretary of the Treasury, had visions of a great industrial nation with large cities and a strong centralized federal government. These views, so much at

Figure 2–1   This nineteenth century Currier and Ives print,
American Country Life, Summers Evening, epitomizes the
agrarian outlook that has been a major part of
American history. This prevailing point of view,
in combination with land speculation and the decline
of municipal government, hastened the end of
American colonial town planning.

odds with the rapidly emerging agrarian philosophy, guided the evolution of the
city plan.

L'Enfant's plan focused on the Capital building and the "President's Palace"
(now the White House),[2] both situated on rises of ground commanding views of
the river. These were connected by a large diagonal boulevard, Pennsylvania
Avenue. From this L'Enfant developed a vast radial plan focused on these and
other major public structures and providing large public open spaces and plazas
as well as two vast green malls—one behind the Capital building and the other
behind the President's Palace—intersecting at the water's edge.[3] A small grid
street plan was superimposed over this grand composition of radial streets, public structures, plazas, and vast malls.

When confronted with requests by one of the commissioners for changes to
his plan, L'Enfant became difficult and was ultimately dismissed. Congress offered him $2,500 for his efforts. He demanded $100,000. He received nothing.
The task of laying out the capital city was entrusted to Andrew Ellicott, Surveyor General of the United States, who replicated L'Enfant's scheme and provided the necessary adjustments. Almost immediately the city became the focus
of speculative attention; it was abundantly evident that the municipal authorities
needed to demand compliance with the plan's requirements were seriously lacking. Such a circumstance in the new federal city was a clear indication of the

Date	Event	Comment
Pre-1789	European concept of municipal government powers	Cities were municipal corporations of considerable authority, commonly capable of owning and disposing of all vacant land in the city, of holding monopolies on certain aspects of trade, and of approving or disapproving physical changes to the city.
1785	The Ordinance of 1785	An opening of a century of cheap land that resulted in rampant land speculation for private gain.
1789	U.S. Constitution	American cities become creatures of the state. State gives municipal corporations limited powers; little ability to control land development.
1790–1810	Plans for Washington, D.C., Detroit, and New York	Plans for these cities were rejected, changed, ignored, in keeping with the concept of minimal government responsibility, rampant land speculation, and minimal interference with private property.
1856	Site for Central Park in New York City purchased	The first of a series of municipal purchases made in various cities for park purposes.
1867	New York City Tenement House Law	Legitimized the railroad flat with a few improvements, precluding by law the development of anything worse.
	San Francisco ordinance	Prohibited development of slaughterhouses, hog storage facilities, and hide curing plants in certain districts of the city.
1877	*Munn* v. *Illinois*, 94 U.S. 113, 126 (1877)	A landmark decision that paved the way for future governmental intervention in private development.
1879	New York City Tenement House Law	Known as the Old Law, the ordinance required that new tenement buildings be constructed on a dumbbell plan, providing a narrow air shaft. Also, two toilets were required on each floor.
1893	The World's Columbian Exposition	The White City becomes a model for what is possible in urban America.
1898	Ebenezer Howard, *Tomorrow: A Peaceful Path to Real Reform*	The birth of the concept of the New Town movement, wherein the public took a stand on urban expansion. Greenbelt garden cities were to be constructed, surrounded by greenbelts of publicly held land permanently committed to agriculture, thus precluding urban expansion and eliminating speculative land costs.
1907	The Hartford Commission on a City Plan	The first official, local, and permanent town planning board in the United States.
1909	Burnham's plan for Chicago	The generally acknowledged beginning of modern city planning. Proposed public housing as a proper government function, but early city plans proposed no changes to or control over private property.
	Welch v. *Swasey*, 214 U.S. 91 (1909)	The first clear-cut nationwide authority for communities to regulate development of private property through limitation of building heights, and to vary these heights by zone.
	Wisconsin Planning Enabling Act	The first enabling act granting a clear right to cities to engage in city planning.
	Land use zoning ordinance passed in Los Angeles	The beginning of the zoning concept.

Figure 2–2   Development of public intervention in private property.

Date	Event	Comment
1912	*Eubank* v. *City of Richmond,* 226 U.S. 137 (1912)	Setback legislation declared constitutional.
1915	*Hadacheck* v. *Sebastian,* 239 U.S. 394, 408 (1915)	Provided that the restriction of future profitable uses was not a taking of property without just compensation.
1916	New York City Zoning Code adopted	The first comprehensive zoning code in America, prepared under the leadership of Edward Bassett.
1920	*Town of Windsor* v. *Whitney,* 95 Conn. 357, 111 A.3 54 (1920)	Made land subdivision regulations possible by holding that dedication of streets as a prerequisite to platting was possible.
1925	Cincinnati adopts comprehensive plan	The first officially adopted plan; a legal connection between zoning and the plan.
1926	*Village of Euclid* v. *Ambler Realty Company,* 272 U.S. 365 (1926)	Established the constitutionality of comprehensive zoning—the Supreme Court's basic constitutional building block for American city planning and zoning.
1928	Radburn, New Jersey	One of the first and most influential of American new towns.
	Standard City Planning Enabling Act	Provided the basic model ordinance adopted by city councils for the next fifty years.
1934	U.S. Housing Act of 1934	The federal government enters the housing field.
1937	U.S. Housing Act of 1937	The foundation for most federal public housing programs for the next forty years. Local housing authorities use state granted eminent domain to acquire housing sites.
1949	U.S. Housing Act of 1949	The beginning of urban redevelopment whereby cities interfere substantially in the local private land market.
1954	U.S. Housing Act of 1954	Extended the clearance program of the 1949 act to include rehabilitation and conservation, thus increasing the degree of public involvement in land use decisions.
Late 1960s– 1970s	The Quiet Revolution	A movement in states such as Hawaii, Massachusetts, California, Oregon, and Florida, in which state government reasserted its involvement in local land use decisions. Examples: Florida established the concept of developments of regional impact and areas of critical concern wherein the state participated in local land use decisions; Massachusetts passed a law authorizing the state to review and override local zoning ordinances if they discriminated against low income families.
1975	*A Model Land Development Code* adopted by the American Law Institute	A new model code that "replaces" the standard enabling acts of the 1920s. Considerable emphasis on the relationship between state and local governments in the land use control regulatory system.

Figure 2–2   (continued).

urban future that lay before the country in the century ahead as the new capital city opened for occupancy in 1800.

Elsewhere in the country, at the beginning of the nineteenth century, large scale city plans developed along the lines of traditional American colonial town planning fared badly. The governor and judges' plan for Detroit, authorized by Congress in 1806 after a fire leveled the settlement on 11 June 1805, was a vast radial plan of boulevards, parade grounds, and "circuses" planned to cover the burned out area of the original city and an additional area of more than 4,000 hectares of the adjoining wilderness of the Michigan Territory. When disagreements developed between the creator of the plan, Judge Woodward, and the governor and the other judges, the plan was repealed and replaced by a grid system more amenable to minimal government expenditure and maximum potential for land speculation.

Similarly, the plan by Joseph Mangin (surveyor and architect for the city of New York) for the expansion of New York City—a plan based on public squares, public structures, and wide boulevards—was rejected in favor of a plan that was more in keeping with the new urban realities of minimal governmental responsibility, rampant land speculation, and minimal interference with private property. New York City had grown so rapidly during the first few years of the nineteenth century that in 1807 a commission was charged with laying out the undeveloped area of Manhattan Island—"in such a manner as to promote the health of the city." The commissioners' plan, filed in 1811, was an unbroken grid street plan extending to the north for over 100 blocks, irrespective of the rough terrain of the island, relieved by just one small parade ground, a single public market, and five very small parks commonly sited on terrain undesirable for private development. This plan, providing for a minimum number of public amenities and activities and a maximum number of identical speculative building lots, promoted the health of the speculative land market and was clearly symbolic of the new era.

Also in 1811, the Cumberland Road (the National Road)[4] was begun. This road, the first major road in the United States constructed with federal funds, became a conduit for immigration from the East Coast to the seemingly limitless farmlands of the interior.

By 1820 the factory system of industrial production was clearly evident as a force for economic and demographic concentration in the United States. The early factories, usually multistory brick mills located at the fall line, as they were based on water power, absorbed some of the local agricultural unemployment that resulted from improvements in agricultural production methods. These factories were shortly augmented by mills that were free of river-based geographic constraints, as they were powered by descendants of the steam engine invented by James Watt in 1763.

The Erie Canal, begun in 1817 and operational in 1825, complemented the National Road as the way to the American West. For a brief period settlements vied with each other to be on the main line and the feeder lines of canal systems, but the canal was soon to be supplanted as a major means of transportation by the railroad. The railroad corporations which ultimately became the New York Central, the Pennsylvania, and the Baltimore and Ohio railroad lines were formed between 1823 and 1831. Railroad track in the United States increased from 37 kilometers in 1830 to over 4,500 kilometers in 1840.

Expansion: its rapidity and its results

A small grid plan town was laid out on the site of present-day Chicago[5] in 1830, at which time the first tenement houses were being built in New York City. These tenements would be occupied in the 1840s by the first of the massive waves of European immigration that swelled the size of American cities. In 1840 only three American cities had populations of more than 100,000. By 1850 there were nine such cities, and over 4.5 million Americans lived in cities and towns.

The three major ports of entry for the immigrants of the nineteenth century were New York City, which had been provided with a grid plan in 1811; Philadelphia, which was founded as a grid city in the 1680s; and the new grid city of Chicago. This form of street planning was generally unfamiliar to the Northern European peasants and to the residents of the European medieval organic towns who began to flock to our shores in mid-century. To most of these immigrants the plan of these ports of entry was symbolic of their new lives in the New World. As they passed through these ports and moved inland they carried this grid plan with them and created thousands of grid plan communities west of the Appalachians. This development was also reinforced by the rectangular land survey system established by the Ordinance of 1785 and by the greed of land speculators who preplanned grid settlements and sold deeds on the streets of New York.

In addition to these frontier agricultural settlements, another form of city was evolving in America in the mid-nineteenth century—the great industrial city. These cities were focused on railroad transportation, as the public road system was scarcely developed. Such cities contained center city factories surrounding power sources; their extent was circumscribed by the efficient transmission of power by belts. In this way, large brick industrial mills, usually three to six stories high, arose near the core of the city. This system, which employed a vast amount of cheap labor, demanded a population within easy walking distance of the mill—usually no more than a kilometer (0.62 miles) or two—and resulted in large concentrations of tenement flats around factory sites.

The residence of the worker in New York City and other large industrial cities in the United States in 1850 was frequently the "railroad flat,"[6] a walk-up structure that was generally five to seven stories high, 7.6 meters wide (1 meter = 39.37 inches), and 22 to 24 meters long on a 7.6 meter by 30.5 meter lot. Constructed solidly in rows across entire block faces, these units had four apartments on each floor surrounding a central common staircase. The rooms in these apartments were constructed in tandem, with just one room in each apartment provided with a window or two for light and air. No sanitary facilities or water supply were provided for in these structures. The small rear yard contained a multiseat outhouse and often a well, resulting in deplorable conditions of sanitation and public health.

During the first half of the nineteenth century virtually no governmental actions were initiated to ameliorate the worsening of housing and living conditions in America through control or redirection of private development. Court injunctions were occasionally issued against specific establishments, but these were few and far between. As a result of this laissez-faire philosophy of private enterprise, of the weak municipal authorities of the new state-centered political system, and of the political tenets and antiurban biases of the agrarian philosophy, some of the worst housing and living conditions experienced by modern man were created in America during the coming half century.

The rapid growth of New York City in the early 1850s brought the lack of public open space in the plan of 1811 to public attention. This lack was rectified in 1853 when purchase of a site for a "central park" was authorized by the New York State legislature. This site, purchased in 1856, extended east and west from Fifth Avenue to Eighth Avenue, and from 59th Street in the south to 106th Street—and later to 110th Street—in the north.

Frederick Law Olmsted, Sr., was appointed superintendent of construction in 1857 and in the following year, in association with Calvert Vaux, he won the competition for the design of the park. His "greensward" plan for Central Park consisted of a vast English garden of "natural" terrain and lakes, curved paths, and irregular plantings. This first English garden to be realized in America on so large a scale became the model for all city parks and remains so to this day. By 1867 park planning was under way in Baltimore, Philadelphia, Cincinnati, and St. Louis. Shortly thereafter, Chicago purchased 770 hectares of land (1 hectare = 2.47 acres) for park purposes.

The postwar era:
to the turn of the century

American cities of the North grew enormously during the Civil War under the impetus of war production, intensifying already serious housing problems. Housing reformers arose, denouncing the do-nothing attitudes of government and demanding public control of housing conditions. In 1867 the first New York City Tenement House Law was enacted, legitimizing the railroad flat with a few improvements and precluding by law the development of anything worse. In the same year a San Francisco ordinance prohibited development of slaughterhouses, hog storage facilities, and hide curing plants in certain districts of the city. This 1867 ordinance, being preventive rather than after-the-fact and restricting land uses by physical areas of the city, set the stage for the further evolution of land use zoning in the United States. The West Coast communities generally took the lead in the development of land use controls, whereas East Coast communities focused on legislation regulating the physical characteristics of tenements and other urban structures.

The period 1860–70 also saw the beginning of suburbanization in the United States, with the creation of small settlements beyond the cities for the residences of owner–managers capable of affording them. Riverside, Illinois, west of Chicago on the Des Plaines River, was planned by Frederick Law Olmsted, Sr., in 1869. Here, as in Central Park, he applied English garden concepts and produced a system of gently curving tree lined streets, single family detached houses with deep setbacks of lawn and shade trees, and large areas of informal parkland, both along the river bank and interspersed throughout the community. This suburban[7] quasi-rural, and exclusively residential pattern of perimeter development became the status symbol of the owner–manager class in the United States. The Riverside pattern has been copied in the suburban development of virtually every major city in the country and still dominates concepts of land subdivision for single family detached units.

After the Civil War mass transit was at first commonly provided by horse drawn vehicles. The horsecar remained the primary means of urban transportation until 1890, although the elevated steam railroad was introduced in New York in 1869, and in 1873 the first cable car line was constructed in San Francisco.

In 1877 the Supreme Court of the United States made the following ruling:

When, therefore, one devotes his property to a use in which the public has an interest, he, in effect, grants to the public an interest in that use, and must submit to be controlled by the public for the common good, to the extent of the interest he has thus created.[8]

This decision paved the way for future governmental intervention in private development, implying the legitimacy of the development control ordinances passed in San Francisco and New York in 1867.

The development controls enacted in the New York Tenement House Law of 1867 were expanded in 1879 to require that new tenements be constructed on a dumbbell plan, providing a narrow air shaft between adjacent structures with windows opening onto this air shaft from the interior rooms. This law, known as the "Old Law," also required two toilets on each floor accessible from the common stair hall, at least seventeen cubic meters of air per occupant, a window opening of at least one square meter in each room, and no more than 65 percent land coverage of other than corner lots.

The United States census of the following year, 1880, disclosed that New York had become the first American city of over a million population. The massive immigration of the next decade[9] flooded the urban fabric of every major American city, resulting in increased congestion and the rapid construction of tenement structures. In Chicago new business buildings rose to sixteen or more stories in response to the soaring land values of the 1880s, introducing the now commonplace vertical character of downtown business areas. By 1890 Chicago as well as New York had a population of over a million, and the metropolis gained increasing significance as a factor in American life.

In addition to entering the established communities, this wave of immigration also populated the "model" company towns built by the large American corporations to serve their industrial plants. (Such a town was Pullman, Illinois, built by George Pullman in 1881.)

While the 1880s saw the development of extensive tenement house slums, they also witnessed the expansion of suburbanization for the owner–managers. This expansion, brought about by significant improvements in railroad service for commuting, included Greenwich, Connecticut; Chestnut Hill, Pennsylvania; and Lake Forest, Illinois. The first social center for affluent suburbanites, "the Country Club," was built at Brookline, Massachusetts, in this period; while the first practical electric trolley—soon to become the dominant means of urban transportation in America—moved over the streets of Richmond, Virginia, in 1888.

At the beginning of the 1890s, business and industrial uses were intermixed throughout the core of the American city, often occupying parts of, or directly adjacent to, tenement houses. On the congested streets of the city—frequently of mud and often strewn with garbage—the contrast between the personal wealth of the few and the abject poverty of the many was startling. Political corruption of the worst sort generated little enthusiasm for increased governmental responsibilities in a system where *public* meant *of poor quality,* as there was little in the public area to stimulate pride or to engender confidence.

The deplorable conditions of tenement house life in New York City were exposed by the journalist Jacob Riis in *How the Other Half Lives* (1890) and *The Children of the Poor* (1892).[10] These disclosures outraged the public, with the result that in 1892 the United States Congress appropriated $20,000 for an investigation of slums in cities of over 200,000 population. This study was the first federal recognition of the problems of slums and urban housing in America and was the harbinger of extensive twentieth century programs of the federal government.

In the last decade of the nineteenth century, when municipal government in the United States was probably at its lowest state in the history of the country, the National Municipal League was founded (1894) as a citizen based group for the reform of state and local government, especially that of cities. The league's influence in the decades to follow was notable, especially in the referendum and recall and in the adoption of the council-manager form of government.

To commemorate the anniversary of the discovery of America, Congress in 1890 designated Chicago as the site of a great world's fair. This fair, the World's Columbian Exposition, opened 1 May 1893. It was designed by a team headed by the Chicago architect Daniel H. Burnham and including Charles Follen McKim of the architectural firm of McKim, Mead and White; Frederick Law Olmsted, Sr., the landscape architect; and Augustus St. Gaudens, the sculptor. This team produced the first example in the United States of a great group of public buildings and public spaces designed in relation to each other, and specifically designed to delight and impress the citizen–visitor and to fulfill that visitor's every need. For the first time, in America, a large scale area was built at one time and on the basis of a unified design with the guidance of a detailed general plan. This fair, also known as the "White City,"[11] was a model for urban America. Well over 2 million Americans flocked to see the "White City," and many left committed to realizing some portion of that citizen centered good order in their home communities. Burnham came to be known as "the father of

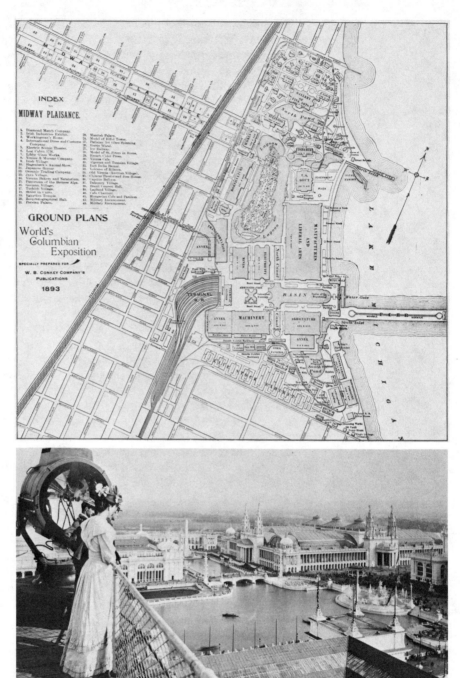

Figure 2–3 The World's Columbian Exposition, 1893.
Built on the lakefront eight miles south of
Chicago's central business district, the exposition
had an enormous and a long-term influence on
city planning in the United States. The
visitors' perceptions were of a handsome,
gleaming white city, a stark contrast to the
urban areas of the time.

city planning in the United States" for his contributions to American city planning during the first decade of the twentieth century; these contributions were based on his experiences at Chicago in 1893.

Upon the termination of the Columbian Exposition, the economic recession experienced by the rest of the nation at that time, which had been temporarily forestalled in Chicago by the exposition, became a serious reality. A violent confrontation developed in the "model" city of Pullman, Illinois, a short distance from Chicago, and federal troops were called in. This Pullman strike of 1894 intensified social discord in Chicago and effectively halted the creation of other such "model" communities in America for decades.

In the spring of 1897, with the social discord and economic conditions relative to the Pullman strike still fresh in mind, Burnham urged that public works planning be undertaken in Chicago on a massive scale, both for the creation of employment and for a socially unifying civic pride. Much to Burnham's disappointment the city's commercial and political leadership failed to act on his suggestions and this concept of socioeconomic reform through large scale construction of public facilities was to lie dormant for several years.[12]

Ebenezer Howard, a stenographer to the British Parliament, wrote *Tomorrow: A Peaceful Path to Real Reform,* published in 1898.[13] This book had a considerable impact on American cities in the twentieth century. Howard proposed to solve the industrial slum problems of the Western World through creation of small self-sufficient garden cities of finite population, surrounded by greenbelts of publicly held land permanently committed to agriculture, thus precluding urban expansion and eliminating speculative land costs. These garden cities focused on green open spaces and public buildings, with schools provided at the center of subunits separated by major streets and with limited industrial establishments located at the perimeter, which was immediately adjacent to the open countryside of the greenbelt. Urban growth was to be accommodated through addition of such static satellite units around a similarly limited and structured central city providing common services. The neighborhood unit concept, the basic building block of the American city following World War II, and the greenbelt towns constructed by the United States government during the Great Depression, evolved from Howard's concepts propounded in 1898.

The American city became increasingly congested and complex at the turn of the century. An elevated railroad wound around the downtown section of Chicago to form the Loop, and the first electric underground railroad subway system was constructed in Boston in 1897. Tall buildings, rising everywhere in response to rising land values, blocked sunlight and inhibited the free flow of air to the streets below. In 1898 a Massachusetts statute was passed limiting the height of buildings around Boston's Copley Square to 27.4 meters. Such actions were commonly viewed during the nineteenth century as invasions of property rights. In 1899, in a landmark decision,[14] the Massachusetts Supreme Court upheld the statute, establishing the public's right to protect and preserve light and air through enactment of maximum building height regulations.

The year 1899 saw the close of a century of extraordinary national and urban population growth, during which time the population of the United States grew from 5 million to 76 million. In 1900, 40 percent of that population lived in cities, thirty-eight of which had more than 100,000 inhabitants.

From 1900 to 1920

In spite of the efforts toward tenement house control made in New York City during the nineteenth century, that city's tenement conditions at the turn of the century were appalling. Lawrence Veiller, a New York housing reformer,[15] led a massive effort to improve these conditions; this resulted in a voluminous report on the conditions of housing in the city and the passage in 1901 of a "New

Law" that Veiller wrote. Unlike earlier tenement laws, the New Law was vigorously enforced. It provided for *required* permits for construction, alteration, and conversion; inspection upon completion; penalties for noncompliance; and, most significantly, a permanent tenement house department to administer and enforce the law. Among other conditions, it required construction on two New York City lots, wide light and air courts between structures, and a toilet and running water in each apartment. The New Law, which became the model for tenement laws throughout the United States, was one of the forerunners of the various reforms that would affect American cities in the twentieth century.

A new era of plans

Although the "White City" of 1893 had made a profound impression on Americans, the economic recession of the mid-1890s suppressed the new enthusiasm for citywide planning. With the increased prosperity that followed the Spanish-American War (1898), this interest again emerged. In 1900 an annual meeting of the American Institute of Architects was held in Washington, D.C., to commemorate the centennial of the capital city. This meeting called attention to L'Enfant's plan, to the "White City" of the Columbian Exposition, and to the disorderly condition of the city in 1900, a result of unrestrained free enterprise, land speculation, and public neglect. Senator James McMillan, impressed by this meeting, appointed a subcommittee to the Senate Committee on the District of Columbia, charging this subcommittee with the restoration of L'Enfant's plan. This McMillan Committee, headed by Daniel Burnham, was the same basic team that had designed the World's Columbian Exposition.[16] It was the first group in America to be identified as experts on city planning and given the status of professional city planning consultants. The McMillan Committee Plan, reported in 1902, focused on restoration of the Mall, the siting of new public buildings, the creation of a regional park system, and the location of monuments. The plan was enthusiastically endorsed by President Theodore Roosevelt, thus establishing a federal sanction for engaging in city planning. The planning movement resulting from the McMillan Plan was a reform movement. Burnham considered himself a leader of the American Republican Progressive movement, which attempted, through the establishment of public works siting and design by public policy, to reduce graft in public building placement and construction, to improve the public environment for all to enjoy, and to effect a transfer of surplus wealth from the rich to all citizens through investment in public structures, plazas, and parks that would be available to all, owned by all, and objects of a socially unifying civic pride.

In 1902 Tom Johnson, reform mayor of Cleveland, convinced Burnham to head a team charged with preparing a plan for a group of public buildings in downtown Cleveland. Johnson intended this project to eliminate a notorious slum area, to provide necessary public facilities, and to stimulate Cleveland citizens to an intense civic pride resulting in an identity with the city and its government. The result of this work, the Cleveland Group Plan of 1903, was the first plan for an American city to be realized after the McMillan Plan for the capital. It stimulated similar "civic center" plans throughout the United States.

In 1904 a civic association in San Francisco, headed by a former mayor, James D. Phelan, invited Burnham to prepare a plan for the city. Burnham and his new planning assistant, Edward H. Bennett, produced a plan that was not limited to a grouping of structures in the civic center: it was a plan of radial and concentric highways, a highway outer belt, extensive shoreline parks, and a mass transit subway.[17] Smoke-producing industry was to be located on the basis of wind-drift patterns and existing and future residential areas were to be planned to produce residential districts bounded by major streets, thus reducing through traffic. These aspects of this plan became city planning dogma in America for the next three generations. This plan, the first application of Burnham's principles to an entire large American city, was published in 1906.

The first official, local, and permanent town planning board in the United States, the Hartford Commission on a City Plan, was created by the Connecticut legislature in 1907. This was followed by the creation of similar boards in Milwaukee in 1908 and in Chicago, Detroit, and Baltimore in 1909. These early boards, commonly consisting of municipal officials and citizen appointees, successful businessmen and bankers, plus a large complement of architects and landscape architects, had little funds, even less authority, and an unclear role in the hierarchy of government. These early boards were created to sponsor the development of a city plan, to oversee its execution, and to encourage financial support of public construction projects. Lacking departmental status, these boards had little direct contact with operating agencies of city government, and the chairmen of the boards lacked equal status with department heads in dealing with the municipal executive officer. These early boards were generally advisory to the city council and were really not branches of municipal government at all.

Ebenezer Howard's garden city concept was realized for the first time at Letchworth, England, begun in 1903. Letchworth was designed as a city for some 35,000 people, surrounded by an extensive greenbelt. This new town was planned in full detail by Barry Parker and Raymond Unwin. Shortly thereafter, Unwin was challenged by a wealthy social worker to create an area of London with healthy housing available to a wide income range and provided with a full range of civic activities. The result of his efforts was Hampstead Garden Suburb, built at the northern terminus of the London subway system in 1907, the first comprehensive neighborhood design. Unwin applied Howard's concepts of satellite towns to the idea of small satellite residential districts that would never grow, being bounded by major streets, with segregated industry (in Howard's scheme at the perimeter, in Unwin's in London) and with the entire project area focused on major green open spaces and public facilities.

In 1907 the United States experienced its highest record for immigration: 1,285,000 people in one year. These immigrants flooded into the New Law tenements of New York City and into every other major city of America, including the steel city of Pittsburgh, where housing and public health were in deplorable condition. In 1907 the first systematic statistical city survey in America was begun in Pittsburgh. In this study, housing, health, and social conditions were carefully surveyed, compiled, and plotted as to geographic location. Correlations and analyses were then made, establishing the foundation for a kind of data based city planning that was to emerge in the United States a generation later.

Burnham, having completed a 1906 plan of San Francisco, spent virtually all of 1907 and 1908 working on a plan of Chicago commissioned by the Commercial Club, a prestigious businessmen's association. This plan, released with symbolic intent on 4 July 1909, was the first metropolitan–regional plan in the United States. Burnham's daring proposals covered a vast area—a radius of forty-eight kilometers from the Loop, projecting a great outer belt of regional parks and reservations, an intricate web of radial and concentric highways,[18] and a lakefront park system of more than thirty kilometers. The plan also grouped and relocated railroad lines and terminals, created many center city parks and broad radial tree lined boulevards, straightened the Chicago River, and projected a vast new civic center and a two level boulevard (now Wacker Drive) paralleling the Chicago River. Burnham also suggested that the city might be required in the near future to initiate a public housing program. In 1909 no such housing existed anywhere in the United States. In the context of the times, the plan was visionary in its outlook. Even today, after almost three-

Make no little plans, they have no magic   (Burnham Plan 1909).   The Burnham Plan [is] that great planning spectacular which marked the last hurrah of the Age of Titans shortly before those worthies retreated to Lake Forest and left the town to the Irish. . . .

The Burnham Plan was nothing if not transcendent. With a shout of "I will!" its makers rose above reality and roared off after "order and sanity" like a crusader pursuing the Turk, and with a common motive: diversion. Immersed in the old plan's messianic rhetoric and gorgeous visionary drawings—detailed to the last neoclassic pilaster—you would never know the town was in a social and economic convulsion, that poverty, squalor and disease ruled great portions of it and corrupt politicians the rest, that

anarchists were raving and socialists organizing, and that muckrakers, investigating committees and labor unions were harassing the very business barons whose Commercial Club fathered the "Plan of Chicago."

There was method in this esthetic madness, of course: surface symbols—grand boulevards and parks, a splendid lakefront, brassy public monuments—were to rouse "civic patriotism" and lower social pressure. But it did not work. After a brave start, circumstance overwhelmed the Burnham Plan—a fact that obsesses the modern planner.

Source: Comment by Bud Botts, Chicago City Missionary Society, in *Journal of the American Institute of Planners* 33 (September 1967): 357–58.

quarters of a century, many of its recommendations and guidelines are still being followed.

The fact that the plans for Chicago (1909), San Francisco (1906), Cleveland (1903), and Washington, D.C. (1902), dealt almost exclusively with public buildings, parks, and streets, proposing no changes to or control over private property, was neither accidental nor solely a function of the nature of Burnham's planning theories. Control of private development by public law lacked clear widespread state and federal supreme court support during this period. Publicly owned lands and facilities, on the other hand, were clearly susceptible to public control. These practical plans were based on a known ability to implement their proposals. But in 1909, in *Welch* v. *Swasey*,[19] the U.S. Supreme Court established the first clearcut nationwide authority for communities to regulate the development of private property through limitation of building heights, and to vary these heights by zone.

The first state enabling act granting a clear right to municipalities within its borders to engage in city planning activities was passed by the state of Wisconsin in 1909. In the same year the first formal course in city planning was offered at Harvard, followed shortly thereafter by a course at the University of Illinois.

A land use zoning ordinance was passed in Los Angeles in 1909 that created a multitude of use zones applicable to large areas of undeveloped land.[20] Virtually all previous land use zoning had been established to protect existing patterns of development. This ordinance signaled the beginning of the use of this zoning concept to control future urban development. The year 1909 also saw the first national conference on city planning, held in Washington, D.C., to determine what was happening in city planning in the United States and to publicize these efforts.

Expansion in the second decade

By 1910 there were almost 92 million Americans, 46 percent of whom were urban, and over fifty cities of more than 100,000 inhabitants. There were also 500,000 automobiles registered in the United States. This plaything of the rich was about to flood the urban fabric of cities built for horsecars, trolleys, and foot traffic. These same cities were about to experience a vast pre–World War I growth based on extended railroad access and an expansion of trolley routes. In reaction to this growth the Russell Sage Foundation, impressed by Unwin's neighborhood design at Hampstead Garden Suburb, sponsored the first demonstration of this concept in the United States. This project, Forest Hills Gardens, located at a site along the Long Island Railroad near New York City, was designed by Frederick Law Olmsted, Jr., and Grosvenor Atterbury, with the advisory services of Unwin. Initiated in 1910 and completed in 1913, it served as a model for American suburban land development.

When Daniel Burnham died in 1912, leadership in American city planning passed to Frederick Law Olmsted, Jr. Unlike Burnham, Olmsted believed that the city plan should include all uses of land, private as well as public, and that the act of planning should involve continuous updating to assure that the city plan maintained a relevance to both current urban issues and the evolving long-range aspirations of citizens. Such municipal planning and control of private development gained momentum in 1912 when the U.S. Supreme Court declared the constitutionality of municipal control of the horizontal location of buildings on private property, via setback legislation, in *Eubank* v. *City of Richmond*.[21]

Eighteen cities in America had planning boards in 1913. Shortly thereafter this number increased markedly, as state after state passed enabling acts permitting their municipalities to engage in planning. In 1913 New Jersey required the referral of all land subdivision plats to the local planning board for review. This was the beginning of land subdivision control as a function of city planning in the United States. Massachusetts in 1913 made planning mandatory for its local governments.

Numerous significant steps were taken in the years immediately preceding World War I to eliminate the graft, corruption, and simple incompetence that characterized American local government and that influenced the vesting of city planning responsibilities in semi-independent politically detached citizen advisory commissions.

The council-manager form of government, initiated in Staunton, Virginia, in 1908, and first gaining national attention in Dayton, Ohio, in 1914, was substantially promoted at that time by the National Municipal League as a means toward urban reform.

Land use zoning, which developed in the West Coast communities and which was of critical importance to the concept of planning for and municipal control of private land development, came to the U.S. Supreme Court in 1915 in *Hadacheck* v. *Sebastian*. Few American communities had enacted land use control ordinances, as the Court might well have held that restriction of higher future profit uses was an unconstitutional taking of property without just compensation. In *Hadacheck* v. *Sebastian* the Court agreed with the California Supreme Court that "regulation was not precluded by the fact 'that . . . the value of investments made . . . prior to any legislative action will be greatly diminished.' "[22]

If the Court did not consider reduction in value of real prior investments to be valid grounds for declaring the ordinance unconstitutional, it was highly improbable that a reduction of potential future value would be held to invalidate an ordinance. Many municipal leaders interpreted this case as granting the Supreme Court's implicit approval to land use zoning and began to prepare land use control programs.

A New York commission had been created in 1913 to devise a scheme for the effective control of future urban development of the city. Under the leadership of Edward M. Bassett, this commission arrived at the concept of a comprehensive zoning code—a device in which land use controls, controls on building height, and control of building setbacks and yards are integrated in a single ordinance. With the *Hadacheck* decision in 1915, all three of these elements had been given constitutional approval, explicit or implied, by the U.S. Supreme Court (height control by zone in *Welch* v. *Swasey;* building setback control in *Eubank* v. *City of Richmond;* land use control in *Hadacheck* v. *Sebastian*). This New York City Zoning Code, the first comprehensive zoning code in the United States was adopted in 1916. This zoning code tended to freeze current land uses rather than propose beneficial change; in addition, it was unrelated to a general plan for the fulfillment of community aspirations (in fact, it was a substitute for such a plan), was generally protective of current land interests, and was totally unrelated to any reasonable forecasts or projections of future land use demand. This "comprehensive" zoning ordinance was rapidly copied and adopted by many other large American cities, signaling a major shift away from governmental alteration of urban form in the public interest through public works and toward a highly conservative legal and administrative control of private construction.

Another significant event in 1916 was the signing by President Wilson of the Federal-Aid Road Act. At that time the nation's intercity road system was barely passable. This act assisted state highway construction, providing two lane concrete roads in a countrywide interstate system. At that time there were 4.7 million automobiles on the streets of America in 1917, an increase of 4.2 million since 1910.

Approximately 2,000 people attended the ninth national planning conference, held at Kansas City, Missouri, in 1917. At this meeting a small group of members decided to create a professional society to consider "the technical aspects of the new science of city planning." The result was the establishment of the American City Planning Institute (ACPI).[23] The fifty-two charter members included architects, landscape architects, engineers, attorneys, and developers. Frederick Law Olmsted, Jr., served as the institute's first president.

According to statistics the United States became an urban nation as it entered the 1920s. The census of 1920 reported that 51 percent of the 106.4 million persons residing in the United States at that time lived in urban areas.

From 1920 to 1940

An era of unprecedented growth

The 1920s, a period of great prosperity, witnessed a considerable expansion in automobile ownership in the United States. By 1930 there would be 26 million automobiles in America, approximately one for every five people—an increase of over 20 million automobiles since 1917. The combination of prosperity and the automobile resulted in the first massive wave of middle income migrants from the central city to the suburbs, as this group became free for the first time of dependence on public transit. In this period of massive suburbanization, the emphasis in city planning was of necessity placed on control of the development of land areas at the perimeter of the city and on immediate public works planning, particularly the construction and widening of streets to accommodate the automobile. Land use zoning of undeveloped areas, land subdivision controls, and other legal and administrative regulative devices made up most planning activities, as engineers, lawyers, and administrators rose to positions of planning leadership.

The basic legal framework for the control of private development in the United States was created in the 1920s. This framework emphasized control and protection, by ordinance, of the physical character of the new middle income residential areas constructed at the perimeter of the city, maintenance of the status quo in the central city, and fulfillment of the interests of business and industry in extensive overzoning for these uses. This land focused, middle-income-oriented, and suburban, business, and industry dominated legal framework that shaped the American suburbs of the 1920s also became the basic framework for the next great wave of suburbanization—that which followed the end of World War II.

By 1920 many American cities required planning board approval of land subdivision plats based on the application of standards for such factors as width of right-of-way, maximum block length, and conformance with the predetermined location of major streets. These standards and mapped locations were established in ordinances creating an official *major street plan*[24] and requiring that all private developments comply with its requirements. These requirements often included dedication of streets to the public prior to the platting of abutting property. The courts upheld this requirement, as in *Town of Windsor* v. *Whitney*[25] in 1920, holding that there is no taking of property as the giving is just a precondition to platting and therefore free of municipal coercion. This logic would be expanded in the 1930s to require the mandatory dedication of parklands through land subdivision control.

Figure 2–4   The threefold increase in automobiles in Knox County, Tennessee, from 1920 to 1925 dramatized the changes taking place across America. "What will it be in 1930?" a report of Harland Bartholomew and Associates asked in 1927.

With the rise in automobile ownership, the suburban expansion of American cities in the 1920s outstripped the speed of municipal annexation and resulted in the development of vast areas at the edges of cities, beyond their municipal boundaries. In addition to fostering extraterritorial controls, this development led to the creation of many county planning authorities capable of dealing with the areas surrounding the central city. Los Angeles County created the first county planning board in the United States in 1922.

The explosive suburban expansion resulted in the initiation of a monumental study of the future of the New York metropolitan area by the Russell Sage Foundation: the *Regional Survey of New York and Its Environs.*[26] Begun in 1922 and undertaken primarily under the direction of Thomas Adams, a distinguished British planner and a charter member of the ACPI, this study was not completed until 1929. Another charter member of the ACPI, J. C. Nichols, responded to this new expansion of the American city by creating the world's first automobile-oriented shopping center, Country Club Plaza, at the outskirts of Kansas City, Missouri, in 1922.

The compact retail sales and business areas of the pre-1920s era, clustered at the core of the city and centered around railroad terminals and trolley stops, began to move outward with the spread of the automobile, making every major street a potential commercial district. Thus, the prosperity of the 1920s, combined with the automobile and generally complemented by commercial zoning of virtually every major street, resulted in extensive lineal strip commercial development. Gross overconstruction for commercial use and street congestion created by a vast increase in automobile traffic resulted in decreased access; this was ultimately reflected in extensive areas of vacant or poorly maintained business facilities along the major streets of the cities—a condition that can still be seen in hundreds of cities.

During the early 1920s most land use zoning was based on broad use categories such as *residence, business,* and *industry.* But many communities were making finer distinctions. Some were creating zones in which the single family detached residence was the only type of residence permitted. State courts supported this concept, generally basing their support, as in *Brett* v. *Building Commissioner of Brookline,*[27] on protection of the public health through reduced danger of fire and increased light and air, and on an inability to find that such control bears no conceivable relationship to the protection of the public health, safety, morals and/or welfare—or, as in *Miller* v. *Board of Public Works of the City of Los Angeles,*[28] on a presumed relationship between inducement of ownership and community stability, interest in public affairs, and good citizenship. Such issues had not been tested in the U.S. Supreme Court—nor had the issue of the application of land use controls to undeveloped land, zoning these areas for uses other than those the free market would indicate. In 1925 the California Supreme Court supported such zoning of undeveloped land areas in *Zahn* v. *Board of Public Works of the City of Los Angeles,* stating, "Zoning . . . looks not only backward . . . but forward to aid in the development of new districts according to a comprehensive plan having as its basis the welfare of the city as a whole."[29]

The first such "comprehensive plan having as its basis the welfare of the city as a whole" to be officially adopted by a major American city took effect in Cincinnati in 1925. Alfred Bettman, a Cincinnati attorney, was heavily involved in the work of the United City Planning Committee of Cincinnati, a citizen group dedicated to integrating urban planning with the ongoing processes of the Cincinnati city government. The pro-planning policies of this citizen committee were adopted as elements of the platform of a reform party, the Charter party, that came to power in 1924 and immediately implemented Bettman's program. A key element in this program was official adoption of a physical statement of the long-term goals and policies of the city with regard to its urban form and structure, including both public and private development; this physical statement was to be followed by the city council in the creation of control devices, such as zoning and subdivision control ordinances, and in the expenditure of public funds. Bettman made the following statement:

The plan should be designed for a considerable period in the future, twenty-five to fifty years. It should be based, therefore, upon a comprehensive and detailed survey of things as they are at the time of the planning, such as the existing distribution of existing developments, both public and private, the trends toward redistribution and growth of population, industry, and business, estimates of future trends of growth and distribution of population and industry, and the allotment of the territory of the city in accordance with all such data and estimated trends, so as to provide the necessary public facilities and the necessary area for private development corresponding to the needs of the community, present and prospective.[30]

The integration of survey data of existing conditions with estimates of future needs and community aspirations in an officially adopted public document was intended not only to produce a better long-range plan but also to place moral power behind the commitment to this plan. The comprehensive plan as pioneered by Bettman and the city of Cincinnati in 1925 was to constitute a cornerstone in American city planning. In this concept, legal control of community development is used as a tool for, and is subservient to, the realization of a set of long-range comprehensive community goals; this is in distinct contrast to the comprehensive zoning concept as realized in the New York City Zoning Code of 1916, in which controls were established without reference to long-range community development policies.

Prior to 1926 the comprehensive zoning concept rested on a weak constitutional foundation in relation to its land use control component. The New York City Zoning Code of 1916 had never been tested in the U.S. Supreme Court, and its land use element had been adopted on the basis of an implied constitutionality in *Hadacheck* v. *Sebastian*. In 1926 the Supreme Court heard *Village of Euclid* v. *Ambler Realty Co.*,[31] in which the constitutionality of comprehensive zoning and all of its parts was contested. The Court had decided, informally, to respond in favor of Ambler, striking down the comprehensive zoning package, when Alfred Bettman, fulfilling a charge from the Ohio State Conference on City Planning, was permitted to file an amicus curiae brief in support of Euclid and comprehensive zoning. Following Bettman's presentation the Court, by a 6 to 3 vote, found in favor of Euclid.

This case established the constitutionality of comprehensive zoning and all of its parts. The Court went out of its way in reporting its findings to effectively cut off the expected flood of future cases revolving about these issues, making the *Euclid* decision the basic constitutional building block of American city planning. For Bettman, however, this was a hollow victory. City after city, armed with the constitutional pronouncements of *Euclid,* proceeded to adopt comprehensive zoning ordinances that were unaccompanied by the comprehensive long-range planning he believed to be essential to the fulfillment of the public welfare.

In 1926 The New York Commission on Housing and Regional Planning, created in 1923 and chaired by Clarence S. Stein, published the first state planning report. This report suggested the creation of a public housing subsidy program. As a result of this study the state of New York passed an act in 1926 establishing a state housing board empowered to provide tax exemptions for twenty years to limited dividend housing corporations willing to provide housing for lower middle income people and to abide by a maximum rent schedule.[32] This first public housing subsidy program in the United States resulted in the construction of 6,000 housing units in fourteen projects and stimulated private investment in rental housing.

Clarence Stein, together with Henry C. Wright, realized a model project in 1926 in the construction of Sunnyside Gardens at a site on Long Island near New York City. Sunnyside provided town houses[33] and garden apartments[34] of varying setback on full block lots, eliminating the narrow side yards and small rear yards of speculative lot-by-lot subdivisions and pooling the land into large common center block parks and playgrounds. These units, models for many future "garden apartment" projects, were two rooms deep and were sited parallel to the street.

The peak year for housing production in the United States during the 1920s was 1927. During that year 810,000 dwelling units were built. During this boom, the City Housing Corporation, sponsors of Sunnyside, took major steps to realize another model project by Stein and Wright, Radburn at Fairlawn, New Jersey. Radburn, constructed in 1928, was built to serve as a model suburban development. Large superblocks were created, containing central block parks bounded by two story single family houses. Pedestrian paths led from the houses through the center block parks to the local school and to a nearby shopping center, thus separating pedestrian and vehicular traffic. This project, an evolution of the neighborhood idea explored at Hampstead in London and Forest Hills Gardens on Long Island, became the prototype for most of the "advanced" American land development planning for the next fifty years.

In 1928 the U.S. Department of Commerce, under Secretary Herbert Hoover, published a new Standard City Planning Enabling Act[35] and recommended its adoption by state legislatures. Publication of this act was useful in that it promoted city planning and directed attention to the comprehensive plan, often ignored in the comprehensive zoning process. But it also confused the comprehensive plan and the zoning plan, leading communities to prepare zoning proposals without reference to long-range integrated public policy issues. The act recommended separate adoption of pieces of the plan, denying its essential quality as an integrated statement of public policies, and also suggested that the planning commission, a semi-independent agency, receive and adopt the comprehensive plan and oversee the planning staff rather than leaving these tasks to the municipal legislative body. The act thus weakened the emerging role of planning as an integral element of government. Many states acted on this suggested enabling act, thus making its provisions the common basis for municipal planning in many states today.

The Regional Plan of New York and Its Environs, prepared by the Russell Sage Foundation, was published in 1929. In this plan emphasis was placed on economic, demographic, and governmental regional problems, as well as on the normal physical elements of a plan, and a vast mass of information on current conditions was coupled with projections of the future. This reliance on data, critical to Bettman's concept of a comprehensive plan, became the norm in the years to come as other cities modeled their plan-making processes after this monumental undertaking. In this regional survey Clarence A. Perry, a resident of Forest Hills Gardens, codified Unwin's neighborhood ideas and propounded the "neighborhood unit" as the basic building block of the city. The neighborhood unit would be based on the elementary school, with other community facilities located at its center and arterial streets at the perimeter. The distance from school to perimeter would be based on a comfortable walking distance for a school age child; there would be no through traffic or industrial or commercial uses.[36] Perry's neighborhood unit concept reinforced a local school-centered pattern, with segregation of uses, that was to become the cornerstone of American suburban development after World War II.

The Depression years

Franklin Delano Roosevelt, pledging a New Deal to the American people, was elected President in 1932. With 13 million people out of work, the main focus of New Deal programs was on unemployment. The New Deal supported planning for the future by means of detailed studies and projections, as well as the careful budgeting of resources, bringing economists, statisticians, and sociologists into the planning profession. Improved housing became a means toward employment as well as a valued by-product. In many ways the New Deal programs resembled application on a national scale of Burnham's program to restore civic pride and confidence through great public projects that provided employment, helped ensure social peace, and tended to redistribute wealth to those in need. The New Deal applied many of the basic planning process concepts of the Regional Plan of New York to comprehensive planning in America, as these processes were essential to the success of New Deal programs.

The National Planning Board, founded in 1933, stimulated state and municipal governments to plan for development over long periods of time and encouraged formulation of twenty year comprehensive plans founded upon statistical projections of probable future conditions. The board also stimulated the creation of state planning boards.

The year 1933 also saw the creation of the Tennessee Valley Authority, an independent multifunctional government agency created for the regional planning and development of the Tennessee River valley. Its programs were extensive, ranging from flood protection and water management to recreational development and power generation.

In 1933 the development of housing in the United States was at its lowest point in a century. The new administration, focusing on employment in the construction trades and on the condition of slum housing, undertook to construct new dwellings in deteriorated central city areas. Its first program—Knickerbocker Village, New York City—provided over 1,500 housing units and was undertaken under the Reconstruction Finance Corporation program created by President Hoover. Its 4 to 5 percent interest loans for ten years were grossly insufficient to forestall economic failure, even when bolstered by a tax exemption by the state of New York. This program was replaced in 1934 by two New Deal programs, the Public Works Administration (PWA) and the Federal Housing Administration (FHA), both created by the federal Housing Act of 1934.

Initially, and for a short time, PWA was authorized to lend up to 85 percent of the cost of housing projects to public and private limited dividend corporations. Only seven housing projects were produced under this program, which was replaced in 1934 by a new and radically restructured PWA Housing Division with authority to make grants and low interest loans to limited dividend housing authorities, usually local housing authorities. The most radical parts of the program were the federal government's power of eminent domain to acquire housing sites and its power to engage directly in the construction of these projects. This program produced fifty projects before it was terminated in 1937.

The FHA was established to attract private funds to the residential construction industry to expand construction jobs for the unskilled. It did this by government insurance of private home loans, removing the financial risk in such investments. It insured loans for up to twenty years at a time when ten years was the normal maximum loan period, and for up to 80 percent of the value of the home at a time when 30 to 50 percent down was common. Extension of the loan period and a reduced down payment made home ownership possible for millions of Americans and effectively stimulated housing construction.

To assure nondefault on these loans, FHA established minimum standards for housing financed under this program that met the housing desires, in purchase and resale, of the upper middle and upper income groups—those least likely to default. These published minimum housing requirements for an FHA loan were the first federal minimum housing "standards" adopted in the United States. They were rapidly reflected in zoning codes, building codes, and private loan manuals as the minimum standards for *all* housing construction in the country. By these means all housing that the middle and lower income groups could afford became a priori "substandard" and undesirable. By its focus on single family detached owner-occupied units, FHA stimulated enormous suburban expansion, especially in the decades of the 1950s and 1960s.

The year 1934 saw the creation of a national citizen focused planning organization, the American Society of Planning Officials (ASPO). This organization was created to bring planning commissioners, city managers, and other officials more actively into the planning movement; to serve as a clearinghouse for information; and to increase communication between planners. (In 1978 ASPO consolidated with the American Institute of Planners to become the American Planning Association [APA].) Alfred Bettman was ASPO's first president.

In 1935 Congress created the Resettlement Administration within the U.S.

Department of Agriculture, as a part of the Emergency Relief Appropriation Act of 1935. The Resettlement Administration undertook to design and construct four communities, collectively referred to as the *greenbelt towns*. These new towns were built to assist in local employment, to resettle relocated farm families, and to create model communities to guide future development. The greenbelt towns, modified neighborhood units in the countryside surrounded by extensive greenbelts of public land and serving as dormitory suburbs for nearby metropolises, were built by the federal government on land acquired through use of the federal power of eminent domain and were operated by the federal government until sold to private enterprise in the 1950s. These four greenbelt towns were Greenbelt, Maryland; Greenhills, Ohio; Greendale, Wisconsin; and Greenbrook, New Jersey. Greenbrook was never built because the U.S. Court of Appeals for the District of Columbia in 1936, in *Township of Franklin* v. *Tugwell*,[37] held the Emergency Relief Appropriation Act to be invalid and ruled that the federal government had no constitutional authority to use its eminent domain power in states for housing purposes.

The entire PWA Housing Division system was abandoned in 1937, as by that time it was clear that the finding in *Tugwell* applied equally to the PWA programs. Local housing authorities also resented federal dominance, and the radical "pump priming" for jobs that was needed in 1934 seemed not so necessary with the emerging economic recovery of 1937. The PWA Housing Division was replaced in the Housing Act of 1937 by the U.S. Housing Authority (USHA). This 1937 act became the foundation for most federal public housing programs for the next forty years. Under USHA, local housing authorities used their state-granted eminent domain power to acquire housing sites.

About 168,000 dwelling units were constructed by local housing authorities under this program between 1937 and the outbreak of World War II. Insofar as New York City alone had over 800,000 Old Law tenements (1879–1901) and railroad flats (pre-1879), it was clear that these New Deal programs revealed the housing problem but actually did little to solve it. In 1938, of all the new housing produced in the United States including public housing, only 14 percent was within the economic reach of the lower 76 percent in income.

A decade after proposing the neighborhood unit concept in the *Regional Survey of New York and Its Environs,* Clarence Perry elaborated on this concept in *Housing for the Machine Age.*[38] Perry held that the neighborhood structure, if it is to create true community, must bring together people of identical background and interests. He also held that the problems of juvenile delinquency could only be coped with by provision of the individual backyard playground at single family detached residences. He therefore recommended that the basic building block of the city, earlier suggested as a fairly high density apartment-based unit, be an area of owner occupied single family detached homes. Thus modified, this concept of the neighborhood unit was to become the basic unit for post–World War II development and the focus of future civil rights suits.

On 1 January 1939 the American City Planning Institute was renamed the American Institute of Planners (AIP). At this time the United States was recovering from the Great Depression and there was much agitation for the elimination of government involvement in housing and other aspects of American life. As the prospect of a European war appeared with increasing clarity, interest in housing and urban development issues subsided.

From 1940 to 1960

The war and after

The United States census of 1940, the first decennial census to include data on housing quality, reported that one out of every eight urban dwellings had no indoor bathing or toilet facilities, that one out of every seven had no running water or plumbing of any kind, and that one out of every seven was in need of major repair. The rapid uncontrolled construction of urban housing units, the pride of the nineteenth century, was becoming the housing crisis of the twentieth century.

The threat of war resulted in the creation in June 1940 of the Office of the Housing Coordinator, which was established to coordinate all federal housing programs and to determine housing needs relative to critical defense industry. The USHA low rent public housing program was abolished, and 100 percent loans were made available to local housing authorities for the construction of defense housing. In this brief period between the depths of the Great Depression and the onslaught of World War II, the International City Managers' Association published *Local Planning Administration*,[39] by Ladislas Segoe, a distinguished planning consultant who played a major role in preparing the Cincinnati plan of 1925. This book codified the planning methods, processes, and standards that had been developed since the early 1920s, becoming both the primary text for students in the planning programs at American universities and the basic municipal reference work that guided community development during the postwar era.

From 1942 to 1945 war planning replaced rather than complemented city planning. Although viewed as essential at the time, this lack of concern for the urban future left the country and its cities totally unprepared for the urban problems that would arise at the end of the war. During the war local planning agencies provided spot assistance to operating agencies (such as developing site plans for military bases), developed plans for war housing projects, and developed a few plans for postwar public works in anticipation of the unemployment that might result from an economic recession at the end of the war. But such foresighted efforts were few and far between. The national commitment to planning for anything but the war effort was at its depths in 1943 when the National Planning Board[40] was effectively abolished by the distribution of its functions among various committees of the U.S. Congress.

In February 1942 all federal housing agencies were consolidated in the National Housing Agency (NHA). Unlike the situation in World War I, when federal government corporations were empowered to build necessary defense industry housing, the approach taken during World War II was to build on the successful 1934 FHA model, stimulating construction of war housing by private enterprise. To assure the success of this program, the Housing Act of 1937 was amended to provide FHA mortgage insurance of 90 percent loans (10 percent down) of twenty-five year duration. Over 1,850,000 dwelling units for war workers were constructed through this wartime mortgage insurance program.

At the end of World War II the nation faced a shortage of over 7 million urban housing units. To meet these needs, especially for returning service personnel, the liberal and highly effective 90 percent/twenty-five year mortgage insurance terms of the war housing program were extended in the FHA and Veterans Administration (VA) housing programs. This action was a major factor in the housing boom of the late 1940s and early 1950s.

Owing to the lack of advanced planning for peacetime, the rapid metropolitan growth of the postwar period generally took place without benefit of comprehensive plan guidelines other than the remnants of long-range plans executed in the 1930s and earlier. A vast expansion of the suburban fringes of American cities occurred after 1945; this was heavily influenced by federal and state highway construction programs, a national prosperity fostering extensive automobile ownership, and the FHA and VA housing programs. Mass transit companies, operating fleets of gasoline powered rubber-tired motorbuses that replaced the electric trolleys in the 1920s and 1930s, began to find it difficult to serve this spread out, low density population pattern.

Figure 2–5   The real estate sales methods
developed in the 1920s served well for the
housing boom after the war. Promotional efforts
such as this one, dating from the mid-1950s, were
widespread, especially in suburban areas.

Well-staffed planning agencies were created in the larger cities to cope with
this postwar suburban explosion. These staffs began to prepare the long-range
comprehensive plans that were lacking in 1945, but devoted most of their time
to the immediate concerns, such as day-to-day zoning and subdivision control.
These agencies also engaged in extensive automobile traffic studies, capital budgeting, and, most significantly, urban redevelopment programs.

Interest in central city redevelopment arose early in the 1940s when the census of 1940 indicated that central cities were beginning to lose population to
their surrounding suburban areas. In response, urban land and business interests agitated for adaptation of the USHA "slum clearance" program, urging
creation of urban redevelopment authorities capable of using their state granted
eminent domain powers to acquire and demolish deteriorated districts for reconstruction by private enterprise for nonhousing purposes. These interests urged
that a federal subsidy be made to private corporations to encourage them to do
this. The advent of the war forestalled further development of this idea, but intense interest in this concept arose again in 1945. In that year the state of Pennsylvania passed the first state urban redevelopment act granting a subsidy for
the reconstruction of deteriorated central city areas for uses other than housing,
which resulted in the Golden Triangle project in Pittsburgh. This project stimulated nationwide interest in such developments.

In 1947 all federal housing programs were relocated to a new Housing and
Home Finance Agency (HHFA), including the FHA mortgage insurance program, which had been an independent federal agency since its establishment in
1934.[41] In 1947 the first of the massive postwar FHA suburban housing projects
to be supported by mortgage insurance emerged at Levittown, New York, followed by Park Forest, Illinois, in the following year.

The neighborhood ideas of Unwin, as developed by Perry in the *Regional
Survey of New York and Its Environs* in 1929 and as modified by him to exclude
all but single family detached units in 1939, became, in effect, minimum national
standards through their inclusion in FHA and VA mortgage insurance requirements. This accrued pattern was codified in the American Public Health Asso-

ciation's *Planning the Neighborhood*[42] in 1948, and was eagerly accepted by municipalities seeking guidance in structuring the extensive suburbs that were appearing at the edges of every major American city. This document was predicated on a value system that gave priority to the single family detached residence; multifamily units were suggested only when they were necessary because of land values or site conditions.

Residential suburban decentralization of the American city in the late 1940s was accompanied by the beginning of the dispersal of manufacturing plants from their long-established locations in the core of the city to locations along major railroads and highways at the perimeter. This dispersal, a reaction to high land costs and transportation congestion at the core of the city, was made possible by major improvements in highway systems, subsidized development of over-the-road freight trucking fleets, and widespread automobile ownership on the part of factory workers. These conditions were pointed up in 1949 with establishment of the first regional shopping center in the United States. In that year Don M. Casto opened the Town and Country Shopping Center[43] at the outskirts of Columbus, Ohio, beyond the new suburban developments.

The Housing Act of 1949 created a federal program for central city redevelopment, fulfilling the program propounded by central city business and land interests in the early 1940s, based on the model of the Pennsylvania act of 1945. Under this program, physically deteriorated areas became eligible for federal support for clearance and redevelopment for any reuse.[44] Huge areas of central cities were cleared by local redevelopment authorities and reconstructed by and for private enterprise, with federal financial subsidy. This act made city planning an important activity in the United States, as it required that any federally aided urban redevelopment program conform to a general plan for the entire community. This stimulated considerable planning activity which resulted in the establishment of many well-staffed planning and urban redevelopment departments in city government and created an instant demand for professionally trained city planners.

Planning concerns at mid-century

The census of 1950 reported a population of 151 million Americans, almost 60 percent urban, owning 48 million automobiles. Suburban fringe areas had increased in population by 35 percent since 1940, whereas central cities had increased by only 13 percent. This census reported that 2.5 million of the 40 million American urban homes were dilapidated, 2.3 million had no running water, 4 million lacked an indoor toilet or bath, and 9 million were substandard. The 1949 Housing Act, as actually appropriated, provided for just 26,000 new low income public housing units a year. At that rate, the 2.5 million dilapidated units occupied by the urban poor would be replaced shortly before 2050 A.D.

At mid-century over 84.5 million of the 151 million Americans were living in metropolitan areas. Much had changed drastically since the beginning of the century, including the methods and processes of city planning, but some basic concepts of development control had barely altered. Land use control by category of use had changed little. This notion of use separation to assure prevention of undesirable effects on surrounding uses was challenged in the early 1950s by an emerging notion of performance controls, applied first to industrial areas and then to other uses. One authority described this in the following words:

Each land use would be tested by its direct and indirect effect on adjacent land use, on governmental services, and on community growth. Under such a standard, industry, business, and homes would be located on any site in any zone so long as the intended use met adequate performance standards. Such a proposition requires a wholesale reexamination of the principle of the use district. Paradoxically, it could result in zoning without zones.[45]

Although slow to gather acceptance and even slower to find widespread application, performance standards came to be viewed by many as the probable planning wave of the future.

But the present in the early 1950s was in the ever-quickening sprawl of suburbia. Many suburban communities, feeling the pressure for residential development, sought to preserve the rural character of their communities, to maintain high land values, and to preserve their social character (excluding all but the reasonably affluent) by enacting minimum lot area requirements of one to two hectares or more, and minimum residential floor areas that would preclude less than substantial construction. In *Lionshead Lake* v. *Township of Wayne,* in 1952, and *Fischer* v. *Township of Bedminster,* in 1953, the New Jersey Supreme Court supported both of these control devices in a fashion similar to the actions of other courts on these issues. In the first case, the court stated that

there are minimums in housing below which one may not go without risk of impairing the health of those that dwell therein. . . . But quite apart from these considerations of public health . . . minimum floor area standards are justified on the ground that they promote the general welfare of the community and . . . the courts . . . take a broad view of what constitutes general welfare.[46]

In the second case the court made the following statement:

The burden of proving the ordinance unreasonable is on the party attacking the ordinance. . . . No case has been presented where a five acre provision has been struck down as unreasonable and arbitrary . . . there would appear to be ample justification for the ordinance in preserving the character of the community, maintaining the value of property therein and devoting the land . . . for its most appropriate use.[47]

Armed with such legal support, and using the neighborhood unit with its focus on single family, detached, owner-occupied homes as a basic structuring system, community after community enacted similar regulations, usually with standards far beyond the minimal protective needs. Over time, this surrounded the central city with suburban ordinances which had the cumulative effect of denying entry to the rapidly increasing number of lower middle and lower income groups—often racial minorities—who were residents of the central city where clearance and redevelopment programs were being undertaken under the terms of the Housing Act of 1949.

The problems of rehabilitating deteriorating areas were addressed in the Housing Act of 1954, which extended the clearance programs of the 1949 act to the rehabilitation of areas in the process of deteriorating and to the conservation of nondeteriorating areas in danger of becoming deteriorated. This three part clearance–rehabilitation–conservation program came to be known as the basic urban renewal program. The focus of this act on conservation vastly stimulated adoption and enforcement of housing codes. The act also required a "workable program" for the elimination of future deterioration, from which the community renewal plan emerged. Among the elements of this program required to be included in an annual report to HHFA were neighborhood analyses, housing for displaced persons, and citizen participation in the renewal process. These emphases led local urban renewal staffs to direct their attention away from commercial redevelopment of the city core and toward efforts to improve the opportunities of inner city residents, primarily the poor and minorities, thus paving the way for the "social advocacy" planning of the 1960s.

The Housing Act of 1954 specifically required that urban renewal projects be a part of a full comprehensive city plan as defined in the Regional Plan of New York tradition, complete with surveys and projections. To ease the financial burden of preparing such plans, Title I, section 701, provided for 50–50 federal–local funding of such plans for communities of under 25,000 people. Since such communities could not afford permanent staffs for this work, it fell to private planning consultants. By means of this act and the "701" program, the federal government not only created vast employment opportunities for planners but also created a major private urban development consulting industry in America. These programs were coordinated through state planning offices, which provided an incentive to rekindling state planning efforts. These increased professional opportunities were immediately reflected in academic systems. Between 1950 and 1960 the number of graduate planning programs in America more than doubled, and student enrollment increased from 187 in 1952 to 645 in 1962.

Between 1950 and 1955, 12.4 million people moved into metropolitan areas in the United States. An average of 2 million persons a year (a total of 10 million of this 12.4 million) located in the suburban automobile-oriented fringes that were served by new highways on which the federal government came to spend over $4 billion a year by 1956.

The latter half of the 1950s saw a major shift of retail centers to the urban perimeter in the form of shopping centers located at or near the intersection of radial and concentric perimeter highways. These new shopping centers provided vast areas of parking space, a unifying architectural design, and pleasant internal landscaped pedestrian shopping plazas. Undoubtedly the most influential of these developments was Northland Shopping Center in Detroit, designed by Victor Gruen and Associates, which opened in March 1954 and served as a model for new shopping centers throughout the country.

In response to the loss of commercial vitality in the historic city core, downtown business groups and city governments initiated efforts to revitalize central areas; these efforts included expanded provision of off-street parking, improved flow of street traffic, and, in the late 1950s, provision of street tree plantings and informal seating areas. Fort Worth, Texas, sponsored a central area plan by Victor Gruen and Associates, presented in 1956, that was aimed at providing the downtown areas with those amenities found only in the new suburban shopping centers. This plan was never implemented, nevertheless it served as the prototype for central business district reconstruction efforts for the next two decades. It provided an inner belt freeway around the commercial core with radial freeways leading to the suburban areas and permitted quick free flow access to the downtown area, large perimeter parking garages, and a central area of street malls reserved solely for pedestrian use, complete with trees, kiosks, benches, and fountains. Many cities adopted the inner belt freeway and radial freeway components of this concept during the next decade as a result of the Interstate Highway Act of 1956, which provided for a $60 billion defense highway construction program consisting of 170,000 kilometers of limited access highways linking every major city in the nation.

With the large-scale relocation of production industry to the perimeter of the city occurring during this period, the concept of the "industrial park" emerged. Highly desirable industrial sites along major rail lines and highways were identified and provided with generous sites and utilities meeting industrial needs. Often there were wide bands of landscaped and earth-bermed open space around the better of such developments, creating highly functional and environmentally attractive industrial accommodations in the suburbs or near the open countryside.

From 1957 until the end of the decade the major planning activities undertaken in the United States included attempts to restructure downtown areas on the Fort Worth model, urban renewal clearance projects, rehabilitation projects, preparation of new long-range (twenty year) comprehensive plans through use of the now classic methods, and day-to-day zoning and subdivision control work. In addition, the planning staffs of some cities, notably of New

York and Washington, D.C., proposed adoption of more flexible building height and bulk controls than simple limits on height and setback. Included among these experimental concepts was control by floor area ratio. In this approach a ratio is set indicating the maximum permitted relationship between building floor area and net site area, allowing virtually any shape and height of building as long as this ratio is not exceeded. It was suggested that such control—a form of emerging flexible performance control—would permit more creative building design and a more vital urban scene.

The Housing Act of 1959 provided federal financial assistance for the preparation of community renewal plans and made matching funds available for the preparation of comprehensive plans on the metropolitan, regional, state, and interstate scales. By 1960 half of the costs of comprehensive planning in America were subsidized by the federal government as an inducement to all levels of government to participate in this activity.

By 1960, 70 percent of the nation's 180 million Americans were living in urbanized areas, and megalopolis, the regional city, was a reality, spreading from Boston to northern Virginia.

Since 1960

New ideas

In the early 1960s two books appeared that were highly influential in planning and public policy during the ensuing decade. In a broad sense they captured some of the dissatisfaction of scholars and intellectuals with the aggressively agrarian and suburban outlook that had pervaded city planning for decades and they challenged the simplistic ideas of the city, community, neighborhood, and family in relation to planning and government.

In 1961 *The Death and Life of Great American Cities*[48] by Jane Jacobs was published and soon became a best-seller. The author attacked some of the major objectives of American city planning and urban policy, arguing that diversity, not uniformity, was essential to the development of self-fulfilling lives; that a mixture of urban land uses was desired, not use segregation by "zone"; that the retention of old buildings was essential; and that a concentration of people was needed rather than suburban dispersal. This bombshell summarized many of the attitudes that were to result in a critical reappraisal and redirection of American city planning during the coming years.

Freedom and *opportunity* were key elements in Lawrence Haworth's *The Good City,*[49] published in 1963, a statement of urban philosophy that stood in stark contrast to the still prevalent agrarian and suburban outlook. This book held that it is the responsibility of planners and politicians to create a society oriented toward human self-fulfillment through assuring a variety of opportunities, permitting a broad range of life-style choices, making as many of these opportunities as possible available to all citizens, and creating "people-centered" institutions. Haworth urged great flexibility to help meet personal needs, voluntary participation in institutions, and a strong citizen–user voice, not only in the operation of these institutions but also in the definition of their purposes. These concepts are central to understanding many of the great changes that have occurred in American urban society and public policy since 1960.

The programs of the 1960s

In 1961 the trend toward more flexible controls resulting in greater diversity, inherent in the floor area ratio and performance control concepts that evolved in the late 1950s, was continued when the New York Zoning Code of 1916 was replaced by a new code that specified site area requirements per room (a room—

density device); incorporated special incentives such as bonuses for provision of plazas, arcades, and pedestrian walkways; created a flexible building setback system; and provided for development control by open space ratio. This code, while protecting light and air, encouraged creation of a variety of quasi-public spaces.

The Housing Act of 1961, in section 221(d)3, provided for an interest subsidy to private nonprofit corporations, limited dividend corporations, cooperatives, and some public agencies for rental housing for low and moderate income families in general. This interest subsidy program became the basic federal housing program in the 1960s and was further expanded in the Housing Act of 1968.

Membership in the American Institute of Planners (AIP), founded in 1917 as the American City Planning Institute with 52 charter members, had grown to over 3,000 by 1962. New Jersey, in 1962, became the first state to license the practice of planning, followed by Michigan in 1966, which licensed use of the title *planner* but not the practice of planning. AIP members generally did not view these actions with enthusiasm since they had the effect of defining the planning profession when dynamic role changes were viewed as needed for effective planning in a rapidly changing society.

In 1963 the community renewal plan efforts of many cities, including New York, Philadelphia, Pittsburgh, and Providence, were redirected toward assisting lower income groups to improve their status and their opportunities and toward bringing about a more effective allocation of city resources to attain these ends. Citizen participants in these programs began to organize to press for planning activities extending far beyond the classic city planning confines of land use, building bulk, and utilities and transportation facilities. The mid-1960s also saw initiation of a new scale in private merchant-builder housing efforts as numerous privately constructed new towns were begun, including Reston, Virginia, and Columbia, Maryland. These new towns were generally satellite dormitory suburbs for the upper middle class.

The U.S. Department of Housing and Urban Development (HUD) was created in 1965, giving urban interests a Cabinet level position, such as rural interests enjoyed through the Department of Agriculture, for the first time in American history. Robert C. Weaver, a black American, was HUD's first Secretary. The Housing and Urban Development Act of 1965, the most comprehensive extension of federal urban development and housing programs since 1949, provided rent supplement payments for those below the local poverty line, 3 percent interest loans for low and moderate income families, and subsidies for an additional 240,000 low rent public housing units. This was followed by enactment of the Model Cities program through the Demonstration Cities and Metropolitan Development Act of 1966.

The Model Cities program, initiated by President Johnson, was unique in the history of American city planning in that it was not a federal program for local implementation in which the problem had been determined and a response—solution devised. Rather, the citizen—residents of city subdistricts designated as Model City districts were to create their own quasi-political organization, to decide on their problems and priorities, and to propose their own means of arriving at solutions. These organizations and their proposed programs were then funded by the federal government. This federal incentive to initiation of local district planning, with urban users defining solutions to their own problems, strongly reflected the values of Jane Jacobs and the philosophy of Lawrence Haworth. Although it encountered serious difficulties, the Model Cities program solidly established citizen policy formulation as an essential part of almost every federal urban development program for the next decade.

In addition, these planning programs were to be built on the almost immediate future (three to five years) instead of the twenty to twenty-five years characteristic of the usual comprehensive plan. Such planning was to use the planning-programming-budgeting system (PPBS), involving an analytical process of defining measurable goals, setting alternatives, evaluating each alternative for cost and effectiveness, and choosing the best means for implementation. Although PPBS in its most complex, technical form did not survive in very many jurisdictions, the goal-oriented approach with citizen involvement in the policy process was a distinct contribution.[50]

The Civil Rights Act of 1968 ended the legality of racial discrimination in the sale or rental of 80 percent of American housing. Later in that same year the Supreme Court, in *Jones* v. *Alfred H. Mayer Co.,* ruled that section 1982 of the Civil Rights Act of 1866 prohibits racial discrimination in all housing in America:

When racial discrimination herds men into ghettos and makes their ability to buy property turn on the color of their skin, then it too is a relic of slavery.[51]

In recognition of the need for more and better housing for low and moderate income families, the Housing and Urban Development Act of 1968 included programs for the construction of 6 million subsidized housing units over the next ten years. Section 235 extended home ownership to low and moderate income families with FHA mortgage insured loans by means of a monthly payment from HUD to the mortgage holder, reducing the owner's monthly costs. Section 236 provided federal interest supplements for multifamily rental and cooperative housing mortgages, thus reducing these rentals.

In recognition of the way in which many communities had used their zoning power to lock out low income groups, the state of Massachusetts passed a Law for Low- and Moderate-Income Housing in 1969. This law authorized the state to review and to override local zoning ordinances when they had the effect of making it uneconomical to build housing for low income families. As a result many communities then set aside zoned land areas for housing for low and moderate income families. The New York Urban Development Corporation (UDC) was also created in 1969. The UDC was charged with the task of redeveloping the state's substandard areas and was empowered to override local zoning and building codes, to condemn and acquire land, and to build buildings, and even entire towns if necessary, to accomplish this end.

In 1961 Congress passed a law permitting states to legalize ownership of a housing unit without title to the land on which the site is located. This stimulated condominium developments throughout the United States in the late 1960s. Through individual ownership of the home—usually but not always row house units—but shared ownership of the common site of a number of related units, creative site planning is encouraged, the cost of common community facilities is shared, and home ownership is possible at reduced cost and with no site maintenance responsibilities. In 1969, four times as many condominium units were built as in 1968. This increase in condominium sales was merely one indicator of a major shift in American housing development that was taking place at that time.

In the early 1950s single family detached housing units, the basic building block of the neighborhood unit concept, had accounted for more than 90 percent of the nation's new housing starts, a proportion that decreased to 60 percent in the late 1960s and to less than 50 percent in the early 1970s. One of the major reasons for the drop was the rising cost of the new detached single family house, which by the late 1970s was beyond the reach of about 70 percent of American family units through a combination of rising minimum standards, land costs, costs of financing, property taxes, and building materials costs. Other factors included major shifts in the housing market. Three are of particular note, namely: a leveling of the demographic curve so that there were fewer families in the house buying age group; population mobility, which often favors attached housing and apartments during certain stages of the life cycle; and wider consumer choice in types of housing.

Planned unit development (PUD) zoning provisions had begun to appear in response to the new scale of residential development following World War II. Existing zoning standards assumed lot-by-lot development and not area development all at one time. Interest in large scale condominium development (where there are no individual unit lot lines) and cluster patterns led to the establishment of special PUD zones in which normal development controls were waived upon special approval of the project. In order to evaluate these alternative proposals, communities turned to performance standards. Among the earliest devices used was the land use intensity (LUI) technique originally devised for evaluating large scale FHA financed developments in the early 1960s. In this LUI system the number of dwelling units, the total project floor area, the amount of recreation area, and the number of parking spaces were derived from indices of land quantity and usability. Once experience proved such flexible project planning zones desirable, variable density provisions were created, allowing experimentation, and provisions for varied residential types and mixed land use followed, continuing the evolution toward flexible performance control of urban development.

In 1969, implementing the Intergovernmental Cooperation Act of 1968, the U.S. Office of Management and Budget issued Circular A–95, which required areawide regional planning agency review of all proposals for local participation in federal development programs. This stimulated the creation of a network of regional clearinghouses charged with receiving and disseminating project information as well as coordinating among applicants for federal assistance. Circular A–95 helped establish the administrative base for the regional planning and coordination thrust of the 1970s. During this closing year of the 1960s the Douglas Commission reported the need for the production of an average of 2.6 million housing units per year each year until 1980 (over two and a half times the housing production of the boom years at the end of World War II) to meet the increasing American urban housing deficit in terms of both quantity and quality.[52]

New directions in the 1970s

In his State of the Union message in 1970 President Nixon stressed the need to save the environment, consistent with an increasing public concern for clean air, clean water, and loss of natural environmental areas. These interests, which came to constitute the ecology movement, began to replace the civil rights movement as the main thematic thrust of American life in the early 1970s, to be replaced by the energy crisis and concern for the recessional qualities of the American economy in mid-decade.

In response to heated public concern for the environment, and also to create an alternative focus for highly visible government action that would replace the Johnson administration's civil rights/urban affairs centered Office of Economic Opportunity, President Nixon established the Environmental Protection Agency (EPA). He also created the President's Council on Environmental Quality to set policy to carry out the provisions of the National Environmental Policy Act of 1970. The major provision of this act was the directive that all government agencies and licensees must file an environmental impact statement when new construction was contemplated, documenting the probable impact of the undertaking. This major step toward nationwide regulation on the basis of measurable performance became the basis for nebulous concepts of development control by socioeconomic impact statement.

The U.S. Census of 1970 reported that more Americans were living in the suburban fringes of metropolitan areas than in their central cities. (In 1970 there were approximately 205 million Americans, 69 percent residing in 230 standard metropolitan statistical areas [SMSAs].) Lower income families, particularly racial minorities, generally did not share in this suburban dispersal of American housing. This fact can be attributed in considerable degree to exclusionary zoning practices. Mary Brooks brought this subject into the open in *Exclusionary Zoning,*[53] published in 1970. In the same year Dale Bertsch, executive director of the Miami Valley Regional Planning Commission,[54] prepared a Regional Housing Dispersal Plan, which came to be known as the Dayton Plan. This plan resulted in an allocation of needed new low and middle income housing units throughout a five county regional metropolitan area on a "regional fair share" basis. Much would be heard of exclusionary zoning practices and the segregating effects of neighborhood unit based suburban residential areas as desegregation suits were filed in city after city in the mid-1970s. The regional fair share concept would become central to a milestone New Jersey Supreme Court decision five years later.

The social action advocates of opening suburban areas to the less affluent collided with the conservation/ecology-oriented environmentalists who propounded no growth or slow growth policies for the metropolitan fringes. In *Golden* v. *Planning Board of Ramapo,* the New York Court of Appeals upheld a zoning ordinance that made issuance of a development permit contingent on meeting performance standards on a point system relative to utilities, drainage facilities, parks, road access, and firehouses. The court stated that

far from being exclusionary, the present amendments merely seek, by the implementation of sequential development and time growth, to provide a balanced cohesive community dedicated to the efficient utilization of land. The restrictions conform to the community's considered land use policies as expressed in its comprehensive plan and represent a bona fide effort to maximize population density, consistent with orderly growth.[55]

Ramapo reported in 1974 that housing starts had been reduced by one half as a result of this program.

The suburban dispersion of federally assisted housing projects, undertaken by HUD in the late 1960s as a means toward opening the suburbs, was often effectively blocked by the requirement of a referendum in support of the issue in the local area prior to initiation of the project. Current white and generally relatively affluent residents of suburban areas tended to vote to exclude such projects, whereas the only districts in which minorities and the poor could count on heavy support were those areas they currently occupied. Article XXXIV of the California Constitution provided that no low rent housing project could be developed, constructed, or acquired by a state public body until the project was approved by referendum in a local election. The California Supreme Court held that Article XXXIV denied the disadvantaged the equal protection of the law. In the *Valtierra* cases (1971) the U.S. Supreme Court upheld the California referendum requirements, stating:

California's entire history demonstrates the repeated use of referendums to give citizens a vote on questions of public policy. Provisions for referendums demonstrate devotion to democracy, not to bias, discrimination or prejudice.[56]

San Francisco's Bay Area Rapid Transit System (BART) made its first run in September 1972; it was the first regional rapid transit system built specifically to provide fast, fully automated, center-to-center transit service and the first new rapid transit system built for a major city in the United States since the 1920s. Its subway portion in downtown San Francisco runs up Market Street, as proposed by Daniel Burnham in 1906.

The Nixon administration announced in 1972 that, in fulfillment of its New Federalism programs, many federal government urban development programs would be terminated and would be replaced with a new system of community development based on decentralized programs and federal revenue sharing. In

October President Nixon signed the State and Local Fiscal Assistance Act of 1972, creating a multibillion-dollar general revenue sharing program.

In the midst of emerging public awareness of political scandal and corruption in the executive branch of the federal government, the section 235 and section 236 housing subsidy programs, created in the Housing Act of 1968, were abruptly suspended on 5 January 1973. The section 235 home ownership assistance program had had a 43 percent default rate in 1972. In Detroit alone, FHA foreclosures had risen to an average of 381 a month in 1971. The section 236 rental unit subsidy program had had 8 percent of its units in default in 1972. Speculators purchased deteriorated central city units, made a few repairs, and then sold them under section 235 at inflated prices to low income families who could not afford to maintain their occupancy.[57] High overrun costs in constructing section 236 rental units, builder padding, and high operating costs raised rents, forcing the poor out.

National land use legislation, first introduced in the U.S. Congress by Senator Jackson (D–Wash.) in 1972, was generally responsive to the environment/ecology interests of the beginning of the decade and focused on state planning processes oriented toward protection of critical areas, natural resource conservation, and the preservation of natural areas. In 1973 the Nixon administration proposed its own national land use planning bill, which failed in the fall of 1973 when the Nixon administration removed its support from the bill in order to gain votes in a potentially impending impeachment trial. Following this fiasco, national land use legislation became stalled in committees and had not reemerged by 1979. The omnipotent New York Urban Redevelopment Corporation (UDC) also collapsed in 1973, the legislature trimming its power to override local zoning ordinances as a result of UDC involvement in a heated public controversy over proposed low income housing projects in wealthy Westchester County.

President Nixon, in the face of an impending impeachment trial and having lost the confidence of the American people through the Watergate election scandal and the subsequent executive cover-up, resigned the Presidency on 8 August 1974. President Ford signed the Housing and Community Development Act of 1974, which abolished categorical, purpose-specific grants and replaced them with a block grant system merging the previous separate grant programs into a lump sum with funds allocated on a formula basis. This act required, as part of a Housing Assistance Plan (HAP), submission of a three year development plan identifying "both short- and long-term community development objectives which have been developed in accordance with areawide development planning."[58]

This reinforced the policy plan nature of emerging American city planning, encouraged in the earlier Model Cities program and in the role of councils of governments (COGs) and other areawide regional review agencies created under Circular A–95. The act also required that the Housing Assistance Plan

survey the condition of the housing stock in the community and assess the housing assistance needs of lower-income persons . . . residing in or expected to reside in the community [to] promote a greater choice of housing opportunities and [to] avoid undue concentrations of assisted persons in areas containing a high proportion of low income persons.[59]

The act further indicated its primary objective as

the development of viable urban communities by providing decent housing and a suitable environment and expanding economic opportunities, principally for persons of low and moderate income. . . . The federal assistance is for the support of . . . reduction of the isolation of income groups within communities and geographical areas and the promotion of an increase in the diversity and vitality of neighborhoods through the spatial deconcentration of housing opportunities for persons of lower income.[60]

This marked the first time that Congressional action was directed toward economic as well as racial segregation (a result of the Douglas Commission report).

In the wake of *Ramapo* (discussed earlier) many communities at the perimeter of metropolitan areas undertook no growth/slow growth programs, usually under the euphemism *managed growth*. Petaluma, California, in the San Francisco area, approached this directly, adopting an Official Statement of Development Policy in 1971 that specified a geographically balanced strategy of new residential construction based on a quota of 500 building permits per year. In the previous year 2,000 had been granted. These 500 building permits were allocated to different sectors of the city and issued under a rating system based on the availability of public services and the quality of design and construction. The Ninth U.S. Circuit Court of Appeals upheld this process in 1975, stating that "the concept of the public welfare is sufficiently broad to uphold Petaluma's desire to preserve its small-town character, its open spaces and low density of population and to grow at an orderly and deliberate pace." The court also stated that the Petaluma plan "does not have the undesirable effect of walling out any particular income class nor any racial minority group."[61]

The Southern Burlington County NAACP brought suit against the township of Mount Laurel, New Jersey, holding that the developing suburban township had adopted a zoning ordinance that failed to provide for a variety and choice of housing for its regional fair share of classes of individuals possibly wishing to live there, particularly families of low and moderate income. In 1975 the New Jersey Supreme Court found in favor of the NAACP, holding that Mount Laurel and every other developing municipality in New Jersey

must, by its land-use regulations, presumptively make realistically possible an appropriate variety and choice of housing. More specifically, presumptively it cannot foreclose the opportunity of classes of people mentioned for low and moderate income housing and in its regulations must affirmatively afford that opportunity, at least to the extent of the municipalities' fair share of the present and prospective regional need therefor.[62]

The court gave Mount Laurel ninety days to revise its zoning ordinance so as to correct these deficiencies, thereby becoming the first state supreme court to impose an affirmative "inclusionary" land use obligation on local government.

The Community Development Block Grant programs, established in 1974, were in trouble in the mid-1970s, as the Ford administration had not implemented the act's requirements that the Housing Assistance Plan provide for the regional distribution of low and moderate income housing and primarily benefit low income persons and racial minorities. Community Development Block Grants had been made to suburban communities free of these obligations, many of which used these funds for entirely different purposes. In early 1976, in *City of Hartford et al.* v. *Carla A. Hills et al.*, a U.S. District court found that HUD had acted contrary to law when it approved six suburban block grants in the Hartford area "without requiring the towns to make any assessment whatsoever of the housing needs of low and moderate income persons who might be 'expected to reside' within their borders." The court also said, "When HUD offered the towns the . . . option . . . to submit no figure at all, and they all selected that option, they acted contrary to the clear implication of the statute, that the HAP could not be waived by the Secretary."[63]

The Cleveland City Planning Commission's Cleveland Policy Planning Report, published in 1975, was indicative of a new type of general planning effort that was emerging throughout the United States. This policy plan, unlike the classic community comprehensive plan, deemphasized the physical elements of community development in favor of clear community commitments to the attainment of certain goals, and statement of public policies on critical urban issues.

Numerous referenda against public housing, against low income housing, and against multifamily housing followed the U.S. Supreme Court decision in the *Valtierra* cases of 1971. In northeastern Ohio, in the regional area surrounding Cleveland, land use change came virtually to a halt as one community after another saw referenda introduced to stop developments of various kinds. Eastlake, Ohio, amended its zoning ordinance to require a 55 percent or greater voter approval of any change in existing land use legislation through a citywide referendum. In 1975 the Ohio Supreme Court struck down the Eastlake ordinance,[64] and on 21 June 1976 the U.S. Supreme Court reversed this decision, upholding Eastlake's referendum requirement.[65] This decision stimulated many suburban communities to adopt similar referendum requirements.

Sixty years after its founding at Kansas City in 1917, the American Institute of Planners had grown to over 12,000 members in forty chapters, and there were over fifty degree granting planning programs in American colleges and universities. In mid-1978 the members of the American Institute of Planners, along with the members of the American Society of Planning Officials, voted to consolidate the two organizations into a single organization—the American Planning Association (APA). At this time the new association had a total membership of about 20,000 planning commissioners, professionals, students, and interested citizens.

Conclusion

Planning for American urban settlements is as old as the settlements themselves. The physical form of American cities was often of great concern to the founding fathers, who carefully set down those community forms they believed most conducive to realizing functional and humanly self-fulfilling settlements. The coming of industrialism and massive immigration in the nineteenth century seriously compounded the country's urban problems when it was politically least capable of coping with them. Nevertheless, the nineteenth century saw significant accomplishments in the development of large city parks, the first attempts to control the worst kinds of housing and development conditions, the beginning of planned suburbs, the development of mass transit and commuter railroads, and, at the end of the century, the first federal government programs and legal authorities to deal with urban development problems.

The years from 1900 to 1920 saw the advent of the automobile as a major factor in American cities, the birth of the planning profession in the creation of the American City Planning Institute (subsequently the American Institute of Planners), the development and expansion of land use zoning and comprehensive zoning, the formation of the first official citizen planning commissions, and the design of civic centers and long-range city plans. The most notable by far of these last was Daniel Burnham's bold proposal for Chicago (1909), calling for a metropolitan approach.

The years of prosperity and Depression, 1920 to 1940, saw the rapid spread of comprehensive zoning (sanctioned unequivocally by the U.S. Supreme Court) and land subdivision controls. The extraordinary growth in automobile production, along with the growth of streets and highways, created new land development problems for the as yet new planning field. During the 1920s several model housing developments were undertaken, including Sunnyside, New York, and Radburn, New Jersey, which influenced much of the land development in this country for years to come. During the 1930s employment and housing received attention with the passage of federal laws in 1934 and 1937 that laid the base for public housing in America and, through the Federal Housing Administration, for mortgage insurance programs that established the standards for the millions of single family detached houses that were to be built in suburban America after World War II.

After the war the nation saw a vast expansion of suburban housing, the growth of planning as an ongoing role of local governments, the development of more technically refined zoning and subdivision controls, a significant growth in the number of planning schools, large scale urban renewal activities, extensive citizen participation processes, and the development of the interstate highway system which affected cities and towns almost everywhere.

Today urban and regional planners work across the entire range of local government, especially in management and finance, as they deal with critical social, functional, and economic urban development issues. The constantly changing world of the planners, in a professional and functional sense, is set forth in the balance of this book to help meet the changing needs of urban development for America in the 1980s.

1   For an eloquent exposition of this agrarian philosophy in the words of a party writing in 1782, see: J. Hector de Crèvecoeur, *Letters from an American Farmer* (New York: Fox-Duffield, 1945).
2   Possibly so named after it was burned by the British in 1814 and whitewashed to cover the smoke stains.
3   This intersection is now far inland, as a vast area of land was later reclaimed from the tidal flats of the Potomac River.
4   The National Road, currently U.S. 40, began at Cumberland, Maryland, in 1811, reached Columbus, Ohio, in 1833, and terminated at Vandalia, Illinois, in 1840. It was constructed at a cost of approximately $7 million.
5   *Chi-kak-quwa* was Piankashaw Indian, meaning ''the place of the skunk smells.'' The swampy site of Chicago at the edge of Lake Michigan originally contained large quantities of wild onions and skunk cabbages.
6   So named because, in these long narrow apartments, going from one room to another required passage through consecutive spaces, as in a railroad passenger train.
7   Sub-urban: below the level of urbanism.
8   *Munn* v. *Illinois,* 94 U.S. 113, 126 (1877).
9   Between 1880 and 1890 some 5 million people entered the United States—as many as the total population of the country in 1800.
10 These books are available as follows: Jacob Riis, *How the Other Half Lives* (New York: Dover, 1971); and Jacob Riis, *The Children of the Poor* (New York: Arno Press, 1971).
11 The team could not agree on a color scheme; therefore, everything was painted white. The effect was overwhelming, particularly at night when the fair was illuminated with electric bulbs recently invented by Edison.
12 These concepts were virtually identical to those of Napoleon III and his administrator for Paris, Baron Haussmann, implemented in Paris between 1851 and 1872. They reconstructed the city, slashing broad tree-lined avenues through the slums and constructing huge public works projects such as the Paris Opera House to assure continued employment, while generating projects conducive not only to a socially unifying civic pride but also to a continued economic expansion and prosperity. This highly successful program was well known to Burnham, who constantly referred to it. Paris was known as ''the City Beautiful.'' Efforts undertaken in America during the early years of the twentieth century to replicate Haussmann's programs became known collectively as the ''City Beautiful'' movement.

13 Reissued in 1902 as *Garden Cities of Tomorrow* (Cambridge, Mass.: The M.I.T. Press, 1965).
14 *Attorney General* v. *Williams,* 174 Mass. 476, 55 N.E. 77 (1899).
15 The first full-time housing reformer in America, and founder of the National Housing Association.
16 With the substitution of Frederick Law Olmsted, Jr., for Frederick Law Olmsted, Sr., who was in ill health at the time. The senior Olmsted died in 1903.
17 At the time of the preparation of the San Francisco plan (1904), the first subway line was opened in New York City, extending from City Hall, on Manhattan's southern tip, to 145th Street, in the north.
18 It is worth noting that Henry Ford introduced the Model T just one year earlier. There were relatively few automobiles in America in 1909.
19 *Welch* v. *Swasey,* 214 U.S. 91 (1909).
20 Untested in the U.S. Supreme Court.
21 *Eubank* v. *City of Richmond,* 266 U.S. 137 (1912).
22 *Hadacheck* v. *Sebastian,* 239 U.S. 394, 408 (1915).
23 The ACPI eventually changed its name to the American Institute of Planners (AIP). In October 1978 it consolidated with the American Society of Planning Officials (ASPO) to form the American Planning Association (APA).
24 Also commonly termed an *official map.*
25 *Town of Windsor* v. *Whitney,* 95 Conn. 357, 111 A.3 54 (1920).
26 The study, bearing the overall title *Regional Survey of New York and Its Environs* (New York: Russell Sage Foundation, 1927–31), included eight volumes on separate topics, plus the Regional Plan in two volumes; the contents were as follows: vol. 1, *Major Economic Factors in Metropolitan Growth and Arrangement;* vol. 2, *Population, Land Values and Government;* vol. 3, *Highway Traffic;* vol. 4, *Transit and Transportation;* vol. 5, *Public Recreation;* vol. 6, *Buildings: Their Uses and the Spaces about Them;* vol. 7, *Neighborhood and Community Planning,* vol. 8, *Physical Conditions and Public Services;* Regional Plan, vol. 1, *The Graphic Plan;* Regional Plan, vol. 2, *The Building of the City.*
27 *Brett* v. *Building Commissioner of Brookline,* 250 Mass. 73, 145 N.E. 269 (1924).
28 *Miller* v. *Board of Public Works of the City of Los Angeles,* 195 Cal. 477, 234, P. 281 (1925).
29 *Zahn* v. *Board of Public Works of the City of Los Angeles,* 234 P. 388, 395 (Calif. 1925), affd. 274 U.S. 325 (1927).
30 Alfred Bettman, ''The Relationship of the Functions and Powers of the City Planning Commission to the Legislative, Executive, and Administrative

Departments of City Government," in *Planning Problems of Town, City, and Region: Papers and Discussions of the Twentieth National Conference on City Planning, Held at Dallas and Forth Worth, Texas, May 7 to 10, 1928* (Philadelphia: William F. Fill Co., 1928), p. 142.

31 *Village of Euclid* v. *Ambler Realty Co.,* 272 U.S. 365 (1926).

32 This was $12.50 per room per month in the core of New York City and $11.00 per room per month elsewhere in the state.

33 Two story dwelling units built side by side, sharing common side walls.

34 Two story structures containing one floor dwelling units, each with its own entry door at the ground level.

35 U.S., Department of Commerce, Advisory Committee on City Planning and Zoning, *A Standard City Planning Enabling Act* (Washington, D.C.: Government Printing Office, 1928).

36 Clarence A. Perry, "The Neighborhood Unit," in *Neighborhood and Community Planning,* vol. 7 of *Regional Survey of New York and Its Environs* (New York: Russell Sage Foundation, 1929).

37 *Township of Franklin* v. *Tugwell,* 85 F.2d 208 (1936).

38 Clarence A. Perry, *Housing for the Machine Age* (New York: Russell Sage Foundation, 1939).

39 Ladislas Segoe, *Local Planning Administration* (Chicago: International City Managers' Association, 1941).

40 Previously reconstituted as the National Resources Planning Board.

41 FHA remained in HHFA until HHFA was superseded by the U.S. Department of Housing and Urban Development (HUD) in 1965. The forty year longevity of this program may well have been partially influenced by the fact that FHA operating expenses are met from fees and insurance premiums paid by the mortgagors, making FHA one of the few self-supporting federal government agencies.

42 American Public Health Association, Committee on the Hygiene of Housing, *Planning the Neighborhood* (Chicago: Public Administration Service, 1948).

43 More commonly known at the time as "the Miracle Mile."

44 This program was tied to housing, permitting it to be included in a Housing Act, by requiring that the project area be *either* 55 percent residential at the time of clearance *or* 55 percent residential as redeveloped.

45 Frank E. Horack, Jr., "Performance Standards in

Residential Zoning," in *Planning 1952: The Proceedings of the Annual National Planning Conference at Boston, Massachusetts,* ed. American Society of Planning Officials (Chicago: American Society of Planning Officials, 1952), p. 154.

46 *Lionshead Lake, Inc.,* v. *Township of Wayne,* 10 N.J. 165, 173–174; 89 A.2d 693 (1952); app. dismd. 344 U.S. 919 (1953).

47 *Fischer* v. *Township of Bedminster,* 11 N.J. 194, 204–205; 93 A.2d 378 (1953).

48 Jane Jacobs, *The Death and Life of Great American Cities* (New York: Random House, 1961).

49 Lawrence Haworth, *The Good City* (Bloomington, Ind.: Indiana University Press, 1963).

50 Charles Lindblom, *The Intelligence of Democracy* (New York: The Macmillan Company, 1965).

51 *Jones* v. *Alfred H. Mayer Co.,* 392 U.S. 409 (1968).

52 U.S., Congress, House, *Report of the National Commission on Urban Problems to the Congress and to the President of the United States: Building the American City,* H. Doc. 91–34, 91st Cong., 1st sess., 1968.

53 Mary Brooks, *Exclusionary Zoning,* Planning Advisory Report no. 254 (Chicago: American Society of Planning Officials, 1970).

54 The regional area surrounding Dayton, Ohio.

55 *Golden* v. *Planning Board of the Township of Ramapo,* 30 N.Y. 2d 359, 334 N.Y. S.2d 138, 285 N.E.2d 391 (1972).

56 *Ronald James* v. *Anita Valtierra; Virginia C. Shaffer* v. *Anita Valtierra,* 402 U.S. 137 (1971).

57 In 1975 HUD announced that it had foreclosed on 200,000 government insured mortgages worth $2.7 billion, becoming the owner of more than 64,000 central city housing units.

58 U.S. Code 1970, Title 42, section 5301 et seq.

59 Ibid.

60 Ibid.

61 *Construction Industry Ass'n of Sonoma County* v. *City of Petaluma,* 522 F.2d 897, 908–909 (9th Cir., 1975). Upon appeal, the U.S. Supreme Court refused to review this case, upholding the circuit court opinion.

62 *Southern Burlington County NAACP* v. *Township of Mount Laurel,* 67 N.J. 161, 336 A.2d 713, 724 (1975).

63 *City of Hartford et al.* v. *Carla A. Hills et al.,* No. H-75-258, 408 F. Supp. 879, 902 (U.S.D.C. Conn., 1975).

64 *Forest City Enterprises* v. *Eastlake,* 41 Ohio St. 2d 187, 324 N.E.2d 740 (1975).

65 *Eastlake* v. *Forest City Enterprises,* 44 U.S.L.W. 4919 (1976).

Part two: Management, information, finance

3 Planning agency management

Planning is important, because it affects the quality of community life. Planning is exciting and interesting, because it grapples with problems, because it involves the world of ideas, and because it gives us a sense of influencing our future. But planning is also a form of work. For planning to take place in today's society, offices must be rented, meetings must be arranged, and reports must be published. These activities do not occur by chance. The work of planning requires an organizational structure. It should have official standing, a known purpose, a line of authority, and financial and human resources.

The need for an organizational structure is more than housekeeping. The official status of a planning agency can affect the weight given to its proposals. The line of authority can affect who hears professional recommendations and in what form. The way in which an agency's work is allocated and supervised can affect the efficiency with which it functions internally and its impact on the community at large. For these reasons and many more, it is important to consider how the work of planning is done and the setting in which it is carried out. Such matters are intimately bound up in the output of the profession.

This is not to say that quality planning can be guaranteed by a particular organizational structure. Dedicated and competent personnel will usually be able to overcome most of the problems of poor organization and administration. But their work will be enhanced if it can be focused on the substance of planning rather than squandered in duplication of effort and other inefficiencies.

This chapter will examine the ways in which planning work is organized and will explore some of the issues in planning administration. It begins with a discussion of agency activities and proceeds to review the planning function in local government and the governmental context. This leads to a discussion of the organizational placement of planning in local government (illustrated by four alternative organizational models), and then to a discussion of the internal organization of the agency. Attention is next shifted to the personal aspects of planning agency administration: agency relations with other groups; and agency staffing, with emphasis on the role of the planning director. The chapter concludes with observations on three key administrative topics and a look at some innovations.

Planning agency activities

Planning organizations should be shaped and equipped to carry out the tasks required of them—in other words, form follows function. In order to better understand potential organizational and staff needs it is useful to understand the range of potential tasks. This section presents a brief overview of potential planning agency activities. It does not include closely related tasks, such as building code enforcement, which might be conducted in a department of development. No attempt is made here to describe how or why all of the activities are conducted. These matters are covered in detail in other chapters in this book. The intent here is to provide an inventory of the kinds of staff activities that can be found in a planning agency.

Plan preparation

The preparation of plans is a major activity of planning agencies. Local planning agencies have historically emphasized the preparation of long-range plans for the overall physical development of the community. Land use, transportation, and public facilities have been primary elements of such plans. In recent years the emphasis has been swinging away from these plans, known variously as master plans, comprehensive plans, and general plans. The current emphasis is on the management of a continuing planning process designed to provide advice and counsel when and where it is needed.

Project planning

Project planning is a specialized type of short-range physical planning for small areas. Often associated with redevelopment schemes, it includes detailed proposals for such activities as street and parking layout, building design, and proposed uses.

Community development planning

The evolution of urban renewal programs away from large clearance programs and the initiation of federal revenue sharing are producing a new orientation for planning. In particular, the Community Development Block Grant program of the U.S. Department of Housing and Urban Development (HUD) has required local planning agencies to spend more time in planning the allocation of federal community development funds among competing local needs. In addition, more attention has been given to the coordination of such funding with ongoing redevelopment work. This planning often emphasizes the use of public funds and redevelopment activities as catalysts to promote private development that will support community goals. (See Chapter 20 for an extensive discussion of this new program orientation.)

Land use development management

This term encompasses a range of activities. Virtually all local planning agencies are involved in regulating land development and land use. This activity involves the administration of zoning ordinances and subdivision regulations. It usually includes the preparation of staff recommendations on all petitions to amend the text or map of the zoning ordinance and the preparation of recommendations on all appeals to the board of zoning adjustment. At a more advanced level it involves growth management activities that link land use controls to budgeting and capital improvement. A related activity is the undertaking of studies leading to the adoption or major revision of the zoning ordinance.

Coordination and review

Coordination interrelates projects or activities so as to avoid conflicts and to provide opportunities that are mutually supportive wherever possible. The primary device used to foster coordination is the review of projects by a central group, the planning agency. Several types of coordination are attempted through planning agency review:

1. Coordination of proposed projects with public plans so that schools, utility extensions, and other public improvements are located properly according to overall development plans.

2. Coordination of local public projects with each other so that, for example, the designer of a fire station is made aware of impending realignment of adjacent streets.
3. Coordination among different levels of government. A city, for example, wants the location of a state highway to be supportive of its own development plans.
4. Coordination among adjacent local governments. Here an umbrella group such as a regional planning agency seeks cooperation in plans or projects of one city that will have a spillover effect in adjacent communities.

Budgeting

Budgeting, once seen as little more than an extension of governmental accounting, is now of vital interest to the planning agency. Budgeting is a process used for allocating scarce resources among competing demands. The planning agency may have primary responsibility for preparation of the capital budget—the spending program concerned with major public improvements. Often the agency will work with the budget office in preparation of capital and operating budgets. This is especially true where the planning function is closely linked to the chief executive. It is less likely to be the case when the staff is responsible to the independent planning commission. The importance of the budget function to planning is reflected by the action of Atlanta where the two functions have been placed under one cabinet level officer. An annual development plan, including goals, policies, and programs and policies, is used as the basis for preparing the annual budget. Philadelphia and Baltimore, as well as Dayton, Ohio, have established mechanisms to link physical and financial planning.

Program planning

Program planning is the devising of organized activities that produce a desired service. It involves the identification of the clients to be served, the description of services to be provided, and the specification of funds, personnel, equipment, and activities necessary to produce the desired service.

Program planning is important to the planning agency, even when it is still the primary concern of the operating department. This is so for the following three reasons. First, it is necessary to have some understanding of the program to be conducted in a public facility, such as a school or a park, in order to properly plan the appropriate location, size, and other characteristics of the facility. Second, the planning agency may be called upon to provide technical assistance for program planning to operating departments that have traditionally undertaken program planning on a very informal basis. Finally, the planning agency may serve in a staff capacity to the chief executive in devising new programs that are not readily available from existing line departments.

Policy analysis

Decision makers often evolve strategies or approaches to certain persistent problems. These strategies or policies provide a guideline or basic approach to a situation. What level of public service shall a community provide to scattered fringe area development? How should law enforcement officers respond to large scale lawbreaking involving civil disobedience? What can be done to halt the abandonment of inner city housing? A multitude of similar issues could be identified to illustrate the need for governmental policy.

Planning is closely linked to policy analysis, although the terms are not synonymous. They have evolved together in recent years with a common set of tools and often with attention to the same subjects. Policy analysis is the use of scientific methods to derive policy. Kenneth Kraemer has identified the essential features of policy analysis as: "(1) a comprehensive or systems approach; (2) scientific tradition and method; (3) the use of mixed teams; and (4) an action orientation."[1]

Research

Much planning and policy analysis could be characterized as research. The planning agency tends to have a unique role in local government research as a major source of data and information. Both the public and the various units of local government have a need for information about population and development trends that may be readily supplied by the planning agency.

Public participation

Many of the above activities of the planning agency will result in some contact between the public and the agency. Land use controls require frequent public hearings. The development of long-range plans requires solicitation of public views on community objectives. The request for information by groups or individuals requires staff time and resources. Public participation and contact are woven through many of the day-to-day activities of the agency. They involve public service, public education, and education of the agency by the public.

Unofficial activities Many . . . activities of the planning department are not recorded in any official list of duties. They include assuming the role of advocate for various groups and interests and geographic areas; generating new ideas about the physical environment and testing them before the public; and giving citizens a forum for voicing their complaints. Research into local physical, social, and economic conditions and the continuous provision of timely, easily understood information, regardless of whose cause it might help or hinder, can bring prestige and a measure of influence to those who provide it. It may be inherent in the nature of government that the more informal or voluntary activities serve the citizens as well as those that are required by law.

Source: Excerpted from Allan B. Jacobs, *Making City Planning Work* (Chicago: American Society of Planning Officials, 1978), p. 46.

The planning function

The nature of the planning function depends on the type of community the agency serves. Variations in a planning program may stem from the characteristics of the individual community; they may reflect the level of the governmental unit involved; or they may respond to the values and goals of the population involved. The cumulative effect of these influences may be summarized in the view that the planning organization will tend to reflect the community perception of the scope of the planning function. Unfortunately, the organizational structure usually does not change nearly as rapidly as the views of the planning function change.

The historical background

Many planning agencies were first established during the 1930s and 1940s. The City Beautiful movement strongly influenced the prevailing views of planning agency work: this work was seen as primarily concerned with the physical development of the city. Such attitudes influenced the composition of early professional staffs and the perception of their role. The early agencies were also strongly influenced by another force—the effort to avoid corruption and politics; thus the independent "blue ribbon" planning commission was a popular form of organization.

Although planning agencies were widespread by the 1930s, pioneer efforts had begun earlier. New Haven, Connecticut, established the first municipal planning board in 1909. By the late 1920s there were numerous planning boards in existence and the basic legal framework for planning had been shaped. Many of the leaders of the early planning movement had lived through and participated in the good government movement of the preceding years. A reaction to corruption and ineptitude in local government, the good government movement had fostered such governmental innovations as the recall, the initiative, and the referendum. It had been fed by the perception, often justified in that day, that politics were corrupt.

Honest graft Many of the early city planning commissions were established as "blue ribbon" groups in reaction to widespread corruption in local government which had carried over from the nineteenth century. "Tammany Hall" was the term widely used for cronyism and machine politics. George Washington Plunkitt, who operated in New York County, now the Borough of Manhattan in New York City, epitomized the times, and there is a present-day revelance to Tammany leader Plunkitt's description of honest graft:

"There's an honest graft, and I'm an example of how it works. I might sum up the whole thing by sayin': 'I seen my opportunities and I took 'em.'

"Just let me explain by examples. My party's in power in the city, and it's goin'

to undertake a lot of public improvements. Well, I'm tipped off, say, that they're going to lay out a new park in a certain place.

"I see my opportunity and I take it. I go to that place and I buy up all the land I can in the neighborhood. Then the board of this or that makes its plan public, and there is a rush to get my land, which nobody cared particular for before.

"Ain't it perfectly honest to charge a good price and make a profit on my investment and foresight? Of course, it is. Well, that's honest graft."

Source: Partly abstracted and partly excerpted from William L. Riordan, *Plunkitt of Tammany Hall* (New York: E. P. Dutton & Co., 1963), p. 3. Original edition 1905.

One of the tendencies of the reform movement, given its distrust of old style politics, was to separate important matters from political control. The device for accomplishing this was the citizen board or commission. Thus, local public utilities and school systems were often removed from direct control of mayors or city councils and placed under the oversight of a commission. The commission, a "blue ribbon" citizen board, acted much as a corporate board of directors, establishing policy and hiring capable managers to oversee operations. The commission model was seized upon by leaders of the planning movement as the desired organizational pattern.

The early planning agencies were thus characterized by three basic features: a focus of their work on the physical development of the city; an official status that tended to ensure some separation from the day-to-day operations of local government; and the insertion of a lay citizen board between professional planners and elected public officials. It is important to recognize that these features were mutually supportive. So long as the scope of the planners' concern was with long-range physical development, political leaders and the heads of operating departments were content to let the planners live in their own world, guided by the oversight of selfless citizen boards. Since the planners were committed to the importance of the citizen commission, the planners had an incentive to maintain their work in the traditional mold.

The wisdom of limiting city planning to a focus on physical development came under serious challenge with the publication in 1941 of Robert Walker's *The Planning Function in Urban Government.*[2] After reviewing the history of the planning movement and doing field studies in thirty-seven cities, Walker argued strongly for reconsideration of the scope and, of necessity, the organization of planning:

> The scope of city planning is properly as broad as the scope of city government. It seems inevitable that the concept of city planning which limited it to streets, parks, transportation, zoning, etc., will give way to a concept of governmental planning which will include these things and the more recent additions to municipal services as well. Insofar as city governments continue to be concerned with them, so should the planning agency be concerned with them; but as urban government expands its sphere of activity into new fields the activities of the planning agency should be correspondingly expanded. This will be clear if it is borne in mind that high city officials can, and do, plan their work without the aid of a separate agency. Planning is essentially their responsibility, and a planning agency can do little more than aid them in exercising it more competently. Thus, the existence of an agency with broad interests does not mean that all planning activity will be carried on by one agency. On the contrary, an important part of the work of a central planning agency should be the coordination of departmental planning in the light of general-policy considerations.[3]

Having recast the scope of planning work, Walker then addressed the need to reshape the organizational arrangement to accommodate the work agenda:

> In the light of these considerations and of the present unsatisfactory situation as regards the independent planning commission, it is believed that the most fruitful line of development for the future would be the replacement of these commissions by a department or bureau attached to the office of mayor or city manager.[4]

Walker both identified and fostered significant reassessment of the scope and organization of planning. The debates and experiments continue. Those involved agree only that no one arrangement is the best for all situations. Clearly, the day is past when planning organization is a simple or a uniform matter.

The planning network

There are very few communities in which all the planning is done by one agency acting alone. Rather, planning activities have expanded in a number of ways, both formally and informally. The result is a loose network of planning activities that permeates public institutions. The parts of this network include the following:

1. Planning within different units and levels of general government. This includes central cities, suburban municipalities, counties, townships, and state governments. This planning is usually general overall planning with a historical tendency to emphasize physical development.
2. Planning within the operating departments of general governments. This includes the planning that occurs within such departments as highways, health, recreation, and education at both the local and state levels. This planning is concerned primarily with the provision of a particular kind of service or facility.
3. Planning by regional agencies not responsible to a single general government. This includes such agencies as councils of governments, economic development districts, and other regional planning

organizations. These agencies are primarily concerned with the coordination of plans and programs among various units of local government within a region.

4. Special purpose planning agencies. These agencies, although they may vary widely in specific characteristics, have in common the fact that they deal with a particular service or program at a level which cuts across the boundaries of various units of government or the agencies within them. These special purpose agencies include such organizations as areawide health planning councils and regional transportation study agencies.

There are certain important factors to bear in mind regarding this planning network. First, some planning operations are formal—that is, they are labeled planning operations and they regularly produce plans and programs subject to public review and adoption. Others are informal: they carry out work that makes choices about the future, but they may not label their work planning. Instead, planning is a part of managing their service area. Second, the links between the various parts of the planning network are not complete. In some cases the links between planning agencies may be quite formal, involving contracts and legal powers to review and comment on plans. In other instances there may be only informal contacts primarily dependent on the personal contacts among staff members in various units. The complexity of planning operations is not the result of mere insensitivity or ignorance. It reflects the fact that planning is an activity practiced on an increasingly broad scale within a complex governmental system.

This chapter is concerned primarily with the work of the local government planning agency. This is the agency most readily identified at the local level with overall policies affecting community development. Its effectiveness and its organization are profoundly affected by the nature of the planning network in which it is located, and its role in that network. The local government planning agency is concerned with the coordination of various plans produced within the network with each other and with an overall plan for the future. Therefore, as the attributes and the work of the planning agency are discussed, it should be recognized that many of the comments may apply to other units in a planning network and that very few units will exhibit all the features described here. Each agency needs to be fitted to its setting. The work of each unit is conditioned to some extent by the work of other units in its area, as well as by the needs of the community.

Line and staff functions

Administrators sometimes categorize organizational units as either *line* or *staff* units. Line units are those whose work is primarily concerned with direct service or production. Police, fire, and public works departments fall into this group. Staff units are primarily devoted to provision of general services within the organization. They provide some services used by the line departments, or advice and service to the chief administrator. Personnel, budget, and policy advisory units are examples of staff units.

One of the factors contributing to the variations and the debate within planning organizations is the fact that planning involves both line and staff functions. Line activities include such matters as day-to-day zoning and subdivision administration. Staff functions include such activities as provision of research and planning services to line departments. The preparation of a long-range community plan is a technical process that would usually be viewed as a staff function. The interpretation of that plan and its use to give advice to decision makers is also a staff function. The nature of both line and staff elements will be seen more fully as the work of the planning agency is described below.

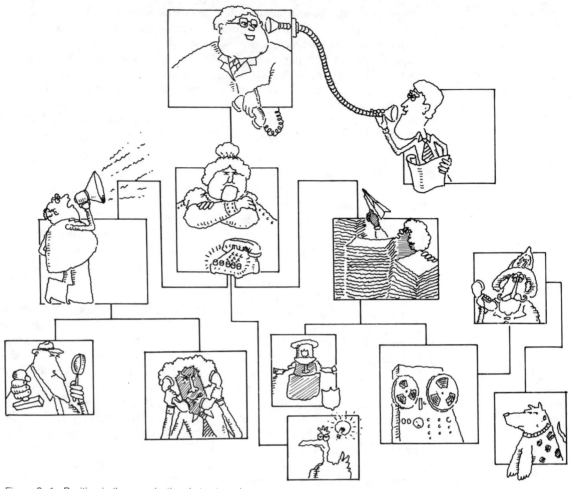

Figure 3–1   Position in the organizational structure does make a difference.

Alternative organizational models

Four organizational models are presented below. They do not represent actual agencies. Their purpose is to show alternative ways of locating the planning agency within the structure of the local government. Both the lay planning commission and the professional staff are shown in each model. The location of the professional staff and its relationship to decision makers is a key feature in each model.

The independent planning commission

The independent planning commission has been the basic pattern of planning organization for many years. It was fostered by the Standard City Planning Enabling Act published by the U.S. Department of Commerce in 1928 (see Chapter 2). Many states patterned their legislation after this standard act. Accordingly, local communities were required to follow the prescription of their state legislation when they set up their own planning operations.

The commission members are usually appointed by the chief executive subject to confirmation by the council, or they are appointed by the council directly. The arrangement is illustrated in Figure 3–2. Terms of membership are usually arranged so that only a few members' terms expire each year. This is

Planning under a commission City planning under a commission need not be out of the mainstream of decision making if the commission and the staff choose not to be. There is little to stop them from being involved and responsive to the needs of the city. City planners under a commission can have considerable freedom to innovate and to work for their own plans and those causes they conclude to be consistent with their city planning charge. They can explore ways of implementing plans on their own, yet within the framework of the government that establishes the planning department in the first place.

Source: Excerpted from Allan B. Jacobs, *Making City Planning Work* (Chicago: American Society of Planning Officials, 1978), pp. 308–9.

intended to foster a continuity of activities. In some cities the mayor and one or more members of the local legislative body are ex officio members whose terms are coterminous with their terms of office. Professional staff, when employed, are appointed by and are responsible to the commission. Typically, the planning commission has the power to approve subdivision plats and must be consulted on all zoning amendments and a variety of public improvement projects.

Most of the benefits attributed to this lay commission are summarized by an early writer in the following words:

The planning commission represents a cross section of community interests, serves as a sounding board or trial balloon for new ideas, acts as a buffer between the technicians and the public, and relieves the city council of many details. Planning commissions may also be instrumental in securing community participation, promoting public interest in planning, and by virtue of their status in the community are able to get planning effectuated.[5]

Another writer has classed their functions in three ways, as

(1) the *representation* roles, bringing detailed knowledge of the community and the attitudes and values of its citizens to bear upon public actions to guide development; (2) the *interpretive* roles, seeking to inform, promote, and stimulate interest in planning and to protect the professional staff from public misunderstanding; and (3) the *advisory* roles, involving assistance in formulating development policy and helping to coordinate the total governmental planning effort.[6]

These supposed positive attributes of planning commissions have been broadly challenged. It has been noted, for example, that these planning commissions are frequently dominated by business and real estate interests, which are hardly representative of the community, and are sometimes at odds with the basic concept of conflict of interest.[7] The separation of these commissions from politics, and thus from the major interests of public decision makers, may cause planning to actually be accomplished elsewhere in local government. Thus, the mayor or manager can rely on the executive staff, on the budget office, and on informal executive committees.

Despite its shortcomings, the independent commission is useful in small cities. These communities frequently depend on consultants for technical assistance. The personal knowledge of local situations and the continuity provided by a planning commission can be quite helpful. Separation from political leaders and operating departments is also less of a problem in small cities, where informal personal contacts allow discussion of issues and information exchange to cut across the full scope of local government.

Another situation in which the independent commission may be an advantage is that of the joint city–county planning effort. In many jurisdictions a city–county planning commission allows one agency to deal with the development issues of both a city and its developing fringe. In addition to being economical,

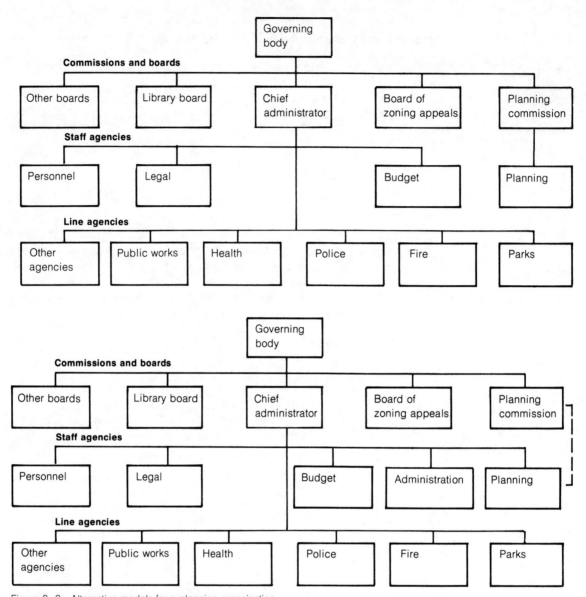

Figure 3–2   Alternative models for a planning organization:
the independent planning commission (top, this page),
the planning department (bottom, this page), the community
development department (top, facing page), and the line and staff
planning department (bottom, facing page).

this arrangement tends to foster the growth of a more coherent set of development policies than would occur with separate planning agencies in each jurisdiction. Both the city and county governments may be willing to support a joint program over which they have some control, while neither would accept a complete monopoly of the planning program by the other party.

The growth of professional staffs and the increasing acceptance of the criticisms of independent planning commissions has resulted in a variety of alternative organizational models. The independent planning commission is still present in virtually all of them, but its role and influence are altered.

The planning department

A popular arrangement of the planning function is the shifting of the planning staff from a position of reporting to the planning commission to one of reporting

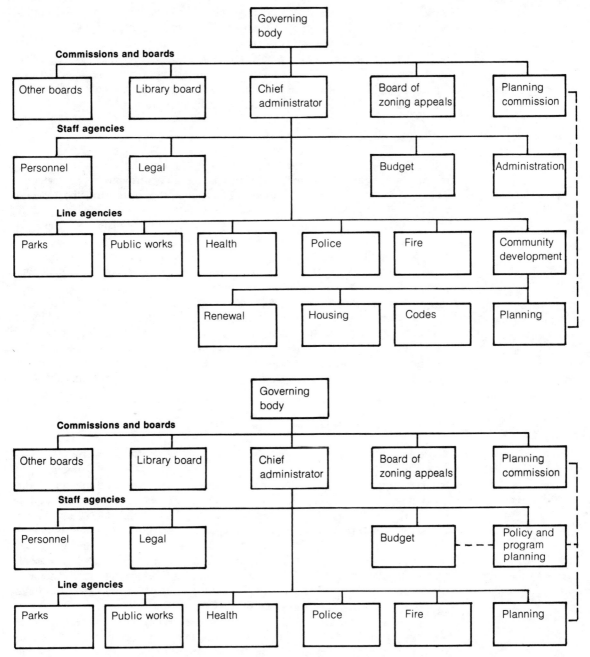

Figure 3–2   (continued).

to the chief executive in either a line or a staff agency. Planning departments (Figure 3–2) conduct both staff and line functions; the important issue is that the planning director works for the executive. The planning commission is usually retained, although its role may be modified. In some instances it may retain the same advisory and regulatory powers as described in the model above. The more recent tendency, although the shift is gradual, is to give the planning staff more direct operational power and limit the work of the commission to an advisory role on policy issues.

The planning department arrangement has the potential advantage of having the chief executive become the champion of planning recommendations. As the staff serves the chief executive, the chief executive selectively appropriates the plans and suggestions of the planners as his or her own. The chief's support of these matters before the council or his or her incorporation of them into budget proposals may greatly enhance the possibility of having long-range plans implemented. These advantages are most readily achieved in a strong mayor or council-manager form of government.

The planning department can be susceptible to the experience of serving two masters simultaneously. It is subject to the oversight of the chief executive in day-to-day affairs, but it is also subject to the advice and influence of the planning commission. This can be a problem if the two are in conflict.

The community development department

The community development department has many of the characteristics and the advantages and disadvantages of the planning department. As indicated in Figure 3–2, the department is an umbrella agency that brings together several agencies affecting community development. In addition to planning, this agency may include the public housing agency, the building and housing code enforcement agency, and the urban redevelopment agency. In this agency, land use controls administration may be given a separate status alongside of planning.

The advantage of such an umbrella agency is the coordination that can be promoted among the related agencies. Planning is directly united with a number of implementation activities. Such coordination may be particularly useful in central cities where urban redevelopment, housing, and other activities intended to combat blight are particularly critical. Boston and Milwaukee, as well as Columbus, Ohio, have adopted variations of this arrangement. The disadvantage of this arrangement is that staff planners may be too far down the organizational ladder to have ready access to the mayor and manager or other key policymakers.

Separate line and staff planning departments

Some communities are institutionalizing planning of a broad scope by setting up two separate planning agencies. The traditional agency is a line function primarily concerned with planning for the orderly physical development of the community. The staff agency, sometimes called *policy planning,* is directly advisory to the chief executive on programs and policies affecting all the operations of the local government. It might be used, for example, to examine issues as diverse as the method of allocating federal Community Development funds among competing local needs, or the preparation of a plan for phasing out one system of solid waste collection in favor of another. This line and staff scheme is illustrated in Figure 3–2. Memphis, New Orleans, Seattle, and Houston have experimented with this arrangement.

An obvious weakness of this scheme is the opportunity for two planning agencies to compete for influence or to work in an uncoordinated fashion. On the other hand, the arrangement does foster more explicit attention to the full range of planning needs in the community.

Commission and staff relationships

Two major factors are present in the organizational models presented above. First, the planning commission is present, exerting more or less official power. Second, the professional staff is also present. The relationship between these two forces is an important factor in the day-to-day operations and the success of local planning. There are indications that the professional staffs are growing in power and gradually forging stronger ties to the executive functions of local government.

A 1971 survey of 2,074 cities by the International City Management Association found that 71 percent of all reporting cities had a professional planning staff.[8] All reporting cities with populations above 100,000 had a professional staff. Most of the cities that did not have a resident professional staff were those with populations below 25,000. In contrast, a 1948 survey reported that only 17 percent of all reporting cities above 10,000 employed one or more professionally trained planners.[9]

Organizational arrangements are also shifting away from the independent planning commission. In 1948, for example, over 50 percent of all planning directors in reporting cities over 25,000 were appointed by planning commissions.[10] By 1971 only 18 percent were appointed by these commissions. Most are appointed by the chief executive. Similarly, there has been an increase in the number of planning departments and development departments while the number of staff directors reporting to independent commissions has decreased.[11] There are some notable variations in these trends according to geographic location and type of city. The direction of the trends is clear, however. The planning staff is being drawn into a closer working relationship with the chief executive. As will be seen below, this can have important impacts on the scope of the work of the planning agency.

These shifts may have the effect of allowing the planning commission to fulfill some of its original purposes. A constant criticism of the planning commission has been that it has been called upon to act as a body of experts—in the review of subdivision plats, for example—when its members have not in fact been experts. To the extent that the professional staff can be allowed to take over those functions requiring technical expertise, the planning commission can be used more for purposes of representation and policy review.

The ebb and flow of power and influence between the professional staff and the planning commission is influenced by more than formal organizational arrangements. An aggressive and technically competent staff may enlarge its influence by the timely offer of advice to city managers and heads of operating departments. The planning commission will gain or lose influence with political leaders and the public by the integrity, representativeness, and prominence of its members. Conflicts of interest, as, for example, a planning commission that is dominated by the developers whom it is supposed to regulate, will tend to inhibit recruitment of a strong professional staff because potential staff members will assume that their work will be subverted to other interests—in this case to the development industry. Conflict of interest situations will also tend to undermine public support of the planning agency. These examples illustrate the many factors that can influence the relative strengths of the planning commission and the staff, as well as the relationship between them. The key point is that such influences are not constant, nor are they unique to a particular organizational model.

Planning agency organization

The internal organization of the planning agency may vary. Here, again, no single model fits all situations. The organization of the agency will be influenced by such factors as size, the place of the planning agency within the organizational framework of the city, and the planning needs of the community. Figure 3–3 shows a typical organization of a planning agency.

In very small communities the staff may consist of a professional planner, an assistant planner, a draftsman, and a secretary. In such a small office the assignment of work is extremely flexible. Each staff member will be involved in some way in almost all the activities of the office. As the number of staff people increases it becomes necessary to give various staff members the primary responsibility for certain kinds of work. The director, for example, will be responsible for public functions, such as interaction with the mayor's office and the planning commission. One assistant planner will be responsible for collection of data for long-range plans. Another assistant planner will review subdivision plats and zoning petitions. One secretary will serve as receptionist and typist. Another will do all the filing and will keep the financial records. As the office continues to grow it will gradually become necessary to subdivide the agency into divisions, each with explicit responsibilities. The subdivision of an agency has several advantages.

The division of an agency into units promotes efficiency by clarifying the responsibilities of each individual. It promotes the development of skills through specialization. Personnel may be selected with training and experience suited to the needs of a particular unit: a landscape architect for the subdivision plat review division; an economist for the research division. Also, persons with gen-

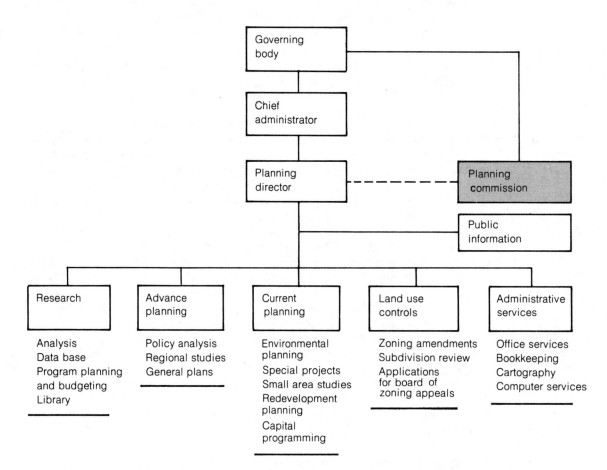

Figure 3–3   Typical organization of a city planning agency showing divisions that are common to many agencies.

eral skills may become specialists in particular aspects of agency work by experience in a unit. The on-the-job training that is possible in a specialized unit also makes it possible to use subprofessional personnel effectively.

Another advantage of subdividing an agency into specialized units is that it allows easier identification and contact of key staff people by outsiders. In a loosely organized agency there will be a tendency for all persons seeking a service from the agency to go to the director. In an agency that has units with specific responsibilities outsiders will go to the unit that relates to their needs. A developer, for example, would go to the unit responsible for subdivision plat review. A school superintendent interested in population forecasts would go directly to the research division. Such direct contacts tend to foster a more efficient communications network between the agency and the various groups with which it needs to maintain contact, both in and out of government.

One of the most important advantages of subdividing an agency is that it protects the continuity of long-range work assignments. Some agency work may require more than a year for the completion of an assignment. Preparation of major reports and updating of comprehensive plan elements fall into this category. Every agency also has work that may be called "brushfire" work. It requires immediate attention. An unexpected request from the manager for information is one example. Another could occur if the state government announces that it will build a new state office building in the city and the manager asks the planning department to assess the impact of the location in terms of city development policy.

Brushfire work is usually no more important than other agency work, but its immediacy and public visibility often result in the shifting of staff from other tasks to work on the immediate problem. One consequence can be the virtual elimination of long-range planning. This is one of the most common complaints of agency directors. One solution is to have certain units responsible for long-range work and not subject to response to brushfires. The organization of the agency can provide a mechanism to protect certain staffs from the disruption of day-to-day issues.

The subdivision of an agency is not without hazard. It can reduce needed flexibility in the use of personnel if unit boundaries are observed too rigidly. Needs often arise which do not fit the responsibilities of one unit. Then it is necessary to create task forces that may cut across several units.

The subdivision of an agency can also hamper as well as help in personnel development. If division directors and their staffs are allowed to concentrate exclusively on the work of their division, they may lose the broader comprehensive view of agency work that is necessary if each unit is to be truly supportive of the work of the agency. Moreover, a professional planner having a broad range of skills can be used so long in a narrowly specialized unit that these general skills become rusty and out-of-date; also, the ability to move upward or to another unit in the organization may be lost.

The most important hazard in agency organization is that the organization can become so rigid that its organization predetermines the agency work program. It should be remembered that the purpose of each division is to serve the overall mission of the agency as it responds to community needs. As community needs change, the agency mission will need to change and its internal organization may need to adjust. If the personnel within each subunit of the organization view their unit as an end in itself, the organization loses its ability to adapt to new situations.

There are several ways of subdividing an agency into divisions; these are as follows:

1. By function: the planning agency can be organized around the major urban functions with which it is concerned. In this case land use, transportation, and recreation would be examples of its internal units.
2. By process: the agency can be organized around the processes or skills necessary to carry out its work. In this case research and design would be examples of its internal units.
3. By time: the agency can be organized according to the increments of time associated with its work. In this case, long-range planning, current planning, and continuing services would be examples of its internal units.
4. By area: the agency can be organized around the major geographic units for which it has responsibility. In this case central business district planning, neighborhood area planning, and waterfront planning might be examples of its internal units.

Few agencies would be organized purely on one of these bases. In actual practice there would be a blending of these factors to produce an organization that is most responsive to the needs of a particular community. Thus, the specifics of internal organization will vary widely from one community to another. There are certain divisions that are common to many agencies (see Figure 3–3); these are advance planning, current planning, land use controls, research, and administration. These divisions are often subdivided into sections.

Advance planning

This division is responsible for the development and maintenance of long-range plans. This may include the development of general plans or the updating of specific elements (for example, land use or transportation). The work of this division is heavily oriented to goal formulation and the definition of broad policies; it provides a framework or point of reference for other divisions in the agency.

Current planning

This division is responsible for short-range developmental planning and brush-fire situations. It may have sections responsible for small area project plans, an urban design section, and a task force section specifically designed to work on brushfire problems. It responds to the need for concrete advice on specific issues. Its work tends to be specific and visible to decision makers.

Land use controls

This division is responsible for administering the land use control mechanisms and for recommending periodic amendments to improve these mechanisms. Its personnel would review all subdivision plats, zoning petitions, and applications to the board of zoning adjustments.

Research

This division supports the work of other divisions in a variety of ways. It often includes a section specifically responsible for maintaining a data base in such areas as population and housing. Its forecasts are used by other planning divisions and by a variety of other agencies of government. It may be called on to do in-depth studies in a policy analysis made to support the decision-oriented work of current planning, or it may do general background studies in new technology, hillside development, housing abandonment, or other issues that are of interest to advance planning in the establishment of policy.

Administrative services

This division provides the support services necessary to the other divisions of the agency. It includes such sections as stenography, drafting, library services, personnel, and office budgeting.

Agency relationships: operating in the planning network

The communications between a planning agency and other units in the governmental system are important contributors to the agency's effectiveness. The day-to-day contacts between a planning agency and other units are important

Figure 3–4　The formal and the informal organization. People will not stay put on the organization chart— the formal organization, that is. The real challenge is to bring the formal and informal organizations together.

sources of information for plan formulation and are also mechanisms for feedback on the merit of various plan proposals.

　The nature of agency relationships is better understood if the organizational charts and other formal aspects of governmental structure discussed in the preceding sections are set aside momentarily. Instead of agency relationships, consider the person-to-person relationships that occur. The official reports, news releases, laws, and other paraphernalia of a planning agency are only a part of the sum of the factors that influence public and private decisions in a community. The other part consists largely of informal contacts among people: the lunch meeting between a planner and an assistant director of the recreation department; a planner's sidewalk meeting with a developer; the telephone calls between members of a planning staff and employees in the line departments and in state agencies; and other similar contacts. It is this informal ebb and flow of information throughout the planning network and the local government that lies near the heart of an agency's vitality.

　If informal contacts between people are the real substance of agency relationships, they are nevertheless conditioned by formal relationships. A planning agency established as a staff level unit reporting to a city manager will tend to have a relationship to line departments of the city that is different from that of a planning agency organized as a line unit.

　The following six sections review the relationships of the planning agency to those individuals, agencies, and groups with which it has its most frequent and important contacts.

The chief administrator

Relations between the planning agency and the chief administrator are extremely important, especially in cities with the council-manager or strong mayor form of government. The chief administrator is the person most likely to affect the broad range of decisions in the community. This is the person who can initiate new programs, lead publicly in the reconsideration of priorities, and throw the full weight of the local government administrative machinery behind an investigation. The influence of the chief administrator ranges from immediate operational issues to major policy questions with a long-range impact. The strong chief administrator is the chief planner for a community in the sense that strategies and action plans are developed to respond to a broad range of community needs. Thus the chief administrator who values planning will be especially interested in the staff aspect of this activity. One authority has described this role as follows:

The notion of a staff role for planning is built on the assumption that the executive has central responsibility for developing policy, for coordination, and for directing and supervising the local government machinery through which development plans are carried into effect.[12]

It was noted earlier that program planning often occurs in line departments. This is the planning for more effective delivery of services. It may involve relatively simple tasks such as planning the summer recreation program in order to anticipate personnel and equipment needs; it may also involve developing entirely new programs such as the initiation of a public emergency rescue squad. The latter example of program planning, that which involves initiation of new programs, is likely to be conducted at the staff level in association with the chief administrator. The same would be true of program planning which considers the relative merit of alternative programs in order to better allocate resources. In this context, administrative program planning is a necessary prerequisite to budgeting. One authority has stated that

the annual budget, combining capital and operating budgets, is an important element in the administrative planning process for the achievement of community goals. Properly used, the operating and capital budgets authorize current action to meet community needs. They assign responsibility to various agencies and departments for accomplishing specific objectives, and allocate the resources necessary for accomplishing those objectives.[13]

The planning–budgeting linkage has grown much stronger as planning has been accepted as an integral part of government operations. It is important to note that this emphasis on budgeting is more than the traditional emphasis on capital budgeting. In the traditional view, the planning interest in budgeting was to assure that provision was made to schedule land acquisition and construction of major public facilities, such as schools, so that they would be in place when needed. The larger view concerns itself, in addition, with the operational costs that will be incurred year by year as programs in education, garbage collection, police protection, and other areas are initiated or altered.

The local legislative body

The city council—or its counterpart—interacts with the planning agency in several ways. The most frequent contact is not necessarily the most important.

The council is the final decision maker on the most fundamental policy issues in the community. It adopts the budget and it passes the local laws. The chief administrator will develop and propose the budget or make recommendations on the programs which the budget supports, but the council must approve. In this sense the council is the ultimate audience for the recommendations that emerge from program planning activities.

The council also has a vital policymaking role in developmental issues. It may adopt the general plan, it makes capital budget decisions that affect implementation of the plan, and it makes zoning decisions that allow development activity to occur. These are some of the reasons why one authority has suggested that the planning agency should be responsible primarily to the local legislative body.[14]

The interaction of the planning agency and legislative body in the context of zoning decisions is important for two reasons. First, the cumulative effect of legislative zoning actions has a profound impact on the physical development of the community. Second, zoning actions are an important area of contact with the planning agency because of their frequency and intensity. Zoning decisions tend to be time-consuming and distasteful to the legislative body. They are often surrounded with controversy. It is primarily in this setting that the members of the legislative body observe the planning staff in action. The opinions they form here about planning staff competence and integrity may influence their willingness to accept planning agency advice in other contexts.

Local boards and commissions

There are numerous boards and commissions in the governmental fabric of every urban community. Many of them have responsibilities that relate to community growth and development. They would typically include local school district boards, park and recreation commissions, and water or sewer utility district boards.

A major objective of planning agency contact with such boards and commissions is to influence them to pursue policies that support the overall plans for the community. A new fringe area school, for example, needs to be located so that it will serve a future—as well as a present—population distribution pattern. Care needs to be taken to see that this school is not placed on a site that will be adversely affected by planned changes in the street network. Moreover, the location of a new school, the extension of public utilities, and the modification of bus services are all examples of "priming actions." They are actions which influence many other developmental decisions. New home construction, for example, tends to take place in areas with public sewers. For reasons such as these, it is important for the policies of independent boards and commissions to be supportive of overall development boards.

Line departments

The line departments are the front lines of local government. They are the departments that collect garbage, repair the streets, and fight the fires. Although the planning agency has little or no contact with their day-to-day affairs, important relationships do exist.

The planning agency is frequently concerned about capital projects initiated in the line departments. Where should a new fire station be located? What size facility should be built? These and similar questions come up in at least two contexts, mandatory referral and capital budgeting.

In mandatory referral state law or local ordinance may mandate that the planning agency has the opportunity to review proposals of city departments and comment on their appropriateness to overall development plans. If a good relationship exists between the planning agency and the line department, the review may take the form of a continuing consultation between the two agencies that begins early in the consideration of the project and continues through the selection of a site to design of a facility and funding by the legislative body. If relations are poor, the review may occur only after project plans have become so detailed that the line department is very reluctant to alter them.

The planning agency can solicit the cooperation of the line departments in at least two ways. First, it can emphasize its service role to the line departments. It can furnish information on population forecasts, development trends, and other matters that are of real value to the line department in its own plan formulation. In a service role the planning agency presents itself as a resource of information and skills that can be used by the line department to do a better job.

The second way of obtaining cooperation from the line departments is to have the chief executive require it. A chief executive who wants a strong staff level planning function will insist that department heads cooperate. This can be effective and it may be necessary, but coercion is a poor substitute for voluntary cooperation.

Figure 3–5   The transportation department and the planning department plan a subway.

Development management

In numerous cities throughout the nation, in both suburban and mature city contexts, a more intimate relationship is emerging between the planning agency and other officials, administrators, and departments. Some planners refer to such efforts as *development management*. What is emerging is the realization that effective development (and redevelopment or revitalization) requires a management team effort. In the suburban context, for example, a growth management "system" may require that the planning agency conduct environmental assessments of new development; that the budget officer conduct cost–revenue studies measuring the fiscal impact of that development; that careful study and consultation with the city attorney be undertaken to determine the legal boundaries of city action to control growth; and that the public works departments be closely involved in programming and scheduling the construction of utility systems that will serve the development.

In the older city the goal is stabilization, revitalization, and renewal. Here the planning agency will be in close working relationships with a housing authority; the local economic development agency; social service agencies; numerous federal officials in regional offices who oversee federally funded programs of local governments; and quasi-public and private groups involved with commercial and industrial investments, job programs, or historic preservation.

In a certain sense every local agency is a planning agency and all must work together if public policy objectives are to be achieved.

Intergovernmental relations

Today's planner works in a very complex intergovernmental context in which decision-making authority is extremely fragmented. What other governments at the local, metropolitan, state, and national levels do affects a particular local government in profound ways. A few illustrations merely begin to scratch the surface. Special districts may plan and operate sewerage systems, provide water supply, collect and dispose of refuse, operate ports and toll roads, and operate hospitals and health facilities. Counties provide some police protection, build roads, operate social welfare services, run court systems, control land use in unincorporated areas, and manage open space and recreation facilities. Metropolitan councils of governments and planning agencies plan and administer intergovernmental programs. Of great importance is the A–95 review process wherein designated metropolitan agencies must comment on local federal aid applications for a host of facilities. State governments build highways, are responsible for higher education facilities, manage state recreation systems, and administer a growing number of environmental regulations related to air, water, and land.

The practical implications for the local planning agency are that it must spend a considerable amount of time monitoring the programs and actions of others, preparing analyses of plans prepared by others, preparing position papers for local government, attending meetings, serving on advisory committees, and in general providing the technical backup for the local manager and mayor who must take public positions on areawide and intergovernmental policies.

Agency staffing

The work of the planning agency is done by people. No organizational arrangement and no degree of moral support will substitute for professional skills and hard work. The pool of professional planners available to agencies has grown substantially in recent years, and there is no reason why adequately funded agencies cannot be adequately staffed. What kind of staff will they employ and how will that staff be used?

The planning director

The position of the planning director is pivotal. Those who view the agency from the outside, whether citizens, political leaders, or other government employees, see the director as the person who speaks for the agency. The director speaks for the professional staff when making statements about public issues in the community. The director is responsible for the performance and conduct of the staff. Those who view the agency from within, whether professional planners or supporting staff, see the director as the person who makes major decisions for the agency, establishes overall work priorities, and allocates work among the staff. By action and example the director affects both the tone and the substance of the agency's performance.

The work of the director is complex, especially in a large agency. It includes several roles and may be approached with a variety of strategies.

One of the most important functions of the director is to provide leadership. The director must influence those inside and outside the agency to cooperate

The politics of city planning Certainly I was involved in the politics of city planning. Every city planner is. Overall, however, the best "politics" is top professional work, forcefully presented and defended.

City planners should not be neutral, and I do not believe their clients, at the level of local government, expect them to be without values or opinions. After they have arrived at some position, some point of view, some desired direction, one would hope to see it reflected in both public plans and day-to-day recommendations. Why hide it? Further, city planners should be willing to stand up for their points of view if they want to be effective. They should be prepared to "mix it up." They must do more than recommend. Within a democratic process they should advocate and search for ways to carry out their plans. I believe, too, that they should value and nurture their utopian predilections. They are nothing to be ashamed of.

Source: Excerpted from Allan B. Jacobs, *Making City Planning Work* (Chicago: American Society of Planning Officials, 1978), p. 313.

with one another in order to achieve common goals. Leadership within the agency includes at least the following four elements:

1. Communication of goals to subordinates. This involves more than writing directives or memos. The director seeks to ensure that staff members understand agency objectives. Also, the director seeks to have the staff adopt agency goals as their own and believe that they are worthwhile. This involves the use of persuasion and explanation more often than it involves the exercise of authority. It is an attempt to have persons on the staff develop personal objectives that are supportive of agency objectives.
2. Motivation of subordinates. Here the director seeks to instill in staff the desire to get the job done. It can involve the quantity and quality of work. It may be promoted by such means as personal example, incentive, or clarity of direction. It often depends on intangibles such as office atmosphere and rapport between the staff leaders and others.
3. Coordination of efforts in the agency. Few situations are more frustrating to a staff than to discover that they are working at cross-purposes to one another. The director is responsible for allocating work so that it is mutually supporting. This involves proper timing of work assignments to ensure that the product of one task is ready when it is needed as input to another task. It also involves the maintenance of common goals so that overlapping or conflicting work is avoided. In a poorly coordinated agency, for example, one might find the land use planning section and the zoning section both working on a study of how to accommodate a rapidly growing fringe area with neither section being aware of the work of the other.
4. Reporting on agency work and accomplishments. The director will need to make periodic reports on agency work to political leaders, the planning commission, and the public at large. This is necessary to maintain public support for continuing reassessment of whether agency objectives continue to reflect community objectives. Feedback from such reporting can be used to inform employees in the agency about acceptance of their work. If the work is well accepted, morale will be improved and future work will be approached with increased dedication.[15]

The leadership function also includes a political aspect in the broad sense. The acceptance of the work of the planning agency is influenced by the degree to which the community perception of the public interest is mirrored in the work of the agency. In exercising the leadership function in the agency the director articulates the public interest in planning issues. If this is done well it will tend to promote both public esteem for the agency and pride among agency employees.

The planning director plays a variety of roles in carrying out all these responsibilities. These roles will vary in importance depending on the nature of the community, the work priorities of the agency, and the composition of the staff. One means of enhancing an agency's chances for success is to have a director whose personal strong points match the most critical needs of the agency. Few persons will fulfill all the roles equally well. Daland and Parker have summarized the roles as follows:

1. Institutional and administrative leadership
2. Professional planner
3. Instigator of political innovation
4. Citizen educator.[16]

The typical planning director must give some attention to all these roles but usually finds that progress in some roles is achieved at the expense of progress in others. Typically, a person appointed as director has previously served in lower positions which emphasize the role of professional planner. The rise through the ranks may reflect a history of achievement in largely technical roles. Yet the planning director's technical role is different. The director of a large agency can seldom indulge in significant involvement in the details of programming a data collection system, revising a complex site design proposal, or writing a technical report on the impact of freeway locations on community air quality. Instead, the director is called upon to review the work of other staff members, to coordinate that work within the agency, and to present it to decision makers with maximum impact. Ironically, successful directors often find that they must allow some personal technical skills to wither to some degree in order to give an appropriate breadth of attention to a wide variety of agency activities.

The director who is conscious of the various roles required by the position will be especially attentive to the image and relationship projected toward key decision makers. A variety of strategies may be adopted by the director in establishing such relationships; among them are the following:

1. The technical expert strategy. Here the planner emphasizes the use of planning techniques and skills to present objective advice to the political decision makers. The strategy tends to emphasize a nonpolitical or nonadvocacy role among the staff. It presumes both the presence of a high level of technical skill on the part of the staff and the willingness of public decision makers to value technical information as a basis for decisions.
2. The strategy of confidential adviser. It may be possible for the director to establish personal relationships with key decision makers in which significant influence rests on personal trust in the director. This situation occurs when the decision makers have faith in the director's personal judgment. It usually comes about only after some years of successful performance in which the director comes to be viewed as trustworthy, discreet, and knowledgeable about community attitudes.
3. The strategy of innovator. Some communities may benefit most from a director who is willing to suggest bold solutions to problems. Here the planning director tends to be highly visible to the public as an advocate of actions not previously considered. The political leaders of the community can observe community reaction to new ideas and then adopt as their own those that gain broad acceptance. The risk of rejection is

borne by the planner, an asset to the politician who is willing to endure the initiation of controversy.[17]

These strategies do not exclude one another entirely, but a director will tend to emphasize one at the expense of others. The choice will reflect personal style, the needs of the community, the past history of the agency, and the preferences or styles of political leaders.

Staff composition

The composition of the agency staff should be tailored to the needs of the community and to the role of the agency in that community. A rapidly growing medium-sized city, for example, would probably want substantial skills related to land use controls, both in its legal and in its design aspects. A rural multicounty planning agency might be especially interested in having some staff with skills in economic analysis. A central city agency in an older city might want staff with special skills in housing, policy analysis, or planning for social services delivery.

Planning agency staff can usually be grouped into three broad classes: support, paraprofessional, and professional. Support staff includes secretaries, bookkeepers, drafting room personnel, and similar positions. These positions are usually filled under personnel guidelines or civil service procedures that are uniform for the community.

Paraprofessionals may be used in significant numbers to collect data, prepare rezoning application forms, conduct field surveys, and carry out other similar tasks. Such tasks do not require degrees in planning. Such positions may be filled by persons who hold a college degree that is not related to planning. Training occurs on the job.

Professional personnel typically consist of two groups at the entry level. Most will be persons holding a master's degree in planning. This degree is widely accepted as the basis for entry at a professional level. Other persons will occupy professional positions who have undergraduate professional degrees in engineering, architecture, or landscape architecture, or who have graduate degrees in such related fields as economics, sociology, geography, or public administration. Full professional status is usually accorded those who meet the qualifications of Certified Planner in the American Planning Association (formerly, full member of the American Institute of Planners).

Consultants

Most planning agencies occasionally find a need to go outside for professional help. Even large agencies with specialists on their staffs will encounter the need for specialized skills not available in house. The use of a consultant is a way of meeting such a situation.

Consultants are often specialized by both training and experience. Transportation planning, economic analysis, historic preservation, and health systems planning are just a few of the subject areas in which consultant specialists may be found. The agency using a specialist consultant not only gets the benefit of a product; it may also profit by having some staff members acquire informal training as a result of contact with the consultant.

A traditional role for consultants is the provision of planning services to those communities that do not have a resident professional staff. Consultants are very important to such communities. It is relatively easy to have consultants prepare studies and long-range plans; a major difficulty is in providing arrangements in which the consultant is available for the frequent advice and comment that are often necessary to implementation of a plan.

Agency administration

The daily administration of an agency requires attention to many details and activities. Meetings must be set up, agendas prepared, and reports published. No attempt is made to deal with all such issues here. But certain aspects of administration are of critical importance to the success of the agency. They include the following issues.

Work programming

It is important that the planning agency apply to its own activities the same rational forethought it seeks to foster in others. The major activities of the coming year should be identified so that provision can be made for personnel, consultants, equipment, and the financial support necessary to accomplish the work. This will not preclude unexpected problems and work items from arising, but it will substantially increase the likelihood that needed work will be done well and on time.

The planning director has initial responsibility for preparation of the work program. But the program should also have the review and support of other groups whose support is vital to it. These groups will usually include the planning commission, the chief executive of the community, and the governing body. The planning director should consult with these groups and attempt to blend their objectives for the agency into the initial draft of the work program. It is important that these groups do more than "rubber stamp" the work program. They should understand the need for the proposed work. This is necessary to ensure their support in funding the work and to enhance the likelihood of their using the results of that work.

The work program fits together a plan of agency activities based on the needs of the community and an agency budget designed to provide funds for personnel and other necessary resources. At a minimum, the work program identifies major tasks for the coming year, funding needs, and potential funding sources. A broadly conceived work program, often called an *overall program design,* is more extensive. It would consider the role of the agency in the community, major agency objectives, alternative strategies, and specific program recommendations for the next five years. Various public officials would be consulted in developing the program design and the commission would be asked to adopt it as an official guide for agency personnel. It is a plan for planning.

Agency financing

The need for financial support is readily apparent to those communities that seriously desire the benefits of planning. Officials accustomed to private or public management can see that planning costs money. Budgets should be developed that reflect traditional operational costs, as follows:

1. Personnel and fringe benefits. This includes all resident staff, professional and nonprofessional, plus consultants' fees.
2. Overhead. This includes the cost of office space, transportation, and supplies.
3. Equipment. This includes furniture, typewriters, and other items that are purchased on a nonrecurring basis.

This general view of the costs associated with planning does not include the cost of having staff attend professional conferences, the cost of acquiring technical publications, or any number of other legitimate expenditures. But many persons would be comfortable with a line item budget which categorizes expenditures according to type of expenditure, whether broken down into general or detailed categories. The deficiency inherent in their way of looking at planning costs is that it does not relate cost to specific activities.

In order to be effective over the long run, the planning agency will need adequate funds for its work program. Where significant changes are made in the work program, the needs for staff, equipment, travel, and other cost factors will be affected. A performance budget which associates costs with specific activities will give an indication of the type and amount of adjustment needed. Unfortunately, too many agencies arrive at estimates of funding needs by simply making crude adjustments in the previous year's salary, overhead, and equipment costs.

Consider, for example, an agency in which the work emphasis for several years past has been on preparation of regional plans affecting land use, transportation, and public utilities. Much of the data have been collected through aerial photography in conjunction with a regional mapping program. Much of the past work has been supported on a matching basis by federal dollars. As the agency prepares to enter the new fiscal year there are demands for more attention to neighborhood level planning and support for the internal planning within operating departments. The work contemplated will require more public hearings, more local travel, and more resident staff, but less will be needed for consultants and equipment. In addition, a much smaller portion of the program will be eligible for outside aid. If the community in this situation arrives at its budget by simply taking last year's budget and adding a percentage increase to take care of inflation, there can easily be a mismatch between needs and resources.

Authority and dissent

The work of an agency is the product of efforts on the part of many individuals. Support staff, paraprofessionals, and professionals all make important contributions. Work is assigned by the agency director or according to the director's instructions. Most aspects of supervision are sufficiently similar to those of other organizations that managerial and supervisory staff can readily be guided by a wide body of knowledge in the field of management. It is a well-known rule of management, for example, that the amount of responsibility delegated to an individual should be accompanied by the delegation of a corresponding level of authority. But one issue does not fall into normal personnel relationships.

A subject of particular difficulty in planning is the management of professional dissent. Some planning work is sufficiently objective and technical that different planners of reasonable competence would almost always come to the same professional conclusion. But some issues involve professional judgments and are influenced by personal as well as professional values. In addition, some issues may be fundamentally political in nature. The following two illustrations may be instructive. In one case, a planner working on a cost–benefit analysis of alternative transportation policies feels that certain qualitative assumptions are being used so that (he suspects) a predetermined outcome will result. Or, in another case, a planner has been assigned to a neighborhood planning project and has been intimately working with residents. The planner translates the goals of, for example, disadvantaged residents into a neighborhood plan that contains a series of recommendations for substantial city expenditures. However, when the city council adopts the next budget few if any of the recommendations are followed.

When should these differences of professional opinion be expressed? How visible should they be to the public or to public officials? These are difficult questions. A complete lack of restraint could produce such a variety of views on public issues that public confidence in the agency would be seriously impaired. Yet it is unreasonable to expect independent individuals who have been trained to think for themselves to always subvert their own views to an official position without a murmur. Such individuals are likely to either become discouraged and leave or to stop thinking for themselves. This type of strain may be felt by professional staff within an agency who differ with the director, or by a director who must represent the planning commission's positions when the commission disregards staff recommendations.

These issues have been treated in depth by Earl Finkler.[18] The Professional Code of Conduct of the American Institute of Planners is also a useful reference. Regardless of the position taken on such issues in a particular agency, it is important that such questions be addressed openly. Everyone in the agency should understand the type of professional behavior expected.

Innovations

The field of planning has been subject to substantial change in recent years. This can be seen in the scope of the issues subject to planning agency scrutiny and in the increase in the quantitative skills used in issue analysis. The shifts in agency organization have been less dramatic. The most widespread changes have already been noted: the shift from independent planning commissions to planning departments and the increase in the influence of professional staff.

The most likely source of widespread changes in agency organization would be amendments to state enabling legislation. The *Model Land Development Code* of the American Law Institute would produce some important changes if adopted by many states.[19] The code provides a land development agency as the primary planning and regulatory unit at the local level. A citizen commission would be optional. A key feature of the agency is its relative increase in direct regulatory power. Many actions now handled by other bodies as quasi-judicial or legislative actions would be handled by the new agency as administrative actions. Early indications are that few states are going to adopt more than selective sections of the code.

Most of the innovations in planning agency organization and administration are not attracting widespread notice because they are diverse and incremental. In general, they reflect a tendency to adapt to the special needs of individual communities. The greatest pressure to seek effective planning mechanisms is in those communities faced with severe problems.

The city of Baltimore was faced with declining inner city neighborhoods and other problems common to the older central cities of the Eastern Seaboard. Provision of housing for low and moderate income families and maintenance of well-established neighborhoods were major concerns. Beginning in 1968 the city took several steps to better organize itself for these tasks. A department of housing and community development was created, headed by a commissioner and reporting directly to the mayor. Its functions include project planning, urban redevelopment, public housing construction and management, and code enforcement. Overall community planning is still handled by the planning commission. Urban renewal authority has since been delegated by contract to the Charles Center–Inner Harbor Management Corporation to provide for direct involvement of the business community in downtown renewal. A similar arrangement exists for the Baltimore Economic Development Corporation. Both are under the supervision of the commissioner.[20]

In Cleveland the planning agency responded to the problems of its community by redirecting its programs to policy planning. The staff has taken a role in such issues as transit management, property tax reform, solid waste management, health delivery systems, and incentives for inner city housing investment. The most unusual aspect of the agency's work is the strong advocacy role of its staff. Rather than being content to make technical recommendations to a commission, this staff frequently advises the mayor, the city council, or other decision making units. The agency has publicly advocated the city's position in regional transportation policy and has worked for an increase in the city representation on the regional planning agency. The much stronger policy emphasis of the agency has required the addition of staff skills in municipal finance, law, management, and the social issues. This group has been organized into a separate section of the agency. It requires additional funds, some of which have been "hustled" by subcontracts with other city agencies and the securing of a foundation grant. The reliance on outside funding creates a need for advance work programming. Yet the thrust of the new effort is to respond to important issues as they emerge. Thus, the commitment to affecting the outcome of public issues in the most forceful way possible makes it necessary to juggle the internal resources of the agency in a nondoctrinaire way.[21]

A very different set of public issues has been present in Montgomery County, Maryland, and in the San Diego region of California. Both have been faced in recent years with a need to manage very rapid fringe area growth. Montgomery County has responded with the development of a sophisticated growth management policy framework in which both public and private decision makers are furnished with substantial technical information along with planning staff recommendations. The delivery of this high quality information to decision makers has been made possible by the assembly of highly qualified staff specialists who are used on a task force basis. The composition of this task force changes from time to time as needs vary.[22]

In San Diego the Comprehensive Planning Organization of the San Diego Region has sought to have each city and county in its region adopt its ten and twenty year population and employment forecasts and use them to assess the need for all public services. The broad use of the common information base then makes it possible for water quality and other areawide plans to better guide and accommodate regional growth.[23]

The joining of planning and budget offices has been mentioned early in this chapter with the example of Atlanta. In Richmond, Virginia, the planning and budget functions have been consolidated under an assistant city manager. The office there serves three broad functions: planning, budgeting and program evaluation, and community development. This type of arrangement fosters better policy analysis and strategy planning as budget officers and planners share each other's perspectives.

While innovations are quite diverse in scope and intent, several trends are emerging:

1. Planning is being applied to an increasingly broad range of activities involving program as well as physical planning. This creates the need to link traditional physical planning with program and policy planning.
2. Planning for social and economic objectives is becoming explicit rather than remaining an adjunct of physical planning.
3. Efforts are being made to build stronger ties between planning and implementation activities. This is especially evident in the links that are developing between planning and budgeting. It is also seen in the relative growth of professional staff influence and the adjustment in the role of the lay commission.

These trends reflect influences that tend to occur together rather than in isolation. They are widely viewed as healthy moves and can be expected to become increasingly visible in agency organization and work programs.

1   Kenneth L. Kraemer, *Policy Analysis in Local Government: A Systems Approach to Decision Making* (Washington, D.C.: International City Management Association, 1973), p. 21.
2   Robert A. Walker, *The Planning Function in Urban Government* (Chicago: University of Chicago Press, 1941).
3   Robert A. Walker, *The Planning Function in Urban Government*, 2nd ed. (Chicago: University of Chicago Press, 1950), pp. 110–11.

4 Ibid., p. 177.

5 Donald H. Webster, *Urban Planning and Municipal Public Policy* (New York: Harper & Brothers, Publishers, 1958), p. 105.

6 Frederic N. Cleaveland, "Organization and Administration of Local Planning Agencies," in *Local Planning Administration*, 3rd ed., ed. Mary McLean (Chicago: International City Managers' Association, 1959), p. 58.

7 See: ibid., pp. 59–60; also Walker, *The Planning Function in Urban Government.*

8 B. Douglas Harman, *Administration of Local Planning: Analysis of Structures and Functions*, Urban Data Service Reports, vol. 3 no. 12 (Washington, D.C.: International City Management Association, December 1971), p. 2, Table 1.

9 International City Managers' Association, "City Planning Data," in *The Municipal Year Book 1948* (Chicago: International City Managers' Association, 1948), p. 247.

10 Ibid., p. 246.

11 Harman, *Administration of Local Planning*, pp. 3–6.

12 James H. Pickford, "The Local Planning Agency: Organization and Structure," in *Principles and Practice of Urban Planning*, ed. William I. Goodman and Eric C. Freund (Washington, D.C.: International City Managers' Association, 1968), p. 540.

13 John K. Parker, "Administrative Planning," in *Managing the Modern City*, ed. James M. Banovetz (Washington, D.C.: International City Management Association, 1971), p. 246.

14 T. J. Kent, Jr., *The Urban General Plan* (San Francisco: Chandler Publishing Company, 1964).

15 Adapted from: James M. Banovetz et al., "Leadership Styles and Strategies," in *Managing the Modern City*, ed. Banovetz, p. 113.

16 Robert T. Daland and John A. Parker, "Roles of the Planner in Urban Development," in *Urban Growth Dynamics in a Regional Cluster of Cities*, ed. F. Stuart Chapin, Jr., and Shirley F. Weiss (New York: John Wiley & Sons, Inc., 1962, pp. 188–225.

17 Alan A. Altshuler, *The City Planning Process: A Political Analysis* (Ithaca, N.Y.: Cornell University Press, 1969), pp. 334–49.

18 See: Earl Finkler, *Dissent and Independent Initiative in Planning Offices*, Planning Advisory Service Report no. 269 (Chicago: American Society of Planning Officials, 1971).

19 American Law Institute, *A Model Land Development Code*, complete text, adopted by the American Law Institute 21 May 1975, with Reporter's Commentary (Philadelphia: American Law Institute, 1976).

20 See: City of Baltimore, Mayor's Committee on the Administration of Code Enforcement, *Organization for Housing and Community Development* (Baltimore, Md.: City of Baltimore, 1967); and City of Baltimore, Department of Housing and Community Development, *Baltimore's Housing Programs* (Baltimore Md.: City of Baltimore, 1977).

21 See: Cleveland City Planning Commission, *Cleveland Policy Planning Report*, vol. 1 (Cleveland, Ohio: Cleveland City Planning Commission, 1975); and Letter from Norman Krumholz, Planning Director, Cleveland City Planning Commission, 2 February 1977.

22 See: Maryland–National Capital Park and Planning Commission, *Annual Budget, FY 1977–1978* (Silver Spring, Md.: Maryland–National Capital Park and Planning Commission, 1977), p. 4.

23 See: Comprehensive Planning Organization of the San Diego Region, *Overall Work Program, FY 1978–1981* (San Diego, Calif.: Comprehensive Planning Organization of the San Diego Region, 1977); and Letter from Stuart R. Shaffer, Associate Director, Comprehensive Planning Organization of the San Diego Region, January 1977.

4 Information for planning

Here are three planning situations which occurred in a large midwestern city in the United States.

An alderwoman was concerned about the fact that middle income families in her affluent district could no longer afford single family homes. A university professor suggested property reassessment to increase the tax burden of owners and thus put a lid on inflationary price increases. She asked the planning staff for an analysis—especially to consider the possibility that the plan might backfire and lead eventually to suburban flight.

The state highway department had been using traffic volume predictions and their spillover effects as the reason for proposing an airport connector freeway which would run through an ethnic neighborhood. Alarmed residents and environmentalists received technical assistance and advice from advocacy planners, and they came up with projections showing that a boulevard would handle the traffic and at the same time would preserve neighborhood and environmental values. Faced with conflicting estimates and projections from two seemingly qualified sources, a perplexed governor ordered an independent review of the situation by a well-known planning consultant.

The city housing agency proposed scattered sites for publicly assisted housing developments for low income families. Some of these sites were within incorporated areas of the suburbs. As expected an opposition quickly formed and found support, curiously enough, from the regional planning commission. The planning commissioners argued that they had expected massive public opposition to any such housing and that they had to represent their constituencies. The basis for this opinion had been a single public hearing held at a suburban elementary school.

Any one of these or similar situations could occur on any day in any part of the country. Quite often, planners who have gained the confidence of decision makers will be asked to provide that commodity which is the stock-in-trade of the profession—*information*.

In the first of the above situations there appeared to be little basic information on values, trends, and projections. Planners could assist in collecting and analyzing such information prior to adoption of the proposed public policy. The second situation would require the sort of independent review called for by the governor. It appeared that the basic information was available, but it was used in a different manner by each group, perhaps because of a biased perspective. The third situation falls in that area between fact and misconception which requires a softer approach to gathering information. Such an approach might be survey research, which can accurately assess both attitudes and public understanding of the issues. In all three cases, the planner can play a useful role by gathering and using information.

Some would argue that this is appropriate for technicians but that the advocacy and politically involved planners need be concerned only with *values*. They would argue that armed with such values the planners could develop strategies to attain objectives without resorting to quantification, measurements, or other such methods.

There may be some isolated instances in which this value-oriented approach could work, but it would seem to be a limited and even elitist professional approach.

Professional planners, even those cast in the action-oriented molds of the advocate and politically involved, should provide the foundation for decision making that is essential in most public policy questions as well as in private decisions. As George Sternlieb once remarked, "Let's face it, when you get right down to it, the best we can do is give them the numbers." Many planners can probably do even more, but all planners as a minimum should be able to "give them the numbers."

Figure 4–1   Communication has evolved from age-old methods—
letters, semaphore signals, oral expression, etc.—
to a highly mechanistic setting that relies on technology.

Some planners may wish to specialize in this area and reduce the time they spend on implementation, while other planners may consider this area as merely a starting point or basic tool for professional practice. The planning profession is sufficiently broad to allow such variations, but the core of knowledge and competency of the profession invariably includes getting and using information.

What is information?

While it is normal to use the term information in a generic and comprehensive sense, a rigorous discussion requires some distinctions to be drawn. A hierarchy of *data, information,* and *intelligence* (Figure 4–2) is intrinsic to such distinctions.

The basis of the hierarchy is *data*. Data are the unitary relationships between observations and real world phenomena. In other words, in order to describe the real world we devise a one-to-one relationship between observations and realities—between what we see and what is actually there—whether the realities are cars, people, dollars, or trees. When we want to observe population characteristics, for example, our data may be one person, one group, one race, or any other unit.

In essence, we can use data to mean facts. Furthermore, as with any other type of foundation, faults or cracks in the data will not serve well. Some perceived or unperceived errors always occur in data collection, but poor techniques or sloppiness make the data of doubtful value. We can estimate statistically the amount of error in data that are sound, since a 100 percent observation of the real world is neither statistically nor philosophically possible. Sloppy data —data with defects and missing observations—are not salvageable. If we have learned anything from the computer age, it is that maxim of good data: GIGO— garbage in, garbage out.

Information is the result of aggregation, manipulation, permutation (change in lineal order), or any other set of statistical, mathematical, or algorithmic change designed to reach some desired level of understanding. Information is what we get when we use data to come up with succinct and salient knowledge that is needed to solve a problem or to show patterns or directions. For example, in our first situation we would probably show the alderwoman the average assessed values, selling prices, improvements, or other grouping of data for her ward blocks rather than the raw data for each house.

Traditional and quantified approaches to communication Communication is a social affair, the act of transmitting news, data, attitudes, values, and other forms of information. Communication may be interpersonal, small group, organizational, or mass media. Communication includes messages which may be transmitted by letter, telephone, face-to-face interchange, facial expressions, and in many other ways. Communication means organization, enabling society to function.

Communication has evolved historically from age-old methods—letters, semaphore signals, oral expression, etc.—to a highly mechanistic setting that relies on technology. And it is technology that provides computers, telecommunications, video display terminals, data banks, and data storage. These communication processors of today's society, both admired and distrusted, depend on programming—"that is, . . . the breaking down of the mathematical operations into elementary steps and the logical feeding of the steps into the machine together with prior data referring to the particular calculation." Programming provides the instruction and the logic, and this is the significant distinction from earlier machines and methods that relied on observation and limited input. It is programming that facilitates quantification, storage, sequential operations, recall, feedback, and "especially the facility of changing the sequence of operations according to criteria evaluated during the course of calculation."

Source: Partly abstracted and partly excerpted from Colin Cherry, *On Human Communication: A Review, a Survey, and a Criticism,* 2nd ed. (Cambridge, Mass.: The M.I.T. Press, 1966), pp. 3, 53, 54.

The most highly developed level of knowledge is *intelligence,* which is that ability of our system to seize the essential factors from complex information and data. It is this ability, whether expressed as models, simulations, indicator series, or trends, that provides the decision makers with what they need to know —and no more. Obviously, many issues and values surround the ethical and moral transgressions that are possible with the use of intelligence. Assuming these issues are not at stake for the moment, we can see that a decision maker, like the governor in our second situation, wants intelligence from the planning consultant rather than the data and information that led to different conclusions from different groups.

It should be noted that the logic flow arrows in Figure 4–2 are vertical and circular. This is not a tautological trick of logic just to bring you back where you started. It is a *feedback loop,* which means that any level in the hierarchy may generate problems, needs, or omissions that can only be resolved at another level. For example, an indicator series at the intelligence level may not work because missing data are suspected. Or a model of traffic flow at the information level may generate volumes with large error factors that make their use at the intelligence level somewhat dubious. In such cases, rather than explaining away the problems or presenting incomplete results, it may be necessary to make corrections at other levels and recycle the analysis.

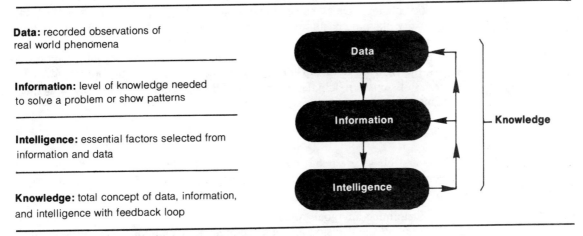

Data: recorded observations of real world phenomena

Information: level of knowledge needed to solve a problem or show patterns

Intelligence: essential factors selected from information and data

Knowledge: total concept of data, information, and intelligence with feedback loop

Figure 4–2   Hierarchy of data, information, and intelligence.

The people for whom planners work may not have the time, the skill, or perhaps the desire to gather and use data, information, and intelligence on their own, but there are many instances where planners can help in the effort. In extreme cases where activist groups gather and use data, information, and intelligence on their own, only to find suspicion and doubt among decision makers hearing their arguments, planners are better suited to undertake these work efforts.

Planners do not collect data, as a general rule. Planners seek out data, when the data are good and the collecting source is appropriate. Planners are generally data users rather than data collectors, for two basic reasons: (1) many other professionals and groups can better collect data; and (2) the planner's time is better spent on information and intelligence matters. As a rule, the planner should avoid collecting data—the only exception would be when unusual timing and conditions require it. Even then, the professional planner will need assistance from other professionals.

Planners spend their time best when they use data to form information and intelligence needed by decision makers. Planners can use a variety of techniques and methods for assistance, most of which have been developed by other professions and disciplines. For example, predictive and estimating models, optimizing models, simulation, gaming, and indicator series can be used to analyze data and reach levels of knowledge that are important for decision makers.

Asking the right questions

Having defined our terms, we should proceed no further until we gain a sense of direction as to the design of planning studies. One of the problems in getting and using information is that too often the right question is not asked. This problem takes on several guises. In one guise, the wrong question is asked and the resulting information or intelligence is useless to the decision maker. In another guise, the question may be proper but it has no answer in the format posed. For example, in our third situation, the question: How does the public feel about scattered housing sites? may not be answerable. There is no real way of measuring feelings for an amorphous public. This sort of question should be broken down into measurable components.

Finally, perhaps the most troublesome situation is that involving a set of data or a group of techniques in search of an application. In this guise, the question is sometimes posed in a manner which provides a response from the data already selected or the technique already in mind. This approach is not acceptable to the serious planner. Data availability and favorite techniques are neither gimmicks to justify planning positions nor commodities to be sold—they are simply tools to assist the planner.

The most important step for the planner in getting and using information is to ask the right questions. There is no simple way to do that, but the following series of steps can help the planner: (1) defining problems, (2) formulating questions, and (3) formulating hypotheses.

Problem definition

The first phase of such a process is problem definition. While this involves a combination of analysis, judgment, and perhaps intuition, there are some guidelines:

1. Determine any goals and objectives
2. Identify the decision makers, the areas they can control, and the factors they cannot control
3. Determine the constraints on the problem as the boundaries within which solutions must be formed
4. Identify other participants who may influence the decisions
5. Determine the goals and objectives of other participants
6. Understand the system for decision making and the environment in which the system operates for the period of time involved.

When such a series of guidelines has been drawn up, a reasonable set of problems could be defined.

Question formulation

It is next necessary to formulate the right questions, perhaps using the following guidelines:

1. Determine the alternative courses of action available to the decision makers
2. Determine the alternative courses of action available to other participants in the process
3. Screen out or eliminate infeasible solutions.

As can be seen, question formulation is derived from alternative courses of action to resolve the problems defined. Some sort of screening mechanism should be employed to eliminate solutions that are obviously infeasible. This saves both time and resources. Having determined such alternative courses of action, the planner can then pose questions that best meet the goals and objectives of decision makers as well as other participants.

Hypothesis formulation

The next step is the translation of these questions into hypotheses or tentative assumptions about the questions and their responses. This is done solely for the purpose of testing. This testing takes two directions. The first direction is logical in the sense that the hypothesis must address both the problems and questions in a clear, efficient, and economical manner—that is, the most direct approach. The second direction is empirical in the sense that the hypothesis can be tested using the data, information, and intelligence at hand or otherwise available. To develop such hypotheses, the following guidelines may be useful:

1. Define the terms and measures to be used to determine if goals and objectives will be met
2. Select common measurements, standards, or criteria by means of which testing of alternative hypotheses based upon courses of action can be undertaken; these may be objective or subjective or some combination of both
3. Select or formulate the testing mechanism to be used
4. Select tests for the validity and reliability of the results.

When these guidelines have been used to formulate the hypotheses, the analysis can then be undertaken. Through a feedback process, answers to the questions and evaluations of how goals and objectives might be met can be made. In a sophisticated analysis there will be probabilities associated with the results to better indicate the extent of chance occurrences or errors that may affect the outcomes. In less sophisticated analyses, or analyses with high degrees of subjective measures, it is often possible to account for uncertainties by use of priority ranking of the results.

The testing of these hypotheses could lead to answers to the questions raised and problems defined. It is essential to consider this in a restrained manner, however. The process described has limitations upon inferences, implications, or speculations which must be made clear. For example, in our first situation if we are to speculate on the future of the housing quality in the alderwoman's ward on the basis of testing hypotheses, it is prerequisite to such speculation to define our assumptions, measures, and criteria. Using the concept of *ceteris paribus*—which means to hold all other factors, elements, or things not found in our hypotheses to be equal in force and unchanging—we can make such speculations. In other words, it is acceptable to make inferences, speculations, and implications on the basis of hypothesis testing as long as all assumptions, measures, and criteria are made known and we do not try to make more out of the hypotheses than is justifiable in this set of constraints. Self-restraint is necessary, because there have been many abuses made in this area in recent practice.

Gathering the data

After the hypotheses have been formulated and tests have been devised, it is time to gather data for the information or intelligence desired. Since we have already stated that planners should be data users rather than data collectors, this process becomes largely a search and screen operation: to search for the most current and relevant data and then to screen them for validity and reliability.

Most of the principles of data collection were developed in Western Europe in the nineteenth century and have not changed. Today we use many governmental and private sector personnel, large-capacity computers, and exotic devices to store and display data, but the principles are unchanged and universal.

There are basically two types of data. *Primary data* are those collected from the original source. We go out and directly observe what is happening and record the results according to our already determined measurements and criteria. For example, we may count houses, births, cars, or people.

Secondary data are data collected by someone else that are available and appropriate for our use. For example, most data in the United States are collected by the Bureau of the Census for such items as houses, births, cars, or people. If such data are available and if they fit our needs, it makes more sense to use them than to try and collect new data.

There may even be a category of data we can call *tertiary data*, or original data that have been used by someone else to create information which we can in turn use to test our hypotheses. In a strict sense, however, tertiary data would be considered information rather than data in our vocabulary.

Data must be evaluated for validity and reliability. This is an entire field of specialization within the field of statistics. Suffice it to say that planners are looking for good data with a minimal amount of *bias*. In a statistical sense bias means that a consistent error has been made over and over in the data collection—usually unknowingly. This could lead to bad data which purport to represent a real world phenomenon but really do not. The way to minimize bias in primary data is to use strict techniques and procedures for collection. In using secondary data, it is necessary to evaluate the techniques and procedures used to collect the data. The data should be used only if the planner believes they fit the needs for hypothesis testing and never solely because they are easily available.

There is a practical side to data collection which relates to planning practice. There is a region of diminishing returns in data collection costs beyond which there is little justification for such expenditures. If it is assumed that no complex set of data will ever be totally free of error and devoid of bias, the planner must make a reasonable decision as to the level of validity and reliability that is necessary as a function of the costs. Other factors to consider include timing, personnel, and seriousness of the question at hand.

There is a certain time when bias is good. That occurs when only a select part of the possible universe of observations is desired. For example, we may want to observe shopping patterns only for black people in a predominantly white neighborhood, in which case the total neighborhood data are not needed. In that situation data must be collected with a biased set of techniques and procedures. It should be emphasized, however, that biased data should be carefully handled and utilized.

A few rules of thumb are useful for gathering the data. In the collection of primary data the techniques and procedures should be unbiased and strictly employed. The resulting data should be tested for reliability and validity and kept within cost restraints. It often makes sense to use statistical specialists for complex problems. For secondary data it is always best to use standard sources with known track records. Even then, it is always necessary to review the techniques and procedures used as well as the results of statistical analysis of validity and reliability. In general, unless references to other sources are needed, tertiary data should be avoided. This is not because of suspicion of the source but because of the inevitability of errors creeping into such collections—errors that are not always known.

Many guides to sources of planning-oriented data are available. Such guides are useful for the beginning planner and the student. It is apparent, however, that the overwhelming amount of primary planning data is collected by the federal government, with state and local governments contributing to the effort. Rather than attempting to duplicate these guides, we will discuss some illustrative examples of primary data for planning purposes.

Population data

There are two broad types of population data collected by government: enumeration and characteristics. Population enumeration is an inherent function of the federal government by constitutional mandate, which requires it for congressional districts. As early as 1820 the census was also collecting data on migration and the work force. Hence, the census remains the paramount source for population enumeration on a decennial basis (soon this will be on a quinquennial basis).

The enumerations provided by these data range from national counts to block faces and should satisfy most needs. The census also provides data on births, deaths, marriages, divorces, as well as population trends and projections.

Population characteristics, such as race, age, sex, occupation, income, education, and mobility, are also found in the census. Other useful sources are vital statistics reports from the U.S. Public Health Service and similar reports from state and county health agencies. City directories, either publicly or privately produced, are sometimes useful.

While the preponderance of population data is governmental, some private sector data are useful. Companies such as R. L. Polk and Company produce annual canvasses for city blocks that supplement the census. Similarly, insurance companies and banks sometimes collect annual data for actuarial purposes that are useful for some planning problems.

The most difficult population data to obtain, validate, and analyze are those related to migration. The variable and sensitive movements of families are difficult to locate and measure, since, unlike births, deaths, and marriages, they are seldom recorded. While the above sources are useful, certain situations require inventive approaches for small areas—for example, using utility and phone connections and disconnections, as well as postal and tax records, where allowable.

Economic data

Economic data are also within the province of federal governmental programs; these data often include state collected data. Data for labor force, banking, employment, unemployment, labor markets, personal income, consumption, production, commerce, sales, and location are collected by the federal government. In addition to the census, major sources are the U.S. Department of Commerce, largely through the Bureau of Labor Statistics, the U.S. Department of Health, Education, and Welfare (HEW), and the U.S. Department of Labor. Most states publish similar reports through related agencies. There are many county and local government data sources for small area details.

Quite a few privately collected data sources are available for purchase. For example, Dodge Reports provide much data on construction and marketing. Dun's market identifiers provide extensive files on marketing data. Many specialized data sets for radio, television, and newspaper marketing exist. Some increasingly good sources of local economic data are metropolitan and large city associations of commerce, which regularly collect such data.

Social data

There are many sources of social data. Housing data are usually found in census reports as well as in reports issued by state and local governments, including housing authorities. Most enumeration and supply data are found in such sources. Good data on housing demand, structural characteristics, condition, and costs are found in the census as well as in periodic data releases from the U.S. Department of Housing and Urban Development (HUD). Several private sources, such as Dun, Dow, Dodge, and McGraw-Hill, offer regular housing data. Interest groups such as the American Institute of Real Estate Appraisers and the National Housing Conference, as well as the federal and state banking and savings and loan associations, provide a wealth of housing data.

The principal source for most health, education, and welfare data is HEW. Equivalent agencies at the state and local levels provide detailed data for small areas. The elusive areas of crime and public safety data are available from the census and through the Uniform Crime Reports published periodically by the Federal Bureau of Investigation. Local crime reporting varies widely with police departments, as does the quality of such data. Several public interest groups collect useful data on prisoners.

Environmental data

There are several sources and types of environmental data. The primary sources for air quality data are the U.S. Public Health Service and the Environmental Protection Agency. The related state and local counterparts usually provide similar data for pollutants by type, sources, measurements, and levels. Similar data are available for water uses, collection, and treatment as well as pollutants. Related data sources covering land use and soils are available through the Soil Conservation Service. Meteorological and oceanic data are available from the National Oceanic and Atmospheric Administration. The same agencies usually collect data on specialized aspects of the environment. For example, data on noise pollution, thermal pollution, plants, and wildlife are available from environmental and natural resource agencies at the federal, state, and local levels.

Using data for information and intelligence

Planners use many methods for converting data into information and intelligence. Most of those methods that are quantitative are borrowed from statistics, operations research, and systems analysis. A summary description of such techniques and methods follows, emphasizing those that are more quantitative and more commonly used.

Descriptive statistics

The elementary use of data in the hypothesis testing process is to analyze and define relationships. This is usually done by employing the basic tools from descriptive statistics. The most elementary descriptive statistics are the *frequency* and *distribution* of data as *variables*. There are arrays of variables in the data according to some measure of distribution. There are many familiar types of distributions (i.e., normal, bimodal, Poisson, etc.) which can be helpful.

The next level of analysis involves the dispersal of data about the central tendencies, usually the *mean, median,* and *mode.* The most typical descriptive statistics are the *mean, variance,* and *standard deviation.* The mean is the sum of the values of the data observations divided by the total number of observations. The variance and the standard deviation are the most common measures of the average dispersal about the mean.

The most commonly found use of descriptive statistics is in the *cross tabulation* of data—sometimes called a *matrix,* table, or array. As can be seen in Figure 4–3, common types of data displays using descriptive statistics range from matrix or array cross tabulations to interval scale distributions or *scattergrams* to nominal/ordinal scale distributions or *bar charts.* These and other displays are familiar to planners. The development of computer display terminals has further increased their use.

Another kind of descriptive statistic that is useful for planners is the identification of relationships among data variables. For example, the *chi square test* may be used to determine relationships between two variables. *Correlation coefficients* provide indicators of the *strength* of any relationships among variables. Also useful is the general area of statistics dealing with the *significance* of

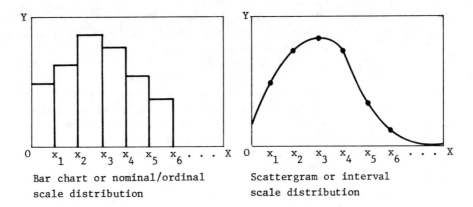

Figure 4–3 Typical displays of planning data.

Bar chart or nominal/ordinal scale distribution

Scattergram or interval scale distribution

Matrix or array

relationships among variables, which is usually called *analysis of variance.* Such uses of descriptive statistics can be helpful for testing hypotheses.

Survey research

A final area of interest to planners is gathering data, either primary or secondary data, through a survey or through direct observation. This often involves telephone calls, mail-out/mail-back, or personal interviews working with carefully developed questionnaires. Many questions of cost, efficiency, and accuracy come into play in the decision on which type of survey to use. This is compounded by the fact that many surveys involve "soft" or qualitative data.

For convenience, we can discuss the softer types of surveys as dealing with human reactions to the stimulus or the question asked. A *perception* tends to be a quick or almost reflexive response to a question that a person does not have strong feelings about. An *opinion* reflects a stronger set of preferences among the choices allowable in response to a question. An *attitude* is a strong and long-lasting response to a question that is ingrained in the person responding. Hence, we can consider questionnaires, opinion polls, or any other type of survey research in such a way as to determine whether responses are perceptions, opinions, or attitudes.

While perceptions may be useful for marketing and trend analysis and opinion polls are useful for political questions and preferences, attitudinal surveys appear to be most useful for most planning purposes; this should be obvious for long-term planning issues. Furthermore, attitudinal surveys may aid the planner in determining the validity of hypotheses as well as the feasibility of implementation of the course of action chosen.

Many aspects of survey research are important for planners, but the correct selection of the sample precedes every survey that is done well.

Random sampling is most common for planning purposes and involves the selection of a sample that represents the group in general. This is usually undertaken by some method based on a random choice of a person or household from a group, using, let us say, a random number table, as long as every other person or household has the same chance of being selected. This method usually requires a complete listing of all persons or households and a standard method of selection. Sample size becomes an arguable point, limited by time and resources available, but a true random sample need not be large if the universe is large. There are more definitive rules available in basic reference sources.

Other types of samples are sometimes used for planning purposes. *Systematic sampling* is a variation of random sampling in which we start selecting every k^{th} person or household from a randomly selected starting point. This works well if every person or household has an equal chance of being selected —that is, if there is no bias in the listing.

Stratified sampling is a way of dealing with the problems encountered when we seek only a special group from the universe of possibilities. Basically, this type of sampling requires stratification, or breaking down the listing into homogeneous groups and then using systematic or random sampling within the groups. A variation of this would be *cluster sampling,* in which we break large listings down into heterogeneous groups that are reflective of the universe. This allows us to keep the sample small yet reliable, thereby reducing time and costs.

Citizen surveys are a significant part of the work of local government, especially for obtaining feedback on the effectiveness of local services, the potential demand for new services, and opinion on issues. When surveys are undertaken on a regular basis they are especially useful to managers and elected officials for program and policy planning and for major budget decisions.[1]

To make citizen surveys effective and reliable, professional services are needed—at least in the development of survey forms, methods, and procedures, and in the training of interviewers. In addition, it is prudent to use professionals to audit the survey results. The major purposes are to cross-check the work to prevent misuse of data and to maintain credibility.

Survey research based upon appropriate sampling methods would enable the planner to deal with some of the less quantifiable aspects of the third situation presented at the beginning of this chapter. The planner could assess perceptions, opinions, and attitudes in order to determine public awareness, understanding, and feelings toward such complex issues as scattered site housing. Such survey research enables the planner to add dimensions to hypothesis testing that may not be available from harder data and standard sources.

Techniques and methods for using data

Normally, when we consider ways of using data so as to come up with the information and intelligence needed to answer the right questions we enter into the areas of models, simulations, and systems analysis. While all of these areas are highly interrelated, they can be described individually. It should be stressed that models, simulations, and systems analysis are simply tools to assist in analysis; they should be used cautiously and only when they can help the planner use data in a better way.

Models

Russell L. Ackoff has defined models in the most appropriate manner as being symbolic representations of real world phenomena in which

$$v = f(x_i, y_i)$$

where v equals some measure of performance; x_i is a set of variables that can be controlled by the decision makers; y_i is a set of variables that represent conditions, decisions, or environmental factors not subject to control by the decision makers; and f is a functional relationship that can be determined or can be predicted.[2]

Such models can be useful for planners when they seek to use data in a manner that represents the real world, can yield information or intelligence for those variables subject to the control of decision makers, and also can be useful for predicting the impact or effects of noncontrollable variables.

Models are used in an attempt to set up a representation of a defined piece of the real world. Kenneth L. Kraemer has pointed out that questions can be asked of the model (in experiments). If the model works well, the answers will provide guidelines for dealing with that part of the real world which the model corresponds to.[3] A model this broadly defined could include mathematical formulas, computer programs, games, planning maps, budgets, scenarios, and architectural models. Planning agencies usually work with models that use mathematical and logical symbols based on beginning algebra and (occasionally) beginning calculus.[4] The following discussion therefore covers the most common models for planning agencies, starting with the simple linear models and progressing to the more complex aspects of dynamic and stochastic programming.

Predictive and estimating models are the most common types used by planners to simply estimate or predict existing relationships between variables in the data or future trends. In other words, these models are designed to explain how the real world phenomena work and what patterns may occur over time. They almost always rely upon existing and past data and hence tend to reflect a continuity, albeit variable in itself, of past and present states and conditions. This requires caution for predicting the future (i.e., conditions may change and make the model ineffective).

Normally, estimating and predicting models used in planning are standard curves fitted to the appropriate data. For example, it is common to find such models used to explain and predict future trends for such variables as population, housing, traffic, and income over time. In these cases, historical data are gathered and an appropriate curve is fitted to the data. The *goodness of fit* of the curve is tested through the use of a number of statistical techniques, and that curve which minimizes deviations from the data is selected for estimation and prediction.

Simple linear models, such as that seen in Figure 4–4, are most common for many planning operations. These models are simply straight line approximations of historical data or observations. The dependent variable, $f(x)$, is calculated by adding a slope or b parameter (which is an inherent characteristic of the relationship used for curve fitting) to an intercept or a parameter. This means that the relationship is linear to some reasonable level of acceptance. As long as the standard error of the fitted linear trend is not large, such a relationship can be used to estimate the changes and predict future values for $f(x)$.

Complex linear models, or *multiple regression models,* use the same basic concept except that more than one independent variable may be used. This extends the space of the resulting trend to n space, which results in an estimating plane rather than a single line. Such models are useful where several variables from the data are known to affect the dependent variable desired. This model is far more complex and difficult to use than the simple linear trend.

Simple and complex linear models are familiar to planners because of the ease of calculation of parameters for curve fitting and the simplicity of assumptions inherent in them. For many problems and for hypotheses testing in which the relationships are linear or near linear, such models are perfectly acceptable.

There are several dangers to keep in mind, however. Linear models assume that the future is simply an extension or repetition of the past. While that may be true for many planning problems, it appears generally dubious to make long-term predictions using linear models. Another danger is that linear models are

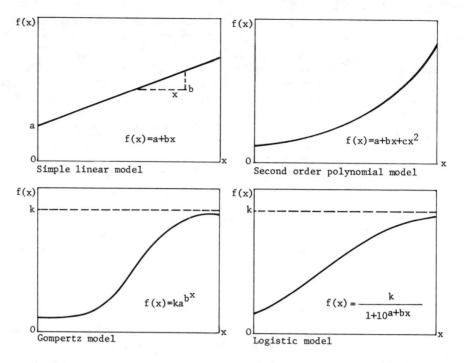

Figure 4–4   Common estimating and predicting models.

based on correlation of variables and not on cause-and-effect relationships. Many errors in planning are possible if cause and effect is mistaken for correlation. Finally, because of the statistical nature of linear models, an averaging out occurs in order to make the linearity assumption work. This means that many real world problems or conditions are virtually ignored by such models, to better deal with the whole. Many planners have learned of the dangers of presenting information or intelligence for the whole which ignores certain parts. Although the common linear model can be used and can be helpful for planning analysis, extreme care should be exercised in its use.

Nonlinear models include a number of standard curves that can be used when linearity does not appear to explain relationships between variables. There are many kinds of nonlinear models that employ curve fitting techniques to explain the observations from the data base. Some of the more common models used in planning, especially to estimate and predict population over time or variables related to population over time, are shown in Figure 4–4.

The *second order polynomial model* accounts for nonlinearity by adding a second order term and parameter (this would be cx^2, the example shown in Figure 4–4) to the simple linear model (which is technically a first order polynomial). By the solving of a series of standard normal equations, the a, b, and c parameters can be calculated in order to fit the curve. For larger data sets, a number of computer programs are available to compute these terms. The model should then be tested by comparing standard error terms with other curves and seeking a curve which has the least amount of error associated with it. Incidentally, there are third, fourth, fifth, etc., order polynomials which can take a variety of curves and bends that can be used for certain data sets. One computer program successively calculates N-order polynomials from data until it reaches a specified level of accuracy. The problem of using higher order polynomials is the difficulty of calculating values for dependent variables higher than the second order.

The *Gompertz model* is a familiar curve that is used for relationships that have periods of growth, stagnation, and decline, usually over time. As can be seen in Figure 4–4, this model usually takes on an S-shaped appearance. The Gompertz model also has an upper *asymptote* (k in the example in Figure 4–4) or threshold beyond which the dependent variable will never extend, which has great potential for certain planning hypothesis testing.

The Gompertz model has been in use since the nineteenth century in many demographic and organic applications. This makes it useful for related planning problems, especially those related to population growth and decline. While the mathematical formulation is difficult to work with because of the double exponentiation, it is a familiar model to most statistical specialists.

The *logistic model* is quite similar to the Gompertz model in appearance and concept. As can be seen in Figure 4–4 it can also take an S-shaped appearance. It is different from the Gompertz model in that it was developed to describe growth and decline in biological systems, hence it tends to show a higher stagnation period. It also uses an upper asymptote (*k* in Figure 4–4) and tends to predict more conservative or lower values for long-term growth than does the Gompertz model.

It is also difficult to use because of its mathematical form, yet it is quite commonly used in census estimating and predicting series, thus allowing for convenient reference. It is commonly found in estimating and predicting population, housing, income, traffic, and other factors related to population growth and stagnation.

Optimizing models are a broad group of techniques which can be used to estimate the best solution to a problem that is subject to constraints. This means that a hypothesis can be described, often using estimating and predicting models, within a set of restraints from the environment or context within which it functions—quite like the real world. The answer to the right question could be considered as optimal if it provides the best solution within the defined limits.

Classical calculus has been used to solve many types of optimizing model problems. This is especially the case when a minimal or maximal answer to a problem within an allowable range of solutions is desired.

Linear programming is a useful model to use when a hypothesis can be stated in linear terms and the solution is subject to a number of constraints which are themselves linear in nature. When a problem is complex yet can be approximated in linear terms it may be possible to use this approach. Interesting examples of the linear programming approach have been made in land use, housing, economic, and transportation problems by planners.

Nonlinear programming is a complex form of optimizing model in which the hypothesis and/or its constraints take on nonlinear characteristics. This makes both the formulation and the solution of the problem formidable. While there have been a few applications in public investment and transportation, this approach to optimizing models is rare in planning.

Dynamic programming is a highly sophisticated optimizing approach which deals with multistage planning periods with incremental or step-by-step optimal solutions. It uses calculus and numeric search routines requiring extensive mathematical manipulation. There have been a few applications of the technique in the area of land use and transportation planning in which public and private costs were to be minimized for new development. Nonetheless, this complex technique remains at the cutting edge of planning practice. It holds great potential for the future because of its planning orientation toward step-by-step optimization.

Stochastic programming is a form of optimizing which is based on hypotheses that are expressed in probabilistic terms and constraints. In other words, the hypothesis and its set of constraints are expressed in terms of uncertainty, with varying outcomes. This requires probability models and processes that are difficult for most planners. While these models reflect the real world, which is indeed probabilistic, that very complexity makes for limited usefulness. Simpler representations of the real world in models are more useful for planning, as long as care is taken in drawing conclusions. Incidentally, one well-developed field of probability is *queuing models,* which are found most frequently in traffic analysis.

Simulation

While models may be considered as representations—that is, likenesses or images—of the real world, *simulations* are considered as imitations of it. There are three types of simulation. An *analog simulation* uses some physical characteristic, such as water in pipes or electrons in a channel, to imitate a real world phenomenon such as money flows or traffic. *Iconic simulation* uses scale models of the real world, such as model airplanes, in some imitative environment such as a wind tunnel. *Symbolic simulation* uses models, usually numerical rather than analytical, to imitate the real world. While all three types are found in planning, the last is most prevalent. In essence, for planning purposes, simulation can be considered a way of using models to generate numerical information from data which imitate real world phenomena. This can help planners test hypotheses and generate intelligence.

The mathematical formulation for a symbolic simulation is similar to that for models: that is,

$$W = F(U_i, U_j)$$

where: W is the set of numerical characteristics of the hypothesis of the problem; U_i represents controllable or noncontrollable variables that generate numerical values; U_j represents other independent variables and constraints; and F is a numerical function. In many cases the U_i variables involve a random sampling or selection process to generate values from the data that imitate the characteristics of W or the problem under consideration. The U_j factors tend to be variables and constants (parameters) that generate probabilistic distributions for computing values for W.

A typical simulation problem could involve traffic flows between two interchanges on an expressway. The data on traffic would be gathered and grouped in some appropriate classes for use in calculating probability distributions. An appropriate random number generating algorithm would then be used to imitate real world observations. This would serve as input to the observed probability distributions which would yield a set of simulated numerical values for W, which would be traffic volumes for the segment in this case. The usefulness of this simulation could be for predicting past, present, and future traffic; testing changes in traffic by manipulating the generating functions; estimating optimal values; or evaluating physical changes in the capacity of the roadway.

Most simulations in planning have been relatively large scale, complex undertakings. They have required tremendous amounts of data and prodigious numerical calculations. Some of the better known examples include the Pittsburgh urban renewal simulation, which attempted to simulate residential and employment land use; the San Francisco housing simulation, which dealt with housing supply and demand under various conditions and types of public policies; the Bay Area simulation study, which was a mammoth effort to simulate economic conditions and residential location; and, later, the National Bureau of Economic Research efforts to simulate urban development. All of these efforts have been very expensive, time-consuming, and controversial.

Perhaps the most controversial set of simulations has been the extensions of the industrial dynamics approach of Jay W. Forrester. These applications resulted in his *Urban Dynamics* and *World Dynamics* works, as well as the famous *Limits to Growth* book.[5] These simulations all employed the basic concepts of growth, stagnation, and decline as inherent characteristics of any urban or resources system. Hence, the simulations assumed that there would be limitations to growth and eventual decay in growth rates. This led to many controversial and dubious conclusions.

These efforts point to a major problem with simulation. In order to work, simulations must be based on a foundation of assumptions about the hypothesis or problem under study. If these assumptions are clearly stated and acceptable to all, there may be value in the numerical values generated. If the assumptions are unclear, are not well stated, and are debatable, as are many variables in planning, then a contentious set of values may be generated. Because of this, the utility of simulation is largely for hypothesis testing and alternative plan evaluation, when used with caution and concern. There appears to be disutility in simulation for prediction and policy analysis in many cases involving major public issues.

An additional field of simulation that appears to have value for teaching and learning is *operational gaming*. This is like simulation in that real world hypotheses and problems are imitated, but it tends to be less concerned with numerical values and more concerned with learning through role playing. For example, the most widely used land planning game is still the Community Land Use Game (CLUG). In universities, citizen groups, and private meetings, participants break up into four teams to develop an area for housing, employment, and shopping within the constraints of utilities, transportation, financing, and taxation. While the CLUG game is a simplification of real world processes, it allows for a simulated learning experience that might not be easily available. For example, the participant can learn the rudimentary decision-making conditions for a major real estate project in a manner far more interesting than learning it from a book and virtually impossible from the real world of development.

There are several other games of interest to planners. The APEX and Metropolis games are more sophisticated and computerized versions of development simulation. The City and Region games offer economic, social, and political characteristics and different area scales ranging from region to neighborhood. The SIMSOC game remains an interesting simulation of national characteristics of social, economic, and political consequences.

Operational gaming has much utility for learning through role playing, as long as one remembers that the situation may be different when it is one's own money. The dubious claims about operational gaming as a tool for plan evaluation, policy analysis, and prediction about decision making should be received with skepticism. We have seen little evidence to support such claims.

Systems analysis

In a sense, one can see a hierarchy of techniques ranging from the specific (i.e., models) to the general (i.e., simulation) to the elusive (i.e., gaming). At the highest levels of complexity we must deal with problems that are so difficult that we can deal with them only by breaking them down into their constituent parts. This is the area of *systems analysis*. A *system* is any entity, physical or conceptual, composed of interrelated parts. These interrelated parts, or *subsystems,* operate together to create a whole that may be greater than the sum of its parts. For example, we know that an urban area may be *systemic* in that it is composed of physical, economic, social, and political subsystems which form an urban complex. These subsystems themselves are composed of interrelated parts. For example, the physical subsystem is composed of transportation, housing, shopping, and other parts, all interrelated and interactive.

Basic systems theory holds that such a complex system must be broken down into parts so that we can analyze it and make decisions about its overall optimal performance. The problem is to avoid *suboptimization* or the optimal performance of some parts at the expense of overall system optimal performance.

Basically, all systems can be considered a *conversion mechanism* which changes input to output. The output has a feedback loop to the input so that a cyclical effect takes place; this is sometimes called *system dynamics*. The system operates within an environment which affects and constrains it.

The application of this theory to planning has been widespread. Systems analysis is essentially process-oriented and is often related to problem solving as well as to optimal performance. It is rather an elaborate technique for hypothesis testing, but it is so employed at times. In terms of techniques and methods, systems analysis often incorporates both models and simulations.

Much of the impetus for planning applications of systems analysis came from the apparent successes of the aerospace and defense programs of the 1960s. Subsequent applications in industry and government during the late 1960s, including the planning-programming-budgeting systems (PPBS) of the federal government, were rated successes by proponents, but many would disagree and would point out the rather modest applications that exist today. Systems analysis has been used extensively in transportation planning, and to a lesser extent it has been tried for housing, social services, health care, and law enforcement planning. There have been several attempts to impose systems analysis as a broad concept for public management as well.

All of these efforts have been fraught with problems. Planning programs have not enjoyed the tremendous resources, technological advances, and unitary decision making of the space programs of the 1960s. These advantages, plus a national commitment to achieve preeminence in space, made systems analysis a major method of making decisions for those programs. That is unlikely ever to occur in the subjective, inefficient, and pluralistic conditions in urban areas in which planning takes place.

Systems analysis has more form than substance in contemporary planning. The basic vocabulary—system, subsystem, optimal, suboptimal, etc.—is used widely in a planning context. Yet there is little of the substantive techniques and methods from the earlier space and defense programs. Hence, the importance of systems analysis may be more as a way of thinking about planning and approaching problems than as substantive techniques and methods.

Intelligence indicators

A number of tools have been developed and applied in planning that are generally oriented toward the provision of intelligence for decision makers. Four types of tools for generating intelligence are commonly used in planning: indicator series, scheduling, group techniques, and information systems.

Indicator series

Indicator series are perhaps the purest example of how planners use tools to provide decision makers with intelligence. In the 1920s a movement started in the United States to take the pulse of the economic and social condition of the nation. Public and private organizations became intrigued with such a notion and have invested millions of dollars to date for research on the development of economic and social indicator series. The basic concept is simply that a regular, consistent, and accurate compendium of measurements of the key indicators of economic and social conditions will provide decision makers with the intelligence they need, when they need it.

The familiar example of economic analysts such as the Council of Economic Advisers providing the President with economic indicators that indicate tax policies as ways of improving the economy has long fascinated planners. While much research has gone into social indicators, the successes have been more modest.

Several indicators have become an established part of American life and tend to have an influence on public opinion as well as on decision makers. For example, the unemployment rate, issued monthly by the federal government, has significant influences on decision makers at all levels of government and within the private sector. The rises and falls of this bit of intelligence often make front page news and affect political careers. To a lesser extent the family budgets for several income levels and the consumer price index are regularly released by federal agencies and tend to have important effects on public policy. A more dubious indicator series is the crime index that has been kept for many years by the Federal Bureau of Investigation and which has been criticized as inaccurate, incomplete, and statistically suspect yet still attracts great interest and attention as the major measure of the "crime problem."

In recent years there has been much attention and developmental research directed toward the extension of social and economic indicators to such areas as environmental quality, educational achievement, occupational growth, and the indefinite area of quality of life. Indeed, a basic problem with indicator series is: What should be included? Some would argue that a social balance sheet should be developed using such indicators as the following:

1. Social costs and benefits of economic innovation
2. Social ills (crime, family disruption, etc.)
3. Social needs (housing, education, etc.)
4. Economic opportunity and mobility.

Yet there is not widespread agreement that such a balance sheet is feasible or useful for public policy analysis. The search for the best indicator series will continue for some time.

Despite the debates over form and content, there seems to be agreement that three functions of indicators would be useful for planning: (1) pulse-taking for the state of the area; (2) monitoring of changes; and (3) evaluation of plan and program implementation.

The guidelines for indicator series should be based on availability and accuracy of data and information; longitudinal characteristics; and relevant indicators. The last point means simply that the indicator series must be a realistic measurement of a social condition based on accepted conceptions of the problems. This would imply a directness and succinctness that go to the heart of the problem. Too often we find planning studies that seem to confuse social conditions through informational overkill and irrelevant measurements.

For the most part, the indicator series movement is national in scale. Some efforts at state planning indicators were undertaken in such states as New York, Wisconsin, and Washington. There are some planning-oriented indicator series in such large cities as New York and Chicago. There has been little application of the technique in medium-sized and small cities, but interest in the subject continues to grow.

Scheduling

During the implementation of a planning program or the implementation of plans themselves, decision makers need a special kind of intelligence. If a project is off track, or if the timing is going poorly, there may be a need to shift schedules or resources, or to crash certain phases. Two techniques which provide such intelligence are the critical path method (CPM) and program evaluation and review technique (PERT).

CPM was developed in 1956 for the evaluation of performance time and total cost of projects with well-defined activities. PERT was developed in 1958 for use in more complicated projects on larger scales, in which degrees of uncertainty were involved.

Both CPM and PERT use a graphic technique called an *arrow network* to describe how *activities* lead to certain *nodes* or *milestones,* as seen in Figure 4–5. In the upper diagram the arrow network shows that node A is the starting point, with nodes B and C being branches to the next milestones. The arrow from A to B is called an activity and takes 2 units of time to complete. In such a simple network the critical path would be the longest time required to go from the starting point, A, to the completion point, F. This would be A-B-D-E-F, which requires 7 units. Usually, in serious applications three time estimates—optimistic, likely, and pessimistic—are used, and a weighted mean time is calculated.

The CPM allows calculations for varying starting and finishing times for activities based on the need for precedence of the nodes. This leads to *float* or leeway in the network. By manipulation of float time, it may be feasible to free resources in order to ensure that the critical path is kept on schedule and to divert unused resources on float activities (if excessive) to other projects.

Figure 4–5   Arrow network.

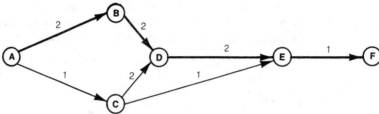

PERT deals with more flexible nodes and activities by manipulating resources and times to reduce the critical path where possible. Thus PERT allows for more complex intelligence to be generated by greater manipulation of time, resources, and personnel for projects with variable requirements.

In order to be useful, CPM and PERT require several prerequisites. The first is that the project must have a clearly stated set of activities with definable starting and end points. With PERT, especially, it is essential that resources be capable of being shifted between activities. Finally, accurate data and information must be available at prescribed periods to allow the manipulation of the network. Given these conditions and a commitment on the part of decision makers to actively seek economical and efficient implementation, these intelligence tools are quite useful.

Group techniques

A recent and peculiar form of intelligence tool is called *group techniques,* which usually refers to the Delphi process and nominal group techniques (NGT). The Delphi technique was developed at the Rand Corporation in 1950 as a systematic way of pooling judgments on a set of topics. The method is based on a set of sequential questionnaires that provide summaries of judgments and opinions from earlier rounds. It is a written, repetitive process that allows participants to change or revise judgments as they go along. NGT is a variation of the Delphi process that uses a structured group meeting to generate ideas. It involves feedback, clarification, and evaluation of ideas, followed by a rank ordering of ideas with individual voting.

Group techniques have been especially useful for local government application in zero-base budgeting and capital budgeting.

The use of intelligence generated through group techniques is valid when a pooled or collective judgment from expert or nominal groups is desired. Group techniques allow for exploratory approaches to generating intelligence for hypotheses, alternatives, and strategy; these are newer and more refined approaches than brainstorming, yet they serve similar purposes. Delphi techniques are especially good for the collating of expert opinion, while NGT allows for multidisciplinary generation of judgments by experts from different fields. Another use of group techniques could be for review of alternative proposals, similar to peer group reviews for research proposals. Through group techniques, also, citizen participation in planning analysis can be made more effective.

Information systems

An important component of the hierarchy of data, information, and intelligence is the physical capability for processing data to information and intelligence. An *information system* is a complex of people, equipment, and processes interacting to provide information and intelligence from input data for assistance in decision making.

The term interaction is critical in this definition, since popular science fiction might lead some to believe that computers and other machines can become independent and self-sustaining. This is not true in general, and it is completely false for planning. The equipment in information systems is simply a useful tool for people to employ for their prescribed processes.

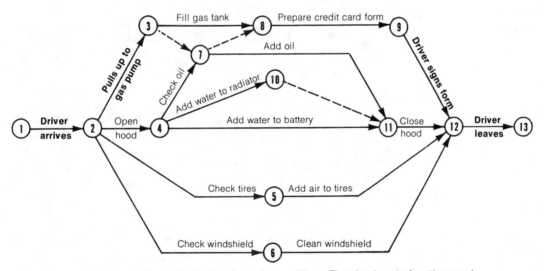

Figure 4–6 Flowchart of a gas fill-up. The simple act of putting gas in an automobile is susceptible to systematic analysis; this approach suggests that certain planning tasks can also be analyzed systematically.

In Figure 4–7 a configuration for such an information system is shown. People develop the problems, questions, and hypotheses which serve as input to the information system. They interpret the output and use a feedback loop to determine whether the system has provided information and intelligence for the hypotheses translated from questions and problems. If it has not, the cycle starts over again. The processes for our purposes can be considered as models, simulations and gaming, and indicator series. The equipment involves a central processing unit and input and output mechanisms. The input mechanism draws upon control and handling equipment and the data storage system being used. Such a configuration is clearly inoperable without the interaction of people, processes, and equipment.

Information systems have become a well-established part of government. The first fully operational system, in terms of planning significance, was in operation in Alexandria, Virginia, as early as 1964. Also in the early 1960s, the Metropolitan Data Project was operating as a federally funded demonstration project in

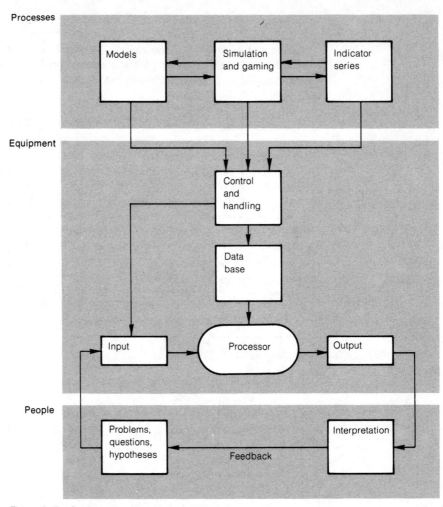

Figure 4–7   Configuration for an information system.

Denver, Fort Worth, Little Rock, Tulsa, and Wichita for selected data sets in each city. A number of important experiments took place in applying aerospace and defense information systems to planning problems in California in the mid-1960s. In the late 1960s and the 1970s the federal government funded a major research and development program in several cities, under the acronym USAC, which was guided by a consortium of federal agencies.

After a history of overblown promises and unrealistic goals, information systems appear to be entering a stage of maturation and acceptability in planning. More modest goals are being pursued, and realistic commitments of time and resources are being allocated. This has the effect of making their utility much more valuable for planners.

The USAC program has developed prototype information systems—Wichita Falls, Texas, is an example—that can be transferred with a minimum of effort. Combining, essentially, street location and basic parcel and building information in a computer file with maps as a visual edit, the planning agency has concise information for development of a "system."[6] It is a step forward from the urban data bank that was tried in the 1960s and was generally disappointing because of lack of agreement on a core data base, lack of top management involvement, failure to integrate information into ongoing operations, and failure to keep data on a continuing basis.[7]

Problems and potentials

What can we conclude about getting and using information for planning, using the vantage point of our original three situations? For the alderwoman, we could gather data and generate information on the housing costs she is worried about. Some models might be used to predict future costs under varying inflationary conditions. Perhaps, given the time and resources, we could simulate the effects of reassessment and alternative taxation schemes. Such information and intelligence should be useful to the alderwoman, especially since the decisions would be made within a highly political atmosphere with much emotional involvement. The decision might be political, but information would ease some of the pain involved.

The consultant working for the governor has a variety of techniques and methods to use for his evaluation of the two sets of projections. The information can be checked for both calculations and data validity. The appropriateness of the models used should be judged. Any indications of bias in the data or their manipulation should be reported. Finally, the consultant should provide intelligence to the governor that could help resolve the conflict. Obviously, the governor would have to weigh such intelligence along with the social, economic, and environmental issues that surround expressways. The decision would be made within a political context.

The third situation requires data collection that would probably be made through survey research. The degree of public knowledge of the issues of scattered site housing should be assessed, and the nature of perceptions, opinions, and attitudes determined. Some information is needed on the characteristics of housing needs in the region, and alternative strategies should be analyzed. Obviously, this intelligence is needed by decision makers acting within a highly charged political atmosphere.

In all three situations a paradox is present. On one side, we realize that complex politics and economics are involved in the decisions. These are not readily susceptible to quantification. On the other hand, there is a dearth of information and intelligence available for the decision makers. This requires quantification. The planner should be familiar with this seeming paradox and should understand that such seemingly political decisions require data, information, and intelligence. Every good politician knows that. The planner who can skillfully analyze data to generate good information and vital intelligence has a great deal of influence on complex political decisions.

Problems remain with getting and using information for planning. It is clear that there are many variables in everyday planning situations which have limited characteristics for measurement, despite the arguments of some theoreticians that anything capable of conceptualization is capable of measurement. We can conceive or sense beauty in cities, but it remains vexing to measure it. Much time and effort have been spent on such pursuits, but the results have been unconvincing. Similar concepts such as freedom, equality, and justice, all of which should be factors in planning, defy convincing quantification. We should stop wasting our time on such spurious measurements and should accept the reality that certain concepts and ideas cannot be measured or quantified. As such, planning will always be both art and science, both quantitative and qualitative. We should temper our analysis with the conviction that some things are better left to fate, belief, and emotion. This does not eliminate planning analysis. It puts it in perspective.

Another problem is the use of values in planning. We have emerged from a period of planning history which attempted to place planners above the fray in large part by developing value neutral techniques and methods. We now know that planning, like other professions, includes beliefs and commitments to inherent values. To pretend that planning is a field devoid of values, seeking only a value neutral solution to problems, severely limits the potential of the field and belittles the dedication of people engaged in the practice. Values do at times find their way into data, information, and intelligence. Rather than seeking sterile means to cancel out values, it is better to make clear what values went into such data, information, and intelligence. For example, if one group argues that x percent pollution discharge is bearable and another argues that x percent pollution discharge is intolerable, the situation presents a conflict for resolution. It does not demean the information if it is good. Values are inherent in data, information, and intelligence and as such are perfectly acceptable as long as they are made quite explicit.

A more serious problem has to do with the cumulation of error in complex models and simulations which invariably accompanies increasing specification and sophistication. In the classical article on the subject, William Alonso has demonstrated how error cumulates with measurement and specification.[8] For example, if we are using data in a model that is at least 80 percent accurate, the manipulation of such data four times in a model results in a decrease of 30 percent of its accuracy. This means that no matter how good the data are, too much specification, manipulation, and sophistication can lead to enormous error terms. At some point error cumulation reaches a level where it exceeds the value of specification. Hence, sometimes imperfect data—which means most planning data—require simpler models with simpler mathematical manipulations if the information generated is to be useful. Failure to recognize this is to inadvertently present decision makers with information that does not really represent the most likely occurrences. Such a fallacious basis for decision making can be disastrous.

In a similar vein, Douglass B. Lee evaluated serious flaws in attempts to construct and use large scale models and simulations in planning.[9] He identified what he considered "the seven sins of large-scale models" as follows:

1. Hypercomprehensiveness: an overly comprehensive structure
2. Grossness: too coarse results for decision makers
3. Hungriness: enormous appetites for data
4. Wrongheadedness: deviation between claimed model behavior and actual equations
5. Complicatedness: the error propagation problem from Alonso
6. Mechanicalness: the illusion that machines make for rigor and order
7. Expensiveness: a full scale land use model alone costs a half million dollars.

Lee argued that planners had lost track of the real policy issues and had made models largely unintelligible to decision makers. He argued for "transparency" in models, so that the information generated is readily understood. This could also lead to consensus on the assumptions and values, so that even though a model is wrong there may be agreement on what to do with its results. In short, Lee concluded that models and simulations will be valuable for planning only if they deal with particular problems that are susceptible to measurement, and only by using simple models and simulations.

Lee's arguments appeared at about the same time as Forrester's urban dynamics simulation, the National Bureau of Economic Research's urban development simulation, and the Projective Land Use Model (PLUM) which was used in the Bay Area and San Diego. All three were large scale, expensive undertakings.

Lee's arguments were apparently sound even though they were castigated by many persons involved in modeling and simulation. In recent years most models and simulations have been smaller, simpler, and less expensive, and have been directed toward specific problems and hypotheses.

As for the future, we suspect that Michael B. Teitz was right in his assertion that analytical techniques and methods in planning will be widely used and valuable only if they are *responsive* to policy problems.[10] By that he meant that models and simulations can generate information and intelligence from data in a useful manner only under the following conditions:

1. If they are sufficiently flexible to adjust to differences among problems
2. If they allow for growth and refinement
3. If they are mutually complementary
4. If they respond to multidimensional problems.

Teitz argues that this would include design as well as management and facilitation. He foresees a future when such techniques and methods will lead to new ideas and inventiveness.

It is clear that the future of planning will involve more rather than less data, information, and intelligence. The skilled practitioner, with a commitment to implementation, should be able to weave information and intelligence into the decision-making and policymaking processes by openly stated, direct, and simple devices. The limitations of techniques and methods should be known and made explicit. Values that have been incorporated into assumptions and manipulations should be clearly stated. Information and intelligence should be seen in their proper perspective as aids to the solution of planning problems, and they should never be allowed to dominate recommendations. That is the optimal way to get and use information for planning in the real world.

Conclusion

This chapter began with three planning situations involving property taxes, the effects of an airport connector throughway, and the location of scattered sites for publicly assisted housing. Without attempts to "answer" these questions, the generic term information was more rigorously defined as a hierarchy of intelligence, information, and data. Within that framework the importance of asking the right questions was shown as a matter of problem definition, question formulation, and hypothesis formulation prior to the analysis of the problem. Gathering data was next described, and then primary attention was given to using data and to techniques and methods of applying data. This included coverage of statistics, survey research, models, simulations, and other tools and applications which planners need for at least three reasons: (1) to help unravel complex problems, not all of which are subject to quantification; (2) where possible, to build replicas of these problems and test them to see what might happen in the real world; and (3) to try to offer some options for administrators and elected officials. Other kinds of tools for planners are shown under the section on Intelligence Indicators, including scheduling methods and group techniques which have been used quite successfully by many public agencies. The chapter concludes by showing how the three issues posed at the beginning of the chapter might have been resolved and then goes on to cover other information issues and potentials that can be explored by planning agencies.

1 A recommended how-to-do-it manual for planning agencies is: Kenneth Webb and Harry P. Hatry, *Obtaining Citizen Feedback: The Application of Citizen Surveys to Local Governments* (Washington, D.C.: The Urban Institute, 1973).
2 Russell L. Ackoff, *Scientific Method* (New York: John Wiley & Sons, Inc., 1962), p. 108.
3 Kenneth L. Kraemer, *Policy Analysis in Local Government: A Systems Approach to Decision Making* (Washington, D.C.: International City Management Association, 1973), p. 97.
4 Almost all college and university graduates from the mid-1960s on who have majored in the social sciences should have little difficulty with the math-

ematical portions of the following discussions in this chapter.

5   Jay W. Forrester, *Urban Dynamics* (1961); *World Dynamics* (1969); *Limits to Growth* (1974) (all Cambridge, Mass.: The M.I.T. Press).

6   Stephen J. Ondrejas and Stephen R. Morath, "Urban Planning in Wichita Falls, Texas: One Year after USAC," paper presented at the 1976 Annual Conference of the Urban and Regional Information Systems Association, Atlanta, Georgia.

7   Kenneth L. Kraemer, William H. Mitchel, Myron E. Weiner, and O. E. Dial, *Integrated Municipal Information Systems: The Use of the Computer in*

Local Government (New York: Praeger Publishers, 1974), p. 4.

8   William Alonso, "Predicting Best with Imperfect Data," *Journal of the American Institute of Planners* 34 (July 1968): 248–55.

9   Douglass B. Lee, Jr., "Requiem for Large-Scale Models," *Journal of the American Institute of Planners* 39 (May 1973): 163–78.

10 Michael B. Teitz, "Toward a Responsive Planning Methodology," in *Planning in America: Learning from Turbulence,* ed. David R. Godschalk (Washington, D.C.: American Institute of Planners, 1974), pp. 86–111.

5 Finance and budgeting

"There's an urban policy coming out—it's called the budget," was the observation of a major West Coast city official.

New York Times, 6 December 1977

The purpose of this chapter is to provide a general introduction to the public finance aspects of urban planning.[1] Particular emphasis is placed on the role of the planning agency in local government finance management and decision making. The chapter contains discussions of where local governments obtain funds, how the budgeting process works, how the capital improvements program is a powerful planning implementation tool, and how to use cost–revenue analyses in planning.

Sources of revenue

Local public officials and experts in the public finance field spend vast amounts of time thinking and worrying about how government revenues will be found to pay for a growing number of public services. This includes the programs and projects that planning agencies propose. However, the literature on taxes and revenue is so large that this overview is very general and provides only an outline of the subject. Emphasis will be placed on basic principles, the more important current issues, and relevance to the urban planning function.

There is a legal foundation to the raising of revenue. Federal and state constitutions have provisions concerning governmental authority to raise revenues, as well as standards for equity and due process. Local governments derive power to tax from state constitutions and state statutes. While some home rule cities may have some flexibility in revenue policy, generally most municipalities may not impose a tax or fee without specific state authorization. State laws, statutes, and court decisions may govern the types of taxes that may be imposed, maximum rates, principles involved in uniform assessments, requirements for local ordinances or referenda, what a community may borrow in terms of both purpose and amount, and a large number of other requirements.

Revenue can be classified in terms of whether it is a tax, a user charge, an administrative fee, a license, a debt service, or a grant-in-aid. Some taxes go into a community's general fund and may be used for any lawful purpose. Other taxes or fees may be earmarked—that is, may only be spent for a particular service.

The equity and fairness of a tax depends on outcomes of the relationship between a *tax base* and a *tax rate*. Most taxes—such as property and income taxes—are stated in terms of a rate that is applied to a base. The base may be the value of a property, the amount of gross personal income, or an expenditure. Property taxes are usually stated as a percentage, or a mill (one-tenth of one cent), or sometimes as dollars per $100 or $1,000 of value. A tax rate on income may be either a flat rate or a progressive rate as income rises. The sales tax is an example of a percentage applied to a particular expenditure.

An important issue concerning any tax is the degree to which it is progressive, proportional, or regressive. If a tax rate increases as tax base increases (for example, federal income taxes) then the tax is considered to be progressive. A proportional tax would be one in which all persons paid the same percentage on a base and there was no cutoff as to the base. Thus, if all persons pay the same rate of income tax for every dollar they earn, the tax would be considered proportional. A regressive tax is one in which persons with low incomes spend a larger proportion of their income on taxes than higher income persons spend. For example, sales taxes are typically considered regressive, as is the United States social security tax.

There is also a set of issues relating to equity and to distributional and economic effects. Some of these issues will be discussed in the section on the property tax. Others, however, are beyond the scope of this book. Some illustrations of these issues are as follows. What are the impacts created because owners of single family houses must pay their own taxes while owners of rental units can shift their taxes to those persons renting units? And what happens when business fees and taxes are simply passed on to the consumer in the form of higher prices? Finally, there is continual debate concerning the impacts of city and state tax rates on industrial and commercial location decisions.

The property tax

The property tax has historically been one of the most important sources of local government revenue. Although state and federal grants have been increasing, the property tax remains an extremely important element of local revenue. State laws classify property as real property and personal property and further classify personal property as tangible and intangible. Generally speaking, real property is defined as land and all structural improvements. It is the real property tax that is of greatest concern to urban planners because of potential impacts on urban development patterns.

The three essential steps in administering a property tax are assessing the value, setting the tax rate, and collecting the tax. The assessment function in local government involves the technical and administrative processes needed for locating, keeping track of, and recording all real property and improvements through maps, aerial photographs, and computer data banks. The act of assessment is partially an art in that real value, or market value, must be determined. State laws normally prescribe how assessors conduct their work. However, real property in the United States is seldom assessed at its full value for tax purposes. State law may establish assessment ratios for various classes of property, but the general rule is that all property is in a single classification. The assessed value figure may be further changed through the use of exemptions (for example, for veterans and the elderly) and may also be further changed through the use of equalization ratios that attempt to ensure that all properties in a given state are treated more or less equally regardless of which governmental jurisdiction does the assessing. Finally, some state financial aid may be based on local assessments.

The tax rate is set by governments that have the power to tax real property. The rate is usually stated in mills or in dollars per $100 or $1,000 units. This rate is applied to the net value, following all exemptions and equalization ratios.

While the real property tax has been one of the most commonly used local taxes, it is also one of the most controversial. Some of the major issues are discussed in this section.

One such issue is the degree to which property assessment is fair and equitable. Local taxpayers are constantly comparing their assessed valuations with those of others in similar circumstances, and residents of rental properties may feel they are paying higher taxes than residents of owner occupied properties

Guide to property assessment Step 1: The assessor appraises and determines the market value of your property. The basis for all assessments in Cook County is *Market Value*. . . . This means the Assessor determines what a willing buyer would pay you, as a willing seller, for your property. When this price is established, the *Market Value* of your property has been determined.

How is this done? Each year the Assessor received copies of all Real Estate Transfer Declarations, or sales, for all properties bought and sold in the County. These declarations indicate to the Assessor what type of property was sold and the full sale price paid.

The Assessor then matches these sales with their corresponding assessments through the use of sophisticated computers. He compares the assessments of similar homes in the same neighborhood where the sales took place. After analyzing this information, the Assessor can predict what similar homes will sell for on the open market. This, then, would determine the *Market Value* of those properties which had not recently been sold.

Step 2: The classification system. Next, the Assessor employs a technique called *The Classification System*. The system allows him to assess different types of properties at different percentages of full *Market Value*. This means that the Assessor differentiates between properties, placing higher assessments on commercial/industrial properties and lower assessments on homes, in relation to the *Market Value* of those properties. In simpler terms, the Assessor first determines the full *Market Value* of a property and then lowers that full value by a percentage determined by law.

Step 3: Your tax is computed. These definitions will assist you in better

understanding the terminology used in computing taxes.

Assessed valuation: This is a percentage of the total value which the Assessor places on property. It includes land and building(s).

Equalization factor: The Illinois Department of Local Governmental Affairs requires that all assessed valuations in Cook County be multiplied by this factor in order to make assessments uniform throughout the state.

Equalized valuation: The result of the Assessed Valuation being multiplied by the *Equalization Factor*.

Tax rate: The rate is established as a result of levies by the local governmental bodies which have the authority to impose taxes on property which is located within that community.

Market value: Another term for market value is *fair cash value*—that is what a willing buyer would pay a willing seller if a property is offered for sale on the open market.

Tax levy: This is the actual amount of dollars which a local school district or local taxing agency requires to operate in any given year.

Example: single family residence

Market value $40,000
Classification system ratio.................16%
Assessed valuation.........................$6,400
Equalization factor 1.4153
Equalized value............................$9,052
Tax rate..8.78%
Tax bill...$795

Source: Excerpted from Cook County Assessor, *Homeowner's Guide to Property Assessment* (Chicago: Cook County Assessor, n.d.), pp. 7–12.

because assessment ratios in some states can be higher on income producing properties.

The interrelation between periodic reassessment of real property and the rampant inflation characteristic of the 1970s has resulted in tax revolts in some parts of the country. Owners of single family dwellings have discovered that inflation has increased the value of their homes (doubling of value in less than a decade has been common). However, as reassessments have taken into account the increased value of real estate, property taxes have soared. This is a particular problem to elderly persons who have no intention of selling their homes for large profits but must nevertheless pay taxes far above originally anticipated levels.

Another problem is that real estate taxes tend to be regressive to the disadvantage of low income people. That is, a high income family with a large, expensive house can afford to pay taxes, presumably. Moreover, housing costs do not make up a high proportion of the family's budget. The low income or moderate income family pays a higher percentage of its income for housing costs, and therefore real estate taxes represent a higher proportion of its family income.

Local government's reliance on the property tax can cause serious problems in metropolitan areas when the wealth of communities (and therefore the taxes generated) varies considerably. Declining central cities and blue collar suburbs find they cannot support essential public services, especially public schools, to the levels financed by high income suburbs. Concern with the potential resulting educational inequalities has led civic and civil rights groups to institute legal action in numerous states. A number of state courts (for example, in *Serrano* v. *Priest*)[2] have held that relying on the property tax for school finance is discriminatory and therefore unconstitutional. Even the U.S. Supreme Court, while not ruling in favor of such groups (*Rodriguez* v. *San Antonio School District*),[3] described the reliance on the property tax as inequitable and chaotic. Efforts to solve these problems of school finance are still being made. One of the most popular solutions is to increase state aid to local schools on the assumption that the state has the widest possible tax base.

The fragmented governmental system and the property tax also cause a considerable amount of "fiscal zoning." On one hand there is competition between communities for "high ratables"—that is, industrial and commercial properties that pay proportionately higher taxes than the costs to service them. This competition does not lead particularly toward well-planned land use patterns in a metropolitan area as a whole. Moreover, the negotiating tactics used by some communities include "sweeteners" whereby the community as a whole installs expensive utilities. On the other hand communities are as vigorous in trying to keep out certain land uses (such as low and moderate income housing) that do not "pay their way." A variety of tactics are used, such as large lot zoning, exclusion of apartments, unrealistically high building code standards, and the requirement of excessive public improvement costs. These practices have created a substantial amount of litigation (see Chapter 15) that is beyond the scope of this discussion. The point here is that taxing and planning mechanisms need to be found that will lessen reliance on these inequitable and questionable practices.

One interesting attempt to alleviate some of the problems created by tax competition and fiscal zoning is being made in Minnesota through a state fiscal disparities law.[4] The law provides that taxes obtained from existing industrial and commercial properties within a broad geographic area may still go to the governmental unit in which the facility is located. However, a portion of the new tax revenues is put into an areawide pool to be distributed among all governmental units. Over a period of time this should tend to equalize the tax benefits accruing to local communities, whether or not they have industry or commercial land uses.

The property tax has also been widely criticized as having undesirable impacts on urban land development patterns. In the suburban context a situation takes place wherein urban sprawl and the pressures of the suburban land market drive up the value of vacant land that is being used for agriculture or that may contain environmentally sensitive systems, such as stream valleys. When a tax assessor observes the land conversion process from rural to urban, he or she assigns a higher land value to land that he or she believes is ripe for development. Thus, a farmer, whether interested or not in urban land development, is faced with higher taxes. A number of techniques are being used in many states to either halt or slow down this process of premature conversion. One technique is the use of open space or conservation easements whereby a community buys the development rights of a piece of property, thereby lowering its value. Another technique is a state law that allows preferential tax assessment for farmland. Under this system the assessor is required to assess farmland for its present use, not its potential use.

In the central city context the problem of the property tax is that the owner of a deteriorating property is faced with strong disincentives to improve or rehabilitate the property since if the value of improvements increases property tax also increases. The concept of the site value or land value tax (which has been with us for three-quarters of a century) addresses this problem as well as the suburban one. The land tax or site value tax has as its basis the concept that the value of land, and not the value of buildings, ought to be taxed. It is argued that in this way land value would increase at the urban fringe and therefore would raise taxes and in turn would create incentives to develop a compact pattern. In the central city context, it is argued, rehabilitation would be easier in that an owner would not be penalized. However, this idea has not caught hold in the United States.

In summary, criticisms of the property tax are substantial. However, the tax has persisted as a primary means through which local governments finance expenditures.

The sales tax

The second largest locally generated source of revenue for cities is the local sales tax. It should be noted that state sales tax may be collected from a consumer at the same time. The latter rate can be, and usually is, substantially higher. A number of states also permit separate local taxes to be levied on cigarettes and gasoline.

Cities are turning to the sales tax as a form of revenue primarily because the property tax is reaching its practical and political limit as a revenue generator. The payment of a sales tax usually comes in small doses, and therefore this may be an easier tax for local government to impose than the property tax.

An important planning issue arises when the sales tax is used as a revenue source. It is a tax source that can skew land use decisions. In states with local sales taxes there is competition between communities to obtain the land use "plums," such as major regional shopping centers which, in addition to producing healthy real estate tax revenues, also contribute substantially to local sales tax revenues.

Income taxes

By the mid-1970s some local governments were collecting approximately $2.5 billion in local income taxes. As is the case with the sales tax, the use of the income tax came about because of the limits of the revenue producing potential of the property tax. But the income tax has not spread to as many states as the sales tax has: only ten states and the District of Columbia were using income taxes as of 1976. Most such taxes have a flat rate, but a few have progressive rates. While the use of the income tax has not increased rapidly, if cities continue to find difficulty in raising revenues through the traditional sources then the income tax may become more popular.

As is the case with any tax, several issues need to be considered when local governments use income taxes. One issue relates to the tax base; that issue is whether it includes only personal income or also includes income from stocks, bonds, and a variety of nonlabor sources.

Another troublesome issue relates to taxation of nonresidents. In fragmented metropolitan areas and in interstate metropolitan areas there are numerous arguments concerning the equity of working in one community and living in another community when either one or both have income taxes. State laws on local income taxes handle these problems in a variety of ways, including using a different rate structure for nonresidents or having reciprocal tax credits between jurisdictions.

Miscellaneous local revenues

One major category of miscellaneous revenues is taxes and fees other than property, sales, or income taxes. There is a bewildering variety of such taxes; the purpose here is simply to identify a number of the more common ones. Localities can impose a variety of taxes on tobacco products, alcoholic beverages, utility services, and theater admissions. Also, cities can impose fees for business licenses which are a combination of regulatory and revenue producing mechanisms.

Another group of fees consists of largely administrative–regulatory fees such as building permit fees, fees for zoning and land subdivision changes, and plumbing and electrical fees. A few communities have tried to use these fees as impact taxes (that is, they have set fees well above regulatory costs as a revenue source), but it has become a relatively well-established point of law that such fees are intended to cover the costs of regulation and should not be used as revenue raising devices.

Cities and counties obtain revenues from a variety of user fees. For example, charges are usually made for water use and other services provided by the municipality, such as electric or gas supply, transit fares, bridge and tunnel tolls, parking fees, airport facilities, and sewerage. Unless subsidized or defrayed by intergovernmental transfers, most user fees are used to pay operating expenses of a facility and to retire revenue bonds that financed construction.

Another category of tax revenues relates in part to the local level and in part to the county or metropolitan level. Local governments have created a host of special districts that carry out certain public functions. Sometimes these districts have been created to serve more than one governmental unit. Sometimes they have been created as a method of avoiding state imposed tax limits on local governments. These special districts often have their own elected officials and separate taxing power. The services they provide include public schools, housing and urban redevelopment, libraries, flood control, sewer and water supply, parks and recreation, health facilities and hospitals, libraries, cemeteries, and airports, to name a few.

Two issues deserve mention here. First, creating a special district does not necessarily solve all financial problems. In both the short run and the long run, the public must pay the taxes. The overall tax load and accumulated debt are watched carefully by the financial community. A city's borrowing power may be limited if special districts already have an excessive amount of overlapping taxes and debt on the same taxpayers. Second, while special districts have been created to carry out a public function and are presumably responsible to the public through either elected or publicly appointed governing boards, they have a tendency to be "out of control" in terms of urban development policy. For example, a community or metropolitan area can adopt a particular kind of growth plan, but this growth plan may or may not be supported by the special districts that build sewer and water lines—a key element in any growth control or planning strategy. One solution to this problem is for special districts to be legally affiliated with a metropolitan council of governments (COG). (In addition, an officially adopted plan of such a COG may require that special districts follow publicly adopted plans.)

Intergovernmental grants-in-aid

The dependence of local government on state and federal aid is considerable, and there has been a sustained growth in such programs for the past several decades. It is beyond this chapter to delve into the details of the federal–state–local grant-in-aid system. Funds are now available to carry out local projects and services from almost every federal executive department that deals with domestic issues. In addition, the general revenue sharing program has funneled several billion dollars a year to local governments.

Local government has a relatively free hand in spending such funds in comparison with the situation regarding the traditional categorical programs related to a single function. By the mid-1970s there was some movement toward a type of special revenue sharing whereby numerous categorical grants within a single federal department were consolidated into a block grant program. Two important programs of this type are the Community Development Block Grant program administered by the U.S. Department of Housing and Urban Development (HUD) and the U.S. Department of Justice's grants for criminal justice planning. The importance of federal aid to localities is demonstrated by the fact that many local governments have "development coordinators" on city staffs whose primary responsibility is to seek federal funds. A few large cities even have Washington lobbyists.

By the late 1970s a number of communities, particularly larger cities, were becoming extremely skillful at seeking federal funds and blending funds from several different sources into coordinated local programs. Thus, a downtown renewal program aimed at industrial and business job expansion might use Community Development funds from HUD, mass transit funds from the Urban Mass Transportation Administration of the U.S. Department of Transportation, public works money from the Economic Development Administration of the U.S. Department of Commerce, and Comprehensive Employment and Training Act (CETA) funds from the Department of Commerce. Cities are showing a growing sophistication in analyzing their needs and using investment policies to accomplish their objectives. We may be entering an era of the urban governmental entrepreneur.

The budgetary process

This section focuses on the budgetary process in general, with emphasis on the operating budget. The budgetary process for capital improvements will be discussed at greater length later in this chapter. Here, the emphasis is on the planning of expenditures for current operating expenses for city programs and services, personnel costs, and other noncapital expenditures. It is during the budgetary process that *choices* are made among competing demands for resources.

The major purposes of a management-oriented budgetary process are financial control, management information, and planning and policy implementation. Financial control relates to the traditional and legal requirements for assuring that government funds are properly spent for public purposes. A good budgetary process requires the generation and manipulation of large quantities of data on manpower, activities, equipment, and similar subjects, and therefore becomes a key management tool. In recent years the planning policy implementation purpose has been growing in importance. This represents an important shift from an "accountant mentality" to a policy orientation—that is, the idea that government spending should be used as a key method of carrying out goals and objectives of the community.

Modern local government budgeting practice should be seen as part of an overall management system. One useful concept of a management system defines it as having three levels of planning: strategic planning, management planning, and operational control.[5] Strategic planning deals with the setting of goals and objectives and the policies for reaching those objectives. Management planning is a level at which more detailed programs (such as budgets) are evaluated so as to make choices that are in line with the adopted policies. Finally, operational control involves the carrying out of tasks and programs.

This general scheme of planning can apply to most kinds of planning activities within government. For example, the typical planning department would be involved in all three levels: at the strategic planning level in terms of fundamental goals and objectives studies and the formulation of proposed policies; at the management planning level through traditional comprehensive planning activities and capital improvements programming; and at the operational level through management of renewal or revitalization projects or the administration of land use controls.

What concerns us here is the interrelation of physical and fiscal planning in this management system. In local governments throughout the nation the distribution of tasks varies considerably. The tasks can be distributed among the manager's office, the planning department, and the budget office. In a few cities there may be a combined planning and budget office, or in still other cities there may be offices of management and budget. Whatever organizational form the city chooses, it is essential that two perspectives permeate the process. For the planning department involved in the budgetary process it is essential that policies and plans be sensitive to financial considerations as early in the planning process as possible. For the budgetary office it is essential that financial management and planning be permeated with policy considerations. These subjects are discussed in a management context in Chapter 3.

Steps in the budgetary process

The actual steps a particular governmental unit follows in preparing its annual budget may vary considerably depending on its organizational structure, its size, and the availability of technical personnel. The following discussion focuses on the steps that normally take place in a budget cycle.

In general, a larger community is more sophisticated in each step, and more emphasis is placed on the early steps which emphasize policy analysis. The eight essential steps in the budgeting process are: (1) fiscal analysis and policy choices; (2) expenditure estimates; (3) review of expenditure estimates; (4) revenue estimates; (5) budgetary forecasting; (6) preparation of the budget document; (7) budget review and adoption; and (8) budget execution.[6]

Fiscal analysis and policy choices   If a budgetary process is to be sensitive to policy local government cannot simply send out forms and ask what various departments want in the coming fiscal year. It is necessary to conduct an analysis of some essential factors before general policies can be set. Such an analysis has several components.

First, it is essential that the budgetary process be based on a sound understanding of local population and economic conditions. Whether a community is growing, stable, or declining will have significant impacts on the revenues available to that community, as well as on service demands. Forecasting economic and population trends can point out a need to adopt particular fiscal policies. For example, a rapidly growing community may have to embark on a heavy capital investment program to provide the utilities and public facilities for an expanding population; however, its capacity to finance these facilities may be limited by the degree to which the local government has the power to borrow funds to serve a future population that may not as yet be paying taxes. A mature or declining community may be faced with a declining population and economic base, which in turn leads to a declining local revenue; however, declining cities do not necessarily have declining service demands, particularly if the population contains a high proportion of low income citizens.

Another step is to review current local government finances. This analysis investigates the revenues and expenditures generated by trends in tax assessments, sales or income tax trends, grants-in-aid from other governmental levels, and potential changes in state laws concerning revenue sources. The key issue is whether the city's financial structure can support the forecast service demands.

Another key element of the analysis is the review of major jurisdictional programs. For example, during the past several decades local governments, in addition to their physical housekeeping functions, have been involved increasingly in "people-oriented" programs in the fields of health, social welfare, and criminal justice. However, the amount of resources available for such programs can vary from year to year depending on changes in federal or state programs, the degree to which local funds can be appropriated, and the launching of new programs or the winding down of certain programs such as Model Cities. If a local government has an effective management system it is at this point that previously conducted program evaluations can contribute to determining the future of present programs.

Areas that are receiving increasing attention from local governments are labor relations and wage and price trends. Thus, as the union movement spreads throughout state and local government, labor relations plays an important part in budgetary policy. Local governments are discovering, as is private industry, that the cost of conducting local government affairs consistently is increasing in an era of inflation. Even national and international problems, such as energy policy, can significantly influence local expenditures.

Expenditure estimates In the policy analysis of the first stage some gross estimates are made concerning major movements in the local government's revenues and expenditures. At this stage departments become much more involved in the detailed estimates. These estimates must, of course, be based on fundamental fiscal policies that have been set by the local government's administration and also must be based on work programs prepared by the departments. It is at this point that departments will need to make detailed analyses of programs and services, staffing and organization charts, salary costs, new equipment, level of effort for various programs, proposed new staff positions, and operating costs of recently completed capital facilities.

Review of expenditure estimates It is at this point that budget making becomes a political and advocacy process on the part of department heads and others; these others sometimes include council members and others representing the local government. The task at this point is "to hammer out the allocation of resources among competing demands."[7] In other words, "rationality" is secondary to traditional bureaucratic infighting. In the larger community budget officers are assisted by budget analysts who go through these requests very carefully. In the smaller community the manager may rely far more on his or her own policy judgments and intuition as to how much of what a department wants it actually gets.

From a policy point of view this may be the most important step in that it is possible to determine the extent to which specific expenditure proposals either do or do not relate to policy objectives. Recent experience suggests that a program budget approach may be the most effective way of achieving this policy-oriented budgetary process. (An example is discussed later in the chapter.) That is, every department head is aware of basic policies and of specific program categories and subcategories that relate to carrying out the policies, together with expenditures allocated by program function.

Revenue estimates Revenue estimates actually take place simultaneously with expenditure estimates. However, most of the responsibility for making revenue estimates rests not so much with the department heads as with the budget officer and the specific revenue collecting departments. These revenue estimates go into the details of the specific means the city uses to raise revenue: building permits, administrative fees, income taxes, sales taxes, fines, revenues from water and utility services, property taxes, business and license fees, regular state grants from such sources as motor vehicle taxes, and specific state and federal grant-in-aid programs that will be implemented during the coming budget year.

It is also essential that judgments and estimates be made concerning trends in revenue sources. Revenue sources of the city itself can be estimated and forecast by the use of city records. These are compared to population and economic forecasts, and further judgments are then made. In addition, it is necessary to carefully monitor changing state and federal grant-in-aid programs in terms of program and regulatory trends; for example: How many years into the future is a particular federal program going to run on the basis of authorizations and appropriation history? What are the purposes to which block grants may be put? Most important in this regard is that many federal and state grants require local matching funds. Can the local government raise the matching funds needed for the additional outside revenue?

Budgetary forecasting While most state laws merely require the adoption of the budget for one year, it is increasingly apparent to local government administrators that it is essential to forecast budget trends for a four or five year period into the future. This is particularly essential in planning for capital facilities (discussed later in this chapter) and it is becoming increasingly important for operating budget purposes as well. The result of such a forecast in a growing city may be reassuring in that "all is well." However, for the more mature city, particularly in the East and Midwest, such an analysis may show that some hard budgetary choices need to be made. For example, some older cities are no longer committing themselves to new programs, and some cities are even funding their capital improvements only on a pay-as-you-go basis.

The longer-range look at the operating budget also has the benefit of exposing long-term trends to the city's legislative body. Such forecasts may, for example, generate a discussion (if not a debate) of potential new revenue sources and of how current capital investments could create future operating costs and may make it possible to avoid unpleasant surprises—such as budget deficits.

The budget document The budget document represents the vast accumulation of estimates, projections, administrative decisions, and proposals presented by the local government administration to the legislative body. A good budget document ought to contain, in addition to the summaries of proposed expenditures by department, function, and program, the backup materials, policies, forecasts, and similar items that would enable the reader to reach an independent judgment concerning the soundness of the document. The budget document may contain supporting material such as a budget message, which emphasizes policy; a summary of the major fiscal analysis that has taken place concerning revenue and expenditure estimates; forecasts of where the local government is headed financially; justifications for either expanding or contracting programs and services; and an accompanying narrative in text, tabular, and graphic form that helps explain the policy choices that are being proposed.

Budget review and adoption   Budget review time is hectic for local legislative bodies. There are more work sessions, evening meetings, and public hearings than at any other time of the year. It is at this point that the mayor or the local government manager may make oral presentations, complemented by presentations by the budget officer and major department heads. Some councils have finance committees that do a great deal of this work.

It is at this point that formal public hearings are held. These hearings are normally dominated by relatively general presentations coupled with the constraints of time (given the fact that budgets must be adopted by specific legal dates). The participation of the public as a whole varies considerably from community to community. In larger jurisdictions public hearings are dominated by testimony and comments from Chambers of Commerce, labor unions, citywide citizen and civic associations, and a sprinkling of neighborhood groups. Citizen participation in budgetary matters seldom takes place at this late stage of the process. Department heads, particularly the head of the planning department, have long since been meeting with neighborhood groups and discussing proposed plans and improvements. (Astute department heads in service agencies such as the park and recreation department and even police departments know that they must be out in the community at all times of the year listening for complaints, floating new program ideas, and engaging in partnership discussions in designing city programs at the earliest stages, not merely when the budget is published.)

The final step in the process is a legal requirement: the council, by ordinance, will adopt the annual budget. In some jurisdictions the capital budget may be adopted at the same time.

Budget execution   This final step takes place all year long and is the responsibility of the manager, the budget officer, and every department head. The technical functions of budget execution—such as accounting controls or audit systems—are beyond the scope of this chapter.

Evolving budget systems

The concept of a budget can be traced as far back as the medieval English Parliament. The historical root of the word *budget* comes from *bougette,* a leather bag carried by the monarch's treasurer. The bag contained papers and documents dealing with needs and resources of the nation.[8] Balancing needs and resources remains the modern purpose of budgeting.

In the United States the concept of municipal budgeting began around the turn of the twentieth century in an age of urban reform. Good government groups realized that some method was needed to control the rampant corruption in the handling of municipal revenues and expenditures. Early work, such as the model municipal charter and budget system proposed by the New York Bureau of Municipal Research, emphasized accountability and feasibility. Thus there was an extensive emphasizing of where money was to come from, how much of it was there, and precisely how it would be spent. Detailed accounting procedures (for example, account numbers and categories) eventually developed. However, early municipal budgets followed a line item approach whereby categories of expenditure were divided into classes such as personnel, equipment, and insurance. This type of budget does not lend itself to serving as a management tool.

In later years budgets and budgetary concepts evolved to the point where budgetary systems emphasized the performance of particular services—thus the concept of the performance budget. In this type of budget, programs and services were divided into categories such as police protection, parks and recreation, traffic control, and other functions of government.

The PPBS experience   During the mid-1960s and early 1970s local government budgeting concepts went through a frustrating and agonizing experience. This was the era in which the planning-programming-budgeting system (PPBS) was supposed to revolutionize municipal decision making. In fact, it did not.

In the early 1960s the U.S. Department of Defense began to evolve a system of analytical techniques based on systems analysis, operations research, and decision-making theory. The Pentagon "whiz kids" were less interested in how much a private is paid or how much a rifle costs than in the *mission* of a particular segment of the military. For example, if a particular mission of a branch of the Navy was "to protect vital sea lanes for commerce and military supply," how was that mission to be accomplished? What were the resources required? What were the alternative ways in which the mission could be accomplished? Which alternative was most cost-effective or cost-efficient?

The PPBS approach has four distinctive characteristics: (1) it focuses on identifying the fundamental objectives of a program; (2) future year implications are explicitly identified; (3) all costs are considered; and (4) systematic analysis of alternatives is performed.

In the mid-1960s an attempt was made to adapt the PPBS system to all departments of the federal government. (In subsequent years the effort faded away.) Proposals to have states and local governments adopt PPBS were made in the late 1960s. Any government that considered itself modern and well managed created PPBS systems. City staffs scurried about preparing "program memoranda" and spent sleepless nights inventing programs, activities, functions, and subcategories. Many technicians felt they were going through a meaningless ritual.

The experience with PPBS taught cities that highly structured, artificial, make-work systems cannot work if they depreciate the human element in government. Systems must be understandable to elected officials, must be accepted by the bureaucracy, and must contribute to a feeling among local government officials and technicians that they know what they are doing. Some good things came out of the PPBS experience, however. In particular, far more attention is being paid to basic goals and objectives; to the identifying of affordable approaches to programs that meet the objectives; to a greater sense of measuring what is being accomplished; and to a better understanding of what is being achieved.

The Dayton system   A number of cities have developed budgeting systems that evolved out of the PPBS experience. One notable example is Dayton, Ohio, which has a long history of management experience. Dayton's budget method is called *program strategies*. The purpose of the system is to describe municipal services in a language elected officials and the community understand while at the same time allocating resources (local, state, and federal) in such a way as to classify expenditures on the basis of policies and programs.

Dayton's 1977 program strategies, for example, identified broad policy categories of policy development, economic development, neighborhood development, land use, community security, human development, transportation, and administrative services. Under the category of, for example, neighborhood development, the general goal was to improve the quality of life of neighborhoods through four major policies: (1) encouraging citizen involvement in neighborhood affairs; (2) preserving unique advantages of city neighborhoods; (3) providing adequate, safe, and sanitary housing in desirable neighborhoods; and (4) preventing neighborhood deterioration by eliminating unsightly and unsanitary conditions.

These general program categories were further subdivided in a program strategies document. For example, the total resource allocation for neighborhood development for 1977 was $9,529,620, or 8.49 percent of the total budget. Figure 5–1 shows the several programs and activities under a single component, housing services, which accounts for almost $3 million of the $9.5 million total. It should be noted that this budget looks back two years and ahead two years because the local income tax has a life span of five years. Moreover, it specifically identifies 1977 resources by revenue source: the general operating fund which is locally derived, Community Development Block Grants, and other federal programs such as CETA and Title XX of the Social Security Act.

PROGRAM HOUSING SERVICES	1975 ACTUAL	1976 BUDGET	1977 RESOURCE ALLOCATION					1978 BUDGET	1979 BUDGET
			General Operating Fund	C.D.B.G.	Federal C.E.T.A. HUD TITLE XX	TOTAL		
No.									
1 Geographic Housing Inspection	1,038,120	1,182,370	420,000	919,110	-0-	1,339,110	1,406,070	1,476,380
2 Rehabilitation Loans/ CWDC	825,000	800,000	30,000	905,000	-0-	935,000	1,028,000	1,130,800
3 Homesteading/CWDC	1,150,000	375,000	150,000	-0-	-0-	150,000	-0-	-0-
4 Home Improvement Counseling/312 Loans	-0-	108,660	-0-	128,230	150,000	278,230	291,060	305,160
5 Residential Relocation	96,700	117,060	-0-	149,520	-0-	149,520	164,470	180,920
6 Dayfare Housing Services	103,030	55,000	-0-	21,880	67,610	89,490	-0-	-0-
7 Dayton Metropolitan Housing Authority	21,580	27,780	-0-	-0-	22,000	22,000	-0-	-0-
8 Emergency Repair Loans/ Income Tax/CWDC	-0-	208,000	-0-	-0-	-0-	-0-	-0-	-0-
PROGRAM TOTAL	3,234,430	2,873,870	600,000	2,123,740	239,610	2,963,350	2,889,600	3,093,260

Figure 5–1 Program strategies and 1977 resource allocations for housing services, Dayton, Ohio.

Figure 5–2 goes into further detail on two specific activities under housing services. It can be seen that specific objectives are presented in significant detail. This detail allows Dayton to determine, during the year, whether or not it is meeting its objectives by keeping track of the performance criteria.

The budgetary program structure also involves preparing "condition statements," (narrative statements based on scientific public opinion surveys and statistical data from each major program element). The program rests on an administrative management structure that involves an office of management and budget and a "strategic planning group" which includes the city manager, the deputy city manager, the planning director, and three assistant city managers who have responsibility for all city programs. In addition, the city is organized into a system of neighborhoods, with citizen priority boards in each area that provide citizen input into the budgetary process. Finally, and perhaps most

KEY 33-3	ACTIVITY Homesteading/CWDC	RANK 2.81	RESPONSIBLE AGENCY Assistant City Manager for Development Services	STAFF 0	1977 BUDGET $150,000

OBJECTIVES	PERFORMANCE CRITERIA	UNITS 76 EST.	77 EST.
1. To purchase, repair and resell vacant, and deteriorated housing units in order to improve neighborhoods and increase home ownership.	1a. Number of properties purchased b. Number of properties rehabilitated c. Number of properties sold	150 100 N/A	100 90 72
2. To reduce the holding period on homestead properties from 12 1/2 months to 11 months.	2. Number of months homestead property held	N/A	11

KEY 33-4	ACTIVITY Home Improvement Counseling/ 312 Loans	RANK 2.33	RESPONSIBLE AGENCY Housing and Neighborhood Affairs	STAFF 7	1977 BUDGET $278,230

OBJECTIVES	PERFORMANCE CRITERIA	UNITS 76 EST.	77 EST.
1. To provide all cost estimates and job specifications necessary to CWDC to make interest loans to owners unable to obtain funds at market rates.	1a. Number of cost estimates b. Number of job specifications c. Number of loans closed	20 20 N/A	40 40 25
2. To provide upon request cost estimates and job specifications to CWDC for all emergency repair loans to City residents.	2a. Number of requests received b. Number of job specifications	80 80	80 80
3. To prepare for CWDC cost estimates and job specifications for all structures to be rehabilitated under CWDC Homestead and Loan Programs.	3a. Number of cost estimates b. Number of job specifications	N/A N/A	300 300
4. To obtain contractor bids for job specifications upon request of CWDC.	4a. Number of bids requested b. Number of bids received	N/A	100
5. To process and complete the rehabilitation of 48 homes under section 312 financing.	5a. Number of applicants processed b. Number of loans closed c. Number of homes in process of rehabilitation d. Number of home rehabilitations completed	N/A 24	60 48
6. To provide cost estimates, job specifications and contractor bids for residential improvements in the Wolf Creek and Northwest Neighborhood Identity programs.	6a. Number of cost estimates prepared for Wolf Creek b. Number of job specifications prepared for Wolf Creek c. Number of cost estimates prepared for Northwest d. Number of job specifications prepared for Northwest	N/A	
7. To make security assessments on all structures involved in the CWDC Homestead and Loan Programs.	7a. Number of structures in Homestead and Loan programs b. Percent receiving security assessments	400 N/A	380 100%

Figure 5–2   Homesteading objectives within program strategies, Dayton, Ohio.

important, the system, while complex in structure, is straightforward in language and thereby gives the city commission, Dayton's legislative body, an opportunity to simultaneously discuss policies and dollars.

Zero-base budgeting During the late 1970s yet another budget system was receiving attention. This was the concept of zero-base budgeting (ZBB). First developed by a private industry (by Texas Instruments), the concept was adopted by a number of state agencies and governments. Perhaps the most famous example of the adoption of zero-base budgeting was Georgia under then Governor Jimmy Carter.

The essence of ZBB strikes at the heart of traditional "nonrational" budget making: the practice of taking last year's budget as a given and adding a little for inflation and expanding programs. Under ZBB, last year is a closed book; *everything* must be justified as though it were a new program.

The major steps and elements of ZBB are as follows:

1. The isolating of "decision units."
2. The analysis of the decision units and the documentation of the analysis into "decision packages."
3. The ranking of the decision packages in order of priority by management.
4. The final compilation of the budget, based on the rankings.[9]

A decision unit is a cost center or activity that makes sense as an analytical unit. For each unit, goals and objectives must be specified, costs estimated, and performance criteria identified. Of critical importance is the definition of different levels of service so that decision makers can choose the level of service that the community wants to support. Under ZBB it thus becomes possible to choose levels of service that are *lower* than last year's, or at least to prevent automatic cost increases. In addition, it may be possible to perform the service in an alternative way.

One cannot predict the degree to which ZBB will be adopted by local governments. But it may be an attractive system to both mature cities with shrinking tax bases and rapidly growing cities whose service demands may grow at an exceedingly rapid rate if they are not well managed.

Capital improvements programming

The 1909 Burnham plan of Chicago is the traditional benchmark for the beginning of modern city planning. The plan is usually mentioned together with the City Beautiful movement. What generally is not said is that the plan contained a discussion of how bond issues would be required to finance the plan's public works proposals. One urban historian has noted that Chicago built $300 million (about $2 billion in 1980 dollars) of public improvements to implement the plan in the first fifteen years.[10] In retrospect, it was an astonishing achievement.

While the Chicago experience taught the significant principle that public expenditures are an important link in implementing comprehensive plans, it was not until the late 1920s that the concept of capital improvements programming began to emerge as a *continuing* element of municipal planning and fiscal management. A number of cities began to realize that the planning of capital improvements was a distinctly different process from annual budgeting. In essence, as capital improvements were increasingly financed by public borrowing it was necessary to undertake financial analyses that projected the community's ability to pay in the future; that analyzed and projected ways in which debt was to be amortized; and that analyzed the choices to be made when the number of potential improvements exceeded the financial capacity of a community.

The experiences of cities in the Great Depression of the 1930s, when numerous cities became bankrupt, and during World War II, when many cities postponed public improvements, gave a fresh impetus to the careful planning of public facilities. Basic concepts of capital improvements programming have come down to the present generally intact. Thus, the capital improvements program (CIP) has become a thoroughly tested, useful planning tool.

This quick glance at the history of the CIP needs to be supplemented by an observation: the CIP and land use controls such as zoning and land subdivision regulations evolved at roughly the same time. However, the number of cities that used land use controls grew much more rapidly than the number of cities that used the CIP. When the planning community was at the crossroads between regulation and budgeting, it took the regulation route and virtually ignored the budgetary route. Given modern insights of political science that show the importance of governmental budgeting and decision making, it is evident that the planning community took a crucial turn toward regulation when it should have been moving along both avenues simultaneously. The resulting imbalance in implementation tools has not been corrected even today, except in a few central cities where regulation is no longer as important, and a growing number of suburban communities that are integrating budgetary decision making within growth management systems.

Definitions

Capital improvements programming is the multiyear scheduling of public physical improvements. The scheduling is based on studies of fiscal resources available and the choice of specific improvements to be constructed for a period of five or six years into the future. The capital improvements *budget* refers to those facilities that are programmed for the next fiscal year. A capital improvements *program* refers to the improvements that are scheduled in the succeeding four or five year period. An important distinction between the capital budget and the capital improvements program is that the one year budget may become a part of the legally adopted annual operating budget, while the longer-term program does not necessarily have legal significance, nor does it necessarily commit a government to a particular expenditure in a particular year.

The definition of a *capital improvement* may be different in different cities. The common definition of a capital improvement includes new or expanded physical facilities that are relatively large size, expensive, and permanent. Some common examples include streets and expressways, public libraries, water and sewer lines, and park and recreation facilities. In smaller communities certain expenditures, such as the purchase of a fire engine, may also be considered a capital expenditure. There is an extremely important fiscal planning principle underlying this definition, which is that capital improvements should include *only* those expenditures for physical facilities with relatively long-term usefulness and permanence. Capital improvements *should not* include expenditures for equipment or services that prudent management defines as operating budget items and which ought to be financed out of current revenues. A number of large cities that invented financial "gimmicks" by placing noncapital expenditures into the capital budget during the late 1960s and early 1970s found themselves in serious financial difficulties by the late 1970s.

The benefits of a CIP

An effective capital improvements programming process can lead to many benefits to local government. Specifically, the CIP can ensure that plans for community facilities are carried out; can allow improvement proposals to be tested against a set of policies; can better schedule public improvements that require more than one year to construct; can provide an opportunity, assuming funds are available, to purchase land before costs go up; can provide an opportunity for long-range financial planning and management; can help stabilize tax rates through intelligent debt management; can avoid such mismanagement as paving a street one year and tearing it up the next to build a sewer; can offer an opportunity for citizens and public interest groups to participate in decision making; and can contribute to a better overall management of city affairs.

How capital improvements are financed

Because most capital investments involve the outlay of substantial funds, local government can seldom pay for these facilities through annual appropriations in the annual operating budget. Therefore, numerous techniques have evolved to enable local government to pay for capital improvements over a longer period of time than a single year. Most but not all of the techniques involve financial instruments, such as bonds, in which a government borrows money from investors (both institutional and individual) and pays the principal and interest over a number of years. Most of these techniques are carefully prescribed by state law. In addition, whether a governmental unit uses these techniques may depend on such financial factors as bond ratings given cities by bond rating services, current interest rates for municipal securities, and the current outstanding debt that the unit is already obligated to pay.

State laws governing local government finance and the literature of public finance classify techniques that are used to finance capital improvements. These techniques are discussed below.

Current revenue (pay-as-you-go)   Pay-as-you-go is the financing of improvements from current revenues such as general taxation, fees, service charges, special funds, or special assessments.

Reserve funds   In reserve fund financing, funds are accumulated in advance for capital construction or purchase. The accumulation may result from surplus or earmarked operational revenues, funds in depreciation reserves, or the sale of capital assets.

General obligation bonds   Some projects may be financed by general obligation bonds. Through this method, the taxing power of the jurisdiction is pledged to pay interest and principal to retire the debt. General obligation bonds can be sold to finance permanent types of improvements such as schools, municipal buildings, parks, and recreation facilities. Voter approval may be required.

Revenue bonds   Revenue bonds frequently are sold for projects, such as water and sewer systems, that produce revenues. Such bonds usually are not included in state imposed debt limits, as are general obligation bonds, because they are not backed by the full faith and credit of the local jurisdiction but are financed in the long run through service charges or fees. However, these bonds may have supplemental guarantees. The interest rates are almost always higher than those of general obligation bonds, and voter approval is seldom required.

Lease-purchase   Local governments using the lease-purchase method prepare specifications for a needed public works project that is constructed by a private company or authority. The facility is then leased to the jurisdiction. At the end of the lease period the title to the facility can be conveyed to the local government without any future payments. The rental over the years will have paid the total original cost plus interest.

Authorities and special districts   Special authorities or districts may be created, usually to provide a single service such as schools, water, sewage treatment, toll roads, or parks. Sometimes these authorities are formed to avoid restrictive local government debt limits and also to finance facilities serving more than one jurisdiction. They may be financed through revenue bonds retired by user charges, although some authorities have the power to tax.

Special assessments   Public works that benefit particular properties may be financed more equitably by special assessment: that is, they are financed by those who directly benefit. Local improvements often financed by this method include street paving, sanitary sewers, and water mains.

State and federal grants   State and federal grants-in-aid are available to finance a large number of programs. These may include streets, water and sewer facilities, airports, and parks and playgrounds. The cost of funding these facilities may be borne completely by grant funds, or a local share may be required. Federal revenue sharing and Community Development Block Grants have given local governments more choice in how to spend their grant money. Much of this money has been used to finance capital improvements.

Tax increment financing   Tax increment financing may be used to provide front end funds in an area where large scale redevelopment is feasible. A district around the proposed development is designated with a tax base equivalent to the values of all the property within the area. The tax revenues paid to taxing units are computed on the initially established tax base during the redevelopment period, which is usually the expected life of the project. The area is then redeveloped with funds from the sale of tax increment bonds. These bonds are sold by the municipality or a specially created taxing district for acquisition, relocation, demolition, administration, and site improvements. Because of the higher value of the newly developed property in the district, more tax revenue is collected and the tax "increment" above the initially established level goes into a fund to retire the bonds. After the development is completed and the bonds are retired, the tax revenues from the enhanced tax base are distributed normally.

Fiscal policies

Careful fiscal analysis and the adoption of specific fiscal policies must be the foundation of a local CIP. Long-range financial studies and forecasts must be made. Typically, they are conducted by the jurisdiction's finance officer, or in small communities by the local government manager's office. At the minimum such analysis should include the preparation of tables showing the amortization of all outstanding debt. Since local government can issue bonds that mature over long periods of time, this analysis will have to look ahead for more than a decade. As a practical matter, more intensive analysis and forecasting are done for the next five year period. These forecasts focus on the local general economic situation and the extent to which it may affect long-term local government revenues. For growing communities the analysis may show the degree to which various categories of revenue—property taxes, fees and licenses, state aid, income taxes, and other sources—will grow in the future. For stable or declining communities, such as mature central cities, such an analysis may show that because the economic base of the city is declining (for example, manufacturing and retailing establishments are moving to the suburbs) the local tax base may also be declining.

Anticipated revenues must then be compared with anticipated expenditures for capital improvements, personnel services, and pension plans, and other costs must be projected to determine whether projected revenues and expenditures are in balance or whether surpluses or deficits are forecast. The financial analysis can provide useful information. However, it is essential that the analysis leads to the development of fiscal policies. These policies should address the major problems or implications identified in the financial analysis and should provide more specific guidance to the budget and planning departments as well as the operating departments that propose capital improvements. Policies would address such issues as: the maximum amount of debt the local government is willing to take on; the types of revenue devices that will or will not be used; the annual amount of debt service that the operating budget can absorb; the specific types of projects or facilities that must be self-sufficient through user fees or other charges; and the degree to which local government will seek state or federal grants-in-aid.

In recent years a number of communities have begun to adopt fiscal policies that are related to strategic community objectives. For example, mature central cities are increasingly adopting policies that relate expenditures to economic development objectives. These cities may adopt policies to finance those improvements that are most likely to maintain or attract an industrial or commercial base, create new jobs for local residents, or generate private investments in neighborhood revitalization. Older cities that are in serious financial difficulty are even debating policies that target expenditures to certain neighborhoods or areas and consciously write off those areas that may be beyond help.

In rapidly developing newer communities fiscal policies are being adopted that will, for example, ensure environmental objectives by purchasing critical environmental areas, by purchasing parklands, or by creating greenbelts that will help shape urban growth. These communities are also paying more attention to the secondary impacts of capital investments so that capital facilities, such as major sewer trunks and major expressways, are located and programmed in areas where the community wants growth to occur and denied or delayed in those areas the community does not want to see developed.

The CIP administrative process

Earlier in this chapter the annual budgeting process was described. The capital improvements portion of that process is often a distinct element that flows through local government in separate channels. In some communities the CIP process may actually occur earlier in the annual cycle. The separate channels for the CIP come about principally because the planning agency may be the key coordinator for capital expenditures, while a budget office or city manager's office may be the coordinator for all operating expenditures. The CIP process may also involve additional public hearings by the planning commission. Whatever procedure is used, the process normally takes several months to complete. Obviously, the process varies from city to city, but the description below should be considered relatively typical.

The first step in a CIP process is the analysis of the fiscal resources of the community—the revenue and expenditure projections discussed above. This is typically conducted by the finance office. After this analysis the local government manager or mayor will meet with key aides and legislators to discuss the implications of the analysis for setting fiscal policies.

The next step is the directive issued by the chief executive officer to all department heads requiring that they submit proposed capital improvements projects to the agency administering the CIP. This is usually the planning agency or finance office. The directive is accompanied by forms, deadline dates, and the identification of key meeting dates. The directive will also contain the fiscal policies discussed above.

The planning agency will then usually provide the detailed project forms, and instructions to departments for completing the project forms. If new procedures have been adopted there may also be a CIP manual that describes the process and the products to be submitted. The reason for this internal red tape is to en-

A. IDENTIFICATION AND CODING INFORMATION

1 Project Number: 703149   Update Code: _____   2. Date FEB. 20, 1976   DO NOT USE

3. Project Name: SILVER SPRING PKNG FACILITY 7B   5. Agency: TRANSPORTATION

4. Program: TRANSPORTATION   6. Planning Area: SILVER SPRING

B. EXPENDITURE SCHEDULE (000'S)

Cost Elements	(8) Total	(9) Thru FY 75	(10) Estimate FY 76	(11) Total 6 Years	(12) Year 1 FY 77	(13) Year 2 FY 78	(14) Year 3 FY 79	(15) Year 4 FY 80	(16) Year 5 FY 81	(17) Year 6 FY 82	(18) Beyond 6 Years
1. Planning, Design and Supervision	32	15	17								
2. Land	540			540				140	100	300	
3. Site Improvements and Utilities											
4. Construction											
5. Furniture and Equipment											
6. Total	572	15	17	540				140	100	300	

C. FUNDING SCHEDULE (000'S)

	(8)	(9)	(10)	(11)				(15)	(16)	(17)	
CO BONDS	557	15	17	540				140	100	300	
CU REC-PK	15	15									

D. DESCRIPTION & JUSTIFICATION   PROJECT NO. 703149   PROJECT NAME SILVER SPRING PARKING FACILITY 7B

1. DESCRIPTION. This project is a feasibility study to: 1) define future development potential in areas to be served by Parking Facility No. 7B; 2) optimize use of public land in relation to development criteria for the sector to be served; 3) examine impact on parking program of improved transportation and proposed development; 4) recommend site for land acquisition, construction and character of project complete with cost estimate and funding arrangements. Project delayed one (1) year awaiting adoption of Silver Spring Sector Plan. Service Area: The Sector of the Silver Spring Parking Lot District bounded by Spring Street, Georgia Avenue, Colesville Road and B&O Railroad.

2. JUSTIFICATION. Plans and Studies: County Council policy statement in FY 73-78 adopted CIP resolutions (No. 7-736): "One of the vital objectives of the public parking program is to support comprehensive development plans for the Central Business Districts. To that end multi-use development of parking lots and garages is to be undertaken where appropriate and feasible after consultation with the Maryland-National Capital Park and Planning Commission." Silver Spring Sector Plan endorses 7B multi-use study concept. Specific Data: Study of ultimate design concept is being expedited because existing 500 space deficiency and acute future deficiency in parking spaces in this sector based upon possible land use development. Forty-nine spaces within Parking Lot No. 22 will be lost with the widening of Second Avenue.

3. STATUS. Feasibility Study. The consulting firm of Raymond, Pine, Parrish & Plavnick have prepared a final draft of this study. Final report was pending approval of Silver Spring CBD Sector Plan. Recent approval will permit completion of report.

4. OTHER. Not applicable.

E. ANNUAL OPERATING BUDGET IMPACT (000's)

Program Costs: Staff 0   Other 0

Facility Costs: Maintenance 56   Debt Service 56

Total Costs _____

Offsetting Revenue or Cost Savings (15)

F. APPROPRIATION AND EXPENDITURE DATA (000's)

Date First In Capital Program   FY 70

Date First Appropriation   FY 73

Initial Cost Estimate   2,700

Present Cost Estimate   572

Cumulative Appropriation	Expenditures and Encumbrances	Unencumbered Balance
572	27	545

Appropriation Request, Budget Year   FY 77

Appropriation Reduction (532)

Supplemental Appropriation Request, Current Year   FY 76

G. RELOCATION INFORMATION

Families 0   Individuals 0   Businesses 0

H. MAP   Map Reference Code: D17R

I. COORDINATION INFORMATION

1. Maryland-National Capital Park and Planning Commission Silver Spring Central Business District Sector Plan

2. Widening of Second Avenue.

Figure 5–3   Capital improvement project request, Montgomery County, Maryland.

sure that essential information about each project be prepared and submitted in standard ways. Of particular importance, in addition to the obvious importance of cost estimates, is that statements of project justification be made. For coordination purposes it is also essential that relationships between projects be cited. For example, a particular new water main will be constructed in the right-of-way of a vacated street within a particular neighborhood conservation project. In addition, departments should be required to discuss how a particular project relates to previously adopted plans and policies.

Departments will usually place priorities on proposals being submitted. Thus, a great many choices are actually made within functional areas, and therefore it is essential that the planning agency work particularly closely with departments.

Following the submission of all project proposals to the CIP agency, numerous meetings are held at which time the planning director, finance officer, local government manager, mayor, and department heads discuss, critique, and hammer out project proposals. The objective at this juncture is to pull together a CIP that is sensitive to the policies that have been adopted; that contains projects related to city development objectives; and that results in a product that the manager or mayor can submit to the city's legislative body. In some communities the administration's proposals are first presented to the planning commission, and public hearings are held. Normally, the general public seldom attends such public hearings. The typical audience includes speakers and representatives from citywide citizen groups, neighborhood associations, Chambers of Commerce, downtown improvement interests, and similar groups.

Communities that are trying to foster more effective citizen participation in the CIP process will typically use a variety of techniques. Some communities, for example, may appoint special ad hoc citizen committees to assist the planning commission or legislative body. If these committees are to function adequately they require extensive staff support and frequent meetings—during the entire CIP process and not just at the end. Some cities also will hold public hearings at the neighborhood level to give an opportunity for more detailed small area input. A fundamental problem in all these efforts is that schedules are, by necessity and by law, rigid and exact—and the citizen input cannot always be accomplished quickly. Also, typical citizen groups are far more interested in their own neighborhoods than in citywide or areawide decision-making processes that deal with broad policy.

The CIP is presented to the jurisdiction's legislative body by the chief executive officer together with any special budget messages. Depending on local practice, the CIP and the operating budget may be discussed separately or together at this point. Normally, the legislative body holds numerous meetings and public hearings. For a legislative body the budget making time of year is the busiest and most hectic time.

After the legislative body determines its own expenditure priorities and choices, the CIP is adopted. By "adopted" it should be understood that there is a significant difference between the first year of the program—the capital budget—and the remaining years. The choices for the first year are relatively firm. For future years the adoption of a CIP should be considered basically as a policy direction rather than a specific and firm choice about projects. It should also be understood that even though the CIP may be adopted with the annual operating budget it will still be necessary for the legislative body to pass ordinances appropriating specific funds during the budget year for specific projects. Ordinances will also be required authorizing the issuance of bonds or other financial instruments.

The problem of choice: priorities

The planning and management fields have had decades of experience with the CIP process. Nevertheless, the setting of priorities continues to be a vexing problem. Choosing what projects will be built and what projects will not be built is the most crucial step in the CIP process, yet it continues to be troublesome. For example, how does a city decide which is more important—enlarging a waterline, building a new library, purchasing more parkland, or repaving a street? In a more "quaint" era planners thought that one simply evaluated each project in terms of the coverage of the comprehensive plan and the facility plans (that is, the park plan); the project was either in the plan or not. However, plans never specifically identified all the potential projects that can come up through the line departments of city government. Moreover, as comprehensive plans have become more policy-oriented they rarely identify specific projects. And some communities have plans that are completely out-of-date or are still under preparation. Communities have responded to this problem in a variety of ways, some of which will be discussed here.

One traditional and still widely used priority system divides proposed projects into four categories: essential, desirable, acceptable, and deferrable. These categories are usually further defined in terms of whether a project contributes to public safety, prevents hazards, satisfies a critical need, or would be of benefit but is not essential. Another type of priority system labels projects in terms of criteria such as protection of life, public health maintenance, conservation of natural resources, and replacement of obsolete facilities.

A moment's reflection on these types of systems leads one to the conclusion that they cannot be particularly helpful since the real criteria remain unarticulated. What is the dividing line between essential and desirable? Is it more important to reduce operating costs or to replace obsolete facilities?

One response to the priority problem that has been tried by some communities is the construction of scoring or point systems whereby a project is evaluated in terms of a particular criterion (for example, contributing to public safety) and a score of between, for example, 1 and 10. Using the internal logic of such systems, it is to be assumed that projects that get a high score are more desirable. It cannot be overemphasized that such numerical systems should be very cautiously used. They cannot be used as a substitute for judgment and, if not carefully constructed and applied, they can do more harm than good.

Recently, a number of communities have been reexamining the ways in which they set priorities. These communities demonstrate a renewed interest in coordinating capital investments with community development policies. A frequently heard word—*linkage*—demonstrates increasing effort to explicitly link community development policies with capital investment decisions. The Dayton illustration given earlier in this chapter is one example.

The CIP of Memphis, Tennessee, is an illustration of recent efforts to link priority systems to development policies. In Memphis, as is true in many other mature cities, available public funds are shrinking. Therefore, the Memphis criteria are based on the idea that it is necessary to more precisely focus limited available funds in projects and neighborhoods where they will do the most good. These criteria are based on high priority areas for investment identified by the city staff and are related to adopted neighborhood plans. The concept of high priority areas for investment is based on the following concepts:

(1) Geographic areas of the City experiencing preliminary or advanced deterioration have multiple problems which tend to be interrelated; (2) by treating problems simultaneously or in a coordinated manner, a greater impact can be made on an area than by treating each problem independently; (3) priority areas can be identified based on the current conditions and needs of these areas along with goals and objectives of the Administration; (4) since funds and manpower are limited in each program area and City division, these limited funds should be directed to the same accepted priority areas so that, for example, streets and drainage are improved and housing rehabilitated as other capital and operating projects are implemented; (5) by concentrating improvements within designated priority areas, fragmentation is reduced and impact is maximized.[11]

Memphis also has a clearly articulated policy concerning service extensions at the urban fringe. That is, when capital projects are considered the first priority is assigned to fully servicing substantially developed areas within the city. The second priority is assigned to projects that serve newly developed areas contiguous to the city. The purpose of these two criteria is the avoidance of costly urban sprawl.

Minneapolis has a priority evaluation rating system that its planning office believes is invaluable in achieving a balanced program. The Capital Long-Range Improvements Committee (CLIC) uses citizen task forces to evaluate capital improvements proposals. The CLIC considers the city's financial capability and annually makes project recommendations, including bond expenditure limits. Proposals are rated on a scale of 0 to 50 points according to fourteen factors. Among the community objectives are economic development, further defined as the extent to which the proposed capital improvements "will encourage capital investment, improve the City's tax base, improve job opportunities, attract consumers to the City, or produce public or private revenues," and public benefit, defined as the extent to which the proposed capital improvement "is justified in terms of number of people to be benefited." The CLIC also receives advice and recommendations on capital improvements from the city planning commission. The planning commission prepares a checklist that contains many policy-related items for departments to follow in making referrals to the commission. This checklist is contained in Figure 5–4.

Priority setting is a particular problem for the small community that has few professional staff members and must rely more on lay persons for decision making. An example (Figure 5–5) prepared by a consultant for Franklin, Massachusetts, shows how it is possible to use a simple easy-to-use checklist for priority setting.

The CIP process and intergovernmental relations

The pattern of intergovernmental relations in metropolitan areas has profound effects on urban planning. The literature on metropolitan area problems and intergovernmental relations is vast and cannot even be reviewed here. However, several circumstances rise out of this fragmented pattern and have profound impacts on the local CIP process. What is relevant for purposes of this chapter are two basic factors and the implications that flow from them. First is the fact that the vast majority of metropolitan areas contain small fragmented municipal governments and a number of separate special districts; and second is the very substantial growth, if not dependence, of cities on state and federal grant-in-aid programs.

The issue of governmental fragmentation that relates to the CIP process is that certain important facilities, especially sewage treatment plants and their related major sewer trunk lines, and major expressways and highways, are built by either state or special district governments and not by local governments. There is a growing understanding on the part of urban scholars and officials that these key facilities can trigger, accelerate, or retard the speed and pattern of urban growth—in other words, they are the growth shapers. The decisions of the governmental bodies that plan and construct these facilities have a profound impact on local government and it is the local government that must then provide the local capital facilities and public services to serve the growth thus generated. Thus, local government may not always have complete control over its destiny.

A number of steps have been taken to coordinate such planning and development at the metropolitan level. Many metropolitan planning agencies are adopting metropolitan development policies and trying (often struggling) to influence these key investment decisions. However, even though many metropolitan

Project	Factor
Goals and objectives	Extent proposal contributes to the goals and objectives of the requesting agency and/or governing authority
Standards and criteria	Extent proposal conforms to criteria and standards established by requesting agency and/or governing authority
Service limits	Extent that existence (or absence) of public or private facilities limits (or denies) the provision of adequate services in area
Environmental quality	Extent proposal may improve environmental quality of the city and its neighborhoods
Quality of life	Extent proposal would offer opportunities for improving the quality of life for residents in terms of personal enrichment and living conditions
Special need	Extent proposal meets a community obligation to serve a special need of a segment of the city's population, including low/moderate income, aged, minorities, handicapped, etc.
Health, safety, general welfare	Extent proposal eliminates conditions detrimental to health, safety, and general welfare of the community
Service distribution	Extent proposal improves the citywide distribution of related services
Economic development	Extent proposal will encourage capital investment, improve the city's tax base, improve job opportunities, attract consumers to the city, or produce public or private revenues
Public benefit	Extent proposal cost is justified in terms of number of persons to be benefited
Cost-effective	Extent proposal may be cost-effective in terms of capital and probable operating costs
Commitment	Extent proposal is acceptable in terms of possible future commitments to provide similar improvements in other areas of the city
Coordination	Extent proposal appears to be coordinated with other public or private projects or facilities
Neighborhood involvement	Extent of efforts made to inform area residents about proposal and involve them in its planning
Total priority points:	

Figure 5–4   Priority evaluation formula, rated on a scale of 0 to 50 points, according to fourteen factors. Where application of priority formula does not seem to result in adequate score for a project, the task force may request CLIC to add up to 50 points.

agencies are governed by locally elected officials, the primary focus of the metropolitan agency is on areawide problems and not necessarily on local impacts of capital investment decisions. Another technique that has been used is the A–95 metropolitan review process whereby federally funded projects must receive comments from a metropolitan agency. Here, again, comments are usually focused on policy issues of metropolitan significance and not necessarily on local impacts. In some metropolitan areas the local impact problem may be overlooked when the metropolitan planning agency itself does not control the trans-

The following checklist should help in considering the secondary consequences of building capital facilities or making other capital outlays. All questions are structured so that yes answers indicate an impact consistent with town policy as expressed in "Planning for Franklin," the Residents' Master Plan Studies, 1974–76.

	Yes	**No**	**Not applicable**
1. Will this project either leave unchanged or slow the rate of population growth in Franklin?	——	——	——
2. Is the amount of growth that this project is designed to serve consistent with the most recent projections of the planning board?	——	——	——
3. Will this project either leave unchanged or increase the ratio of jobs in Franklin to residents of Franklin?	——	——	——
4. If the project is likely to stimulate residential development in an area, as opposed to townwide,			
a) Will that development be totally in the center or suburban district?	——	——	——
b) Will that development be partially in the center or suburban district?	——	——	——
c) Can the stimulated growth in that area be serviced with roads, schools, utilities, etc., without further town investments?	——	——	——
d) Are existing development controls adequate to relieve all other concerns about the stimulated growth in that area?	——	——	——
5. If the project is likely to slow residential development in an area, as opposed to townwide,			
a) Is that area in the rural district?	——	——	——
b) Are one or more public service systems in the area being used at or near capacity?	——	——	——
6. If the project is likely to stimulate commercial or industrial development in an area, as opposed to townwide,			
a) Is that area now zoned for commerce or industry?	——	——	——
b) Can the stimulated development be adequately serviced with roads, utilities, etc., without further town investments?	——	——	——
c) Are existing development controls adequate to relieve all other concerns about the stimulated growth?	——	——	——
7. If located in a rural district, will this project itself be free of characteristics leading to an urbanized "character"?	——	——	——

Figure 5–5   Priority setting checklist proposed for the town of Franklin, Massachusetts.

portation planning process, or when it does not have influence over special districts that construct sewage treatment facilities. A handful of metropolitan agencies have begun areawide capital improvements programs. These programs attempt to at least identify capital investments being made by various governmental levels and then inform major decision-making units of government. These projects are demonstration projects that, as yet, have not demonstrated their sensitivity to local policy problems.

At the local government level a number of steps can be taken to at least exchange information. A local governmental unit can survey capital investment plans of overlapping governments and special districts that will be built within the jurisdiction. This activity can at least inform local officials, who then may want to take political action; it also provides an opportunity to coordinate projects that will be built by different units in the same part of the community. Some communities have organized intergovernmental bonding committees that attempt to keep each other informed as to bonds that will be issued by the governments involved. This is a particularly important step, because when a community's bonds are rated by investment services the amount of overlapping debt on taxpayers is a relevant factor in the safety of the security.

State and federal grants-in-aid present another set of problems for local government. While local governments react favorably to state and federal programs that can help them undertake capital improvements projects, there are some problems that require careful attention from local officials and planners dealing with capital investments.

One such problem is that grant programs can distort economic choices and can skew local decision making. Federal money may be available for certain capital improvements but not for others. The tendency is for local governments to choose those projects that can be funded in part through federal or state programs. Capital facilities that do not have a grant program to support them may go begging. The grant formula for the balance between federal or state and local cost can also skew decision making. For example, for more than a decade the federal urban mass transportation system program provided that the federal government would pay up to 80 percent of the cost of a transit capital program. On the other hand, an interstate highway going through a locality would be funded by a federal formula that provided for the federal government to pay 90 percent of a highway project. Clearly, it can cost local government more to choose transit instead of highways.

The U.S. Congress's cycle of providing authorizations and appropriations or grant-in-aid programs can also be troublesome to local government. For example, Congress may pass a new grant program with a span of five years and with a total authorization of a lump sum or up to certain amounts for each year of the program. However, until Congress appropriates the money for a particular program in a particular year, that money is not available. Moreover, appropriations may be below annual authorization levels. To add to the misery of local government financial planners Congress also has the habit of appropriating money several months into a fiscal year, and then local governments are forced to try to carry out programs and spend money designed for a twelve month period in, for example, seven or eight months.

During the 1950s and the 1960s the number of categorical grant programs—that is programs for a single function or program—grew to the point where federal, state, and local officials realized that coordinating multiple programs at the local level is a serious problem. Two of the most significant pieces of federal legislation—general revenue sharing and the Community Development Block Grant program—have enabled local governments to have a far greater voice in spending federal money. Moreover, the flow of funds has become more regular, thus allowing better programming of capital investments. These federal programs have also been supplemented by other funds for public works such as funds administered by the U.S. Department of Commerce's Economic Development Administration. A significant development in the area of federal transportation policy has (as mentioned earlier) enabled local officials to choose between federal aid for mass transit or for highways.

The local CIP process is also very heavily influenced by other types of impacts of federal programs. For example, as both major metropolitan areas and small communities have discovered, environmental standards for water quality management have resulted in the requirement that local government agencies spend enormous amounts of money to help maintain and improve water quality. New and major improvements in sewage treatment plants and the construction of major trunk sewer lines may require local communities to postpone other capital investments. In addition, the secondary impacts of federal, capital-related programs are not yet well understood, let alone controlled. For example, a federal or state environmental requirement may force a local government unit to build a trunk sewer line in a particular location. While this capital investment achieves certain environmental objectives, the construction of it can also open up vast areas of land for urban development. Local land use plans may not have proposed such development.

As can be seen even from this short discussion, local government capital investments can be greatly influenced by other levels of government. The degree to which local government units can use capital investments to shape urban growth will determine the extent to which the CIP serves as an effective management tool.

The CIP process and the political process

The procedures discussed in this chapter for the CIP and the local budget emphasize concepts, techniques, and bureaucratic routines that are essential to a well-managed local government. The neat, rational process described does not really explain completely the complex political process that is taking place simultaneously, often outside the bureaucratic technical process. A favorite pastime of some academics (albeit unsophisticated ones) is to take planning and management literature describing such routines and then compare real world case studies to the routines. These analyses always come to the conclusion that "things don't always work that way." However, this does not mean budgetary processes are obsolete, unrealistic, or naive—it simply means that the process is more complicated.

The purpose of this section is to make some generalizations from the literature (see the bibliography to this chapter) that describe the richness of local government budgetary decision making.

One set of observations that have been made relates to common patterns of action within a government's technical bureaucracy. For example, heads of operating departments are far more interested in their own departmental priorities than they are in citywide policy issues. Thus, the public works director is more interested in sewer construction than in park acquisition. Also, given the fact that most department heads are running ongoing programs and services, they are more interested in solving current problems than in building an infrastructure for an urban land use policy program. Generally, but not always, the department administrator's time horizon may be shorter than the planner's. Naturally, all department heads ask for more than they expect to get: therefore, projects listed near the bottom of a priority list may be of next to no importance. Moreover, politically astute department heads frequently establish informal relationships with elected officials, especially council committees related to their own areas of interest; therefore, they have built a consensus on certain projects.

Another general observation relates to *when* capital investment decisions are made. Many investment decisions are made outside the annual CIP process. For example, emergencies can occur in the middle of the budget year and expenditures must be made. Decisions on capital investments may be made as political promises during campaigns and then implemented after new officials take office. A few major capital investment decisions may be made when a comprehensive plan is adopted. More commonly, however, many key investment decisions are made at the time when neighborhood or district plans are prepared. Also, new programs and projects become possible because of a new state law or federal program. The point here is that not all decision making is postponed until that time of year when the CIP is being prepared.

Some of the literature deals with the role of elected officials in the budgetary process. In general, elected officials are engaged in a constant negotiating process with public and private interests that want improvements or that oppose certain improvements. The continuing bargaining process makes the elected official reluctant to commit himself or herself for too many years in advance. Therefore, programs for future years are not as firm as they appear. In fact, one of the bargaining devices that is frequently resorted to is to program a particular improvement for a particular future year. As the next budget cycle comes around the project may "move up" a year, and sometimes can be moved back a year. It should be understood that many projects bounce from year to year in the capital program but never arrive in the capital budget. Because elected officials are involved in this negotiating process, they also have some reluctance to explicitly identify and publicly announce all capital investment policies and priorities. They want to maintain flexibility and the opportunity to change their minds.

There are certain investment decisions and styles of decision making that are irresistible to elected officials and, therefore, are inevitable. These are: a desire to keep tax rates down; a desire to spread capital improvements throughout the city so that each neighborhood "gets something"; a tendency to "give in" to vocal community and neighborhood groups—and sometimes ignore such opinion; a tendency to balance expenditures and allocate cuts and additions "across the board" among all city departments; a tendency at times to avoid seeking certain federal or state grants if there are too many strings attached; and a strong tendency to jealously guard the capital investment decision-making process to the point where technicians do not really participate and often do not know why certain decisions are made.

The relationship of the CIP to other planning tools

Comprehensive planning   At one time "master" plans were so specific that particular facilities were identified. Now, as plans become more policy-oriented they may provide only a very general guide to investment decisions. On the other hand, community or neighborhood level plans and plans for small communities may still contain a degree of specificity that makes it easy to know whether a particular improvement does or does not conform to policy.

Plans prepared for particular functional elements—the park plan and the public library plan, for example—can also be quite specific as to improvements. In fact, some plans go so far as to make broad cost estimates as to implementation of proposals. This practice is to be recommended because it gives elected officials a far better idea of what it might cost to follow a planner's recommendations.

What may be the beginning of some new trends is illustrated by recent developments concerning the relationship of the CIP to comprehensive planning. At the suburban fringe a growing number of communities are constructing so-called growth management systems in which the CIP is an important component. Thus, communities such as Ramapo, New York, carefully try to relate this comprehensive plan to the CIP and to zoning and subdivision regulation. Permits for development are based on whether or not certain community facilities either are in place or are programmed in the CIP.

It is also interesting to note that in several older central cities (as in Philadelphia, Baltimore, and Pittsburgh) the CIP is the "centerpiece" of the planning program. In these cities the CIP is a very important activity and annual and multiyear development programs and policies are developed so as to be interrelated with annual capital budget decisions.

The relationship between the planning function and the budgeting function has been taken a step further in Atlanta. A department of planning and budget was created that is responsible for both urban planning and financial planning.

The ordinance creating the department specifically requires the preparation of development programs relating to capital investments for one, five, and ten year horizons.

The relationship between the CIP and traditional zoning and land subdivision regulation administration is also growing more intimate in many suburban communities. In addition to the Ramapo example, cited above, a growing number of communities are adopting either ordinances or policies that permit or deny zoning and subdivision permits on the basis of whether there are adequate public facilities. These policies and ordinances are based on the desire to extend utilities in the most efficient way and to prevent urban sprawl. A number of growth management systems may permit private developers to install public facilities at their own expense if these facilities are not scheduled until later years.

Subdivision regulation administration (see Chapter 14) also relates to the CIP in that there has been a historical trend to require developers to install utilities and other public facilities at their own expense. This policy in effect shifts some of the public costs for capital facilities out of the public budget and into the budget of the private developer and, therefore, to the eventual home buyer. In addition, while state laws are relatively silent on the point, it is widely known that extensive negotiations go on between private developers and public bodies as to who pays for major public facilities required by new urban development. This is particularly the case in planned unit developments and other large scale developments such as shopping centers and industrial parks. When local government perceives that there are economic development or tax advantages to encouraging industrial and commercial development, local government will frequently pay the cost of utility extensions in order to promote private investment.

Special assessments   In more mature communities special assessments are the principal way of financing purely local street and utility improvements. Special assessment districts are set up whereby properties that benefit from a particular improvement (for example, a new street) actually share the costs of providing it. This is another technique that shifts capital facility costs away from public budgets.

Community development and renewal   Community development and renewal projects often require large capital investments such as new streets, utilities, and parks. Chapter 16 covers many of the substantive issues that community development raises. The point here is that an extensive amount of coordination is required between the CIP and federal and state funds and private funds to be expended in a particular area. One recent trend in large cities is the coordination and coupling of a variety of programs in community development, transportation, and public works—incorporating CETA funds—with the objective of stabilizing neighborhoods, renewing business and industrial districts, and creating new jobs (see Chapter 20). It should be noted that extensive negotiations may also go on between public bodies and private developers in joint public developments. Public bodies again may be willing to pay for certain improvements in order to make private investment possible. The Dearborn Park project in Chicago, where vast areas of railroad yard land are being redeveloped into a "new town in town," is but one example.

Mandatory referral   A number of state enabling acts and local charters provide that, when capital facilities are built by either the governmental unit or independent special districts, the plans for such capital facilities be referred to the local planning commission or planning department for comment. When the capital facility is being built by the governmental unit itself, the planning agency comments may have some force. However, when independent governmental units are constructing facilities, the advice is usually only advisory.

Annexation   At the urban fringe, newly developing areas seek to be annexed to a municipality so as to save on certain urban services, such as police protection, fire protection, and public utilities. A few states, such as Illinois, permit the execution of annexation agreements whereby local governments and private developers may negotiate as to public facility improvement costs. Even in states without such enabling laws, governments frequently have exercised such negotiating powers because of their strong bargaining position. Again, the issue here is the shifts and balances between private and public expenditures for capital facilities.

Official maps   Several states have provisions whereby local government can adopt official map ordinances. These ordinances permit local governments to specify the location of particular improvements—such as future park sites or the right-of-way for a future street—on a map. The designation of such a site on the official map puts private property owners on notice of a government's intention to construct a public facility. Placement of land within such an area may permit governments to deny zoning and building permits so that the eventual cost of acquisition may not become prohibitive. However, there is usually a strict time limit (between one and three years) by the end of which a public body must purchase or condemn the land.

Cost–revenue studies as a management tool[13]

Up to this point the emphasis in this chapter has been on public revenue and cost issues, relating to planning, that focus on citywide policy issues. Sources of revenue, intergovernmental aid, the budgeting function, and capital improvements programming tend to be comprehensive views that relate to fundamental broad policy issues. This section deals with the public revenue and cost factors involved when government is regulating new development or redevelopment. These techniques are used to help analyze or manage a particular development at a specific time and place.

The concept of comparing public costs and revenues of a particular development proposal had its modern roots in the planning field in the late 1930s. The 1920s had seen a large amount of subdividing of properties into residential neighborhoods that were "premature" in that they remained forever vacant. A number of communities were trying to renew these "dead" subdivisions and would prepare simple analyses that showed how much more money would flow into the city treasury if the land were developed with improvements instead of remaining tax delinquent.

Beginning in the late 1940s and the 1950s cost–revenue concepts were used in both central city and suburban planning situations. In the central city context urban renewal project reports would frequently contain estimates showing how little tax revenue was now being generated by a deteriorated neighborhood and how much it cost to service that neighborhood; these reports would then compare revenues and expenditures of the area after renewal.

In the suburban context the 1950s was a time of aggressive annexation in many communities. Because planning agencies did not control the precise location of urban development, they had to take annexation requests from wherever they came and in whatever location. The cost of extending major sewer and water lines and serving new populations encouraged planners and public administrators to study the costs and revenues of annexing a particular area.

By the late 1960s and early 1970s the focus of cost–revenue studies shifted to the problem of growth management. This came about through a combination of factors: inflation and the resulting increasing public costs for all services; a greater desire to manage growth; shifts in the housing market from single family dwellings to multiple dwelling units; and the increasing popularity of planned unit developments with combinations of uses. These developments all contributed to a growing concern and awareness on the part of planners and urban administrators that it was necessary to more carefully measure potential tax revenues and potential public costs at the time that new development was being approved through the land use controls administration process.

The growth of interest in the fiscal factors of development accompanies the concurrent development concepts in environmental planning, wherein development proposals are analyzed to determine their *impact* on a variety of natural, economic, and social systems. Thus, these types of studies are increasingly referred to as examples of *fiscal impact analysis*.

Basic concepts

A recent comprehensive study of impact analyses, undertaken at Rutgers, defines the fiscal impact study as "a projection of the direct, current public costs and revenues resulting from population or employment change to the local jurisdiction(s) in which this change is taking place."[14] Researchers intimately familiar with the techniques emphasize the conceptual limits and boundaries of such studies. For example, fiscal impact analyses usually consider only *direct* impact and not secondary impacts that may take place as money flows through the local economy. No one knows how to do this, in any event. There is also an emphasis on *current* dollar costs, and this emphasis is limited to *public,* not necessarily *private,* costs of public actions. In essence, fiscal impact analysis is the estimation of, the tallying of, and the comparison of costs and revenues. Most fiscal impact studies limit themselves to the costs and revenues related to the local jurisdiction, and not necessarily to other or higher levels of government. The bottom line on any analysis is either positive or negative. It is positive if the revenues that a particular development will generate are larger than the public service costs. It is negative if the public service costs are larger than the anticipated revenues. Thus, stating the obvious, local governments are reluctant to approve developments unless there is a positive fiscal impact on the community.

Cost–revenue analysis, which focuses on municipal revenues and services, should not be confused with cost–benefit analysis, which tries to assess nonmonetary issues as well, or with cost-effective analysis, which tries to assess the most economical way of carrying out a particular public service.

Another technical factor that deserves mention is the difference between average and marginal costs. An analysis can come up with one result when one tries to estimate the average cost of providing some public service which takes in all present and future residents, and with a different result when one does a marginal cost analysis, which tries to specify how much more it will cost to service the next increment of population growth. Over the long run the average cost is more relevant; over the short run the marginal cost may be more important to a governmental unit.

The Rutgers study identifies six basic types of fiscal impact analyses: per capita multiplier, case study, service standard, comparable city, proportional valuation (these represent average costing approaches), and employment anticipation (representing marginal costing methods).

The per capita multiplier method of analysis is the most common (over 70 percent of the studies in the Rutgers study used this method). Forecasting of future costs and revenues is based on average cost per person and average school cost per pupil, which in turn is based on population of pupils residing in particular housing types. Highly reliable population and school data are needed to support this method.

In the case study method a particular development—the case at hand—is analyzed by examining the characteristics of the development. Then a series of interviews is held with various city department heads to determine the range of possible future local costs to serve that development.

The third method, the service standard, is fundamentally a more detailed approach similar to the per capita multiplier method. Thus the service standard method goes into the details of manpower requirements within the specific service categories. Data are derived from the U.S. census of governments.

The comparable city method is only used on occasion, but may be used more frequently in the future if data about particular cities increase. Basically, the method emphasizes changes in population size or growth rate by comparing the community at hand with other communities of similar size, growth patterns, etc.

The proportional valuation method is used for nonresidential studies. The fundamental basis of the method is that the study assigns a proportion of municipal costs to a new nonresidential facility on the basis of its real property valuation in comparison with that of the community as a whole.

The employment anticipation method is another technique relating to nonresidential developments. This method is based on the assumption that municipal costs are related to the number of employees of an establishment and that this is the best measure for determining public costs.

The classifying of types of studies into the six categories described above is based more on the varying ways in which *cost* is calculated. The calculation of revenues is similar in all study types.

The per capita multiplier method

A comprehensive manual that would explain the technical detail of fiscal impact studies would be as long as this entire book. This chapter can only highlight some of the general procedural and data requirements for but a single method—the per capita multiplier method. The series of study steps relates to calculating the costs that a particular development might generate.

The first step in calculating costs is to determine the amount of locally generated data available. Both municipal and school district budgets should be obtained and analyzed. In particular, it is useful to know school district populations. These are frequently divided into elementary and high school, and can also be divided by specific grade. The local government expenditures should be divided into service categories—for example, general government, public safety, public works, health and welfare, and recreation and culture—and should be separated into operating expenses and debt service expenses.

The next series of steps relates to analyzing the characteristics of the development. For example, what is the total size in area, and what portion is residential and what portion is nonresidential? Within the residential portion the dwelling units need to be classified by type (single family, town house, apartment) and should be further classified by the number of bedrooms. It is also essential to classify the dwelling units as to cost and rental per dwelling unit. Using these data together with previously generated data from the school district, it is then possible to use basic multipliers for each housing type. For example, data collected at the local (and sometimes state) level will show the mean number of children that can be expected to reside in various types of dwelling units. These multipliers can then be applied to the development that is being analyzed to determine the number of school children that will be generated. Then, using average per pupil expenditures from the local school district, it is possible to calculate the total costs that will be generated by the development for public schools.

While school costs are typically calculated on a per pupil basis, a different base is used to calculate municipal costs. These total municipal costs are analyzed in terms of what proportion can be assigned to existing residential and nonresidential facilities. Those costs that can be assigned to residential areas, on the basis of the proportion of their property value to total local real property value, can then be divided by the local population to determine a per capita cost multiplier. The cost multipliers for various municipal functions are then applied to the development. Data from the U.S. census that show multipliers for various housing types can then be used to determine the total population of the development. The total population times the per capita cost is then calculated for each public service category.

If the development contains nonresidential uses, such as a shopping center, it is necessary to assign costs to that portion. Previously, when total municipal cost data were being analyzed costs were allocated to both residential and nonresidential uses. This allocation was based on real property value. The real property value of the use at hand is then compared with the total nonresidential value in the community. If, for example, the value is 1 percent of the total property value of residential uses in a community, then 1 percent of the costs of municipal services can be allocated to that use.

Finally, computation is made of all estimated and projected costs that can be assigned to the development. Now the analyst's attention turns to estimating revenues that the development will produce. In calculating revenues major emphasis is placed on general revenue categories such as the property tax. Revenues for utility services are typically not considered since they are user charges and almost by definition cover the cost of operating services.

The most important source of revenue to be calculated is, of course, the property tax. This needs to be allocated to the school district and to the municipality. In addition, there are a variety of miscellaneous revenues, such as building and zoning permits, that come from the development. Estimation of real property income is based on calculating the costs of the dwelling units and applying the various ratios and multipliers that were discussed in the revenue section of this chapter. Thus far the analyst is dealing with sources of revenue that go to the governmental unit or to the school district directly from the resident.

A second, more complex, set of calculations must be made concerning intergovernmental transfers. Many grant-in-aid programs on both the federal and state levels are based on population. If the development increases the population of a community then the community will be getting more aid, such as federal revenue sharing or state motor fuel tax funds. Similarly, for a school district the amount of state aid is dependent on enrollment or attendance. If enrollment increases, then state aid will also increase.

All revenues are then tabulated; these include both revenues going directly to the municipality or the school district and the governmental transfers to both units. The analyst is now at the point where total revenues can be compared to total costs.

How are the results of such a study used? If the study result is positive then both the developer and the community are presumably happy. If the result is negative, however, there still are some steps that can be taken. For example, a number of models of such impact analyses have been developed through which it is possible to change some of the inputs so as to change the outcome. For example, since it is generally acknowledged that multifamily dwelling units have fewer school age children than single family dwelling units, a developer might decrease the number of single family units and increase the number of apartment units. This alone might change the balance. Or, if it is largely a multifamily development, it is possible to change the mixture of dwelling unit sizes so as to have fewer large apartments with children.

Some policy issues

The sketchy description presented above cannot do justice to the complex technical and analytical steps involved in fiscal impact analyses. But it can provide a basis for some consideration of policy issues that are raised when these techniques are used.

One issue relates to the technical validity of such studies. Typically, they are carried out by municipal personnel who are not necessarily familiar with the intricacies of analysis, methodological pitfalls, and data limitations. The probability of making errors is high enough to require that the analyst be very careful. All assumptions must be stated; all data sources must be identified; and data sources, particularly local ones, should be described so that it is known whether data are based on a long-term history of data collection and analysis or on a one shot look at a current fiscal year.

Another issue relates to how a particular development might fare in various communities. For example, a moderate income development that is planned for a high income community may receive a negative result in an impact analysis. That same development in a moderate income community may generate a small surplus.

The use of fiscal impact analysis raises profound equity issues fundamental to a democratic society. While the effective municipal planner and urban administrator must manage the community's resources efficiently, can they do so at the cost of individual constitutional rights? While fiscal impact analysis can provide more information for more rational decisions, local planners and administrators cannot blindly ignore social implications. One authority has observed that the user of fiscal impact analysis must realize that, in fact, every land use cannot be a municipal benefit, and while local governments may assess relative fiscal merit, it does not follow that those lands uses that impose a liability can then necessarily be excluded. Moreover, "Courts have recognized that municipalities also have to provide housing for those who work nearby, answer regional as well as local needs, and provide residential opportunities for those who are economically disadvantaged."[15]

In short, we do not need an analytical tool that will discriminate against people. Yet the tool will be used more in the future if, as it now appears, the public is less willing to make transfer payments or invest in public goods.

Conclusion

This chapter has introduced the main elements of local government finance and budgeting as they relate to urban planning and the local government planning agency.

How does a local government find the revenues to pay for the increasing number of programs and projects in the planning field? Sources of revenue are discussed, with emphasis on taxes of various kinds and on grants-in-aid.

The next section contains a discussion of the budgetary process in general, with emphasis on the operating budget. A step-by-step outline of the budgetary process is given, and various budget systems are described and evaluated.

Capital improvements programming is then discussed in detail with regard to the benefits of such programming, its financing, its fiscal policies, and the administrative process involved. The influences of intergovernmental relations and the political process on capital improvements programming are considerable and should be well understood by decision makers in the planning field. Therefore, these influences are taken up in some detail. The section ends by relating capital improvements programming to a number of other planning tools.

The final section discusses the importance to planning of cost–revenue studies. The emphasis here is on the role of fiscal impact analyses. One method of this type of analysis is outlined, and policy issues involved in these analyses are discussed—particularly those equity issues fundamental to our society that will continue to confront decision makers faced with increasing urban growth and, frequently, dwindling resources.

1 For detailed coverage of local government finance, see the following book in the Municipal Management Series: J. Richard Aronson and Eli Schwartz, eds., *Management Policies in Local Government Finance* (Washington, D.C.: International City Management Association, 1975).

2 *Serrano* v. *Priest*, 487 P.2d 1241 (1971), 96 Cal. Rptr. 601.

3 *Rodriguez* v. *San Antonio School District*, 411 U.S. 1, 93 S.Ct. 1278 (1973).

4 Minn. Ex. Sess. Laws 1971 Ch. 24. Codified at Minn. Stat. Ch. 483F (1974).

5 James C. Snyder, *Fiscal Planning and Management in Local Government* (Lexington, Mass.: Lexington Books, D. C. Heath and Company, 1977), pp. 78 ff.

6 The organization of this discussion is based on: Richard W. Lindholm, David S. Arnold, and Richard R. Herbert, "The Budgetary Process," in *Management Policies in Local Government Finance*, ed. Aronson and Schwartz, pp. 68–87.

7 Ibid., p. 72.

8 Lennox L. Moak and Kathryn W. Killian, *A Manual of Techniques for the Preparation, Consideration, Adoption, and Administration of Operating Budgets* (Chicago: Municipal Finance Officers Association, 1973), p. 5.

9 David L. Leininger and Ronald C. Wong, *Zero-Base Budgeting in Garland, Texas*, Management Information Service Reports, vol. 8 no. 4A (Washington, D.C.: International City Management Association, April 1976), p. 2.

10 Mel Scott, *American City Planning since 1890* (Berkeley: University of California Press, 1969), p. 102.

11 City of Memphis, *Procedures Manual for the City of Memphis Capital Improvements Budget and Program* (Memphis, Tenn.: City of Memphis, 1974), pp. iv–v.

12 City of Minneapolis, Capital Long-Range Improvements Committee, *CLIC* (Minneapolis: City of Minneapolis, 1971).

13 This section draws on the following work: Robert W. Burchell and David Listokin, *The Fiscal Impact Handbook: Estimating Local Costs and Revenues of Land Development* (New Brunswick, N.J.: Rutgers University, Center for Urban Policy Research, 1978).

14 Ibid., p. 1.

15 Ibid., p. 8.

Part three:
Making plans
and programs

6 City development plans

The city development plan has been the cornerstone of American planning theory and practice since the early 1900s. During this century there has been a continuing redefinition of what a plan is and what it does. The concept of the plan has evolved to keep pace with changing needs and new theories of public decision making. As a result, a plan of the 1980s will bear little resemblance to the typical city plan prepared at the turn of the century.

City plans have masqueraded under a variety of names—development plan, urban plan, master plan, general plan, growth management plan, comprehensive plan, policy plan, and many more. These name changes reflect, in part, the evolution of what the plan is supposed to do. In some cases, the name change is a public relations effort on the part of one city administration to disassociate itself from the planning efforts of a previous administration. Largely for convenience, this chapter will use the term *city development plan,* or the more convenient term *city plan*.

Despite changes in name and concept, some consistent threads characterize the city plan. First, it is a *physical plan*. Although a reflection of social and economic values, the plan is fundamentally a guide to the physical development of the city. It is the translation of values into a scheme that describes how, why, when, and where to build, rebuild, or preserve the city. This emphasis on the physical has been the source of much controversy and debate. Some have argued that the physical emphasis ignores people, but this argument has by and large been put to rest. The point to be remembered is that the city development plan is not a social service delivery plan, or a health plan, or a plan for economic promotion, although it may reflect or incorporate elements of all of these.

A second characteristic of the city plan is that it is *long range*. By that we mean it covers a time period greater than one year, usually five years or more. In years past the city plan was largely a snapshot or frozen image of what the city would look like twenty, thirty, or forty years later, but there was, unfortunately, little guidance as to how to get from the present to the utopian future. It is now recognized that an effective plan will express current policies that will shape the future rather than show a rigid image of the future itself. Nevertheless, a good plan should be slightly utopian. It should challenge and inspire us with a vision of what might be. It should also tell us how to get there.

A third characteristic of a city development plan is that it is *comprehensive*. It covers the entire city geographically—not merely one or more sections of the city. It is also comprehensive in functions—that is, it encompasses all the functions that make a city work, such as transportation, housing, land use, utility systems, and recreation. Moreover, the plan considers the interrelationships of functions.

Fourth, the city plan is a *statement of policy,* covering such community desires as quantity, character, location, and rate of growth (be it no growth, slow growth, rapid growth, or decline) and indicates how these desires are to be achieved.

In some states the city plan has essentially no legal status. It is a piece of advice that can be ignored with little or no penalty. In other states its standing

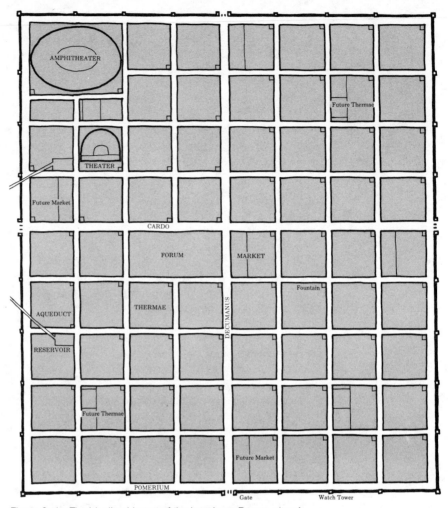

Figure 6–1   The idealized layout of the imaginary Roman city of
Verbonia (circa 25 B.C.) (above) is a striking contrast to the
suburban villages with forest preserves and other undeveloped land
in the Barrington area (facing page), northwest of Chicago. The
Verbonia master plan, designed to accommodate about 50,000
people, shows the sites for the entertainment complex (top left), the
forum, the public market, the public baths, and the major water line
serving the city.

has been enhanced by new laws or judicial rulings that give it substantial authority to compel action. While the plan is not a zoning ordinance, a subdivision
regulation, an official map, a budget, or a capital improvements program, it
should be a guide to the preparation and the execution of these components of
the planning process.

Finally, a plan is a guide to decision making by the planning commission, the
city council, and the mayor or manager.

This chapter reviews evolving concepts of the city plan from its origins in the
United States in the City Beautiful movement to the concerns of the present
day; analyzes major functions of the plan with respect to policy, decision
making, and legal requirements; and reviews the steps in preparing a plan, including considerations of policy, procedure, intergovernmental relations, technical processes, review processes, and major kinds of coverage. There is a brief
evaluative conclusion.

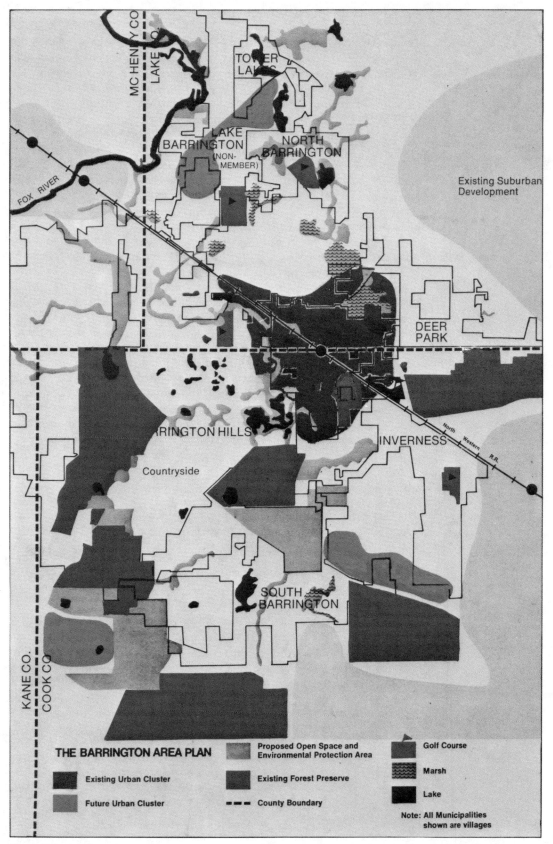

Figure 6–1   (continued).

Evolving concepts of the city plan

The modern city plan has developed over time and has been shaped by numerous legal, political, and social forces. Understanding these root forces is a prerequisite to understanding what the plan is and what it can and cannot accomplish. The essential point of this review is that the city plan both reflects and is a reflection of the social and cultural values of the times. The city plan can only be understood by understanding the community that prepares it and the social environment of the times. (The history of city planning in general in the United States is reviewed in detail in Chapter 2.)

The conscious design of cities and towns is a practice as ancient as civilized humanity. Our most familiar and admired roots in city design are the Greek and Roman cities. These cities were planned with well-developed ideas of city function in mind, and were built with great engineering skill. The earliest American plans reflected some of these ancient roots in that they were primarily concerned with the layout of new communities. These plans ranged from the simple gridiron of the land surveyor to the visions of L'Enfant and William Penn for the cities of Washington and Philadelphia.[1]

In the latter part of the nineteenth century the major cities of the United States experienced remarkable population growth, and planners shifted their attention from design of new communities to methods of improving conditions in existing cities. Immigrants streamed into such cities as Boston, New York, Chicago, and Philadelphia, along with the young from the farms looking for work. Older cities doubled or tripled in population,[2] and this growth brought the attendant difficulties of land speculation, residential overcrowding, inadequate sanitary systems, traffic congestion, and rapid, unplanned construction and land subdivision. In the early part of this century there were two major responses to these conditions—the City Beautiful movement and the social reform movement—that have greatly influenced city planning to the present day.

The City Beautiful movement and social reform

The City Beautiful, epitomized by the Chicago world's fair of 1893 (officially the World's Columbian Exposition) created an "ideal" city of broad streets and monumental public buildings. This generated demand throughout the country for replanning of the ugly mix of factory and tenement, and the congested, smelly streets of the "real city." The talents of architects, landscape architects, and engineers were sought for citywide improvement plans that focused on aesthetics.

The most important plan to emerge from this movement was Daniel Burnham's plan for Chicago in 1909 (Figure 6–2). It was characteristic of the City Beautiful movement in depicting an aesthetic vision of the city, but it also contained chapters on rapid transit, suburban growth, a comprehensive park system, transportation and terminals, streets and subdivision control, and problems in the central city. The chapter on the central city treats not only civic

Figure 6–2 Daniel Burnham's 1909 Chicago plan, probably the most influential general plan ever drafted in the United States, provided for traffic circulation, railway stations, parks, boulevards, public recreation areas, a yacht harbor, and a civic center. Developed by Daniel H. Burnham and Edward H. Bennett, it has been a constant reference point in both the history and the current practice of planning. Many of the features shown in the diagram (top) have been built, including the major parks, yacht harbor, and other facilities along the lake front; major streets (now freeways); and the straightening of the South Branch of the Chicago River. The photo (bottom) is from a point approximating the lower left portion of the diagram with the yacht harbor clearly shown.

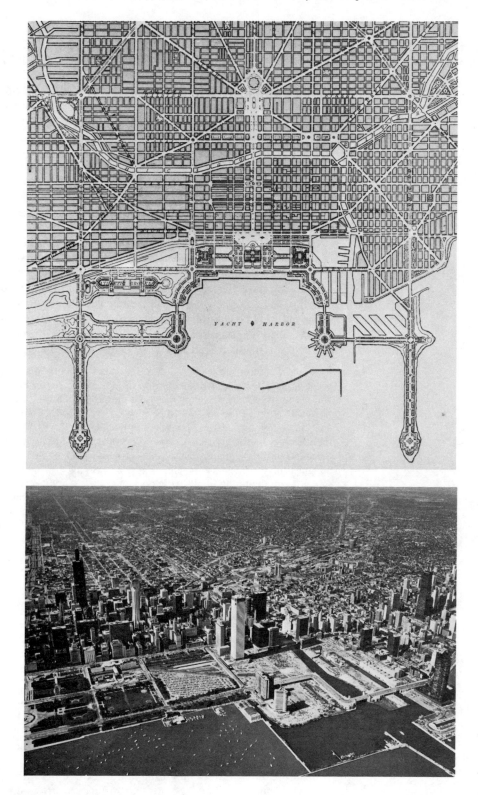

buildings but the problems of congestion and the menace to the health of the community posed by the slums.

The condition of the slums was the generating force of the second major response to the burgeoning city. A social reform movement concerned with the unwholesome effects of overcrowding in windowless tenements, infant mortality, and frequent epidemics grew up during this same period. Jacob Riis, a police reporter in New York, was its most dramatic spokesman in his book *How the Other Half Lives.*[3]

The reformers saw the interrelated problems of congestion and crime, unemployment and transit, density and recreation space. Their efforts were aimed at coordinated and comprehensive approaches based on surveys of existing conditions. The solutions to the social and physical needs were sought in physical change: street widening, rehabilitation, and zoning (which was then practiced in German cities).

By 1917 city planning was enough of a profession to stimulate the formation of a professional organization, the American City Planning Institute. By this time the City Beautiful was giving way to the "city practical" or city functional, with an emphasis on scientific data analysis and efficient management. Regional planning and a popular interest in zoning also characterized planning in the age of the automobile and the skyscraper (the 1920s). The extent to which comprehensive planning concepts had developed had been articulated by the distinguished city planner Frederick Law Olmsted, Jr., in 1911:

> We must disabuse the public mind of the idea that a city plan means a fixed record upon paper of a desire by some group of individuals prescribing, out of their wisdom and authority, where and how the more important changes and improvements in the physical layout of the city are to be made—a plan to be completed and put on file and followed more or less faithfully and mechanically, much as a contractor follows the architect's drawings for a house. We must cultivate in our own minds and in the mind of the people the conception of a city plan as a device or piece of administrative machinery for preparing, and keeping constantly up to date, a unified forecast and definition of all the important changes, additions and extensions of the physical equipment and arrangement of the city which a sound judgement holds likely to become desirable and practicable in the course of time, so as to avoid so far as possible both ignorantly wasteful action and ignorantly wasteful inaction in the control of the city's physical growth.[4]

The standard zoning and planning enabling acts

The model zoning and city planning enabling acts which were published by the U.S. Department of Commerce in the 1920s[5] have had an extraordinary influence in defining the city plan. These model acts were eventually adopted by almost all the states, and for more than fifty years they have served as the principal *legal* description of the city plan. (See Chapters 2 and 15 for further discussion of these acts.)

Although these model acts did much to promote local zoning and planning efforts throughout the country, they are most notable for three weaknesses: failing to define the relationship between planning and zoning; establishing incomplete coverage of the plan; and sanctioning piecemeal adoption of plan components.

The Standard State Zoning Enabling Act came first in 1922 and provided that zoning regulations must be in "accordance with a comprehensive plan." However, the nature of a comprehensive plan was not yet clear.

The Standard City Planning Enabling Act, which followed in 1928, indicated that a zoning plan should be included in the master plan and that the zoning commission should become part of the planning commission. However, there is no indication of the essential difference between zoning as regulation of existing land uses and comprehensive planning as a long-range view of what uses should be. Perhaps even more important, there was no indication of how the two activities should be related. The drafters were of the view that zoning should be based on a comprehensive understanding of current land uses and future needs. However, the timing of the two model laws and a lack of clarity did little to stop a trend in many cities to adopt a zoning ordinance without any comprehensive planning at all.

Another weakness of the planning act was that the content of plans was not defined. Only five areas of concern were cited: streets, other public grounds, public buildings, public utilities, and zoning. A footnote indicates that at least some of the drafters had a more comprehensive view of the plan elements.[6] However, in many cities planning was limited to the five areas cited in the act. Many cities also followed the practice of preparing and adopting master functional plans such as a master transportation plan. While the act indicates the interrelated nature of the planning activities, it also allows for adoption and publication of portions of the plan. This inadvertantly encouraged uncoordinated functional planning.[7]

The 1930s and early 1940s were characterized by major national and state involvement in planning activities related to New Deal public works programs and the war effort. David Lilienthal in his book on TVA says:

Here is the life principle of democratic planning—an awakening in the whole people of a sense of this common moral purpose. Not one goal, but a direction. Not one plan, once and for all, but the conscious selection by the people of a succession of plans.[8]

Toward the end of World War II there was a resurgence of interest in city planning efforts in many municipalities as they anticipated postwar adjustments. The focus of these efforts was on questions of employment and industrial development.[9]

Postwar: The housing acts

After World War II American cities again were teeming with overcrowded slums. The industrialized cities had attracted migration from southern and rural areas. Housing was in short supply and there was great interest in eliminating blight, rebuilding central cities, and expanding the housing supply.

All of these aims were addressed in the Housing Act of 1949. The focus of the act was on redevelopment projects. The act contained language requiring redevelopment to conform to "general plans for the development of the locality as a whole." When the limits of the redevelopment approach became apparent, additional emphasis was given in federal legislation to citywide planning efforts, land use regulations, and maintenance of the housing stock. The Housing Act of 1954 required "workable programs" from cities applying for urban renewal assistance. One of the requirements of the workable program was a long-range general plan (zoning, subdivision regulations, code enforcement, and citizen participation were also required). By 1959 money for comprehensive planning was available to cities, counties, and state and interstate agencies. As a result of federal financial support there was "more urban planning in the U.S. in the latter half of the 1950's than at any previous time in history."[10]

The support of the federal government spawned a library of "701" plans, named after the section of the federal Housing Act that authorized the funding. Many of these plans were of immense value to the cities and villages that sponsored them; others, however, were prepared only because they were required as a condition of eligibility for urban renewal funds. Planners suffered much criticism for the rather mechanical and unimaginative way in which the plans were prepared. Many of these plans ended up on the proverbial shelf to gather dust.

While the "typical" "701" plan was being turned out by the hundreds in the 1950s and 1960s, the traditional approaches to developing the plan were being reexamined. It was a time of ferment within the profession as it became more and more apparent that the static, goal-oriented master plan approach was not working. Planners were aware that the shape of urban centers was being determined by forces outside the control of the local government planning function, and that efforts to reshape the city had social and economic consequences that had not been well anticipated. Moreover, the planners were increasingly aware that the long-range, general policy guidance of the classic plan was having little influence on the short-term, incremental decision making characteristic of most city governments.

The bridging of this gap between long-range goal setting and short-term implementation was the focus of much of the reexamination of planning during this period. Martin Meyerson, in 1956, issued a call for a "middle-range bridge" between decision making and long-range planning.[11] Others stressed the need for a planning "process" with emphasis on efficient gathering and integrating of data on which to base alternative courses of action.[12] There was increasing interest in examining the social and economic consequences of physical planning.[13]

These new perspectives resulted in the creation of development departments in a number of large cities, which combined planning and development functions. Other planning departments turned to vast data collection efforts made more feasible by new computer technology. Some departments gave up the traditional planning document that described the city of the future graphically and verbally and focused instead on general goal statements accompanied by budgeting and programming procedures.[14] This was the period in which the policy plan was developed.[15]

The 1960s was also a time of considerable debate concerning social versus physical planning. Social activists argued that the physical planners ignored people. The physical planners responded by arguing that their plans took into account social values. In the end the debate was neither won nor lost but was replaced with new controversies as both sides grudgingly accepted some of the points made by their adversaries. A great interest in social planning was one result of the attention given to human problems during President Johnson's War on Poverty and the Model Cities program. The broader concept of planning was institutionalized by the American Institute of Planners in its definition of the professional planner in 1967. No longer did the professional planner have to be concerned primarily with physical development and land use.

By the late 1960s and the early 1970s the whole concept of the plan and planning was rather battered and beleaguered. Critics were sniping at "cookie cutter" plans that were not responsive to city needs, at elitist plans prepared and adopted by "establishment" planning commissions, and at plans that ignored the needs of minorities and low income families. Critics argued that no one could or should try to articulate the goals for something as complex as a city. The idea of advocacy planning was developed in the 1960s, and participation in plan making became as important as the plan itself. In retrospect it is easy to see that the turmoil that characterized the nation during the 1960s was reflected in the planning profession. Sacred cows were attacked, respected practices were considered suspect, and conventional wisdoms were disregarded.

The changes of the 1970s

In the 1970s a variety of forces combined to breathe new life into the idea of the city plan. The forces included the beginnings of growth management, mandatory planning requirements, court challenges to land use controls not based on a plan, and the publication by the American Law Institute of its *Model Land Development Code*.[16]

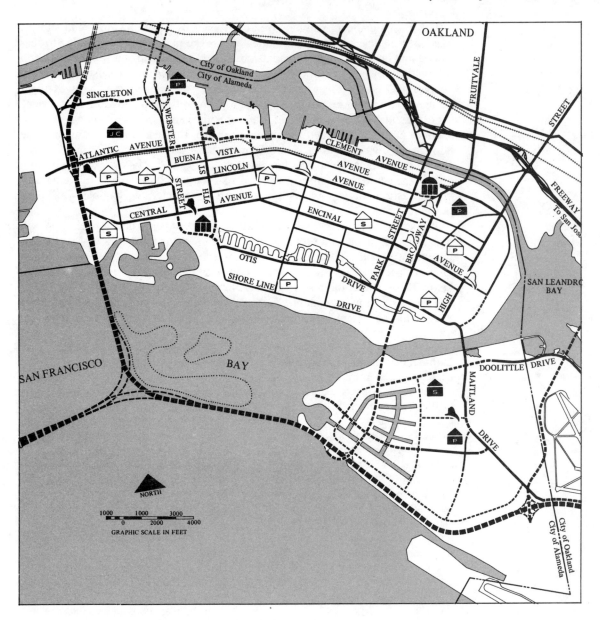

EXISTING   PROPOSED

P	P	PRIMARY SCHOOLS
S	S	SECONDARY SCHOOLS
JC	JC	JUNIOR COLLEGE
		CULTURAL CENTER
		FIRE STATION
		CIVIC CENTER

EXISTING   PROPOSED

▬▬▬	▪▪▪▪▪	FREEWAY
▬▬▬	▪▪▪▪	PRIMARY HIGHWAY
▬▬▬	▪▪▪▪	SECONDARY HIGHWAY

Figure 6–3   Public buildings and transportation elements of the general plan for Alameda, California, prepared in 1968. This is the horizon (broad overview) for just two elements of the general plan proposed for development by 1990. Other plan elements included land use, urban aesthetics, circulation, public buildings, recreation, and utilities.

The most significant planning trend of the 1970s was the widespread interest in growth management. Communities across the nation were beginning to recognize that growth inevitably had its costs and that growth at any cost was not a reasonable objective. In the 1960s every town wanted new industry and more people. In the 1970s this growth ethic was being questioned. New growth might bring new tax revenues but it also brought with it new demands for new services such as roads, schools, libraries, fire protection, and sewers. The cost of these services at times exceeded the revenues gained through taxes. Even when the new growth was not a fiscal problem for local governments, it caused other kinds of problems. New developments might destroy a favorite wooded area, disrupt the ecology of a marsh, overcrowd a school, cause pollution, create traffic congestion, or simply disrupt a way of life that townspeople wanted to preserve.

This effort to preserve a "way of life" has been the Achilles' heel of growth management, since some towns were using their apparent concern for the environment and the municipal treasury as an excuse to keep out the "wrong kind" of people. The "wrong kind" could mean anyone with a family income below theirs and could also mean a member of a minority group.

Early growth management efforts were labeled *nongrowth,* as some towns wanted to put an absolute stop to all new growth. Later efforts were more so-

---

Elements of growth management

Local growth management is . . . a conscious government program intended to influence the rate, amount, type, location, and/or quality of future development within a local jurisdiction. Growth management programs may include a statement of growth policy, a development plan, and various traditional and innovative implementation tools—regulations, administrative devices, taxation schemes, public investment programs, and land acquisition techniques. . . . It should be noted that this definition, which in fact focuses on actively guiding growth, differs from the popular notion of stopping growth completely.

As defined, the growth management process attempts to influence the "primary" characteristics of growth: rate, amount, type, location, and quality. These are the essential input features of urban growth—the major avenues through which the overall form and nature of development can be affected. It is also possible to distinguish a secondary set of growth features that could be called "impact" characteristics. These features, such as environmental impact, fiscal impact, or impact on regional parity, are outputs that result from the development process itself. Analyzing the impacts of development is one way to judge the effectiveness and equity of growth management. A local government may attempt to limit negative growth impacts by managing primary growth characteristics—by minimizing the fiscal impact of new growth, for example, by directing it to locations already served by water and sewer systems and limiting its rate to a level that can be accommodated by planned public facilities.

Source: Excerpted from David R. Godschalk, David J. Brower, Larry D. McBennett, and Barbara A. Vestal, *Constitutional Issues of Growth Management* (Chicago: American Society of Planning Officials, 1977), pp. 8–9.

---

phisticated and sought to control the amount, timing, and location of new growth on an annual basis by establishing some form of quota or by tying each increment of new growth to the installation of sewers or the provision of other expensive municipal services.

When viewed from one perspective, there is very little new about growth management other than a label. One of the purposes of planning has always been to influence, manage, and direct the growth of cities. What is distinctive is that past planning assumed that growth was good and bigger was better. Today communities want growth on their own terms. The difference today is that growth management is viewed not as a new *activity* but as a new *goal* of city government.

There is, however, another perspective, a perspective that suggests that growth management is really the coming of age of planning. Growth management finally brings together the plan and the tools of implementation. Growth management programs have designed and implemented new ways to control growth—new ways to use the traditional powers of zoning and capital investment. The interest in growth management has enhanced the status of the city plan. It is the plan that forms the foundation for political acceptance. The public, the builder, and political leaders will accept the restrictions of a growth management program if they can be certain that it has been soundly conceived (that is, based on a plan). As will be indicated later in this chapter, the courts, too, are insisting that community efforts to manage growth must be based on a plan.

Another major event of the 1970s was the adoption in 1975 of the American Law Institute's *A Model Land Development Code* (mentioned above). The code promises to have a major effect on all our land development practices in the next several decades, much as the model codes of the 1920s have had. The article on local (municipal) planning reflects the challenges to the traditional comprehensive planning process made in the 1950s and 1960s. It stresses the use of long-term goal setting and data collection and analysis as bases for public action. Social and economic impacts are recognized and study of them is required (although physical development is the central concern). Planning is clearly viewed as a continuing process intended to serve those who must take public action.

The code provides for a "local land development plan" that contains long-term policies and goals regarding the use and development of land. However, these goals "are primarily important as a framework for the short-term programming"[17] required in other sections. The code's major concern is with the "preparation and evaluation of specific programs of public action."[18] A short-term program of one to five years is required; it identifies publications, their sequence, and the agency responsible.

The organizational location of planning in local government is not specified in the model code, but the client for the plan is the legislative body of the municipality and adoption of the plan by that body is necessary to give the plan legal standing. The requirement of adoption is to focus the attention of legislators on "problems of physical development and location of activities that use land and on concrete programs aimed at their solution."[19]

Updating requirements in the code are designed to ensure that a continuing planning process is maintained and that the plan continues to reflect relevant trends and viewpoints. Periodic local land development reports must be adopted within a year from the end of the short-term program period to maintain the legal status of the plan.

The drafters of the code are clearly interested in a close and comprehensible relationship between planning efforts and short-term land use regulation, including zoning. Unlike the Standard Planning Enabling Act of 1928, which sanctioned both but did not link them well, this code is designed to provide the broader perspective necessary for noncapricious land regulation, as well as a shorter-term program that gives a clear indication of the intentions of public agencies in carrying out the goals.

The functions of a general plan

Court strikes down city zoning decision—no general plan.

Civic organization decries city decline—calls for coordinated approach.

Plan commission announces new plan as required by state law.

Developers call city plan outmoded—stops new investment.

City loses federal dollars for lack of development plan.

State coastal zone planning to be turned back to cities and counties.

Utility announces site for nuclear power plant—village board calls for impact assessment.

These are some of the headlines that might appear in the local press indicating a city's need for a city plan. We can see from the list that cities are likely to undertake plans in response to a combination of local circumstances or to the requirements of state and federal laws or regulations.

As indicated in these fictitious headlines, conditions within a municipality itself are an important generating force for a comprehensive planning effort. Burgeoning growth or rapid decline may ignite the concern of both private citizens and public servants.

A major new facility such as an oil refinery may require a comprehensive plan for the future of a city or town. The boom towns of the West have initiated city plans as they struggle to define the short- and long-term impacts of coal mining on their communities.

A local resource such as an attractive coastal location, a lake, or a historic site may generate development pressures that require a plan. It may become apparent that new growth is destroying the resource that attracted development in the first place. Pressures may arise to restrict new growth in order to preserve the resource. A general plan becomes a useful tool for sorting out what the community wants, whether limits should be imposed, and what interests are being served by such action.

The courts increasingly have looked for a rationale behind a city's zoning ordinance that can be used to weigh the relative merits of zoning changes or to justify the costs that compliance with a zoning ordinance may require. The general plan articulates long-range development goals for the community, against which shorter-term zoning administration can be measured.

Federal requirements for comprehensive plans have varied over the years, but there has been a consistent interest at the federal level in encouraging or requiring municipalities to coordinate public and private investment. A comprehensive development plan for a municipality, whether as part of a workable program, a community renewal program, a "701" comprehensive planning grant, or an urban strategy, was and is considered a basic coordinating tool. The availability of federal money to pay for a comprehensive plan has been perhaps *the* most important motivating force for undertaking the activity.

The functions performed by a city plan are many and complex, but they can be grouped under three principal categories:

1. First, the plan is an expression of what a community wants. It is a statement of goals, a listing of objectives, and a vision of what might be.
2. Second, the plan, once prepared, serves as a guide to decision making. It provides the means for guiding and influencing the many public and private decisions that create the future city.
3. Third, the plan in some cases may represent the fulfillment of a legal requirement. It may be a necessary obligation. Such a mandated plan can, of course, still fulfill the first two functions, but the fact that it is required adds a distinctive dimension to the planning process.

How, one might ask, can a single document fulfill such broad and complex functions. The answer, of course, is that the plan document by itself does not do the job. The value is derived from the *process* of preparing the plan and the *use* of the plan after its preparation.

Planners like to point out that planning is a process. By that they mean it is naive to assume that you can publish a single document that answers all the questions or solves all the problems. Conditions change, resources are shifted, and goals are altered, making it necessary to revise, adapt, and update the plan. The point of a plan is to focus attention on the process—to create a basis for debate, discussion, and conflict resolution. Planning must be a continuous and continuing activity designed to produce the best possible decisions about the future of the city. The *plan* represents a periodic bringing together of the activities of planning. The essence of a plan is that it is a statement of policy, an expression of community intentions and aspirations. When recognized as a statement of policy the plan can have tremendous influence, but that influence is only realized within the context of a total planning program.

The plan as a statement of policy

Central to all notions of the city plan is that the plan is a statement of what the community wants. It is a statement of goals, a listing of desires, an expression of ambitions. A good plan should be all these things. However, while there is widespread agreement as to the importance of goal setting, actual practice often falls short of ideal expectations. This is not surprising when one considers the immense difficulty of setting goals for something as large and diverse as a city. How can conflicts between the goals of competing interest groups be resolved? Is it possible to define goals that are specific enough to be useful? Can long-term planning goals be made compatible with short-term political goals?

The problems of goal setting are many and complex, but since 1960 there has been continuing and substantial improvement in the ability of local governments to prepare plans that embody meaningful statements of policy. Part of this improvement is the result of the changing context of city planning. Traditional planning methods are being replaced in response to new demands.

To a considerable degree the traditional methods of planning were borrowed from work done in architects' offices, single function government agencies, or private corporations. These methods were well suited to the single site and the unitary setting, but they have not been as well suited to the complex and mercurial city. Traditional planning method was predicated on such factors as basic agreement on goals, ability to predict the future with precision, and centralized control over the resources needed to achieve the goals. Early city planning, of course, was privately supported and was under the control of respected community leaders who shared a common vision of the future of their city. In this consensus, environmental goals were implied rather than stated, since the leadership agreed and everyone else either did not care or did not have the power to be heard.

Today we plan in a different political and social environment. Decision-making processes are more open and more democratic. A more sophisticated citizenry wants to know what the city administration "plans" to do, and wants to be part of the plan-making process.

Traditional planning was essentially a technical exercise. Modern planning practice is both normative and technical, concerned with both ends and means. Normative planning develops the broad, general basis for action, whereas technical planning is concerned with specific, established purposes and the procedures employed in achieving those purposes. One is concerned with values, the other with methods.

An effective plan should deal equally with the normative and the technical, since a planning department has a dual role in the affairs of government. A planner should function in a middle zone between the politician (a normative planner) and the bureaucrat (a technical planner). The planner has special competence and training in both areas and his or her plans should reflect both.

The policies or goals that are contained in a plan may already exist in various forms or places within a community and may simply be brought together and organized. Or they may be the result of a long and sophisticated goal-setting process. In either case they must be sufficiently unified to express clear direction and purpose so that the citizen has little doubt as to what the community believes in and stands for.

Some will resist using a plan as a statement of policy. Elected officials may be reluctant to commit themselves too far into the future, preferring instead to keep their options open. Special interest groups may also see some danger in using the plan as an expression of policy. If the adopted policies are antithetical to their perceived interests they would prefer to have no plan at all. It should be kept in mind, however, that a good plan does not foreclose future decision making by prescribing the future in detail. The policies of the plan say, in effect, "When we encounter this situation we will probably act this way for these reasons." This approach has the advantage of stating a position in advance of heated controversy. To deviate from a policy in the plan will require an argument and a rationale as convincing as the one in the plan. Departing from the precepts of a plan should always be possible although not necessarily easy.

The advantages of reviewing the plan as an instrument of policy include the following:

1. The essential and uncluttered statements of policy facilitate public participation in and understanding of the planning process
2. A plan that is a statement of policy encourages or even demands involvement on the part of public officials
3. The plan as policy provides stability and a consistency in that it is less likely to be made obsolete by changing conditions
4. Finally, the plan is a guide to the legislative bodies responsible for adopting land use controls, the commissions or boards that administer them, and the courts which must judge their fairness and reasonableness.

The plan as a guide to decision making

If the first function of a plan is to express community goals and objectives, then the second is to serve as a guide to decision making. A plan needs to make a difference. Those who make decisions about the city need to take account of what the plan says.

The ways in which a plan can make a difference are many and complex. Sometimes the relationship between a plan and the community decision is clear, direct, and formal. At other times the relationship is ambiguous and indirect. And, unfortunately, there are too many cases in which the decisions are made without any reference to the plan. The most common way in which the plan is used as a guide to decision making is in the zoning process. Certainly, the enactment and amendment of a zoning ordinance should be guided by the contents of the plan. In addition, the week-to-week administration of the zoning process is best done through reference to the policies and principles set forth in a comprehensive plan. As will be indicated later in this chapter, this relationship between the plan and the zoning ordinance is being defined by law rather than by convention. Some state legislatures are requiring that the zoning ordinance be consistent with the city or county plan, and some courts are hesitant to uphold a land use control measure that is not supported by a plan.

Subdivision regulations, like the zoning ordinance, should also be designed and administered in accordance with the recommendations of a plan. In the same way, the official map is another tool of community development that is designed to reflect the goals set forth in the plan.

The capital improvements program and budget have traditionally been thought of as implementation devices that were guided by the contents of a plan.

The worth of the comprehensive plan

Ever since I was awarded a degree in city planning from a school that stressed, I thought, the worthiness of comprehensive, long-range physical planning for urban areas, I have heard that whole notion criticized. Repeatedly, I have heard the quality, content, usefulness, and effectiveness of the comprehensive plan challenged, as often as not by those who teach city planning. The critics say that the comprehensive plan is too vague, too subjective, too biased, too specific. It is elitist and divorced from the people, . . . full of end-state visions that are unrelated to the real issues of a dynamic world. . . .

There are certainly elements of truth in these assertions. But, in general, they coincide neither with my sense of reality nor with the centrality of the idea. Comprehensive plans have always been policy documents, even if they have not been read that way. They have become less and less end-state, static pictures of the future. They regularly deal with pressing current issues: housing, transportation, jobs, public services, open space, urban design. . . . Any planning efforts are remarkable in a society that could never be accused of having a bias toward city planning in the first place, a society that has tended to look at land and urban environments as little more than high-priced consumable commodities. And isn't it grand that plans are visionary! Why shouldn't a community have a view, a vision of what it wants to be, and then try to achieve it?

Source: Excerpted from Allan B. Jacobs, *Making City Planning Work* (Chicago: American Society of Planning Officials, 1978), p. 307.

Planning departments are frequently responsible for putting together the capital improvements program and setting priorities among the competing demands for a share of the capital budget.

A rather dramatic illustration of the plan as a guide to decision making as reflected in budgeting exists in Atlanta, Georgia. In 1974 a new city charter integrated the planning and budgeting process in a new department of budget and planning. The city's plan, known as the Comprehensive Development Plan, is the cornerstone of an elaborate and continuing process that relates the city's goals to its budgets. According to the 1974 charter amendment, the operating and capital budgets *must* be based on the Comprehensive Development Plan (CDP). Public hearings are required for both the Comprehensive Development Plan and the budgets, and the city council must formally adopt each of these each year. The introduction to the 1978 Comprehensive Development Plan states that the plan "is : . . mandated by the city charter and published annually for frequent use by citizens, city officials and organizations interested in the development and improvement of Atlanta."[20]

The Comprehensive Development Plan includes "plans" for one, five, and fifteen years in a program format. Summary information on current or proposed projects and programs to achieve those plans, and cost figures, are also included in the document. The major sections of the 1979 Atlanta CDP are as follows:

1. *Issues and General Goals* is a statement of the most important current issues, problems, and opportunities confronting the city of Atlanta. Citywide goals, which would establish what kind of city its people are attempting to build, are set forth in this section.
2. *Major Directions* indicates the focus of the Comprehensive Development Plan. The 1979 CDP identifies six major directions toward which city resources will be directed during 1979 and over the next five years.
3. *Development Policies* translates the CDP's Major Direction statements into recommended city policies for seven of the eight functional areas.
4. *Program Areas* lists recommended programs and projects, by functional

area and by goal, objective, and action. The one, five, and fifteen year funding priority and Neighborhood Planning Unit (NPU) location of each action are also indicated.

5. *Official Maps* are included. There are two kinds of maps: those that are citywide, which include narrative notations drawing from the material in the main body of the document; and those that cover a single Neighborhood Planning Unit and show proposed land use patterns, together with one and five year actions for the NPU.

Few, if any, cities are as advanced in this process as is Atlanta, but Atlanta's experience is indicative of a trend, a trend toward making the plan a significant document that will be used to guide the many decisions controlling city development. It is clear that by integrating planning and budgeting, and by requiring that no budget be adopted without reference to an adopted city plan, a city plan takes on major significance in Atlanta. In short, it does indeed function as a guide to decision making.

A city plan can and should be used to guide or influence a variety of decisions. Allan Jacobs illustrates the importance of the plan as he reviews his experiences as the former planning director of the city of San Francisco:

As time passed and with a growing and more solidly based set of plans to rely upon, individual short-range proposals . . . . could be viewed in the light of long-range

---

How to use development plans The good planning agency does not keep its plans on dusty shelves but uses plans in day-to-day decision making. This example shows how planning agencies use plans.

Let us say that a private developer wants to build a 150 acre development that is predominantly residential (135 acres) and partly commercial (15 acres). Let us assume that a mixture of housing types —single family homes, rental apartments, and condominium apartments— is proposed. How does the planning agency use plans in reviewing such a development?

The agency would first check the land use plan to determine whether the general area is designated residential, then examine the proposed densities to see how well they fit with the plan's proposals and projections. The planning staff would also check to determine any physiographic characteristics—soil conditions, stream profiles, and important stands of trees—to see the environmental constraints that will influence site planning. The staff will also determine the land use plan policies concerning the amount and location of commercial space in the center of the community.

On the basis of the land uses and anticipated population to be served, the staff will, in turn, check other plans for sanitary sewers, storm runoff, major and minor streets, and public facilities to determine how well the proposed development "fits into" the community's plans. For example, the parks and recreation plan may call for a neighborhood park site within this general area. Or the school plan may have identified the area as being served by an existing school; therefore, no additional school facilities are anticipated. The staff will also examine the capital improvements program to determine how public facilities that are or are not programmed in the future will serve the new development.

There will be times when the development raises major policy issues not covered by general plans. Perhaps the plan is out-of-date, or perhaps it was not detailed enough to make a judgment. In these cases planning staffs will carry out supplemental studies that amplify or update a plan element.

Finally, the planning staff will prepare a staff report that will be presented to various decision makers in government, such as the planning commission, the mayor, the city manager, and the city council.

considerations. . . . We could review the location of a subsidized housing development in the context of the housing plan element. We could measure a neighborhood re-zoning proposal against the housing and urban design elements. When a piece of public land was to be sold or leased, we could check it against a policy of the plan, as we could the vacation or widening of a street. We could relate a small renewal project in Chinatown to both the city-wide and neighborhood plans that we had prepared and we could advocate such a project. City planning was especially pleasing when the projects and programs were clearly the outcome of our plans. We were exhilarated when all our research, meetings, presentations, reconsiderations, confrontations and responses to demands led to concrete actions, or even when all we knew was that the ideas had a fighting chance of becoming reality.[21]

Jacobs goes on to say that the functions of coordination, zoning administration, subdivision regulation, design review, and the design of renewal and redevelopment projects are extremely important activities; but all require some framework within which to function and make recommendations.

That framework is the general or master plan. Without it, city planners have a much harder time explaining why their ideas and their proposals are preferable to anyone else's. There were times when I might have argued otherwise, most notably in the early San Francisco months when I was impatient to get on with the action, to respond to the burning issues. . . . Taking the time to decide what we want our communities to be and then acting to achieve those goals seemed more and more worthwhile in San Francisco as time passed. It was a route that proved more practical as well.[22]

Most often a plan is used to guide the decisions of the planning department itself, the planning commission, the city council, and the mayor or manager. However, there are others who use the plan as a guide. Other departments of city government, for example, might have need for the guidance offered by a plan. A fire department might use it in designing its service areas. And state government and metropolitan planning commissions may have occasion to use the plan. What is perhaps most important is that a well-designed plan should influence the decisions of the private sector. Builders, land developers, and businesses can learn of the city's intentions as indicated by the plan and be guided accordingly.

Obviously, a plan that is used to guide decision making must be well prepared. It must be specific, must outline clear programs and priorities, and must avoid the trap of vague generalities.

The plan as a legal document

Increasingly, cities are preparing plans because they have to, not necessarily because they want to. This is a fairly recent phenomenon that has resulted from states mandating their local governments to plan, or courts insisting that some form of planning document be presented as the basis for land use controls.

This trend toward the required plan gained considerable momentum during the decade of the 1970s and promises to have a profound and lasting effect on our views of planning and plans. The trend reflects, more than anything else, a coming of age of planning and a recognition that a plan can and should really mean something. It reflects a change in attitudes toward the plan. The plan is no longer a formality, to be prepared and forgotten. It is rapidly becoming a requirement—and one that must contain certain elements; it is becoming a requirement that has for all practical purposes the force of law, or a requirement that must be fulfilled if the city is to receive federal or state funds or other benefits.

This trend appears to result primarily from a shifting attitude on the part of the courts as they review land use regulations. The Standard State Zoning Enabling

Act of the 1920s stated that zoning "shall be in accordance with a comprehensive plan." For decades this language has been the subject of intensive debate, but for decades the courts rendered their opinions on zoning matters without requiring that a city have a plan, or requiring the zoning to be consistent with a plan if there should be one.

This judicial attitude was not surprising considering the rather static nature of the early zoning practice. It was in those days assumed that a city would prepare a zoning map which outlined areas of residential, commercial, or industrial use and that any amendments to or variances from the zoning map would be few and far between. Property owners needed only to look at the map and the zoning text to determine what they could or could not do with their property. In short, the zoning map and text became the plan and the courts needed to look no further to determine what the city wanted.

Two major changes have occurred in land use control practices which have eroded the willingness of the courts to accept a zoning ordinance without reference to a city plan. The first change was the increasing use of flexible land use controls. Cities are no longer willing to specify in advance where everything will be or what it will look like. They have adopted a "wait and see" attitude toward development by using such devices as floating zones, planned unit developments, large lot zoning, special use permits, and wholesale amendments or variances. Property owners can no longer know in advance exactly what they can do with their property. They expect to go before the city authorities and negotiate an agreement.

This trend toward negotiated agreements is in part a result of an appreciation of our inability to predict the future. It seemed that no matter how carefully a city would prepare its zoning ordinance something unanticipated would happen to make it inappropriate or out-of-date. The other reason for negotiated agreements was that cities wanted to be able to attract the right kind of use and prohibit the wrong kind. The flexible controls allowed them to say yes to electronics factories, and stately homes on two acre lots, and no to smelting plants and low income apartment buildings. While this may have suited a city's need to control its own destiny, the courts began to doubt the fundamental fairness of the system. The zoning ordinance was no longer prescriptive on its face but was merely a set of procedures one had to go through to find out what might be done with one's property. It was a system that could be subject to abuse.

The second change in land use control practice has been the increasing adoption of growth management programs. Traditionally, planning and land use control systems have been concerned with the location and character of growth. In the 1970s planners added a third dimension: timing. It was no longer assumed that all growth was good. Growth had its negative consequences and some cities went so far as to adopt a no growth policy. Most, however, were satisfied to control the rate of growth (for example, x number of housing units per year).

Again, the courts have begun to say that if a city wants to control the rate of growth it will have to show some evidence of a coordinated approach in order to avoid charges of arbitrary and capricious enforcement. In short, they would like to see a plan.

When vast acres of land were zoned for all manner of uses far in advance of need, it did not matter that much whether there was a plan. Now that land use control has become a finely tuned flexible tool for controlling the most minute detail of development, including timing, a plan has become increasingly more important.

One of the best-known cases in which the judiciary has recognized a plan as a valid defense of a local growth program is *Golden* v. *Planning Board of the Township of Ramapo*.[23] Ramapo Township amended its zoning ordinance to implement a permit system for all new residential development. A permit would be granted only if the development were adequately served by public facilities; adequacy was determined by a point system based on the proximity of the development to available services such as sewage treatment or water supply. In upholding the timing control system, the court relied heavily on the fact that the challenged ordinance was implementing a well-designed general plan for the community. In the absence of the plan, it is unlikely the court would have ruled in favor of the township.

Two Oregon cases further illustrate the judicial interest in the plan. In *Fasano* v. *Board of County Commissioners* the Oregon Supreme Court rejected the notion that amendments to the zoning ordinance are legislative and instead determined that they were quasi-judicial, thus completely shifting the presumption of validity usually applied to all legislative acts. The court's opinion placed heavy weight on the comprehensive plan as a justification for zoning amendments, and noted that "the more drastic the change, the greater will be the burden of showing that it is in conformance with the comprehensive plan as implemented by the ordinance."[24]

In *Baker* v. *City of Milwaukie* the Oregon Supreme Court unequivocally gave the city plan a central role in local zoning:

We conclude that a comprehensive plan is the controlling land use planning instrument for a city. Upon passage of a comprehensive plan, a city assumes a responsibility to effectuate that plan and conform prior conflicting zoning ordinances to it. We further hold that the zoning decisions of a city must be in accord with that plan.[25]

The issues that are being raised in the courts concerning the status of the city plan are also being debated in state capitols. A number of states have begun to *require* local governments to prepare plans, or *require* zoning and other land use control measures to be consistent with local plans, or both. State legislatures are being pushed and pulled into this posture. They are being pushed by the courts and pulled by their own desire to gain greater control over the development process.

California was one of the first states to enact legislation requiring local governments to adopt a plan. California also requires local zoning to be consistent with the adopted plan. The Florida Local Government Comprehensive Planning Act of 1975 mandates planning by counties, municipalities, and special districts. It further requires that all land development regulations enacted or amended be consistent with these comprehensive plans. Kentucky, Nebraska, Colorado, and Oregon also have some form of mandatory planning or "consistency" requirements.

Not everyone agrees with this movement to require cities to plan. Some argue that the only meaningful plan is one that is generated from local needs and desires, not one imposed by some higher level of government. The debate on this issue will doubtless continue, but it is probable that the decade of the 1980s will see the plan emerge as an "impermanent constitution," a term coined a quarter of a century ago by Charles M. Haar. Haar argued as follows in 1955:

If the plan is regarded not as the vestpocket tool of the planning commission, but as a broad statement to be adopted by the most representative municipal body—the local legislature—then the plan becomes a law through such adoption. A unique type of law, it should be noted, in that it purports to bind future legislatures when they enact implementary materials.[26]

The implications of the mandated plan and the rulings that the control of land use be consistent with the plan are far-reaching. The plan ceases to be an exercise in platitudes. It must do more than be for motherhood and against sin. It must be carefully and accurately crafted, for it will have the force of law. This is not to suggest that the traditional functions of a plan, those of education, information, persuasion, and coordination, are lost. On the contrary, these functions will always be a central purpose of the plan. However, as the status of the plan changes increasingly toward that of the impermanent constitution, it will become more important, it will be taken more seriously, and it will have a greater effect on people's lives.

Preparing a city plan

Who initiates?

The development of a local city plan is most often initiated by the local public authority—the city council, mayor, city plan commission, city manager, or city planner (not necessarily in that order). The reason for undertaking the plan *in theory,* and perhaps in best practice, is local concern over the future orderly growth and development of the city. Concern may stem from lagging growth, burgeoning growth, or stagnation.

In fact, federal and state requirements for and funding of comprehensive plans may be the most important motivating force for undertaking a plan. Federal requirements for comprehensive plans have varied over the years, but some coordinative plan has been a requirement for federal city development monies, and federal monies have been available in greater and lesser amounts to pay for plans.

We have already discussed the trend in state enabling legislation to require plans for cities. While there is increasing national concern about rational use of land and protection of farmland and natural resources (such as coastal zones), there is a continuing political pressure to maintain the "local" nature of land use decisions. The result is state planning efforts that delegate comprehensive planning responsibility to local municipalities. One of many examples is the coastal zone planning program in Oregon, where coastal cities were required to prepare master plans that included provisions for use of the coastal area. Massachusetts has recently proposed growth policy requirements for localities that tie local and regional growth plans to statewide capital investment programming.

It is important to note that there is also a long American tradition of initiation of comprehensive planning efforts by concerned citizens as well as public servants. The Burnham plan is the best-known historical example. There are many recent instances. For example, in Rockport, Massachusetts, a comprehensive plan was undertaken by a group called Citizens for Rockport who "met . . . to map out plans for documenting the consequence of rapid and unplanned growth, to design more effective recommendations for shaping new development and to involve as many people as possible in the formulation of an overall growth strategy for the town of Rockport, Massachusetts."[27]

There may be a combination of public and private effort, such as the startlingly determined new growth plan for La Jolla, California. This is a joint effort of a nonprofit corporation of La Jolla citizens (La Jollans, Inc.) and the city of San Diego.[28]

The initiation of a comprehensive planning effort in response to public concern over the future of the municipality is, in many ways, the ideal circumstance for the undertaking. One of the aims of the planning effort is to generate widespread discussion of the future development of the municipality. As many planners have discovered, it is often difficult to gain the attention of any but a few of the public. This is particularly true of plans generated by a planning department or commission simply in response to federal or state requirements.

Who directs the work?
And who else should be involved?

While a comprehensive planning effort may be financed and directed wholly outside the public sector, this is the exception and not the rule. The majority of municipalities over 25,000 in population now have planning departments or commissions with paid staff, one of whose tasks is to prepare comprehensive development plans for their municipalities.[29]

It is evident that the locus of responsibility for planning will vary from one community to another and that a city planning staff must often serve a combination of local elected officials, appointed advisers, and hired managers.

As Black so aptly puts it:

The planning function does not fall neatly into either the "line" or "staff" activities in government. The proper placement of planning in the municipal organization chart has long been a matter of dispute.[30]

The dispute over the placement of planning is commonly traced to the fears of the reformers of the 1920s of corrupt municipal government. These reformers are often depicted as somewhat romantic proponents of the notion that rational men outside of political influence could create a future vision for improvement of the municipality. It is now a commonplace to emphasize the need to bring the planning function closer to those who make public investment decisions (the legislator and/or the mayor).

This approach to the planning function is reflected in a slow but definite trend favoring planning or planning/development departments over independent planning commissions. This trend is particularly evident in the West where many cities have only recently come into existence.[31] There are many situations in which the staff is responsible to the chief executive of the city but also has a planning commission advising it. There is also a small but significant number of cities with joint city–county commissions.[32]

The city manager's role in the planning function is especially prominent in smaller cities, where he or she is most likely to have major responsibility. This is also true in many larger cities.

If the plan is going to be "used" following its preparation—to guide zoning decisions, to provide the basis for planning community development activities, to set priorities for street improvements, it is essential that those who are expected to use it be involved in its preparation. Local elected and appointed officials who will be ruling on zoning changes should have been through the process of examining population trends, housing patterns, and commercial development, and should have had to sort out goals for future patterns of development. And officials who will be developing and adopting the capital improvements program should be familiar with the city's long-range goals.

If the planning function is located in a city department, the staff will have to seek input from private investors (lending institutions, real estate developers, businessmen, industrialists, and others with a vital interest). Also, it behooves the staff to seek the involvement of city department heads, local elected officials, or the mayor's office as necessary to gain support for required public investment.

There is another large group of people who need to be involved who are not only individual investors but are also the major consumers of the plan—the public. The public comes in several forms. It can include individual citizens with a particular interest in plan making, and it can include the organized public. The latter includes a broad range of groups—labor unions and minority organizations, promoters of environmental quality or historic sites, neighborhood groups, to name a few. Both the individual citizen and organized publics should have an opportunity to participate in plan development. Advisory committees, radio and television presentations and call-in shows, surveys, and public meetings are some of the many techniques for gaining public participation in a plan. Now that participation has become widely recognized as an integral part of the planning process, there are many highly developed techniques available to the planner. (Some of these techniques are discussed in Chapter 19.) It is also known that the timing of plan preparation must reflect the amount of time that it takes to gain the interest and involvement of the larger community.

Neighborhood participation

Depending on the size and character of the city or town, neighborhoods will be an important factor in plan development. Some larger Western cities, according to work by Lawrence Susskind,[33] have taken a building block approach to the comprehensive plans. Within the framework of general policies for the city, neighborhood residents have been asked to determine their future needs. In other cities, such as San Diego, there is a comprehensive plan for the entire city but the major emphasis of the planning work is on neighborhood plans, which show the specific improvements needed to achieve the goals of the overall plan. The city of Chicago focuses its efforts on "opportunity areas." Where neighborhood groups exist, they are involved in the planning—sometimes as partners with the city and sometimes with a parallel "advocacy" planning effort, financed by the community to reflect the particular concerns of the current residents.

Where the city is working in partnership with a community group or in a more adversary role, the involvement of neighborhood residents in self-assessment of neighborhood conditions and needs is a helpful process. It builds a broadened understanding at the community level of the factors involved in neighborhood decay. In this way it can bring about, for example, a heightened interest in maintaining the flow of home financing monies into neighborhoods that is reflected in "antiredlining" laws. It provides insights for the planner into "how things work" in a particular neighborhood, insights that can be important to the design of new housing sites, street layout, and location of commercial facilities.

Relationship to county, metropolitan, and regional planning

What about the other end of the spectrum? How should the comprehensive planning effort of a municipality be related to the larger context of which it is a part—the county, the metropolitan area, the region?

The development of most cities is immediately affected by the surrounding environs of those cities. Depending on prevailing annexation laws and practices, and the history of development, cities may be struggling with a declining tax base as new development occurs outside their city limits. Cities may be members of councils of governments or may have intermunicipal arrangements for the provision of services ranging from water supply to schools.

The planning context in which the municipal planning effort is undertaken is an increasingly complex one. Counties, metropolitan areas, states, and interstate regions may all have comprehensive planning efforts which to a greater or lesser extent must be considered by the local municipality.

State involvement in land use planning is relatively new and varies greatly from state to state. Some municipalities will find themselves undertaking comprehensive planning efforts because of state programs delegated to them. The greatest impact of state planning on individual localities over the next decade may be in revised state planning acts and in the identification of areas of particular concern to the state because of their unique ecological, historical, or economic significance. Should such sites be identified in or near municipalities undertaking a planning effort, they would be important considerations in the planning effort.

Regional or metropolitan planning programs encompassing a city will certainly have important implications for local transportation, growth projections, overall land use allocations, competing business centers, housing distribution, and natural resources management. Other issues of importance to the locality that may be addressed at a regional level include water supply, solid waste disposal, and flood control.

Many cities work closely with regional agencies in plan development. Smaller cities may even rely on a regional planning staff to prepare the plans, as is the case with Bridgeport, Alabama, whose comprehensive plan was made by the Top–of–Alabama Regional Council of Governments. There are also numerous instances of city–county joint plans, prepared by joint staff and adopted by both city council and county commission.

Differences of perspective at the local and regional levels mean that there is often some friction between the two planning efforts. Large older central cities very often feel underrepresented on regional commissions whose membership is not always (or even usually) based on population. Suburban communities experiencing growth pressures may or may not find regional estimates of growth acceptable or even reasonable. Discussion of the need for and location of low and moderate income housing is very often controversial.

One of the greatest challenges for the planners of the next decade will be to sort out the jurisdictional level at which to plan various services and land uses. Our greater understanding of ecological systems, our communication technology, and our national energy needs are a few of the factors that have heightened our awareness of interdependence. At the same time we have a continuing commitment to local community control over decision making and to involvement of people in the decisions which will affect their lives.

Municipal plans should identify the city's role in the region of which it is a part and should describe how that role may be changing because of growth or decline. A realistic assessment of the alternative futures open to a city must take into account regional trends. However, it is the city's planners who should know best the particular strengths and weaknesses of the city that will influence its future development.

Who does the technical work in plan preparation?

When a city has a planning staff, it will be their responsibility to prepare plans. However, given the diverse technical skill necessary to identify environmental, transportation, utilities, and other needs of the city, most planning staffs will require additional assistance. In some cases this assistance can be provided from other city departments such as public works or engineering. Consultant help is also frequently used in the preparation of particular components of the plan. In small cities consultants may undertake all of the technical work under the direction of the planning staff, planning commission, or city manager.

It is important when consultants are used that the local staff and policymakers stay closely involved in the evolution of the plan—examining data, formulating policy, and reviewing alternative schemes. If the consultants prepare all the material on their own and present a finished product to the community, it is much less likely to be useful to the city. In addition, it is often useful to involve consultants in some aspects of plan implementation. This is a way of guarding against planning work that is irrelevant to the particular needs of a particular community and to the mechanisms available to it for implementation.

How much money is needed?

Planning is certainly not an expensive task of city government compared with providing services such as police and fire protection. Plans rarely cost more than 0.5 percent of the cost of the city capital investments which the plan intends to guide. However, because the payoffs from planning are not seen as immediate and tangible, the planning budget is often considered expendable.

This is particularly true in times when funds are short. It can, of course, be argued that when money is short it is most important for city officials to know the anticipated impact of public investment. However, it is exactly at this point that planning is often seen as a luxury.

As has been indicated, federal funding has often been available for planning. Over the years the funds have been related to particular types of federal grant programs such as highways or urban renewal. In the last decade monies were available to municipalities specifically for comprehensive planning. In the next decade it is difficult to predict whether such funds will be available. The current trend is away from categorical grant programs toward provision of revenues for general purpose and community development. This will mean that each locality will have to make its own case for planning. This task will be easiest in those localities experiencing major growth or decline. It is also likely to succeed where the planning effort is designed to give city officials assistance in making investment decisions. A clear link between the planning effort and the management of the municipality must be established.

How much time is needed?

The length of time needed to prepare a development plan will vary with the following factors:

	More time	Less time
1. Is it an initial effort?	X	
2. Are there highly technical elements to be prepared, such as analysis of hazard areas?	X	
3. Will widespread public involvement be sought?	X	
4. Is there a critical investment decision contingent upon plan completion?		X
5. Are there legislative requirements?		X
6. Are there rewards for early completion?		X
7. Are staff available and on board?		X
8. Are commissioners', council members', or mayors' terms coincident with the planning period?		X
9. Is there an imminent changeover in the city administration?	X	
10. Is there information available on the municipality in regional or state planning agencies?		X
11. Does the plan have to be consistent with a regional or state plan?	X	
12. Are things changing very rapidly in the municipality which make the planning of high interest?		X
13. Are there deep divisions in the municipality about what the future of the community should be?	X	
14. Is there more than one city agency with significant planning responsibilities?	X	

Since there are at least as many incentives for prolonging the planning process as for shortening it, it is essential that deadlines be set at the outset that specify the availability of specific products. Such deadlines must, on one hand, be realistic about the time it takes to collect and process information; on the other hand they must recognize that planning efforts that become prolonged may find themselves obsolete by the time their findings are printed.

One useful technique for providing a city development plan in a timely manner where a short time frame is required is to use an interim plan. This allows for a statement of goals and objectives, subject to further refinement upon completion of more complex and time-consuming studies.

In determining the timing of a plan it is important to remember that planning is an ongoing process. No comprehensive plan can be the "last word" on the future development of the city. Factors beyond the influence of city administrators and beyond their predictive capacities are likely to cause change and to require new plans. There is a tendency in being comprehensive to be instead exhaustive. Exhaustive data that are known only to the planning director and his or her staff and are never used to formulate policies or describe trends are neither helpful nor worthy of the expenditure.

Who adopts the plan?

How important is formal adoption of the city development plan by the city council, or formal endorsement by the mayor? If, indeed, the intent of the plan is to make a public statement of the city's policies with regard to the future physical development of the city, formal adoption or endorsement is *the* act of political support.

As we know, adoption is no guarantee of implementation or even full support. However, it is an important step in the process of articulating, publicizing, and endorsing municipal goals and objectives for physical development. Adoption does ensure that those adopting will be informed of the plan's goals and policies. (It is to be hoped, of course, that at least some of them have been actively involved in their preparation.) The plan also can provide strong leverage for zoning ordinance revision (if necessary) and enforcement.

It is essential that a plan give the user an understanding of the conditions that require public action—hence the need for a public policy. The drafters of the plan should not assume that the user knows why the city needs a plan at all. The plan should describe the current situation in the city: the city's growth trends, functions, and population mix, as well as the adequacy of its infrastructure to serve those who live there and those expected to come there. A brief history is often useful for understanding the current situation.

What that is inherent in the current situation requires public action? If matters continue as they are with no attempt to influence them, what consequences will follow that are considered undesirable? The shortfalls in the city's housing stock, abandoned neighborhoods, scattered development of agricultural land, overuse of a local natural resource that threatens its future—these are some of the conditions that should be presented to the reader to show the necessity for a plan.

What is the policy?

The overall strategy A city plan contains a series of policies concerning land uses, provision of housing, location of new transportation facilities, etc. These individual policies should reflect an overall strategy for the city's development that is articulated at the outset. In growing cities this strategy may center on approaches to affecting the rate and location of growth and new development or on schemes for slowing or directing growth. In older cities with stable or declining populations the focus of the strategy will concern the public resource and investment priorities that will help in maintaining and upgrading the city.

The policies in a city plan are often supported by a series of goals for the city's development, including the amenities the city should provide and to whom it should provide them.

Because of the comprehensive nature of the plan and the consensus approach to policy formulation often inherent in plan development, goals statements often have an *inclusive* quality that makes it difficult to determine real priorities for action. Improvement of "quality of life" and provision of "decent, safe, and sanitary housing for all" are typical planning goals that are not specific enough.

A good plan is one that pushes beyond a laundry list of generalized goals to a series of more concrete policy recommendations. Priorities should be clear. Goals must be translated, to borrow a federal phrase, into "specific and measurable" objectives. For example, in the now famous Petaluma, California, plan the determination to retain a small town character has been pursued by setting an upper limit on new development that can take place in the town annually and issuing building permits accordingly. In Cleveland, priority was given to making resources more available to the poorest segments of the population. Thus, strategies in the plan are aimed at the redistribution of resources to overcome inequities. It is interesting to note that this plan does not focus on land use questions but on poverty and income distribution.

The larger the city is, the more difficult it is to determine priorities. Many activities are going forward at the same time in both the public and private sectors. One approach to such complexity is to build an overall development strategy out of a series of neighborhood plans. In Atlanta, for example, all public investments contained in the capital improvements program must first be reflected in neighborhood plans.

In St. Louis an attempt was made to face squarely the disparity between the needs of various communities and the resources available plus the long-term payoff of investments. Neighborhoods that were clearly "beyond saving" were approached with a strategy of eventual land banking and redevelopment and substantial investments were reserved for neighborhoods that had sufficient vitality to resist further deterioration.[34]

Whatever the approach and direction of the plan's overall strategy, the strategy should be stated at the outset and it should be possible to relate the recommendations of individual plan components to it.

Plan components In addition to an overall statement of a development strategy, the plan must contain more detailed recommendations regarding the particular aspects of the city's infrastructure and land uses which, together, determine the shape of the city's development (or redevelopment). These more detailed recommendations concern such "functional" plan elements as transportation and community facilities.

What functions should definitely be a part of the city plan? The list of plan components changes with the ebb and flow of federal policy, and urban programs and amenities of interest at a particular time and in a particular place. Recently the U.S. Department of Housing and Urban Development required every plan to have a land use and housing element. Many plans of the 1970s contain components on the environment.

It can be useful to look at elements that ought to be covered in any plan in terms of two categories: (1) the use of land, and (2) the provision of urban services (or infrastructure).

The first category includes the availability of land for development, its suitability for development (including environmental sensitivity, subsoil conditions, and the presence of steep slopes), compatibility of uses, and potential for changes in use. The land use element or chapter of the plan will provide the basic policy guidance for the zoning ordinance, for consideration of major public investments in land development (or land banking activities), and for encouraging or discouraging alternative private land development.

City plan elements

1. The current circumstances of the city and why a plan for the city's development is needed
2. What the city's strategy for future physical development is including:
   a) The overall development and/or redevelopment strategy and more specific policies for:
      (1) The use of land
      (2) The provision of urban services and infrastructure including but not limited to:
         (a) Transportation
         (b) Utilities
         (c) Community facilities
         (d) Recreation and open space
         (e) Housing
         (f) Social services
         (g) Natural resources
         (h) Economic development
      b) Particular areas of the city of particular importance (optional)
3. What should be done in the short run, what it will cost, and where the money will come from (not always the same document)
4. Who developed the plan and how it can be changed.

Urban services or infrastructure have traditionally included transportation, utilities (sewer, water, gas, electricity, telephone), community facilities (libraries, schools, government buildings), and recreation facilities (parks, playgrounds, open space). Housing is increasingly viewed as a basic part of the infrastructure that must be considered. Solid as well as liquid waste disposal is also of growing concern as a basic urban service.

The entire range of social services, including health, education, and law enforcement, come within the purview of many city plans. Also of common concern are historic preservation and the identification and preservation of natural resources.

Recently, in response to national economic trends and interregional shifts, city planners have become more concerned with economic development and its relationship to physical development. Employment and tax base, which have always been implicit concerns of city development, may become explicit elements of urban infrastructure to be considered in future city plans.

Which of the many urban services are addressed in the plan will depend, of course, on the particular concerns of the city and the resources open to it. In some states, such as California and Florida, plan elements are determined by state law. In a coastal New England plan there may be a chapter on tourism. In coastal California the plans must address hazard areas such as land prone to earthquakes. Whichever are included, each element should contain information on what exists, what will be needed (or wanted), how it may be provided, where it should be located (if relevant), and how the functional plan will reinforce the city's overall development policy.

Keeping functional planning elements consistent with each other is, of course, a primary aim of a city plan. However, it is not easily accomplished, especially if the plan is not built on a clear strategy. It is necessary to consider the consequences of one policy recommendation on others and to make explicit any trade-offs required between policies. For example, in the plan for La Jolla cited earlier it is recognized that a slow growth policy will have very direct consequences for the already limited supply of low and moderate income housing. Specific provision is made for setting aside land for such development in order to offset this consequence.

Site specific components of the plan In some cities there is a desire to include in the plan site specific recommendations about such parts of the city as the central business district, a university complex, or neighborhoods. These portions of the plan would treat both land uses and infrastructure in terms of the needs of a particular area.

As with recreation, transportation, and other functional plans, it is important to show clearly how plans for a particular area fit into the larger scheme of things. The inclusion of site specific plan recommendations depends on their importance to a particular city and whether their inclusion will unduly lengthen the plan document.

What is the policy intended to accomplish?

The desired ends of the plan are inherent in the goals statements in the policy recommendations both for an overall strategy and in individual plan elements. Most people reading a city plan have an instinctive desire to know what *actions* should be taken to carry out the goals, policies, and strategies articulated in the plan. A purpose of the plan, after all, is to integrate short-term actions with long-range goals.

In smaller cities it is often possible (and highly desirable) to include a section of short-, medium-, and long-range action recommendations. In larger cities these recommendations may be contained in a capital improvements program or other budgeting documents or in more detailed plans for particular parts of the city. It is important in the latter case to reference these other documents.

People also want to know where the money will come from to carry out the actions recommended in the plan. The anticipation of revenue sources for major investments as well as the costs and benefits of such investments are, at the present time, part of only a few plans. If it is desired that the plan influence short-run actions, inclusion of such material is important.

Who developed the plan? Can it be changed?

The city plan should include a section covering the process by which it was developed, outlining the reasons for its preparation, identifying persons and agencies responsible for its preparation, and showing agencies that have endorsed it. This section should also include a statement of the methods and timetable for updating the plan to reflect new trends.

What should the plan look like?

Plans come in more varied sizes and shapes than most public documents, perhaps because of the design training of many of those responsible for them. Many plans are printed in a series of volumes so that no one document is unwieldy. Many are summarized in short pamphlets for wide public distribution. The Los Angeles and Fremont, California, agencies use a loose-leaf notebook in which individual plan components may be added (or substracted) as they are completed or updated. This is a visual reflection of the ongoing nature of plan making.

Should maps be used?

Maps have always been a primary communication tool for planners. They can be very helpful in making graphic and site specific the policies contained in the plan. Some cities, such as Philadelphia, report that their maps are the tools most heavily used by those trying to relate specific proposals to the plan. However, they also report difficulties in keeping the map updated.

There is also a point of view that people come to rely too heavily on the maps and ignore important policy statements. Some plans specifically state that if there is a conflict between the map and the policy statements, the written word rules.

Conclusion

One of the major themes of this chapter is that a city plan both reflects and is a reflection of the times. A good plan must be responsive to the social and cultural mix that characterizes each particular place and era. How else can we explain the wide range and character of the various plans that have been produced during the last half century? Yet within that variation the essence of the idea of a plan has remained intact, and we must conclude that it will continue to survive.

Declarations of what the city plan of the 1980s and 1990s will be like are risky. Declarations of what they should be like are foolish. Nevertheless, there is merit in attempting to look ahead and project some of the current trends to see what might be in store.

First, and most important, we will continue to see city plans produced, regardless of what they are called, because the compelling logic behind them will not subside. That logic is simply that it is wise to look ahead, to anticipate rather than to react, to coordinate rather than to compete, and to make decisions that are based on shared community objectives.

Second, the production of the city plan will be better integrated into city government and will no longer be the exclusive province of the planning department or commission. Many of the major principles of planning are becoming commonplace in city management. No longer is the planner seemingly the only spokesman for the long-range, comprehensive point of view. Managers, budget officers, and department heads increasingly espouse and practice a form of planning that the planning profession has long advocated. This trend toward greater acceptance of planning principles is a welcome sign and a challenge to the planning profession. If the profession does not continue to grow and advance, it will be swallowed up by its own success. It will have no special skills or principles to offer to the city management agenda. The challenge will be to continue to lead in the development of tools and techniques of planning and management.

Third, it is likely that future city plans will focus increasingly on issues of resource management—be they water, energy, land, or air. The nation is becoming increasingly sensitive to the limits of these finite resources and the constraints that these limits impose on future development. The concept of carrying capacity will cease to be an academic constraint and will become a central feature of a growing number of city plans.

Finally, we will continue to see more efforts to define the legal dimensions of the city plan. The trend toward mandated plans will no doubt continue. There will be increasing experimentation with laws that require that development regulations be "consistent" with published plans. And the basic themes espoused in the American Law Institute's *Model Land Development Code* will proliferate as more and more states review their planning and development acts. The result will be the production of city plans that carry the authority of the law as well as the authority of their own logic.

1   John W. Reps, *The Making of Urban America: A History of City Planning in the United States* (Princeton, N.J.: Princeton University Press, 1965).

2   Mel Scott, *American City Planning since 1890* (Berkeley: University of California Press, 1969) p. 2.

3   Jacob Riis, *How the Other Half Lives* (New York: Dover, 1971).

4   From a speech presented by Frederick Law Olmsted, Jr., at the Third National Conference on City Planning, Philadelphia, 15–17 May 1911, quoted in Scott, *American City Planning*, p. 141.

5   U.S., Department of Commerce, Advisory Committee on Zoning, *A Standard State Zoning Enabling Act* (Washington, D.C.: Government Printing Office, 1922); and U.S., Department of Commerce, Advisory Committee on City Planning and Zoning, *A Standard City Planning Enabling Act* (Washington, D.C.: Government Printing Office, 1928).

6   Bassett's view of a plan as limited to several elements probably dominated over the broader views of Olmsted and Bettman.

7   Alan Black, "The Comprehensive Plan," in *Principles and Practice of Urban Planning*, ed. William I. Goodman and Eric C. Freund (Washington, D.C.: International City Management Association, 1968), pp. 353–55.

8   David Lilienthal. *TVA: Democracy on the March*

(New York: Harper & Brothers, Publishers, 1954), quoted in: Charles M. Haar, *Land Use Planning: A Casebook on the Use, Misuse and Reuse of Urban Land* (Boston: Little, Brown and Company, 1971), p. 712.

9 Scott, *American City Planning*, p. 397.

10 Ibid.

11 Martin Meyerson, "Building the Middle-Range Bridge for Comprehensive Planning," *Journal of the American Institute of Planners* 22 (Spring 1956): 58–64.

12 Melville C. Branch, *Continuous City Planning*, Planning Advisory Service Report no. 290 (Chicago: American Society of Planning Officials, April 1973). There were also challenges to the planner's claim to comprehensive understanding of the functions of the city (Altschuler; Braybrooke and Lindblom) and the planner's predictive capacities. Others asked whose goals were being articulated and challenged the activity as promoting the interests of those in power—often in conflict with the interests of those affected (Davidoff; Gans). The effects of general plans on particular neighborhoods and on city life-styles were also pointed out by Herbert Gans and Jane Jacobs. See: Alan Altshuler, "The Goals of Comprehensive Planning," *Journal of the American Institute of Planners* 31 (August 1965): 186–95; David Braybrooke and Charles Lindblom, *A Strategy of Decision* (Glencoe, Ill.: The Free Press, 1963); Paul Davidoff, "Advocacy and Pluralism in Planning," *Journal of the American Institute of Planners* 31 (November 1965): 331–38; Herbert Gans, *The Urban Villagers: Group and Class Life of Italian Americans* (Glencoe, Ill.: The Free Press, 1965); and Jane Jacobs, *The Death and Life of Great American Cities* (New York: Random House, 1961).

13 See: Melvin M. Webber, "The Role of Intelligence Systems in Urban Systems Planning," *Journal of the American Institute of Planners* 31 (November 1965): 289–96; and William L. C. Wheaton and Margaret Wheaton, "Identifying the Public Interest: Values and Goals," in *Urban Planning in Transition*, ed. Ernest Erber (New York: Grossman Publishers, 1970).

14 Scott, *American City Planning*, p. 560.

15 Franklyn H. Beal, "Defining Development Objectives," in *Principles and Practice of Urban Planning*, ed. Goodman and Freund, pp. 335–40.

16 American Law Institute, *A Model Land Development Code*, complete text, adopted by the American Law Institute May 21, 1975, with Reporter's Commentary (Philadelphia: American Law Institute, 1976).

17 Ibid., Article III, p. 136.

18 Ibid.

19 Ibid., p. 155.

20 American Society of Planning Officials, *Local Capital Improvements and Development Management: Case Study Draft Report—Atlanta*, prepared by the American Society of Planning Officials under contract to the U.S. Department of Housing and Urban Development and the National Science Foundation (Chicago: American Society of Planning Officials, 1978), p. 4.

21 Allan B. Jacobs, *Making City Planning Work* (Chicago: American Planning Association, 1978), pp. 304–5.

22 Ibid., p. 306.

23 *Golden* v. *Planning Board of the Township of Ramapo*, 30 N.Y. 2d 359, 285 N.E.2d 291, 409 U.S. 1003 (1972).

24 *Fasano* v. *Board of County Commissioners of Washington County*, 264 Ore. 574, 582, 507 P.2d 23, 27 (1973).

25 *Baker* v. *City of Milwaukie*, 533 P.2d 772 (1975).

26 Charles M. Haar, "The Master Plan: An Impermanent Constitution," *Law and Contemporary Problems* 20 (Summer 1955): 375.

27 Massachusetts Institute of Technology, Department of Urban Studies and Planning, *Planning for the Future of Rockport; An Analysis of Community Needs and Recommendations for Action* (Cambridge, Mass.: Massachusetts Institute of Technology, Department of Urban Studies and Planning, 1974), p. 7. This effort was neither initiated nor carried out by municipal officials and employees, although the regular involvement of the town council was sought.

28 Two plans were created, one in 1967 and an update in 1975. What is startling is to see such items as automobile congestion in the downtown area cited as an issue, and improvement of pedestrian access given a suggested response.

29 As of 1971 the International City Management Association found that only 12 percent of the cities over 25,000 that responded to a joint International City Management Association/American Society of Planning Officials survey *did not* have a professional planning staff. See: B. Douglas Harman, "City Planning Agencies: Organization, Staffing, and Functions," in *The Municipal Year Book 1972* (Washington, D.C.: International City Management Association, 1972), p. 55.

30 Black, "The Comprehensive Plan," p. 357.

31 Harman, "City Planning Agencies," p. 56.

32 Ibid., p. 57.

33 Lawrence Susskind, Chapter 5 and Appendix in *Housing for All under Law: New Directions in Housing, Land Use and Planning Law*, a report of the American Bar Association Advisory Commission on Housing and Urban Growth, ed. Richard P. Fishman (Cambridge, Mass., Ballinger Publishing Co., 1978).

34 For an interesting discussion of the political difficulties that such a strategy involves, see: S. Jerome Pratton, "Strategies for City Investment," in *How Cities Can Grow Old Gracefully*, U.S., Congress, House, Subcommittee on Banking, Finance, and Urban Affairs, Subcommittee on the City (Washington, D.C.: Government Printing Office, 1977), pp. 79–90.

7 Utility services

The provision of clean water and the removal of both waterborne and solid wastes has been a responsibility of urban governments since at least Roman times. We know that Sextus Julius Frontinus was water commissioner of Rome in A.D. 97, at which time he reported nine major aqueducts in the city ranging in length from ten to fifty miles and in cross section from seven to fifteen square feet. At that time the major drain for both storm water and sewage from Rome was the same as it is today, the *cloaca maxima*. Removal of solid wastes from the large urban areas has also been a problem since early times, though in the past (as in many developing nations today) it has frequently been handled through "scavenging" rather than through a highly organized refuse removal process. In the United States today, water supply systems are planned to supply every citizen with roughly 100 gallons of water per day; sewerage systems are planned to remove 100 gallons from the household as wastewater; and solid waste disposal systems are planned to remove and dispose of, in an environmentally acceptable manner, roughly five and one-half pounds of solid waste per capita per day.

Environmental decisions that were once the responsibility of the local community or of the individual property owner have now been redefined to become broader social concerns and to be subject to federal regulation. In a span of just thirteen years we have seen the passage of the Solid Waste Disposal Act of 1965 (P.L. 89–272), the Resource Conservation and Recovery Act of 1970 (RCRA) (P.L. 91–512), the Federal Water Pollution Control Act Amendments of 1972 (P.L. 92–500) and 1977 (Clean Water Act of 1977, P.L. 95–217), and the Safe Drinking Water Act of 1974 (P.L. 93–523). With the passage of each ensuing piece of legislation the requirements of local government have changed from complete autonomy to operation within relatively stringent federal guidelines. With each change the role of the planner has evolved from back seat to driver's seat in the generation of projections and criteria upon which to base decisions on investment in environmental infrastructure. To fulfill this role well the planner must understand the physical constraints, economic trade-offs, and significant secondary impacts of extensive infrastructure development in the areas of wastewater management, solid waste management, and provision of potable water supply.

The purpose of this chapter is to introduce the urban and regional planner to the concepts and criteria used in the design and construction of environmental infrastructure systems, focusing on those areas in which the skills of the planner will be most in demand and/or those in which the planner can exercise the greatest leverage. The chapter first covers the planning information and tools common to all three environmental areas: service area definition, population projection, and financial analysis. The major portion of the chapter then reviews the physical and land use parameters of each of the three environmental services (water supply, then wastewater, and finally solid waste), concentrating on those aspects of each service in which the planner has maximum leverage. Finally, there is a brief discussion of environmental planning.

This chapter seeks to present the accepted criteria and coefficients for planning, the special problems and methods of financing for major environmental infrastructure facilities,[1] and a sound understanding of the complex issues of environmental planning within American cities. In this chapter references are made to basic working volumes which can be of use to planners as they deal with the more complex issues of water supply, wastewater, and solid waste management.

Infrastructure planning

Many of the design criteria for infrastructure investments in urban areas in the United States have been reduced to engineering rules of thumb and standard off-the-shelf designs for purification systems, sewage treatment plants, and solid waste disposal facilities. While many of these rules have simplified design choices for engineering firms, they may also have removed planners and local government officials from an active part in the decision process. The initial design parameters for water, wastewater, and solid waste disposal systems (projections of future population and selection and planning of service areas) are more within the realm of the planner than that of the design engineer. There are, for example, issues of system sizing in which the financial and/or population impacts on a given community may be severe. As an example, system sizing for wastewater facilities has been shown to be significant in directing the growth of communities. This has been discussed in such volumes as *The Costs of Sprawl*[2] and, more recently and with greater focus on specific examples, in *Interceptor Sewers and Urban Sprawl*[3] and *Land Use and the Pipe: Planning for Sewerage.*[4]

Three design parameters determine to a large extent the sizing of any environmental infrastructure facility: (1) the ultimate extent of the service area; (2) the ultimate service area population; and (3) the projected per capita service level requirements. While the third parameter *may* fall more within the purview of the engineer than that of the planner, responsibility for estimating the first two parameters lies directly with the planner. Even though it is frequently argued that one is ''better safe than sorry'' in sizing infrastructure facilities, such conservatism carries a cost in excess capacity which may place an unreasonable payment burden on initial system users or, in the case of excess interceptor sewer capacity, may allow for unplanned sprawl or expansive development along the lines of the interceptor systems not ''planned for'' as a portion of the growth path of the community. This unplanned growth frequently costs the community in terms of increased service requirements of new arrivals (schools) whose incremental costs outweigh the incremental addition to the property tax base.

While there is no perfect solution to the sizing issue, only a thorough understanding of the mechanisms which go into sizing a system can give the planner the confidence and expertise required to present a strong case for controlled development and planned facility expansion. The remainder of this section highlights the significant decision parameters associated with sizing of environmental infrastructure: definition of service area; projection of population; and estimation of per capita consumption/generation.

Geographic service area

Choice of service area for water supply, sewerage, and solid waste varies considerably. Water supply service areas depend on the availability of sufficient quantities of potable water within a reasonable distance of the point of demand. For a smaller urban area this may mean little or no long distance transport as water may be supplied from deep wells, free running streams, or lakes in close proximity to the community. In contrast, water for larger urban areas is frequently transported over great distances. The Metropolitan Water District of

Southern California carries water to Los Angeles and environs through the Colorado River aqueduct, 242 miles in 92 miles of graded tunnel, 53 miles of canal, 54 miles of graded aqueduct, 29 miles of inverted siphon, and 4 miles of forced main.

Water Because clean water is a basic requirement for public health and because with increased density there is an increased possibility of contamination of on-site water supplies with on-site wastewater disposal facilities (septic tanks and cesspools), public water supplies tend to extend into any periurban area likely to have major residential developments. All water systems are maintained under pressure; most maintain pressure from a water tower or a hill mounted tank. As a result, water lines do not follow topography as closely as do sewer lines. Water supplies to cities and towns within larger metropolitan regions tend to be interlinked and to expand as required to cover suburbanizing communities if this can be done within existing supplies.

Within the Boston metropolitan area, the Metropolitan Water Board (now amalgamated into the Metropolitan District Commission) was established in 1895 to provide water to cities and towns in the eastern portion of Massachusetts; it now contains forty-three member communities. The Metropolitan Water District of Southern California, with its elaborate aqueducts, was also developed to provide water at wholesale rates to communities and small water companies in southern California. Water supply systems are, within bounds of supplies, expandable to adjacent communities. Unlike wastewater collection systems, they are not significantly bound by topography nor do they act as significant contributors to the process of urban sprawl. Many suburban communities have developed that use public water systems but on-site sewage disposal.

Wastewater Unlike fresh water supplies, which must be kept under pressure, wastewater systems are often least expensive and most practical when they can be designed as gravity flow systems. The most economical means of designing sewerage systems is to have them follow natural drainage basin areas within communities or across community boundaries. While the vocabulary of water supply is "metropolitan," the vocabulary of wastewater removal is "basin," so that one finds the Saw Mill Creek Sanitary District, the Haikey Creek interceptor system, etc. Stream and river basins seldom are coterminous with community boundaries.

Recognition of health hazards associated with high density use of on-site disposal systems, increased land costs (which encourage more concentrated development), and increased awareness of need for water quality improvements have led to the expansion of sewerage systems into areas previously served by on-site systems as well as into areas identified for future large scale moderate density residential development. In recent years such expansion has been greatly assisted by funding provided by Federal Water Pollution Control Act amendments. With the development pressures for expansion of sewerage systems, the presence or absence of such systems frequently has meant the financial success or failure of land development activities.[5] Under these circumstances the delineation of the service area for any sewerage system can be a highly political decision within a community, and a major development investment, once begun, cannot be easily stopped or diverted, as has been amply shown in the development of land within Fairfax County, Virginia.[6]

While sewer districts may be constrained (if they are gravity systems) to follow topographic boundaries, they are not constrained to service the entire basin or to exclude acceptance of wastes from other basin areas if these wastes can be pumped across the basin divides. As a result the precise delineation of the sewerage district is a significant planning variable for encouraging, discouraging, or directing growth within a developing community. Delineation of a sewer district is a tool for land use planning only at the initial stages. Once a sewer is in operation within a service area, it is an individual's right to be connected to that sewer. The sewer district must then provide the expansion in treatment capacity brought about by this additional sewer connection (again, a lesson learned from the expansion of facilities in Fairfax, Virginia).

Solid waste   While the service area vocabulary of water supply is most frequently metropolitan and that of sewerage systems is basin, the vocabulary of solid waste disposal is uniquely local. While there are examples of successful regional solid waste operations such as those in the San Francisco area, in most other areas of the nation solid waste disposal is handled and frequently reaches its final disposition within the confines of a community. The plan for one community to be the ''sink'' or recipient for a region is accepted by all voters except those in the receiving community, with the result that efforts in regional cooperation have frequently ended in a stalemate. While the major cost determinant of solid waste is frequently the cost of transportation, geographic constraints play a far less significant role in determining the final boundaries of a service area than do political constraints.

A word on growth   The definition of the service area for the environmental infrastructure is most critical in sewerage planning, is significant in water system planning, and is least critical (unless there is an ability to create a regional solid waste facility) in solid waste management. In planning for sewerage, definition of the service area boundary can affect the eventual growth pattern of the community, as sewers become the precursors of development of moderate density, single family land use patterns. While there are no hard and fast rules for setting service area boundaries for infrastructure, defining these boundaries is (as mentioned earlier) within the purview of the planner, who has the responsibilities of providing the data on which service area boundaries are based, of analyzing potential secondary impacts of service extensions, and of using the extension of the service area to complement community growth plans rather than allowing the extension of environmental infrastructure to determine the direction and magnitude of future growth.

Projection of population[7]

In the course of planning for water, sewerage, or solid waste disposal systems no calculation is more important in the sizing of the system than the projection of future ''ultimate'' population. Population size frequently depends on infrastructure development as much as the size of infrastructure investment depends on the size of the population.

Particular services act as leading indicators of population growth. Highways have filled this role; now sewers and water supply fill much the same role of providing the preconditions for development. This section of the chapter is concerned with the projection of population size at some point in the future within a specified service area.

While the techniques of demography are well developed for projection of the populations of major political or geographic areas, they are poorly developed for the small area population projections required for sewerage system planning. In general, the smaller the geographic area is, the more important are the nonbiological determinants of population growth: economic growth and migration.

Because of this, population projection for minor areas has become more of an art than a science. All methods used in local projections are necessarily crude and range from an assumption of constant incremental growth (straight line projections) to more complex component methods of projection which look to economic growth and land carrying capacity as constraints to total population size. It is important to note that at the local level methods referred to as *straight lining* frequently produce results nearly as good as those of the more sophisticated demographic models at far less cost and without the need for computers.

The significance of assumptions and methods concerning population growth can be seen in *Interceptor Sewers and Urban Sprawl,* which investigated fifty-two interceptor sewer projects.

In the majority of the case study projects, there was great uncertainty in the population forecasts. In each case where uncertainty existed, the population projections ultimately used in sizing the interceptors were very high—far in excess of past growth trends for similar areas. For example, in Fulton County, Georgia, the engineer predicted levels of population well in excess of those predicted by the regional planning agency. . . . In the Horn Lake Creek/Southaven, Tennessee, projects, there is a feeling of inevitability about the prospects for growth. The projected figures used in sizing the interceptor were over ten times the current population. . . . Connection fees will finance the project and there will be a great incentive to permit any and all new development.[8]

Standard methods for population projection are available to the engineer and planner. The most useful of these techniques are listed below and are also summarized in Table 7–1. Most traditional sanitary engineering and land use planning texts and references contain summaries of population projection methods similar to those listed immediately below.[9]

Arithmetic method   The arithmetic method is the simplest projection method. It assumes that the population will grow by the same number of people each year. This is also known as linear growth.

Geometric method   Geometric growth is growth at a constant rate. It is the same principle as compound interest in a savings account. The growth rate is the percent change in population each year.

Decreasing rate of increase method   The rate of population growth, particularly in larger cities, is seen to decrease with increasing population. This method allows the planner to set a saturation population on the basis of existing zoning or other information and project a population growth path which approaches the saturation population at a decreasing rate.

Logistic S method   The logistic method, in principle, is similar to the decreasing rate of increase method in that population growth is projected to increase at a decreasing rate to a saturation population. Unlike the above method, however, the logistic method calculates the saturation population from previous growth data. One specific caution must be applied to use of the logistic method. The growth rate between t_0 and t_1 must be greater than the growth rate between t_1 and t_2 for this method to yield meaningful results.

Ratio and correlation method   Population projections at the state or regional level are frequently available to the planner. These may be stepped down to local areas by assuming that the local population will remain a fixed proportion of the larger population.

Component method   The component method of projection requires detailed information on each of the major components of population growth: births, deaths, and migration (both in and out). The most commonly used component method is cohort survival with a side calculation for migration. This method requires relatively complex calculations and data frequently not available at the local level.

Table 7–1 Population projection methods and equations.

Method	Basic equation	Definition of terms	Evaluation of constants
Arithmetic	$\dfrac{dP}{dt} = k_a$ $P = k_a t + P_o$	P_o = initial population ($t = 0$) P = population at time t t = time k_a = arithmetic growth constant	$k_a = \dfrac{P_2 - P_1}{t_2 - t_1}$
Geometric	$\dfrac{dP}{dt} = k_g P$ $P = P_o e^{k_g t}$	k_g = geometric growth constant	$k_g = \dfrac{ln(P_2) - ln(P_1)}{t_2 - t_1}$
Decreasing rate of increase	$\dfrac{dP}{dt} = k_d(S - P)$ $P = S\,(S - P_o)e^{-k_d t}$	S = saturation population k_d = decreasing-rate-of-increase constant	$k_d = \dfrac{-ln\left(\dfrac{S - P_2}{S - P_1}\right)}{t_2 - t_1}$
Logistic S	$P = \dfrac{S}{1 + me^{bt}}$	S = saturation population m, b = constants P_0, P_1, P_2 = populations at times t_0, t_1, t_2 n = interval between t_0, t_1, t_2 $t = t_x - t_0$ in years	$S = \dfrac{2P_0 P_1 P_2 - P_1^2(P_0 + P_2)}{P_0 P_2 - P_1^2}$ $m = \dfrac{S - P_0}{P_0}$ $b = \dfrac{1}{n} ln\left(\dfrac{P_0(S - P_1)}{P_1(S - P_0)}\right)$
Ratio and correlation	$\dfrac{P_2}{P_{2R}} = \dfrac{P_1}{P_{1R}} = k_r$	P_2 = projected population P_{2R} = projected population of a larger region P_1 = population at last census P_{1R} = population of larger region at last census k_r = ratio constant	$k_r = \dfrac{P_1}{P_{1R}}$

Source: Adapted from Metcalf and Eddy, *Wastewater Engineering: Collection, Treatment and Disposal* (New York: McGraw-Hill Book Company, © 1972 by McGraw-Hill Book Company), p. 19. Used with permission of McGraw-Hill Book Company. As used in Richard D. Tabors, Michael H. Shapiro, and Peter P. Rogers, *Land Use and the Pipe: Planning for Sewerage* (Lexington, Mass.: Lexington Books, D. C. Heath and Company, 1976), pp. 22–23.

Choice of techniques The art of population projection lies in knowing enough about the local conditions within a region or community to choose the most appropriate projection technique or techniques. Working with a range of techniques and a range of population projections frequently allows the planner and others concerned with evaluation of system design to identify areas of excess capacity in the system and therefore areas of potential savings in total system costs.

Financing

This section introduces the concepts which underlie the economic evaluation (analysis) of alternative investments in environmental infrastructure. While it is generally not possible to quantify the benefits to be gained from infrastructure investments, it is necessary that an analysis be made of the relative costs. This section highlights the conceptual framework and methodology for cost comparisons but does not deal explicitly with alternative costs of development.

The annual cost of any investment in infrastructure is a combination of three variables: the annualized cost of capital; the cost of operation and maintenance for a given year; and either the annualized value of any "once only" capital subsidy raised through another level of government or the annual subsidy provided through another unit of government (both cost decreasing). Evaluation of these terms is necessary if one is to look at the life cycle cost of a set of options rather than only the first cost. Trade-offs can be made between high first costs with low operating and maintenance costs and low first costs with a relatively high operation and maintenance component. An example of such a trade-off might be the purchase of new or used equipment for refuse collection. A community unable to raise sufficient funding to purchase a fleet of new compacting vehicles may be able to purchase these used from adjoining communities. While the first cost may be reasonable, the costs of maintenance will be greater given the age of the equipment.

Federal and state subsidy or grant programs may alter significantly the locally perceived cost of any given alternative. State and federal capital grants reduce the initial capital costs of a project; an example of such a grant program is P.L. 92–500, which has provided up to 75 percent federal funding for wastewater projects. Under such circumstances capital becomes relatively inexpensive when viewed from the standpoint of the community. On the other hand, operating subsidies make operation and maintenance appear relatively less expensive to the local community.

Comparative costing methodology[10] All financial analyses begin from the conceptual base of present value (or present dollars' worth) of an investment. If one were guaranteed 5 percent ($r = 0.05$) interest on an investment of $100.00 which one was about to place in the bank, one would expect to have $105.00 at the end of the year, as $(1 + 0.05)(\$100) = \$105.00$. In the second year one would expect a return of an additional 5 percent on the investment (now $105.00), or

$$(1 + 0.05)(\$105.00) = \$110.25$$

or

$$(1 + 0.05)(1 + 0.05)(\$100.00) = \$110.25$$

or

$$(1 + 0.05)^2(\$100.00) = \$110.25.$$

If this is carried out for n years one would expect to receive

$$(1 + 0.05)^n(\$100.00) = \$.$$

In much the same way one can calculate the present value of $100.00 one year from now given an interest rate of 5 percent. An investment of $95.24 today will be equal to $100.00 ($1.05 \times \$95.24 = \$100.00$) in the bank one year from today. As a result, given that one wants $100.00 in a year, one should be indifferent to receiving $95.24 today or receiving $100.00 one year from today, because $95.24 is the present value of $100.00 at 5 percent one year hence. Again, it is possible to generalize the calculation to any point in the future and any rate of interest, as

$$PV = \frac{1}{(1 + r)^n} \cdot K$$

where n = years
r = interest rate   100
K = future investment in capital.

If one is interested in calculating the total cost of a project over its lifetime, one should add the present value (PV) of the yearly investments in capital to the present value of the operation and maintenance charges (OM). This total present value can be calculated as

$$PV_t = K_0 + K_1\left(\frac{1}{(1 + r)^1}\right) + OM_1\left(\frac{1}{(1 + r)^1}\right)$$
$$+ K_2\left(\frac{1}{(1 + r)^2}\right) + OM_2\left(\frac{1}{(1 + r)^2}\right) + \cdots$$
$$+ K_n\left(\frac{1}{(1 + r)^n}\right) + OM_n\left(\frac{1}{(1 + r)^n}\right).$$

PV_t is equal to the present value of all expenditures both in capital and in operating and maintenance costs incurred over the length of a project.

A second and equally useful concept is the annualized cost of a project (that is, the cost which would have to be paid out each year to exactly equal the costs of capital, interest, and operations and maintenance for the lifetime of the project). This concept is the same in principle as the monthly payments that one makes on a mortgage:

$$\text{annualized costs} = \frac{(PV)(r)}{1 - \left[\dfrac{1}{1+r}\right]^t}.$$

From the concepts and equations presented above it is possible to calculate either the total cost (present value) of any project or the annualized cost of a project as a means of evaluating the cost of an infrastructure provision. This type of analysis is frequently sufficient when one is comparing systems which will provide an identical service with no difference in benefits which would accrue to one as opposed to the other. This analysis is not sufficient for evaluating the costs of systems providing unequal services or benefits—such as a system of solid waste removal which would pick up two days a week as opposed to one which would pick up on only one day. A complete discussion of these concepts of cost–benefit analysis is beyond the scope of this chapter; the interested reader should seek out texts in public finance or engineering economics for a more complete discussion.[11]

Determinants of total costs Much of the art of urban and regional planning is incorporated in projections. This chapter has already discussed population projections. The sections which follow include discussions of projections of consumption (production) of water (and wastes) needed to estimate future requirements of infrastructure services.

All of these efforts at projection would be merely academic were it not for the fact that construction—provision of services—represents a "lumpy" investment. If we were able to add a single unit of additional capacity when that unit was required, and if that unit were to cost the same amount regardless of when it was added *and* how many were added at the same time, there would be little economic advantage to careful projection of the timing and size of our investments. In fact, this is clearly not the case. Few major investments in services do not contain economies of scale: the average cost (per capita or per unit of service provided) declines as the total size of the facility (sewage treatment plant, water purification plant, incineration facility, or sewerage or water pipes) increases. This occurs for a number of reasons—probably the most significant of which deal with either the basic "lumpiness" of specific portions of the operation or the capital structure—or because of basic physical properties of the systems themselves.

Most infrastructure facilities require land based operations. To a large extent the quantity of land is not directly related to the capacity of the facility. Thus, doubling the size of a sewage treatment facility does not require doubling the amount of land. For sewer pipes, water mains, or refuse trucks, there are frequently minimum sizes set by law (8 inch pipes) or by manufacturers (16 to 32 cubic yards for a compactor). With this lumpiness, the average cost of operation declines until the system reaches capacity. In much the same way the operation and management of a facility do not expand linearly with the capacity of the facility. The number of specialized operators required is a set minimum which does not vary as much with the capacity of the plant as with the number of shifts worked and the basic indivisibility of the manpower involved. One plant manager is required per plant, regardless of plant size, though the manager of a large plant may be paid more for skills in management. Size represents an advantage in supply of required chemicals and other inputs as well. A large water purification plant pays less per unit of chlorine when it receives it by the rail carload at its back door than does the smaller plant that requires intermittent deliveries by truck.

A second area of economies of scale is that of the actual size relationships inherent in the facilities themselves. Sewer and water pipes offer an excellent example of this relationship. The volume carried in a given pipe is proportional to the cross sectional area (r^2) of the pipe, while the materials required for construction of the pipe itself are *more nearly* proportional to the circumference of the pipe ($2r$). Trenching costs are even less sensitive to volume carried, as the hole dug for most smaller pipe sizes is most often a function of the equipment used rather than the pipe size.

Economies of scale become particularly important as we consider the trade-offs between investments in large scale facilities (those that will contain excess capacity for a considerable period in the future) and development of facilities that are smaller and less costly. Figure 7–1 presents in simplified form a linear growth path in total sewage flows for a hypothetical community. The assumption in all service systems is that demand will always be satisfied (in Figure 7–1

Figure 7–1   Sewage flow capacity expansion paths for a hypothetical community.

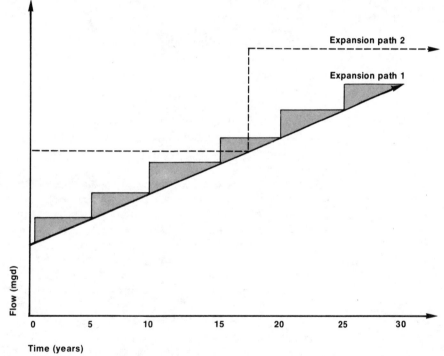

that the system will always expand ahead—above and to the left—of the demand). With this requirement it is possible to choose an infinite number of different paths to fulfilling demand. As discussed earlier, the value of future dollars is less than that of a dollar spent today. Were there no economies of scale working, path 1 in the figure would be superior to path 2.

Small increments to systems are frequently far more costly per unit of service delivered than are large additions to capacity. This is true in water supply and wastewater systems and less true in solid waste systems where collection system costs tend not to be subject as much to economies of scale. In addition, construction of a second, parallel pipe costs more than did construction of the first, as areas have built up along water and sewer lines. In solid waste management the same phenomenon may be seen in the cost of additional landfilling capacity. While in the short run it may be less expensive to maintain a landfill site with limited capacity, in the long run owning a larger site will reduce the cost—and may allow for the existence of a landfill operation whose location more nearly minimizes total transport costs.

The final area in which economies of scale play a significant role in the development of environmental infrastructure is in the decision to develop regional facilities. Through the capital funding that has been guaranteed with P.L. 92–500, and through mandatory regional considerations (section 208) for wastewater facilities, a number of small and medium-size communities have found regional wastewater solutions to their economic advantage. The trade-offs for decisions to construct one regional facility or a set of local facilities for wastewater, water supply, or solid waste disposal are those between savings in capital through economies of scale, and costs in operation (or additional capital) required to transport water or wastes over a greater distance.

In the case of wastewater facilities the trade-off is between capital costs in the treatment plant and the cost of interceptor sewers to connect together the two service areas to a single plant. In the case of water supply the concerns are roughly the same. In solid waste management the regionalization issue, from an economic vantage point, is again the trade-off between the capital savings in a larger disposal facility and the operating costs of a greater haul to the disposal site. At a more practical level the issues related to regionalization of solid waste are more closely related to location of the disposal facility/site than to economics. The concept of the "sink" community is one that has been discussed in the literature and will be mentioned later in this chapter; even though the economics may be persuasive for a regional solid waste disposal facility, the sociology and politics are more difficult to predict.

In summary, the issues concerning financial analysis of environmental infrastructure investment are centered around two closely linked concepts. The first is that of present value or annualized costs, which can be used to compare service systems providing the same service from a combination of capital and operating and maintenance costs and over varying lifetimes. The second concept is at least as critical and is one of economies of scale associated with investments in environmental infrastructure. As discussed, larger facilities provide lower average (unit) costs, thus arguing for larger, more expensive facilities. At the same time, present value considerations place a lower value on future dollars than on present dollars, which reduces the apparent cost of investments made in the future and thereby encourages the deferral of capacity expansions and the construction of smaller, less expensive facilities in the present.

The purpose of the three sections which follow (covering, in turn, water supply, wastewater, and solid waste) is to make the reader a more informed critic of the design, sizing, and investment criteria of environmental infrastructure. No portion of a chapter can develop technical design expertise on the part of the reader; rather, the remainder of this chapter is intended to focus attention on those specific questions not covered earlier in the chapter which are of concern to the planner or are decision variables over which the planner has some control. Each of the sections which follow covers the issue of the effects of per capita generation of wastes (or demand for water) on the technical design criteria required for understanding the total system and also identifies the specific points in the planning/decision process over which the planner, by virtue of training, has the greatest control.

Water supply[12]

The uniform and protected supply of drinking water has been an urban necessity since populations began to come together in large groups. Rome was famous for its miles of aqueducts, and cities such as Fatehpur Sikri in central

India became ghost towns when supplies of potable water ceased. While we consume an estimated 1.6 liters (0.42 gallons) of water per capita per day for drinking purposes, our total need may be as much as 100 to 125 gallons per capita per day. (Heavy industrial areas may average over 150 gallons per capita per day). This section is divided into two main parts: the first briefly discusses the primary issues in water supply planning; the second introduces the engineering design criteria for water supply systems. The section also considers one of the secondary impacts of P.L. 93–523, the Safe Drinking Water Act of 1974 —the availability of reservoirs for recreational activities.

Major issues

How much water to whom?   Municipal water supplies far more than the drinking and bathing needs of the citizenry. Within the United States roughly 43 percent of the water supplied in cities of over 25,000 goes to residential uses while 19 percent goes to commercial uses, 25 percent to industrial uses, and 13 percent to public and other uses. Requirements for fire protection affect both the average consumption of urban water and, more significantly, the planned system capacity. Hardenburgh and Rodie make the following statement:

For instance in a city of 10,000 population with an average consumption of 125 gpcd, the total consumption is 1,250,000 gpd or about 875 gpm, while the required fire flow is 3,000 gpm. . . . Therefore the fire rate determines the sizes of water mains and pumps, if used, and the reservoir capacity in small cities [GPCD = gallons per capita per day; GPD = gallons per day; GPM = gallons per minute].[13]

As shown in Table 7–2, the population must increase by a factor of four for the fire supply requirements to double and by a factor of ten for the requirements to treble.

Table 7–2 Fire flow required by the National Board of Fire Underwriters.

Population	Required fire flow in average city (GPM)	Population	Required fire flow in average city (GPM)
1,000	1,000	28,000	5,000
2,000	1,500	40,000	6,000
4,000	2,000	60,000	7,000
6,000	2,500	80,000	8,000
10,000	3,000	100,000	9,000
13,000	3,500	125,000	10,000
17,000	4,000	150,000	11,000
22,000	4,500	200,000	12,000

Source: W. A. Hardenburgh and E. R. Rodie, *Water Supply and Waste Disposal* (Scranton, Pa.: International Textbook Company, 1961), p. 45.

While for planning purposes average daily water requirements per capita range between 100 and 200 GPCD (depending on nonresidential requirements), most flows, particularly those to residences, are not smooth throughout the day. Figure 7–2 shows the peaked nature of water use in residences. The result is that the peak demand for water (and the requirements for the carrying off of wastewater) is considerably greater than the hourly average.

While this is significant in the design of water systems, the fact they these systems are under pressure allows for the delivery of increased quantities with little increase in pipe size above the minimum. This unevenness of demand does, however, require that supplies be available to the system at the periods of

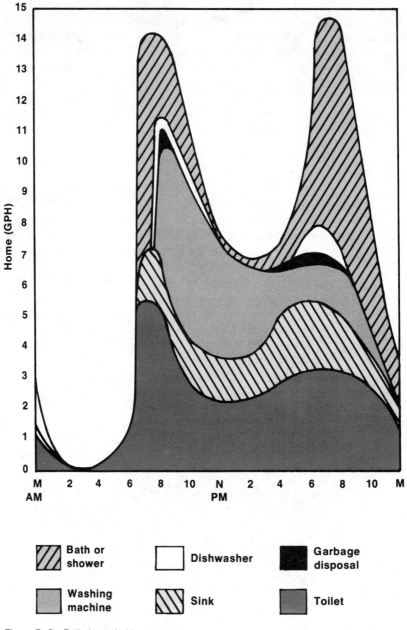

Figure 7–2 Daily household water use.

high demand. Local reservoirs or water tanks are generally available with roughly one full day's capacity to maintain both pressure and quantity during peak periods.

When to provide public supplies and why In the United States central water supply systems exist in nearly all cities and towns and in most villages and unincorporated places down to systems serving a small set of households. In spite of this, however, a significant number of outlying areas, particularly those experiencing rapid suburbanization, are initially supplied by individual wells and must face the decision of provision of central water supplies.

The decision to extend or to create central water systems is based on a series of factors. The most significant have always been and will continue to be fire protection and public health. One work states that water supplies should be "wholesome and palatable, . . . attractive to the senses of sight, taste and smell . . . [and] . . . free from disease organisms, poisonous substances, and excessive amounts of mineral and organic matter."[14]

Public water supplies are provided when densities increase in suburban areas to an extent where it is no longer possible to provide both on-site water supply and on-site sewage disposal, when there is a danger of contamination of the water supply by the sewage disposal system, and/or when requirements for fire-fighting necessitate a reliable high pressure water system.

Provision of potable water supplies The source of all potable water is initially the same: it is rainwater, which (1) may be collected for use; (2) may be allowed to run off, then collected (river/stream intake systems) and stored in a natural or manmade reservoir; or (3) may be allowed to infiltrate into the ground from which it may be pumped (a well) or from which it once again emerges (a spring). While collection of rainwater is seldom used for major water requirements, in areas in which groundwater is brackish or scarce this method may offer the only option. More common systems of water supply rely on combinations of river flows, storage reservoirs, and wells.

The majority of municipal water supplies are from surface water either from continuous draft (or selective draft) systems or from impoundage systems. Continuous draft or selective draft systems remove quantities of water from flowing water bodies such as rivers and streams, as well as from ponds or lakes whose capacities are sufficient to allow for year-round fresh supplies. Because such continuous water sources are frequently also used for industrial or for sanitary waste removal from upstream communities, they frequently require major purification works.

In areas in which continuous draft water supply systems are not possible, communities have traditionally maintained protected impoundments at a distance from the community and have carried clean water through aqueducts to the community. Boston brings the majority of its water (320 million GPD) from the Quabbin Reservoir, a 25,000 acre preserve in central Massachusetts. Three of the major supplies for New York City (the Croton River, the Catskills, and the Delaware River) are protected impoundments which have been used virtually untreated by their respective water districts. There is a long-standing tradition of protection of upland watersheds to prevent contamination and thus to obviate any need for purification other than chlorination. This desire for impoundment protection has virtually eliminated the use of reservoirs as recreational sites and has, in many areas, isolated these watersheds from hiking and camping. As will be discussed below, the Safe Drinking Water Act of 1974 may have put an end to the protected reservoir as a means of providing untreated water to a populace and as a result may have changed both the land use patterns around the reservoir areas and the basic arguments against employing reservoir waters for contact and surface uses.

The final source of potable water available to some communities is groundwater. Where water tables are sufficiently close to the surface, and where infiltration rates are sufficiently great to ensure recharge with a minimum of drawdown or where potable surface water is not available, groundwater may offer a viable water supply or augmentation source. Memphis, Tennessee, is supplied entirely from thirty wells, while a number of other communities such as New Haven, Connecticut, derive a portion of their requirements from well water.

The source of potable water is a major concern for all communities. Costs of providing water vary greatly depending on the combination of protected source, transport requirements, and purification works. While well water is generally clean, it frequently contains minerals in solution which make it hard, discolored, or flavored. Protected watersheds located in areas at a distance from the demand point require high capital expenditures and land costs in impoundments and easements for aqueducts. Investments in water supplies have become exceedingly high as communities or groups of communities are forced to go further or deeper for adequate supplies or are required to treat extensively water sources not previously used as potable water. All of these factors point toward conservation as a significant economic concern.

Water purification   The Safe Drinking Water Act of 1974 (P.L. 93–523) for the first time charged the U.S. Environmental Protection Agency (EPA) with setting primary drinking water regulations. These regulations were set in preliminary form in December 1975 and were made final in 1977 to establish maximum contamination levels for ten inorganic constituents, turbidity, coliform organisms, six pesticides, and radionuclides.

With the passage of P.L. 93–523 the federal government accepted the regulatory responsibility for guaranteeing safe drinking water to all citizens and included within the jurisdiction of EPA not only the setting of standards but also the development and dissemination of information concerning the methods of treatment available for removal of major water supply contaminants. For many communities the passage of the act dramatically affected their treatment procedures, requiring purification of water from impounded ''safe'' systems. The secondary impacts of this law are discussed in greater detail under Protection of Water Supplies.

Filters have been used for water purification since the early 1800s.[15] Traditional purification works were one of, or a combination of, the following:

1. Filtration plants that remove objectionable color, turbidity, and bacteria as well as other potentially harmful organisms by filtration through sand or other granular substances after necessary preparation of the water by coagulation and sedimentation.
2. Deferrization and demanganization plants that remove excessive amounts of iron and manganese by oxidizing the dissolved metals and converting them into insoluble flocs removable by sedimentation and filtration.
3. Softening plants that remove excessive amounts of scale-forming, soap-consuming ingredients, chiefly calcium and magnesium ions (a) by the addition of lime and soda ash which precipitate calcium as a carbonate and magnesium as a hydrate, or (b) by passage of the water through cation-exchange media that substitute sodium for calcium and magnesium ions and are themselves regenerated by brine.[16]

With the advent of P.L. 93–523, the complexities of purification have increased dramatically. While there are chemical processes such as lime softening which are effective for a number of inorganic contaminants, the chemicals selenium and fluoride require specific processes for their removal.[17]

Protection of water supplies   The advent of P.L. 93–523 and its amendments has altered the amount of leeway that communities have in deciding on the precise source and the quality of their water supply. Many elements, organic, inorganic, and radioactive, which were not considered harmful in the past or for which there were no standards within localities or within states, are now subject to federal regulation. A number of the substances now subject to standards are not kept out by a ''secure and protected watershed.'' If these substances occur in sufficient quantity they will require communities that in the past have not treated their water to now invest in large purification and treatment facilities.

Abandonment of the concept of a secure and protected water supply not requiring treatment has meant that planners must now face two significant new issues associated with the secondary impacts of new federal drinking water standards: (1) the demand for full recreational use of the reservoirs previously closed for public health reasons, and (2) the potential sale and development of watersheds for residential or second home development. These changes can bring both benefits and potential dangers to the water supply system in addition to any changes that may be required for meeting federal standards.

By far the lesser danger to water supply is the opening of reservoirs to recreational uses. It has long been argued that controlled recreational uses of water supply areas can do little to damage the water quality in large reservoirs whose ecosystems are sufficiently robust to accommodate any inadvertent organic or inorganic addition to the water. Sportsmen have long pushed for the opening to fishing and surface sports of many of the closed reservoirs. Recreational use of Lake Whitney, serving New Haven, Connecticut, and located throughout the bedroom community of Hamden, is denied to residents even though all of its water is filtered prior to distribution. Other reservoirs, such as the immense Quabbin Reservoir of the Metropolitan District Commission of Boston, which is open to fishing under controlled conditions, could, it has frequently been argued, be opened to far more water based recreation without harm to the water carried to the Boston area.

The second issue is more difficult to analyze and is potentially more harmful. Communities with protected watersheds frequently have maintained them not within their own boundaries but within the boundaries of other towns. For example, the majority of the impounded water supply for the city of Cambridge, Massachusetts, is located to the west in Lincoln, where Cambridge owns (and pays taxes on) more land than there is to the city of Cambridge itself. It must be pointed out that Cambridge has for some time had a filtration plant at Fresh Pond for all of its water supply.

Formerly "protected" watershed lands are now being sold or leased by communities attempting to recover a portion of their fixed capital investment. A number of communities, such as Newark, New Jersey, have been considering or have implemented development projects within their watersheds. The potential secondary impacts of such projects must be considered in terms of additional siltation of impoundments and of the introduction into the watershed of pesticides or other organic and inorganic chemicals not previously present and, significantly, not previously planned for in the design of the purification facility. Both the land use patterns and the design of the purification facility must be considered with a view to the longer-term equilibrium point in the water supply when the impacts of changing land use and increased surface and/or contact recreation are fully realized.

Water conservation   A final issue not being fully addressed in the literature to date is water conservation. Many portions of the country are now water poor and to them conservation appears a potential "source" of additional supplies.

Conservation, however, is only a partial solution to water supply problems. As Table 7–3 indicates, simple water conservation devices such as water saving toilets, flow restricting shower heads, and faucet aerators can make a dramatic difference in total consumption, accounting for, at the average (assuming consumption of 100 GPCD), roughly 24 percent savings in consumption using these devices alone. Combining use of such water conserving devices with behavioral changes such as curtailment of lawn watering and car washing can account for savings in particular seasons and geographic areas well above the 24 percent mentioned above. Modification in basic structures and design is required for additional savings. Certainly, recycling of "gray" water (water used in washing) is one such option, but an option requiring extensive investment in dual piping systems and storage of water. Appliance standards which encourage more water—and energy—efficient appliances would be another structural change that would have a significant impact on water supply requirements and, indeed, on wastewater flows as well.

The final solution in water conservation may lie in behavioral changes that cause consumers to use less water in many of their daily activities. The bumper sticker saying, "Save Water, Shower with a Friend," might well be replaced with, "Save Water, Take a Quick Shower with a Water Saving Shower Head."

Table 7–3 Water saving devices for homes.

Device	Consumption per unit (gallons)	Annual savings per person per year (gallons)
Standard toilet	5–7 gal.	
Water saving toilet	3.5 gal.	1,950–6,390
Standard shower head	8–10 GPM	
Flow restricting shower head	3.5 GPM	3,280–5,930
Faucet aerators	Save 25% of faucet flow	

Source: Man L. Chan et al., *Household Water Conservation and Wastewater Flow Reduction*, prepared for the U.S. Environmental Protection Agency, Office of Water Planning and Standards (Cambridge, Mass.: Energy Resources Co., Inc., July 1976), pp. 19–21.

Design of water supply systems

A complete water supply system, for simplicity, may be seen as containing four elements: a source, an aqueduct or conduit from the source to the purification plant, a purification plant, and a distribution system. Both the source of supply and the methods and requirements of purification have been discussed above. This section covers, primarily, the concerns of sizing and configuration of conduits and water distribution systems.

Aqueducts, from the source to the storage point within the community or to the purification plant, may be force systems or gravity flow systems. Both Boston and San Francisco are served by over twenty-five miles of force aqueduct. A greater number of cities are served by gravity systems. These pipes are generally designed to carry roughly 50 percent more than the average daily requirements of the community to allow for rapid drawdown by fire or excessive demand from summer uses such as sprinkling or air conditioning. Such large pipes tend to follow the shortest distance principle constrained only by access to rights-of-way and natural impediments such as major water courses or difficult terrain.

Distribution systems within a community are generally classed as one of two types. The preferred system is a gridiron system (Figure 7–3) in which any point on the system may be fed from more than one supply source. In larger systems the gridiron pattern is frequently nested so that the principal mains themselves feed from more than one direction within the inner loop or central business district area. The less preferred distribution system is a "dead end" system (Figure 7–3) designed in a tree branching pattern with increasingly smaller branches leading away from the main supply lines.

The gridiron pattern is preferred for several reasons. Most important is that in the gridiron water is supplied from more than one direction to any user, thus minimizing the potential for interruption in case of line breakage or other repair requirements. In addition, the dead end system leaves a large number of ending points at which water can stagnate and as a result can develop undesirable odors, tastes, coloration, or bacterial or algae growth. Inability to design for a perfect gridiron system requires utility access to end points that can be opened to prevent excessive stagnation.

As has been mentioned, in metropolitan areas water supplies may be required for fire use nearly as much as for public health. To a limited extent fire requirements determine the dimensions of the system itself. Hardenburgh and Rodie state: "[While] a 4-in. pipe will carry enough water for the domestic needs of about 1,000 people [it] . . . will barely supply a single fire hose. . . . Moreover, the cost of laying 6-in. or even 8-in. pipe is not materially greater."[18] As a result, it is argued that a 6 inch pipe should be used only when there is a good reason to do so and that otherwise an 8 inch pipe should always be chosen.

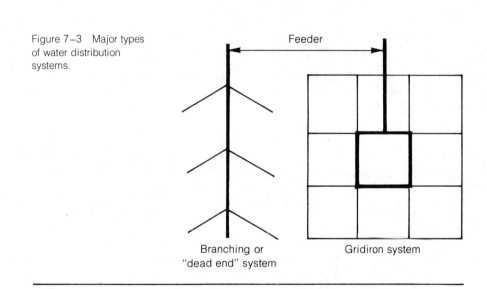

Figure 7–3   Major types of water distribution systems.

When one considers the number of individuals in residences served by a 4 inch pipe, it becomes apparent that an 8 inch pipe will service 6.28 times as many people. This suggests that most residential systems have sufficient excess capacity in the water system to allow for considerable additions to the residential stock without putting undue pressure on the distribution system. It should be noted, however, that this calculation says nothing about either large increases in the service area or about the availability of increased supplies.

Summary

Planning issues associated with supplying fresh water within major urban areas are focused more heavily on supply than on distribution. Distribution networks are largely fixed by public safety (fire) requirements on the smaller end and by a relatively fixed central business/high density demand pattern on the upper end. The more critical issues of water supply today and in the future are those associated first with the number of inhabitants and the location and adequacy of supply to serve the projected population, and second with the new requirements for extensive treatment of municipal water supplies which make the maintenance of protected watersheds and impoundments less attractive finally and less necessary for public health. The use of water supply reservoirs and the use of water supply watersheds are likely to be the major issues in this area facing planners in the near future.

Wastewater[19]

While the provision of sewerage has long been recognized as a major factor influencing suburbanization, the increased awareness of environmental quality has now made this provision a major investment required for land development. This preeminence, combined with the large federal grants program under P.L. 92–500, has brought the possibility for large scale sewerage development to virtually every small community and suburban area in the United States; with it goes a challenge to local planners to see the provision of sewerage as a potential tool for the guidance and direction of land use. Where sewerage planning has traditionally been the responsibility of civil and sanitary engineers, planners must now assume a significant role if phased and directed growth is to take place at the urban fringe.

The role of the planner is strongest early in the sewerage system design process and diminishes as the process moves closer to the final system design. The planner's role is particularly important in the issues of service area definition and population projections. It begins to diminish in overall contribution in the issues of per capita flows and allowances for peak to average flow. The role of the planner is minimal in system sizing and in selection of type or design of treatment facility.[20]

Major issues

How much sewage is generated?   Planned sewerage system capacity depends critically on the assumed number of GPCD generated. Errors in estimation contribute significantly to excess capacity (conservatism in system design). Such excess capacity frequently allows for "unplanned" developments within the community and may create unreasonable financial burdens on the existing population.

Existing estimates and rules of thumb for per capita daily waste flow generation vary widely. In areas with metered public water supplies, wastewater flows have been shown to be between 60 and 80 percent of metered water. Values for average water use vary as a function of the season of the year because of water uses that do not enter the sewage stream, such as watering of lawns and washing of automobiles during the summer months and running of taps to prevent freezing water lines in the northern areas of the United States during the cold months.

Other inaccuracies in projection of water use per capita are generated when per capita flows are set to be equal to total water dispatched divided by population. In this calculation, losses due to leakage, fire flow, and unmetered use are attributed to the average household. In addition, in areas in which homes are on septic tanks but with public water systems, past experience has shown that when these areas are sewered there is a tendency for water use to increase with acquisition of new water using appliances. As a result, even for communities in which there has been public water supply, estimates of future wastewater flows from present water use may be low. In areas in which there are no available records on water use, engineers fall back on comparative figures for similar communities or on generalized rules.

One hundred gallons per capita per day is a figure generally accepted by EPA for sizing interceptor sewer systems. Two studies, one in 1960 and one in 1976, raise questions concerning the rationality of assuming per capita flows as high as 100 GPCD. In 1960 the U.S. Public Health Service, in a report to the Senate Select Committee on Natural Resources, estimated residential water use to be 60 GPCD, with wastewater roughly 42 GPCD.[21] No authoritative study has been conducted since that time, but in 1976 Tabors, Shapiro, and Rogers (in

Land Use and the Pipe) attempted to estimate wastewater generation on the basis of work done by Ligman et al.[22] to analyze the composition of waste flows.

By building a "worst" case (assuming maximum water use by appliance type), Tabors, Shapiro, and Rogers arrived at a figure of only 89 GPCD as maximum per capita generation.[23] With present trends in increased appliance and plumbing efficiency, it is unlikely that it would be possible to generate an average of the estimated 89 GPCD, less so the 100 GPCD suggested by EPA standards. While higher values of per capita flows ensure sufficient capacity into the future, that capacity may encourage additional unplanned population increase or may cause an unnecessary burden in debt support on the part of the present users of the system.

The design flow for a sewerage system is generally calculated as

$$Q = \text{(population)} \times \text{(GPCD)} \times \text{(peaking factor)}.$$

With this relationship, it is possible to see that any errors or overestimates of the variables on the right hand side of the equation are multiplicative to quantity Q, so that an error of, for example, x percent in population creates an error greater than x percent in Q.

Why sewer?   A number of strong forces are at work pushing communities, particularly those in the suburbs, toward major investments in sewerage facilities. Probably the strongest such force was the passage of P.L. 92–500. This legislation provided for a standard of quality in treatment by 1977 and for a sizable purse of federal funding to develop the collection systems and the treatment facilities required to improve water quality nationally. Within any given community the pressure for extension of sewers or development of large scale sewerage facilities is predicated in large part on the requirements for public health, which no longer allow for on-site sewage disposal through either septic tanks or cesspools on lots smaller than one acre. With the economics of large scale developments, lot sizes of a quarter of an acre are now accepted as necessary for developer success. Therefore, development now requires guaranteed sewerage facilities.

The decision to sewer or not to sewer depends to a large extent on the alternatives available within any specific community and geographic/geological environment.

In areas in which development that uses on-site systems has already occurred and in which soil and ground water conditions cannot support on-site disposal, the decision is frequently mandated by a state or local health agency, although the precise specifications of the decision may be open to negotiation. In areas of new development the requirement that lots be roughly a quarter of an acre per housing unit for the development to be financially successful necessitates some form of sewerage facility.

In areas in which homes are being served by on-site disposal systems which operate relatively well, and in which future development is anticipated in the form of higher priced single family dwellings only, it is possible to maintain environmental quality without requiring large scale sewerage facilities (through large lot zoning combined with organized inspection and maintenance of on-site systems). Such "nonstructural alternatives" to development of large scale sewerage facilities are now being considered by many communities that can afford dispersed development, as well as by selected other communities that are able to combine small package treatment facilities with monitored on-site systems.

Each community is different in its needs and options. That there are options in each instance must be kept firmly in mind, as large treatment facilities may create more problems—even for water quality—than they solve.

Treatment alternatives While it is beyond the scope of this chapter to discuss fully the alternatives for sewage treatment, it is significant to identify the three major groupings of treatment facilities. It should be noted that P.L. 92–500 mandated that all municipal wastes would receive at least secondary treatment. While this effort is progressing, there are major areas in which this standard has not been met. Boston represents one such area, in which a series of studies is under way and a set of arguments is taking place concerning whether the improvement in facilities from primary to secondary will, in fact, improve water quality in Boston Harbor and whether a "deep ocean outfall" will accomplish the same objective—or possibly improve on it—with no additional treatment and lower overall expenditures.

Primary, secondary, and tertiary treatment may be defined as follows:

Primary Treatment: Primary treatment refers to the removal of between 30 and 35 percent of the organic pollutants and up to one-half of the suspended solids. Generally, the processes involved are a screening process for removal of heavy solids, a skimming process which removes floating solids, and a settling period to remove heavier suspended materials. The cost is generally between $0.05 and $0.25 per 1,000 gallons treated.

Secondary Treatment: Secondary treatment removes between 80 and 90 percent of the organic materials and over 80 percent of the suspended solids. It generally requires a multiple-step process involving one biological process and one or more processes for settling of suspended solids. Biological processes include activated sludge, stabilization ponds, and trickling filters. The objective of all of the steps in the secondary treatment process is to increase the amount of both organic and suspended matter which is removed. The cost is generally between $0.10 and $0.70 per 1,000 gallons treated.

Tertiary Treatment: Because of the large quantities of synthetic organic compounds and inorganic ions in the waste stream, many localities are being asked to extend their treatment processes. Tertiary or advanced waste treatment adds additional steps to primary and secondary treatment in order to provide additional removal of standard organic pollutants or to remove one or more specific organic compounds or inorganic ions from the stream. Common pollutants removed are phosphate and nitrate. The actual process chosen depends upon the ions or synthetic organic compounds to be removed. Phosphorus removal costs an additional $0.10 to $0.20 per 1,000 gallons treated.[24]

Potential land use impacts The three essential elements in the process of suburbanization and land development in the United States are highways, water supply, and sewerage. To a large extent highways have been completed with the final linkages in the interstate system and with a partial halt to new construction around many of the major urban areas. As has been discussed, water systems are seen as essential to public health and as a result tend to be available when required. In addition, managers of water supply systems frequently see these systems as utilities actively seeking new customers. Sewers are a different matter: they are expensive and are public goods provided by tax dollars. As a result, at present the battle over land use and land use planning is centering on the extension of sewerage facilities before large scale, moderate density, single family housing developments—frequently described as sprawl—can begin.[25]

Where suburbanization and increasing land values once were said to follow the major feeder highways into the countryside, these developments now seem to follow the extensions of interceptor sewers. The primary impacts are relatively clear: increased development of single family dwellings on one-quarter acre lots and the potential for multiple dwelling units and commercial "strips." The secondary environmental impacts are less easily identified although these frequently are decreased water quality through nonpoint source pollution (fertilizer and highway runoff), poorer air quality because of increased automotive emissions, and lowered visual quality through intensive development. Many of

Wastewater definitions

Sewage: Sewage refers to the wastewater flow from residential, commercial, and industrial establishments which flows through the pipes to a treatment plant.

Sewerage: Sewerage refers to the system of sewers, physical facilities employed to transport, treat, and discharge sewage.

Sewer: Sewer refers to the pipe, conduit, or other physical facility used to carry off wastewater.

House connection: Sometimes referred to as house laterals, house connections are the points of contact between the individual dwelling unit and the sewerage system.

Lateral: A lateral is the pipe to which individual houses and business establishments attach. If one considers the analogy of a tree, the laterals represent twigs.

Main/submain: The word *main* is frequently used loosely to indicate a large pipe which is not a lateral and not an interceptor. Like a trunk, a main or submain frequently forms one of the larger branches of a complex collection system.

Trunk: A trunk sewer is one of a set of large pipes which form the branches of the sewerage system. In many communities, it would be the pipe which collects sewage from a large portion of a community and then discharges it into an interceptor.

Interceptor: Interceptor sewers derive their name from their original design purpose in older cities in which they intercepted the flow of smaller trunk sewers that was going directly and untreated into a river or a stream and carried that flow to a downstream treatment facility. Interceptor now refers to any pipe, regardless of size, that carries wastewater to the treatment plant.

Sewer outfalls: Sewer outfalls, or effluent outfalls, are interceptor-sized pipes which transport, after treatment, the effluent of the sewage treatment plant to the final receiving body.

Source: Excerpted from Richard D. Tabors, Michael H. Shapiro, and Peter P. Rogers, *Land Use and the Pipe: Planning for Sewerage* (Lexington, Mass.: Lexington Books, D. C. Heath and Company, 1976), pp. 13, 15–16.

---

these impacts can be lessened or avoided through more attention to the phasing of sewerage development and to the use of sewerage development as a tool for land use planning. The summary to this section of the chapter discusses in greater detail the options for positive land use impacts from sewerage development.

Alternatives to sewers The alternatives to large scale sewerage systems are frequently not well articulated in the sewerage planning process. While they cannot apply to all applications, they do offer points of economic and environmental comparison with the large sewerage systems.

In many suburban communities in which on-site systems are used extensively, consideration of extension of sewers is made on the basis of septic tank failures. While there are areas where soil characteristics are not suitable for septic systems, the more normal problem is poor maintenance and insufficiently frequent pumping. Where the alternative exists, establishment of an enforced septic tank inspection, maintenance, and pumping program can offer a cost-effective alternative to sewer extension, as can actual ownership of on-site systems by local governments. In such areas there may be a need for a septage treatment facility or for specific arrangements with adjoining communities with large scale sewage treatment facilities that might handle the septage.

A second alternative to large scale sewerage systems is the package treatment plant, a small scale, frequently prefabricated, secondary treatment facility that can be readily installed and easily maintained and is cost-effective for groups of homes or small commercial or institutional establishments. To date, package treatment facilities have received insufficient attention for evaluation of their long run reliability. They require a means of disposing of the effluent from the plant as well as systematic disposal of the sludge. Effluent disposal can be to a flowing water body or, in some instances, to the ground in large leaching fields. Sludge disposal requires the same precautions and concerns for these small plants as for the larger treatment plants. Package systems are designed to operate with minimum supervision, although some states require full-time operators, which makes the economics of operation less advantageous.

While the above are two major alternatives to large sewerage systems, there are others, ranging from large holding tanks to on-site tertiary treatment facilities. The significance of any of the alternatives is that they would give the planner the opportunity of comparing, on the basis of cost, performance, and risk, a set of alternative strategies for accomplishing the same objective.

Design of sewerage systems

Wastewater treatment systems are made up of three components: a collection system, a treatment facility, and a disposal system. Wastewater is generated from a number of sources which, when added up, equal the total flow of the systems. These are wastes from residences and commercial establishments, wastes from industrial establishments, storm waters (in combined systems), and infiltration or exfiltration, depending on the groundwater pattern and the quality of the jointing between sections of interceptor and/or collector piping. Projection of the quantity of wastewater which will be collected and processed (for sanitary sewers only) requires an estimate of residential population within the service area multiplied by this population's average daily production. The calculation for commercial areas generally takes into consideration the population of the service area multiplied by a coefficient representing an average number of stores, offices, etc. Projection of industrial wastewater loads must be done on a community by community, industry by industry basis for any large scale wastewater producing firms, and is again frequently estimated as "population equivalents" for smaller nonwater-using firms. The last component of wastewater flow is the estimate of infiltration into the pipes from surrounding groundwater or exfiltration (leakage) to the surrounding soil.

The carrying capacity of the sewers (pipes) within a sewerage system must be planned to accommodate the peak flows. As was seen in Figure 7–2, the ratio of maximum to minimum flows can be more than an order of magnitude. For small residential systems these peaks can be great, although as a system grows the peaks tend to smooth out, as a function of different use patterns (the addition of industrial flows or commercial flows) and because of the greater distances over which sewage must flow within the pipes themselves. There is a clear time dimension to sewage flows, just as there is to traffic flows within a city. It takes longer for traffic to travel from the rural areas than from the central suburbs, and the impact of the additional car arriving at any point is diminished as the road system increases in size. This is roughly analogous to the distance smoothing effect within a large sewerage system.

In general, the requirements for sizing the pipes within a sewerage system vary with the size of the upstream population. The smaller this population is, the larger the ratio of peak to average flow should be. The same logic holds for minimum to average flows. While planners have less control over the determination of the appropriate value of peak or minimum to average flow, it is necessary that they be aware of the relative range. As can be seen in Figure 7–4, for small populations the minimum to average flow ratio is 0.3, with the peak to average 4.0; for larger systems the ratio is from 0.8 to 1.45.[26]

From the perspective of the planner the most significant engineering variable is that of minimum pipe size set by state law. The minimum diameter for street laterals and downstream collectors is set at 8 inches for most states, with house connections of either 4 or 6 inch minimum size. At 100 GPCD an 8 inch pipe in moderately sloping terrain can service roughly sixty acres of one-quarter acre lot development before reaching capacity; thus, for many sewer systems built in suburban areas the vast majority of the system is frequently made up of the minimum size pipe—8 inches in diameter.

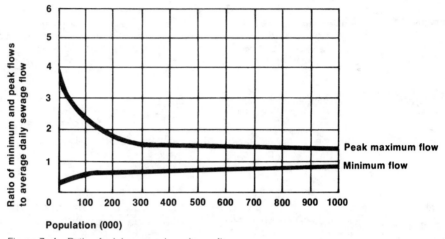

Figure 7–4 Ratio of minimum and maximum flows to average daily sewage flow.

The remaining engineering criteria for sewerage system design center on the exact location of the system and on the material from which the system is constructed. Because sewage is waterborne, it is most economically collected with a gravity system. (Discussion of two other systems, force mains and pressure systems, are beyond the scope of this chapter.) Gravity systems must maintain a minimum flow within the pipes which is sufficient to prevent sedimentation in pipes while not being so fast as to cause erosion in the pipes. As a result, for gravity systems the slope of the pipes is calculated so that the flow is between 2 feet and 10 feet per second. While there are frequent trade-offs between costs of different system components which are exceedingly smooth and not subject to erosion, the most common piping systems are concrete with a rubber or synthetic gasket between sections of pipe.

Summary

Through the greater part of this discussion of planning for sewerage, the focus has been on planning criteria and hardware. This final section of the discussion of wastewater management summarizes the potential for using infrastructure investment as an active tool for land use planning. Several chapters in this book discuss the options and techniques available for land use planning. Here we are concerned only with the potential use to which sewerage policies may be placed in land use planning.

Figure 7–5 summarizes the policy options for using the provision of environmental infrastructure—in particular, availability of sewerage—for land use control. These policies have been divided along two axes. The first is by type of action (restrictive or incentive), and the second is by means of operation (physical or financial). As can be seen, the majority of the policy options exercised to date have been restrictive and physical, ranging from refusal to sewer and sewer moratoria to policies of carefully delimited expansion through staging of investments. In addition, there have been capital subsidies for construction provided by both state and federal governments to encourage the development of large scale wastewater sysems to accommodate existing and planned growth and development. Such capital grants carry with them restrictions as to the criteria for system design and review through the National Environmental Policy Act (NEPA). In addition, P.L. 92–500 provides planners with what is probably their

Policy	Principal mechanisms	Governmental level	Time horizon for planning	Actual or proposed applications
Sewer moratorium	Ban or quota on new sewers, connections, building permits, subdivision approval, rezoning	State or local	Usually less than two years	Over two hundred, concentrated primarily in N.J., Fla., Cal., Ohio
Refusal to sewer	Rural fringe and community refuses to provide sewerage	Local; may be overriden by state	. . .	Massachusetts
NEPA review	Mandatory agency and public review of federally funded projects to encourage consideration of secondary impacts	Federal; all levels involved in review process	Up to fifty years	Rockland County, N.Y., Delaware
Facility design	Select physical options to encourage certain types of land use, e.g., force mains, smaller treatment plants	County/regional	Twenty to fifty years	Sewerage plan for York County, Pa.
Facility sizing	Limit excess capacity in projects to preserve future land use options	Local, county/regional	Ten to twenty years	California
Service area	Establish "urban service area" within which public services will be provided	County/regional	Ten to twenty years	Lexington, Ky., Prince George's County, Toronto, Canada
Staging policy	Staging of individual facilities to promote certain development patterns	County/regional	Five years	Minneapolis–St. Paul, Minn., Ramapo, N.Y.

Figure 7–5   Sewerage/land use policies.

most intensely focused opportunity for input into the sewerage planning process through sections 208, 209, and 303, which provide for states to develop comprehensive plans for water quality maintenance through an ongoing planning process.

Sewerage planning has traditionally been the realm of the engineer, not the planner. What has become increasingly apparent is that the planner must be involved in the decisions surrounding construction of such systems if the systems are to complement the development activities of communities rather than themselves determining the directions and extent of community development.

Solid waste management[27]

As is the case with water supply and wastewater management, in solid waste planning the role of the planner occurs early and is critical to the development of facilities which lead rather than follow the demand created by the expansion of urban areas. In this section two major issues will arise several times: the question of land use and land values associated with sanitary landfills or other final disposal sites for solid wastes, and the question of the costs and alternatives available for disposal of solid wastes. The issues discussed here are primarily those of urban and suburban rather than rural areas.

Major issues

Not in my backyard Major land use issues in solid waste management (as is the case with sewage treatment plants) have most frequently been associated with the stigma of having a major solid waste facility in the neighborhood. The popular consensus seems to be, "They are fine, but not in my backyard." This general attitude toward solid waste facilities may be based on the fact that these facilities can be hazardous and an eyesore if improperly run. On the other hand, the general image of an open dump—with frequent burning of refuse, blowing of paper, and severe rodent problems—is an image that is closer to the solid waste situation of the 1950s and earlier (the town dump) than to conditions today (the sanitary landfill).

The development of regional solid waste management facilities brings another set of concerns. Regionalization of solid waste facilities may offer the only economically acceptable alternative for communities forced to find higher cost solutions, such as more advanced waste processing systems (that is, incineration). The attitude of "not in my backyard" has extended to one of "not in my community" for many more suburban and even rural communities facing the possibility of becoming the sink community for a regional solid waste system. There are many examples of public officials and citizen groups lying down in front of refuse trucks as they are about to enter the community.

One well documented set of analyses of the prospects and problems associated with regional solid waste facilities was carried out for the region of Syracuse, New York. Despite the formation of the Onondaga County Solid Waste Authority, each of the smaller towns, largely for political reasons, refused to accept the solid waste of Syracuse or Salina, forcing these larger communities to seek more expensive alternatives for disposal of their wastes.[28]

Land values in proximity to solid waste facilities have traditionally been depressed. The question of whether facility location was based on low land values or whether land values dropped as a result has never been fully documented. Unlike either sewers or water supply, however, solid waste removal and transfer requires trucking, any large quantity of which will cause environmental problems through noise and litter.

Land use Easily the most important portion of solid waste planning from the point of view of long-range interests of the community is the location, operation, and use of the landfill site. While in many communities the landfill site has been operated as an open and burning dump and has been kept open for long periods of time, new federal and local regulations which prohibit burning of dumps and enforce nightly covering of the waste with a minimum of six inches of soil have had the effect of filling sites more rapidly and creating both the demand for new sites and, significantly, a resource for development at the now completed site. Careful advance planning of final disposition of landfill sites has the advantage of preparing a neighborhood or a community for a resource—after the filling has been completed—and thereby making the filling itself somewhat more palatable.

Planning for final disposal has taken on a different appearance in recent years. During an interview an official of a community in the Syracuse, New York, region that was about to open a new landfill area commented that the community had no plan to either complete the old fill or develop it. Within six months of the original interview, however, the same official was proud of the planned athletic facilities and canal front park which were to be developed on the completed site with the assistance of local service groups. Whether a development will be for a university, for a sledding/tobogganing/skiing slope, or for golf courses and playing fields, advance planning will improve attitudes on the part of neighbors and will aid in the smooth transition from a potential liability to a land based asset.

Increasing costs of disposal   Increasing costs brought about by exhaustion of inexpensive disposal sites, increased regulation by either state or federal agencies, and inability of communities to agree on the site of regional facilities for landfills or for resource recovery or advanced processing have been a major issue in solid waste management. The choice of a system for final disposal generates the greatest interest on the part of citizens and political leaders but represents only a relatively small proportion of the total costs of the overall system (between 70 and 85 percent of costs are in labor costs for collection). Collection costs are perceived as fixed, yet method of collection, point of pickup, frequency of collection, truck size and type, size of district, and bags versus cans contribute significantly to overall system costs.

How much must be removed?   The discussion of solid waste disposal which follows focuses on four major issues: collection, transportation, processing (if required), and disposal. Figure 7–6 is a flow diagram of the choices to be made and the basic steps through which the analysis must proceed in designing and evaluating a solid waste disposal system.[29]

The generation of solid waste is seasonal and is related to the affluence of the individual. Christmas cleanup, spring cleaning, fall leaves, and heavy months of moving such as June and July bring slightly higher than average quantities per capita of solid wastes. In general, however, total (residential, commercial, and industrial) solid waste generation per capita has been increasing from roughly 2.75 pounds per capita per day in 1920 to 5.3 in 1968.[30] Estimated levels of nonagricultural wastes for Massachusetts in 1972 were 7 pounds per capita per day,[31] and estimated national figures for commercial, municipal, and other urban wastes (excluding industrial, mining, and agriculture) for 1973 were 6.25 pounds per capita per day.[32] These increases can be accounted for largely by increases in disposable packaging and a dramatic increase in paper product consumption.

Collection   With the exception of the New England town social and political tradition of the Saturday morning trip to the dump, most communities provide for collection of solid waste on a regular basis. The decision on the point of collection and the material to be collected may determine many of the costs of service. Many communities collect garbage (food wastes) separately from rubbish (paper and other combustible and noncombustible wastes), necessitating collection directly from the backyard or alley. Labor now represents the largest component of collection costs; as a result most communities have shifted from backyard collection and separate collection of garbage and refuse to combined curbside pickup from standard containers or plastic bags.

The question of how frequently refuse will be collected is again one of cost. There are trade-offs in operating equipment, routes taken, and crews associated with once weekly or biweekly collection which require analysis for each com-

Figure 7–6   Decision alternatives for residential solid waste management. This flowchart shows the decisions that must be made for the four major solid waste functions: collection, including storage, level of service, and home separation for recycling; transport; processing, including volume reduction and resource recovery; and ultimate disposal.

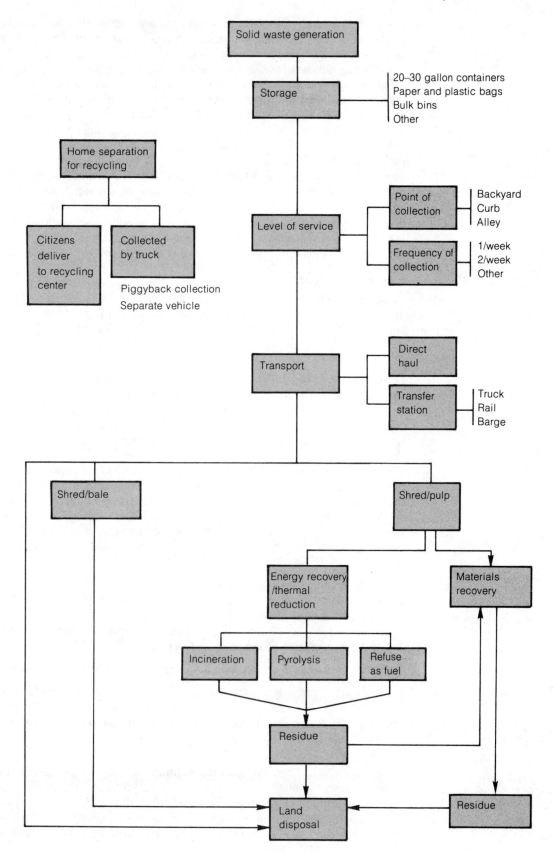

munity.[33] It is likely that some areas will require greater coverage than others. Traditionally, central business districts with high densities of commercial establishments and restaurants require daily pickup. This, too, may depend on the communities studied, as larger establishments frequently maintain their own "dumpsters" or compactors as an on-site convenience or necessity.

One of the more interesting issues in solid waste management is recycling. While the economics of recycling facilities which separate at the "sink" at present are marginal, recycling via separation at the source appears far more favorable. The actual economics of such a program depend to a large extent on local conditions and on the means of collection. A number of communities have begun source separation/collection (Somerville, Massachusetts, for example) involving collection equipment with special bins for separated materials (glass, aluminum, newspapers) distinct from the compactor into which all other rubbish is thrown. The analysis completed to date on source separation schemes is interesting in that it shows that participation in the program tends to increase over time. Throughout, however, there is a need to generate and maintain citizen interest.[34]

Collection vehicles for residential systems range in size from 13 to 41 cubic yards and may be either open or compacting. Because of both length of haul and litter from noncompacting vehicles, compactors are far more common. There is considerable range in quantity and cost, although the 20 cubic yard rear loader was nearly ubiquitous on urban and suburban routes as of the late 1970s.

Transportation   After collection of solid waste there are a number of options for transportation to the point of final disposal or processing. These options depend largely on the relative costs of equipment and labor associated with each. In the case of a community that controls a convenient landfill or disposal facility, it is likely that the collection vehicles and their crews will deliver the waste to the site.

In communities in which there is a considerable distance between the collection point and the point of final disposal there is frequently a transfer station in the system which allows for the aggregation of the contents of a number of smaller collection vehicles into a large, specifically designed, frequently compressing tractor–trailer vehicle which will then transport the materials to their point of disposition.[35] Such transfer systems are desirable for the following reasons:

1. They minimize wear on collection vehicles
2. They minimize crew time spent on long rides to and from the disposal site
3. Changes in disposal sites will not change the optimal collection routes, only the operation of the transfer trucking.

At the same time, there are two disadvantages to transfer stations, namely:

1. They are expensive to establish; as a result, they require careful analysis of the benefits to be gained over a significant future time
2. They can arouse public opposition, a problem common to almost all solid waste management facilities.

Processing options   There are few options for final disposition of solid waste, and in all instances the final repository for at least a portion of the material will be the sanitary landfill. The options for final disposal may be grouped into three general categories: marginal volume reduction on site; baling and shredding for volume reduction; and resource recovery, combined with one or both of the above.

As has been mentioned above, the most difficult political and planning decisions associated with solid waste management are those dealing with the choice of landfill or final disposal site. Once a site has been chosen there is a considerable incentive to operate it as long as possible. Any system which bales, or shreds and bales, the wastes into uniform blocks which can minimize the need for clean (expensive) cover will dramatically reduce the economic and political costs associated with the dedication of new landfill sites. For this reason, volume reduction schemes have become attractive. Such methods as baling will achieve densities of from 1,000 to 1,700 pounds per cubic yard or roughly double the densities available from standard compacting equipment used at a landfill site. Other advantages of baling include ease of shipment; savings in transport costs where baling is done at a transfer station; and stability in a landfill after the fill has been closed, because bales allow for more rapid reuse of the site.

Shredding offers a second method of volume reduction which is frequently combined with baling as a means of achieving smaller volumes of wastes. In addition, shredded wastes are frequently the input to a resource recovery operation which allows small particles of various materials to be separated at specific points in the processing of the waste stream. Shredding involves some form of grinding of the wastes into a nearly homogeneous solid. It has frequently been argued that shredded wastes are odor free and do not support either combustion or vectors of disease—both common problems within traditional sanitary landfills.[36] Shredding is not cheap, however; Syracuse, New York, reported $110.60 per ton treated for shredding alone in the first year of operation.

Final disposal Among the methods available for final disposal of solid wastes, there is a considerable range in overall costs and in the processes available. Whenever there is an option for a low cost landfill, a community generally should and will opt for it. Even given the noncomparability of figures, the preprocessing by shredding followed by landfilling becomes an option which, in current dollars, will be as expensive as (if not more expensive than) incineration.

Choice of final disposition depends, therefore, on the options available to the community. Where no landfilling possibilities are available, advanced and expensive treatment will be the only option. It should be remembered that in older, densely populated areas such as the Northeast, the larger cities within an urban area are frequently landlocked politically by their own suburban rings. The tensions between central city and suburb have created solutions which are not economically efficient but which represent political necessity. The Syracuse region offers one such example. With one political party controlling the city and the other controlling the suburban ring, locating a landfill site for a "regional" solid waste authority has become virtually impossible. Even with county operation of the solid waste authority cooperation with the surrounding towns was not fully possible.

Resource recovery from urban solid wastes has become an attractive possibility for the recycling of scarce metals and, significantly, for the saving of energy (production of aluminum from existing aluminum requires 5 percent of the energy needed for production of aluminum from bauxite) and for the generation of heat through controlled incineration of wastes. Two primary forces have maintained these programs at lower levels than had been predicted by their proponents. First, recovering materials from solid wastes at the sink is expensive, and the market for recycled materials is highly variable, thus making the operation of such systems subject to high risk. Second, because most resource recovery systems depend at least in part on incineration for volume reduction and solids separation, the solid waste operation comes into direct contact with the air quality regulations controlling particulates and the emissions of the combustion products of plastics, rubber, and heavy metals. Owing to the uncertainties associated with the setting and regulation of federal clean air requirements, processes involving incineration of solid wastes within air quality control regions have become highly uncertain.

The most inexpensive means of recovering resources for recycling is at the source before they become intermingled. Whether they are cans, bottles, or newspapers, these wastes are most conveniently collected separately through independent pickups or through the use of combined pickup vehicles designed specifically for the purpose. While this requires active participation on the part of the citizenry, the cost in operations and capital on the tax dollar appears to more than make up for the inconvenience.

Summary

Critical planning issues in solid waste management have been discussed in this section, with emphasis on sanitary landfills and other final disposal sites, on collection and processing, and on costs and alternatives for final disposal. Here, as in earlier sections of this chapter, the importance of environmental planning has been considered throughout.

Environmental planning

Environmental planning is a new area of concern for the professional planner and the planning student. It is an area traditionally controlled by civil and sanitary engineers but is one in which there is increasing need for integration with the more traditional areas of planning if environmental infrastructure is to complement rather than lead the development of communities. This chapter has attempted to point to the areas in which planners are likely to have the maximum leverage—those areas early in the facilities development process when locations are being considered and when such significant parameters as population projections and future land use and density patterns are being discussed. As the process of environmental infrastructure development continues, the planner's role diminishes. The planner's input into systems design and operation is small. With the exception of solid waste planning—in which the planner has a significant role at the end, when the landfill site is ready for redevelopment—the role of the planner may be relegated to trying to work around an environmental infrastructure that has been inherited or has been allowed to develop without the planner's direct participation. The technical information concerning the design and construction of environmental infrastructure facilities contained in this chapter is not intended to make the reader an environmental engineer, but it attempts to offer the first steps in making the reader an informed consumer of consulting engineering reports.

1   In some sections this chapter will present estimates of the costs of capital facilities and operation. These are presented as indications of average relative costs at a given point in time. Caution in their use is advised: first, they are averages and as with all measures of central tendency only poorly represent the actual range of values which would apply to specific applications; second, the figures presented are for one point in time. The cost of providing environmental infrastructure has been increasing dramatically, as have most construction costs; therefore, recent editions of those sources referenced should be consulted for up-to-date "average" figures.

2   Real Estate Research Corporation, *The Costs of Sprawl: Environmental and Economic Costs of Alternative Residential Development Patterns at the Urban Fringe,* prepared for the U.S. Council on Environmental Quality, the U.S. Department of Housing and Urban Development, and the U.S. Environmental Protection Agency (Washington, D.C.: Government Printing Office, 1974).

3   Clark S. Binkley et al., *Interceptor Sewers and Urban Sprawl* (Lexington, Mass.: Lexington Books, D. C. Heath and Company, 1975).

4   Richard D. Tabors, Michael H. Shapiro, and Peter P. Rogers, *Land Use and the Pipe: Planning for Sewerage* (Lexington, Mass.: Lexington Books, D. C. Heath and Company, 1976).

5   See: ibid., pp. 152–68.

6   See: ibid., pp. 133–45.

7   The section which follows is excerpted in large part from: ibid., pp. 20–23.

8   Binkley et al., *Interceptor Sewers and Urban Sprawl,* p. 5.

9   For additional methods suitable for small area projections, see: P. M. Meier, "Stochastic Population Projection at Design Level," *Journal of the*

Sanitary Engineering Division, ASCE 98, SA6 Proc. Paper 9436 (December 1972): 883–96.

10 The discussions which follow assume that an analyst is working in constant dollars (that is, that there is *no* inflation); these same calculations apply when working in current dollars (with inflation), although generally such calculations do little to clarify the concepts and add an additional variable—inflation—to the calculation.

11 For additional references, see: Richard A. Musgrave and Peggy B. Musgrave, *Public Finance in Theory and Practice,* 2nd ed. (New York: McGraw-Hill Book Company, 1975); E. J. Mishan, *Cost Benefit Analysis,* rev. ed. (New York: Praeger Publishers, 1976); and Eugene L. Grant and W. Grant Reson, *Principles of Engineering Economy* (New York: The Ronald Press Company, 1974).

12 The majority of the materials presented in the water and wastewater portions of this chapter have been derived from a set of basic texts on water and wastewater engineering. The most complete of these are the following: G. M. Fair et al., *Water and Wastewater Engineering,* 2 vols. (New York: John Wiley & Sons, Inc., 1966, 1968); W. A. Hardenburgh and E. R. Rodie, *Water Supply and Waste Disposal* (Scranton, Pa.: International Textbook Company, 1961); and Metcalf and Eddy, Inc., *Wastewater Engineering: Collection, Treatment, Disposal* (New York: McGraw-Hill Book Company, 1972). While these works are useful detailed references, they are written for the engineering student, not for the planner. There are a number of publications on rural water supply and sanitation prepared by the U.S. Public Health Service and the Extension Service of the U.S. Department of Agriculture, although these are seldom informative for the planner more interested in urban supply and removal issues. Tabors, Shapiro, and Rogers, in *Land Use and the Pipe,* have attempted to bring together a number of the major issues associated with wastewater planning. Their discussion of projection techniques, financing, and land use are of importance beyond sewerage planning.

13 Hardenburgh and Rodie, *Water Supply and Waste Disposal,* p. 45.

14 Fair et al., *Water and Wastewater Engineering,* vol. 1, p. 1-8.

15 John Gibb in 1804 in Paisley, Scotland, and James Simpson in 1829 in Chelsea, London.

16 Fair et al. *Water and Wastewater Engineering,* vol. 1, p. 2-15.

17 For more detailed information on treatment requirements and estimated costs for purification works required under P.L. 93–523 and its subsequent amendments, readers should refer to such volumes as: U.S., Environmental Protection Agency, Office of Research and Development, Municipal Environmental Research Laboratory, Water Supply Research Division, *Manual of Treatment Techniques for Meeting the Interim Primary Drinking Water Regulations* (Cincinnati: U.S. Environmental Protection Agency, May 1977).

18 Hardenburgh and Rodie, *Water Supply and Waste Disposal,* pp. 133–34.

19 Parts of this section draw on: Tabors, Shapiro, and Rogers, *Land Use and the Pipe.* See also note 12.

20 Thorough discussions of the engineering criteria for design of wastewater systems may be found in: Metcalf and Eddy, *Wastewater Engineering,* and Fair et al., *Water and Wastewater Engineering.* A nontechnical discussion of the engineering criteria may also be found in Tabors, Shapiro, and Rogers, *Land Use and the Pipe.*

21 U.S., Senate, Select Committee on Natural Resources, *Water Resource Activities in the United States* (Washington, D.C.: Government Printing Office, 1960).

22 Kenneth Ligman, Neil Hutzler, and William C. Boyle, "Household Wastewater Characterization," *Journal of the Environmental Engineering Division, ASCE* 100, No. EE 1 (February 1974): 201–13.

23 Tabors, Shapiro, and Rogers, *Land Use and the Pipe,* p. 29.

24 Ibid., p. 16.

25 Examples of the land use impact of sewer extensions are documented in the three case studies in: ibid., pp. 133–63, and in Real Estate Research Corporation, *The Costs of Sprawl.*

26 Additional details on carrying capacity and flows may be found in such sources as Tabors, Shapiro, and Rogers, *Land Use and the Pipe,* and Metcalf and Eddy, *Wastewater Engineering.*

27 Information and references on solid waste management are widely available. An excellent source of detailed technical and economic data is: U.S., Environmental Protection Agency, Office of Solid Waste Management Programs, *Decision-Makers Guide in Solid Waste Management,* 2nd ed. (Washington, D.C.: Government Printing Office, 1976).

28 See: Bernard Heiler and Shih-Hsiung Chen, "Paretian Analysis of Solid Waste Management in the Onondaga County—Syracuse Area," paper delivered at the Environmental Systems Program, Harvard University, 14 February 1974.

29 See, for example: U.S., Office of Solid Waste Management Programs, *Decision-Makers Guide in Solid Waste Management.*

30 Michael R. Greenberg et al., *Solid Waste Planning in Metropolitan Regions* (New Brunswick, N.J.: Rutgers University, Center for Urban Policy Research, 1976), p. 8.

31 Commonwealth of Massachusetts, Department of Public Works, Bureau of Solid Waste Disposal, *Solid Waste Management Study Report,* vol. 1 (Boston: Massachusetts State Printer, 1972), p. 1.

32 "Solid Waste: Disposal, Reuse Present Major Problems," *Congressional Quarterly,* 28 April 1973, p. 1019.

33 In general, the cost of weekly collection is between 13 and 19 percent less than biweekly. (ACT Systems, Inc., *Residential Collection Systems,* vol. 1, EPA Publication SW–97c.1 [Washington, D.C.: U.S. Environmental Protection Agency, 1974].)

34 SCS Engineers (Long Beach, California), *Analysis of Source Separate Collection of Recyclable Solid Waste: Separate Collection Studies.* EPA Publication SW–95c.1 (Washington, D.C.: U.S. Environmental Protection Agency, 1974), available from National Technical Information Service, Springfield, Virginia, 22151.

35 While some cities such as New York and Seattle use barges for transport of wastes, there appears to be little potential for expansion of this mode. Considerable attention has also focused on rail haul, although problems of transport through communities and of location of the sink community have limited its development.

36 U.S., Office of Solid Waste Management Programs, *Decision-Makers Guide in Solid Waste Management,* p. 79.

8 Urban transportation

Transportation is a vital service function in urban areas along with sewers, water supply, schools, and recreational facilities. The transportation system is the framework upon which the city is built. In the years preceding the automobile the range and speed of available transportation modes had a significant effect on urban form. The transit age produced dense, compact urban areas that still dominate the core of many cities. The advent of the automobile–freeway system (and, in some cities, of heavy rail rapid transit) provided urban travelers with an essentially unconstrained range, allowing growth to occur with fewer restrictions than before. Today, when other conditions have been fulfilled, transportation can be the key to another step in urbanization.

The purposes of transportation are to enable people to move among various sections of the city for many purposes, and to move goods. Although essential for the workings of a metropolitan area, transportation is a service, not an end in itself. A transportation system provides the means by which people can get to work, can shop, and can spend their leisure hours. Thus the system should support the collective mobility goals of the people in the area covered by the system.

Therefore, a transportation system must be a part of the urban plan. It should be designed to support the overall goals of the region, whether these goals are physical, social, or economic. Ideally, transportation planning should be part of the total planning process. Usually the metropolitan planning organization (MPO) assures that this is done, although often transportation planning is carried out as a separate activity within the overall planning process. The primary reason is that special funds are set up for these activities from the state and from the U.S. Department of Transportation.

For many years transportation planning focused on overall metropolitan issues, the extent of the transit system, the extent of the highway system, the location of airports, and the railroad system. Now that many of these large scale transportation facilities have been built in metropolitan areas, there is a growing public resistance to additional facilities. Transportation planning efforts therefore are now concentrating on managing the transportation system, particularly at the smaller community level. This has paralleled the desire of many people to be involved in the decision-making process, which is most effective at a "microscale" where the citizens can more readily understand the issues. Thus, the transportation planning process is now linked more with community planning than with metropolitan planning, although regional transportation planning must continue to provide the framework for studies of smaller areas.

This chapter, therefore, is aimed at discussing circulation at the community level—how the transportation system works and how it should fit in with the overall plan for a community. The chapter covers street systems, traffic engineering, land use trip generation, transit systems, parking, pedestrian systems, and the relationship between transportation and land development (including the role of various types of roads in land development), as well as the measurement of the social, economic, and environmental impacts of transportation improvements.

Street systems

Automobile travel in cities tends to be concentrated on certain streets. Generally, about 80 percent of the travel is concentrated on about 20 percent of the streets, and this ratio tends to carry over to rural highways as well.

City streets serve many purposes in addition to carrying automobiles and trucks. As many are aware, they also serve for a large volume of vehicle parking and, in recent years, for a significant amount of motorcycle and bicycle traffic. In addition to vehicle movement and storage, city streets both open up the city and link it together in functional and symbolic ways. Streets provide for location and right-of-way, both above ground and below ground, for major public utilities, including gas, liquid waste, electric power, and telephone lines. Streets provide much of the space and opportunity for public landscaping, monuments, malls, and public sculpture. Much of urban design is built on the street plan. Much of a city's history, character, and symbolic value is associated with its street layout, especially in a central area. Streets need to be planned and built for fire equipment, emergency vehicles, and police patrol cars as well as for cyclists, pedestrians, and parades.

The advent of classification

In the 1920s and 1930s, as highway programs developed, there were great political pressures to improve every rural road in the country. This was repugnant to the professionals who felt that priorities should be established on the basis of needs. To counteract this, the professionals devised road classifications and recommended that appropriate financing be established for each class. For example, the most important roads would be designated the trunk line system and thus would receive the bulk of the money. This would sharply reduce the money spent on lightly traveled local roads. Thus, in the 1930s the states started to develop a functional classification of roads—primary, secondary, local—each with its own special use and its own special funds. This proved very effective in getting the byroads built in rural America. The ultimate in this type of thinking was the development of the Interstate Highway System, which was designated a supersystem, to be built throughout the country with federal monies allocated to the states to build this system to a very high standard.

The classification concept was applied in two ways, one functional and the other administrative. The functional breakdown was related to how the facilities were used or how they would be used: in rural areas, primary and secondary routes, farm to market roads, etc.; in urban areas, arterial, collector, and local streets. Then design standards were often set up for each class by the federal government or the state, county, or city.

The administrative concept was related to the authority responsible—federal, state, county, or local. Then the financing of the road or street would reflect the varying responsibilities.

This classification approach received the support of the political leaders, and it proved to be an effective way of getting things done. It got the farmer out of the mud in the 1930s by building what was basically a country road system throughout rural America; it assured the development of a very advanced primary system administered by state highway departments. With the designation of the Interstate Highway System came the development of the finest national road network in the world.

However, when the Interstate System was originally conceived it was intended to link metropolitan areas—not to go into cities. Cities, however, decided that freeways built into the metropolitan areas would be an asset. To obtain the city support for the Interstate System, Interstate legs were designated to urban areas. The first phase of the Interstate System was concentrated in rural areas with the development of some urban sections. But with the development of additional urban Interstate links, resistance developed. There was a feeling that the Interstate System extensions were tearing cities apart, spreading them out, and making them less desirable places to live in. People were saying that the social and economic costs to the community were greater than the travel benefits. Because of this attitude, many freeway sections were halted or greatly slowed down.

This reaction pointed up some of the weaknesses of highway classification, particularly when accepted uncritically. It is dangerous in urban areas to designate a street in a given section and then to say that it should be operated or built to certain standards related to that class. In rural areas this is not as much of a problem, but in urban areas a multitude of social and economic factors must be considered in operating or designing a particular facility. In many cases a more appropriate solution may call for lower standards than the class norm—perhaps calling for lower operating speeds or arterial street design standards instead of freeway standards, to reflect the character of the area. In other words, some compromises or other adjustments may have to be made between objective highway standards and the immediate land use needs of those living contiguous to the street or highway or owning commercial property that has access to the street or highway.

There are limitations, then, to a street classification approach in urban areas. Still, if it is applied with caution, classification can be a useful technique for developing a good street system in built up areas.

Development of the classification plan

The first step in developing a street classification is to group all streets by present functions. This involves drawing on the experience of those with a working knowledge of the streets and of traffic patterns. As a start it is useful to look at the four classifications recommended by the National Committee on Urban Transportation, which are listed below.[1]

Expressway This class is devoted entirely to traffic movement with little or no land service function. Thus, it is characterized by at least some degree of access control. Except in rare instances, this classification should be reserved for multilane, divided roads with few, if any, intersections at grade. Expressways serve large volumes of light speed traffic and are primarily intended to serve long trips.

Arterial This class of streets brings traffic to and from the expressway and serves those major movements of traffic within or through the urban area that are not served by expressways. Arterials interconnect the principal traffic generators within the city as well as important rural routes. Arterials handle trips between different areas of the city and should form a reasonably integrated system. The length of the typical trip on the system should exceed one mile.

Collector This class of streets serves internal traffic movements within an area of the city, such as a subdivision, and connects this area with the arterial system. Collectors do not handle long through trips and are not, of necessity, continuous for any great length. In gridiron street patterns, however, a street of several miles in length may serve as a collector rather than an arterial if the predominant use is to reach the next junction with an arterial and there turn off.

Local The sole function of local streets is to provide access to adjacent land. These streets make up a large percentage of the total street mileage of the city but carry a small proportion of the vehicle miles of travel. In and around the central business district (CBD) local streets may carry traffic volumes measured in thousands, but this is the exception. Local residential streets in most cases carry daily volumes of 1,000 or less.

Criteria for establishing systems

A good classification plan calls for a network of streets that integrates commercial and industrial development, schools, parks, residential areas, and highways. In effect, it supports land use objectives and at the same time provides improved traffic circulation.

Some of the factors involved in designating streets for appropriate systems are the travel desires of automobile, truck, and transit users; the access needs of adjacent land development; the network pattern of existing streets; and existing and proposed land uses.

A street classification plan should reflect the location of traffic generators, the amount and location of through traffic movement, and the access needs of abutting property. In evaluating these factors, consideration must be given to present and future traffic requirements and land use plans of the area.

Information helpful in classifying streets into systems will be obtained from origin–destination data, traffic volume counts, street inventories, and parking studies. Other information, such as land use data and prospective commercial, industrial, and residential development, will indicate requirements for access.

The preservation of neighborhoods by diverting through traffic should also be a basic objective. Collection and distribution of local traffic within a neighborhood, as well as access to abutting property, should be provided by a collector street system which interconnects through traffic arteries with local access streets.

On the basis of past studies, the breakdown of street mileage in Table 8–1 is suggested as a starting point in establishing a street classification plan in a community. The percentages shown are typical of a classification plan that can be established on the basis of street patterns found in most cities. In planning new areas, different apportionments of system mileages might be found more suitable. Table 8–2 summarizes the recommended criteria for each class of street.

The quality of service that a street system provides depends on how well each street is performing in relation to its primary purposes and in relation to operational characteristics and design. The highest quality of service will be obtained when there is complete compatibility between these factors.

The purpose of the system reflects whether speed of movement or direct access to property is the main service requirement. Movement or access should be obtained with maximum safety. Accident rates are an index of safety and are one of the factors used to adjust operational controls and design features on each system. Table 8–3 outlines quality of service criteria for each class of street.

Street class

In new areas it is possible to design the street system to reflect more effectively the classification concept and the desired land use objectives of the community. In such areas it should be recognized that streets structure the neighborhood, form the entrance to each home and the front edge of most yards, provide the paths of communication between homes, and set the visual framework for the whole area. Therefore, their design should conform to and harmonize with structures and landscape.

The street system represents one of the three or four major public investments in a community. Obviously, it should be a good investment—a permanent, enduring asset to the community. Since the total investment is limited, any

Table 8–1 Suggested division of street system mileage.

Population of metropolitan area	% mileage in each system		
	Expressways[1]	Major arterial and collector streets	Local streets
Under 25,000	. . .	25–35	65–75
25,000–150,000	. . .	20–30	70–80
150,000–500,000	2–5	20–25	75–80
Over 500,000	5–8	20–25	75–80

Source: National Committee on Urban Transportation, *Criteria for Establishing Systems* (Chicago: Public Administration Service, 1958).

1 The percentage of expressway system mileage will vary from city to city depending on amount of through traffic, deficiencies in the street systems, topography, population density, and other factors.

Table 8–2 Summary of street system classification criteria.

Element	Expressway	Major arterial	Collector	Local
Service Function				
Movement	Primary	Primary	Equal	Secondary
Access	None	Secondary	Equal	Primary
Principal trip length	Over 3 miles	Over 1 mile	Under 1 mile	Under ½ mile
Use by transit	Express	Regular	Regular	None except CBD
Linkage				
Land uses	Major generators and CBD	Secondary generators and CBD	Local areas	Individual sites

Source: National Committee on Urban Transportation, *Criteria for Establishing Systems* (Chicago: Public Administration Service, 1958).

Table 8–3 Minimum desirable operating characteristics of existing streets.

Type of street	Overall speed		Accident rates per 100 million vehicle miles	
	Peak hour	Off-peak	Fatal	Injury[1]
Expressway	35	35–50	1.5–3.0	50–100
Major arterial	25	25–35	2.0–6.0	75–200
Collector	20	20–25	2.0–4.0	60–80
Local	10	10–20	0.0–1.0	1.0–20

Source: National Committee on Urban Transportation, *Standards for Street Facilities and Services* (Chicago: Public Administration Service, 1958).

1 Injury accidents include all fatal and nonfatal injuries.

economies which can be made are available for other facilities—parks, play-grounds, schools, and water and sanitary systems, for example.

With these thoughts in mind—efficiency, safety, appearance, and economy—a proposed street system should be developed to appropriate design standards. In new areas it is appropriate to have more street types than in older areas, perhaps as many as ten types of streets, each requiring special specifications in operation and development. Regardless of the types selected, streets can be grouped into three classes: traffic, service, and connector. These are described below.[2]

Traffic streets   This class consists of those streets predominantly carrying traffic: freeways, major arterials, and arterials.

Freeways   These are streets with complete control of access (i.e., no access from commercial or residential property). These streets generally carry over 40,000 trips per day.

Major arterials   These streets have very little facing commercial or residential property; they should be served from side streets. These streets carry 25,000 to 40,000 trips per day.

Arterials   These streets will have facing commercial development. Residential property generally does not have direct access but is served from side streets. Arterials generally carry traffic in the 10,000 to 25,000 trip range.

Service streets   This class of street carries traffic and serves adjacent land use; it consists of major collectors, minor collectors, loop streets, and culs-de-sac.

Major collectors   These streets serve more than 150 dwelling units.

Minor collectors   These are streets that serve less than 150 dwelling units.

Loop streets   These are streets without outlets connecting single streets or adjoining streets, any portion of which does not serve more than 25 dwelling units.

The cul-de-sac   This type of street provides outlet at one end only, with special provision for a turnaround, and serves less than 25 dwelling units.

Connectors   This class of street does not serve adjacent land uses but does connect land development with traffic streets; it consists of major connectors, minor connectors, and parking connectors.

Major connectors   These streets do not serve adjoining land development, but the traffic using them is generated by more than 150 dwelling units.

Minor connectors   These streets do not have any adjacent land development and serve less than 150 dwelling units.

Parking connectors   These streets do not have any adjacent land development but they provide direct access to a parking area.

Street specifications

The streets described here have been divided into categories according to the amount of traffic they will carry—the lowest class being streets serving 25 dwelling units or less. On such streets it has been shown that the chances of meeting another car where two cars are parked opposite each other will occur only about once a month for an average driver. This would indicate that on such streets two parking lanes and one moving lane should be sufficient (see Table 8–4).

However, when a street serves more than 25 dwelling units, two moving lanes should be provided. When the traffic is generated by between 25 and 150 dwelling units (250 to 1,500 trips per day), the probability of traffic meeting is slight and two 10 foot lanes will suffice. Where the volumes are over 1,500, the chances of traffic meeting are much greater, and the design characteristics of the street should be improved to provide for better operational conditions. In these cases, two 12 foot lanes are recommended.

As traffic builds up in urban areas two major changes occur. One is that the amount of commercial development along the street increases. From an examination of commercial development examples it would appear that commercial property usually develops on streets carrying 10,000 vehicles or more per day. Commercial development on streets with lighter volumes tends to occur when those streets intersect with streets having larger volumes.

Table 8–4 Functional requirements of streets.

Classification	Moving lane width[1]	Parking lane width[1]	Total street width	Design speed
Freeway	4–8 @ 12	2 @ 12[2]	112–160	60
Major arterial	4–6 @ 12	2 @ 12[3]	92–116	50
Arterial	4 @ 12	2 @ 10	68	40
Major collector	2 @ 12	2 @ 8	40[4]	35
Minor collector	2 @ 10	2 @ 8	36[4]	30
Loop	1 @ 10	2 @ 8	26	25
Cul-de-sac	1 @ 10	2 @ 8	26	25
Major connector	2 @ 12	. . .	24	35
Minor connector	2 @ 10	. . .	20	30
Parking connector	2 @ 10	. . .	20	25

Source: Alan M. Voorhees & Associates, Inc., *Principles and Standards for Street Development in Broward County* (McLean, Va.: Alan M. Voorhees & Associates, Inc., 1966).
1 Shows number of lanes required and the width of each lane in feet.
2 Emergency parking only, plus a 40 foot median.
3 Plus a 20 foot median.
4 Eight feet less if parking is required on only one side.

Secondly, as traffic volume increases, noise on the streets increases as well. The noise on streets carrying 10,000 vehicles per day is around 65 decibels; as commercial traffic builds up this level rises to 80 decibels or more. Generally, from a residential point of view, 70 decibels is considered the maximum tolerable level.

Therefore, attempts should be made to discourage residential property directly adjacent to streets carrying or expected to carry 10,000 vehicles per day. Property on these streets should be set back 100 feet. Certainly such setbacks should be mandatory when the volume reaches 25,000 trips a day.

As the traffic volume approaches or is predicted to approach 25,000 trips per day, more and more access controls should be applied. Most of the access should be prohibited on streets over this volume except where the traffic conditions will be improved by directing traffic away from the nearest intersection to access points a block or more away.

The functional requirements of the classes of streets listed earlier are summarized in the following paragraphs.

Freeways   Since these streets will be serving over 40,000 trips a day, they should be built to freeway design standards. Careful attention should be given to all the details related to their design and the surrounding land. These streets should have 12 foot moving lanes, 40 foot medians should be encouraged, and design speeds of 60 miles per hour (mph) should be provided.

Major arterials   Since the volumes on these streets will be between 25,000 and 40,000 trips a day, there should be at least four moving lanes of 12 feet, two breakdown lanes of 12 feet, and a divider of 20 feet. The design speed should be 50 mph. Access should be controlled very carefully. Residential development should be served from side streets, and a detailed traffic analysis should be made to determine how best to serve the commercial property—whether from service roads, special entrances, or side streets.

Arterials   Since these streets will be carrying from 10,000 to 25,000 vehicles per day, they should have four moving lanes of 12 feet and two storage lanes for breakdowns. The design speed should be around 40 mph. Residential development should be discouraged from abutting on these streets; commercial property can have direct access.

Major collectors   Since this type of street will be serving over 1,500 vehicles per day, there should be two moving lanes of 12 feet each in addition to the parking lanes. Normally, this would mean a total street width of 40 feet. However, if the development adjoining such a street requires parking on only one side, one 8 foot parking lane is all that is required, in which case a 32 foot street will be adequate. A design speed of 35 mph will be sufficient.

Minor collectors   There are local streets which serve adjoining property but do not serve more than 150 dwelling units. This means that such streets should not have more than 1,500 trips per day. Two moving lanes should be sufficient, and parking lanes should be provided. The moving lanes should be 10 feet in width and the parking lanes 8 feet, which will call for a 36 foot street. However, if the street is located in relation to development requiring only one side of the street for parking, then only one parking lane will be needed, allowing the street to be only 28 feet wide. Design speeds of 30 mph should be provided.

Loop streets and culs-de-sac   These are short streets which serve abutting property. Since no portion of the street serves more than 25 dwelling units, its traffic volume will be low—up to 250 trips per day. Since a driver will seldom have to stop to allow a car to pass, a 10 foot moving lane should be adequate if two 8 foot parking lanes are provided. In apartment house areas two moving lanes should be provided. The need or desire for speed will certainly be limited; therefore, a design speed of 25 mph should be adequate.

Major connectors   These streets will not serve adequate land use but will serve more than 150 dwelling units. This means that traffic will be heavier and there will be more frequent meeting of vehicles; thus, a wider land width will be required. The moving lane width should be 12 feet. Thus, a 24 foot street will be adequate since no parking lanes are required. Design speeds on such a street would be higher to assure maximum safety. A speed of 35 mph is recommended.

Minor connectors   Since these are local streets which do not serve adjoining development, parking lanes will not be required; only two moving lanes will be necessary. Since 150 dwelling units will generate only about 1,500 trips per day, 10 foot moving lanes should be adequate, or a total width of 20 feet. Design speeds should be 30 mph.

Parking connectors This class of street is likely to be very short, but it should provide ample room for two vehicles to meet and pass each other. This can be accomplished with two 10 foot lanes. Design speeds of 25 mph should be provided.

It is suggested that every traffic street section built be designed especially to fit in with the land uses that it accommodates. The design principles and standards that have been set forth take into consideration not only the traffic and economic factors but also the impact that such streets will have on the residential development. The use of streets solely to move traffic, such as parking connectors and minor and major connectors, reduces cost and tends to enhance residential development. This use removes traffic from residential development, thereby increasing safety and enhancing the amenities of the residential area.

The use of streets primarily for serving residential development permits designing a street solely for this purpose. In essence, this provides for greater efficiency as well as more amenities.

Traffic engineering and system management

During the late 1950s and early 1960s, transportation planning was dominated by the now traditional "3–C" comprehensive, coordinated, and continuing transportation planning process. This process starts with an inventory of travel and existing system conditions. This is followed by the selection and calibration of models for trip generation, trip distribution, modal split, and network assignment. The results of this process are used to test alternative regional networks and evaluate alternative facilities, producing capital programs for expansion of the highway and rapid transit system.

This familiar process is still of great value in the younger, still developing urban areas. It is also being extensively applied in corridor studies, and many of its methodologies have been adapted to the newer and parallel "transportation system management" process.

Transportation system management (TSM) recognizes that investment in highway and rapid transit systems is nearly complete in many of our urban areas and that the expansion of these systems is limited by financial resources and the adverse community reactions generated in recent years. TSM is a new process, focusing on "service-oriented" actions. TSM attempts to achieve the same community goals as the capital-oriented 3–C process, but TSM attempts to reach these goals by extracting more efficiency and effectiveness from existing highway and transit systems.

TSM can be contrasted to the 3–C process in the following ways:

1. It provides many alternatives (versus a few)
2. It provides alternatives of differing character (versus similar alternatives)
3. It provides alternatives designed to modify demand (versus use of a relatively fixed demand level)
4. It provides for implementation by both public and private sectors (versus public investment only)
5. It provides consideration of all travel modes (versus a single mode orientation).

TSM usually involves lower capital costs and shorter lines, but this is not necessarily so. For example, the acquisition of new buses can represent a substantial capital investment and yet be classified as a TSM action. Some TSM actions, such as carpooling programs, will have long and productive life cycles.

TSM is also feedback-oriented, as contrasted to the prediction orientation in the 3–C process. Experience may prove that the monitoring of system performance will be the single most important characteristic of the new process.

While the more traditional transportation planning activities have been assigned to the metropolitan planning organizations (MPOs) (and were a principal reason for the initial organization of many MPOs), the TSM process makes the local government agency at least an equal partner in the process with the MPO, and many times the dominant agency. While the MPO has an important role to play in the analysis of interjurisdictional and multimodal TSM actions, the greater share of planning and implementing of TSM actions is likely to lie with such agencies as cities, counties, and transit agencies. It is at this local level that the traffic engineer and the transit operator come into the mainstream of planning and management. The traffic engineer is no longer exclusively concerned with the improvement of highway capacity and safety but now must give consideration to action packages that simultaneously decrease travel demands while increasing system capacity. As the traffic engineer functions in this broadened environment, he or she will be giving increasing attention to impacts on the social and physical environments. As participants in the TSM process, the traffic engineer and the transit operator have an opportunity to generate proposed TSM actions, to participate in the joint review and classification of these actions, to assess possible action effects, and to take an active part in the joint selection of actions and development of implementation programs. A major role for the traffic engineer and the transit operator lies in the implementation of TSM action and the subsequent monitoring and adjustment of actions to achieve the final increments of system efficiency.

In areas of the city where new growth is taking place, application of sound design principles for new street systems (as discussed earlier in this chapter) will basically meet social, economic, and physical environmental goals. In this case, the function of the traffic engineer lies in monitoring performance, adding traffic control devices as demand grows on new streets, and making adjustments in original designs when events vary from predictions.

It is in the older areas of the cities that TSM is likely to be concentrated. Here, the traffic engineer will be applying his or her skills to preserve street capacity, ensure smooth traffic flow, and increase safety. The traffic engineer will also be aiding transit by providing priorities of movement through the street system. He or she will be encouraging carpooling through promotion and rider-matching programs, and will be attempting to reduce vehicle demand through work rescheduling and, in severe cases, pricing disincentives.

Figure 8–1 lists potential TSM actions by goal class. Transportation system management will be guided by the same community goals that guided the more capital-intensive improvements. In Figure 8–1 these goals have been aggregated into two simple concepts of increasing mobility and enhancing conservation—the latter through reduction of air pollutant emissions and reduction of energy requirements. On these lists actions such as ride-sharing promotion and signal improvements are likely to be the more cost-effective. In contrast, improvements in local transit and "take-a-lane" high occupancy vehicle (HOV) preferential facilities will have a high cost per unit of effectiveness gained.

Not all of this long list of TSM candidate actions will be universally applicable. Figure 8–1 also contains an abridged list of actions that might be more suitable for implementation in cities that are among the newer, smaller, and less congested ones. Shorter trip lengths in these cities might, for example, make park–ride with express transit impractical. Transit improvements will be most effective where a healthy transit riding habit already exists, and this is not usually the case in these younger urban areas. The effectiveness of truck restrictions and enhancements, as well as work rescheduling, will depend on particular situations.

Any process striving to achieve maximum use of existing streets will require selection and application of measures of effectiveness. Measures of effectiveness (MOEs) can be used to describe existing system performance and to provide the format and units for standards and criteria, prediction-of-action impact,

Mobility dominant goal	Conservation dominant goal
Larger cities	
"Add-a-lane" preferential facilities for high occupancy vehicles (HOV)	"Add-a-lane" preferential facilities for high occupancy vehicles (HOV)
Preferential parking for HOV	Preferential parking for HOV
Ride-sharing promotion	Ride-sharing promotion
Improvements in local bus fares, routes, and schedules	Improvements in local bus fares, routes, and schedules
Park–ride with express bus	Park–ride with express bus
Express bus operations	Express bus operations
Bicycle paths	Bicycle paths
Signal improvements	Ramp metering with HOV bypass
Pedestrian separations	Automobile restricted zones with HOV preference
One way streets	Exclusive HOV ramps
Reversible streets	Through traffic restrictions with HOV preference
Turn restrictions	"Take-a-lane" HOV preferential facilities
Ramp metering	Parking duration limit with HOV preference
Channelization and widening	Facility and area tolls and taxes with HOV preference
Curb parking restrictions	Parking duration pricing with HOV preference
Bus stop relocation	
Loading zones	
Speed limits	
Truck enhancements, controls	
Work rescheduling	
Motorists' aids, advisories	
Smaller, less congested cities	
Ride-sharing promotion	Ride-sharing promotion
Improvements in local bus fares, routes, and schedules	Improvements in local bus fares, routes, and schedules
Bicycle paths	Bicycle paths
Signal improvements	
Pedestrian separations	
One way streets	
Turn restrictions	
Right turn on red	
Channelization and widening	
Curb parking restrictions	
Bus stop relocation	
Loading zones	
Speed limits	

Figure 8–1 TSM actions by goals category.

and before-and-after studies. For example, accident rate (accidents per million vehicle miles) has been suggested as an MOE for safety. The accident rate MOE can be used to identify problems; it also allows a before-and-after assessment of the results of implementing TSM actions to enhance safety.

For a simple, bottom line figure, other MOEs could include vehicle miles of travel, vehicle hours of travel, and vehicle occupancy. For more elaborate and specific measurements, more specialized MOEs can be developed and applied.

Land use trip generation[3]

Although TSM has surfaced in response to a shift away from urban growth and toward urban enhancement, new development will continue to occur. One of the more important functions of the traffic engineer and the transportation planner still will be the analysis of new and changing land uses, and this usually involves the application of land use trip generation planning.

Numerous transportation studies have shown that trip generation characteristics are similar for comparable types of land use. This type of data makes it possible to estimate future traffic volumes on various transportation facilities and thus provides a means to evaluate alternative solutions and thereby plan transportation systems effectively.

The trip generation characteristics for various types of land use are set forth in Tables 8–5 to 8–9, in which the land uses are divided into four principal categories: residential, commercial, industrial, and public and semipublic uses. In addition, each category is subdivided into several density classes having comparable trip generation characteristics. These tables also use a common base of acreage, by which all land uses can be compared, and a specific base for each land use that more accurately reflects trip generation for that land use in terms of daily vehicle trips to or from the area.

Residential trip generation

In low density residential development (less than one dwelling unit per acre) traffic generation may be as low as 5 daily vehicle trips per acre. High density residential development, such as high rise apartment housing, may sustain as many as 400 daily trips per acre. Traffic generation varies directly with the number of persons living within the particular unit of area; the number of vehicle trips per person tends to remain fairly constant. Since the number of persons per dwelling unit often decreases in higher density housing, the number of vehicle trips per dwelling unit tends to decrease with higher densities. Table 8–5 shows these variations. Three separate residential density categories are used in the trip generation tables, indicating typical rates in vehicle trips per acre and in vehicle trips per dwelling unit. Although there are variations in traffic generation with family income, car ownership, family composition, etc., the rates illustrated are for average suburban communities.

Peak hour trip generation has the greatest effect on the highway system. The peak hour rate is approximately 10 percent of the average daily volume, with the evening peak substantially higher than the morning peak. Typical studies of single family residential areas have found average weekday peak hour generation to be as shown in Table 8–10. Directional splits vary considerably between areas; in some cases, the directional proportions are more unbalanced.

Commercial trip generation

Commercial land exhibits a high intensity of trip generation (Tables 8–6 and 8–7). Trip generation rates range widely, especially when expressed in terms of acreage. A more meaningful measure is in terms of floor area and type of usage.

The commercial classification has two principal subclassifications: retail (Table 8–6) and office (Table 8–7). Retail development is divided into five subclassifications. Trip generation rates are indicated in vehicle trips per acre for purposes of comparison with other land uses, and in vehicle trips per thousand square feet of floor area. The density measure for office buildings is the ratio of floor area to land area. The density of development of office buildings is divided into five classifications.

Peak periods are especially critical in commercial areas. There are three possible peak periods. These generally run from 8 to 10 percent of the daily traffic. The entering peak period occurs most frequently in the early afternoon or early evening. The peak traffic hours, occurring generally between 4:00 P.M. and 6:00 P.M., combine entering and leaving traffic with peak travel for home-

Table 8–5 Trip generation characteristics by residential land use.

Land use	Density by dwelling units per acre	Daily traffic generation rate			
		Vehicle trip-ends per acre		Vehicle trip-ends per dwelling unit	
		Range	Typical	Range	Typical
Low density (single family homes)	1–5	5–65	40	7–12	9
Medium density (patio houses, duplexes, town houses)	5–15	40–150	75	5–8	7
High density (apartments)	15–60	85–400	180	3–7	5

Source: Harold Marks, *Traffic Circulation Planning for Communities* (Los Angeles: Gruen Associates, 1974).

Table 8–6 Trip generation characteristics by commercial–retail land use.

Land use	Density by site	Daily traffic generation rate			
		Vehicle trip-ends per acre		Vehicle trip-ends per 1,000 sq. ft. floor area	
		Range	Typical	Range	Typical
Neighborhood retail (supermarket)	10 acres	800–1,400	1,000	70–240	130
Community retail (junior department store)	10–30 acres	700–1,000	900	60–140	80
Regional retail (regional shopping center)	30 acres	400–700	600	30–50	40
Central area retail	High density	600–1,300	900	10–50	40
Highway-oriented commercial (motels, service stations)	Low density	100–300	240	4–12	10

Source: See Table 8–5.

bound employees. The leaving peak occurs at store closing time. Each of these three peaks may control the design of individual elements of the circulation system adjoining a shopping center. The peak period for office buildings is in the morning or evening and generally runs about 20 percent of the daily traffic.

Industrial trip generation

Industrial trip generation can best be correlated with employment. Floor space sometimes reflects the number of workers, but it is not consistent since it varies with the type of industrial use. Industrial development has been divided into five subclassifications in Table 8–8, using the principal density measure of employees per acre. Traffic generation rates are indicated in vehicle trips per acre and in vehicle trips per thousand square feet of floor area.

Industrial traffic, because of the shortness and sharpness of its peak periods and its very high directional orientation, frequently constitutes a much more serious problem to the adjoining highway than does traffic from other land uses. Industrial traffic peaks are related to the working hours, but generally 80 percent of all the inbound traffic will be during the morning peak. The same ratio generally holds true for the evening peak.

Public and semipublic trip generation

This category covers a wide variety of facilities with no common density measures. Density components include area of land used and the number of persons affected. Trip generation rates in Table 8–9 are indicated in daily vehicle trips per acre and in other base measurements that most accurately characterize the land use.

Mass transit

While grade separated rapid transit continues to attract attention, buses operating on surface streets and freeways are the backbone of urban transit. As with other elements of the transportation system, goals, objectives, and priorities are the starting point for planning new or improved mass transit services. Transit today often acts in an environment of conflicting policies. Improvements in transit service are often paralleled by improvements in the street and parking systems; these often negate any potential that transit might have for relieving congestion and improving the environment. An analysis of priorities will at least identify this type of situation and allow choices between transit and highway improvements to be made on a rational basis.

Nearly all mass transit services today are conventional, fixed route, fixed schedule bus operations, often augmented by express service. Long favorable experience has shown that transit must furnish service with cost and speed characteristics that can be traded off against highway costs and speeds in order to attract riders from automobile to bus. The difficulties of achieving such a situation have left transit in the position of serving mostly social goals (instead of mobility goals), such as providing for nonauto-transportation owners, the elderly, the young, the poor, and the handicapped.

Bus service planning

A good starting point for planning transit is to survey the coverage provided by the system. This coverage can be expressed as the percent of population covered, the percent of elderly, the percent of poor, or the percent of other market groups. Since the maximum acceptable walking distance to a bus stop is about a quarter of a mile, a half mile band centered on the transit route establishes the coverage. In the mid-1970s the coverage for transit systems in the United States ranged from 50 to 100 percent of the population.

The hours and days when service is provided are another key characteristic. Except for the larger cities, few jurisdictions have service before 6:00 A.M. or after 8:00 P.M. Service cutbacks of 50 percent or more are made on Saturdays, and often Sunday service is not offered at all.

The frequency of transit service is usually a policy decision. A common starting point is thirty minutes between buses during peak periods and sixty minutes for the middle of the day and the evening. In some large systems, where heavy peak passenger loads are encountered, the frequency for bus service is determined by limiting the number of passengers per bus. During peak periods the number of buses serving routes is adjusted so that the number of standees plus seated riders never exceeds a certain ratio of the number of seats. This ratio, called the *load factor,* can vary from 1.0 (no standees) to 1.5 (one-third of the passengers are standees).

Table 8–7 Trip generation characteristics by commercial–office land use.

| Land use | Density by floor area ratio | Daily traffic generation rate | | | |
| | | Vehicle trip-ends per acre | | Vehicle trip-ends per 1,000 sq. ft. floor area | |
		Range	Typical	Range	Typical
Single story bldg. with surface parking	0.5:1	120– 1,200	300	6–60	14
2 story bldg. with surface parking	1:1	240– 2,400	600	6–60	14
3 to 4 story bldg. with deck parking	2:1	360– 6,000	1,200	6–60	14
3 to 6 story bldg. with structure parking	5:1	1,200–12,000	2,600	6–60	14
High rise office bldg. with structure parking, over 10 stories	10:1	2,400–20,000	. . .	6–60	14

Source: See Table 8–5.

Table 8–8 Trip generation characteristics by industrial land use.

| Land use | Density by employees per acre | Daily traffic generation rate | | | |
| | | Vehicle trip-ends per acre | | Vehicle trip-ends per 1,000 sq. ft. floor area | |
		Range	Typical	Range	Typical
Highly automated industry, low employee density (refinery, warehouse)	5	2– 8	4	0.2–1.0	0.6
Light service industry, single lot industry (lumberyard)	5– 20	6– 30	16	0.4–1.2	0.8
Industrial tract (5 acres) (machinery factory)	20–100	30–160	70	0.6–4.0	2.0
Office, campus; research and development (research industry)	100	150–200	170	3–8	4
Mixed central area industry, small industrial plants	varies	10–100	. . .	1–4	. . .

Source: See Table 8–5.

Table 8-9
Trip generation characteristics by public and semipublic land use.

| Land use | Density measure | Daily traffic generation rate | | | |
| | | Vehicle trip-ends per acre | | Vehicle trip-ends | |
		Range	Typical	Range	Typical
Schools and colleges	No. of students	Colleges: 7–600	60	0.4–1.0[1] Veh. trip-ends/ student	0.8[1]
Places of public assembly (theater, stadium, convention center)	No. in attendance			Stadia[2] 2-veh. trip-ends/ 4 seats	
Administration facilities (city hall, state offices, post offices)	Floor area ratio	70–600	200	10–60[3] Veh. trip-ends/ 1000 sq. ft. floor area	20[3]
Recreation facilities (park, zoo, beach, golf course)		Parks: 1–10	4	Golf Course: 2–10[4] Veh. trip-ends/acre	8[4]
Terminals (bus terminal, airport)	No. of con- veyances	3–30	15	Local Airport: 6–12[5] Veh. trip-ends/ based aircraft	8[5]
Hospitals	No. of beds	16–70	40	6–16[6] person trip-ends/ bed	10[6]

Source: See Table 8-5.
1 Trip-ends per student.
2 Four seats per 2 vehicle trip-ends.
3 Trip-ends per 1,000 square feet of floor area.
4 Trip-ends per acre.
5 Trip-ends per based aircraft.
6 Person trip-ends per bed.

Various sizes of buses are available with capacities ranging from twenty to fifty-two seats. Most domestic manufacturing expertise has gone into the larger buses so that these have often proved to be the more reliable and are therefore more attractive to many operators.

Other characteristics of transit service to be considered in bus service planning include the percentage of transfers in the system (averaging 20 percent, but with a wide range), the peak-to-base ratio (varying from 1 to 4 peak buses for each midday bus, with a mean of 1.8), and the location and frequency of stops. In the more formal systems stops are often located at quarter mile intervals and are provided with signs and sometimes with schedule information and benches. In some smaller systems the actual location of stopping is often left to the discretion of the bus driver, thereby providing a more tailored service for bus riders.

Fares are another central issue. In the mid-1970s fares averaged twenty-five cents but were increasing rapidly. There are variable methods of payment including single flat fares, tokens, passes, and zone fare schemes.

Bus transit is not a rapid mode; the average speed is between 13 and 14 mph.

Nearly all transit is now under public ownership, with bus systems owned and operated by cities, counties, or special districts. Sometimes actual operation is contracted to private management groups although ownership and subsidization remain public.

The costs of providing transit service are critical and have been rising in the 1970s. The cost of a full-size bus in the mid-1970s was $80,000 to $100,000. Capital investment is also required for bus storage facilities, garages and repair bays, shops, parts storage facilities, washing and cleaning facilities, offices, and employee and driver facilities. Operating costs must cover drivers' wages, fuel and oil, equipment maintenance, repair costs, tires, scheduling and inspection, marketing, insurance and claims, fringe benefits, and taxes and licenses.

Federal, state, and local assistance have formed a larger part of transit budgets in recent years, with subsidy rates ranging from 20 to 80 percent of annual budgets. In other words, practical policy decisions have held down fare increases in the face of increasing service demands and rising unit costs. Transit financing remains one of the most critical urban transportation issues, since deficits must be met with federal and state funds plus such local funds as general funds, sales or payroll taxes, gasoline taxes, property taxes, or utility taxes.

The planning of a bus transit line starts with the measuring of the desired route. The probable average operating speed (probably 13 to 14 mph) can then be used to establish the round trip time. Then, using the policy service frequency, the number of buses can be determined along with the vehicle miles and vehicle hours of travel. Service costs can be estimated from the operating data and revenue from patronage estimates. A variety of methods can be used to estimate passengers; these methods range from application of "passengers per vehicle mile" rates to elaborate, computerized mode-use models.

Most transit systems are radial in nature and are centered on central business districts. This is the result of a self-fulfilling historical trend in which transit follows areas of higher population densities and lower automobile ownership. Crosstown services have been successful only in rare cases. Buses are commonly operated along one spoke of the radial system—from or through downtown and out to the end of another spoke. The selection of which radial routes to link in this manner depends on the through passenger volume.

Table 8-10　Peak hour traffic and trip generation

Time	% of daily traffic		Vehicle trips per dwelling unit		% of Directional split	
	Range	Mean	Range	Mean	Outbound	Inbound
A.M. peak	5–15	8	0.5–1.4	0.8	75	25
P.M. peak	8–19	12	0.8–1.8	1.1	40	60

Source: See Table 8-5.

Transit ridership followed a steep decline after World War II, a decline that was really a continuation of a downward trend which began in the 1930s. In recent years large federal capital investments in transit have occurred within the same time as a flattening of the demand trend. Considerable increases in ridership have been experienced by some systems. In a study of seven bus systems that achieved a high percentage of gains in riders, the following factors were found significant:

1. Strong public and political support for transit
2. Stable financial resources
3. A large service expansion, especially into areas previously not served or poorly served
4. Readily available transit information.[4]

Fares in these systems are either constant or reduced, but this was not considered a significant factor.

Minibus and Dial-A-Ride systems

Recent development in mass transit has been in two directions. One direction is toward high capacity, corridor mass transit using heavy rail, light rail, or bus transit. The other direction is toward "paratransit," which includes pooling (car, van, and buspooling) and use of common carriers such as jitneys and demand-responsive bus operations. Demand-responsive service, often called Dial-A-Ride, calls for abandonment of all or part of the fixed route, fixed schedule operation. In one version of Dial-A-Ride, called *deviation*, vehicles depart from their specified routes to provide door-to-door pickup and delivery of passengers in response to telephone requests. Full demand-responsive service provides door-to-door service in specific areas with no routes and no schedules. Service is requested from a central dispatch facility and the user is customarily told what the expected wait will be (this may be a half hour or more).

Full demand-responsive services have been characterized as "many-to-many" and "many-to-one." The first generally allows for a trip between any two points in a service area, and the latter is a collector type of service with connections to popular destinations such as a shopping center, an arterial bus route, or a rapid transit station. The latter has usually evolved into a regular peak hour, door-to-door pickup and delivery for commuter work trips.

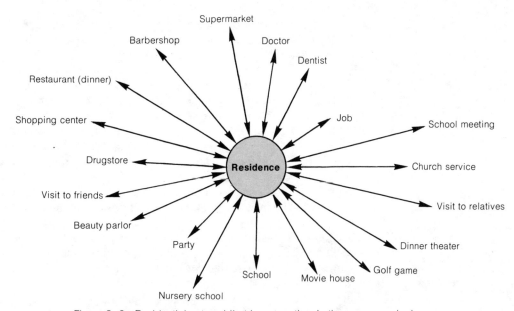

Figure 8-2   Residential automobile trip generation. In the average suburban community, traffic generation may be as low as five vehicle trips per day per acre in low density residential areas. A datum such as this, however, does not show, from the resident's point of view, how important these trips are.

Dial-A-Ride is considered most suitable for low density areas and for service to the elderly and handicapped. Service areas have varied from three to ten square miles in size, with populations of from 13,000 to 44,000. Fleet size has varied from one to twenty. The use of small buses has generally enabled demand-responsive service to operate at a cost per vehicle mile equal to or less than that of regularly scheduled services. However, the very low vehicle occupancy rate found in this type of service has pushed the cost per passenger to levels three times that of more traditional types of mass transit.

Among other paratransit modes, carpools, vanpools, and buspools have proved effective and appear to have a large potential for use in urban areas. Another form of paratransit, as mentioned above, is the jitney. Jitneys are usually cars or vans operating on a fixed route but with a flexible schedule. Scheduling is usually not an important consideration since service frequency is generally very high. The potential for jitney use is largely unexplored in the United States, but jitneys have been successful in Latin America.

Station planning and design

When grade-separated rapid transit exists in a community, an important local government planning function is minimizing the impact of rapid transit stations and integrating these stations into the community fabric. The planning process for the rapid transit line will furnish information on alignment, station location, and access volumes by mode. Station planning should then take into consideration land availability, topography, rights-of-way, and adjacent land uses. The most significant factor will be the access network, including facilities for pedestrians, bicycles, surface buses, and automobiles.

Station design principles will require that access priority be given in the following order: pedestrians; bicycles; buses; taxis; kiss–rides; park–rides.[5]

Station design should provide adequate capacity for these modes, should separate the modes (especially pedestrians), and should minimize access travel distances. Direct access paths should be provided to the greatest extent possible. When possible, more than one choice of access path should be provided (particularly for automobiles) so that the arriving passenger has a second choice in case he or she misses the first.

A key factor in providing access for buses will be the amount of curb space for loading and unloading. A sawtooth type design will allow buses to stop, load and unload, and bypass other stopped buses on the way out. Each berth in the bus loading and unloading area will probably accommodate eight to ten buses an hour.[6] Where the volume is very high, buses from one route can be required to use the same berth each time and those stops can be designated by route to organize pedestrian flow.

Automobile access and egress should be to an arterial. Adding the fourth leg to an existing T intersection is a handy device, but new intersections with signals should not be closer to adjacent signals than the intersection spacing already encountered in that area.

The movement into the station is probably the more critical for the auto volumes and should be planned around the peak five or ten minutes to avoid queueing on the streets.

In addition to the effects of traffic, station design should consider the impacts of such factors as air pollution, noise, vibration, and visual intrusion. Although these impacts must be assessed with existing land uses in mind, a more significant factor will probably the land use changes created by the location of the station. Experience in Toronto has shown that subway stations have little impact in blighted areas, since rapid transit cannot markedly affect market trends already in operation. On the other hand, when market factors are favorable, major commercial development can be expected at stations served by major arterials with large tributary areas. Apartments often develop within sight of stations. Strong commercial gains can also be expected at the rapid transit terminal if economics provide a basic impetus.

Parking

Parking is an integral part of the overall traffic problem. A fundamental factor to consider in examining the perennial parking shortage is trip purpose. Studies conducted in the early 1950s by the U.S. Bureau of Public Roads and the state highway departments serving seventeen cities provided interesting corroboration for a condition probably existing in many other cities in the late 1970s.[7]

The studies showed that although the magnitude of the parking problem varied generally with city size, the percentage of work and business trips was constant and was 50 to 60 percent of all trips. On the other hand, shopping trips decreased proportionately by city size, even though there was little variation in the absolute number of trips. Other trips (doctor, dentist, theater, etc.) increased sharply in number and percent as city size increased. However, the

Figure 8–3 A major shopping street on Chicago's South Side in 1925 is seen above; the stores in this strip commercial district were served not only by the last of the horses and wagons and the early automobiles, but, most important of all, by the elevated rapid transit. This may be contrasted with the acres of free car parking provided at Woodfield Mall, northwest of Chicago, seen below.

most important findings were the combined demands in peak and off-peak hours for space for those who worked in the central business district and those who had business to transact there. These are the all-day and long-term parkers who tie up the space the shoppers are looking for—at least that is the way the argument goes until data are compiled for planning recommendations and policy decisions.

In the development of any effective parking program it is of paramount importance that due consideration be given to these other types of trips, particularly the work trip, for if the worker's parking needs are neglected the program will not be successful. A good example was seen in Allentown, Pennsylvania, where the merchants had developed a cooperative parking program called Park and Shop. Through this program they obtained a series of lots near their stores in an excellent position for the shopper. As soon as these lots were opened it was discovered that the all-day parkers were using them. With the help of the city, the merchants then established a series of outlying lots for the sole purpose of providing space for the workers. This space was provided at a very low rate. Consequently, the Park and Shop lots became available for their original purpose. The plan had the additional advantage of keeping the all-day worker away from the main shopping streets and thereby reducing traffic congestion.

Because parking on the street affects the traffic capacity of the street system, most cities tend to limit parking during the peak hours on key traffic arteries. During off-peak hours parking is allowed on most streets under certain time restrictions, basically in line with the needs of the area. Certain streets have short-term needs; in such cases, parking regulations should be aimed at providing rapid turnover. It is not uncommon near banks and post offices to have ten or fifteen minute meters. In areas with more convenience goods shopping or numerous trips for service purposes (as with laundries and dry cleaners), half hour parking is quite adequate. However, in areas where there is more selective shopping, one hour or two hour parking is often allowed. Parking should be related to the needs of the area to assure that people who visit the area for a given purpose can find a space suitable to their needs.

Parking programs should, of course, be tied in with the availability of off-street parking. Where this is available and the charges are appropriate for the use of the area, street parking regulations can be established. Certainly, transit availability must be considered in these analyses. Bus routes and transit stops should be evaluated. Such stops should reflect the general pedestrian pattern and the accessibility of key traffic generators in the downtown area.

A wide variety of means have been employed to fund parking facilities,[8] including benefit districts or assessments, city improvement programs, general revenues, and revenue bonds. More and more, however, cities are turning the financial aspects of parking programs over to the private sector.

Some larger cities are deliberately discouraging parking in the downtown area. The subsidizing of parking in the downtown area tends to encourage greater automobile use in the area. Some cities now levy parking taxes in the downtown area. Since parking costs are a critical factor in affecting the mode of travel that people use to the downtown area, it is not surprising to find areas that are using parking policies to induce greater transit usage.

Singapore has adopted what is generally referred to as *road pricing,* in which a permit is needed to bring a car into the downtown area at a given period of the day. Motorists must pay a high fee for this permit. This policy has had a significant impact on the downtown area: it has cleared the streets of traffic and has forced greater transit usage. However, this idea would not win approval in the United States, where many would consider it to be discriminating against those who could not afford the price. In the United States, parking fees in larger cities are largely dictated by the marketplace and few cities wish to tamper with them.

Pedestrian systems

Considerable attention is being given to pedestrian systems either in the downtown area or in other concentrated areas in a few large cities. In many cases it has been felt that a mall was the answer for the downtown area because it tended to create a pleasant environment for walking in the area. It has become quite clear from experiments in the United States and elsewhere that if integral traffic problems are not adequately solved these malls will not be effective. In other words, unless people can get to the mall in less time (in terms of total elapsed time) than previously, the mall is not likely to be a success. This reflects the "Reilly law of gravity," which indicates that there are two things that affect shopping patterns: (1) the selection and variety of goods in competitive areas, and (2) the time it takes to get to one shopping area compared to another. Since malls usually do not bring in new stores immediately, and since they do not tend

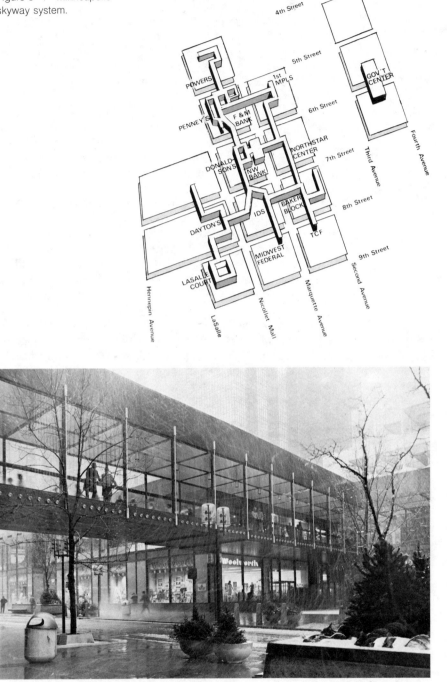

Figure 8–4   Minneapolis
skyway system.

to improve variety in the downtown area, the key to a mall's success is improved access. Therefore, any proposed mall should be checked out in terms of its impact on traffic access and egress.

In the 1970s pedestrian systems in metropolitan areas have been tried out both above ground and below ground. Probably the most significant above ground system is in Minneapolis, where many activities have been linked via the second stories of key buildings in the downtown area (Figure 8–4). This has been carried out over a period of years as part of an overall plan for the area. In both Toronto and Montreal extensive underground pedestrian systems have been built that tie together the stores and buildings, linking major activities in the downtown area.

The Montreal and Toronto systems have been greatly accelerated by the development of multiuse projects—buildings housing many uses, which are linked together to a large degree by the transportation system. St. Bonaventure in Montreal is a good example; Dominion Complex is an example in Toronto. The systems in Toronto and Montreal are well planned and have brought new interest and activity to the downtown area.

Many believe that the underground systems do not make much sense in areas with attractive weather. However, in the cold climates of Montreal and Toronto the underground pedestrian systems have an additional appeal.

In some cities improvements in pedestrian systems have been at street level; some of these have been combined with urban renewal, as in Charles Center in Baltimore.

Interest has been expressed in the European development of the automobile restricted zone (ARZ). In many ways these zones are demonstrations of programs that were planned for American cities in the 1950s and 1960s. In designing these zones planners have attempted to develop malls, relocate parking, improve access for both transit and automobiles, and generally make the downtown areas more attractive. These schemes have done a great deal to preserve these areas; however, the most effective schemes have cost a great deal of money.

As of the late 1970s such projects were being designed in Boston, Memphis, Phoenix, and some smaller cities such as Burlington, Vermont. But in many large metropolitan areas there seems to be a great reluctance to undertake this on any extensive scale, mainly because there has not been a total traffic improvement and also because merchants are quite reluctant to implement them. Figure 8–5 highlights characteristics of ARZs in the United States.

Transportation and land development

The impact that transportation improvements have on land development depends first on the degree to which transportation service is advanced—how much more capacity is added to the system and the speed at which the system operates. The impact depends secondly on the extent to which the improvements create new economic development opportunities. Is land available for development within a convenient range of transportation facilities? Are there opportunities for redeveloping existing areas in line with the access provided by the new transportation improvements?[9]

It is also quite clear that other market factors must be favorable or transportation will have little or no impact on land development. The exact pattern of development that materializes depends on a series of decisions—whether it is the highway official deciding on a road location, the manufacturer deciding where to locate a plant, the merchant deciding whether to expand a store, a government agency deciding whether to relocate, or a family deciding whether to buy or rent a particular house. But all of these decisions are made in light of the alternatives that are available at a given time.

Obviously, in making these decisions many factors are weighed. For example, in addition to transportation a family will consider such factors as type, size, and kind of house; cost; financial arrangements; neighborhood amenities; distance to stores and schools; and adequacy of government services. An industrialist will look at such factors as accessibility to the labor force, over-the-road transportation, and railroad lines; government services; and land costs. A merchant will have another series of factors to consider, such as the relationship to various residential areas and to competing stores; the price of land; and other kinds of retail and service establishments in the area.[10]

City, mall, year opened	Length of mall	Type of auto restriction
Allentown, Pa. Hamilton Mall, 1973	2,400' length of downtown retail street	Roadbed narrowed to two lanes serving all traffic. Sidewalks widened.
Atchison, Kans. 1963	2½ blocks of downtown retail street	Fully pedestrianized. Traffic on two cross streets.
Burbank, Calif. Golden Mall, 1968	6 blocks of downtown retail street	Fully pedestrianized.
Danville, Ill. 1967	2 blocks of downtown retail street	Fully pedestrianized.
Fresno, Calif. Fulton Mall, 1964	2,800' length of downtown retail street	Fully pedestrianized, including one block length of three cross streets.
Honolulu, Hawaii 1969	1,800' length of downtown mixed retail street	Transitway for buses. Two cross streets carry traffic; three others dead end at mall.
Kalamazoo, Mich. Burdick Mall, 1959	1,200' length of downtown retail street	Fully pedestrianized. Traffic on two cross streets.
Louisville, Ky. River City Mall, 1973	3 blocks of downtown retail street	Fully pedestrianized.
Miami Beach, Fla. Lincoln Road Mall, 1960	8 blocks of retail street	Fully pedestrianized. Traffic on six cross streets.
Minneapolis, Minn. Nicollet Mall, 1968	8 blocks of downtown retail street	Two lane transitway for buses and cabs. Cross streets open to all traffic.
Oakland, Calif. 1961	5 blocks of neighborhood shopping street	Sidewalk widening; all traffic allowed on one way, two lane roadbed.
Pomona, Calif. Pomona Mall, 1962	3,000' length of downtown retail street	Fully pedestrianized. Traffic on cross streets.
Providence, R.I. Westminster Mall, 1965	1,000' length of downtown retail street	Fully pedestrianized. Traffic on cross streets.
Riverside, Calif. Main Street Mall, 1966	4 blocks of downtown retail street	Fully pedestrianized.
Salisbury, Md. Downtown Plaza, 1968	900' length of downtown mixed retail street	Fully pedestrianized. Side street pedestrian plazas give additional depth.
Washington, D.C. F Street Mall, 1966	2 blocks of downtown retail street	Sidewalk widening. Narrowed roadbed serves all traffic.

Figure 8–5   Automobile restricted zones in the United States, 1977.

Transportation and urban structure

In an attempt to understand the role of various social and economic factors on city growth, particularly the role of transportation, a series of studies was carried out which evaluated the changes that have occurred in cities and which tried to relate these changes to those factors. The results of these studies can probably best be summarized by looking at the overall impact that transportation facilities have had on the overall structure of the city, and then considering the role that roads and transit have had on land development and on alternative urban forms.

Figure 8–6   Coordination of automobile and transit planning can be seen in the Dan Ryan Expressway in Chicago, where the median is used for rapid transit.

It is clear that transportation is one of the key links in determining the overall structure of the metropolitan area. During the transit age, North American cities developed at high densities. For example, although there is considerable variation, most of the development that occurred during the transit age developed at over 100 people per acre. This generally occurred within two to four miles of the central business district. During the automobile age the development has been occurring at between fifteen and twenty persons per acre. Such density patterns were made possible by the automobile, yet they reflect a strong preference for lower residential density. People were willing to increase travel so that they could have these lower densities. For example, the work trip length increased 18 percent in Detroit between 1953 and 1965.[11]

As another example, a large number of freeways were built in the Detroit area between 1953 and 1965. Overall development during this period, in terms of population and employment, showed little difference in the inner portions of the city where the area was fairly well developed, but beyond two miles there was considerable increase in population and employment. What had taken place was the development of the vacant land found largely between the transit corridors.[12]

Roads and land development

The greatest impact of transportation facilities on major land uses—residential, commercial, and industrial—is in the commercial and residential areas.

Freeways Intensive research into land values at the time of freeway construction in Chicago showed dramatic increases in value on a before-and-after basis. The study included land immediately adjacent to the freeway (one block), land within eight blocks, and land beyond eight blocks which was designated the control area. Data compiled in the late 1960s showed dramatic increases in land values for both residential and commercial properties, especially within one block of the freeway.[13] Industrial land also jumped in value but not as much proportionately. All land included in the study, however, at least doubled in value.

These healthy increases in land values along the freeways were not always maintained. About 25 percent of the areas through which these freeways pass did not show positive increase in land values, regardless of whether they were residential, industrial, or commercial. In some cases land values grew at only half the rate of the control areas, particularly in areas where there was poor housing or where racial issues were developing—or in commercial and industrial areas where there was considerable deterioration of existing shops or industries. In most cases in which there was a relative slippage, this slippage was related to all types of land uses. Again, this would seem to indicate that, although generally transportation facilities can have a positive impact on an area, they cannot override blighted conditions or deteriorating situations.

A series of studies has been undertaken in different metropolitan areas on selected routes. Probably one of the most famous of these studies is that related to Route 128 which circumscribes the Boston area. With the development of this route, over ninety-six plants located themselves along its boundaries; these plants employed over 17,000 people. A large number of these workers came from inner portions of the city seeking more room to expand.

Of the industries that moved to Route 128, 54 percent indicated they did so for expansion purposes; 25 percent had been displaced for public improvements such as highways; 14 percent had been displaced by private parties; and 7 percent had found the old facilities too expensive to operate. Although these industries had a positive impact on the areas they moved into, they also created many hardships that the control areas are still faced with.[14]

The housing market expanded near the facility, generally growing by 20 to 40 percent more than at other locations. A factor that often shows up in these studies is that when residential quality or prestige is combined with improved access, substantial growth is usually assured. The very positive impact that Route 128 had on residential development was quite surprising. It was felt at first that highways of this type would primarily encourage commercial or industrial development.

A study of the Gulf Freeway running southeast of Houston showed that it greatly stimulated growth in its corridor, particularly in residential development. Two quarter-mile bands of properties—one adjacent to the freeway and another adjoining the first—were compared with control areas beyond the immediate range of the freeway. The land value in the first band grew 585 percent in a fifteen year period. The second band grew 240 percent, while the control areas grew about 251 percent (very close to the second band).[15]

Similar studies of the Dallas freeway showed a growth in land value of 405 percent for the band along the freeway, 110 percent for the band second from the freeway, and 231 percent for a third band. The control areas had growths of about 125 percent.

In these cases the land values along the freeway itself grew two to three times as fast as the control areas, and the second band grew at about the same rate as the control areas. Land values clearly were influenced by the development of the freeway, but in every case there were always other factors that generated particular changes in land use.

One of the major hopes of the development of a freeway system in a metropolitan area is to try to strengthen the downtown area. Most of the systems were designed to serve this area effectively. However, one thing that has become clear is that these radial freeways improved accessibility to the suburban areas more than to the downtown areas and, in effect, allowed more growth to occur in the outlying areas than in the downtown areas.

The highway system In addition to freeways, improvement of the highway system itself has an impact on land development. In a series of studies of small cities in Iowa and Connecticut where freeways were not particularly prevalent, it was found that highway accessibility was only one of the many factors involved in determining growth patterns within a metropolitan area. Available land, sewer facilities, and airport accessibility were more important.

Although accessibility was an important consideration, there were many other factors to be considered in development. This undoubtedly reflects the fact that most sections of the metropolitan area are served by highways to some degree. The difference in accessibility from one place to another may be only a few minutes. The automobile has freed individuals to the point where they can afford to weigh other factors in the selection process.

One of the most significant factors observed in the 1960s was the effect that street patterns had on retail locations. This was particularly true in the suburban portions of cities in the United States. In areas where the street system converged for various reasons, it was almost assured that commercial development would follow. Then, as streets were built to bypass an area they would attract more commercial development and would often replace the older commercial areas if the land developed was not adequately controlled. Various studies have shown that there is a direct relationship between traffic volumes and commercial development. It is quite clear that many of these activities prefer to locate on high volume streets, or where they can have wide exposure from traffic.[16]

Transit and land development

Studies of rapid transit systems in Toronto, Montreal, San Francisco, Boston, Chicago, Cleveland, and Philadelphia have provided some insight into the land use impacts of these major facilities.[17] This section focuses on rapid transit, since the impact of the ubiquitous bus transit on land development is of less significance.

Downtown It is clear that rapid transit improvements can help to induce increased downtown development. However, the presence of other supportive factors is essential. Perhaps most important is the presence of effective demand. The availability of land feasible for development is another.

The public sector's need for offices and other high density facilities is a form of leverage which could be used. The location of publicly funded urban renewal projects is another.

The length of time from commitment, construction, or initial operation of a major transit improvement to the generation of significant related land use change is completely unpredictable. In most cases a period of five years or more is involved, and in some others it may be much longer—if ever. Not only must conditions at the site be opportune; the general area's levels of demand for development and capital to meet it must also be healthy.

Outlying stations Transit improvements can help in intensification of land uses around outlying stations. As with impacts in downtown areas, however, many other factors are required. For example, location in low density residential surroundings may completely block land use impacts when low density zoning is supported by residents.

Regional impact Net regional growth impacts directly attributable to new transit improvements will probably not be large in comparison with the transit investment. So many other forces are involved that any net gain in regional wealth or economic vitality is likely to be hard to identify and cannot fairly be attributed to the transit improvement alone. On the other hand, future energy shortages may result in an increased dependence on rapid transit, generating a correspondingly greater influence on interregional locational choices for businesses and individuals.

One of the most significant trends now being observed in American cities is a change in growth patterns. The larger metropolitan areas have slowed down in growth, and more of the growth is now occurring in the medium-size cities of 200,000 to 500,000 population; but even there the growth is modest.

The fact that metropolitan areas are not growing as quickly and are not building roads in the outlying areas is definitely recasting the growth patterns of cities. There is the filling-in of the areas that were bypassed in the 1950s and 1960s, and there will probably be a growing number of policies supporting not only this filling-in process but also development in the older sections of the cities, related to public transport systems.

Joint development

Urban transportation improvements often require the displacement of homes, businesses, and industrial firms. A program for fair and orderly relocation of persons and entities involved is a requirement of federal and state highway laws and regulations.[18]

Transportation facilities may also create or aggravate existing problems of the ambient environment, including air, noise, and water pollution; visual intrusion; and depletion of open space and recreation resources. Programs to remedy and in some cases improve on existing environmental conditions must be an integral part of any transportation facilities construction project.

At the same time, urban transportation improvements can increase accessibility to adjacent lands and improve local traffic circulation patterns, thereby creating opportunities for the joint development of new or replacement facilities along the right-of-way. These replacement facilities may eventually more than compensate local municipalities for the temporary loss of real property tax revenues from lands used for the transportation right-of-way and may provide new taxable sites and structures for displaced residents and businesses.

Joint development is a means of accomplishing the following:

1. Integrating the transportation facility with the needs of, and maintaining the integrity of, affected communities
2. Ensuring that transportation proposals are consistent with comprehensive regional planning goals and with local objectives and development priorities
3. Offsetting the negative impacts of transportation facilities
4. Capitalizing on opportunities to attract private development of the type most desired from each community's perspective
5. Taking advantage of opportunities which may be provided by the introduction of transportation improvements to help solve preexisting problems identified by the communities.

The design approach for highways must take into serious consideration the residential nature of the communities through which the highways pass. To many of the residents of these communities, construction of a highway is perceived as taking local land and thus degrading the community environment. A joint development program undertaken as part of the highway construction program would endeavor to provide the maximum compensation to the abutting communities for temporary and permanent disruptions which the highway would cause. The measures to minimize harm must be conceived in the broadest sense; they must include not only the equitable treatment of persons who are directly adversely affected but also compensation in a more general sense to the communities on either side of the facility.

The physical context of joint development planning activities is the highway corridor, or *general path* of a proposed highway. A corridor may vary from one block to several blocks to several miles in width, depending on the nature of the area through which the highway passes and the manner in which the highway affects that area.

The end product of the joint development planning process is the *corridor joint development plan*. This consists of a proposed pattern of land uses, including the highway improvement, the network of local services associated with scheduled public actions, and proposed funding for which each of the implementing agencies is responsible.

In concept, transit joint development is identical to highway joint development and presents many of the same physical and legal problems and opportunities.

Joint planning and implementation are the essence of an effective joint development program. The scope of such activity for a given project is, of course, a function of the nature and complexity of that project. The overriding principle, however, is that transportation facilities are major infrastructure elements that have the potential capacity for reorganizing—and improving—the corridors through which they pass. The success of joint development depends on securing broad based participation in the planning stage and solid financial commitments in the implementation or execution stage.

Social, economic, and environmental impacts

A transportation project may change regional, corridor, or local scale conditions. The impact may occur at only one level or at all three levels and may vary from project to project. Experience has shown, however, that certain expected effects—technically designated impacts—are repeatedly of concern in evaluating transportation projects.[19] These are social impacts, economic impacts, and environmental impacts.

Social impacts are: community cohesion; accessibility of facilities/services; displacement of people. *Economic impacts* are: employment, income, and business activity; residential activity; effects on property taxes; regional and community plans and growth; resources. *Environmental impacts* are: environmental design, aesthetics, and historical values; terrestrial ecosystems; aquatic ecosystems; air quality; noise.

Assessment should take account of both present and future conditions. Ideally, each alternative would be assessed at two future times: short range and long range. In short-range assessment the focus is on direct construction impacts and first year operating conditions. In long-range assessment the focus is primarily on indirect impacts and design year operating conditions.

Data on the transportation aspects of proposed facilities are a primary input into all of the impact assessment techniques. Transportation factors are of five types. Three of these are factors having direct impacts on people and places abutting the facility; these factors are: (1) *physical design*—physical characteristics and type of construction of the facility; (2) *maintenance/operations* —policies which affect the use or maintenance of the facility; (3) *traffic* —facility use characteristics.

The other two transportation factors are those having indirect impacts through changes in the relative costs of travel; these factors are: (4) *travel demand* —probable changes in trip making because of changes in relative costs and levels of service (these changes indirectly affect social and economic behavior); (5) *accessibility* —(the aggregate effect of an alternative on mobility) the comparative costs and times for travel to and from specific origins and destinations.

Physical design can be determined from typical cross section and right-of-way requirements, from sketch plans and profiles based on preliminary engineering, or from plans and profiles based on refined engineering location documents. Operations and maintenance factors depend on the physical design to a large extent and include such items as speeds, vehicle types, transit frequency, and traffic control. Traffic data can be based on existing traffic counts, subarea traffic assignment, or detailed flow simulation. Travel demand data can be developed from screenline counts and trends at key points, from existing trip tables at district or sector levels or from trip generation and distribution on a small zone basis through the use of gravity models. Mode use can be estimated through the use of manual or automated sketch planning techniques or full zone-to-zone mode choice modeling. Accessibility is summarized from traffic assignments at district, sector, or zone levels.

When adequate forecasts of socioeconomic and land use factors are available (and this is not always the case, which then requires re-forecasts or independent projections), impact estimation is still subjective in many cases. *Community-cohesion* impacts must be value judgments based on physical design characteristics and a knowledge of land use, population, and resident attitudes. *Environmental design, aesthetics,* and *historical values* depend on assessments of "quality." Owing to the location, size, and use of specific examples where facility design creates a conflict, *accessibility* can be more explicitly evaluated, through the use of before-and-after travel times, among selected land uses such as employment, commercial, health care, and recreational.

Displacement and impact on *residential activity* can be directly estimated through the physical design characteristics and should be related to income level for persons displaced. Impacts on *employment, income,* and *business activity,* and on *property taxes,* follow similar lines.

Consideration of *community plans* and *growth* requires a disaggregation of plans and policies into individual items and then an assessment of how the proposed facility relates in terms of direction and qualitative magnitude of impact. Impact on *resources* (other than environmental) will be primarily related to construction materials displaced or altered and to operational effects such as energy consumption.

Ecological impact estimates also tend to fall into the subjective range but should be based on inventory of organisms, climate, and other characteristics.

Air quality and *noise* impacts lie within the limits of numerical analysis. With vehicle miles of travel and speed, and perhaps number of trips involved, useful estimates of pollutant and noise emissions can be produced through manual methods or special computer programs, or as part of automated assignment programs.

The definition of benefits is becoming increasingly broad. In early 1960 a criterion of traffic congestion relief was the motivating force behind most transportation improvements. This was initially broadened to the concept of user cost–benefit criteria. In the late 1960s environmental considerations began to achieve equal consideration. Initial concerns were with the natural environment, but this was rapidly expanded to include the socioeconomic environment as well.

At this point the distribution of benefits and costs became of equal importance with the aggregate values. Concern about unintended negative income transfers put a premium on knowing "who benefits and who pays."

The trend in the 1970s has continued to broaden the stated objectives of transportation improvements and thereby the criteria by which they are judged. A whole series of urban form, quality, and value criteria have been added to the previous cost–benefit, environmental impact, and energy consumption concerns. Criteria relating to improving the economic vitality of central areas, to intensifying and structuring future urban development, and to assessing the net value of induced development are increasingly becoming the motivating forces behind transport programs.

Conclusion

This chapter has dealt with many facets of urban transportation, starting with streets in a systems sense and moving from that to the development of street classifications. Traffic engineering and street system management were covered next, in the context of land use and of the way in which they interact with the generation of travel on the street system. The next major section of the chapter dealt with the nonautomotive aspects of urban transportation that are receiving major attention in transportation planning: mass transit, automobile parking, and pedestrian systems. Transportation and land use planning were then covered; this was followed by a concluding section on socioeconomic and environmental impacts.

Transportation planning in the 1970s has shifted from the massive regional and metropolitan area plans to the community, neighborhood, and district levels. This has occurred principally because most of the large scale transportation planning has been completed in metropolitan areas, but it has also taken place because of adverse reactions to freeways in many areas of the United States. Planning emphasis has shifted to policy and program planning: transportation system management (TSM) is an example. Much of this planning takes place at the state and national levels, but cities and metropolitan areas also are concerned with policy questions that are covered with respect to capital budgeting and development planning in Chapters 5 and 6.

Increasingly, as the last section of the chapter bears out, every transportation service and facility—freeways, arterial streets, parking garages, "people movers," or any other substantial investment—is checked and analyzed much more thoroughly from a cost–benefit standpoint, from the standpoint of broader economic benefit, and from a community benefit point of view.

In all of these multiple uses of transportation—systems; circulation; linkages; access; open space; utility rights-of-way; and movement of goods, people, and vehicles—the planning agency is in the best position to provide the dispassionate analysis that helps resolve the competing demands for the use of limited resources.

1   National Committee on Urban Transportation, *Determining Street Use* (Chicago: Public Administration Service, 1958), pp. 1, 2.

2   Alan M. Voorhees & Associates, Inc., *Principles and Standards for Street Development in Broward County* (McLean, Va.: Alan M. Voorhees & Associates, Inc., 1966).

3   This section is drawn from: Harold Marks, *Traffic Circulation Planning for Communities* (Los Angeles: Gruen Associates, 1974).

4   U.S., Department of Transportation, Urban Mass Transportation Administration, *Increasing Transit Ridership: The Experience of Seven Cities* (Washington, D.C.: Government Printing Office, 1976), pp. 11–23.

5   Vukan R. Vuchic and Shinya Kikuchi, *Design of Outlying Rapid Transit Station Areas,* Transportation Research Record 505 (Washington, D.C.: Transportation Research Board, 1974), p. 4.

6   Wilbur Smith and Associates, *Bus Use of Highways Planning and Design Guidelines,* National Cooperative Highway Research Program Report 155 (Washington, D.C.: Transportation Research Board, 1975), pp. 38–47.

7 See: Alan M. Voorhees, *Parking Facts—What's the Problem?* (Washington, D.C.: Automotive Safety Foundation, 1955).

8 Automotive Safety Foundation, *Parking—How It Is Financed* (Washington, D.C.: Automotive Safety Foundation, 1952), pp. 27–41.

9 Alan M. Voorhees & Associates, Inc., *The Impact of Transportation on Land Development: North American Experience* (McLean, Va.: Alan M. Voorhees & Associates, Inc., 1975).

10 See: Alan M. Voorhees, "Development Patterns in American Cities," in *Urban Transportation Planning: Concepts and Applications,* Highway Research Board Bulletin 293 (Washington, D.C.: Highway Research Board, 1961).

11 Wilbur Smith and Associates, *Future Highways and Urban Growth* (New Haven, Conn.: Wilbur Smith and Associates, 1961), pp. 16–18.

12 Salvatore J. Bellomo, Robert B. Dial, and Alan M. Voorhees, *Factors, Trends, and Guidelines Related to Trip Length,* National Cooperative Highway Research Program Report 89 (Washington, D.C.: Highway Research Board, 1970), p. 15.

13 Jay S. Golden, *Land Values in Chicago: Before and After Expressway Construction* (Chicago: Chicago Area Transportation Study, 1968).

14 See: A. J. Bone and Martin Wohl, "Massachusetts Route 128 Impact Study," in *Highways and Economic Development,* Highway Research Board Bulletin 227 (Washington, D.C.: Highway Research Board, 1959).

15 William G. Adkins, "Land Value Impacts of Expressways in Dallas, Houston, and San Antonio, Texas," in *Highways and Economic Development,* pp. 52–59.

16 Alan M. Voorhees, "Urban Transportation," paper presented at the Symposium on Urban Development Policies and Techniques, Rio de Janeiro, Brazil, August 1973.

17 See: U.S., Department of Transportation, *Land Use Impacts of Rapid Transit: Implications of Recent Experience,* Executive Summary (Washington, D.C.: U.S. Department of Transportation, 1977).

18 Alan M. Voorhees & Associates, *North Shore: Boston Transportation Planning Review* (Boston: Alan M. Voorhees & Associates, August 1972).

19 David A. Crane and Partners/DACP, *Impact Assessment Guidelines: The Rule of the No-Build Alternative in the Evaluation of Transportation Projects,* National Cooperative Highway Research Program 8–11 (Washington, D.C.: David A. Crane and Partners/DACP, Inc.; Economics Research Associates, Inc.; Alan M. Voorhees & Associates, Inc., 1977).

9 Business and industrial development

Planning for business and industrial development is one of the most important aspects of the comprehensive planning process. Except for the most affluent bedroom suburbs, the community typically depends for its economic health on its ability to attract and to hold business establishments and industrial plants. In terms of the cost of essential public facilities and services, residential development seldom pays its own way in tax and fee revenues. The deficit must be made up by the tax yield from commercial and industrial properties which typically produce a net gain to the local government. One of the principal factors in the financial difficulties that so many older central cities face today is their inability to retain stores, offices, and factories, or to attract enterprises. In addition, as cities expand their role to include promoting economic development—the provision of jobs for their citizens—planning for business and industry takes on even more importance.

Even affluent suburbs usually find the tax revenues yielded by their shopping districts, office developments, and industrial parks a welcome source of relief to overburdened residential property taxpayers. On the other hand, businesses and industries that mainly employ unskilled, low paid workers may constitute a financial drain on the community unless the employees live elsewhere and commute to work. Therefore, local governments must face this fact and adopt budgetary and housing policies to ensure that this population is served.

Merely designating areas in which land is available for commercial and/or industrial development on the comprehensive plan map will do little to attract or to hold commercial and industrial enterprises. Relatively few establishments are free to locate wherever they choose. Prevailing wage scales, the local cost of living, land prices, utility rates, and tax levels, as well as transportation costs, are the principal economic factors that typically influence the selection of a new office or plant site. Resource based manufacturing and processing plants must be near their raw materials sources, and proximity to processed materials suppliers and fabricators of components is often an important consideration. Rail or waterborne transportation must be available for shipping bulky products to marketing centers. Where transportation represents a major element of production cost and where other factors permit it, industries tend to select sites close to the markets they serve.

Similar considerations govern the choice of locations of most nonindustrial businesses. Shopping centers and free-standing retail stores must be conveniently accessible to their customers via freeways, arterial streets, or transit lines. Locations of offices are commonly influenced by the presence of financial institutions and other commercial enterprises that these offices frequently contact, although this factor is becoming somewhat less important with advances in communications technology.

The availability of a suitable labor force is also a significant factor in the selection of locations for major office developments and industrial plants. The importance of this factor will vary, depending on employee skills requirements. In addition to transportation costs, prevailing wage scales, the local cost of living, land prices, utilities rates, and tax levels there are the principal economic factors that typically influence selection of a new office or a plant site. A growing proportion of business enterprises are strongly influenced by the character of the community in choosing a location. Among the paramount concerns are an adequate housing supply, freedom from deterioration and blight, the quality of the schools and other public facilities and services, and the availability of cultural and recreational resources. These considerations help to explain why newer suburban communities often attract business and industry away from older central cities and successfully compete with them for new enterprises. (See Chapter 16 for a discussion of the economic development problems faced in older central cities.)

The less dependent a business is on such factors as sources of raw materials, availability of transportation, and proximity to markets, the greater is its concern with the characteristics of the community. Indeed, if a location is chosen that offers a pleasant way of life at a reasonable cost, personnel with necessary skills will usually migrate there to fill available jobs.

It is in the sphere of community character that the comprehensive plan can significantly influence the choice of business and industrial locations. On the other hand, the presence of large office developments, retail centers, and industrial plants has a major impact on the character of the community which, in turn, is reflected in the policies and proposals of the comprehensive plan. Not only will land use patterns and population composition be affected, but future growth and development may also be influenced in important ways. To a considerable extent the aphorism "growth begets growth" is true. A community in which office development, retail centers, or industrial plants thrive is more likely to attract more of the same than is a declining city or a city that has not experienced these types of development.

Of course, suitable sites must be available at reasonable prices. Adequate street access, utilities, and public services must also be available, or it must be possible to extend them to the site without undue cost or delay. While at one time large employers, particularly manufacturers, were greatly concerned with local taxes, today the availability and adequacy of necessary public services is usually a more important consideration. A moderate or even higher level of taxation generally is accepted as the cost of location in a desirable community.

Planning for business

Comprehensive plans and zoning ordinances generally designate locations and prescribe standards for four major classifications of business: (1) offices, (2) retail stores and personal service establishments, (3) commercial services, and (4) wholesaling and distribution. Types of office development vary greatly, ranging from giant metropolitan skyscrapers to single story suburban buildings of an almost residential character. Retail development ranges in scale from regional shopping centers to corner groceries. Personal service establishments include barber and beauty shops, shoe repair shops, cleaners, and similar services commonly found in retail districts. Commercial services, on the other hand, are sometimes referred to as heavy commercial uses because of their semi-industrial character. Automobile sales and repair establishments, plumbing shops, and building supply outlets are classified in this category. The wholesaling/distribution category includes warehouses and other goods storage and shipment enterprises, and sometimes is classified with light industrial uses instead of separately.

Five basically different kinds of business locations are shown on comprehensive plans and zoning maps. With few exceptions, every community has a central business district, commonly referred to by planners as the CBD. Such business centers may differ greatly in size and character. They include major metropolitan centers which contain the largest concentrations of business headquarters and financial institutions, as well as department stores and a wide variety of specialty shops, service establishments, hotels, restaurants, cafes, and theaters. Medium-sized city central business districts, typically serving urban populations of 100,000 to 500,000, are distinctively different from metropolitan centers in scale and character, although they may contain many or all of the same kinds of establishments. Small city CBDs are yet another readily identifiable type. The central business districts of some suburban communities closely resemble their small city counterparts in terms of both scale and types of businesses, but others are distinctly different, containing branches of central city stores and fashionable specialty shops catering to affluent suburbanites.

The second category of business location is strip commercial development, which is largely the product of the automobile era. Arterial streets frequently are zoned for and at least partially built up with almost every conceivable type of business development. Although the location of commercial outlets along arterials makes sense in terms of their accessibility and exposure to large numbers of potential customers, the traffic congestion that strip development generates devalues the public's investment in building and maintaining high capacity streets.

While it takes the same linear form as strip commercial development, highway commercial development, the third principal type of business development, is often classified separately for planning purposes. It is located along highway routes at the edges of or between urban areas. The businesses strung out along highways typically cater to the traveler and include service stations, motels, restaurants, and similar conveniences. In recent years establishments serving the residents of several different but closely related communities can sometimes be found on highway frontage sites. Automobile sales and service centers, furniture and appliance stores, discount stores, and even shopping centers are examples. Outcast commercial enterprises, such as drive-in theaters and lumber yards, that either are unwelcome at more central locations or cannot afford them, are also typical of highway commercial development.

Shopping centers are the fourth principal type of business development. Most new retail development has occured in shopping centers in the past quarter of a century. These planned complexes of stores, usually grouped around pedestrian malls and plazas and surrounded by parking lots, tend to come in three different sizes reflecting the functions they serve.

Regional shopping centers usually contain between 500,000 and 2 million square feet of store space and have from one to four department stores as anchor tenants. A population of at least 150,000 in the service area is necessary to support a regional center.

Community shopping centers, requiring a support area population of 50,000 or more, generally contain 150,000 to 300,000 square feet and have a junior department store (one that does not carry appliances and "hard goods") or a variety store as the principal tenant.

Neighborhood shopping centers consist entirely or primarily of convenience goods outlets with a supermarket as the anchor tenant. Usually containing 100,000 square feet or less, neighborhood centers generally do not have enclosed, air-conditioned malls, elaborate landscaping, and similar amenities typical of recently built larger shopping centers. A population of 5,000 to 40,000 is necessary to support a neighborhood center.

In the 1970s, with the slowdown of urban growth in many parts of the United States, fewer shopping centers were built. Of those major centers that have been constructed in recent years, more have been of the regional type than of the community type, apparently because the larger centers have proved more profitable.

Office parks, the fifth type of commercial development, are groups of as few as one or two or as many as dozens of office buildings in landscaped settings

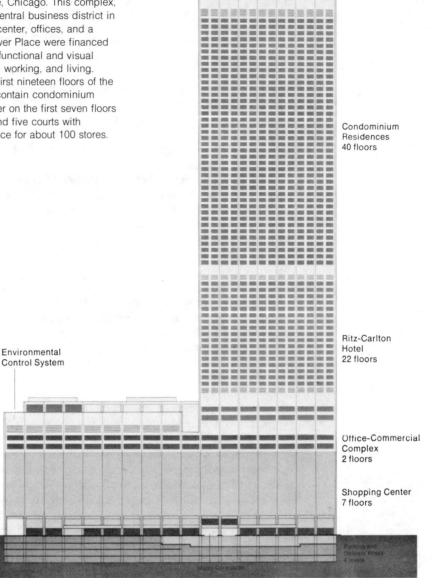

Figure 9–1 Water Tower Place, Chicago. This complex, located two miles north of the central business district in Chicago, includes a shopping center, offices, and a hotel. All elements of Water Tower Place were financed and built at a luxury level for a functional and visual combination of urban shopping, working, and living. Hotel rooms are located in the first nineteen floors of the tower while the top forty floors contain condominium apartments. The shopping center on the first seven floors is built around a large atrium and five courts with 610,000 square feet of floor space for about 100 stores.

Condominium
Residences
40 floors

Environmental
Control System

Ritz-Carlton
Hotel
22 floors

Office-Commercial
Complex
2 floors

Shopping Center
7 floors

with large parking lots or parking structures. These typically suburban developments are the office counterparts of the more common industrial parks. Indeed, the advent of the office park appears to have been inspired by the success of the industrial park. Some industrial parks combine both office and industrial development, while some regional shopping centers have incorporated major office development. Mixed use developments (see Figure 9–1), combining office buildings, retail stores, personal service establishments, restaurants, and apartments, are found in recently built central city urban renewal projects as well as in suburban locations.

Commercial development standards

Central business districts Comprehensive plans frequently propose the expansion or modernization of existing central business districts but seldom call for the creation of new ones. Almost every community already has a CBD, and, however underdeveloped or rundown it may be, the plan must deal with it in its own terms. There is seldom any other economically viable use for an outworn downtown district. Almost without exception, property values are too high to justify any but commercial development. If clearance and redevelopment is proposed, it is usually necessary to write down the price of the land, using public subsidies, in order to make it competitive with other commercial locations. Public improvements such as street widening, provision of off-street parking, conversion of streets to landscaped pedestrian malls, and lesser beautification projects, sometimes integrated into an urban renewal program, are the principal means of revitalizing CBDs. Unless they are combined in a scheduled program to attack downtown problems on a comprehensive basis, such improvement programs are not likely to be cost-effective.

Every central business district is virtually unique; therefore, with a few exceptions, it is not possible to prescribe uniform standards for improvements. One generally applicable principle is that shopping districts should be kept as compact as possible to encourage pedestrian traffic among stores, thus facilitating comparison shopping and impulse buying. The potential customer who has to move his or her car and park a second time is as likely to head for home as to remain downtown and shop. For similar reasons, retail store frontage should be continuous, with minimum interruptions by parking lots, office buildings, or hotels without ground floor stores, or by banks, airline ticket offices, and other nonretail uses. Even building setbacks that place display windows beyond the inspection range of sidewalk passersby should be discouraged. Disruption of pedestrian traffic by closely spaced intersecting streets also is undesirable, but blocks should not be so long as to make it inconvenient for shoppers to cross streets at intersections or to walk between parallel streets. Blocks generally should be 300 to 500 feet in length. Some downtown urban renewal projects have removed pedestrian circulation from the street level to second story malls and plazas connected by pedestrian bridges in order to eliminate conflicts with vehicular traffic.

A central focus to a shopping precinct such as a plaza, mall, or other open space reserved for pedestrians will be desirable if it is a lively, intensively used space that makes downtown visually attractive and gives the footsore shopper a pleasant place to sit down and rest. However, there is nothing more deadly than a sparsely occupied pedestrian space. Another problem that must be recognized is that a sunny central square or mall may become a mecca for human derelicts, driving away the shoppers it was meant to attract.

Parking should be located within easy walking distance of the stores it serves. In most situations 300 to 400 feet is a practical maximum. Pedestrian bridges over streets connecting parking garages with stores may be advantageous, particularly in harsh or rainy climates such as those of Minneapolis and Seattle. However, this kind of arrangement may have the undesirable side effect of minimizing pedestrian circulation throughout the central district. Transit lines should be routed on major shopping streets, with fairly closely spaced stops. Bus shelters and benches should be provided for transit patrons. With varying degrees of success, some cities have experimented with minibus services linking the various parts of their central districts. For the same purpose, moving sidewalks and elevated "people mover" systems have been proposed by many CBD development plans. None has yet been built in a downtown area, but in 1977 the U.S. Department of Transportation made grants to Los Angeles, Houston, Cleveland, and St. Paul to experiment with people movers. Earlier trials of shuttle buses linking peripheral parking lots with the central core yielded disappointing results, and most of these arrangements have been abandoned. Proposals of the 1950s and 1960s for bringing people in automobiles downtown via close-in circumferential freeways with direct ramp connections to parking garages—modeled after Victor Gruen's early plan for Fort Worth—did not prove feasible.

Most of the planning principles applying to shopping precincts of central business districts also are applicable to financial and office precincts. Such districts also thrive on concentration and conveniently short walking distances. The major difference is that continuity of store frontage is less important. Parking may be located further from the business it serves (as far as a quarter of a mile in large cities) because downtown employees are willing to walk longer distances than store customers. Indeed, some large cities have discouraged or even prohibited new parking facilities in financial and office districts in order to reduce traffic congestion by encouraging transit patronage. Such measures are practical, however, only where adequate transit service is available.

New central districts are planned only in new towns, such as Columbia, Maryland, and in exceptional situations such as Fremont, California (in the San Francisco Bay Area), which was incorporated from four existing small communities in the early 1950s. The city's general plan proposed a new central business district on an undeveloped site, and within a decade it was built there. The Fremont center consists of a series of adjoining shopping centers and suburban type office buildings, but it also contains a central park, an imposing city hall, and a Bay Area Rapid Transit station.

Strip and highway development   The community that has no strip commercial development or highway commercial development is singularly blessed. These types of development are almost never proposed where none already exists, but comprehensive plans commonly recognize their existence and sometimes call for their expansion. There are two divergent schools of thought on the layout of strip commercial development. One calls for setting the buildings as far back from the arterial street or the highway as is practical and using the front setback for off-street parking. A minimum depth of fifty-three feet is necessary for two rows of forty-five degree angle parking and a one way access aisle. The depth must be increased to sixty feet for sixty degree angle parking and to sixty-two feet for ninety degree angle parking. If sufficient additional space in front of the buildings is attractively landscaped and properly maintained, and if free-standing signs within the setback area are of reasonable size and are well designed, this type of layout can be visually agreeable, provided that there is continuity of treatment among adjoining sites. However, unless access to the parking areas is exclusively from side streets, entrance and exit driveways on the arterial will have a highly disruptive effect on traffic flow, causing congestion and accidents.

The other approach to the layout of strip commercial development calls for either no setback or preferably a landscaped setback of twenty or thirty feet in front of the buildings, with parking located at the rear. This minimizes conflicts with traffic on the arterial street. It is based on the principle that the more space that lies between commercial buildings and adjoining residential development, the less the adverse impact on the neighborhood will be. (Some planners also believe that parking lots are intrinsically unattractive and should be concealed from public view as much as possible.) Experience has demonstrated, however, that parking at the rear of commercial establishments, particularly those that are open at night, can be extremely annoying to the residents of adjoining homes and apartments. The impact is even greater if access to parking is through an intervening street instead of a side street. Where parking lots are located at the rear of commercial buildings, many zoning ordinances require that the parking be screened by a masonry wall or a fence, with trees and other landscaping on the street side. However, it can be argued that unless the buildings are so high as to loom over nearby residences, it is less disturbing to the occupants to immediately adjoin a commercial building than to adjoin a parking lot, particularly if the rear building wall is screened by landscaping.

The fact that truck deliveries, refuse storage, and other service activities almost of necessity occur at the rear of buildings is a problem intrinsic to strip commercial development. Food markets, the most common type of neighborhood store, are particularly objectionable in this respect. At the very least, truck loading and service areas should be required to be screened; but their inevitable presence tends to strengthen the principle that maximum open space, including parking, should be located at the rear of commercial buildings where it can help to insulate adjoining residential development from the impact of an essentially inharmonious use.

In the allocation of land to strip commercial or highway commercial development, the minimum depth should be sufficient to accommodate the buildings (usually 100 to 200 feet), one or more double rows of parking (53 to 62 feet each), and at least 15 feet of landscaping adjacent to the arterial street, 10 feet in front of the building, and 10 feet at the rear property line—a total of some 200 to 300 feet. The depth of the commercial strip can be reduced if parking is located alongside of buildings, rather than at the front or rear, but parking lot depths may be greater if aisles are laid out at right angles to the arterial street instead of parallel to it.

Regional and community shopping centers Regional and community shopping centers are highly dependent on fast, convenient access from their trade areas. Regional centers usually draw customers from distances of five to fifteen miles and community centers from distances of three to five miles. However, time is a more important consideration than distance in determining areas of attraction. In a metropolitan region with a closely spaced freeway grid, regional shopping centers may be as little as five miles apart. While convenient access is a key element in selecting a location, even more important is the assurance that no competing center of the same type will be able to locate nearby. Unlike individual stores, shopping centers usually seek to attain virtual monopolies in their trade areas. According to the Urban Land Institute, "From the standpoint of location, the site should represent an impregnable economic position."[1] If vacant land suitable for a competing center is available in the vicinity there should be reasonable certainty that the site will not be zoned to permit a second center.

Most shopping center developers agree that visual exposure is another prime location factor, and many believe that for this reason a location adjacent to a freeway is most desirable. The combining of exposure and access requirements has led to the location of many regional shopping centers on arterial streets immediately adjacent to freeway interchanges. However, experience has demonstrated that the advantages of such sites often are more apparent than real. If shopping center access or egress points are located within 600 to 1,000 feet of a freeway ramp, turning movements will cause traffic to back up both on the arterial and on the freeway, particularly during peak business hours. The ideal regional shopping center site would be located a half mile to a mile from a freeway interchange and would be surrounded by arterial streets on all sides, providing maximum potential for dispersal of traffic and maximum choice for automobile access and egress. Special right turn and left turn lanes should be provided on the boundary streets to accommodate shopping center traffic. Entrances to the site should be clearly marked.

Transit service to regional, community, and neighborhood shopping centers is highly desirable. Good transit service can minimize the need for providing employee parking. Where shopping centers are located on arterial streets in urban areas, bus service is often available. A few regional centers have provided on-site bus routes with sheltered bus stops conveniently located near major store entrances. Underground or elevated rapid transit lines with stations within shopping centers have been proposed, but none has been built in the United States. A recent trend is the provision of special access ways and storage facilities for bicycles.

A shopping center site should be regular in shape. Sharp angles, odd projections, or indentations can make site layout difficult. The minimum site dimension should be about 400 feet for a community or regional center. Typically, the site should not be divided by any streets. However, it is often advantageous to have separate though controlled street access to free-standing auxiliary establishments such as automobile service centers, theaters, banks, and drive-in restaurants. Odd-shaped peripheral parcels sometimes can accommodate these kinds of facilities, but it is far easier to plan the traffic circulation system, including necessary streets, from scratch. The classical rule of thumb for the size of a shopping center site is 40,000 square feet (about one acre) for each 10,000 square feet of store space. The 30,000 square feet not occupied by buildings is allocated to parking, truck loading and service areas, and landscaping. While this standard is valid for neighborhood shopping centers and small community shopping centers, larger centers require a lower parking ratio, and site area needs will vary considerably depending on the layout as well as the size of the center.

Shopping center sites generally should be relatively flat, with a slight gradient (less than 5 percent) to facilitate drainage. In some instances more steeply sloping sites have been utilized with ingenuity to accommodate multilevel store buildings with customer access and parking at different levels. Developers of regional centers are best able to justify the relatively large capital investments necessary to deal successfully with sloping sites. Low-lying sites with drainage problems should be avoided unless expensive and time-consuming filling and settling operations are acceptable. Because of the large amounts of impervious surface (building roofs, parking lots, and driveways) created by shopping centers, these centers generate substantial volumes of storm water runoff. This problem must be solved in planning any shopping center and a low-lying site makes the solution more difficult to achieve. Needless to say, water supply, sewerage, and gas and electric services must be available.

A site of fifty acres or more is needed for a regional center, and a site of fifteen to thirty acres is needed for a community shopping center. The layout of these types of centers usually arrays the buildings along a central mall, often with one or more transverse malls. It is increasingly common, particularly in regional centers, to enclose and air condition these malls in order to make the shopping experience painless regardless of the weather. (What effect the current energy crisis will have on this practice remains to be seen.) In addition to being landscaped with elaborate planting, pools, fountains, and sculpture, malls are frequently used for displays of merchandise, fashion shows, automobile shows, art and craft fairs, band concerts, and other entertainment events. Indeed, the mall has become such a paramount feature of large shopping centers that many shopping centers are now referred to simply as *malls*. In some communities the major shopping center mall even has replaced the traditional city square as the principal focus of civic ceremonies.

The standard layout for a regional or community center is a linear pattern with one of the anchor tenants (generally a department store) at either end; this is based on the theory that such an arrangement will bring the maximum pedestrian traffic—and resultant impulse shopping—along the mall. The layout varies where there is only one anchor tenant—or where there are more than two. One of the earliest regional shopping centers (in Framingham, Massachusetts) had stores on two levels, but few others adopted this pattern until recent years when larger centers and more costly land have made two levels a logical design solution. No centers with three or more levels throughout had been built as of the late 1970s, but if escalators are used this is a possibility. Service stations and TBAs (automobile tires, batteries, and accessories outlets) are commonly located in shopping centers but are separated from store buildings. A recent trend in the design of large regional centers is to locate movie theaters,

Figure 9–2 Some of our large shopping centers serve also as
community centers, offering band concerts, musical performances, flower
shows, art exhibits, and other community-oriented activities. Shown here
is the Lyric Opera Company Ballet performing in 1976
in da Vinci Court in the Northbrook Court Shopping Center,
north of Chicago.

banks, offices, and other nonretail uses on portions of the site where they are separate from the store buildings. In certain instances a special type of store, such as a supermarket or a store featuring merchandise in a price bracket different from that of the goods offered by other shops in the center, will seek such a location.

To minimize walking distance to stores, parking is generally laid out on all sides of the store buildings, with automobile access to the site from a number of peripheral points. Experience has shown that the most workable parking layout is to orient the aisles at ninety degrees to store buildings with transverse access driveways at the outer and inner edges of the parking lots and, in very large parking lots, with an additional transverse drive at a midpoint. With the advent of shopping centers having 1.5 million or more square feet of store space, two or more levels of decked parking have been provided at some of the larger regional centers. The well-designed Lloyd Center in rainy Portland, Oregon, and the Alamoana Center in Honolulu pioneered in offering parking under cover to their customers. Some of the early centers provided three or more times as much parking space as store space, but this was found to be excessive. On the basis of a survey of 270 shopping centers, the Urban Land Institute recommends five and a half spaces per 1,000 square feet of gross leasable area (slightly more than twice as much parking space as store space).[2] However, a later study concludes that the largest regional centers (800,000 square feet and over) need only five spaces per 1,000 square feet.[3] Assuming that there is a workable parking layout, the number of cars that can be accommodated can be determined by dividing the square footage devoted to parking on the site by 350 or 400 square feet per car.

In regional shopping centers, truck service areas are frequently located at the basement level with one way access and egress ramps. This tunnel-like layout avoids the need to provide wasteful turning space. In community and neighborhood centers the cost of underground service areas can seldom be justified, and they are usually located at grade. This arrangement requires that the center have only a single tier of stores with service at the rear (usually a workable layout in a neighborhood center) or, if there is a double tier of stores, that screened service areas intrude into parking lots adjacent to the buildings. The latter type of layout interrupts the continuity of display windows, substitutes visually uninteresting screen walls or fences, and sometimes involves conflicts between delivery trucks and customer traffic.

To prevent a shopping center from having the appearance of an island of bulky buildings set in a sea of asphalt, it is essential that it be generously landscaped. In addition to a planted strip at least twenty to thirty feet deep around the outer edge of the parking lots, there should be planted islands within the parking area. A sparse distribution of planter beds or one at each end of the parking aisles usually will not be sufficient to relieve the dreariness of acres of pavement. A better plan places landscaped strips, protected by curbs, between rows of parked cars. These strips should be wide enough to accommodate pedestrian walks and shade trees, which on warm summer days will provide functional as well as visual advantages. Planter beds should also be located adjacent to the buildings. Large trees, mainly evergreens, are desirable to soften the often harsh appearance of great building masses, particularly two and three story windowless department stores. A reasonable standard is for at least 10 percent of a shopping center site to be landscaped and at least 20 percent of the parking areas, excluding peripheral planted strips, to be landscaped.

Neighborhood shopping centers   Neighborhood shopping centers occupy sites of five to ten acres. Unless they have a large volume of walk-in trade, they need a higher ratio of parking lot area to store space (3 to 1 or 3.5 to 1) than do regional and community centers because of their higher rate of customer turnover. The layout of neighborhood centers typically is simpler than that of larger centers. Buildings are often arranged in a simple linear, L-shaped, or U-shaped pattern. Pedestrian areas may be limited to nothing more than paved walks in front of stores. However, in many neighborhood shopping centers it has proved advantageous to include a small landscaped plaza or courtyard with a tot lot for toddlers, where housewives can stop and visit during their shopping trip. Such amenities not only create good customer relations but also cause delays which may lead to unplanned purchases.

Renewal of commercial areas

A major share of the billions of dollars that have been expended on both publicly assisted and privately funded urban renewal has gone to finance the redevelopment of commercial areas. Most of these projects have been located within or adjacent to central business districts. Although the federal aid program under Title I of the federal Housing Act of 1949 was originally aimed exclusively at eliminating residential blight and even required that an urban renewal project area be primarily in residential use either before or after redevelopment, the emphasis gradually shifted. Primarily as the result of pressure from the nation's larger cities, the 1954 Housing Act permitted 10 percent of capital grant funds to be expended on nonresidential renewal (i.e., projects on sites that were in nonresidential use both before and after renewal), and the 1959 Housing Act raised the quota to 20 percent.

Few communities in the nation are not experiencing some degree of decline in their central business districts. Problems resulting from loss of sales to outlying

Figure 9–3   Quincy Market, Boston. By the 1950s this public market was
obsolete, although it had a superb location in the heart of Boston's
waterfront and government areas. The 1826 building was restored and renovated
to provide for a wide variety of public markets as well as shops and restaurants.
At the top, the market is seen beyond Faneuil Hall in the center foreground.
The variety of leisure activities that the market fosters is seen below.

shopping centers and loss of jobs to suburban office developments and industrial parks are nearly universal. Municipal governments have a major stake in the economic health of their CBDs because these districts are, typically, the principal sources of property tax and sales tax revenues. A substantial part of the business establishments, particularly the financial institutions, are tied to downtown as a headquarters location. A declining central district is an embarrassment to them. Merchants are not merely embarrassed; they also suffer financial losses that can be recouped only by the opening of suburban branches. For all of these reasons it is not surprising that a major effort has been made to revitalize the nation's CBDs.

The Chicago stockyards: a comeback The Chicago stockyards, abandoned by all of the meatpacking companies, largely because of changing technology in transportation and distribution, is trying for a comeback. The stockyards area of one square mile is about five miles southwest of the Loop (central business district). Several small manufacturing companies have moved to the stockyards area, and several other companies have made commitments to stay there.

The Chicago Economic Development Commission has several incentives to offer companies considering the stockyards or other areas of Chicago; they show the range of incentives that can be considered by local governments. These are:

Real property tax reduction: The property tax assessment can be reduced from 40 percent to 16 percent of market value for thirteen years on industrial properties "redeveloped or substantially rehabilitated" in areas of high unemployment.

Sales tax relief: The state sales tax on the purchase of equipment and machinery for manufacturing and assembling

tangible personal property is to be phased out over six years.

Industrial revenue bonds: Companies needing financial help can apply for city revenue bond financing at interest rates that are substantially less than commercial rates.

Federal loan guarantees: The U.S. Economic Development Administration can guarantee a certain percentage of business loans to give the business a better interest rate.

Joint ventures: The Chicago Economic Development Commission can develop joint ventures with companies so that the commission can acquire and develop land in certain industrial parks for the company.

Investment tax credit: The 1978 Federal Revenue Act expands the investment tax credit so that it applies to companies that rehabilitate plants that are twenty or more years old. The credit also can be used for construction of new fixed assets.

Source: Abstracted from Bill Barnhart, "Smell of Success Arises from Stockyards," Chicago Sun–Times, 21 January 1979, pp. 59–60.

Few if any downtown renewal projects have aimed to rebuild the entire central district. Such an undertaking would be prohibitively costly, even in a small city, and often would involve more surgery than necessary to cure the patient. Instead, downtown urban renewal projects have been basically of two different types. Both have preserved the essentially healthy portion of the central core and have used it as a springboard for additional development. One type of project has introduced amenity features, such as a pedestrian mall or a landscaped central plaza, into the core and has located new buildings on adjacent underdeveloped properties. A number of projects of this type, such as the malls in Minneapolis, Kalamazoo, Sacramento, and Fresno, and Midtown Plaza in Rochester, New York, have aimed at rejuvenating declining retail areas, some with greater success than others. Provision of additional parking, improved access, and beautification of streets in the surrounding area are common features of this type of project. The other more usual type of project has involved clearance and reconstruction of a major area or major areas close to the core, planned to yield spillover benefits while not drawing business away from the core. Office buildings are generally the predominant use in these projects. Successful examples include Penn Center in Philadelphia, Government Center in Boston, and Constitution Plaza in Hartford.

The range of uses found in downtown urban renewal projects is almost as broad as the range typical of the entire CBD. Only establishments that cannot afford to pay the high rents that new development demands have been excluded. While suburban shopping centers have severely hampered the growth of downtown retailing, decentralization has not cut into the demand for office space in the CBD nearly as deeply. Consequently, most renewal projects contain far more office space than store space. Hotels and convention facilities are features of a considerable number of downtown projects. City halls and other public buildings are included in some, and theaters and concert halls can be found in a few. Apartment buildings have been combined with various harmonious types of commercial development such as ground floor convenience stores, restaurants, and high fashion shops.

Mixed use projects Some of the most successful central district renewal projects have combined a wide variety of uses, although offices generally have been the predominant use. The original CBD renewal project, Rockefeller Center, built in midtown Manhattan in the 1930s and subsequently expanded, offers a prime example of mixed uses: 15.5 million square feet of office space, 1.5 million square feet in more than 200 retail shops, several theaters (including the 6,200 seat Radio City Music Hall), and an outdoor ice skating rink.

In the 1960s two highly successful mixed use central district renewal projects were built in Baltimore (Charles Center) and Atlanta (Peachtree Center). Charles Center combines 1.7 million square feet of office space, 335,000 square feet in retail stores, 650 hotel rooms, 400 apartment units, and two theaters. Baltimore's convention center was built on an adjoining site. Architect–developer John Portman's Peachtree Center includes 2 million square feet of office space, 300,000 square feet in retail stores, 2,200 hotel rooms, and a 2 million square foot merchandise mart.

Portman also designed and was a financial partner in Embarcadero Center, a federally assisted urban renewal project in downtown San Francisco containing 3 million square feet of office and store space and an 800 room hotel with a dramatic twelve story high lobby. A spectacular hotel designed by Portman is also a key element in the still incomplete Bunker Hill Redevelopment Project adjacent to the Los Angeles CBD. In addition to office and apartment towers, this development includes the Music Center, a complex of three civic theaters. Perhaps the most dramatic of all central district renewal projects in the country is Detroit's recently completed Renaissance Center. This $337 million development of the Ford Motor Company, General Motors, and other Detroit industries aims to revitalize the declining CBD of the motor city. Also designed by Portman, the complex includes a seventy-three story, 1,400 room hotel, four office towers, and a three level shopping mall. Renaissance Center may prove to be the most challenging test to date of the efficacy of downtown renewal.

"Old town" projects A very different type of central district revitalization project, both in character and scale, has proved successful in a number of cities. "Old town" projects involve the restoration of one or more blocks of antique buildings to approximate their original character. Ground floor occupants typically are restaurants, cafés, gift shops, and boutiques, although in San Fran-

cisco's Jackson Square the principal use is by wholesale furniture establishments serving interior designers. Office space on the upper floors of "old town" buildings is frequently occupied by small business and professional offices.

The first and still the outstanding example of district-wide rehabilitation in the country is the Georgetown area of Washington, D.C., where residences as well as commercial buildings have been restored. Successful smaller scale "old town" commercial developments include Chicago's Gaslight Square, St. Louis's Laclede Village, Denver's Larimer Square, and Seattle's Pioneer Square. Some neighborhood shopping areas have received similar rehabilitation treatment without changing their basic function. Old Town Mall in Baltimore is an example.

Neighborhood commercial centers   The concern of cities with the decline of their central business districts has frequently caused the plight of neighborhood commercial centers to be ignored. In older cities many are in serious need of assistance, but local governments have been slow to recognize this as a public responsibility. In neighborhoods with largely low income residents, the commercial center often is perceived as unsafe; consequently, insurance rates have increased, rents have risen, and vacancies have resulted. Owners of neighborhood stores seldom have the capital necessary to invest in improvements. Landlords seldom provide more than minimum maintenance. The cities generally ignore the situation. To solve the problem of neighborhood commercial center decay a combination of public and private effort is necessary. Revitalization programs are usually initiated by the public sector, but property owners and merchants will need to participate if the effort is to succeed. Rehabilitation of store buildings is as essential as streets and utilities improvements, provision of parking, and beautification of the business district.

Modernization projects   A recent trend is the remodeling of shopping centers that are less than a quarter of a century old. So that they may compete with newer regional centers, open malls have been enclosed and air conditioned, store buildings have had their faces lifted, parking has been decked, and landscaping and other amenities have been added. While this kind of renewal has been a phenomenon of the late 1970s, the pace can be expected to accelerate as more shopping centers begin to show their age.

The maturation of a regional shopping center   When Northland Center opened in 1954 it was the first major regional shopping center in the United States. Since then it has been extremely influential in the development of hundreds of shopping centers in other parts of the country, and also in the generation of extensive housing and other kinds of development in its own area.

The center was located twelve miles from the central area of Detroit on 409 acres of land in an area that was sparsely populated and showed few signs of urbanization. The center opened with 70 stores, 900,000 square feet of floor space, and parking for almost 10,000 cars. The Northland anchors from the start have been Hudson's department store and J. C. Penney.

Like any other organization, Northland was born (in 1954), grew up, reached "old age," and was renewed (in 1975) when the center was expanded and the malls were enclosed. Over the years a multiplier effect has generated a hospital, hotels, apartment buildings, and ancillary services in adjacent areas. What was open country in 1954 is now the developed city of Southfield, Michigan.

Financing of renewal Whether entirely privately financed or publicly assisted, the renewal of commercial areas cannot be undertaken without first having been demonstrated to be financially feasible. If renewal is proposed as one of the means of implementing the community's comprehensive plan, the preliminary feasibility studies at least will be the responsibility of the local planning agency. The primary requirement is a realistic appraisal of the market demand for the types of commercial enterprises (retail stores, offices, etc.) that the plan seeks to attract. Next, studies need to be made of property values, structural condition of buildings, potential of sites for clearance or rehabilitation of buildings, parking requirements, projected traffic, and needed public improvements. Unless these studies reasonably lead to the conclusion that renewal is likely to be financially feasible, the comprehensive plan should not propose this alternative.

If a renewal project is proposed for public assistance, study of community costs and benefits also is in order. Such questions as these should be answered: What physical improvements are likely to result? How much private investment and how much public investment are likely to be required? What gains can be anticipated in property values and tax revenues, in retail sales volumes, and in employment? What indirect economic benefits to the community (such "ripple effects" as increased sales and jobs in businesses servicing new downtown development) can be anticipated? What social costs, such as the need to relocate marginal businesses or low income people now living in the area, will be involved? If both quantifiable and nonquantifiable benefits to the community cannot reasonably be expected to outweigh comparable cost items, publicly assisted renewal should not be proposed.

Although many commercial renewal projects including such enormously costly ones as Detroit's Renaissance Center are privately financed, the greater number are accomplished with public financial assistance. The federal government is the principal source of these subsidies. Under Title I of the Housing Act of 1949 the U.S. Department of Housing and Urban Development (HUD) made loans to finance urban renewal activities and grants of up to two-thirds of net project costs (three-fourths of net costs in cities of less than 50,000 population). The local share of the cost was permitted to be contributed in the form of public improvements benefiting the project area. It was common practice to gerrymander the boundaries of urban renewal project areas so as to receive credit for the cost of local public improvements that were needed regardless of whether there was a project.

Along with HUD's other categorical grant programs, federal aid to urban renewal was systematically starved by the Nixon and Ford administrations in the early 1970s. However, communities were and still are free to spend their federal revenue sharing funds to help finance renewal projects, although the amounts that can be used for this purpose usually are stringently limited by other more pressing public needs. Since 1974 the Housing and Community Development Act has made funds available to cities specifically to improve housing conditions and remove urban blight. Under this rubric, it is possible to use Community Development Block Grant funds for renewal of commercial areas to the extent that other types of improvement projects do not have higher priorities, and provided that HUD approves the grant application as sufficiently related to the purposes of the act. The problem that remains is that any major renewal project, particularly a large scale commercial project, takes years to accomplish, and the necessary private investment is unlikely to be forthcoming unless the city is firmly committed to a continuing program of public assistance. Such a commitment frequently is not practical because Community Development Block Grant applications are funded annually, on the basis of three year programs.

As an alternative or a supplement to the use of federal grants, a number of states have enacted legislation permitting the financing of urban renewal projects using tax allocation bonds. This procedure involves the diversion of all property tax revenues collected in the project area in excess of the amount collected in the year immediately prior to the initiation of the project into a special fund. This fund is used to amortize the principal and interest on bonds issued in amounts sufficient to cover the public costs of the project. Once the bonds are paid off, the flow of tax increment is rediverted back to the city, the county, the school district, and other local taxing agencies. The tax allocation bonding device is particularly well suited to financing commercial renewal because it typically yields significant increases in real property tax revenues. For example in the relatively small city of Pasadena, California (population 110,000), annual tax increments amounted to $3 million five years after initiation of a downtown project and were projected to rise to $6 million by the tenth year.

Several federal assistance programs are now available to help finance the revitalization of business districts. Because of overall shortages of funds and mandatory limits on the amounts of individual loans and loan guarantees, these programs are most suitable for revitalization of small city CBDs, portions of larger CBDs, or neighborhood commercial centers. It is almost essential to obtain leverage from available public funds in order to acquire sufficient capital to finance a project. One federal program can be piggybacked with another, federal moneys can be combined with local public funds, and federal and/or local funds can be used in conjunction with private capital. Most of the federal sources for financing rehabilitation of private commercial properties can be tapped only if there is city participation in a coordinated improvement program.

Small Business Administration (SBA) section 502 loans and loan guarantees of up to $500,000 per business can be used for rehabilitation, property acquisition, expansion, new construction, or fixtures. The funds available for direct loans are very limited; therefore, the SBA usually guarantees bank loans, or the bank can take a first mortgage and SBA a second mortgage. For businesses to be eligible for section 502 loans or guarantees, a nonprofit Local Development Corporation must be created to serve as a conduit.

The corporation may be citywide in scope or may be organized by the business owners in a particular district. Public funds are usually necessary to assist in setting up and administering the corporation. Loans or guarantees are channeled to the borrower from the Small Business Administration through the Local Development Corporation, which is required to contribute 10 percent of the project cost. The city can contribute all or part of this amount using federal Community Development Block Grant funds or local sources such as bond issue revenues for this purpose. Frequently the private borrower contributes a portion of the required 10 percent share. The Small Business Administration's section 7A program makes loans directly to business owners, but the maximum amount of a loan is only $150,000. Up to 90 percent of a private loan not exceeding $350,000 (or $500,000 in special cases) can be guaranteed by the SBA.

HUD's section 312 low interest loans are available through cities to finance commercial as well as residential rehabilitation. To obtain maximum results, HUD urges the use of this program in combination with local loan programs. Commercial projects must compete with residential projects for available funds, and housing improvement programs have a higher priority in most cities. Use of section 312 programs is most appropriate in situations in which relatively small amounts of capital are needed because loans are limited to $50,000 per business. Unlike the Small Business Administration loan program, only rehabilitation projects are eligible. HUD requires that there be a local code enforcement program in the project area. Baltimore's Old Town Mall project was financed using section 312 loan funds.

Local Development Corporations are eligible to receive federal Economic Development Administration grants and low interest loans if it can be demonstrated that the projects to be financed will improve employment opportunities. Projects must conform with an areawide economic development program.

A city can use Community Development Block Grant funds to make loans to finance rehabilitation of commercial properties, to write down interest rates, or to guarantee a portion of private commercial loans. The city of St. Paul has used these funds to match loan funds provided by local banks for neighborhood commercial center revitalization projects. The city of Baltimore has issued bonds to cover its share of the cost of rehabilitation programs. In Chicago bond issue funds have been used to pay for public improvements in neighborhood business districts. The city of Detroit has established local assessment districts for this purpose.

Another means of publicly assisting commercial construction and rehabilitation projects is to grant tax concessions to property owners by excluding the value of the improvements from assessments over specified time periods. However, such favorable tax treatment is barred by the laws of many states, and there has been relatively little experience with using this device to stimulate commercial development. It has been employed primarily to attract industries to undeveloped sites.

Planning for industry

Location and sites

While the location of commercial development depends almost entirely on local market demand, national and regional markets are more important criteria for industrial location. Proximity to materials sources and components suppliers is essential to the operations of many types of manufacturing and processing plants. However, long distance transmission of electricity and natural gas have freed most industries from having to locate close to their energy sources. The growing versatility of truck transport has reduced dependency on railroad service, but it is still the most economical method of shipping heavy or bulky products over land. It is advantageous and in some cases it is essential for certain types of industries, such as petroleum refineries, to be located at deep water ports.

Industrial development requires large, flat or nearly flat sites with soils having good load-bearing qualities. It is advisable to have rail service available, and truck access via one or more highways or major arterial streets is mandatory. Necessary energy supply must be available or potentially available. Industrial sites should be isolated from existing and potential residential areas and from other land uses on which they might have an adverse impact. Even a totally nuisance-free plant housed in handsome buildings surrounded by well-maintained landscaping will create substantial automobile and truck traffic which will be unwelcome in nearby neighborhoods. Traffic noise and safety hazards are inevitable. Industries typically will not select sites where their operations are likely to result in complaints from nearby residential neighborhoods. Some types of commercial development, such as regional shopping centers and office parks, try to avoid locations close to industrial concentrations so that the traffic they generate will not have to compete with industrial traffic using the same routes.

While in the past thirty years or so commercial development followed the movement of population to the suburbs, industrial development virtually led the way. The relatively small sites available in central cities are unsuitable for the production methods of modern industry.

Early in the century automobile manufacturers introduced the specialization of industrial tasks in a system of continuous flow production. Large one story buildings are necessary to house production lines. Materials storage areas, truck loading berths, and employee parking areas greatly increase the need for spacious sites. These typically are as readily available at reasonable prices in subur-

Figure 9–4 Irvine Industrial Complex, Irvine, California. This 6,300 acre industrial district provides flexibility for many kinds and sizes of enterprises and is served by three transportation modes: air, rail, and freeway.

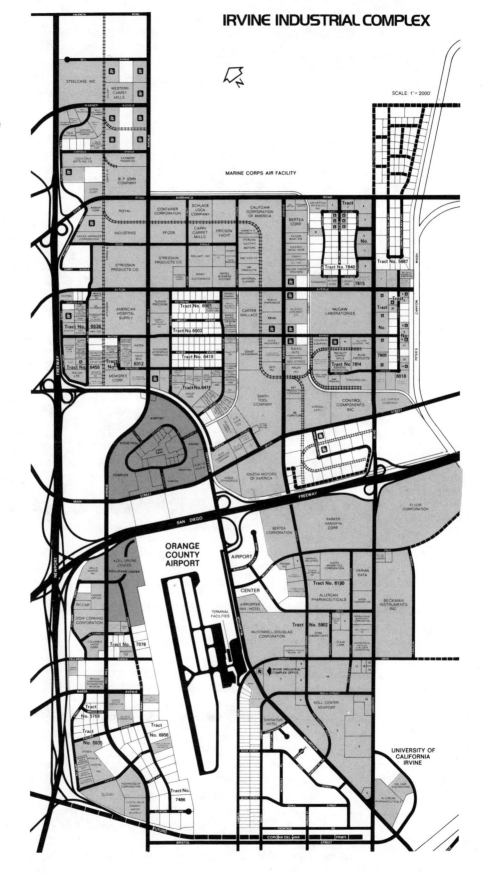

ban locations as they are scarce and costly in central cities. In the period 1954–65, 63 percent of industrial construction in metropolitan areas in the United States occurred in suburbs, and the percentage was even higher (73 percent) in the northeastern states.

Traffic congestion, overburdened public services, high taxes, poverty, crime, and the other ills of central cities have further increased the attractiveness of outlying industrial locations in recent years. Needless to say, the growing suburbanization of industry has also exacerbated the plight of central cities, depriving them of badly needed tax revenues and creating mounting unemployment accompanied by growing welfare rolls and other symptoms of poverty. (These issues are described at some length in Chapter 16.)

Figure 9–5   Technology Park, Atlanta, Georgia, contains both offices and manufacturing. One of the advantages of the planned industrial district is the opportunity to provide attractive landscaping, off-street parking, and horizontal layout.

In the early years of industrial decentralization (1945–55), large subdivisions of moderately priced homes were built within easy commuting distance of most substantial concentrations of suburban industrial development. Some of these residential accommodations were so large as to constitute virtual new communities. For example, Levittown, Pennsylvania, built to house the workers at a nearby U.S. Steel plant, provided 6,200 dwellings as well as necessary shopping centers, schools, parks, and other community facilities. At the other extreme, Stanford Industrial Park in Palo Alto, California, created 18,000 jobs, but very little moderately priced housing was built in the community or nearby. The result was not only long commuting distances for the workers but also the need to build a high capacity expressway through a residential area, accompanied by continuing complaints from local residents about traffic congestion and noise.

More common than this almost all-or-nothing type of situation are instances in which the number of industrial jobs and the supply of suitably priced housing are significantly out of balance. Sites should not be designated for industrial development by the comprehensive plan unless appropriately located lands are earmarked for the construction of housing that will be required by industrial workers. If suitable sites for housing are not available within the community, at least there should be assurance that an adequate supply will be provided within a reasonable time-distance of industrial employment centers. Thirty minutes is often cited as a desirable maximum commuting time, but the energy shortage could cause a reduction of this standard.

In recent years some suburban communities that have welcomed industrial development but have excluded housing suitable for industrial workers have been subjected to law suits demanding zoning changes necessary to provide sites for moderately priced housing. The first successful suits of this kind, in the New Jersey courts, may presage similar attacks on exclusionary zoning in other states.[4]

With the exception of very large plants and those that require free-standing sites because of their need to be close to raw material sources or because of their incompatibility with other plants, industrial parks provide the most advantageous locations because they are designed to meet the requirements of modern industries. Operating efficiencies can be gained and conflicts with neighbors can be avoided when an area is especially planned to accommodate industrial development. Interdependent plants can take advantage of opportunities to cluster in close proximity. For example at Tampa Industrial Park two major breweries are served by a glass manufacturing plant and a brewer's grain supplier located in the same industrial park.

Most industrial parks, particularly large ones (over 500 acres), require rail service. Proximity to airports, both for air shipments and executive travel, is considered desirable by many industries. Locations adjacent to freeways offer several kinds of advantages. Time savings in truck transportation result in lower costs and expanded market areas. The labor market area also expands as the time-distance to the work place decreases. Certain industries benefit from the advertising value of visual exposure to a freeway, particularly if their plants are sources of pride. If an industrial park in an urban area is sufficiently large and intensively developed, it will be able to obtain transit service which can result in significant cost savings both directly for employees and indirectly for employers.

Industrial park sites must be relatively flat and well drained. Land coverage by large buildings, storage areas, and parking lots creates storm water runoff problems that must be solved. Water supply, sewerage, and gas and electric service need to be available or easily extended to the site. Flexibility is the key to planning industrial parks, because it is virtually impossible to predetermine the precise site requirements of individual plants. An industrial park should be sufficiently large and should have a configuration that will accommodate a variety of types and sizes of plants. The area can be as small as fifty acres, or as large as thousands of acres, assuming that it is realistic to anticipate development at such a large scale. It is usually advantageous to estimate the need for industrial sites fairly generously and to plan a number of different locations for industrial parks, unless competing land uses would be shortchanged. An adequate or more than adequate supply of industrial land will ensure that there will not be future shortages and resulting high prices which will discourage development. A variety of locations makes it possible to accommodate different types of plants which may have mutually incompatible features. However, industrial sites should not be so widely scattered or so distant from other planned urbanization as to result in unnecessarily high public costs for street maintenance, utilities, and police and fire protection.

Depending on the size of the site, access to an industrial park should be provided via two or more arterial streets. If there is only a single major access route, the dead-end situation is likely to create traffic congestion. For all but the smaller industrial parks (of 100 acres or less), four lane access streets are necessary. Within the park local streets may have only two lanes, but each lane should be fourteen to sixteen feet wide to accommodate large trucks. Intersections should be designed to handle truck turning movements with ease. A simple gridiron street plan, or a variation featuring ninety degree T intersections instead of four way intersections, is usually the most suitable type of layout. The advantage of a grid plan is that the land can first be subdivided into rectangular sites of the largest size for which there is likely to be a demand, and these sites can subsequently be subdivided into smaller ones of almost any size desired. The layout of individual industrial sites will vary according to the requirements of each particular plant. Adjacent to the building, space must be provided for truck loading and for materials, products, and waste storage. Elsewhere on the site, truck storage and employee parking should be accommodated, along with sufficient space for landscaping. Not to be overlooked is the importance of reserving room on the site for possible future plant expansion.

Despite the attractions of industrial parks and other suburban locations, there still are possibilities for central cities to retain existing industries and to attract new ones. Where good transit service is available so that provision of parking for employees can be minimized, an existing industrial building in sound condition may be a less costly alternative than a suburban site. A comparison should take account of the rising cost of new construction, the relatively low cost of remodeling, increasing suburban land prices, restrictive land use regulations, mounting traffic congestion at outlying industrial sites, potential shortages of utilities capacity, and the impact of the energy crisis.

Older central city loft buildings with space available at low rents can play an important incubator function for infant industrial enterprises. Where buildings are large enough it is often possible to accommodate a production line operation on a single floor. Locating closely related operations on different floors in the same building, with elevators, loading docks, freight handling facilities, and storage areas shared, can result in major gains in production efficiency. Central city industrial sites also can offer certain external economies by reason of their proximity to suppliers; to financial, accounting, and legal services; to resident labor; and to the market for the product itself. The availability of the existing urban infrastructure (streets, transit, utilities, and other public facilities and services) may offer cost advantages.

In addition to the possibilities of adapting aging industrial buildings to meet today's needs, consideration should be given to renewal or new development in areas, such as the corridors along railroad lines and deep water channels, which are particularly suitable for this type of use. A 1972 architectural/cost study in Cleveland involving the design of innovative prototypical multistory industrial buildings suitable for in-city sites demonstrated that they can be competitive in cost with suburban locations.[5] The emphasis of the federally assisted urban renewal program on housing and downtown redevelopment, combined with market conditions of the 1950–75 period, resulted in relatively little industrial renewal. However, as central city sites are becoming more competitive and federal Community Development Block Grant funds are available to write down land assembly and clearance costs, the potential of redevelopment for industrial use in the years ahead appears stronger.

Regulation of industrial development

Industrial development is regulated by two different types of laws: local ordinances, primarily zoning and subdivision ordinances; and federal and state statutes prescribing air and water quality standards. The state laws are designed to meet the requirements of the federal Clean Air Act and Water Pollution Control Act as promulgated by the U.S. Environmental Protection Agency. State air and water quality standards may be more restrictive than federal standards. In addition, some states require the preparation of an environmental impact statement before a new industrial development (or any other type of development) is authorized by a local government, regardless of whether the proposal meets local land use and state air and water quality standards.

Zoning Early zoning ordinances permitted almost any type of use in industrial districts, although industries were not permitted in residential or commercial districts. Later, industrial districts ceased to be treated as dumping grounds for all types of uses when it was recognized that the presence of dwellings in industrial areas can be as detrimental to the health and safety of the residents as the presence of industrial plants in residential areas. Today all types of residential development customarily are excluded from industrial districts and it is not uncommon to bar certain inharmonious types of commercial development as well.

Most zoning ordinances classify manufacturing and processing plants into at least two categories—light industry and heavy industry—and provide a district for each. Often light industries are permitted in heavy industrial districts, but heavy industries are never permitted in light industrial districts. Some ordinances have a third district, commonly termed the industrial park district, in which limitations are even more stringent than in the light industrial district. Sometimes there is a transitional general industrial district between the light and heavy industrial categories. This is particularly appropriate when plants with severe nuisance characteristics or safety hazards, such as slaughterhouses and explosives manufacturing plants, are permitted in the heavy industrial district. It is more common, however, to authorize such uses on a special permit basis, subject to prescribed conditions, in the heavy industrial district, or to bar them from the community entirely.

Traditionally, zoning ordinances have contained a list of uses permitted in each industrial district. The uses are assigned to the districts on the basis of the assumed severity of their impacts. This type of regulation is relatively simple to write and to administer and enforce. However, in this era of rapid technological change it is difficult to keep a use list complete and up-to-date. Such lists are also an unreliable basis for regulation of industrial development because they fail to take account of the impacts resulting from a plant's size and of the possible differences in operating procedures of plants manufacturing the same product.

Performance standards In 1954 Dennis O'Harrow, then executive director of the American Society of Planning Officials, published a landmark study, *Performance Standards in Industrial Zoning,*[6] which recognized the arbitrariness of classifying industries merely by name, on the basis of their traditional methods of operation, and proposed that they be classified on the basis of their actual performance characteristics. This can be accomplished by prescribing specific standards for observable or scientifically measurable industrial plant emissions and other potentially detrimental impacts. Appropriately different levels of performance can be permitted in different districts.

Theoretically, performance standards could be prescribed for nonindustrial uses, but they are less suitable for this purpose. The most serious impact of most commercial development, for example, is the traffic it generates, and this factor cannot be directly controlled by zoning regulations. However, certain features of nonindustrial development, such as emissions from food market incinerators and glare from illuminated signs and parking lot lighting, can appropriately be regulated by prescribing performance standards.

The first zoning ordinance substituting performance standards for the traditional use lists was adopted by the city of Chicago in 1957. Since then, hundreds of cities and urban counties have followed suit. The use of performance standards has a precedent in building codes, which at one time specified materials and construction methods. Now building codes simply prescribe fire resistance, load bearing capacity, and similar performance criteria.

The administration of performance standard regulations occurs in two stages: ensuring that the standards will be met by a proposed industrial plant, and ensuring that they are met after the plant is in operation. In a large city or an urban county the zoning administration staff will usually have sufficient technical knowledge to determine in advance, on the basis of information submitted by the applicant and checked for validity, whether a proposed plant will meet prescribed standards. However, in complex cases or where new products or processes are involved it may be necessary to call upon consultants with special expertise. Smaller communities must depend mainly on the advice of consultants, but this seldom is burdensome because there are relatively few applications for new plants to be reviewed. Many cities and counties shift the cost of consultants' fees to the applicant, just as the latter must pay for staff processing of the application.

Enforcement of performance standards once the new plant is in operation is also a staff responsibility, supplemented by consultant assistance when necessary. Routine monitoring of plants with potential nuisance features may be required, but most enforcement activity occurs in response to public complaints. Performance standard regulations may be applied retroactively to preexisting plants provided that a reasonable amount of time is allowed to bring them into conformity.

This chapter will not deal with the technical contents of industrial performance standards but will merely discuss the various types of standards that appear in most zoning ordinances of this kind.

While regulations prescribing air quality and water quality remain on the books in some zoning ordinances, federal standards administered at the state, regional, or local government level now control air and water pollution. The Clean Air Act of 1970 charges the U.S. Environmental Protection Agency (EPA) with establishing national air quality standards for seven types of pollutants (carbon monoxide, nitrogen oxides, hydrocarbons, ozone, particulates, sulfur oxides, and a miscellaneous group including heavy metals, radioactive agents, and other pollutants). EPA has designated all areas currently not meeting the standards or which may violate them by 1985 as Air Quality Maintenance Areas. Each state is required to formulate an implementation plan to achieve and maintain the federal air quality standards. States that do not contain any Air Quality Maintenance Areas must plan measures to prevent significant deterioration of air quality. States that do contain such areas must also submit a more detailed analysis of the impact of future growth and development on air quality.

The implementation plans are enforced by permit systems. The federal law requires the states to have adequate legal authority to prevent construction or continued operation of a source that emits pollutants in violation of the national standards. In the few states that have not instituted permit systems, EPA does so. Many states have delegated the permit power to regional agencies in metropolitan areas whose boundaries are coterminous with natural air basins. Some states such as California have blanketed the entire state with such air pollution control districts. In other states the permit authority is vested in local governments. EPA classifies air pollution sources as direct (smelters, paper mills, steel mills, etc.) and indirect (facilities that attract mobile sources such as highways, shopping centers, and airports). The effect on air quality of each existing and proposed source requires special study. Analysis and projection of the emissions potential of a particular source is a complex procedure taking account of topographic and meterological conditions as well as the operating characteristics of the source. Existing and potential emissions from other sources in the air basin must also be considered.

The Federal Water Pollution Control Act of 1972 sets goals for the attainment of water suitable for swimming and fishing by 1983 and the elimination of pollution discharges by 1985. Instead of prescribing uniform water quality standards, the law controls the amount of pollutants that may be discharged in each instance. Because there are significant differences in the capacities of water bodies to handle concentrations of pollutants, criteria for each particular body of water are set individually. The law permits the states to administer water quality controls provided that they submit programs that receive EPA approval and that they have legal authority to enforce the controls. As with air quality, water quality is regulated by a permit system. Some states delegate the permit power to regional districts or local governments.

Water pollution discharges are classified as point sources, such as a sewer outfall or an industrial waste outlet, and nonpoint sources, such as runoff from a paved area or from an agricultural operation. The standards that are used in administering water quality regulations are complex and they depend basically on the type of effluent and the absorbtion capacity of the receiving waters. Standards will vary according to the local situation, the quality of the water, the affected fish and wildlife, and the need to protect public health. Every point source is classified according to two standards: a *technology standard* which prescribes what is economically achievable in pollution reduction, and a *water quality standard* which prescribes the additional reduction that is necessary to achieve the environmental goal appropriate for the particular body of water (suitable for drinking, swimming, etc.). Technology standards are used as the base level for limitations, but the discharge of pollutants is governed by water quality standards if they are more stringent. Preparation of regional water quality plans is financed by EPA grants to the states under section 208 of the Water Pollution Control Act.

Noise nuisances have been the subject of considerable recent scientific research because of public concern with airport and highway noise. Measurement of industrial noise is best accomplished by use of a sound level meter meeting the standards of the American National Standards Institute. The meter has a built-in weighting device which corrects the reading (in decibels) to reflect the human ear's greater sensitivity to high pitch than to low pitch sounds. Noise levels are most commonly measured at the site boundary line. Because noise is generally more disturbing to the community at night than during the daytime, more stringent noise level restrictions between 7:00 P.M. and 7:00 A.M. are common. Impact noises of short duration, such as the noise of a forging hammer or a punch press, are usually permitted to exceed by a prescribed amount the limits set for continuous noises.

Vibration refers to ground-transmitted oscillations such as those caused by the dropping of a forge hammer, the driving of piles, or blasting in a quarry. Such earthborne vibrations are measured by a seismograph or an accelerometer. Steady state vibration limits are set in terms of displacement (in thousandths of an inch) in relation to a sliding scale of frequencies (number of oscillations per second of vibration). For discontinuous impact vibrations the maximum permitted displacement may be as much as double the maximum prescribed for steady state vibrations. Like noise, vibrations are usually measured at the plant site boundary line.

Glare caused by industrial processes is generally readily controlled by shielding the light source. Glare is measured in footcandles by a photoelectric photometer with a spectral response similar to that of the human eye. Measurements are taken at the site boundary line.

In some instances zoning ordinances deal with fire and explosion hazards inherent in industrial materials and processes, although such hazards are generally regulated by fire prevention codes. Materials which decompose by detonation (explosives) often are prohibited, or, if permitted, are required to be stored and handled in accordance with the National Fire Codes published by the National Fire Protection Association. Limitations are usually imposed on storage of flammable liquids and gases. The amounts permitted to be stored vary significantly according to the flash point of the liquid or gas and whether it is stored above or below ground.

Performance standards governing electromagnetic radiation, heat, and humidity appear in some zoning ordinances, but industries with these kinds of emissions are relatively uncommon. Standards for discharge of liquid wastes and solid wastes usually are the subjects of separate local ordinances or state statutes.

Many cities and counties, particularly suburban communities that are selective about industrial development, not only have restrictive use lists or high performance standards but also require that industrial plants (and other types of nonresidential development) undergo design review. The site plan, indicating automobile and truck access and circulation, employee parking, truck loading and storage, materials storage, rail access and loading, building locations, landscaped areas, and pedestrian walks, must gain the approval of the local planning commission or a special design committee. In addition, many communities require review of the design of buildings and landscaping. Building materials and colors are often required to be submitted, and the location, size, and design of signs must be approved. Where design review by a public agency is not required it is often imposed by the owner or developer of an industrial park. Indeed, private design standards often surpass public standards in severity.

Environmental impact statements may affect the location and characteristics of industries. If environmental studies identify avoidable adverse impacts, conditions governing operating processes may be imposed in granting a permit. If the environmental impact statement indicates that a proposed plant will have significant unavoidable impacts, the permit may be denied altogether.

Conclusion:
some planning policy issues

Planning for business and industrial uses in the community raises fundamental planning policy issues. Events of the late 1970s make it likely that the attitudes of planners, governmental officials, and citizens toward business and industrial development will be substantially different from the attitudes of only five to ten years earlier.

Perhaps the most important issue is growth itself. In the early 1970s it would have been safe to conclude that all except some suburban bedroom communities defined new commercial and industrial development as "good for the community." Such growth was considered a mark of progress. Yet as concern for environmental values permeated the planning field, many persons began to question whether blind faith in new economic development was warranted. Numerous environmentalists and citizen groups became concerned that the secondary impacts of business and industrial growth might change the size and character of their communities. It is well known that new economic development can cause ripples throughout the local economy. Thus, new industrial jobs not only create income for a community but also create costs as new families move in and public services must be provided for them. (A major influx of employees of a new plant may also significantly change the characteristics of the local population. Such a change would require local government to plan to meet the needs of new population groups.) Larger scale communities are inevitably more complex and, in the opinion of some, less desirable places to live. From these factors stems the concept," Small is beautiful."

If citizens were beginning to question the costs and benefits of new economic growth, governmental decision makers were questioning the impact on city budgets. From this perspective it is not so much a matter of being for or against growth as it is a matter of allocating the capital costs of essential new public facilities and projecting the long-term costs of expanding public services. Thus, local government may attempt to shift some of the capital costs to a new business or industry if the government itself cannot generate sufficient revenues to provide the needed facilities.

If a new commercial or industrial project is large enough, there may be impacts on the local government simply because a threshold point has been reached in a particular service area. For example, new development may be the cause for the construction of a new sewage treatment plant or the expansion of an existing plant. Since such capital costs are seldom incremental (see Chapter 7) serious problems of the timing of public facilities expenditures may occur. In terms of service costs, a new shopping center may require a substantial increase in police services for traffic control and for patrols to prevent vandalism and burglaries.

New commercial and industrial development may also have impacts on existing businesses. For example, a planning agency and a city council may be faced with the agonizing choice of approving a new shopping center on the outskirts of the city that inevitably will hurt retail sales in the community's central business district, or of losing the tax revenues to a neighboring community. Or new industrial plants at the outskirts may simply be a place for relocating industries that are abandoning obsolete central city facilities. What is to be done with the older areas?

Whether a community is experiencing rapid growth or is suffering from decline may seriously affect its ability to plan for and regulate new economic development. Thus, the suburban community that is experiencing rapid growth and, therefore, is attractive to shopping center developers may find that it has a great deal of leverage in bargaining with these developers. Shopping center developers may want to get into the community so badly that they are willing to pay for costly public facilities that serve the center. On the other hand, mature cities or regions that are experiencing decline have little or no leverage and, instead, must offer nonfinancial inducements and financial incentives to persuade businesses to locate in their area.

A number of issues in planning for business and industrial development generate disagreement, and in many situations it is not clear what is the "right" choice for a community. For example, in the late 1970s a major redevelopment proposal for a central business district was made by private interests. The plan called for total clearance of a dozen blocks to provide a clean slate for redevelopment. Some community leaders proposed tax incentives to encourage this project. On the other hand, critics pointed out that very little attention was being paid to the businesses and jobs that would be destroyed. Would, for example, jobs be provided for the same class of workers? And who would really benefit from such a massive infusion of tax write-offs?

Another example that is being debated is whether some of the new economic development planning proposals (discussed in Chapter 20) are really helping local economies. Thus, some critics ask, is it worthwhile to build convention centers and new hotels which provide temporary construction jobs for those who are lucky enough to be in the building trades but, in the long run, provide the community with new jobs only for maids, busboys, and similar low paying occupations?

Finally, it is interesting to speculate what will happen during the 1980s and 1990s as much of the early twentieth century industrial plant begins to wear out. Suburban communities welcome new industrial development as long as it is clean, professional, and white collar. But where will we build the new steel plants, petrochemical refineries, and other industrial facilities that are essential to the economy but that may threaten environmental quality?

272 *The Practice of Local Government Planning*

Clearly, planning for business and industry deals with far more important issues than merely adequate parking lots and attractive landscaping. It deals with fundamental economic and social issues in the nation's cities and metropolitan areas.

1 J. Ross McKeever and Nathaniel M. Griffin, *Shopping Center Development Handbook* (Washington, D.C.: Urban Land Institute, 1977), p. 34.
2 J. Ross McKeever, *Shopping Center Zoning,* Technical Bulletin 69 (Washington, D.C.: Urban Land Institute, 1973), p. 25.
3 Barton-Aschman Associates, "Parking Demand at the Regionals," *Urban Land,* May 1977, pp. 3–11.
4 *South Burlington County NAACP* v. *Township of Mt. Laurel,* 336 A.2d 713 (1975); *Oakwood at Madison* v. *Township of Madison,* 371 A.2d 1192 (1977).
5 William A. Gould, "Can Inner City Multi-Level Buildings Compete?" *Urban Land,* April 1972, pp. 3–13.
6 Dennis O'Harrow, *Performance Standards in Industrial Zoning* (Columbus, Ohio: National Industrial Zoning Committee, 1954).

10 Recreation space, services, and facilities

The responsibility for providing leisure opportunities is normally shared by the public and private sectors in most communities, and planners have a primary role in the location, preservation, and design of open space; the development of recreational facilities; and the delivery of social programs to serve the leisure needs of the public.[1] Planners also work with other professionals in park and recreation agencies who are responsible for managing leisure opportunities.

The preparation of the park, recreation, and open space elements of a comprehensive plan is the responsibility of most local planning agencies. These agencies are also responsible for processing, approving, or preparing public and private recreation development proposals, land use changes, environmental impact statements, and the capital improvement budget that can have a significant effect on the quantity and quality of leisure opportunities. The location and effectiveness of open space and leisure opportunities can have a significant impact on the form and function of cities. These spaces and opportunities can also help to improve the quality of life and environment in urban America.

Leisure needs and resources

The task of translating human needs or leisure behavior into space and opportunities requires an understanding of the process and products of recreation planning and the methods and techniques commonly used to prepare recreation plans. It also requires an understanding of the ways in which recreation planning can be used to solve problems or realize potentials at both the systems and the site planning scales.

The nature of recreation planning

Recreation planning is a process that relates the leisure time of people to space.[2] It is an art and a science that uses the concepts and methods of many disciplines to provide public and private leisure opportunities in cities. In practice, recreation planning blends the knowledge and techniques of environmental design and the social sciences to develop alternatives to the way we use time, space, energy, and money to accommodate human needs.

In the broadest sense recreation planning is concerned with human development and the stewardship of land by helping to relate people to their environment and to each other. In a narrower sense recreation planning is most concerned with the variables of leisure behavior and open space. It is a hybrid of physical and social planning that has evolved from the professional fields of city planning, landscape architecture, and recreation and park administration. It also now includes aspects of public administration, sociology, civil engineering, forestry, geography, and environmental health.

Traditional emphasis Recreation planning has traditionally been identified with resource planning or facility planning. The major emphasis has been on open space preservation and the development of open spaces for outdoor recreation.

Figure 10–1 The park of the nineteenth century was a place for sitting, contemplating, and strolling. The later twentieth century park is a place for games, athletic competitions, picnics, family gatherings, and many other activities.

Before 1970 site design, organized competitive sports, and outdoor public spaces were emphasized in most recreation plans. The philosophical basis of these plans was the social reform or City Beautiful movement of the early 1900s. Public parks were viewed as natural refuges from the evils of the surrounding city—as pastoral retreats or escapes from urban congestion and pollution.

Current emphasis The current emphasis in recreation planning is on the relationship of public recreation opportunities to other types of land use, design, and access at the urban and regional scales. While the primary focus is still on the physical resource, this has been broadened to include social and environmental factors.

An expanded focus on urban beautification, community development, historic preservation, environmental interpretation, multiple use of public and private spaces for recreation, and a broad range of organized recreation programs is now common in most communities. The philosophical justification of most efforts is to beautify or renew the city to make it a desirable place to live in, work in, or visit.

Emerging emphasis   The emerging emphasis of recreation planning is a blend of environmental design, social science, and public administration intended to provide leisure opportunities as part of a human service and environmental management system. Both public and private spaces and services are included in a system of opportunities that is integrated on scales ranging from the neighborhood to the metropolitan area.

This emerging emphasis includes programs for human development, environmental management, systems planning, self-generated design and management, recycling of developed land into open space, noncompetitive self-programmed activities, creative play areas, and integration of arts, culture, senior citizen, day care, and adult education programs with parks and recreation.

Special programs for the mentally retarded and physically handicapped are considered the responsibility of parks and recreation departments.[3] Community gardens, car care clinics, skateboard parks, outdoor education, and New Games[4] and physical fitness programs are activities sponsored by park and recreation agencies. A new generation of spaces is being used to supplement existing resources; it includes: use of rooftops, cemeteries, pneumatic structures, and air rights over parking lots, and conversion of obsolete buildings to public or private recreational uses.

Previous distinctions between indoor and outdoor spaces and public versus private opportunities are fading with a broader view of recreation planning that integrates space and services. The traditional parks or recreation department is becoming part of new agencies with a broader mission, such as human services, life enrichment, and environmental planning and management.

The current and evolving emphasis on recreation planning requires more sensitive and sophisticated methods than the application of arbitrary standards and conventional wisdom of the past. New demands for citizen participation in the planning and design process, environmental and social impact assessment, cost-effectiveness of public investments, and the meeting of human needs will make the traditional emphasis of recreation planning seem romantic. These new demands call for rethinking the objectives, purposes, mission, and methods of recreation planning to meet the needs of the present and the future.

Purposes and objectives   Recreation planning develops alternatives for policy decisions by the public and private sector. It should be representative of what people want, imaginative in projecting what might be, and realistic in recognizing what is possible. It is based on the idea that cities are for people; that change, complexity, and compromise are the essence of cities; and that planning is a means of anticipating, or reacting to, change.

If a city is to provide effective leisure opportunities it needs a way of solving current problems or anticipating future needs. Recreation planning is one means of: (1) obtaining a perspective on these problems; (2) developing realistic alternatives; (3) formulating goals, policies, and recommendations for public and private decisions; (4) developing criteria to measure change; and (5) involving people in the planning, design, and decision processes.

Recreation planning has a mission that distinguishes it from other types of functional planning. This mission can be used to rationalize recreation planning as a function of local government; it can also be used to describe the responsibilities of a recreation planning unit or a consultant to a public agency. This mission includes the following:

1. Providing objective, current, and relevant information to community decision makers about the quantity and quality of existing or potential leisure opportunities
2. Improving the quantity and quality of the leisure experience for residents and visitors to the city
3. Providing an optimum range, mix, and location of leisure opportunities for all people
4. Preserving or developing appropriate recreation resources to serve their highest and best use
5. Relating recreation plans to other types of planning and the comprehensive plan
6. Promoting public understanding of and support for more effective recreation planning at all levels of government
7. Evaluating the effectiveness of existing and proposed public and private recreation development
8. Encouraging public and private cooperation to provide leisure opportunities in or near cities
9. Rationalizing existing and proposed park and recreation facilities
10. Encouraging innovation, demonstration, and research to improve the state-of-the-art.

Concepts, definitions, and principles

The nature of cities and recreation requires an understanding of basic terms, relationships, and issues before applying the methods of recreation planning. There is no consensus on all concepts because of the rapidly changing nature of recreation planning, but precedent and practice suggest these concepts as a place to begin in most communities.

Conceptual framework The overall planning task is to understand the significant relationships among people, cities, leisure, recreation, open space, and urban form. The detailed planning task is to relate time (leisure), activity (behavior), and space (environment) to a geographic area (the city). Both tasks require judgment, calculated risk decisions, and additional research. Both require demonstration to find out what will work best in situations ranging from the inner city to the suburb. In all cases, this conceptual framework is the basis for recreation planning:

1. Public parks, leisure services, and open space are vital aspects of urban form and function
2. Leisure services and spaces that are well designed, properly located, and adequately maintained, and that serve the needs of intended users, can improve the quality of urban life and environment
3. The planning and design process can provide a rational basis for community action to improve the quantity and quality of leisure opportunities in cities
4. Social research techniques can be used to measure leisure behavior in terms of preference or satisfaction for different types of activities or environments
5. These values can be translated into dimensions of time, space, and activity for different population groups
6. These factors can be related to the demand for and supply of existing or

potential leisure opportunities to indicate need in terms of area or services for a specific activity or set of activities

7. This need can be translated into measures of effectiveness or performance standards which reflect the values of people
8. These measures can play an important role in the planning and decision process for the provision of leisure opportunities in cities
9. The provision of leisure opportunities in cities can be a joint effort of the public and private sectors
10. This effort is worthwhile in human terms and can be justified by its social, economic, political, and environmental benefits.

Basic definitions Many recreation planning efforts are not effective because ambiguous terms are used to describe recreation. While no definition can meet all needs, there is general acceptance and common professional understanding of the terms leisure, recreation, outdoor recreation, park, and open space. These terms are described on this page.

Some definitions In the discussion found in this chapter, the following five basic terms are used to describe recreation space, services, and facilities:

Leisure: Any portion of an individual's time not occupied by gainful employment or used in the pursuit of essential activities.

Recreation: Any leisure time activity which is pursued for its own sake or which happens to a person as a result of a recreation experience.

Outdoor recreation: Leisure time activities which use an outdoor public or private space.

Park: Any public or private land set aside for aesthetic, educational, recreational, or cultural use.

Open space: All land and water in an urban area not covered by buildings.

Extensive glossaries and interpretations of these terms are available in many texts, plans, and government documents.[5] Because some terms may have different philosophical or pragmatic meanings in different communities, and because high levels of citizen participation are needed to revise or prepare a recreation plan, it is essential to establish a working set of definitions at the beginning of any planning effort.

Common principles There are some common principles of recreation planning that have been distilled from experience and research in a wide range of typical and extreme situations. These principles should be considered basic to the success of any planning effort and can be used to monitor the quality of the planning process:

1. All people should have access to recreational activities and facilities regardless of interest, age, sex, income, cultural background, housing environment, or handicap
2. Public recreation should be coordinated with other community recreation opportunities to avoid duplication and encourage innovation
3. Public recreation should be integrated with all other public services, such as education, health, and transportation
4. Facilities should be adaptable to future requirements
5. Facilities and programs should be financially feasible at all stages of development; operation and maintenance place a greater financial burden

on the municipality than the initial capital cost; more facilities require more staff
6. Citizens should be involved in all stages of the planning process
7. Planning should be a continuous process of data collection, review, and evaluation
8. Local, regional, and state plans should be integrated
9. Land should be acquired prior to development and dedicated to park and recreation uses
10. Facilities should make the most efficient use of land; should be designed and managed to provide for the convenience, health, safety, and pleasure of intended users; and should represent positive examples of design, energy use, and concern for people and the environment.

Significant relationships

The relationships among the city, people, leisure, outdoor recreation, open space, and urban form have been detailed in many sources.[6] This overview can be used as a justification for the provision of recreation space and services in cities.

People and the city   Our reliance on the city for a livelihood, social interaction, food, shelter, and services has made it the focus of American life. Most people meet their major needs, desires, and ambitions in a metropolitan area. Family life, employment, education, culture, and leisure activities essentially take place in an urban setting. Instead of viewing the city as a place to escape from during leisure, it can be considered a recreation resource with great potential. We can build cities in parks instead of parks in cities.

People and leisure   The prospect of leisure has become an end in itself for many people engaged in dull or meaningless work. Leisure also provides the time and means for human development or life enrichment in a technological, work-oriented society. A major problem for growing numbers of people is how and where to utilize increasing amounts of leisure. How we solve this problem may influence our culture and our society. Leisure can be the blessing or the curse of an urban society.

Leisure and recreation   Leisure and recreation are related but different concepts. While leisure has commonly been thought of as a period of time or state of mind and recreation has been perceived as an activity in space, the prevailing view has become much broader and more humanistic.[7] This view sees leisure as a context for pleasure and self-expression.

Recreation is perceived as what happens to people as a result of activities or experiences. Recreation is not a specific event or point in time or space; it is a state of being or an emotional condition independent of activity, leisure, or social acceptance. Recreation is what happens to people in terms of their self-image, achievement, or satisfaction and can occur at any time in many places. By this definition, the requirements for a recreation experience in cities go beyond traditional public spaces and programs. They include any aspect of a city where an individual can experience freedom, diversity, self-expression, challenge, or enrichment.

Outdoor recreation and open space   The relationship of outdoor recreation to open space is based on a biological need to retain some association with the natural environment in an urban setting and a psychological need for contrast and change in spatial surroundings and activities that most indoor environments do not provide. When these needs are linked with the routine indoor jobs of most people and the sterile, stressful, and ugly outdoor environments of many cities and suburbs, they generate strong desires for escape to open space, especially to those open spaces with a natural character. This is why many people seek recreation opportunities in regional parks, or travel long distances to public wilderness areas or private resorts.

This desire to experience open space also explains why many large urban parks with a natural character are heavily used and essential to those without the means to leave cities for this type of recreation experience. The same holds true at the neighborhood scale, except that the desire here is more for visual contrast to the surrounding area, simple outdoor recreation activities, or a social focus in a landscaped setting.

Open space and urban form Open space can be the "structural framework of a city to produce edges, foci, nodes, districts and regions of different size, scale and character."[8] The opportunity to experience an architectural element from or through open space is an important visual quality. No single design element can better shape and complement urban form than well-placed open space. Its ability to differentiate, integrate, or buffer different types of land use or activities is unsurpassed. Sensitively designed open space can give people a sense of identity and territoriality. It can define urban form and limit the physical size, shape, or density of a city or neighborhood.

Trends and issues

A perspective on the time, space, and municipal budgets devoted to providing public leisure services in urban America includes the following important facts and trends that should be considered in preparing recreation plans:

1. Neighborhood type public parks accommodate only a small proportion (5 percent) of the total population at any given time. Public parks of this type accommodate an insignificant portion of the average leisure time budget (0.1 hour per day), and both the number of users and the time they spend in urban parks is decreasing in relation to their total time budget for leisure and the amount of leisure time spent in nonurban and private recreation places. Most parks are underused or unused by a majority of the population they were intended to serve and the phenomenon of nonuse is common in both urban and suburban areas.[9]
2. Decreasing levels of disposable and real income and increasing levels of unemployment and inflation will decrease the demand for high cost activities (e.g., power boating, resorts, skiing). Conversely, it will increase the demand for simple low cost activities close to home (e.g., walking, bicycling, swimming, canoeing).[10]
3. The increasing cost of gasoline may force many people to change their priorities and seek energy conserving ways to spend their leisure in or near cities. The option of personal transportation will be replaced with mass transit, bicycle, or pedestrian access to local recreation opportunities.[11]
4. Because adequate public transit is not available to most regional and community parks, a significant number of the urban population (30 percent) who cannot drive or do not own cars must rely on local parks for recreation opportunities.[12]
5. Some of the nation's finest leisure resources (e.g., art museums, libraries) are close to low income, central city residents yet are comparatively little used by them. Conversely, many potential suburban users of these regional facilities do not use them because of travel distance or their lack of convenient access to the central city where most of these facilities are located.[13]

The complex problems and issues related to urban parks and recreation are summarized in the *National Urban Recreation Study*.[14] This study describes significant differences between the quality and quantity of opportunities provided by individual cities and major differences between the inner city and suburbs of most metropolitan areas. It supports the findings of other studies[15] that outline these problems and issues for recreation planning at the city and regional levels:

1. Most Americans live in urban areas. The resources for outdoor recreation are not where most people live. Severe inequities exist in the distribution of recreation opportunities and are becoming worse.
2. Federal policy and expenditures for recreation favor nonurban areas which are accessible only to families with automobiles and are used primarily for summer vacations.
3. Public outdoor recreation policies and programs have not changed with the speed of social change and are not meeting the challenge. Most cities continue to develop park and recreation facilities of a traditional type with few innovations in design or construction.
4. There is a serious lack of research and evaluation in urban recreation. The federal government has not provided adequate support to states and metropolitan areas for research and technical assistance.
5. There is a critical lack of open space in central cities and a need for natural areas within metropolitan areas.
6. Existing recreation opportunities in urban areas suffer severely from a shortage of operation and maintenance funds.
7. Preventing vandalism and protecting the safety of park users and staff members has become a serious problem in most major cities.
8. In most cities no concerted effort has been made to coordinate public and voluntary or private recreation services.
9. Many urban parks and playgrounds are empty. Inadequate design, maintenance, and programs prevent them from fulfilling their potential.
10. Most urban leisure spaces and services do not adequately serve the needs of racial or ethnic minorities, children, the elderly, the poor, and the handicapped.

A detailed study of recreation planning problems and issues in the central city has drawn the following conclusions:

1. Location of parks and recreation facilities is a primary factor affecting the success of recreation programs. Consideration must be given to population density and the availability of public transportation in the location of new facilities. The acquisition of large tracts in outlying areas will not meet the recreation needs of the great majority of city residents. Emphasis must be placed on neighborhood facilities.
2. In spite of a virtually unanimous commitment to increased recreation programs and opportunities, cities do not have the financial capability to sustain expanded recreation programs indefinitely. Cities increasingly must look to state and federal government for the additional financial assistance necessary to sustain the desired level of recreation programs.
3. Optimum utilization of potential recreation resources is not being achieved in most of the nation's cities. Publicly owned facilities with existing recreation capabilities are being underused. School facilities in particular, even in jurisdictions having city–school recreation agreements, are not being utilized effectively. Cities must expand the multiple use of facilities, establish park–school complexes, and employ imaginative designs and new construction techniques.
4. Lack of communication among city, county, and private agencies is a

major problem preventing the optimum utilization of existing recreational facilities and programs. Coordination is inadequate between city and county recreation departments and semi-public organizations carrying on recreation activities. Communication between recreation departments and the citizen is frequently inadequate. Citizens not only must be informed of the availability of the various programs, but also convinced that participation and utilization are worthwhile.

5. Cities must take into consideration the recreation needs of special segments of the population in developing priorities. In most cities the needs of all population groups are not being adequately met. Only in recent years have cities begun to recognize an obligation to provide recreation for the handicapped and deprived.

6. Residents of deprived urban neighborhoods are almost entirely dependent on public recreation facilities. Residents of more affluent neighborhoods have a wide range of recreational alternatives. Adequate recreation programs and facilities are considered a high priority item among the deprived.

7. Residents of urban slum neighborhoods frequently charge that too much effort is directed toward park and recreation facilities for the middle and upper income groups, and that recreation planning is being performed by persons having no real knowledge of the needs or desires of the deprived. To overcome this charge, planners should encourage the participation of a wide spectrum of the community in the planning process. To be successful, recreation programs must be what the people want, not what the recreation department believes to be best for the people.[16]

These facts and issues call for changes in the current approach to urban recreation planning. They suggest a departure from the traditional approach to providing urban leisure services and a major emphasis on demonstration or innovation. Repeating the ideas of the past fifty years will not serve the needs of users or suppliers of local recreation facilities.

The past role of public parks and recreation in contributing to the quality of life and environment in urban America is clear, but the future role is not. The survival of many urban park and recreation systems is at stake in a projected era of scarce resources and the competing needs of public support. It is time to question the assumptions, concepts, and techniques used to plan, design, and manage urban parks and to consider *alternatives*, if the urban park is not to become an endangered species.[17]

Changing perspectives

Philosophical and pragmatic changes in American society, the park and recreation movement, and evolving public policy all project many changes for the delivery of leisure services in cities. These changing perspectives provide a context for recreation planning and should condition the preparation of a park and recreation plan.

The cultural revolution in American thought concerning environment, leisure, work, and sense of community is the first change. This "greening of America"[18] places a high value on self-development, *humanism*, and process. It is concerned with the consumer, physical health, and the quality of life. In the emerging view it is not necessarily activities, facilities, or programs that are central— it is what happens to people as a result of a recreation experience. Recreation becomes a dimension of human development that has little to do with programmed activities or social acceptance.[19]

The cost–revenue crisis for local governments is the second change. Drastic

cuts or efficiencies in municipal services will be necessary to keep pace with
inflation. Taxpayers faced with a decline in real income are not likely to approve
bond issues or tax increases for local parks. They will develop a serious interest
in the performance or *effectiveness* of leisure services.[20]

Third, the existing system of recreation spaces in most communities will be
all these communities can afford to maintain. Local funds may not be available
for new spaces, which fact implies making the best use of existing spaces that
need renewal. Many community and especially neighborhood parks or facilities
no longer meet the recreation needs of changing populations. The facilities and
landscaping are obsolete and the programs may not be relevant to the needs of
special populations (e.g., racial or ethnic minorities).

A new spirit of self-help and community involvement is emerging in many
places; this is the fourth change. This spirit recognizes the *limits* of government
in solving many human problems. It senses a degree of personal commitment
and responsibility that can be used by people to help design, develop, and maintain urban parks. The ideas of self-generated and self-maintained urban parks
are being tested in some communities.[21] The expectation of professionals or of
government ''doing everything'' may be outmoded, may be fiscally impossible,
or may not serve the best interests of people.

Fifth, the traditional priorities of land acquisition and development are being
reversed in some cities which are beginning to have a sense of the city as a recreation place in which voluntary program leadership is more effective than are
extensive investments in land and facilities. The philosophy of alternative, noncompetitive recreation programs such as New Games[22] is being tried out in
many places. Community service organizations and the private sector are providing effective recreation opportunities that can complement or replace some
public recreation programs. The community is viewed as a recreation system
for private nonprofit, public, and commercial effort.[23]

Finally, a consolidation of government services is rapidly combining the traditional park and recreation department with other social services or with departments of environmental planning and management. In both cases the traditional
''fun and games'' or ''housekeeper'' images of these departments is dramatically broadened toward life enrichment or human development and environmental change or improvement.

These changing perspectives represent dramatic opportunities for the provision of leisure services. They indicate a growing awareness that the use of leisure time has important implications for human and community development,
mental and physical health, the conservation of resources, the local economy,
and the quality of urban life.

In a planning context these changes imply moving beyond a narrow focus on
recreation activities, buildings, and parks toward a mission of improving the
quality of urban life and environment. At the policy or operational level of local
government these concepts place parks and recreation in the broader context of
a human service and an environmental management system. They recognize the
relationship of leisure spaces and services to the social and physical environments of cities.

Park and recreation plans

The park and recreation plan is an expression of a community's objectives,
needs, and priorities for the provision of leisure space, services, and facilities.
This plan should provide a guide for public policy and private decisions related
to the scope, quality, and location of leisure opportunities to meet the needs of
residents and visitors.

The park and recreation plan should be a long-range, comprehensive, and
policy-oriented document that (1) describes alternatives, recommendations, and

guidelines for public and private decisions related to the use and preservation of open space for recreation, and (2) makes recommendations on the acquisition, development, and management of both public and private spaces or facilities for leisure-oriented uses.

The plan should acknowledge the past leisure patterns of the population, describe the present uses of facilities, and project future needs with words, graphics, or data that communicate the facts, outline alternatives, propose new ideas, and motivate action. The plan should clearly outline what is possible and who can best provide these opportunities, and should project the benefits and costs of alternative opportunities in a time phased implementation program.

The planning process requires a high degree of citizen involvement and an understanding of public opinion at all stages. Although most existing plans have focused on the public sector, outdoor space, and organized program, the trend is toward a balanced emphasis on the public and private sectors, indoor and outdoor opportunities, and the integration of space, services, and facilities.

The recreation planning process results in plans, studies, or information that can be used to make decisions regarding a city's changing leisure needs, problems, and opportunities.[24] Recreation planning is a systematic way of anticipating, causing, preventing, or monitoring change related to the provision of public and private leisure opportunities. It is a continuous process of change in response to new social values, life-style patterns, technology, legislation, and availability of resources. The planning process should be:

1. *Evolutionary* instead of revolutionary: radical changes may be necessary in many instances, but they will have a much greater chance of public acceptance if proposed in an incremental or demonstration program
2. *Pluralistic* instead of authoritarian: the right choice is a matter of value, not fact, based on a consideration of several alternatives from individuals or groups with different objectives
3. *Objective* instead of subjective: the criteria or methodology used to describe alternatives must minimize distortion of the facts even though the final decision may be based on subjective values
4. *Realistic* instead of politically naive: parks and recreation must develop a constituency to compete on their own merits in the decision-making or budget process
5. *Humanistic* instead of bureaucratic: the approach to developing a plan, design, or service must be to serve people instead of the public agency responsible for providing leisure opportunities or preparing the plan.

Changing views of planning   The traditional view of planning is of a static and linear process which follows a series of logical and consecutive steps. Planners begin with the definition of a problem and end with recommendations to solve that problem. The emphasis is on the *output* or product instead of the *input* and process. A primary concern is on the *what* and *how* of planning, rather than *who* participates and *why*. The means often become ends. Implementing the plan becomes the objective instead of the way to achieve an objective.

The traditional planning process attempts to reduce complexity with arbitrary guidelines or standards to produce uniform spaces or services. Professionals superimpose their values on the process. Citizens are asked to participate in a token way by reviewing plans or proposals prepared by experts. Everything is neatly organized and predictable in terms of timing, responsibility, and outcome. The end product of this process is usually a two dimensional physical plan that is relatively inflexible, uniform, and unrepresentative of many community values or needs.

A new view of planning sees the process as dynamic and incremental. It begins with the values, behavior, or priorities of many people and accommodates these through political compromise. The emphasis is on *input* and process. Change, controversy, compromise, and involvement at all stages of the planning process are expected. Ends are used to justify the means. Achieving these ends is more important than the plan and the methods used to prepare it.

The new view encourages diversity with criteria sensitive to the particular needs of a social group or planning area. The objective is to provide *effective* spaces or services. Professionals act as resource persons to translate human values into *alternatives* that citizens or their representatives can consider. Citizen participation is essential and is taken seriously at every step in this process. The outcome of the process is not predictable and the sequence of events may not follow any preconceived pattern. The end product is a set of policies, priorities, or criteria that are relatively flexible, diverse, and representative of community values.

General characteristics The park and recreation plan should detail the aspects of land use, circulation, urban design, and community facilities that describe how and where people use their leisure time in cities. Some communities will have a separate conservation and open space element of the comprehensive plan that focuses on a broader set of objectives such as growth management, managed resource production, or public safety as shown in Figure 10–2. The open space element will also detail the methods, benefits, and costs of preserving open space as shown in Figures 10–3 and 10–4. Many communities are now combining the parks, recreation, and open space elements of the comprehensive plan.

Parks and recreation use, however, represents only *one* possible use of open space. Although parks and recreation use is commonly considered a multipurpose use of all lands designated as open space in the comprehensive plan and zoning ordinance, these lands should not be considered a substitute in the requirements for user-oriented recreation spaces unless they are primarily used for recreational purposes.

This distinction is not intended to discourage the multiple use of open space but, rather, to recognize that certain types of recreation opportunities have special requirements. For example, airport flight paths, freeway buffers, and utility corridors may have multipurpose recreation potentials, but these areas are *not* the equivalent of lands normally considered for *primary* recreational purposes. There may also be serious questions of public health and safety associated with recreational facilities in transportation corridors or near high voltage transmission lines.[25]

The plan should be: (1) balanced to meet present deficiencies and future needs; (2) oriented to the projected population characteristics and economic base of a community; and (3) in scale with a community's fiscal resources or expected federal or state assistance programs to help implement the plan.

An effective plan will: (1) identify problems; (2) present relevant information on the social and physical implications of these problems in measurable human terms; (3) develop problem-solving alternatives; (4) describe the expected results of each alternative in terms of environmental and social impact on the planning area; and (5) rank or recommend alternatives in terms of economic, social, and political feasibility.

The planning period The time horizon for the park and recreation plan should parallel the comprehensive plan. In most communities this will be a twenty year projection of trends with four five year increments that parallel the capital improvement budget cycle. Because leisure patterns are very subject to changes in the economy, in technology, or in life-style, it is important to project future trends with the best available information and to revise or update the plan at least every five years.

Figure 10-2 Functions and classification of open space.

Managed resource production
Agricultural production
Mineral production
Forest production
Energy production

Environment and ecological balance
Fish and wildlife refuges
Watershed areas
Significant geological features
Visual corridors and viewpoints

Public health and safety
Flood control and water supply
Waste disposal areas
Airshed quality improvement
Geological hazard zones
Fire hazard zones
Airport flight path zones
Hazardous storage zones

Community development and social welfare
Parks and recreation areas
Historic preservation districts
Public and institutional building sites
Land use buffers

Urban form
Growth control
Circulation corridors
Utility corridors
Future expansion reserves

Figure 10-3 Methods for preserving open space.

Acquisition of fee
Purchase
    Purchase with life tenancy
    Lease purchase
    Excess condemnation
    Official map
    Purchase and leaseback
Gift with life tenancy
Trade or transfer
Tax foreclosures
Street closing
Redevelopment process
Subdivision dedication
Private purchase or gift

Acquisition of less than fee
Conservation easements
Development rights
Public easements
Scenic easements
Purchase and resale without certain
    rights
Compensable regulations

Zoning
Protective zoning
Aesthetic zoning
Agricultural zoning
Zoning for large lots
Zoning for planned unit development
Private restrictive covenants
Slope conservation restrictions

Property tax concessions
By contract
Tax abatement for hunting/fishing rights
Tax exemptions
Tax deductions for gifts

Long-range park and recreation plans without revision are difficult for the general public to understand and support and for planners to update. Political officials are often reluctant to support or implement long-range plans because tangible results are not evident to potential voters.

The short-range (five year) time horizon is most appropriate for recreation planning in the inner and central cities of metropolitan areas with a high concentration of special populations. Flexibility and results are the measures of success for recreation planning in the inner city. A commitment of money for land, development, and programs at intervals encourages demonstration and continuing public involvement. It also allows people to change their preferences or priorities in process and brings the level of planning to a human scale that neighborhoods can relate to as a logical planning unit.[26]

The planning area   Because of the relative mobility of most users and the specialized nature of many urban park and recreation opportunities, a "problem shed" approach should be used to determine the planning study area. This approach prompts the solution of problems in terms of cause and effect. It describes how and where urban populations will use existing or potential recreation opportunities and has advantages in distributing the cost of specialized facilities (e.g., a zoological park or an arboretum) over a broader tax base.

Figure 10–4   Benefits and costs of open space.

Quantifiable benefits[1]
Recreation user satisfaction
Natural resource and lease income
Savings from compact growth
    Energy conservation
    Reduction in cost of government services
Savings in transportation costs
Preventing development in hazardous area
Tourism and related economic industries or services
Agricultural industries and services
Increased land values of adjacent properties
Decreased levels of crime and violence
Attraction/retention of desirable development

Nonquantifiable benefits[2]
Improvement in mental and physical health
Reduction in levels of air, noise or water pollution
Increased recreation opportunities for the disadvantaged
Maintenance of rural atmosphere
Increased community identity and imageability
Preservation of scenic, historic, or cultural features
Retention of options for future growth

Quantifiable costs[1]
Land acquisition
Development of recreation facilities
Maintenance and operation of recreation facilities

Nonquantifiable costs[2]
Impacts on tax base
Impacts on housing market
Opportunities foregone for development

1 Quantifiable in an objective sense, because of available
  data, measures, or precedent.
2 Nonquantifiable to date because available data, measures,
  or precedent are not objective and generalizable to many
  situations. Developing evidence is available but should be
  used with qualifications.

The problem shed may differ according to a city's demographic character, density, degree of development, and economic base. For example, the planning area or problem shed is dramatically different for a tourist-oriented city with a natural resource focus than it is for a resident-oriented community with a cosmopolitan urban character. In an area with relatively few natural resources, man-made recreation resources would be dominant. For example, the components of wildlife and vegetation for a suburban community might be substituted or supplemented by the components of street life and architecture in the central city.

A comprehensive plan could include the widest range of components that could contribute to a recreation experience in an urban setting. It should include those places traditionally considered public park and recreation opportunities, but it can also include facilities such as shopping centers, amusement parks, theaters, restaurants, libraries, museums, airports, farmers' and flea markets, private yacht and tennis clubs, community colleges, historic districts, hotel and motel districts, waterfront districts, and pedestrian malls and plazas.

This approach views the entire city as a recreation space instead of as a set of isolated spaces and experiences. It integrates space and services, public and private, and indoor and outdoor opportunities where appropriate and possible. It considers any place in which people can experience diversity, pleasure, or enrichment as a potential leisure resource.

The components and the work program The basic planning task is to inventory, analyze, and project valid information that relates people (behavior), time (leisure), and activity (recreation) to space (resources) and to a geographic area (planning unit) using criteria or measures (performance standards/social indicators) that are sensitive to the changing physical character, social needs, and political priorities of a community. This information can be used to identify deficiencies by planning unit and population subgroups for specific activities or spaces. It can also be used to establish regional, citywide, and neighborhood policies and programs.

The detailed requirements for the park and recreation element of a comprehensive plan are described in federal and state guidelines that should be consulted before a work program is established. These general requirements can be used to define the components and work program of the plan. Major topics would include the legal authority and agency responsible, existing conditions, recreation resources, demand and use patterns, needs analysis, goals and objectives, and implementation, including means of financing.[27] Figure 10–5 shows the possible components of the park and recreation element of a comprehensive plan.

Relationship to comprehensive plans The comprehensive plan is a general guide to the future character and development of a community. It identifies significant areas to be preserved or changed for the achievement of social, economic, or environmental goals. The park and recreation plan uses the factual information, policies, and recommendations of the comprehensive plan to develop detailed policies, standards, design, or management criteria and capital improvement programs that will achieve the leisure objectives of residents and visitors.

The comprehensive plan focuses on the overall relationship of open space and leisure services to land use and the quality of urban life and environment. The park and recreation plan details these relationships and translates them into specific sites to acquire or develop for leisure-oriented uses. It also details policies, practices, or criteria related to the design and management of these leisure spaces and services.

The comprehensive plan provides the basis for a community's recreation plan and should be completed first. It provides general concepts and goals for the social and physical development of a city. The recreation plan details a community's recreation needs with specific recommendations for land acquisition, facility development operations, maintenance, and financing that are not normally part of the comprehensive plan. If properly executed, the comprehensive plan and the recreation plan will complement each other and will also satisfy requirements for federal and state assistance.

The preparation of a park and recreation plan is normally the joint responsibility of the planning and recreation agencies. Figure 10–6 shows a typical division of responsibilities. It should be noted that while the planning agency has the prime responsibility and the recreation agency has an advisory responsibility during the preparation of a comprehensive plan, these roles gradually reverse as the community prepares and implements its park and recreation plan.

Figure 10–5 List of components of the park and recreation element of a comprehensive plan.

Introduction
Describe objectives and scope of plan
Define legal authority for federal/state programs
Define agency responsible for preparation of plan
Describe previous and future studies related to plan
State assumptions and qualifications of plan

Existing conditions
Describe regional context of planning area
Describe leisure behavior patterns of population
Describe environmental characteristics of planning area
Describe recreation problems and potentials/planning unit
Describe general character of planning units

Recreation resources
Classify resources and opportunities
Inventory existing land, facilities, and program
Evaluate opportunities by planning unit
Describe potential recreation resources/programs
Evaluate design, access, and public safety

Demand and use patterns
Inventory time budgets of population
Analyze recreation use patterns by demographic groups
Describe user preference/satisfaction
Analyze causes for nonuse of existing opportunities
Describe problems of special populations
Assess impact of nonresidents/tourists
Assess impact of fees and charges on demand patterns
Assess impact of access on use of facilities

Needs analysis
Analyze demand/supply relationships
Develop use concepts, principles, and design criteria
Develop space, development, and program standards
Describe deficiencies by planning unit
Project needs by planning period and planning unit
Describe public/private potentials to accommodate needs

Goals, policies, and alternatives
Describe existing goals, objectives, and policies
Describe desirable goals, objectives, and policies
Analyze alternative ways to achieve desirable goals
Describe the implications of each alternative
Recommend one alternative
Describe social and environmental impact of alternative

Implementation
Describe public/private actions by project/planning unit
Schedule actions by time period, planning unit, responsibility
Estimate benefits and costs of each project or program
Relate costs to general and capital improvements budgets
Describe needed financing
Describe needed new legislation or responsibility
Describe public participation to approve and implement plan
Describe how, when, and who will revise plan

Appendix
Background studies
Data and methodology
Bibliography and sources
Acknowledgments and credits

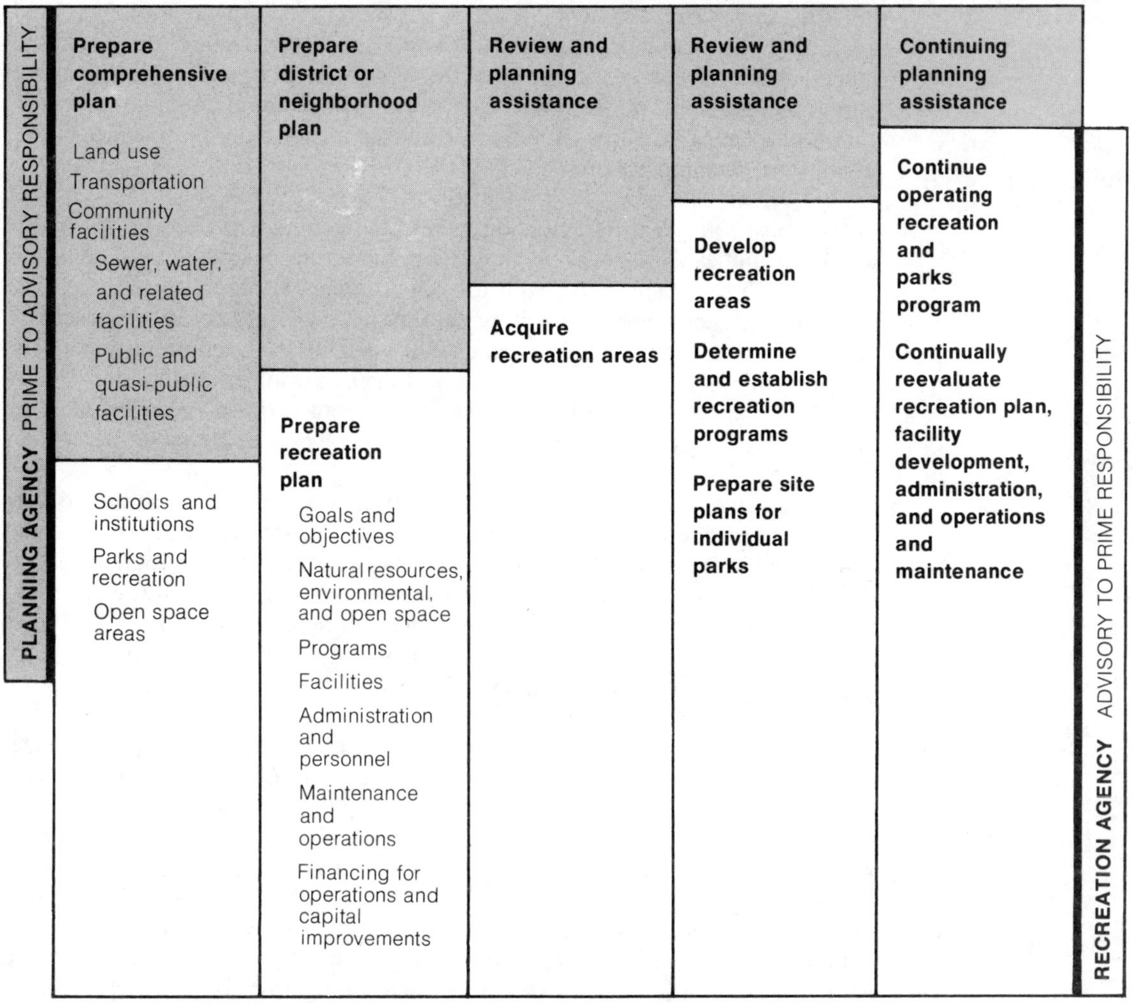

Figure 10–6 Progression of comprehensive planning and recreation planning for areas, facilities, programs, and services.

Planning methods and techniques

The methods and techniques of urban recreation planning have essentially focused on the application of space and facility standards to a population or planning area. Although these standards are commonly qualified as "guidelines," they often become "absolutes,"[28] regardless of significant differences in the demographic character, density, leisure patterns, climate, or economic base of a community.

The problems and implications of a "standards approach" to urban recreation planning are described in many sources, yet this approach persists for lack of accepted alternatives.[29] To perpetuate this methodology in most communities will magnify the problems previously described in this chapter. What is necessary and possible is a more sensitive and systematic approach to the leisure needs of people living in urban and suburban environments.

Determining needs

Needs assessment can be approached in four different ways commonly referred to as the resource, activity, economic, and behavioral approaches to recreation planning. Each approach is briefly described below.

Resource approach Physical or natural resources determine the types and amounts of recreation opportunities. Supply limits the demand or use to the human or natural carrying capacity of the resource. Expressed demand is more important than latent demand which encourages duplication instead of diversification of existing facilities. Supplier or management values are usually dominant in the planning process.

Activity approach Past participation in selected activities is used to determine the opportunities that should be provided in the future. Supply creates demand. The public preference or demand for opportunities is based on participation rates or attendance which usually project more of the same type of opportunities. Because only expressed demand or use is measured, the primary focus is on providing more program leadership instead of self-directed activities. Nonuse, or the latent demand for opportunities, is not seriously considered. The values of users and the supplier are dominant in the planning process.

Economic approach The economic base or fiscal resources of a community are used to determine the amount, type, and location of recreation opportunities. Investment in and responsibility for providing land, facilities, or program is conditioned by measurable costs and benefits or the self-supporting nature of activities. Fees and charges are commonly required for many opportunities. The supply and demand for activities is manipulated by price. User and supplier objectives are balanced in the planning process.

Behavioral approach Human behavior and events in leisure settings influence the choice of how, where, and when people use their free time. Time budgets of individuals and social groups are translated into public and private opportunities that require land, facilities, and program. The focus is on recreation as an experience; it is on why a person participates, what activities are preferred, and what happens to the person as a result of these activities. User preference and satisfaction condition the planning process. Advocacy and pluralism are expected dimensions of the planning, design, and management process. User objectives are dominant and satisfying experiences are the expected product.

Research, practice, and the nature of the problem suggest the *behavioral* approach as the *best* way to understand and provide for the recreation needs of urban populations. This approach is more complex and controversial than the other three approaches because it requires value judgments, the development of credible measures, and high levels of citizen participation. It has great utility, however, for analyzing nonuse, latent demand, future trends, and the needs of special populations at the neighborhood level. This approach complements the advocacy and pluralism of most communities and the trend toward a more humanistic view of leisure services.

Supply and demand analysis The methodological challenge of supply and demand analysis is to relate existing and future recreation behavior (demand) to existing opportunities (supply) with a measure (standard) that indicates need (deficiency). The conceptual challenge is to develop sensitive classification systems to describe space, facilities, and services (supply) and recreation activities or experiences (demand) that can be aggregated at the neighborhood, city, and county levels. Both demand and supply must be related in terms of effectiveness (quality) for general and special populations.

The identification of relative need (deficiency or surplus) should be based on criteria or standards other than the traditional National Recreation and Park Association (NRPA) recreation standards,[30] or, if NRPA standards are used, they should be *adapted* to the special requirements of each planning unit. Any measures used to determine relative need and deficiency should be:

1. Based on the latent and expressed recreation demand of the general and special populations of a planning area
2. Attainable in the planning period by a combination of public and private action or alternatives provided
3. Understood and supported by the public or its elected representatives
4. Based on the leisure behavior, the environment, and the social values of the planning areas
5. Measures of quality, performance, or effectiveness for a given time period, population group, and planning area.

Ten basic methods of supply and demand analysis are in current use. Each method is briefly outlined below and is detailed in the sources cited in the endnotes. The best aspects of each method can be developed into a methodology that fits the special needs and levels of planning expertise in a community.

1. *Innovative approach.* Based on user goals, accommodation, and preference and incremental implementation. It results in a social indicator that reflects only the needs of a neighborhood at a given time. It translates values into space and money.[31]
2. *Measures of effectiveness.* Based on sensitive measures of use, accessibility, preference, and satisfaction for existing facilities that are developed into a needs index for planning future facilities.[32]
3. *Level of service approach.* Based on qualitative measures of effectiveness for a given set of facilities. An acceptable level of service is one that satisfies a given set of values.[33]
4. *Needs–resources index.* Based on the concept that different neighborhoods have different needs and resources which can be ranked in a comparative need index. It uses indicators (e.g., income, poverty level, population density, youth population, crime levels) to calculate comparative needs.[34]
5. *Recreation experience components concept.* Based on performance standards that describe the type of experience and similar activities that support this experience and translate this into space and design requirements.[35]
6. *Population ratio method.* Based on specific ratios of acres, facilities, or program leadership for a general population.[36]
7. *Area percentage method.* Based on a specific percentage of the planning area for public recreational uses.[37]
8. *Carrying capacity approach.* Based on the concept that space or facilities have minimum, desirable, and optimum levels of human and natural carrying capacity and these can be translated into space with standards.[38]
9. *Systems model approach.* Describes and projects existing supply and expressed demand on the basis of participation rates for selected activities and relates this to time-distance impacts on facilities.[39]
10. *User resource planning method.* Based on classifying people into user groups that require certain environmental characteristics, dividing each planning area into resource types, relating the desired recreation experience to resource, and developing planning guidelines on the basis of an analysis of user and resource requirements.[40]

Regardless of the method used, the development of measures, criteria, or performance standards for recreation land, facilities, and program should be based on *objective* quantitative and qualitative factors instead of on arbitrary judgments. The space standards should cover use variables—needs, preference, satisfaction, access, opportunities, weather, crime, and environment—and supply variables—land, design, development, program, management, maintenance, interpretation, and administration. The standards for space, facilities, and program can be classified by orientation as shown in Table 10–1.

The methodology should view supply and demand as a circular process that starts and leads back to the values, wants, and needs of potential users of space and facilities[41] with an emphasis on the *quality* or *effectiveness* of opportunities. The question of *how good* is as important as *how much* in this analysis, because space does *not* constitute service. In many communities, less space with *better* design and management is the most constructive solution to meeting recreation needs.

Table 10–1   Classification of selected types of recreation standards.

Orientation	Specific type	Measurement units	Examples
Use	Population ratio	Area/population	1 ac. neighborhood park per 1000 pop.
	Recreation demand	Area/user group	1 ac. playground per 600 children
	% of area	Area/planning unit	10% of planning unit area
Development	Facility to site	Units per acre	16 picnic tables per acre
	Facility placement	Distance between units	Picnic tables 50 feet apart
	Facility to activity	Units/user group	1 softball diamond per 10,000 pop.
	Facility size	Area/facility	3–5 acre neighborhood playground
Capacity	User to resource	Users/site	400 people per mile of trail per hr.
	User to time	Users/time/site	50 people per mile of trail per hr.
Program	Activity to population	Activity/population	1 arboretum per 10,000 pop.
	Leadership requirements	Leaders/activity	2 leaders per 100 children
Management	Supervision to users	Staff/population	1 supervisor per 1000 users
	Maintenance to site	Degree/area	1 laborer per 10 acre playground

To account for differences in the recreation needs of different neighborhoods or special populations, needs, preference, satisfaction, access, and other use variables, or the equivalent, can be weighted (see Figure 10–7). Both the expressed and latent demands for different types of recreation experiences and spaces—as expressed by acreage, per capita investment, and other criteria—can be described and projected at the community level by aggregating the needs or deficiencies of each neighborhood.

User preference and satisfaction

A consideration of user preference and satisfaction is fundamental to the provision of urban recreation space, services, or facilities. This should be based on concepts of quality, a recreation activity classification system, a recreation space classification system, leisure behavior surveys, and measures of effectiveness that can provide systematic information to planners and decision makers.

Concepts of quality   Two concepts are basic to the urban park experience and measures of user preference and satisfaction associated with this experience. Both concepts are based on the premise that people expect a pleasurable experience in an urban park, appreciate a range of choice in how and where they use their leisure, and have social/psychological needs that can be accommodated as part of a park experience. These basic concepts are commonly expressed as:

1. *Resource quality:* objective measures of factors or conditions a visitor views as part of the permanent natural and man-made physical elements or facilities of an area (e.g., scenery, vegetation, water, toilets, tables, trails)

2. *Use quality:* objective measures of factors or conditions visitors view as constraints (negative) or inducements (positive) to their expectations and satisfaction during a visit to an area (e.g., overcrowding, waiting, noise, conflict, fear, embarrassment, danger; or program leadership, interpretation, information, law enforcement, food service).

The concept of quality is based on a *behavioral* approach to the recreation experience which translates basic human needs into three desires that condition user preference and satisfaction for a given area or activities. These desires are:

1. *Resource directed desires:* contact with a natural resource (e.g., sun, sand, surf, wildlife); the degree of satisfaction depends on the quality of and access to the resource
2. *Image directed desires:* the fulfillment of a desirable image (e.g., jogger, sailor, tennis player); the degree of satisfaction depends not on the resource but on the way others may view the resource, activity, or user
3. *Leisure directed desires:* a pleasurable way to use leisure time (e.g., Sunday drive, window shopping, television, movies); the degree of satisfaction does not depend on the resource or others, but on how effectively the place or activity consumes leisure time.

Figure 10–7 Outline of method for determining neighborhood recreation priorities.

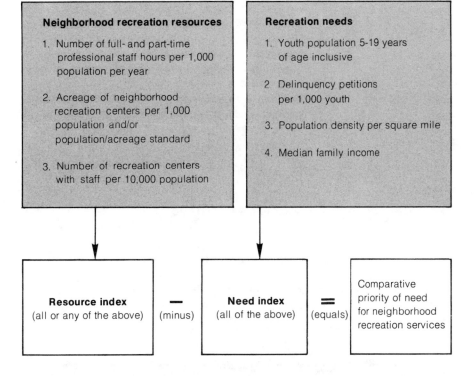

In this context, user preference and user satisfaction for a recreation experience can be described with the following definitions:

1. *User preference:* the voluntary choice of an activity or area to fulfill a desire
2. *User satisfaction:* the fulfillment of a desire and a preference which are normally conditioned by the user's preconceived ideas about the area, the activities available, the natural setting, the man-made facilities, and the management of the area.

The total recreation experience has five phases which can be used to measure user preference and satisfaction for urban parks. These phases are commonly labeled: anticipation, travel to, on-site, travel back, and recollection.[42] Although most recreation planners, designers, and managers are concerned with the on-site phase of the recreation experience, user satisfaction is affected by all phases of this experience. More attention should be given to what happens off-site by providing better information about what to expect in parks, about how to get there, and about what to bring or do.

Recreation activity classification   The wide range of leisure activities in cities can be classified in a way that acknowledges the concepts of quality and is useful for the planning and management of urban recreation spaces. The problem is to analyze existing or potential recreation spaces and ask what people *expect* in terms of a recreation experience, and what they *received* in terms of satisfaction, on the basis of the concepts of resource and use quality that have been described above.

The primary task is to classify and aggregate recreation activities into categories that reflect similar components of experience and resources. A secondary task is to analyze the relationships among the different activities (multiple use), environmental impacts (carrying capacity), space requirements (standards), and support elements (management) required for each category. Most activities can be classified into the following four categories of recreation experience:

1. *Physical recreation,* which requires physical effort as the major experience of the activity
2. *Social recreation,* which requires social interaction as the major experience of the activity
3. *Cognitive recreation,* which includes cultural, educational, and creative or aesthetic activities
4. *Environment-related recreation,* which requires use of a natural resource such as water, trees, scenery, or wildlife to provide the setting or focus for an activity.

Because the total recreation system is not outdoor-based, both *indoor* and *outdoor* experiences are considered. Within each of the four experience categories there are activity clusters which represent *similar* types of activities. These activities generally require the same types of resources to allow for *flexibility* in the application of standards.

Data related to user satisfaction can be classified in terms of *use quality* and *resource quality* and related to each planning unit. This results in an activity classification system that can apply to existing or new parks and can be analyzed for significant relationships between the user and the resource. These broader relationships can provide a *behavioral* basis for planning or management guidelines, minimum standards, and operating policies for each park and for the entire system.

Recreation space classification   The range of existing or potential recreation spaces in a city can be classified in a way that acknowledges different scales or service areas, relates to travel time-distance or access criteria, provides for different levels of design and management, and relates to the natural or human carrying capacity and design load of the area.

The classification of a space should match the functional use and design potentials of a given area. For example, to designate an area as a playground yet not have this space designed or managed to accommodate the behavioral needs of children is absurd. In the same way an area designated as a downtown plaza for office workers requires an appropriate commitment of design and development.

In practice the classification of an area implies a commitment of resources to develop and manage it to an adequate level. It also implies a level of use and satisfaction that can be used in projecting needs. The classification of recreation spaces should be approached seriously or the plan will lack credibility.

Recreation spaces can be classified by function or dominant use, ownership, degree of use density or development, and planning unit orientation. Generally, the planning unit orientation is most appropriate at the community or metropolitan scale because it best relates to use patterns, public recreation systems, and private recreation opportunities. The following categories include most recreation spaces and provide logical planning service areas:

1. *Home-oriented spaces.* Most leisure time (90 percent) is spent in or around the home in private spaces. This type of open space is frequently ignored in most plans and can be made more effective by changes in the zoning ordinance, subdivision regulations, or subdivision planning that acknowledge the potentials of the home as a leisure environment.
2. *Neighborhood spaces.* These spaces are generally associated with an elementary school, are pedestrian-oriented, and normally serve a population of 5,000 people. They should provide a range of active and passive recreation opportunities oriented to the changing needs of a neighborhood.
3. *Community spaces.* These spaces usually serve from three to six neighborhoods, are pedestrian- or mass-transit-oriented, and normally serve a population of 20,000 people. They are usually associated with a junior high or high school complex and a shopping or community center. They provide a range of specialized facilities not possible in neighborhood parks to serve the diverse needs of a planning district.
4. *Citywide spaces.* These spaces serve the entire community, are automobile or mass-transit-oriented, and normally serve a population of 100,000 people or more. They provide a range of intensive and extensive activities and highly specialized facilities not possible in community-oriented spaces.
5. *Regional spaces.* These spaces are commonly resource-oriented areas that serve metropolitan needs with the types of passive, extensive activities not possible or appropriate in citywide parks. Access is by private or public transportation.

A logical extension of this list could include any of the cultural facilities, commercial recreation enterprises, and special districts, events, or spaces described earlier in this chapter.

Leisure behavior surveys The best way to study the leisure behavior of a community is to initiate a continuing program of survey research to measure user preference and satisfaction for recreation activities and spaces, levels of participation or nonuse, and latent demand. Survey research techniques can also be used to assess the recreation needs of special populations, to identify major problems and potentials, to project public opinion, and to determine the effectiveness of existing facilities or programs.

Two types of surveys are required to prepare and revise park and recreation plans: (1) community-wide surveys of leisure patterns describing expressed and latent demand, participation rates, and people's perception of recreation opportunities; and (2) pre- and post-construction evaluation surveys of specific projects describing user and nonuser response to these projects. Both types of surveys should include a probability sample of users and nonusers, and surveys taken on-site and in the home.

Constraints of time and money make it difficult to survey the entire population. Most surveys use a probability sample to represent the entire population. From this representative group planners can make inferences to the total population.

There are many probability sampling techniques, but all are based on the concept of random selection, which implies that every member of a population has an equal chance of being surveyed. This technique minimizes bias and allows the planner to use probability theory to measure the accuracy of the survey, extrapolate or project the results to the total population, and estimate the size of error.

The merits of using survey research as a planning tool are well established in practice and are described in many sources.[43] If a planning agency does not have the time, funds, or expertise to undertake recreation surveys, it can use a combination of consultants and volunteers for many aspects of a survey effort. There are also many survey techniques other than personal interviews which can be less costly and less time-consuming. Many communities have used telephone, mail, and newspaper surveys successfully.

Leisure behavior surveys are an essential aspect of recreation planning. They provide a systematic way of describing, evaluating, and projecting a community's leisure interests, needs, problems, and potentials. They can also establish baselines for monitoring the effectiveness of existing programs, measuring change, and outlining the need for future programs.

Recreation measures of effectiveness   Beyond surveys of leisure behavior, it is essential to measure the effectiveness of existing services to help: (1) provide current information on how recreation services are meeting public needs; (2) provide a baseline from which future progress can be measured; (3) estimate the future effectiveness of proposed recreation programs; (4) determine budgets for recreation-related programs; (5) prepare capital improvements requests; (6) provide annual reports of the effectiveness of community services; and (7) consider public issues.

Traditional recreation measurements have focused on quantifiable factors such as acreage, numbers of facilities, and personnel. These statistics represent inputs (resources) instead of outputs (satisfaction), which are the true measures of recreation effectiveness that meet the needs of people. Measurements in common use include the following:

1. Number of acres, areas, or individual facilities of various types, often expressed as so many per thousand population
2. Amount of recreation staff time spent on individual programs or services
3. Attendance records or number of visits to recreation facilities or activities
4. Number of classes, meetings, or organized programs
5. Number of participant hours for selected activities
6. Number of persons so many minutes or miles from specific types of recreation facilities
7. Attendance and participation categorized by sex and age group
8. Amount of recreation opportunities available at various time periods.

Measuring the effectiveness of recreation services is difficult because of the subjective nature of recreation, but it is possible, and it can provide a useful data source for the planning, design, and management of recreation services. Data can be gathered for a specific facility or activity; for recreation services provided by government and the private sector; or for a geographic area such as a neighborhood, census tract, planning district, or political unit. Illustrative measures can include the following:

1. Total attendance and participant hours or days for each major activity or facility during a given time period (enjoyment)
2. Number and percent of different participants and nonparticipants for each major recreation service during a given time period (enjoyment)

3. Number and percent of persons living within and not within x minutes or y miles of a specific type of recreation facility or activity (accessibility)
4. Waiting times at various facilities and at various times, number of persons deterred from using a facility because of crowdedness during a given time period, ratio of usage to capacity at various times for specific facilities or groups of facilities for a given time period, or number of times that citizens feel too crowded in recreation areas (crowdedness)
5. Number of different activities, facilities, or features available at specific points in time (variety)
6. Number and ranges of accidents, injuries, and criminal attacks for a given time period (safety)
7. Index of physical attractiveness of recreation areas and facilities (physically attractive)
8. Index of overall perceived recreation satisfaction of citizens (overall enjoyableness)
9. Juvenile delinquency and crime rates affected by recreation programs (crime avoidance)
10. Incidence of illnesses affected by recreation services (health)
11. Changes in economic base and property values affected by recreation services (economic well-being)
12. Extent of annoyance to persons living near recreation facilities from noise, traffic, and deviant behavior (public acceptance).

These measures have been applied in several cities with reasonable success.[44] The trend toward public accountability and professional management of leisure services, and an urgent need to assess the social impact of government services, suggest the use of measures of effectiveness in most communities on a continuing basis. They can provide the manager and the public with an *objective* way of evaluating the use of public funds, of revising existing plans, and of preparing new park and recreation plans that meet the needs of people.

Conclusion

This chapter outlines selected aspects of the process and products of urban recreation planning, as well as basic concepts, measures, and methodologies intended to help reshape the direction of urban recreation planning for the 1980s. The prospect of increasing levels of leisure and urbanization suggests an increased demand for recreation space, services, and facilities in cities. The possibility of fuel rationing, decreasing real income, and reduced public budgets can have a significant impact on the use levels of existing federal, state, local, and private recreation opportunities. This impact will be most pronounced at the local level where most people spend most of their leisure time.

The possible impact of increased use levels on existing systems will raise serious questions of funding, user fees, access, design, and multiple use. It will also suggest radical changes in the proposed acquisition and development programs for the provision of public facilities, and significant opportunities for the private sector. These changes will demand a sophisticated level of recreation planning that can dramatically improve the quality of urban life and environment.

Federal, state, and local requirements for comprehensive recreation plans and environmental or social impact statements on proposed public and private recreation areas will also demand a more sophisticated understanding of recreation needs. Arbitrary standards and romantic rationales for the provision of public open space or recreation services are not enough to justify the expenditure of public funds in an era of scarce resources and competing needs. Token or unrealistic recreation plans will lack the credibility to serve as useful guides for decision making.

The changing life-styles and leisure needs of many people living in cities and suburbs will require a revision of the criteria and standards used to establish the existing urban park and recreation systems. They point toward new or different facilities, services, or planning concepts, in order to make more effective use of the existing system. They also point toward imaginative designs and solutions that will integrate recreation space and services into the life and environment of cities.[45]

1 This chapter is based on portions of: Seymour M. Gold, *Recreation Planning and Design* (New York: McGraw-Hill Book Company, 1980).

2 Seymour M. Gold, *Urban Recreation Planning* (Philadelphia: Lea & Febiger, 1973), p. 3.

3 See: Thomas A. Stein and H. Douglas Sessoms, eds., *Recreation and Special Populations*, 2nd ed. (Boston: Holbrook Press, 1977).

4 See: Andrew Fluegman, ed., *The New Games Book* (San Francisco: Headlands Press, 1976).

5 See: Gold, *Urban Recreation Planning*, pp. 317–22, and *Recreation Planning and Design*, Glossary. Also see: H. Douglas Sessoms, *Glossary of Recreation Terms* (Arlington, Va.: National Recreation and Park Association, 1972); and U.S., Department of the Interior, Bureau of Outdoor Recreation, *Glossary of Terms* (Washington, D.C.: Government Printing Office, 1975).

6 These relationships are typically described in: William H. Whyte, Jr., *The Last Landscape* (Garden City, N.Y.: Doubleday and Company, 1968); and August Heckscher, *Open Spaces: The Life of American Cities* (New York: Harper & Row, Publishers, 1978).

7 This view is typically described in: Max Kaplan, *Leisure: Theory and Policy* (New York: John Wiley & Sons, Inc., 1975); Thomas M. Kando, *Leisure and Popular Culture in Transition* (St. Louis: Mosby Company, 1975); James F. Murphy and Dennis R. Howard, *Delivery of Community Leisure Services* (Philadelphia: Lea & Febiger, 1977); Seymour Greben and David E. Gray, "Future Perspectives," *Parks & Recreation*, June 1974, pp. 11–19; and Gold, *Recreation Planning and Design*.

8 Kevin Lynch, *The Image of the City* (Cambridge, Mass.: The M.I.T. Press, 1960), p. 18.

9 Seymour M. Gold, "Nonuse of Neighborhood Parks," *Journal of the American Institute of Planners*, 38 (November 1972): 369–78.

10 U.S., Department of the Interior, Bureau of Outdoor Recreation, *Outdoor Recreation: A Legacy for America* (Washington, D.C.: Government Printing Office, 1973), p. 30.

11 Seymour M. Gold, "Recreation Planning for Energy Conservation," *International Journal of Environmental Studies* 10 (April 1977): 173–89; this article is also in *Parks & Recreation*, September 1977, pp. 61–63, 83–89.

12 U.S., Department of Housing and Urban Development, *Urban Recreation*, prepared for the Nationwide Outdoor Recreation Plan by the Interdepartmental Work Group on Urban Recreation, HUD–CD–41 (Washington, D.C.: Government Printing Office, 1974).

13 Ibid.

14 U.S., Department of the Interior, Heritage Recreation and Conservation Service, *National Urban Recreation Study: Executive Report* (Washington, D.C.: Government Printing Office, 1978).

15 Ibid., see *Bibliography*, Technical Report 13, for a detailed list of studies.

16 U.S., Department of Housing and Urban Development, Office of Community Planning and Development, *Open Space and Recreation Opportunity in America's Inner Cities*, prepared by the National Recreation and Park Association (Washington, D.C.: U.S. Department of Housing and Urban Development, Office of Community Planning and Development, 1974), passim.

17 Seymour M. Gold, "The Fate of Urban Parks," *Parks & Recreation*, October 1976, pp. 13–18.

18 See: Charles A. Reich, *The Greening of America* (New York: Random House, 1970).

19 See: Murphy and Howard, *Delivery of Community Leisure Services;* Greben and Gray, "Future Perspectives"; and Seymour M. Gold, "Deviant Behavior in Urban Parks," *Journal of Health, Physical Education and Recreation* 49 (November 1974); 50–52, for detailed discussions of this concept.

20 See: Harry P. Hatry et al., *How Effective Are Your Community Services? Procedures for Monitoring the Effectiveness of Municipal Services* (Washington, D.C.: The Urban Institute and International City Management Association, 1977), pp. 41–65.

21 See: Randolph T. Hester, Jr., *Neighborhood Space* (New York: Halsted Press, 1975), for detailed case studies and bibliography; also see: *Sunset* (Menlo Park, Calif.: Lane Magazine & Book Co.), for articles on "Community Action" since 1954.

22 See: Fluegman, ed., *The New Games Book*.

23 Murphy and Howard, *Delivery of Community Leisure Services*, pp. 129–66.

24 See Chapter 4 for an extensive discussion of information and decision making in the planning process, including discussions of gathering and using data; of systems analysis; and of modeling and other analytical approaches.

25 See: Michael J. Meshenberg, *Environmental Planning* (Detroit: Gale Research Co., 1976).

26 See: Gold, *Urban Recreation Planning*, Chapters 3, 6, and 7.

27 See: Gold, *Recreation Planning and Design*, Chapters 2, 3, and 4, for a detailed description of concepts, methods, and work program to prepare the park and recreation elements of a comprehensive plan.

28 See: Gold, *Urban Recreation Planning*, Chapter 5, and *Recreation Planning and Design*, Chapter 11.

29 See: Gold, *Urban Recreation Planning*, pp. 143–81, and 185–253.

30 Robert D. Buechner, ed., *National Park Recre-*

ation and Open Space Standards (Washington, D.C.: National Recreation and Park Association, 1971).

31 See: Gold, *Urban Recreation Planning*.

32 See: Harry P. Hatry and Diana Dunn, *Measuring the Effectiveness of Local Government Services* (Washington, D.C.: The Urban Institute, 1971).

33 See: Maryland–National Capital Park and Planning Commission, *Park, Recreation and Open Space Plan* (Silver Spring, Md.: Maryland–National Capital Park and Planning Commission, 1977).

34 See: Edwin J. Staley, "Determining Neighborhood Recreation Priorities: An Instrument," *Journal of Leisure Research* 1 (Winter 1969): 69–74.

35 See: Monty Christiansen, *Application of a Recreation Experience Components Concept for Comprehensive Recreation Planning* (Harrisburg, Pa.: Department of Community Affairs, Bureau of Recreation and Conservation, 1975).

36 See: Buechner, *National Park Recreation and Open Space Standards;* also: Gold, *Recreation Planning and Design,* Appendix G.

37 See: National Recreation and Park Association, *Urban Study Status Report: A Progress Report* (Washington, D.C.: National Recreation and Park Association, 1971).

38 See: U.S., Department of the Interior, Bureau of Outdoor Recreation, *Guidelines for Understanding and Determining Recreation Carrying Capacity* (Washington, D.C.: Bureau of Outdoor Recreation, January 1977).

39 See: State of California, Department of Parks and Recreation, *Park and Recreation Information System* (PARIS), Planning Monograph no. 2 (Sacramento, Calif.: California Department of Parks and Recreation, November 1966).

40 See: National Advisory Council on Regional Recreation Planning, *A User-Resource Planning Method* (Loomis, Calif.: National Advisory Council on Regional Recreation Planning, 1959).

41 See: Thomas L. Burton, *Making Man's Environment: Leisure* (New York: Van Nostrand Reinhold, 1975).

42 Marion Clawson and J. L. Knetsch, *Economics of Outdoor Recreation* (Baltimore: The Johns Hopkins Press, 1966), pp. 33–35.

43 Survey research is typically described in: International City Management Association, *Using Productivity Measurement: A Manager's Guide to More Effective Services,* Management Information Service Special Report no. 4 (Washington, D.C.: International City Management Association, 1979); Kenneth Webb and Harry P. Hatry, *Obtaining Citizen Feedback: The Application of Citizen Surveys to Local Governments* (Washington, D.C.: The Urban Institute, 1973); Hatry and Dunn, *Measuring the Effectiveness of Local Government Services;* and Hatry et al., *How Effective Are Your Community Services?*

44 See the sources cited in note 43. And see Hatry et al., *How Effective Are Your Community Services?;* and Gold, *Recreation Planning and Design,* for comprehensive lists of case studies and extensive bibliographies.

45 Preparation of this chapter was supported by the Beatrix Farrand Fund while the author was a visiting scholar with the Department of Landscape Architecture, University of California, Berkeley.

11 Education services

The city is an organization of people and institutions designed for using information and knowledge. The basic institutions for this purpose are its schools, colleges, universities, research centers, museums, libraries, and other learning centers. These institutions provide education services, process and store information, transmit knowledge to the next generation, advance knowledge, and display the achievements of society. This chapter will cover education services in the planning process, while Chapter 12 will cover planning for the arts, including cultural activities.

This chapter is based on two postulates about the role of educational institutions in communities. The first holds that educational institutions (schools, colleges, universities, museums, libraries) are structures of opportunity which, along with the family, the church, local government, business institutions, etc., are the key determinants of the quality of urban life.[1] The second holds that such institutions are highly valued symbols of community identity and achievement.

The entire community benefits from these institutions and is evaluated on the basis of their quality. The planning process which guides decision making on school size, location, and program therefore should be coordinated with the process which guides all community development.

In the United States planning for the programs and the facilities of educational institutions is for the most part the responsibility of the institutions themselves. Thus it is an activity that is usually separate from local government planning. The degree of its autonomy varies from state to state and even among various municipalities within a state. In most circumstances, however, the proper functioning and the best distribution of education services is possible only when planning for them is part of a larger process of community planning for growth and change.

This chapter will discuss planning for education services, with such services viewed in the following four contexts: (1) as generative or regenerative institutions which contribute to the quality of life by creating opportunities for learning; (2) as symbolic elements in communities which can reinforce socially positive attitudes but can also engender enmity in the face of social and territorial change; (3) as a part of a process of public decision making which responds to the needs and demands of a growing or changing population; and (4) as resource-consuming entities competing with other community needs.

One of the purposes of this chapter is to examine some means for increasing the collaboration between specialized education planners and specialists in other areas; this includes the generalists of local planning agencies responsible for comprehensive community planning. Some large city and metropolitan school districts (i.e., New York City; Fairfax County, Virginia) have specialized planning staffs which include people trained in city planning, but for the most part education planners consist of those who have been drawn from the ranks of school administrators.

The major areas of interaction between local education planners and local community planners have been and will continue to be in the projection of population change and in community decisions about location of, size of, and programs housed in specific physical facilities.

Russell Holy traced the emergence of the "school survey" of enrollments and facilities and the development of the field of education planning in primary and secondary school systems to the period just before World War I.[2] In the 1920s and 1930s primary and secondary education planning evolved and was institutionalized in large city school systems and in some state education agencies. Since World War II, school or education planning has evolved parallel with city planning and state and regional planning.

During the 1970s educational system planning was established as part of institutional decision making. Institutional planning has tended, however, to remain aloof from urban and regional planning processes. (In this respect education planning is not unlike the field of health planning.)

College and university planning, on the other hand, had its origins in the campus planning work of landscape architects and architects in the first half of the twentieth century and flowered in the decade of the 1960s as the nation responded to the needs of a rapidly growing college age population.

This chapter deals first with the overall demographic trends in the United States that influence the scale of education planning. Coverage is then included on planning for the primary and secondary education system; the demographic aspects of school planning; current practice with regard to enrollment projections; site location, size, and other facility planning issues that touch on general community planning; and specific application of education planning in large scale land development projects, including new towns, suburban communities, and central cities. Selected aspects of higher education planning are then discussed, particularly with regard to demographic trends or projections of manpower requirements and the location and development of college and university campuses in relation to social and economic opportunities.

The population basis for education planning

Demographic studies provide the information base for education planning, and the major kinds of studies are those dealing with population growth and population migration. Crude measures of growth, assuming no one moves in or out, can be obtained from the vital statistics on births and deaths that all localities have access to. Such data must be augmented by migration data on the moves in and out that have been, historically, quite difficult to obtain on a small area basis. Increasingly reliable methods are being developed, however, for tracking these data as well as other growth factors which influence school enrollments.

Education service planners generally work deductively in reviewing and analyzing demographic data and information, starting with national trends, reviewing state and regional population information, and then analyzing intensively the local data. The national trend data may include birthrates, categorical age group data, and data on regional migration. State and regional population data usually will include migration and fertility data. The local data may include many kinds of information: birthrate and death rate data, school enrollment trends, past employment data and projections, residential construction data, and social indicators.

Schools at all levels, including higher education institutions, have been affected by broad demographic trends of the past generation. Some of these trends began in the 1940s and are likely to continue to influence public attitudes until the end of the century.

The first and most readily noticed of these demographic trends was the "baby boom" of the 1940s and 1950s. This was followed by a sharp drop in the birthrate in the 1960s. An increase in the number of births in the 1980s is expected because of the larger number of women in childbearing years during this period, but this does not necessarily mean an increase in the birthrate.

The drop in the birthrate from the late 1950s on meant a drop in the 1970s in the number of school age children (ages five to seventeen). During the decade 1975–85 the enrollment in elementary and secondary schools in the United States is projected to drop by about 5 million.

Figure 11–1 Demographic trends are an integral part of education planning.

National and regional trends in population migration will affect school enroll-ments. Undoubtedly the best known has been the movement from central cities to the suburbs and unincorporated portions of metropolitan areas, a movement that has historically been going on for well over fifty years. This movement ac-celerated with the housing boom after World War II. Regional population shifts have included movements from the South to the North and Northeast, from the North to the South and Southwest, and from the Midwest to the West Coast. During the 1970s the U.S. Bureau of the Census has noted a population shift from metropolitan areas to nonmetropolitan locations in small towns and rural, nonfarm locations. In addition, standard metropolitan statistical areas (SMSAs) are growing at a slower pace than was experienced during the 1950s and 1960s and a few are losing population.

Finally, other demographic trends relative to family formation may have a significant impact on school enrollments. These include fewer first marriages, a substantially higher divorce rate, increasing use of sterilization as a means of birth control, and delayed marriages for women.

A final example is a projection after 1980 for a long-term decline in college age population until 1994, which indicates a sharp drop in college enrollments. This would follow the actual beginnings of decline in college enrollments which occurred during the latter part of the 1970s.

The effects of the decline in United States birthrates will not be distributed equally. School enrollments will continue to grow after 1975 in school districts in outer suburban rings and in cities in the southeastern part of the country and in parts of the West. In these regions the most important school/local planning issue will be coping with growth and providing new services. In almost all older central cities and many suburban districts the problem will be enrollment de-cline—what to do with school buildings no longer needed. One recent projection indicates that as many as 5,000 schools in the United States will be declared surplus in the next decade. The planning issue of dealing with these "surplus" schools by demolition or by adaptive reuse is discussed in a later section.

The school age population decline in the decade of the 1980s may not affect higher education institutions as dramatically as it will affect primary and secondary schools. Established colleges and universities in large urban areas will find it easier to maintain their size by increasing enrollment of older and of part-time students. This is, in part, because of an accessible large pool of jobs for part-time students and the availability of child care services. Colleges in smaller places will experience greater difficulties maintaining enrollment targets. A number of private colleges and some of the more isolated public colleges will be closed.

The generation that caused the "bulge" in the school system in the 1950s, then in the higher education systems in 1960s, promises in the late 1970s and in the 1980s to have a large disbursing effect on housing and community service demands along with a smaller concentration effect in and around older cities.

Planning for the physical and educational community

Planning for education services at the primary and secondary levels should be based on two premises: that the physical community or *community of place* supports and reinforces the family and the school in child rearing, and that a full range of educational opportunities is provided to all citizens so that an increasingly diverse set of programs and methods of instruction can be elected by parents on behalf of their children.

Ideally, these two premises work together. Planning for a new or expanding community or communities whose school age populations are decreasing may at any time require that greater emphasis be placed on one of these premises regarding education services—but not to the detriment or neglect of the other.

The schools and the community

The child's world may be thought of as a series of interests that gradually are enlarged—first by the nursery, then by the home, and then by the school and the immediate residential community in which basic daily needs are met. Both child and parent draw support from physical arrangements within these elements according to quality and accessibility. As the child matures, his or her interests may continue to be met within the local community or he or she may join other communities, thus transcending existing physical boundaries. Until the child does this, the depth of his or her experience and thus his or her understanding of the world is bounded by, if not indelibly colored by, the local geography.

Community planning which brings the needs and activities of daily living into reasonable spatial relationships with one another is supportive of the process by which children are educated and integrated into their social environment. The community of place concept takes essential aspects of its identity from the physical presence of the school. This idea was first described in the work of Clarence Perry in the 1930s; it has been reaffirmed and refined by the work of Suttles in the 1970s.[3]

Young parents also have a social stake in the community of place which includes the local school. As Gans has pointed out, friendship formation among neighborhood residents may or may not be enhanced by physical proximity, but it does appear to be closely related to age group and level of educational attainment and is constrained by differences in child-rearing practices.[4] Just as children's early social experiences tend to be "place bound," so young parents may also establish key relationships through school activities and involvement in after hours recreational programs which use school facilities.

New support for the theories of Mumford and Perry on life cycle stages and the neighborhood school have also emerged in new theories of child development, and in the criticism by child development authorities of the physical and social conditions in which children have been and are being reared.

The postwar urban and suburban developments of the 1950s and 1960s have been scored by child development authorities for failure to recognize the developmental needs of children. Inadequate attention, it is felt, has been given in standard community planning practice to certain elements of community once taken for granted in older cities and towns. An emphasis on safety from vehicular traffic, on the quality of light and air, and on freedom from crowding and other deleterious influences characteristic of life in older urban centers has consistently caused parents to seek safer, cleaner living environments in which to raise their children. But these environments have tended to ignore or understate the significance of other key elements of community life, namely the markets and the work places, as well as the manner in which essential community services are delivered.

Figure 11–2 School buildings today are planned for multiple uses and adaptive uses.

Children have been insulated from certain clear and obvious dangers at the expense of being isolated from the essential worlds of adult life. As a 1970 White House conference on children reported:

A host of factors conspires to isolate children from the rest of Society. The fragmentation of the extended family, the separation of residential and business areas, the disappearance of neighborhoods, zoning ordinances, occupational mobility, child labor laws, the abolishment of the apprentice system, consolidated schools, television, separate patterns of social life for different age groups, the working mother, the delegation of child care to specialists—all these manifestations of progress [have] operated to decrease opportunity and incentive for meaningful contact between children and persons older or younger than themselves.[5]

Authorities studying the effect on the adolescent of the separation between school and work, point to single land use "residential only" communities as part of the problem. The physical segregation of home and school from other community elements is a holdover from reforms advocated in the 1920s as "protective insurance" against the evils of rapid industrialization and urbanization. Child development authorities now argue that this segregation has fostered in the young a lack of reality about the world of work. Still other authorities point out that the child's world and the adult's world are becoming increasingly distant, not only in space, but in the time parents have to devote to their children and through the conceptual complexity of the work in which many parents are now engaged. A gulf exists between customary adult work and the tasks and activities parents can share with children.[6]

Noting that the typical child in today's school has not one but two working parents and that an increasing number of children are being brought up in single parent families, a study by the Carnegie Council on Children finds parents assuming an executive rather than a direct role in their children's upbringing, "choosing communities, schools, doctors and special programs that will leave their children in the best possible hands."[7]

Social and educational factors in elementary and secondary education impinge on the community planning process in several ways. At a time when national educational authorities encourage and expect parents to take an active part in the schools, school and family interaction becomes much more difficult when both parents typically are working and an increasing number of children are brought up in single parent families.

Complicating the situation are other factors which contribute to the development of the student's character and subsequent academic achievement, including employment and work schedules of parents, health services, child care, neighbors who care, and the stability or lack of stability of the family.[8]

Solutions that are being advocated by educators are centered on reaching students earlier and encouraging involvement of parents in the daily life of the school.[9] The success of these measures in providing the necessary support will involve various elements of the city plan such as distance between school and home or school and work place, accessibility to public transportation, and accessibility to necessary health and social services.

Integration and neighborhood schools

A major problem affecting schools, which also has implications for land use planning, is school integration. Change in the provision of educational services has been the major vehicle for national social policy with respect to racial integration, but these policies have not always benefited children. Many hold that busing of students, for example, has disrupted existing community life, increased the rate of white family migration to the suburbs, and lessened the prospects of equal opportunity through integrated schools.[10]

In their attempts to provide equal education services, local policymakers sometimes ignore the values of neighborhood schools. In busing controversies values attached to neighborhood schools by residents are sometimes viewed as part of an overall pattern of resistance to integration. Yet both black and white families have resisted efforts to transport small children out of their neighborhoods. Some financially able families—both black and white—have deliberately moved to socially and economically integrated communities in which the neighborhood school concept is prominent and is regarded as "an inalienable right."

Issues for planners

It cannot be proved conclusively that the stability of neighborhoods is important to the functioning of schools or that there is a causal relationship between the decline in school achievement and the disruption of neighborhoods. Nor can the physical deterioration of neighborhoods be attributed to the decline of local schools. But it is evident that parents attach overwhelming importance to the proximity and continuity of local schools. A number of discontinuities result from adding physical distance to the social and cultural distance that may already exist between schools and families. The uncertainties surrounding social policy with respect to schools are further compounded by the realization that changes are occurring in the supply of children and in the nature of families.

In the ideal type formulated by Perry, the school occupied the center of a well-balanced neighborhood with a variety of housing types at medium densities and a reasonable rate of succession and immigration. In this setting schools could be sustained that would allow most children to walk to school provided that facility design, financial support, and staffing would allow for some fluctuation in school population. Ideally, both schools and neighborhoods should be of such form, size, and population as to provide for involvement of resident parents in decisions about the physical conditions and social processes of schools. The consolidation of school districts and creation of larger school areas which occurred in the 1960s and 1970s, has been achieved at the expense of community participation. Larger schools at all levels have provided economies of scale and a greater variety of programs which can be offered to larger, more heterogeneous groups—but at a price.

School administrators who must constantly review staff and program requirements for small schools frequently find themselves at odds with parents over closing existing schools or justifying new schools. Rising energy costs combined with rising costs of local government in general, as well as lower enrollment forecasts, have put pressures on schools for cost cutting.

The case for small schools on the other hand has gained support from recognition of the effect of early learning conditions in the home on school performance. Leggett and others advocate that elementary school size be based on the number of parents that can effectively interact with school staff (size of PTA). Models that draw on the experience of the British infant schools are being advocated in the United States. Such schools accommodate children from the ages of three to eleven in relatively small schools, for approximately 300 children, representing a possible 200 to 250 sets of parents.[11] A trend toward smaller schools may also gain momentum from a renewed emphasis on compact, energy-efficient neighborhoods and on bus transportation cost increases.

Educational plans and programs can to some extent be tailored to the needs of individual neighborhoods. Although much of the strength of public supported systems lies in the similarity of one unit to another, particularly with reference to equity, differentiation of schools should be developed to provide greater opportunity to all. Students whose special needs cannot be met within the confines of their immediate neighborhood should be accommodated without inordinate travel. Schools can vary by adherence to traditional or innovative modes of instruction or by offering special programs such as bilingual education. Alternative schools, magnet schools, programs for the gifted and talented, schools which accommodate earlier admission, and schools which have provision for mainstreaming handicapped children are all part of the kit of tools that enable school boards and school administrators to be responsive to differences.

The ability of school planners and administrators to plan for future enrollments, to establish standards for school size, and to devise programs that respect community differences depends on the quality of the information that has been provided about populations. School planners and administrators need to be apprised about the schooling implications of proposed housing patterns, about the probable impact of zoning and rezoning decisions, and about the effects of the implementation of other plans on existing school communities.

An example of collaboration between city planners and public school planners is seen in the work of the Minneapolis city planning department and the Minneapolis public school system. Their joint planning includes parallel committees which review school facility decisions, with specific guidelines at specified stages of each decision. For example, decisions about new buildings on new sites are made only after review of the function, site, and site design for the project by the city planning staff and a second review when the project is ready for construction. Similar specific guidelines are provided for additions to buildings whether a new site is required or not, for rehabilitation projects, and for disposition of school sites. This procedure has been in operation since the mid-1960s. In addition the long-range education facilities plans for Minneapolis public schools are reviewed by the city planning staff as well as by a citywide advisory facilities committee.

The metropolitan planning provisions for joint school/urban development planning in the Twin Cities (Minneapolis and St. Paul) metropolitan area are also exemplary. The "Development Framework" of the Metropolitan Council of the Twin Cities Area requires that all school districts prepare and adopt facilities plans that are consistent with county and municipal comprehensive plans. School districts and municipalities are to cooperate in planning, staging, and timing development, and in reviewing the need for municipal school facilities. The policy also states that "the school facilities plan should emphasize increased utilization of school facilities, coordination of the school district capital expenditure program with county and municipal capital programming, and increase intradistrict planning and sharing of facilities."

Planning for primary and secondary education

The three major decision points at which local government planners can influence primary and secondary education services are: the location of schools, the number of schools (as well as their size or capacity), and the social and economic characteristics of students to be served.

No land use decision is traditionally of greater importance to residents at the grass roots level than is the location of schools. Schools are widely perceived as focal points for neighborhoods. Although the school community served by any single facility changes over time, the school facility and its playground tend to maintain a symbolic role in social interaction. Even when school enrollments decline, schools and school grounds are used as community centers for many activities such as community meetings, day care, teen and adult sports, adult education, and senior citizen activities.

In the early planning of the new town of Columbia, Maryland, for example, primary consideration was given to the concept of "learning as a basic foundation for human community." Planning and implementation focused on the development of a system of overlapping communities in which school plant and playgrounds served as focal points. Neighborhood centers combined elementary schools with complementary facilities such as day care centers or early childhood education facilities, a swimming pool, a community park and play area, and a convenience store. Secondary schools formed the hub of the village center along with facilities for shopping, religious worship, and passive recreation, and with facilities for community organizations.[12]

To the extent that the general development plan for a community affects the density of population, the range of housing types, and the pace of development activity, it influences the need for schools. Many local planning agencies also have responsibilities for programs of advance land acquisition for public facilities and the administration of subdivision regulations; these activities involve them directly in decisions about the acquisition of school sites.

Education, unlike other elements in local planning, has not been a subject of much concern for local government planners, despite the fact that the urban development process shows a clear relationship between the housing market and the demand for schools, leisure activities, and social services.

The beginning point for collaborative planning is the development of strategies for guiding or intervening in decisions about future settlement. Information

Table 11–1 Demographic multipliers for school age children for housing type and size, 1970: by geographic region and division.

Geographic region and division[1]	Single family				Garden apartments			High rise			
	Two bedroom	Three bedroom	Four bedroom	All unit average	One bedroom	Two bedroom	All unit average	Studio	One bedroom	Two bedroom	All unit average
Northeast											
New England	0.246	1.130	2.068	1.212	0.038	0.150	0.174	0.000	0.015	0.081	0.033
Middle Atlantic	0.288	1.111	1.911	1.211	0.011	0.200	0.156	0.000	0.015	0.318	0.125
North Central											
East North Central	0.355	1.173	2.102	1.249	0.036	0.232	0.219	0.000	0.013	0.290	0.483
West North Central	0.361	1.099	2.063	1.142	0.023	0.165	0.173	0.000	0.068	. . .	0.136
South											
South Atlantic	0.553	1.121	1.760	1.130	0.009	0.269	0.358	. . .	0.000	. . .	0.083
East South Central	0.443	1.066	1.728	1.024	0.035	0.306	0.323	. . .	0.000	. . .	0.021
West South Central	0.604	1.109	1.988	1.161	0.052	0.298	0.274	. . .	0.000	0.200	0.050
West											
Mountain	0.404	1.081	1.825	1.364	0.034	0.246	0.245	0.000	0.000	0.000	0.000
Pacific	0.445	1.106	1.842	1.255	0.040	0.307	0.290	0.023	0.000	0.098	0.069
National (All area average)	0.401	1.104	1.924		0.043	0.271		0.012	0.017	0.182	

about the changing nature of the population of households in communities is essential in all such planning. In the case of schools it is needed in greater detail than in almost any other community planning activity.

The objectives and procedures of most local public growth management programs are very similar. They are to control the use of land, the quality of design, the spatial distribution of activities, and the timing of development. To accomplish this, "prime" developers are required to make detailed estimates of probable community growth rates by type of family and income and by the environmental, economic, and fiscal impacts of this growth. The most highly evolved approaches to integrated community planning and to school planning have emerged from these approaches to large scale urban land development planning, mainly from the methodology of fiscal impact studies.[13]

Education services for large scale development

Where planned large scale residential development is taking place, it is possible, by checking indicators of development activity and past experience, to project the sizes of future households and, therefore, the number of school age children. This can be done by standard cohort survival methods of school enrollment supplemented by tabulations of types of housing to be provided, including unit size (bedroom count) and price or rent levels. This ability to plan education services benefits from the quality of information guiding private sector activity. Presumably the development is being undertaken on the basis of a reliable housing market analysis. Large scale developers may seek to directly influence the identification and the acquisition of school sites. Developers, in consultation with

Table 11–1
(continued).

Geographic region and division	Town houses				Mobile homes			
	One bed-room	Two bed-room	Three bed-room	All unit average	One bed-room	Two bed-room	Three bed-room	All unit average
Northeast								
New England	. . .	0.000	. . .[2]	0.640	. . .	0.268	0.324	0.396
Middle Atlantic	0.115	0.304	1.311	1.187	0.048	0.177	1.022	0.375
North Central								
East North Central	0.000	0.409	1.371	1.078	0.078	0.208	1.148	0.360
West North Central	. . .	0.389	0.750	0.544	0.135	0.233	1.169	0.430
South								
South Atlantic	. . .	0.556	. . .	0.838	0.136	0.194	0.906	0.367
East South Central	0.000	0.267	1.500	0.656	0.323	0.262	0.928	0.422
West South Central	0.087	0.400	1.265	0.570	0.239	0.239	1.207	0.513
West								
Mountain	. . .	0.231	. . .	0.577	0.043	0.283	1.158	0.565
Pacific	0.015	0.322	1.333	0.617	0.031	0.159	1.433	0.192
National (All area average)	0.103	0.345	1.331		0.074	0.207	1.076	

Source: U.S. Census Public Use Sample, 1970, based on housing units built from 1960 to 1970. Shown in Robert W. Burchell and David Listokin, *Impact Handbook: Estimating Local Costs and Revenues of Land Development* (New Brunswick, N.J.: Rutgers University, Center for Urban Policy Research, 1978), p. 35.

1 Geographic regions: Northeast Region, New England Division—Connecticut, Maine, Massachusetts, New Hampshire, Rhode Island, and Vermont; Middle-Atlantic Division—New Jersey, New York, and Pennsylvania. North Central Region, East North Central Division—Illinois, Indiana, Michigan, Ohio, and Wisconsin; West North Central Division—Iowa, Kansas, Minnesota, Missouri, Nebraska, North Dakota, and South Dakota. South Region, South Atlantic Division—Delaware, District of Columbia, Florida, Georgia, Maryland, North Carolina, South Carolina, Virginia, and West Virginia; East South Central Division—Alabama, Kentucky, Mississippi, and Tennessee; West South Central Division—Arkansas, Louisiana, Oklahoma, and Texas. West Region, Mountain Division—Arizona, Colorado, Idaho, Montana, Nevada, New Mexico, Utah, and Wyoming; Pacific Division—Alaska, California, Hawaii, Oregon, and Washington.

2 Insufficient sample size; less than 1,000 units.

school district officials, may set aside sites at current prices for future acquisition or they may identify sites as part of a community development package and assist in site preparation costs.

Determination of the yields (numbers and ages of students per dwelling unit) to be expected from various housing types at any stage of the development—that is, the numbers from single family detached houses, town houses, garden apartments, and high rise apartments—will vary with trends in family formation and family size, but, in general, strong relationships exist between the demographic characteristics of new residents expected and the type and size of housing units. A typical calculation of these relationships is shown in Table 11–1.

Both the school planner and the local planner need to understand the importance of detailed information regarding dwelling unit and housing project characteristics. Both sales and rental housing may be programmed and assigned so as to deliberately influence pupil yields at various grade levels. For example, some studies assume that subsidized housing may tend to produce (at the outset) larger pupil yields on the average than equivalent size nonsubsidized housing. This may be true in areas where subsidized sales or rental projects respond to previously unmet needs of older, more mature families with school age children; on the other hand overall yields from subsidized housing may not be very high where the housing is provided for the elderly or for unmarried single persons or couples without children.

Other factors that can influence projections in new residential developments include the differences in tenure in subsidized apartments compared to market rental housing; the differences in family composition for housing for the elderly, the handicapped, or young single people; the differences in family composition that occur when apartments are converted from rental to condominium; and the kinds of occupants that occupy apartments and town houses in developing parts of areas that are frequently "staging areas" for families which move in a few years to single family detached houses.

School enrollment projections   The projection of school enrollments is the task of the school planning staff. Standardization of demographic data used by school districts and other public agencies is obviously desirable. The centralization now provided by some state agencies also can provide higher quality data for the projections of all agencies.

Many variables are used for school enrollment projections, varying with the locality. For Howard County, Maryland, for example, the factors considered included actual enrollment in public schools; enrollment trends in nonpublic schools; student migration (movement of students into and from the county as well as among schools); open enrollment involving special placements distinct from student migration; new housing starts; number of resident births and trends in birthrates; number of pupils expected per type of dwelling unit constructed; land use pattern changes, which influence enrollment projections for all types of schools; availability or projected availability of public sewer facilities, which influences rates of residential development; mobility of population as shown by analysis of pupil-yield factors by housing type; and enrollments within individual school service areas.

School enrollment projections are also frequently based on a combination of cohort survival projections (which use the ratios between births and later kindergarten and first grade enrollments) and the calculation of upper grade enrollments from first grade enrollments. The ratios and data on past trends provide the basis for successive calculations of the probable size of each age group. The use of such data is usually tempered by knowledge of development trends in each district. The two stages of the projection process involve the development of projections of school age population and school enrollment by grade for the entire district and the projection of enrollments by school service area for each school of each type. The method includes the following steps: (1) first grade enrollment ratios are calculated by past experience from the ratios between births in the district and corresponding first grade enrollments six years afterward; (2) the most current cohort survival ratios for each grade are applied; and (3) analysis is made of school-by-school enrollment from the overall district enrollment projections, by use of past enrollment data and by analysis of building activity (new dwelling units and converted dwelling units) and other change factors in each school service area.

The school district's cohort survival rates are the relationships between the number of children in each grade level in a certain year and the number of children in the next higher grade in the next year. Calculation of the cohort survival rates between all grades for several years must be made to determine the most consistent ratios. In areas where population composition is changing because of the changing characteristics of families moving into existing units or into new dwelling units, the ratio between births and kindergarten or first grade enrollments may be considerably more or less than 100 percent.

School location Enough has been said about the neighborhood school to indicate its importance to people living in any given area. What has not been indicated are the standards or "objective" criteria that help determine where to put the school building. Land use planning is the essential starting point; this provides the framework and the general guidelines. Selection of specific sites then becomes—or should become—a collaborative effort of school and local government planners through use of a combination of education and planning criteria. The criteria developed by school systems are not the same for all jurisdictions, but those proposed for Howard County, Maryland (site of the new town of Columbia), are representative enough to be suggestive:

1. Site locations shall be in conformance with future school needs as shown in the General Plan for Howard County and/or as determined from needs assessment of land use regulations and zoning changes.
2. Sites shall, insofar as practicable and economical, be central to the eventual geographic neighborhood(s) and area of the future school to minimize long-range transportation requirements and to reduce the need for some children to walk disproportionately long distances, and also for easier access to the building or grounds by children and adults during after school hours for recreation.
3. Location near employment centers, industrial complexes, or commercial areas is not desirable and should be avoided to minimize exposure to hazards created by vehicular traffic, to lessen attractive nuisance values, and to lessen disturbance from noise, fumes, odors, etc.
4. Potential need for future redistricting of schools is to be considered, and distances between and among school sites are to be such that if the need for redistricting arises it can be accomplished easily.
5. Whenever practicable, school sites and recreation/park sites are to be adjacent to enhance the potential advantages of shared use facilities.
6. The site is to be suitable for economical development of structure and grounds.
7. The site acreages are such as to enable fulfillment of requirements as set forth in the educational program of requirements and guidelines for acreage:
   a) *Elementary schools:* ten (10) acres plus one (1) acre for each 100 student capacity of the school
   b) *Middle schools:* twenty (20) acres plus one (1) acre for each 100 student capacity of the school
   c) *High schools:* thirty (30) acres plus one (1) acre for each 100 student capacity of the school.
8. The topography of the site is to be such that grading and development costs are economical.
9. The configuration of the site is not to constrict or limit the design of the building structure.
10. Public water and sewer services to the site are desirable at the time of acquisition. If these public facilities are not available, the feasibility of on-site systems must be established.
11. A system of pedestrian pathways or sidewalks to and into the school site shall be considered in the site selection processes.
12. Vehicular access to the school site must be by roads or streets required for, and designed to accommodate, expected traffic.[14]

When urban development plans are implemented with concrete proposals, coordination between at least three sets of planners in Howard County must take place: the school planner, the county planner, and the development team planner, with supplementary input from other county agencies such as public works, parks and recreation, and public safety. Assessment of the need for school sites is continuously evaluated in Howard County and updated in response to land use and subdivision regulations and zoning changes. School planners are also called upon to assess the possible impact on school facilities and enrollments inherent in proposed zoning changes.

The issue of centrality of school location within the eventual geographic neighborhood or service area of the school sometimes generates conflicts between school planners and land planners charged with design and development planning and implementation of specific sites. The socially desirable characteristics of geographic centrality and convenient walking distance must be weighed along with other factors influencing physical design of the neighborhoods, including distinctive housing types, old settlement patterns, land ownership patterns, and place names—factors which historically have influenced residents' perception of "community" but which may not be coterminous with a school service area.

A shared school site contiguous to community parks, conservation areas, or community open space is advocated by many planners. A properly developed site of this kind would provide for a comprehensive outdoor community recreation program with playground and play fields to serve a wide range of age groups. It might also be related to environmental education with the potential for establishing outdoor learning centers.

While school sites should be located in a position central to population served, they should also be located with an eye to possible future redistricting. What is needed is a network of schools neither too near each other nor too far apart. "Too near" and "too far" are determined by fixed and variable factors: state guidelines for walking distances, residential densities and subsequent student yields, the availability of sidewalks or walk systems in dense urban neighborhoods, and logical transportation routes in rural areas.

School districts have a variety of means at their disposal for responding to increases or decreases in school service area populations: permanent or temporary school closings, the development of alternative programs which may attract students from outside the declining service area, changes in school structure (e.g., the range of grade levels served), and use of double sessions or year-round school programs. All of the above can be employed to avoid overbuilding or underuse of specific schools resulting from community growth or change.

School facility planning in most areas is predicated on specific school standards—a grade-level organization pattern (for example, K–5/6–8/9–12) with standards for the number of pupils assigned per school and per class, and site size standards. The instructional programs, teaching methods, and nature and needs of the pupils to be housed represent the context within which such school characteristics are considered when specific projects are planned.

Application of school standards   Standards are not infallible; nor are they intended to be. When used correctly—that is, with prudence and in conjunction with other information, opinions, judgment, and data—they provide benchmarks for specific application in making decisions. Such decisions may involve the location of a school building exactly within a predetermined area, determining the precise size of the school building in terms of the number and size of classrooms, and allocating basic facilities to the building.

Extensive research on the influence of class size on the quality of education reveals no provable causal relationships. Other factors are apparently much more important to educational achievement. The most important question education planners—or any planners—can ask about a set of standards is: What value or values are of greatest importance? Most standards for school size are based largely on administrative efficiency and the practical and empirical factors of class size and very little on educational outcomes. Most jurisdictions will probably continue to base school size standards on these traditional concepts—how many primary grade classes one principal and a principal's staff can administer efficiently—but from time to time new and perhaps less standardized thinking about learning processes and community structure may generate plans for smaller schools with new configurations. Such schools would serve smaller geographic areas, could generate a variety of different service area sizes, and could occupy very flexible, convertible community-core space. Until educational ideas emerge to generate these new educational forms, the standard 400 to 600 student elementary school and similar size standards for middle schools and high schools will continue to dominate the school planning process.

Standardization also dominates expert opinion about school site sizes. Standards recommending larger and larger land area requirements for schools have been developed since World War II. Large site requirements are justified by school administrators by aggregating larger land areas needed for one story buildings; for increased parking needs; and for the need to provide for a wide range of athletic facilities, nature study areas, and buffer areas between schools and their sports areas and the surrounding roads as well as neighboring land uses. However, the era of expanding school site area standards may be ending. High land costs (in part a result of higher community facility standards and higher costs for services), the pressures to increase overall community density to conserve energy, and the growing pressures to conserve all resources may lead to reconsideration of the need for seven to ten acre elementary school sites and forty plus acre high school sites. Adequate schools and sports areas can be and have been provided on much smaller sites.

Mature school systems

Most of the preceding discussion has covered large scale developments—usually residential, occasionally new towns or other endeavors—that involve problems in trying to anticipate population influx and growth but that also provide greater opportunities for planning sites and facilities for years, even generations, ahead.

But what about the smaller communities? The more mature places? The older suburbs? The places where the community cycle is regenerative rather than just beginning? The planning process obviously continues, but the approach is often modified.

In those types of community developments in which the housing market is not dominated by a single, large scale development process, the current activities of land developers and builders are available in other forms. In most communities these will include information from subdivision plans, building permits, and the annual school census, as well as information on the installation of electric and telephone services which utilities make available to local and school planners, and birth data in the district by year from local or state health departments. In addition to making use of these readily available community data, planners will find it useful to keep in touch with local builders and lending institutions for information about the number and types of dwelling units in the planning stage.

In suburban jurisdictions where enrollments are declining local planners may expect problems of adjusting downward from the present high levels of expenditures for education. Local government executives and citizen groups will seek greater control of school expenditures. Accountability for learning outcomes is a related issue in suburban districts. School officials will be pressed to justify expenditures, and local community planners can expect an increasing demand for information about school systems.

Many suburban school systems will close elementary, junior, and middle schools through the 1980s. For these systems, declines in enrollment may create opportunities for catching up—improving the quality of education, renovating older facilities, and achieving more desirable teacher–student ratios. Such system improvements will have to be justified with great care and will require effective program and facility planning.

Declines in enrollment may also, through the availability of additional classroom space, provide the opportunity to alter the ways in which schools are organized and the type of services provided. (For example, shifts from traditional elementary/junior high school organization to kindergarten through grade 5/middle school/high school structure may be possible under no-growth or decline circumstances.) To make use of excess capacity, local school systems may consider the extension of kindergarten to a full day and indeed are likely to lower the age at which students can enter public systems. In this way they may assume further responsibilities for early childhood development by incorporating and expanding such activities as Head Start programs and by taking on greater responsibility for the education of the handicapped.

Whether there is growth or not, school facilities will require modification in accordance with new laws requiring the provision of "the least restrictive environments" for use by persons who are physically and mentally handicapped and whose earlier education may have been provided at home or in separate institutions—or perhaps was totally neglected. The modification, extension, or expansion of the public education system to provide services previously not part of their programs creates pressure for additional expenditures.

An improved capacity to plan for future school enrollment is in evidence in Charles County, Maryland, which completed a five year long-range master plan which integrated all aspects of change which must be taken into account: curriculum planning, development of educational objectives, transportation, food service, school facilities, and administration and management. The future of such programs as special education, education for the gifted and talented, and provisions for the handicapped is dealt with, as are approaches to the typical school issues such as discipline and accountability. All policies are presented and integrated in one document. Preparation of the plan involved eleven key people in the system and approximately eighty people at various levels of leadership in the public and private sectors of Charles County.[15]

Most suburban school planning will continue to focus on problems of enrollment growth and provision of education services to previously underserved school age populations, including the handicapped.

Some older communities, which share with central cities the problems of declining demand for education services, face difficult decisions of planning the closing of selected schools, the adaptation of school buildings to new uses, and the redevelopment of sites for totally new uses. These issues of planning for decline in demand for education services are the subject of the next section.

Education services in central cities

In most central cities the major school problem is not planning for new physical facilities (although many buildings need replacement or substantial renovation) but is, rather, deciding which school facilities should be retained, abandoned, or replaced. Three major kinds of decisions face the community planner in these situations:

1. Selection for retention and renovation of older school facilities, which may involve the joint development of programs for other community services such as day care, services for the elderly, etc.
2. Sale, demolition, or adaptive reuse of school facilities which are no longer needed for educational purposes
3. Location, size, and program mix for schools to be housed in new facilities in connection with neighborhood revitalization programs (these arrangements are likely to include planning for other social services in multicenters or in community schools).

Retention and renovation of school buildings   Decisions to renovate or expand schools because of expectations of stability or continued school age population growth should be reviewed in relation to the long-term stability of the housing stock in the service area, expected changes in land use, and changes in accessibility related to transportation improvements. The role of the local planning agency will be to raise the community issues related to decisions about schools and/or to provide a forum for innovative thinking about each community's school needs.

In most school renovation a basic consideration for conservation is the adaptability of the school structure. Nineteenth century load-bearing walls do not permit much change in spatial arrangements. The potential for increasing a school site size to meet recreational needs of the community also may be a factor in selecting schools to keep. And the relationship of sites to public transportation could be particularly significant, for example, if the proposed school use were a "magnet school" (a school with a special set of programs and special goal structure that would tend to attract people from the large area). Participation in these schools will depend in part on public transportation and the quality of the neighborhood.

The problem of disposing of school buildings is not limited to older cities. It is also a problem in many inner suburbs, but large cities, particularly those in the Northeast, are now experiencing the largest decreases in elementary and secondary school enrollments. From 1970 to 1975 in the fifteen largest cities in the United States public school enrollment declined by 3.8 to 22.6 percent. The smallest drop in percentage was in New York and the greatest in St. Louis. The most important point to keep in mind is that the enrollment dropped in every one of these largest cities during the same five years.

In these cities and in some close-in suburbs that were growing until very recently, a large portion of surplus school capacity is located in specific school service areas. Where this is the case, decisions about school closing and the allocation of facilities to other uses should not be difficult. The decisions are more difficult and planning is most essential in situations where the declines are dispersed over relatively broad areas of the city. These declines may justify closing a large number of schools. In the extreme situations low birthrates, outmigration, and a reduction of housing stock have combined to generate great decreases in school age population. Large numbers of school buildings will be abandoned or sold for alternative uses. The need is to establish criteria for selecting those schools to be preserved and those to be closed. These criteria should deal with the following points:

1. The age and condition of the school facility
2. The adaptability of the school to modern education requirements
3. The availability of excess capacity in adjacent schools
4. The decline in enrollment for the current period and the expected decline in enrollment in relation to other candidate schools
5. The effect of closing specific schools on overall racial integration of the system
6. The presence or absence of community programs including those for which alternative sites would be difficult to secure
7. Mid- and long-term projections of land use changes and neighborhood population composition changes
8. The accessibility and general effect on spacing of each of the schools as candidates for the new system, which will by definition have new and larger service areas.

Sale, demolition, or reuse of school buildings[16] Alternative uses for surplus school buildings include: alternative educational programs (i.e., vocational education or day care), public library or other public services, and a limited range of private sector uses including housing and, in appropriate locations, commercial or even industrial uses. Reuse or sale rather than demolition of abandoned school structures will become increasingly popular. The primary reason is that renovation costs for most uses generally run somewhat less (in terms of capital investment) than new projects. Costs will depend, of course, on the quality of the renovation and the condition of the original structure as well as on the new use. In general, savings on the order of 50 percent up to as high as 75 percent in overall project costs can be expected. A second reason is that retention and renovation may have a positive effect on the quality of the community.

There are three basic options for school boards which have surplus school capacity: the use of some facilities for educational purposes other than their original uses; leasing on a short-term basis; and sale of some buildings to other public agencies or private individuals with or without restrictions in the deeds of sale.

A common and time-consuming legal requirement requires the approval by the voters of leasing or sale of school properties. Some state legislation places restrictions or conditions on leases of school property, including minimum rentals and limitations on length of leases. The sale of no-longer-needed school buildings may be subject to similar restrictions of state law, established to protect the public interest but nevertheless frequently found to slow down the process of decision making.

A school district's decision to close a school and dispose of the building for other uses almost always involves the interests of a larger community and therefore calls for community as well as school planning. The factors to be considered regarding reuse include: first, the needs of the community for other kinds of services and facilities; second, the real estate market in the area for housing and other potential uses; third, the configuration and condition of the building; and fourth, its location in relation to other community uses. These and other local criteria should be evaluated in a full study of alternatives undertaken jointly or by the local planning agency and local school officials. If a decision has been made to dispose of one or more school facilities, an overall study of potential reuses may be undertaken primarily by the local community planning staff. Studies which include the possible private use of school facilities often include the advice of a panel of local real estate developers and market studies by real estate consultants.

After determining the range of potential building or site reuses it may be necessary to carry out special feasibility studies of possible configurations of a building in view of its structural condition and maintenance and the condition of its mechanical systems, as well as the characteristics of its site and its location.

Frequently, communities are surprised that disposition of a school is not a moneymaking proposition. This is particularly true if the intended reuse requires extended renovation including structural changes and modifications or replacement of parts of mechanical systems. In such situations the only two alternatives may be demolition, and conversion of the land to other uses, or sale of the building for a nominal sum.

In almost every case it is in the community's interest to dispose of the property as soon as possible after the decision is made that it is no longer needed. Following such decisions vandalism frequently increases, insurance rates go up, and complaints begin to be made regarding expenditures for minimum maintenance of a nonproductive facility. Sale prices of no-longer-needed schools therefore should be based on the economics of the public or private reuse rather than on the replacement value of the structure itself.

The readaptive use of no-longer-needed school buildings may be of social and symbolic value to the community beyond the economic return to the school district. For example, some old school buildings have architectural character or symbolize some aspect of the history of the educational system. In such cases the decision should not be treated wholly in terms of economics.

Figure 11–3 Before (building exterior and auditorium: top and above) and after (auditorium and classroom: right) views of the Madison-Morgan Cultural Center in Madison, Georgia. Built as a public school in 1895, this structure now provides space for an art gallery, a historical museum, offices, a film room, and an auditorium for the performing arts. The auditorium has been restored, but the original seating, chandelier, and sconces have been retained.

There is no insurance that the reuse cost will be less than the cost of building a new facility for any activity but there are some rather remarkable examples of cost savings in specific instances. The Saint Assumption School in East Boston was converted to housing for $14 per square foot where comparable new construction costs were in excess of $30 per square foot.[17] In 1976 the Haverhill, Massachusetts, city hall occupied the converted Haverhill High School after extensive renovation involving new police headquarters and jail facilities and complete replacement of heating, ventilating, air conditioning, electrical, and other mechanical systems at a cost of about $16 per square foot at a time when the cost of new construction for municipal office buildings was almost $40 per square foot.[18]

Enrollment decline in city districts is frequently accompanied by increased need for other community services. Some schools have leased space to the public agencies providing these services. In other cases joint planning and construction of facilities have provided a realization of the old ideal of the use of schools as community centers for recreational, cultural, and other events in addition to their education uses. Such uses, whether in new or renovated buildings, may arise from the decisions of agencies in large cities to decentralize the provision of services. Therefore, in addition to preschool and adult education programs, one might find in such new community school centers any or all of the following: preventive health services, day care, senior citizen activities, after-school programs for teenagers, and a variety of recreational programs.

Examples of such projects include the conversion of the Kalamazoo Central High School to a multiuse community education center which rents space to a variety of educational and community programs; the structure converted was originally built in 1912 and required extensive renovation. The city of New York converted one of its unneeded elementary schools with a large site to a new community recreation center, while a modern (1954) school building is being used for a temporary district office for the school board, a day care center, and a senior citizen center.

Conversion to such private uses as housing, commercial facilities, offices, and private schools is often best from the community's point of view. Many of the school buildings available for such conversions will have spaces designed as classrooms of from 400 to 800 square feet in area. Such spaces are well suited for adaptation for apartments for single people, including senior citizens.[19] As is the case with public uses, the savings in construction costs for such uses as housing can be substantial. A specific case in Gloucester, Massachusetts, illustrates such economies.

In Gloucester the total construction cost for converting a grammar school to apartments was $1,482,350; the total construction cost for a new high rise was $2,216,712. The cost per unit for apartments in the converted school was $18,530; in the high rise it was $22,850. In addition, the average apartment size in the converted school was 800 square feet, while in the high rise it was 456 square feet.

In addition to the lower cost and more space per dwelling unit, this Gloucester housing has interesting architectural features including granite walls, high ceilings, natural wood floors, oak wainscots and large apartment sizes. There is also, in this school conversion, a greater variety of apartment types than was possible in a new project with which it was compared. The old school's location was a marketing advantage. It is near many community facilities, is near central Gloucester, and has easy access to a variety of shopping facilities, churches, and the waterfront.

Another example of housing reuse is the conversion of the Dewitt Junior High School in Ithaca, New York. The Ithaca school board chose to sell this vintage junior high school building, originally constructed in 1912, for $20,000 to a local architect. The building is located in downtown Ithaca and the remodeling consists of a ground level shopping area that includes clothing stores, a bakery, a delicatessen, a camping goods store, several restaurants, and office space, and upper floors devoted to forty-nine one and two bedroom apartments. The project has preserved a significant local work of architecture and provides a handsome living environment at a cost of approximately $500,000 required for the conversion. This conversion to multiple uses also contributes $40,000 a year in taxes to the city of Ithaca and the Ithaca school district. The project has increased the viability of the downtown whose retail market had been threatened recently by outlying commercial developments and has provided construction jobs and business for local suppliers.[20]

Some other examples of private reuse of surplus school facilities include office space for training schools, vocational schools, private preparatory schools, and private corporations; an inn and retail uses in Claremont, California; a church in Des Moines, Iowa; antique galleries in Atlanta, Georgia; and a nursing home in Abbeville, Georgia.

Improving school facilities   The quality of school systems in old central cities is widely recognized as a key factor in the long term viability of old neighborhoods. Increased prospects for improving the quality of these school systems may lie in court decisions requiring state equalization of expenditures for local public primary and secondary education. Such measures will mean increased state and federal assistance and perhaps greater control of local school systems.

New schools in the old city   School replacement, a long deferred need in many cities, is frequently integrated with the planning agency's capital improvements program. The process used in Baltimore is illustrative. Two instruments guide the provision of school facilities and services in the city: a twenty year plan for school construction in the city, and a management information systems document completed in 1971. An inventory completed in 1967 ranked schools in five categories: of approximately 235 schools, 77 were built before 1920 and were judged to be old, obsolete, and in need of replacement; 31 were deemed usable for a little longer if certain repairs were made; and schools in categories three to five were found to be obsolete but feasible for renovation, or in need of minor repairs, or in satisfactory condition. By 1977 all schools described in the inventory had been scheduled for replacement, renovation, updating, or closing.[21]

Declining enrollments in certain areas of Baltimore have permitted school officials in some instances to replace two, and sometimes three, schools with one somewhat larger, centrally located facility. Schools at the elementary level range in size from 450 to 840 students. Schools whose enrollments drop below 350 become candidates for closure. Some neighborhood elementary schools are maintained with lower enrollments because of the difficulties that would be encountered in serving communities isolated by industrial areas or strong transportation barriers that make the child's journey to school less safe.

Since 1971, thirty-five Baltimore city schools have been replaced or renovated under a unique program of state planning. The emphasis is on replacement of elementary schools and renovation of specialized high schools such as Baltimore's City College, a long time leader as a high school specializing in the humanities.

Sites for replacement schools are hard to find in the built-up older city. Facilities must frequently be accommodated on sites of one and a half acres or less. Availability of the site is the major criterion. School officials seek to avoid acquisition of sites containing good housing. At the same time they seek compatible neighbors. The search for sites is carried out in conjunction with the department of city planning and the department of housing and community development. Sites are evaluated on location with respect to the pupil population to be served; the complexity and costs of development; the potential site-caused compromises or constrictions on building design; the proportions of the site; its capacity to support the educational program; its ability to accommodate projected pedestrian and vehicular traffic; its location; the availability of utilities; the surrounding land uses, projected future land uses, and regulations governing future land uses; drainage, soil conditions, and natural ecological features; as well as possible other uses and possible adverse conditions such as smell or noise.

Reuse of surplus schools is also a problem in Baltimore. Many potential uses and users are contemplated but the costs of maintenance and operation of the many desirable ideas and programs that appear within the community are often prohibitive. The mayor's office has engaged consultants to evaluate the potential for reuse of six schools as housing for luxury, low income, and elderly residents.

Higher education planning

In the years since World War II higher education in the United States has evolved into a complex and diversified structure of colleges, universities, community colleges, on-campus and off campus learning centers, and research institutes. Planners and local government administrators can expect higher educational institutions, especially those that are part of state systems, to strive for decentralization and diversification of their educational offerings, but in the 1980s this will be difficult because society is likely to shift its priorities elsewhere. Innovations will be based on social and technological changes and will occur chiefly because of changes in the age groups that colleges and universities serve.

The demographic basis of planning

The decade of the 1960s was a period of enormous growth in higher education in the United States. The growth was accounted for by two major factors: the rapid increase of the college age population (the result of the "baby boom" of the 1940s and 1950s) and an increasing ratio of the college age population enrolling in colleges and universities. Public policy encouraged the growth of existing institutions, the establishment of new institutions, and the development of entire new systems, including many community colleges. The growth was reflected in the near doubling of enrollment nationally between 1965 and 1975.

From 1975 on enrollments leveled off, and some falling off of enrollments is projected during the 1980s. These are national projections and are subject to regional and local variations which could differ sharply.

The age group that is likely to have the greatest influence on higher education in the 1980s is the post-college-age population. This group will be interested in retraining and upgrading its technical and professional skills in hundreds of employment areas. Another expanding role will be in satisfying the noncareer-related interests of retirement age groups. With the average age of retirement falling, there will be increasing pressure for educational programs to be offered in many fields. Such programs can be offered in a variety of ways, but especially through evening and Saturday programs.

Many retirees are interested in other than leisure time activities, some in second careers and many in further education. Educational institutions which seek to serve the needs of such groups will be brought into closer relations with their immediate communities. Fulfillment of these roles by colleges and universities will involve them in an increasing number of issues in local planning processes.

The nature and importance of the further education function will vary with the basic demographic and economic characteristics of communities. Urban colleges are more likely to develop part-time study than are small town colleges. Communities which have government employment or education as major economic activities may have a large demand for formal college level courses that will increase job skills. And communities with large populations of retired persons will have greater demands for instruction related to the use of leisure time and to arts, literature, and public affairs.

Projections made by the U.S. Department of Health, Education, and Welfare indicated that first time enrollments (freshmen in college) would reach a peak in 1978 of 1,181,000 and would decline by 165,000 or 15 percent by 1985. Some experts predict a drop of 400,000 in college enrollments in the period 1980–90. Because of regional differences in birthrates and net migration these demographic changes will not be uniform across the nation. In areas where the college age population decrease will be greater, smaller private sector colleges may experience sharp enrollment declines. Some will be abandoned. In such regions a few state university campuses may be closed, but the practice of finding adaptive reuses for college facilities will not be as common as it is for secondary schools.

Since government employment represents an increasingly large cohort of the work force (up from 13 percent to 20 percent of all nonagricultural workers from 1950 to 1975), and since promotion in civil service positions in local and state government as well as in the federal government is frequently geared to further education, the demand for higher education services by the older post-college population will probably continue to grow.

Some communities will plan for new and expanded higher educational institutions and campuses which respond to the demographic shifts mentioned above. As has been stated earlier, local government planners can play a role in demographic analysis including projections of needs for community-wide education. In very general terms this may mean provision of age specific population estimates, population projections for small areas, and survey research on needs as a part of planning research by state, county, and local planning agencies. (See Chapter 4 for a detailed discussion of survey research.)

The size of an institution and the degree of its autonomy will greatly influence the need for the extent of joint college/locality planning and decision making. Some of the more advanced statewide university systems such as the University of California have developed policies which encourage and facilitate collaboration with local governments and address the developmental problems of the institutions' immediate environment. This is accomplished through the appointment of specialized community planning staff members on the staff of each campus and through research on impacts of campus growth on localities; student and faculty housing demands; economic effects; university teaching; and research programs.

The structure of higher education

Many kinds of institutions of higher education have evolved in the United States in the past half century, including colleges, universities, and other institutions that have contributed enormously to the richness and diversity of community life. There are three broad classifications of these institutions.

The first group would include universities with major graduate programs, professional schools, and substantial research activity. This group includes old private universities, old and usually large and semiautonomous state universities, the statewide systems of multicampus universities, and a limited number of city universities. Their relationship to the immediate community tends to be intense and immediate in many cases. Many of these large institutions with enrollments of 20,000 to 30,000 students serve national and sometimes international populations. Therefore, they may not be perceived by their local neighborhoods as particularly relevant to the quality of local life except as employers. The politics of joint planning are likely to be very different in these schools from those in the smaller public or private colleges which draw their students largely from the immediate area.

The next group consist of the four year colleges, whether public or private, which usually have much smaller enrollments, ranging from 3,000 to 10,000 students. In some of the state systems these colleges may have evolved from teachers' colleges or normal schools to perform much more diverse educational functions. They are frequently, but not exclusively, found in smaller towns or cities and tend to provide services to a student population that is more local in origin. Their educational programs and cultural activities may fulfill some of the needs of local people who are not part of the student–faculty community. Their educational offerings at the undergraduate level are not likely to be as diverse as those from the university. The four year college can offer only limited graduate work, and the emphasis is overwhelmingly on undergraduate education.

The third group is made up of the community colleges, formerly known as junior colleges, which provide education and training of two years' duration. Decisions about their location can be major regional and local planning issues in which state higher education agencies usually play decisive roles. Many existing community colleges can be expected to grow in response to the educational needs of the older segments of the population.

Where does planning fit in?

Higher education planning and its relationship to the local government obviously vary with the nature of the institution, its enrollment, the size of its resident population, and other characteristics. A few common characteristics can be expected, however, in almost all institution/local government planning relationships.

First, the working relationships of local government planners should be tailored to fit the characteristics of the local educational institutions, including their enrollment, the nature of their student population, campus layout, and similar characteristics.

Second, planners should be sensitive to and should capitalize on the contributions of colleges and universities to the urban social and cultural environment. Sometimes planners can contribute to educational policies in an advisory capacity and should seek opportunities for bringing the advantages of the educational programs to the citizens of the community. Many institutions are receptive to this approach.

Third, planning agencies should develop good working relationships with the administrative offices of colleges and universities, particularly with the finance and planning staffs. This is more difficult (but is certainly not impossible), as major decisions are made in state capitals that may be many miles away.

Fourth, colleges and universities should be viewed by local planners as major employers which need the same kind of support in planning, infrastructure services, and environmental services in their community setting that would be provided for any other major employer. Local planners have direct interests in the development policies and long-range programming of these institutions. These interests include the projected enrollment, the age and sex characteristics of students, and the projected physical form of the campus.

Finally, planners have an immediate and continuing concern with the physical form and daily life of the campus, including the automobile parking and traffic, commuting and travel modes, and student and faculty housing. These questions often have a direct budgetary effect on the city government.

The urban university district[22]

While there are special planning problems for every campus, there is a general type of urban higher education district in many older cities which has clearly defined land use planning problems. These university districts have emerged as special types of communities: in Philadelphia with the West Philadelphia District, including the University of Pennsylvania, Temple University, and several large hospitals; in Cleveland's University Circle District with Case Western Reserve University, the Cleveland Museum of Art, and several large hospitals and research clusters; in Chicago with several such districts including the South Side with the Illinois Institute of Technology and Michael Reese Hospital and the University of Chicago/Hyde Park–Kenwood Woodlawn Districts. Others come to mind in Boston, New York, San Francisco, Columbus, Minneapolis, and Denver.

These special types of urban districts require special attention from local planners. They are one of the significant new urban forms of the twentieth century and offer opportunities for revitalization of cities. They have been the focus of considerable competition for urban space and other scarce resources. During the 1960s local planners sometimes found themselves in adversary roles vis-à-vis university planners when campus expansion plans displaced low income and minority group populations. At least as frequently, joint city–university planning for the renewal of the university districts was a major item on the agenda of city planning agencies and was considered a successful aspect of local renewal programs. The 1980s will provide opportunities to consolidate these gains and in some cases to build onto and refine university district planning organizations as well as the institutions and the support services for such districts.

Traditionally, large cities have been the centers of important intellectual activities. The proximity of libraries, museums, concert halls, hospitals, independent research institutes, business and professional enterprises, industries, and government offices has augmented the cultural, scholarly, and scientific resources of the universities. These institutions have provided research and consultative opportunities for students and teachers. The technological, social, economic, and political ferment of large cities has also been a stimulus for learning and research.

Increasingly the central city areas of metropolitan regions have seen a diminution of their activities in retailing, manufacturing, and wholesaling as a result of changes in transportation and communication. While these formerly dominant economic activities have been moving to the periphery, emergent activities in decision making, information gathering and dissemination, education, and research have grown to become prominent features of the same cities. These "knowledge industries" have provided an increasing number of services as well as employment opportunities for the metropolis.

Analysis of the internal form and the character of the boundaries of a university campus is useful in understanding the interaction between a university and its immediate environment. The form of a university campus affects its ability to expand and change internally. Formal–axial patterns with strongly marked boundaries which seem to assert, "There, it is finished," are difficult to modify internally and are nearly impossible to expand gracefully once the closed design is filled in.

One such static form is the monumental plan made by McKim, Mead and White for Columbia University in the 1890s (Figure 11–4). The finality of this form left little room for the physical expansion of the university. When the time came for Columbia to expand, it was not aided in its dealings with the city government or its neighbors by the completed and imposing visage of its campus. A mode of campus design which permits easy internal modifications, growth by

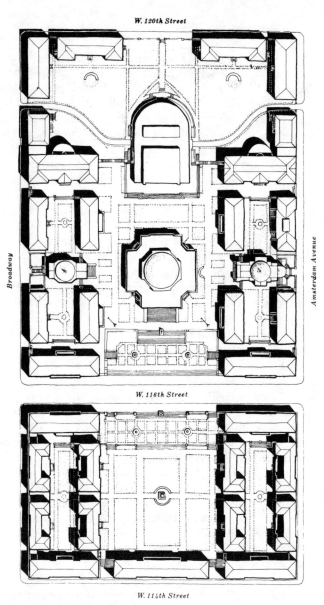

Figure 11–4   Columbia University original site plan, 1898.

filling in, and extension upward, outward, and downward is an important objective of contemporary campus planners. In the same sense, blurred boundaries between the campus and a variegated university district environment can permit varied responses to changed situations and yet permit retention of old forms and values.

The opportunities of the urban university district may be grouped under the following general headings:

1. The opportunity for a planned physical development of the university district: extensive renewal of housing, streets, commercial services, shopping facilities, schools, utilities; coherent and legible design of a public or semipublic space which forms a civic–cultural nucleus of a city; revision of a major mode of transportation

2. Opportunities for social development within the district: a superior urban school or schools which might serve as models for the educational system at large; an opportunity for reducing race and class prejudice and antagonism; an opportunity for a reduced journey to work for certain

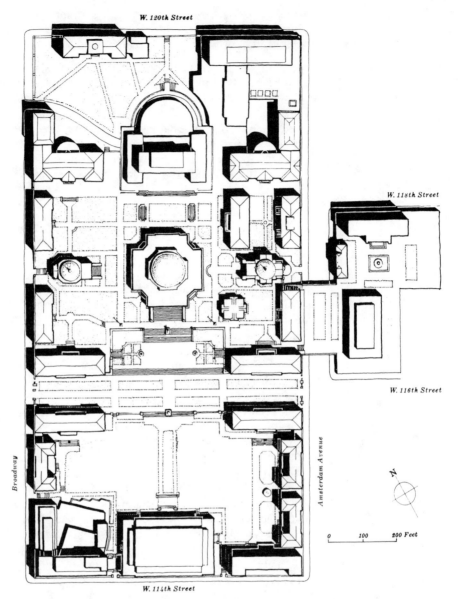

W. 120th Street

W. 118th Street

W. 116th Street

W. 114th Street

Broadway

Amsterdam Avenue

0   100   200 Feet

Figure 11–4   Columbia University site plan, 1970. (See text, page 323.)

types of experts and technicians essential to the operation of the industrial–urban society; an opportunity for new experiences in citizenship; opportunities for preventive approaches to urban problems including community mental health, referral to community services, and improved police protection within the district

3. Opportunities for economic growth of the district with implications for the development of the regional economy, including: opportunities for new product development and the growth of new industries; opportunities to expedite the transfer of technology to existing industrial institutions and their personnel

4. Opportunities for the recruitment and retention of experts who deal with urban problems

5. Opportunities for the creation of new institutions to meet previously unanticipated demands (e.g., direct action corporations, community development, neighborhood improvement, new cultural centers): the cooperative sharing of scarce resources such as teaching and research staff, equipment, and facilities; the revitalization of existing institutions

(e.g., existing social welfare agencies, community protection
associations, organizations for improvement of housing, for the
prevention of juvenile delinquency, and for community mental health).

Large urban university or university–cultural areas such as University Circle in Cleveland are the most complex types of this institutional land use. They
display in magnified form the entire range of problems of accommodating and
integrating higher education into the overall pattern of urban development.
These clusters of educational institutions have large, time-differentiated effects
on traffic and parking; they influence the characteristics of demand for housing in adjacent areas; and they generate demand for retail and service establishments that are different from those of the typical urban residential
neighborhood.

City government relationships

Many of a community's impressions of a college or university will be formed
through day-to-day living: the ebb and flow of students going to classes, parking
on and off campus, living in apartments, rooming houses, and dormitories,
shopping in local stores and shopping centers, and contributing to the local
economy as consumers and taxpayers.

Much of the planning between the college or university, irrespective of size,
and the city government is concerned with accommodating these daily
concerns: parking, housing, shopping, police and other protective services,
public schools, and local government services for students, faculty, and
employees.

A university campus, together with the other educational, research, cultural,
and health service institutions that make up these districts, can create as much
or more traffic than a major industry or a regional shopping center. The number
of automobile and public transit trips to and from the district will depend in part
on the number of students and faculty who live on campus or in or near enough
to the district to walk to their daily activities. Other factors that will affect traffic
and parking loads include the student automobile ownership policy of the universities and colleges; the number, type, and size of cultural events (theater performances, concerts, dance recitals, etc.) that attract public attendance; and the
types of health care—all of which generate some specialized types of short-term
visits (outpatient care, patient visitors, etc.).

Specialized traffic and parking studies will be needed in such districts as a
basis for joint planning by the institutions and local government for traffic, parking, and the provision of bus and mass transit facilities. The coordination of
transportation planning will be a major planning agenda item in these areas.
Traffic patterns in surrounding areas may also be influenced by the large volumes of institutional traffic. The same types of concerns on a smaller scale will
arise near single college and university campuses or adjacent to large hospitals.

Local planning agencies will be particularly concerned with the quality of
housing and commercial services in college and university neighborhoods.
These concerns parallel those of college and university administrators. In campuses located in the older parts of large cities neighborhood decline can have
serious consequences for the quality of the housing stock, for public safety, and
for other characteristics of life in campus-oriented residential neighborhoods.
Many college and university officials have concluded that the desirability of
these neighborhoods for student and faculty residence has a direct effect on the
viability of the institution's academic and research programs.

Community policy expressed through land use controls, building and housing
code enforcement, community services such as police protection, recreation
programs and facilities, schools, and neighborhood revitalization efforts should
be responsive to the needs of college or university communities. Conversion of

large houses to apartments is typical of such areas. Such a process can have positive effects on residential quality. Although the campus usually includes some student housing, the quality varies considerably. And student housing preferences also vary. Students who live off campus but do not commute from their homes seek low rent accommodations. They may be subject to exploitation by entrepreneurs who convert existing single family housing or overcrowded apartment units; some universities establish qualitative standards for off-campus student housing, but they are difficult to enforce. This suggests a stronger role for local housing code enforcement in neighborhoods with large student populations.

The business and service needs of a university or college community grow from specialized characteristics that differentiate it from other parts of the urban area. Almost every campus has an adjacent business area that caters to its faculty and students. Almost every institution also competes in this market with campus food services, with book and supply stores, etc. Relevant local planning issues will include: the division of these markets; the extent to which campus-oriented business districts meet the needs of the population; and the location, design, and traffic and parking arrangements for such services. The convenience goods, fast food, and personal service establishments that dominate university commercial districts are usually marginal compared with other such districts. They are seldom well planned or attractive, but they nevertheless deserve attention from local government as an integral part of the community. Market analysis may show unmet potential in these areas.

Economic impact studies

By the early 1970s a generalized approach to college economic impact had been developed by the American Council on Education (ACE).[23] It is sufficiently flexible to use in most situations with readily available data. Such an impact model is shown in Figure 11–5.

The impact models in use, including those developed by ACE, deal with payments to local business, local government, and local individuals as benefits and with the costs of municipal and educational services that presumably can be allocated to college influence. The allocation of costs is usually in proportion to the college's share, which is generally lower than its share of business and industrial consumers of municipal services.

As the quality of urban life becomes more dependent on knowledge and as more leisure time becomes available to more people, the local role of the community colleges and universities will no doubt change and will perhaps increase. These institutions are extending their benefits to a widening age spectrum in the population. The city of the 1980s may consider its institutions of higher learning as one of its most important resources and their neighborhoods as some of the most desirable places to live.

Summary

In summation, the "costs" to local government for a college or university include such direct items as police, fire, and other protective services; public schools; tax exempt properties; and a wide range of direct and indirect services for students, employees, and faculty. Offsetting such costs are a wide range of community benefits. Some can be estimated or measured quantitatively, including student expenditures for food, clothing, and housing; faculty and employee salaries; and college and university bank deposits. Others are intangible benefits: the value of the institution for a prospective industry; long-term benefits to the local economy of college or university research and technological innovation; provision of a permanent, stable employment base; continuing educational opportunities; and provision of a range of cultural programs and services.

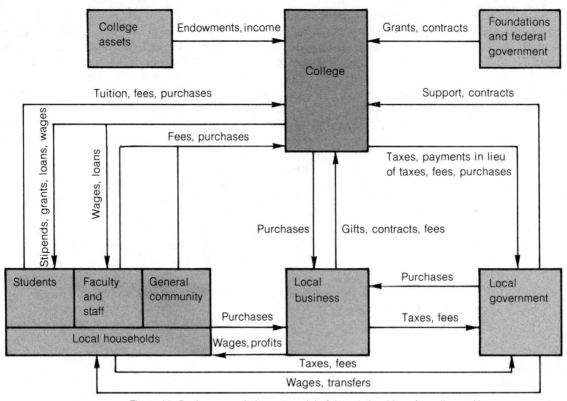

Figure 11–5 An economic impact model of the relationships of a college with the local government and local business. This model shows graphically the economic interaction of the students, faculty, and staff, and of the college itself with the local community. It does not reflect the community costs incurred for the public school system or the community benefits gained from continuing education programs, voluntary student services, and lectures, concerts, and other events presented free or below cost.

Conclusion

Major aspects of planning for education services have been explored in this chapter from the point of view of the city or community planner. Although governmental provision of educational services has traditionally held itself apart from other governmental activities, the community's interests would appear to be best served when education planning is part of a larger process of community planning.

Proceeding from this point of view, this chapter described the population basis of education planning, including demographic studies, the trends of recent years, the prospects for population change during the 1980s, and the ways in which population can be analyzed for planning purposes. Planning for the physical and educational community then was examined; then planning for primary and secondary education was discussed from three major perspectives: large scale development, suburban school systems, and the special problems of educational services in central cities. This discussion occupied the major portion of this chapter and dealt with issues of community growth and change and the intermingling of physical, social, and economic aspects of public schools in many kinds of neighborhoods. Special attention was given to land development policies with respect to the provision of education services.

The final major section of the chapter covered higher education planning—the colleges, universities, and other institutions that provide a special character to thousands of communities in all parts of the United States. Since many of these institutions house a nonresident population, attention was given to the special questions of local government services for housing, traffic and parking, and other services, as well as the costs and benefits of these institutions.

Elementary and secondary schools, and institutions of higher learning as well, have been a neglected area in local government planning. Perhaps planning agencies have reflected the attitude of local educational administrators, school boards, and legislative bodies that education is not their concern. One can only speculate about the reasons for past indifference, but the time is propitious for change.

1   Lawrence Haworth, *The Good City* (Bloomington, Ind.: Indiana University Press, 1963), pp. 25–38.
2   Russell A. Holy, *The Relationship of City Planning to School Plant Planning* (New York: Columbia University, Teachers College, Bureau of Publications, 1935), p. 26.
3   Clarence A. Perry, "The Neighborhood Unit," in *Neighborhood and Community Planning,* vol. 7 of *Regional Survey of New York and Its Environs,* ed. Committee on the Regional Plan of New York and Its Environs (New York: Russell Sage Foundation, 1929); and Gerald D. Suttles, *The Social Construction of Communities* (Chicago: University of Chicago Press, 1972).
4   Herbert Gans "Planning and Social Life: Friendship and Neighbor Relations in Suburban Communities," *Journal of the American Institute of Planners* 27 (May 1961): 134–40.
5   Quoted in Urie Bronfenbrenner, "The Calamitous Decline of the American Family," *Washington Post,* 2 January 1977.
6   Bruno Bettelheim, *Children of the Dream: Communal Child-Rearing and American Education* (New York: The Macmillan Company, 1969), p. 60.
7   Kenneth Keniston and the Carnegie Council of Children, *All Our Children: The American Family under Pressure* (New York: Harcourt Brace Jovanovich, 1977), p. 12.
8   Bronfenbrenner, "The Calamitous Decline of the American Family."
9   Staunton Leggett et al., *Planning Flexible Learning Places* (New York: McGraw-Hill Book Company, 1977), p. 3.
10 See: William G. Coleman, *Cities, Suburbs and States* (New York: The Free Press, 1975), pp. 163–96; and *Washington Post,* 8 January 1978.
11 Leggett et al., *Planning Flexible Learning Places,* p. 5.
12 Morton Hoppenfeld, "A Sketch of the Planning–Building Process for Columbia, Maryland," *Journal of the American Institute of Planners* 33 (November 1967): 398–409.
13 See: Philip S. Schaenman, *Using an Impact Measurement System To Evaluate Land Development* (Washington, D.C.: The Urban Institute, 1976); and Thomas Muller, *Fiscal Impacts of Land Development: A Critique of Methods and Review of Issues* (Washington, D.C.: The Urban Institute, 1976).
14 Howard County [Maryland] Public School System, Office of New School Facilities and Planning, "Proposed Policy: School Site Selection Criteria," memorandum sent to the board, Howard County Public School System, Columbia, Md., 20 May 1977.
15 Interviews with Charles County, Maryland, public school officials.
16 Much of the material in this section is based on research by Marcia W. Dodson, summarized in her "Recycling the Nation's School Buildings" (master's thesis, Cornell University, May 1977).
17 Hendrick S. Holmes, *Surplus Schools: A Study of Adaptive Re-use* (Published privately, 1975).
18 Gene Bunnell, *Built to Last: A Handbook on Recycling Old Buildings* (Washington, D.C.: National Trust for Historic Preservation, 1977).
19 Dodson, "Recycling the Nation's School Buildings," p. 48.
20 Ibid.
21 Interviews with Baltimore public schools staff, October 1977.
22 Much of the material in this section is drawn from research published in: Kermit C. Parsons and Georgia K. Davis, "The Urban University and Its Urban Environment," *Minerva* 10 (July 1971): 361–85.
23 See: John Caffrey and Herbert H. Isaacs, *Estimating the Impact of a College or University on the Local Economy* (Washington, D.C.: American Council on Education, 1971).

12 Planning for the arts

Within the urban environment every citizen should have available accessible avenues of cultural development, expression, and involvement.

National League of Cities
Municipal Policy Statement

The intricate network of art and cultural organizations that provides arts programs in American cities is coming to full maturity in the 1970s and 1980s. Through the establishment by the federal government of the National Endowment for the Arts in 1965 and the subsequent formation of state arts agencies in all fifty states, the District of Columbia, and the five trust territories, public financing has provided for arts programs, which are increasingly being defined as essential public goods. In turn, American cities are providing an increasing amount of direct, tax based financial support to arts programs by establishing city and county arts agencies and by providing arts programs through other agencies of local government.

It is not easy to precisely define *the arts,* since the term encompasses a broad range of activities. The arts include the performing arts of music, dance, and drama. The arts include the visual arts of painting, sculpture, and printmaking. Also included in the arts are literature and the media arts of film, radio, and television. Crafts are considered arts, as are folk arts. Thus, the term no longer draws a distinction between *fine arts* and other arts.

The arts can form a symbiotic relationship with a wide range of community programs and resources, ranging from education to community facilities. Today, for example, fairs and festivals, arts exhibits, and performances are activating downtown areas. The arts can help build broader community programs, and community programs can help support the arts and make them available to a wider audience.

In planning for the arts, a broad range of activities and programs may be considered. Figure 12–1 gives an idea of the variety of arts and other cultural resources that can be made available in American cities.

The purpose of this chapter is to describe arts activities and programs in a planning context. While many of these activities are private in the sense that they are not conducted by government, local government involvement in the funding and planning of arts activities is increasing. This chapter first gives the broad background to government involvement in the arts in this country, including history, funding, responsibilities, and policy questions. The chapter then describes the wide variety of arts facilities, historic resources, and programs; it concludes with a section on planning.

The management of local government services can include diverse arts elements (see Figure 12–1), and line government agencies are finding, increasingly, that the arts are useful in serving the public. Local government agencies are creating arts programs within their own governmental programs and are establishing cooperative programs for specific constituencies with various arts and funding organizations.

The development of government support
for the arts

From the founding days of the United States and the commissioning of the Liberty Bell, government support of the arts has been a part of the American tradition. In the course of the celebration of this country's Bicentennial, the following words of John Adams were often quoted:

I must study politics and war, that my sons may have liberty to study mathematics and philosophy, geography, natural history and naval architecture, navigation, commerce, and agriculture, in order to give their children a right to study painting, poetry, music, architecture, statuary, tapestry, and porcelain.[1]

This generation of American leaders and citizens is carrying out what must have been a dream of our founders—the pursuit of an improved quality of life through the arts.

The Works Progress Administration

Perhaps the best known example of government support in our recent history is the U.S. Works Progress Administration (WPA) arts projects of the 1930s. These federal programs, which involved hundreds of American communities and thousands of American artists, resulted in thousands of works of art, including sculpture and murals. The performing arts were also supported under the WPA's arts projects.

The works created through these projects are significant, but perhaps more important is the evolution of a national consciousness of the constructive place of the arts and the artist in community life. The appreciation of the role of artists and the growth of a unique national culture advanced the status of the arts in this country and helped the United States to ultimately become a leading creative place that could hold and attract quality artists.

Government reorganization and eventual dissolution of the Works Progress Administration's Federal Art Project brought this massive federal support of the arts to an end. However, the project left Americans with a desire to build and nurture a national environment hospitable to creative expression; it also set the stage for a surge of creative activity which was ultimately of international significance.

The WPA came to an end in 1943. Although strong federal support continued to build federal collections and to contribute to research activities such as the Smithsonian Institution and its museums, a broader federal support of the arts in America lay dormant during the later 1940s and the 1950s; this remained the situation until the 1960s.

The National Endowment for the Arts

Because of broad citizen support for decisive federal support of the arts, the National Endowment for the Arts and the National Endowment for the Humanities were created by statute in 1965. What had clearly been a federal initiative in the 1930s became a citizen initiative of the 1960s. Public testimony by cultural, corporate, governmental, and educational leaders provided numerous reasons for federal support of the arts.

In the early days of the National Endowment for the Arts, national policies were structured so as to ensure that leadership of and support for the arts would be a shared partnership between federal and state governments. Thus, a way was provided to permanently cement into the American governmental structure the public financing of the arts.

Arts and cultural resource services
The arts: performing arts (music, dance, drama, opera); visual arts (painting,
     sculpture); media arts (television, radio); intermedia and experimental arts
Cultural institutions: museums (arts, science, historic, botanical, zoological);
     libraries and allied information resources; performing arts centers
Cultural services administration
Financial support of arts and cultural resources

**Economic aspects of the arts and
cultural resources**
Arts and culture-related industry
Economic development programs: travel and tourism, manpower planning
Employment in cultural services
Economic aspects of artists: legal, insurance and retirement coverage, employ-
     ment, loans, artistic freedom, training and experience, collective bargaining
Economic aspects of cultural institutions: information and data, legal, insurance,
     taxation funding, economic impact
Volunteerism in the arts
Planning and coordination

**Government facilities, architectural design
and construction, and public art**
Full utilization of public land and facilities
Excellence in architectural design of government and government financed
     construction
Public art and exhibits in public buildings
Spaces that accommodate the arts in public buildings
Cultural facilities
Historic buildings

Aesthetics: environment and natural beauty
Contribution of aesthetic perceptions of the artist
Environment and natural beauty protection
Arts in environmental education
Cultural institutions of museums, zoological and botanical gardens
Environmental aesthetics: landscape architecture, sign control, urban
     beautification
Parks and open space

Historic resources
Historic preservation of archival material, artifacts, and antiquities, oral history,
     historic museums, and sites
Heritage education

**Cultural resources programs in public education,
communication, and information**
Arts in primary and secondary schools
Arts in universities
Public education through excellence in graphic design, electronic media, and
     exhibitions
Communication of social messages

Cultural resources programs in recreation
Arts as leisure time activity
Arts in recreation programs
Parks
Fairs
Festivals
Cultural facilities

Figure 12–1   Arts and cultural resources in American cities.

Social development programs
Artists as catalysts for human resource development
Public service capabilities of art groups, cultural institutions
Adaptive uses of the arts in emotional health maintenance and problem prevention
Adaptive uses of the arts in social service public education
Creative arts therapies in prisons, probation, mental health services, public
  assistance programs, drug addiction prevention and treatment programs, and
  special education

Figure 12–1 (continued).

State arts agencies

The National Endowment for the Arts provided financial incentives to states to form state arts agencies. In place now is a broad program of federal and state cooperation through state arts agencies in all fifty states, the five trust territories, and the District of Columbia. All jurisdictions provide some direct financial support for their government arts programs.

Community arts agencies

The new surge of federal support brought forth a broad range of community based activities. Community arts councils have been formed throughout the nation in cities of a million and towns of a few hundred. Concurrently, cities and counties are providing government support for arts organizations. Such cities as Miami and San Antonio have created arts councils supported by municipal tax funds.

The methods of financing range from direct appropriations made by city councils to formulas based on hotel taxes (as in San Francisco), to entertainment taxes, to mill levies (as in Dayton, Ohio). San Francisco, Seattle, New York, Atlanta, and Miami, along with many other cities, provide city government funds to their community arts councils.

Within the American political system the arts are supported by many U.S. congressmen, state legislators, city managers, mayors, and city council members. Political leaders have been joined by civic, educational, philanthropic, and corporate leaders to form a broad based partnership in support of the arts in this country.

The importance of the arts to local government was well summed up in the National League of Cities *Municipal Policy Statement* of 1977:

The arts are a critical element in the survival of cities. If we are to achieve an improved quality of life for the nation's urban population, all levels of government must recognize the arts as an essential service. All men, women, and children should have the opportunity to experience the arts in their daily lives.

Many local arts councils are private not-for-profit organizations that are financed by private or state and federal funds. At the time of the formation of the National Endowment for the Arts in 1965, there were about 100 community arts agencies. Now over 2,000 community arts agencies provide arts programs and services. More than 250 of these are local government agencies or have been designated as official arts agencies by local governments. Community arts agencies assume a range of roles. Some simply raise funds for the arts organizations in the community. Others provide programs such as art exhibits and touring performing arts events. Most are increasingly service-oriented and provide such services as community arts calendars and technical assistance in fund raising and program planning.

The New Deal in art Roosevelt's paternalism made possible federal subsidies to the cultural arts. One must hasten to add, however, that other rationales had gained currency which justified national cultural uplift. Political radicalism, which was strong throughout the depression decade, carried with it the idea of mass cultural awareness and of art forms which reflected a radical ideology and served its purposes. And, during the depression, America experienced an upsurge of nationalism accompanied by patriotic self-examination. This phenomenon included a new concern for locale, the vernacular, and the American scene— for a culture which was uniquely American. . . .

The American government channeled its subsidies to artists through two agencies: the Section of Painting and Sculpture (later Section of Fine Arts) in the Treasury Department, and the Federal Art Project in the Works Progress Administration. Both could be justified on grounds that they kept the skills of artists from deteriorating at a time when there were few private commissions and sales. Both units also aspired to make art a larger part of American life and thereby improve the quality of that life. . . .

Each art unit had its special successes and failures. The Treasury unit brought painting and sculpture to more than a thousand American towns,

many of which formerly had no original art. The Federal Art Project returned to the taxpayers well over 2,500 murals, 17,000 sculptures, 108,000 easels, and 11,000 designs. In addition it operated over 100 Community Art Centers, compiled a 20,000 piece Index of American Design, made posters, models, photographs, and many other items. Neither the Treasury nor the Federal Art Project succeeded in convincing the representatives of the American people that federal art patronage was such an uplifting activity that it should be considered as a proper function of government and therefore be continued. The life of the Treasury art unit depended upon money siphoned from the public construction program of the depression—and that atrophied in the 1940s. . . . All of Roosevelt's cultural projects became the focus of the powerful conservative coalition which the voters returned to Congress in 1938. While the art effort survived a few more years, new laws weakened central control and the quality of the work began to decline. The most important questions—about the criteria for "quality" art, the place of art in American life, and the compatibility of the creative temperament with the requirements of bureaucratic efficiency—were never resolved satisfactorily.

Source: Excerpted from Richard D. McKinzie, *The New Deal for Artists* (Princeton, N.J.: Princeton University Press, 1973), pp. x–xi.

The arts as a public good

Broad support of arts financing is made possible by an underlying belief that the arts are a public good—that is, that the arts are for everyone, are supported by taxes in whole or in part, have economic utility, and are an appropriate governmental activity.

Since they are a public good, open access is provided to all members of society. Just as libraries, schools, universities, and other institutions of learning and enrichment belong to the people, so do the arts. Admission or entry fees are generally subsidized. The primary support for many arts and cultural activities comes from artists themselves who often do not charge for their services to community programs. After artists, the private sector is the most substantial supporter of the arts. Federal, state, and municipal support of the arts is increasing significantly.

The 1969 federal tax laws altered the conditions for foundations in the nation. With increasing government regulation of corporate earnings and subsequent decreasing foundation wealth, less funding is available for philanthropic activity. Thus, what was previously financed through private dollars simply cannot survive or flourish through private support alone.

The desire of Americans to participate in arts and cultural programs and the desire of arts leaders to provide these programs are the basis of continued government support. As government funds come increasingly into play, programs are being broadened to include increasing numbers of citizens. Attendance figures at all kinds of arts events are increasing dramatically.

Arts organizations are designing programs intended to reach both broader and groups and small, specific constituency groups. Programs are aimed at the cross section of a community as well as at specialized client groups such as the handicapped, senior citizens, and the economically disadvantaged. The fervent belief that the arts are for everyone provides the incentive for artists, arts leaders, and cultural institutions to provide programs that reach increasing numbers. Thus, they must seek the funds to pay for those services.

Citizens who benefit from arts programs in turn provide broad based advocacy to bring forth increasing funds for the expansion of governmental and private support. Municipal leaders play a key leadership role in assisting citizens to articulate the need for increasing funds as well as for prudent government administration of funds for the arts.

Arts agency structure

Five years before the establishment of the National Endowment for the Arts the New York State Council on the Arts was established in 1960. That agency has served as the pattern for the organizational structure of the National Endowment for the Arts and for state arts agencies. Common characteristics of the federal and state arts agencies are the division of the total organization into program areas. For example, various forms of creative expression are represented by music, dance, literature, and the visual arts. These program areas are assisted by citizen panels that advise on government policy and make recommendations for grants. The federal and state programs make grants to nonprofit organizations that provide arts programs and events to the public. Grants are generally provided on a matching basis, with the applicant providing funds or in-kind resources.

State arts agencies are administered by governor appointed councils or commissions that provide the policy leadership for the arts agency. Broad citizen support for the arts has enabled the National Endowment for the Arts and the state arts agencies to secure increasing amounts of tax based support for their programs that serve local arts and community organizations.

Coordinated arts planning demands clear jurisdictional responsibilities. The National Endowment for the Arts clearly has jurisdictional responsibility for the entire nation. The state arts agencies clearly have jurisdictional responsibility for their entire states. On the substate level jurisdictional responsibilities may be based on: planning regions, standard metropolitan statistical areas (SMSAs), counties, or cities. Although there is rapid formation of community arts agencies, there is a lack of clear administrative structure in many areas.

Clear designation of jurisdictional responsibility saves time, money, and resources, and helps prevent duplication. As a network of service and program delivery is developed the establishment of clear jurisdictional responsibilities can limit administrative costs and thus increase substantive program support. Major metropolitan areas should consider establishing community arts agencies that provide administrative services such as mailing lists and information services to local government agencies. Less populated areas can draw on the administrative and program services of the more developed community arts agencies.

Partnership support of the arts

Government support of the arts will continue to increase. But one of the primary strengths of the American arts is the diversity of the funding base. No one source of support pays the bill; thus the arts are experiencing a unique opportunity to practice free expression. Bold and adventurous expression through the arts is as important an expression of our society as are the classical and traditional. American arts enjoy a privileged position among nations of the world because of the diversity of public and private support. Although the federal per capita support may appear to stand below government support in other nations, the tax incentives for private philanthropic support set in motion a vitality of expression perhaps uniquely possible in America.

Private individuals can enjoy the benefits of membership in cultural organizations, and membership fees and private donations in turn provide some funds. Foundations also support community arts activity. Because business corporations benefit from quality arts programs in their communities, they are providing increasing funds for cultural institutions which, they hope, will attract additional business and economic growth. Labor unions and special interest groups are developing arts programs specifically for their members.

Local government leaders can find allies in and assistance from the federal and local arts service organizations. The National Assembly of Community Arts Agencies, the National Assembly of State Arts Agencies, the American Council for the Arts, the National Symphony Orchestra League, and other national organizations composed of member arts organizations provide research and information services for local arts programs. In addition, such organizations as the International City Management Association (ICMA), the National Governors' Association, the National League of Cities, and other national government service organizations have established committees on the arts.

Public policy for the arts

Government funding of the arts involves as many and as diverse areas of public policy consideration as any other area of public finance. Public policy issues in the arts generally relate to funding, equity, and government control.

Funding the arts

The basic justification for per capita distribution of funds is equity—the assumption that all citizens deserve a similar investment. The analysis of per capita expenditure is used as a monitoring device for informed and conscious decision making. In addition, the monitoring of funds as they flow from a funding source in a current year enables the funding agency to review critically the projects that are recommended for funding. Per capita monitoring is used as an aid in decision making by the National Endowment for the Arts as well as by various state arts agencies such as those of Indiana and New York. In some states a local jurisdiction can obtain data relating to funds allocated to its jurisdiction.

Along with local government support, state and federal dollars contribute to the costs of keeping organizations with large budgets operating. Government, as well as the arts institution itself, must be accountable to the public for services delivered. Ongoing support for operational costs of arts institutions is justified by comparing cultural services to libraries and other public institutions that are open and accessible to citizens. Operating support based on government pur-

Assessing arts needs The different methods to determine needs can be placed on a continuum between the arts planner and the public he/she is serving:

1	2	3	4	5
arts planner				public

The closer the planner comes to point 5, or deriving his/her assessment of needs solely from the public response, the more valid is the planning process. At point 1, the arts planner relies entirely upon his/her own perception of the community needs. He/she says, "I like opera. There is no opera. Therefore, we need opera." This method is not only ethically suspect, but politically suicidal, and is included only for symmetry. At point 2, the planner determines needs through an intuitive grasp of public opinion, rather than upon [his/her] own preferences. This process can be justified only if the planner is qualified to "sense" what the populace wants. Assessing needs by intuition is fraught with pitfalls, among them the planner's biases and previous conditioning. . . .

At point 3, the arts planner relies on the leaders of public opinion to determine needs. These include political leaders, economic leaders, and arts leaders, both patrons and beneficiaries. Each of these individuals has his/her own goals; the only way to democratize the process is to "Tap the opinion of the masses."

The arts planner collaborates with the public in determining needs at point 4. There is a two-way flow of information and opinion, usually accomplished through discussion groups and creative use of the mass media. This method provides strong roles for both the planner and the public, but is flawed because few planners have the resources to listen to all relevant groups, and the most active groups and civic leaders, as opposed to "the masses," tend to be most involved. . . .

At point 5, the planner obtains arts needs directly from the public. This can be accomplished through many avenues, among them direct surveys, which are potentially comprehensive and fair. . . .

Refinements on opinion surveys include analyzing those people currently interacting with the arts, holding "gaming" interviews. . . .

One could analyze how people allocate and spend their money in the arts, but with imperfect consumer knowledge, the influence of advertising and promotion, and limited resources, too many variables can act in the value structure. The political process (referendums, etc.) is rarely appropriate for the arts because it works best for yes/no decisions.

The arts planner makes the initial determination of needs, and translates these needs into applicable programs. He/she gauges community reaction from attendance, questionnaires, and group response. The planner must be prepared to receive this feedback and alter programs accordingly. This process offers the planner a dynamically creative role, while stressing democratic participation. It allows the public to express its preferences for something real and concrete, rather than to evaluate abstractions.

Source: Excerpted from Michael P. Brooks, "Assessing Arts Needs," in *Planning for the Arts: Proceedings of the Third Annual Winter Conference on Planning,* ed. Claire Greene (Urbana, Ill.: Illinois Arts Council and University of Illinois at Urbana–Champaign, Bureau of Planning Research, 1978), pp. 22–24.

chase of services enables the public to hold arts organizations accountable, in addition to enabling arts organizations to exercise free cultural expression.

In addition to the need of arts institutions with large budgets for ongoing support, smaller and more modestly budgeted organizations play an important role in American cultural life and also need to be included in funding. These smaller groups can develop new ideas and program concepts that point to new directions for all arts organizations.

Funding patterns need to be developed which are inclusive in nature. As operating support is accepted increasingly as a community responsibility, such support should be made available to all arts and cultural pursuits within the community. Large and small, traditional and experimental—all arts and cultural resources within the community weave the cultural fabric of American cities.

Government leadership–or government control?

Government support of the arts should be based on partnership support and leadership. Government should permit the arts to be free to practice the arts. In the 1970s there was a proliferation of federal and state guidelines that provided suggestions on applying for government funds. Such guidelines constitute clear government regulation and interference in the arts. The primary concern of federal, state, and local funding agencies should be fiscal and program accountability. Government guidelines that suggest that a particular approach is to be taken in order to receive government funding may deplete and short-circuit the artistic community of America and hamper innovative expression and creative work.

City and county leaders stand closest to their arts organizations and must emerge as local spokesmen for the needs of local art organizations. Such leadership can help in simplifying and minimizing guidelines where they may already be encroaching on local and private sectors. Federal and state government guidelines should receive critical attention from local leaders. Constant vigilance is vital.

Government facilities

Ensuring excellence in architectural design, providing spaces that accommodate the arts, and including public works of art in public buildings and spaces are important to an overall aesthetic–cultural climate.

Government is responsible for the design and construction of public buildings. Government is also a regulator of private construction through building codes and zoning ordinances. Thus, government affects the architectural ambience of American cities.

Public use of public facilities

Full use of public buildings is one of the most important forms of assistance the city can provide to cultural and community groups. All government facilities, particularly meeting rooms and auditoriums, should be available for cultural, educational, and community purposes.

Nonprofit arts and cultural organizations, as well as many other nonprofit organizations, often lack adequate facilities to meet, perform, or exhibit. Many public facilities would be quite suitable for such purposes. To obtain the maximum benefit from the public investment, it is in the public interest to make full use of public facilities for public purposes, including arts and cultural activities. Some facilities are underused; they may remain unoccupied for months at a time or remain closed evenings and weekends. During such periods spaces could be used for the visual and performing arts.

When public facilities are opened for wider public use, rates should be established that cover a portion of the maintenance and custodial costs. A special fund set aside to cover costs for groups unable to pay such fees would reimburse agency budgets for full use of the facilities.

Each local government should have a complete record of all holdings, including buildings and land, indicating which holdings are used (and which are not used) for public purposes. The benefit of a central record would be to identify facilities and land that could be used for arts, educational, recreational, and other cultural and leisure purposes.

Quality design of public architecture

Government agencies are showing an increasing concern for quality in the architectural design of buildings and facilities constructed under their jurisdiction. Government is responsible for vast amounts of public construction for highways, public and private hospitals, schools, recreational facilities, and housing. Review of architectural designs by a design board can help to assure quality use of public funds. Such a review group would advise all agencies in the predesign and conceptual stages of a construction project, before design funds were spent. The aim would be to achieve consistent, high quality public design.

Creative spaces for the arts

Providing physical spaces and facilities for arts and cultural services should be considered in publicly financed buildings, in publicly financed or assisted housing, and in urban development projects. During the initial stages of design, project reviewers should consider spaces that are specifically designed for cultural or adaptive uses. In government office buildings, public office complexes, and public multipurpose centers there should be full consideration of multiuse space for arts and cultural services and special facility needs. For example, Century Center, in South Bend, Indiana, combines a convention and arts complex. The Syracuse, New York, arts–government complex provides another example of multiuse facilities.

Many government agencies sponsor, and encourage local groups to sponsor, exhibitions in their public and lobby areas. This can provide a valuable and stimulating service at little or no cost to government.

Finally, design performance criteria for the arts and for cultural resources should be developed. Performance criteria and planning guides that consider arts and cultural resource needs should be available for all publicly assisted structures; these should outline the accommodations and facilities needed for the arts in public cultural facilities, libraries, educational buildings, convention centers, and other multipurpose facilities. In educational and housing construction programs, spaces can be provided to serve the arts, community cultural needs, and other community functions. Such spaces are especially useful and accessible when planned, programmed, and designed in the initial design stages of the entire building or project.

Public art

A work of art that is readily seen in the course of the daily activities of many citizens is generally referred to as *public art*. Increasingly, artists are interested in creating works of art that are easily accessible to all.

Public sculpture, murals, monuments, and other art forms have been a prominent feature in much of the world throughout historical times. The importance of the private collector and the museum is a relatively recent phenomenon. Today, there is a resurgence of interest in creating works of art where everyone can enjoy them, and can enjoy them as a part of daily living.

Artists today are painting large outdoor murals on the sides of buildings and are setting up neighborhood programs in which artists have worked with residents to create public sculptures. These contemporary works of art are placed on public property. From the World Trade Center in New York City to Seattle,

Chicago, Atlanta, Baltimore, and Detroit, examples of public art are visible throughout the nation.

In numerous government building projects 1 percent of the total construction cost of a public project is specifically allocated for works of art. Public buildings provide a viewing area for the works of art and the architecture of the generation during which the building was built. Outdoor sculptures, indoor murals, and other works of art, then, contribute to the permanent record in addition to enriching community life.

As with facility design, such works of art should be incorporated into the planning process from the beginning of the project design. It is important that an open procedure be established for the selection of artists for these public works

Municipal agencies for the arts Local city and county governments have a number of options in creating arts agencies. One alternative is to create an arts commission by ordinance, as was done in Seattle. Fifteen commissioners, appointed by the mayor, represent the arts, business, labor, and minority groups. The commission can hire an executive director who has the power to retain staff. Another option is a cultural affairs office, such as Boston has, placed in the executive branch of government. The office is run by a director of cultural affairs and, interestingly, was not created by ordinance or charter. Palo Alto, California, created a municipal arts department. The department is a separate entity but is in a division of social and community services, which also contains parks and recreation departments. The office is run by an arts director and the director is responsible to an assistant city manager. Another organizational alternative is the independent authority approach. For example, the Arts Council of Tampa–Hillsborough County in Florida was created by the state legislature. The authority can float bonds or present tax referenda to voters. A city or county can also place an arts program and planning function within another city department. For example, Waterloo, Iowa, administers its art programs through a municipal recreation department.

Source: Abstracted from American Council for the Arts, *Cities, Counties and the Arts* (New York: Interbook, Inc., 1976), pp. 3–10.

of art. Full notice of publicly financed construction projects using public art should be fully advertised. Such projects should also be open to presentations from any artist.

Historical resources

Strengthening municipal responsibility for historical resources helps preserve the heritage of American cities. Archival material, artifacts, oral history, and historical museums and groups constitute a major aspect of the cultural resources of cities. Cities such as Indianapolis and San Antonio have provided decisive public–private planning leadership in historic site development as part of downtown revitalization.

Historic sites and districts

The National Register of Historic Places of the U.S. National Park Service provides assistance for the protection of historic sites. The National Historic Preservation Act of 1966 is a significant tool for preserving historic resources at the federal level. It provides an expanded National Register of Historic Places; grants-in-aid for historic preservation; and an Advisory Council on Historic

Preservation. Placement on the National Register provides a degree of protection from demolition for a historic site and in many cases makes the site eligible for federal assistance in preservation.

Across the nation imaginative adaptive uses have been devised for a wide variety of structures. For example, county courthouses that are outstanding examples of late nineteenth century architecture, abandoned by their governments

Figure 12–2   Mount Royal Station, Baltimore, built in the late nineteenth century by the Baltimore and Ohio Railroad, has been restored and renovated for the Maryland Institute College of Art, with space for classrooms, library, gallery, and other uses. Top: the building when it was used as a railroad station; lower left: the entrance to the gallery and library; lower right: the library.

for glass and curtain wall buildings, are once again becoming an integral part of the community.

To provide local help in historic preservation, state and local governments can provide property tax relief to privately or commercially maintained historic sites on the federal or state register. Municipal designation of historical zones and architectural districts can provide community control over façades in such areas. Special zoning and planning regulations offer protection to unique areas of a community as well as to individual historic properties. Historic districts in Savannah and Philadelphia are just two examples of historic district development that have spurred a return to the city and have increased real estate value in older areas of cities.

To encourage community preservation action, municipalities can provide for planning and architectural design assistance. Local governments should use historic structures for public purposes and should work with private interests in the rehabilitation of such structures.

Community libraries and archives

County historians and historical societies contribute to the preservation of local historical data. Oral history programs with taped documentation enrich a community history program. Many senior residents have themselves been prime contributors to our cultural heritage and are important resources for oral history programs.

Archival records are held by public libraries and community agencies. Official public records of permanent value can provide historical value to research and educational programs. Centralized archives and records management can help ensure a systematic channeling of appropriate records and documents into community archives.

In addition to providing research material and information storage and retrieval, public libraries can serve as resources for rare books and manuscripts. Exhibitions of rare materials help broaden a community's appreciation of its heritage.

Parks

Many parks departments operate and maintain historic sites and museums, including battlefield sites, log cabins, and buildings of early historic significance. Tours are often given at these sites. A new approach to old sites is being taken that encourages adaptive use for community meetings, weddings, and other occasions. Pittsburgh, Nashville, San Antonio, St. Petersburg, and Fort Wayne exemplify the tourist appeal of early forts restored as educational park–museums.

Urban development projects

Urban development projects in major cities have primarily demolished old structures and built new ones. There is a growing movement, however, to preserve and rehabilitate historic structures within project boundaries. These historic structures can house many different types of arts and cultural activities.

The many roles of community arts

Government social programs and cultural activities can be mutually self-supportive. The arts are being included in programs for youth and senior citizens, in community mental health programs, and in prison rehabilitation. The arts have proved that they can sensitize and humanize, can provide social involvement, and can assist in education, communication, personality development, and community well-being.

Arts in the community

One of the most significant aspects of the burgeoning governmental arts programs is the enthusiasm, organizing ability, and creative talent contributed by artists themselves to a wide variety of community programs. Artists for some time have contributed ideas, time, and talent: have worked in schools, inner city neighborhoods, hospitals, and prisons; they have worked with the young and the old, and they have been largely responsible for establishing community art centers that are sensitive to community needs. Effective use of the artist and of arts techniques in educational, social, and health programs will require compensation for the artist in a professional capacity. Budgeting for supplies, and selling arts events tickets, will help strengthen these programs.

The National Endowment for the Arts and the state arts agencies have gained recognition for supporting cultural programs that extend the arts to broader communities. Through arts grants, inner city school and community arts activities have been supported and stimulated; poetry readings and concerts have been held in city parks; and ethnic and minority group art forms have been given added impetus.

Community art and cultural centers, art workshops, and minority group professional performing arts companies have been particularly successful in promoting appreciation of the cultural resources of communities. Wide-ranging ethnic arts programs have been developed in Cleveland, New York City, and Los Angeles.

Programs for the development of the cultural resources of inner city communities promote such activities as touring programs with professional performances that relate to the everyday life of the neighborhoods.

The National Endowment for the Arts and the state arts agencies have sponsored the Artists in the Schools program as a way in which artists can provide services within community programs. This significant government program has helped establish the important link between artistic expression and educational development. Programs in cities in Oklahoma, Indiana, New York, and other states provide outstanding examples.

Arts in colleges and universities

American colleges and universities provide a myriad of educational programs and services, including many humanities and professional art courses and degree programs. The enormous scope of cultural and arts activities on the campuses today makes the college or university an important resource for the community. Public and private cooperation in support and use of arts and cultural resources should be considered. University student community involvement in many instances serves as a valuable learning experience and also constitutes an important contribution by the university to its surrounding community.

Inner city art programs initiated and conducted by college art students have provided programs for youth and adults and have established university–community liaison. At the same time, special university art exhibits and performing arts events geared to community and ethnic interests have served constituencies previously unrecognized in American culture. University art museums and performing arts facilities provide community cultural centers of great importance.

The creation of student internships for academic credit for work in community centers teaching the arts, together with the provision of tuition scholarships and stipends for ethnic artists to work with students inside the university, is an arrangement that promotes a two way exchange. In addition, financial support can be given to the artistic endeavors of students who are members of the university community.

Continuing education programs are another way of fulfilling a college or university commitment to citizens. Many short courses, conferences, institutes, and workshops can be sponsored. Although many of the courses will be oriented toward basic education and business techniques, cultural programs also contribute to the social well-being of the community.

Local government funding While it is possible for local government to appropriate general fund monies for arts activities, a number of communities have established various forms of designated or special taxes to support the arts. For example, San Francisco provides money to major cultural institutions from a fund created by a local 6 percent tax on hotel rooms. In St. Louis the St. Louis Art Museum, the Museum of Science and Natural History, and the St. Louis Zoo are supported by a special property tax. The tax is levied by a taxing district that covers both the city and the county. Another financial tool is the bond issue, exemplified by Salt Lake City which used the proceeds from bonds to construct a combined concert hall and visual arts center and to restore an old theater. One of the most common methods of raising money for the arts is the "1 percent for art" law. In fact, the actual percentage can vary from 0.5 to 2 percent. In essence, such an ordinance requires that construction of public buildings include a set-aside of a certain percentage of the budget for commissioning art works.

Source: Abstracted from American Council for the Arts, *Cities, Counties and the Arts* (New York: Interbook, Inc., 1976), pp. 25–29.

Arts in recreation

Arts and cultural resources are a valuable element in developing leisure time policy and recreation programs and facilities. The arts offer variety and vitality to both indoor and outdoor recreation in both densely populated and less urbanized areas.

While the investment of public funds for this arts purpose has become a recognized responsibility of government, the provision of recreation services nevertheless continues to focus largely on outdoor/nature-oriented activities.

A more interesting and balanced recreation program can be planned by supporting the activity preferences of ethnic and racial groups and exposing the public to the music and art of different folk cultures. The disadvantaged and minority group people who frequently constitute large dynamic communities in central cities often do not have basic public recreational programs available or within easy geographic access.

Many arts, cultural, historic, and environmental education functions are included in the programs of area recreation agencies. For example, Art Park, New York (a state facility), and National Gateway East and West in New York and San Francisco, show the potential of culturally-oriented public parks. Cultural programming in numerous city parks has extended to the provision of theater, concert, and museum facilities.

Arts in social development

Many examples of successful arts programs can be found in rehabilitation and the social services. The arts can act as a tool for providing individual insight and perception in mental and physical rehabilitation and can be equally effective in problem prevention by offering an individual a constructive path toward personal development.

Increasingly, programs are demonstrating that creative arts techniques have provided a breakthrough in reaching the mentally retarded child, the mentally ill, the prison inmate, and the socially deprived. Often, learning through nonverbal means such as dance, drama, or visual art has proved successful in these areas.

Programs for older Americans As people are living longer, there is an increased need for the community to take a sensitive look at the needs of the elderly,

Figure 12–3 The performing arts are also a part of a community's cultural expression.

which include a full range of social services and in-community alternatives. New societal roles for people in retirement are emerging. Such roles include use of older volunteers in community programs and cultural organizations. Education and training programs for the development of new skills, including the arts, strengthen programs to develop alternative life-styles for older people. Many older people have themselves been prime contributors to our cultural heritage. And programs involving the senior citizens with the young could provide a needed link between the past, the present, and the future.

Creative arts therapies   Art and music therapies have long proved to be effective methods in emotional health maintenance, mental rehabilitation, and crisis intervention. Agencies have successfully provided art and music programs to help develop positive self-images and self-confidence among the emotionally ill. People who are specifically trained, certified, and employed in art, music, dance, and drama therapies can help develop public and private creative art therapy programs.

Counseling programs   Various agencies maintain a corps of people who deal directly with the public in counseling and law enforcement. These people have daily contact with the public and reflect the responsiveness of government to human needs. Counseling or rehabilitation personnel should be familiar with arts events and opportunities in the area in which their clients live. Training programs for counseling personnel should include the use of community and cultural resources and familiarity with the arts as educational and rehabilitative techniques.

Programs for institutionalized citizens   The institutional population represents a clientele that is isolated from the rest of society. While there is a trend away from institutionalization and toward outpatient and community based care and facilities, there are millions of citizens who are residents in government operated institutions and hospitals. The arts and creative techniques are being used increasingly as a breakthrough in rehabilitation programs, in many cases, where other methods of therapy have failed.

Zoning for artists' studios   Zoning, the workhorse of planning, can be used as a tool to help the arts. In New York City the Soho neighborhood was at one time the city's center for the dry goods industry. The area contained large loft spaces in nineteenth century cast iron structures of some architectural and historic significance. As industries began to move out to the suburbs, building owners began to rent space to artists for living–studio space. Unfortunately, this was in violation of both state laws and local zoning codes. Through the efforts of the Soho Tenants Association, the New York State legislature amended the multiple dwelling law to enable artists to reside in their studios. At the city level the zoning ordinance was amended to permit artists to combine studios and living areas as long as certain minimum and maximum space standards were met. While health and sanitary restrictions were maintained, fire and building code restrictions were liberalized.

Source: Abstracted from American Council for the Arts, *Cities, Counties and the Arts* (New York: Interbook, Inc., 1976), pp. 38–40.

Programs in the criminal justice system   Community based resources for the prevention of criminal and delinquent behavior by adults and youth are needed. Cultural enrichment programs can be used for this purpose in conjunction with other programs. For example, more extensive use of probation as a community based service provides a less expensive and more effective method of dealing with those who come before the courts. Meaningful use of leisure time is part of a total rehabilitation process, and involvement in the arts can present varied activities for positive treatment.

The prison inmate educational system can provide an academic program which encompasses all levels of instruction. Within both academic and vocational education programs the arts can serve as an important learning tool.

Prison art programs have been a major and highly publicized attempt on the part of the corrections system to involve inmates in art activity. Art programs are viewed by correctional agencies as an acceptable avenue of expression that promotes an individual's self-expression and as a technique that can reveal latent artistic talent. Art shows document the talent of inmates in correctional institutions. The New York State prisons at Auburn and Ossining are outstanding examples of successful prison art programs.

Planning and studies in the arts

Local planning and research in the arts are growing as arts programs grow but arts planning as a technical and analytical activity is still in its infancy. A conceptual framework for conducting a comprehensive arts and cultural study and

Arts opportunities in small towns The small town presents special problems and special opportunities in planning for the arts. Not only is the population base frequently small, but some small towns serve as the center of a large agriculturally based geographic area. Nevertheless, many small communities have formed arts councils and conduct a variety of services and programs. Arts opportunities include the following:

1. Farmhouses, barns, outbuildings, and store fronts can be preserved or redecorated
2. Existing social institutions such as the Grange, social service organizations, public health and medical facilities, and religious organizations provide useful links to the community and provide arts outlets
3. A regional cultural center can be established
4. Schools, churches, and civic build-ings can be used for exhibits and activities
5. Clubs can be formed for persons with common arts interests
6. Small town historical societies have been formed which create museums or special displays, identify old historic industrial or public sites, and help preserve landmarks
7. Special events can emphasize the arts of ethnic and folk groups
8. Businesses and groups and associations can help form and promote businesses such as antique shops that help the development of small town downtown areas.

Source: Abstracted from University of Wisconsin, Office of Community Arts Development, *The Arts in the Small Community: A National Plan* (Madison: University of Wisconsin, University Extension, Office of Community Arts Development, 1978).

arriving at a plan or set of policies does not exist; there is no single model. Thus far the planning emphasis can be characterized as an activity which involves surveying existing programs, setting some goals, and developing some programs. Also, the emphasis is on current programs and general guidelines rather than on long-range planning.

This portion of the chapter covers some basic types of studies. Previous sections on facilities and programs have described the *substance* of what is being studied and planned for. It should be understood that the organization and content of a local arts study and plan present some practical conceptual difficulties. For example, the arts planner must decide the structure of the study and analysis: there are *activities*, there are *programs*, there are *economic impacts* of arts activities; there are *physical facilities* (both single and multiple purpose); there are *private* and *public agencies* that provide arts opportunities as either a *primary* or a *secondary* function; and there is a wide range of sources for *financial* assistance.

Responsibility for planning

There are three major types of agencies with responsibility for planning for the arts, and all of them should proceed with coordinated planning activity. These three types of agencies are: community arts organizations, planning agencies, and line agencies of government.

Many kinds of community arts organizations, some of which are local government agencies, are invaluable in the earlier stages of arts planning. Some of these organizations are often experienced at developing long-range approaches for financial support and program development. They generally have direct and immediate access to artists and other arts groups and have developed several kinds of inventory information. Such organizations may also have done their homework on needs assessment and goal setting in relation to financial and program projections. Such information is indispensable in policy and program development.

Planning agencies are now establishing arts planning components within their planning programs. In the requests for federal funds, the review of planning agencies for arts and cultural impact is being made along with economic and environmental impact review. Thus, local planning agencies can lead in community and functional area coordination of arts funding as it relates to local sources of support. Continuous coordination with the community arts organization can provide new, broader opportunities for arts funding and development.

Line agencies also maintain a responsibility for the arts. Many agencies, such as parks and libraries, provide extensive programs. Line agencies are finding that the arts are helping them to reach their own agency goals. Many such agencies form arts committees, arts units, or arts service divisions. While this activity helps to open up opportunities for citizens to participate and enjoy the arts, it also increases the need for the sharing of planning and information.

Research, surveys, and analysis

Now that the arts are being recognized increasingly as one of the elements in building a good community, local government needs to exercise leadership in research. City and county planning agencies are conducting research in the arts just as they are in educational, transportation, and environmental factors. Government planning efforts should focus on the structures for financial support and the administration of arts programs, while the administration of arts programs should continue to be conducted by arts organizations.

Increasing amounts of data are available on the arts, including attendance figures, expenditures, and lists of arts activities.

During the early 1970s the National Endowment for the Arts commissioned detailed statistical profiles of the arts and arts organizations by a leading public opinion firm. These studies provided valuable data on the arts in America. During the late 1970s the National Endowment for the Arts and the state arts agencies made increasing use of expert advisory panelists to consider policy and long-range development of the arts. The National Endowment for the Arts and many state arts agencies have original source data provided by arts groups on grant applications which could be used for building statistical profiles on government support of the arts.

Linking arts information into municipal record systems is beneficial for the arts as well as for local government. Information on government funds and events can be correlated with other socioeconomic data. Public expenditures in the arts, for example, may have significant relationship to public expenditures made in other areas of public investment. By systematically building dollar investments and attendance figures into community information systems, local governments will be able to learn more about how to plan for arts programs.

Surveys A basic inventory of names, addresses, and phone numbers of arts organizations is the obvious starting point on arts planning. Such inventories have already been made by a myriad of national, state, and local arts organizations. Therefore, the local arts planning agency should check first with the National Endowment for the Arts and the state arts agency for applicable (1) directories of organizations and persons, (2) inventories of programs, services, facilities, etc., in various arts areas, and (3) studies and reports conducted in other cities.

Various survey methods are available, ranging from reviewing the local telephone book to questionnaire mailings and face-to-face interviews. Once the basic list of arts organizations is compiled, it is possible to gather information on programs, services, facilities, etc., and proceed to preliminary analysis; further information gathering; final analysis; and development of goals, objectives, facility needs, program needs, financial forecasts, and other elements that were set forth before the entire process was started. Figures 12–4 and 12–5 show the kinds of information typically collected in local government surveys. (Survey research is discussed in detail in Chapter 4.)

Analysis Equipped with such basic information, arts planning organizations can base public policy decisions on information. In a field where program possibilities are unlimited and needs are great, information is an essential tool in setting goals, objectives, and priorities.

Group discussions with arts leaders can assist in issue identification. In an increasing number of cities, including New York and Indianapolis, mayors have appointed arts committees. Such committees, as well as community arts councils, can provide invaluable leadership in identifying priorities for local government action and in promoting team efforts in support of the arts. Broad participation and involvement also build future support for program goals.

As goals are established, cost and budget projections can be made for projected programs. Establishing the total program cost of accomplishing the goals enables the community to develop short- and long-term plans for the arts. Grant applications to federal and state funding sources, as well as to corporate, foundation, and private funding sources, should be based on this financial planning.

Economics and the arts

Today's many arts and cultural activities contribute substantially to the economy of American cities. As more people become interested in the arts there is a rapid growth of new arts organizations. Massive increases in museum atten-

---

1. Name of organization
2. Address
3. History of organization
4. Type of organization (profit or nonprofit)
5. Arts category (What art form or activity does the organization represent?)
6. Programs offered (classes, concerts, exhibits, services, with schedules)
7. Geographic area served
8. Size of audience (Arts groups collect this information in different ways.)
9. Membership, organization, leadership
   Size
   Qualifications, if any (practicing artist, patron, etc.)
   Staff (how many, what positions)
   Liaison with other arts organizations
10. Facilities
    Location
    Year of construction
    Condition of structure
    Kind of occupancy (owned, rented, shared)
    Adequacy for program delivery
11. Budget (This will be one of the more difficult sections under which to obtain uniform information; budget and finances of organizations are likely to be drawn and audited differently, and some

organizations will be hesitant to give a full financial disclosure.)
Revenue—earned income:
   Admissions or fees
   Endowment
   Tuition
Revenue—unearned income:
   Individual donations
   Business contributions
   Foundation support
   Fund-raising activities
   Loans
   Government support (federal, state, local)
   Miscellaneous
Expenditures:
   Salaries
   Accessions
   Nonsalary administrative and plant operation
   Nonsalary production costs
   Capital expenditures
   Debt service
   Student aid
   Miscellaneous
12. Needs of the organization
    Space
    Financing
    Other

Figure 12–4   Illustrative directory and inventory information to be obtained in a survey of arts organizations.

dance, increases in audiences for the performing arts, and the rapid growth of community arts groups have a direct economic effect on the community.

While government agencies conduct numerous economic surveys, data are not specifically collected for the "arts and culture" classification and are thus not readily available. Economic and labor statistical reporting systems do not (but should) include a specific category for the "culture industry" so that statistical profiles can be obtained.

Economic impact studies Economic impact studies show a clear relationship between expenditures in the arts and economic development.[2] Arts budgets in a community are added up and then multiplied by a "multiplier" factor to determine the economic effect of the arts. These studies have been perhaps the most important research tool in promoting increased public and private support for the arts. Thus, if it can be shown that art and culture "pay off" in terms of economic growth, both government and business are more likely to support expenditures for a "frill." Because there is extensive peripheral activity in the arts, ranging from increased tourism to increased art supply purchases, the arts are emerging as a constructive and lucrative community investment. Economic impact studies carried out in cities such as Baltimore and Indianapolis document the economic contribution of the arts to a city. (The arts are, for example, a factor in attracting business and industry to a community.)

---

1. Age
2. Highest level of education
3. Occupation
4. Income level
5. Ethnic group, if significant
6. Arts organization memberships
7. Frequency of attendance by breakdowns of kinds of cultural events
8. Frequency of participation by breakdowns of kinds of arts activities
9. Distance traveled to event
10. Mode of transportation
11. Type of attendance: drop-in with no prior intent, visit in conjunction with other activities, sole purpose visit
12. Type of housing by zip code
13. Per cent of budget spent on arts and leisure time activities and maximum user is willing to spend

---

Figure 12–5 Illustrative information to be obtained in a user group survey.

Economic development planning That the arts are a nonprofit activity that stimulates the economy is accepted as an important factor in local economic development. Moreover, the arts are being seen as a market sector in themselves. Many artists are small business persons possessing a salable product or service. Arts organizations can establish allied arts marketing activities for recordings, art reproductions, and development services. Such allied activities assist the support of less lucrative arts programs. Also, small businesses that provide products or services, such as booking agencies, art galleries, and recording and advertising studios, are emerging. The U.S. Small Business Administration provides services and loans for these businesses as for other businesses.

Government support for the arts can stimulate the opportunity for arts practitioners to market their goods and services in the open market system by providing development workshops that train artists and arts organizations to market their products. Government agencies can also assist by establishing liaison with economic development agencies which might provide loans and other assistance.

Part of the vital strength of the arts in the United States is the diverse mixture of not-for-profit and commercial arts activities. As government programs stimulate private commercial activity in the arts, so momentum in the arts will increase.

As a major attraction for settlement and tourism the arts are one of the intangible assets for economic growth. The nonprofit cultural organizations maintain

Adapting and reusing buildings for the arts Perhaps the fact that many arts activities survive on small budgets may help cities in unexpected ways. Old buildings and spaces are being used increasingly by arts organizations. The resulting space not only provides arts opportunities but frequently preserves buildings that otherwise would be torn down. In addition, abandoned commercial buildings also provide new uses for old spaces. Some examples include:

1. The former State Savings and Loan and Trust Company in Quincy, Illinois, has been renovated as an office building and the former main banking room is used for art exhibits, concerts, poetry readings, and lectures
2. A former pawnshop and run-down hotel in Lincoln, Nebraska, is now the Haymarket Art Gallery, with classrooms, kitchen, and studios
3. A bakery in Cambridge, Massachusetts, has been converted into a small theater
4. A Vassar, Kansas, barn is now a playhouse
5. The Hartford Stage Company occupies a converted drugstore/warehouse
6. A World War I and II torpedo factory in Alexandria, Virginia, is now an art center that serves about 1,000 artists and 350 students
7. Other opportunities have been taken in churches, movie theaters, banks, railroad stations, social halls, and even roller rinks.

Source: Abstracted from Education Facilities Laboratories, *The Arts in Found Places* (New York: Education Facilities Laboratories, 1976).

a level of economic activity that in itself is important. In addition they are the foundations of an auxiliary culture-related industry generating billions in economic activity. Clearly, art institutions and cultural activities such as museums, galleries, and theaters are major tourist attractions in New York City, Chicago, San Francisco, and Washington, D.C.

Local tax incentives Several financing alternatives can be explored on the local level. Tax benefits to property owners who permit nonprofit organizations to use their property can be established. Such property owners would receive property tax exemptions on that property that is basically available to and used by the public. Local governments and organizations, including cultural institutions, should explore with local taxing authorities and with state departments of taxation the possibility of obtaining property tax exemptions on those buildings, or parts of buildings, which are permitted to be used free of charge or below market rental by nonprofit organizations. Such a provision would serve as an incentive to property owners to make their facilities available to the public. And public purpose use of private facilities would decrease the need for public facilities and thus reduce local government's financial demands.

A potential benefit to the performing arts is repeal of local admissions taxes. In the 1970s Washington, D.C., repealed its 5 percent tax and Chicago repealed its 3 percent tax. Chicago also changed some building code regulations and decreased its licensing fees for nonprofit theaters. In Washington, the total amount that had been collected from the eight major performing arts organizations ($235,000) was equal to one-half of their combined deficits.

These are only two of the options that might be used to increase public participation and support of cultural resources.

The arts plan and program

As was discussed earlier, there is no model format for an arts study or plan. Most arts planning reports consist of surveys of existing conditions and institu-

Cultural tithing for the arts   The Cambridge (Massachusetts) Arts Council, concerned about limited access to major cultural resources in the community at Harvard and Massachusetts Institute of Technology (M.I.T.), has taken steps to open up both of these schools. The council has proposed "cultural tithing," a sharing program that has financial support from major foundations, as well as federal sources. The program has resulted in M.I.T. students performing at the opening week ceremonies for a new mixed income housing project; Harvard donating a store front office for the Cambridge River Festival; M.I.T. providing logistical support for environmental work; M.I.T. offering tickets to the community for student performances and jointly sponsoring, with the arts council, a children's opera; and Harvard lending a photographic exhibit for the opening of a mixed income housing project.

The arts council is working with both universities in other ways to encourage community and university interaction. The following are either under consideration or in effect: student performances at locations outside the university; revolving exhibitions of photographs and other relatively nonfragile exhibits; resource workshops for high school teachers; and the Community Box Office, the allocation of a portion of the tickets to most cultural events to a box office in the local high school where they will be more readily accessible: these tickets will be offered free or at reduced rate.

Source: Abstracted from Ronald L. Fleming, *Local Government and the Arts: The Cambridge Arts Council,* Management Information Service Reports, vol. 10 no. 12 (Washington, D.C.: International City Management Association, December 1978).

tions, followed by a chapter on recommendations.[3] When one compares these reports to planning reports in other subject areas, it becomes clear that there needs to be more of a relationship between goals, policies, programs, and expenditure criteria, and implementation techniques. (There is extensive discussion of the purpose, content, and format of a plan in Chapter 6.)

As an example of an arts planning report that emphasizes a planning approach, the format and content of a plan prepared for Metropolitan Dade County, Florida,[4] is instructive. Following a rather traditional examination of existing conditions, an historical review of cultural development in Dade County, and a discussion of local needs, goals, and objectives, their plan is structured into three major sections: recommendations of the plan, implementation, and recommendations for a continuing arts planning program.

The plan portion is subdivided into three major areas: services, facilities, and financial assistance.[5] Under the implementation section, the document goes on to identify in a highly organized manner the goals, objectives, and policies of the plan.[6] Under a continuing program, the plan calls for a better way of measuring the need for cultural arts and leisure time activities. It also identifies the need for data on such factors as attendance at cultural events and socioeconomic characteristics.[7]

Some planning agencies elsewhere, pursuing a more modest work program objective, combine cultural or arts studies and recommendations with a variety of other plans and studies. For example, plans for arts and cultural activities are frequently included in plans for civic centers, recreation and open space, community facilities, public schools, libraries, and other traditional interests of planning agencies. One characteristic of such efforts is a continuing emphasis on the physical facilities that house the programs and activities. As arts planning matures in the practice of public planning agencies, functional and service-oriented plans undoubtedly will be prepared that have perspectives beyond the physical facility that houses an activity.

Conclusion

Local government leadership of and support for the arts will play an increasingly important role in American cultural life. Mayors, city managers, planners, and civic leaders will increasingly articulate the needs and dreams for the arts in communities throughout the nation. City neighborhoods and community groups will play an ever more active role in the arts. This diversity and broad involvement in the arts should be encouraged as an essential element in building programs.

Diverse cultural expression will emerge from all parts of the community. Minority and ethnic groups, the handicapped, and other special interest groups will develop their own arts programs. This kind of activity will be the surest sign of success of the arts in America.

Excellent arts institutions will expand activities to serve increasingly diverse elements of the society and will receive major support to accomplish this service. Excellent programs will receive increased support thus allowing major arts institutions in the United States to further expand their international activities in the arts.

As the arts assume an indigenous role within the community, a broad range of institutions will emerge to work together. Increased interagency cooperation involving government agencies, universities, and schools will augment increasing enthusiasm on the part of the private sector—corporations and citizens—for the arts.

1   John Adams, *Letters of John Adams Addressed to His Wife,* ed. Charles Francis Adams (1841), vol. 2, letter 78 (1780), as quoted in: John Bartlett, *Familiar Quotations,* 14th ed. (Boston: Little, Brown and Company, 1968), p. 463.

2   See, as examples of such studies: David Cwi and Katharine Lyall, *Economic Impacts of Arts and Cultural Institutions: A Model for Assessment and a Case Study in Baltimore,* National Endowment for the Arts Research Division Report no. 6 (Baltimore: Johns Hopkins University Center for Metropolitan Planning and Research, 1977); and Hammer, Siler, George Associates, *Economic Impact of Selected Arts Organizations on the Dallas Economy* (Dallas, Tex.: City of Dallas, 1977).

3   American Council for the Arts, *Cities Counties and the Arts* (New York: Interbook, Inc., 1976), pp 37–40.

4   Metropolitan Dade County Planning Department, *Proposed Cultural Facilities and Activities Plan* (Miami, Fla.: Metropolitan Dade County Planning Department, 1976).

5   Among the major policy recommendations of the plan are: creating a cultural arts advisory council; providing staff services and a cultural affairs coordinator to the arts council; establishing a congress of artists; recommending that more detailed plans be prepared for a visual arts complex; and identifying specific sites for historic preservation.

6   For example, one of the general goals is to provide proper facilities for all types of arts and cultural expression. Three objectives are identified to help carry out this goal: obtaining better use of existing facilities, upgrading or modifying existing facilities, and identifying the need for new facilities. Under policies the document gives specific directives to various government agencies. For example, the cultural affairs coordinator is directed to survey existing programs at existing sites to determine the degree to which each facility has suited the program being offered.

7   In addition, the plan identifies a general work program for further studies and plans. Some of the subjects to be studied include the degree to which business is involved in the arts, public and audience preferences, the degree of concern of local government for the arts, and general public reaction to nontraditional forms of arts.

13 Urban design

Urban design is that branch of planning primarily concerned with the functional and visual relationships between people and their physical environment and the ways in which those relationships can be consciously improved. As such, urban design is directly involved with many substantive areas of planning, including housing, transportation, open space, institutional services, commerce, and industry.

The practice of urban design is based on the assumption that the physical environment can be designed, and that a desired physical form can be created through the use of various design methods. It assumes that economic and political forces can be influenced within the urban design process described in this chapter. Urban design is generally understood to function as part of the public sector, where it can serve to stimulate, guide, and influence actions of the private sector.

Historically, urban design has had a public sector emphasis which continues to be stressed, though by no means exclusively. The emphasis is based on the public sector's traditional responsibility for open space, transportation, community services, and utilities. Guiding the physical design character of these public sector uses is an important means for improving environmental quality and an incentive for private sector investment. As a group, these public sector uses establish an overall framework for the separate, smaller, and mostly privately developed uses of housing, commerce, and industry.

This chapter briefly describes the role of urban design in urban government and then sets forth the nature of physical development and the ways in which it affects urban design. The chapter outlines a process of urban design; provides examples of design products in city, district, and project settings; discusses implementation methods and approaches; and concludes with a section on management that covers basic questions and requirements, organizational considerations for the planning agency, and staffing, citizen participation, and other special issues.

The role of urban design in city government

Urban design to many is such an amorphous term that it is desirable to show how it fits into the framework of city government—as a legal, political, and administrative institution—before dealing with design from the process point of view which dominates this chapter.

The city as a municipal corporation has significant planning powers that have a direct effect on urban design. These are typically expressed through zoning ordinances and subdivision regulations and may also be expressed through sign ordinances, historic preservation programs, design review procedures, and other actions.

In addition, through the comprehensive planning process, expressed in a wide variety of ways, the city strongly influences the type, location, and character of both private and public development. Finally, the city government can directly control, if it chooses to do so, the design of public facilities such as governmental offices, branch libraries, transit systems, streets, and open spaces at scales ranging from citywide to specific projects.

The city can also influence the facilities of other governmental levels—school district, county, state, and federal. With requirements for environmental impact statements, such influence is more than perfunctory. To do this, however, means assignment of strong urban design responsibility to an agency of the city government, most probably the planning agency, with coordinating and review responsibilities for all public facilities.

The city government, through its commitment to urban design, provides an institutional framework for the following: (1) legal controls and incentives for private development that reflect local urban design concerns; (2) planning processes that support urban design activities; (3) coordination of public facility planning; (4) methods for working with the private sector on its development proposals; (5) methods for conducting formal and informal public meetings so as to get information and feedback; and (6) acquisition of administrative and professional staff who will work with urban design consultants, architects, landscape architects, and other design professionals in the ongoing development and preservation process.

The nature of physical development

Urban design's contribution to the larger field of planning is in providing tools to help create a satisfactory balance between pressures for new development and pressures for conservation. The activities of urban design, in attempting to achieve this balance, tend to fall within three general categories: the determination of what is to be protected, or *conservation;* the determination of where and how development investments are to be located, or *development focus;* and the determination of appropriate physical forms and types of use, or *development character.*

Conservation

Conservation involves the use of nonrenewable resources to achieve a workable, comfortable environment. This includes consideration of almost every aspect of the environment: the conservation of valuable, nonreplaceable open land; the conservation of energy through efficient transportation options as well as through climate responsive building design; and the conservation of historic, scenic, or otherwise serviceable buildings and landscape.

Development focus

Development focus involves the strategic location of development and conservation investments so as to produce a positive environmental, social, and economic impact on adjoining uses. In a declining urban environment public and private investments can be located so as to make the most of positive economic impacts. A vivid example of this principle is the similarity in size of most American downtowns. Virtually all central business districts, regardless of their total square footage, tend to concentrate within 150 acres of land, or a twenty minute walk cross dimension. Within this convenient walking range there is maximum opportunity for a variety of interrelated uses and services to economically support each other.

In areas experiencing vigorous development activity there must be consideration of locations that are nondisruptive to either the existing infrastructure of roads and community services or perceived assets such as views, historically important buildings, landscape, and patterns of neighborhood access and identity. The correlation between development focus and conservation suggests that wherever new settlements or buildings are located care must be taken to protect adjacent lands, buildings, and open space.

Development character

Development character establishes the appropriate quality of development with regard to three dimensional physical form as well as to type and location of uses. The desire for compatibility of physical character grows from the wish to reduce the disruptive impacts of new buildings inappropriately related to their surroundings. Compatibility means that there should be visual harmony between existing and new development. Normally, this is qualified by explicit standards for building height, use, location, and materials. It is based on the principle that similar elements existing together establish an easily recognizable and identifiable place. For example, a group of tall buildings may identify downtown while the repetition of scale and architectural detail of a housing type may identify different residential districts. Compatibility does not mean absolute replication. It seeks to establish the limits for a range of visual tolerances that are nondisruptive to the visual character and quality of a particular district.

What is designing? J. Christopher Jones begins his book on design with a string of diverse definitions in an attempt to narrow down the definition he will find useful for his book. Some of these definitions are:

"Finding the right physical components of a physical structure."

"A goal-directed problem-solving activity."

"Decision making, in the face of uncertainty."

"Simulating what we want to make (or do) before we make it (or do) it."

"Relating product with situation to give satisfaction."

"The optimum solution to the sum of the true needs of a particular set of circumstances."

"The imaginative jump from present facts to future possibilities."

Jones points out that although these definitions differ widely they have one common element: they refer not to the outcome of designing but to its ingredients. He then proposes a contemporary definition based on products, effects, and end results: "The effect of designing is to initiate change in man-made things."

Source: Abstracted and excerpted from J. Christopher Jones, *Design Methods: Seeds of Human Futures* (New York: Wiley–Interscience, 1970), pp. 3–4.

The desire for individuality of physical character grows out of the need to establish and maintain a special identity, focal points, and landmarks within the fabric of a city. A cluster of tall buildings may mark a place of easy transportation access, amenity, or community services. Special landscape, graphic identification, and street furniture may establish the identity of a shopping street. In some instances building heights may be limited to protect the visibility of an existing landmark or structures may be prohibited altogether to protect open space. Landmarks share the qualities of being distinctive and of providing visual diversity and points of orientation.

Development character is also determined by the mix, type, and intensity of use. Through observation one may speculate that diversity of uses in close and convenient proximity enhances the quality of life for cities and their inhabitants. Nevertheless, most city planning and governmental actions over the past thirty years have tended toward simplification and homogeneity. This attitude is due, at least in part, to the inherent administrative difficulty associated with integrating mixed uses within large scale projects. The resultant homogeneity of use has been troublesome in American cities. Traffic congestion increases as places of living and working grow further apart, and downtowns, lacking housing, are empty after dark. At a smaller scale, however, the reverse may be true. Homogeneity may be essential to the health of a particular land use. For example, interrupting the continuity of a shopping street with other uses may erode the ability of individual shops to function as a convenient and identifiable place.

Geographic scale of design

Since urban design deals broadly with environmental quality, a particular design problem can exist at a number of different geographic scales. Three levels are set forth for purposes of this chapter: these are city design, district design, and project design.[1]

City design   City urban design is concerned with land within already urbanized areas. It is typically administered within a city's jurisdiction. Its purpose is to provide design guidance in the public interest for all the substantive subjects of city planning. It provides a physical design context for citywide planning decisions and for the coordination of public and private development. Where appropriate, it may designate special districts or projects for more detailed design consideration.

District design   District urban design is concerned with functionally or environmentally cohesive areas within a city. A district may be identified either by function, as in a retail district, or by geographic area, as in a residential neighborhood. The purpose of district design is to establish procedures and techniques for protecting and enhancing the special natural or man-made assets of a particular area that have demonstrable value to the city as a whole. Additionally, after district design investigation, it may be necessary to designate special public or private projects for more detailed design consideration.

Project design   Project design is concerned with site and program specific development. The purpose of project design is to develop sign controls that satisfy district and citywide objectives. Along with visual and functional considerations, project design may take the form of a feasibility study that establishes site adequacy and market demand, and public and private joint development incentives, in order to accomplish larger environmental objectives. Also, project design may focus on a specific site or may extend over a considerable area such as an expressway right-of-way location and design or the landscape of special streets.

Though a particular urban design problem may relate to one of these three scales, its solution may require consideration of the larger scale context or the smaller scale part. For example, the solution to a downtown district-wide parking problem may require consideration of region-wide transportation programs that provide convenient options to the use of private automobiles. The solution may also require analysis of parking structure design at the project scale in order to test the parking program's physical impact on the district.

Process

An urban design problem is complex because it involves so many elements, including diverse community interests, the development of interrelated subjects at one time, and the blending of interdisciplinary skills. It is a process-oriented approach that many people are not familiar with, especially those who have highly specialized experience and training.

Typically, the urban design process has four parts. First, *context* is examined and defined by subjects and geographic area as well as by the requirements for community participation and background data. Second, *alternatives* are developed that describe various approaches to solving the same problem. Third, *choices* are made between alternatives on the basis of their relative social, environmental, and economic consequences. Finally, *implementation* techniques are selected which fit the administrative capability of the local government.

The emphasis of urban design is on learning what to do rather than on the creation of the built artifact. This point should be underscored since it differentiates urban design from the practice of architecture. Urban design is an interacting process that involves one or more governmental agencies, decisions on public facilities, consultation with public and private organizations, the development of data and other information, the measurement of public and private benefits both quantitatively and qualitatively, and consideration of as many of these factors as is feasible within a given physical environment. The urban design process typically establishes a physical design program, related design policies, and means of implementation. Though intimately related to the design process, the architectural process begins at this point and carries on through definitive design, contract documents, and construction.

Other design activities may also be carried on as part of the urban design process, including graphic design programs, public sculpture, the regulation of signs through zoning ordinances, the preservation of historic buildings by ordinance regulations, and other programs for preserving the environment.

Context

Beyond subject and scale, an urban design problem is pragmatically defined by the limits of time and budget available to solve it. These additional constraints must take into account the nature of people participating in the design process as well as the particular needs for data and the background information that apply to the problem.

Although it is possible to bring an almost unlimited number of participants into the design process, it is wise to set boundaries to avoid subverting the energy, time, and purpose of those more directly involved. Six general groups define the range of those most likely to contribute to the process:

1. Clients or client groups to set or maintain the boundaries of the work by defining scope and providing ongoing reviews at points of decision
2. Related planning disciplines whose members may become part of the design team, including such special skills as economics, social services, legal services, transportation, construction management, engineering, environmental assessment, landscape architecture, and architecture
3. Governmental agencies involved, including school districts, state highway agencies, county highway agencies, public works departments, and similar agencies
4. Resource groups with direct interest and expertise
5. Individuals who make up important user interests (transit riders might be an example) but who must be organized to create a representative response group
6. Broad based community organizations that have an interest in the nature of change within the community.

The need for background data varies significantly from problem to problem. The appropriate kind and amount are constrained by the problem type as well as the time and budget available. Typically, urban design data contribute visual and measured surveys of the built and natural environment, space standards, functional criteria, and other descriptions of the problem's physical aspects. Often urban design provides a coordination role in the data collection of other specialty disciplines. The costs involved in collecting data suggest organizing the collection process in stages. Thus, as the problem focuses increasingly on particular subjects or geographic areas, the investment in more detailed data can shift accordingly and with reasonable efficiency. (The collecting and handling of data are dealt with in detail in Chapter 4.)

Alternatives

Developing alternative solutions to a problem provides the principal means of describing the choices available. There are many methods for generating alternatives. Listed immediately below are four examples. They may be used separately or together at different points in the design process.

Case studies   It can be hypothesized that somewhere there exists a successful prototype solution to every environmental problem. Adapting these successful prior solutions to a new situation is an effective way of starting a dialogue about the problem. It serves to help show that, however unsolvable a problem may seem, there exists a comparable solution. It also takes advantage of the considerable costs already invested in solving a similar problem. An important aspect of this technique is identifying and comparing the context differences between the case study and the actual problem situation.

Sketch design   Sketch design begins as an initial probe into a problem based on minimum data and is designed specifically to generate discussion. This can be undertaken at minimum expense and can be enormously helpful in determining what further data are necessary. Continuous recycling of sketch designs will successively elevate the problem to higher levels of resolution. In an overall design effort this is a serious and effective technique which provides the opportunity to monitor, discontinue, or redirect the work at minimum cost.

Sub-problem design   This technique involves breaking a complex problem down into a series of separate more easily solved parts. This method is clearly useful if undertaken with the methods mentioned above.

Meetings   Many kinds of formal and informal meetings are desirable for the exchange of views and the soliciting of responses from resource groups and other organizations. These meetings can be structured around formal procedures for generating or selecting alternatives or they can be organized so as to attempt to resolve conflicts or at least to narrow down conflicting issues. Such meetings, when planned carefully, announced well in advance, and conducted in a genuinely open manner, are an asset to the design process.

Choices

In the course of the decision-making process choices must be made between alternative solutions. With few exceptions, choices must also be made between the parts of a large urban design project. For example, in situations of limited resources or limited public support few large projects can be totally accomplished at one time. Some design proposals must wait for markets to develop; others must take place in a sequence that allows market confidence to slowly mature. Some actions are dependent on others, such as the revitalization of retail districts and their need for easy access and parking.

In the selection process the clients have to evaluate both their short-term desires and the efficacy and cost of the alternatives. This can happen in a number of ways, from a quick intuitive judgment to a careful and articulate assessment of the underlying values surrounding the decision. The latter is almost a requisite in decisions that involve the participation of diverse interest groups or large public or private investments. A suggested framework for this selection process would consist of the three parts listed immediately below.

Cost-effectiveness   Each alternative is first rated by the environmental, social, and economic benefits it yields in relation to local public costs in order to establish an initial ordering of priorities. A particular action is scored in terms of its benefits with respect to other actions. Since the costs of different actions can be estimated, each can be given a dollar per point value and they can be compared.

Attractiveness   Other aspects of each alternative, such as degree of popular support, ease of implementation, and ability to attract outside funding, can substantially modify the feasibility and desirability of a project after the initial cost-effectiveness analysis. These factors are evaluated to establish each alternative's attractiveness rating.

Budget emphasis   Taken together, the previous two factors allow an overall evaluation of the relative funding emphasis to be placed on each alternative by phases or annual budgeting. For example, a proposal with a high rating on cost-effectiveness may have associated public support or implementation drawbacks and may be lowered in funding priority. This could elevate another alternative which yields less per dollar spent but can be immediately implemented. The organizational framework established by this process is useful in the structuring of the discussion of alternatives by the response groups involved. Figure 13–1 shows one way of formalizing and structuring this process, as used in the city of San Antonio, Texas.

Implementation

The final major step in the urban design process is implementation, which is based on feasibility, continuity, and incrementalism. These three ideas mean an approach and a point of view that will undergird urban design so that it gains strength from the governing body, the chief executive, the planning agency, and other agencies of the local government. Without this kind of support urban design cannot be nearly as effective in either the public or the private sector.

The first idea is that urban design must be based on reasonable limits of feasibility. This involves an understanding of public awareness and support, public and private administrative capability, and the limits of public and private funding. There have been too many examples of urban development proposals in the United States that have set goals well beyond any public or private means of achievement. In pursuit of a more prosperous future, vast areas of central business districts have been cleared and still lie vacant in anticipation of markets that never materialize. This, of course, was never the intention of urban design and, indeed, is almost a corruption of the term.

During the long-term implementation process, original design objectives may alter and the urban design plan may be subject to change. This implies a process of resolving the problem on the basis of new information. This requires continuity of planning and management in order to avoid the inefficiencies of starting over.

A development plan should be designed to allow for subsequent phases to adapt to changing information and emphasis. Each project should be designed as a complete entity at each phase of development. The incremental approach

Chart 3: Investment Decision Framework

EVALUATION CRITERIA   PROPOSALS

I. COST EFFECTIVENESS

A. EVALUATION OF GOAL FULFILLMENT
   (Rating Scale: 0-5, low to high)

   Environmental

   1. Enhance visual quality of
      man-made environment   _____ _____

   2. Enhance natural environment   _____ _____

   3. Protect environment from
      physical disaster   _____ _____

   4. Reduce pollution and effects _____ _____

   5. Maximize variety of environ-
      ments   _____ _____

         Average Score   _____ _____
         (Total divided by 5)

   Social

   1. Provide needed basic services _____ _____

   2. Maximize opportunity for soc-
      ial and intellectual growth   _____ _____

   3. Attract to Corridor variety
      of people and income groups   _____ _____

   4. Insure safety to residents   _____ _____

   5. Enhance personal self-
      sufficiency   _____ _____

         Average Score   _____ _____
         (Total divided by 5)

   Economic

   1. Maximize earning opportuniti-
      ties by increasing employment
      in Corridor   _____ _____

   2. Preserve and enhance existing
      capital investments in Cor-
      ridor   _____ _____

   3. Encourage private investment _____ _____

   4. Expand City's tax base   _____ _____

   5. Minimize transportation costs _____ _____

         Average Score   _____ _____
         (Total divided by 5)

TOTAL BENEFIT SCORE   _____ _____

B. EVALUATION OF LOCAL PUBLIC COSTS

   Capital Costs
   ($000's/yr)   _____ _____

   Operating Costs
   ($000's/yr)   _____ _____

   COST SCORE
   (Rating Scale: 0-5, low to high) _____ _____

C. BENEFIT/COST RATING

   Benefit Score divided by Cost
   Score   _____ _____
   (Rating Scale:
    High Yield   Over 3.0
    Low Yield   2.0 - 3.0
                 1.0 - 2.0
                 Under 1.0

II. ATTRACTIVENESS RATING
    (Rating Scale: 1-5, low to high)

   1. Evident public interest   _____ _____

   2. Demonstrable business support _____ _____

   3. Easy to implement; few bar-
      riers   _____ _____

   4. Visible impact   _____ _____

   5. Quick completion   _____ _____

   6. Required to permit other
      programs   _____ _____

   7. Not dependent on other pro-
      grams   _____ _____

   8. Low demand on City budget   _____ _____

   9. Draws other funding - state,
      federal, private   _____ _____

         Average Score   _____ _____
         (Total divided by 9)

III. OVERALL EVALUATION

A. FINAL PROGRAM RATING:

   Benefit/Cost Rating X Attractiveness Rating   _____ _____

B. EMPHASIS IN CORRIDOR BUDGET

   Emphasis Rating: _____ _____
                        Overall
   Rating Scale   Evaluation
   Highest
     Emphasis   Over 12.0
                       6.0 - 12.0
                       2.0 - 6.0
   Lowest
     Emphasis   Under 2.0

Figure 13-1   Investment decision scoring, San Antonio River Corridor.

ensures future flexibility should the project direction change. It also provides for a sense of completeness should the project stop at any time. This will help avoid the large unfinished projects that characterized some developments of the 1960s and the early 1970s.

These approaches—feasibility, continuity, and incrementalism—provide a management and planning point of view toward urban design that are deliberately modest—nonutopian, if you will—in outlook. They set forth a point of view for the much more specific devices and methods for implementation that are covered in a subsequent section of this chapter.

Products

Perhaps the most powerful end product of urban design is the development of solutions through images, drawings, diagrams, and models. These images develop and communicate the sensory and physical quality of design policy. They provide the principal context of an urban design language and distinguish urban design products from those of other urban planning disciplines. The use of images serves two important purposes—the testing of design concepts and the communication of design agreements. For example, design concepts may be tested in terms of sites, development programs, and three dimensional physical forms. As such, the alternative images summarize different policy positions and serve as a basis for evaluation and decision making. The image is also a means of communicating design agreements. When a decision has been made the design image, together with verbal and numerical descriptions, serves as a guide to those who will implement the plan. Later these products serve as a reference for those who must review the proposal for conformance to the plan. Figure 13–2 suggests the range of urban design program activities that are product-oriented.

In conjunction with images, urban design products define programs, policies, guidelines, related effects, and implementation techniques. Together, these descriptions can communicate virtually all the qualities of a proposed environment from general principles to detailed implementation proposals. They can describe a desired development program, phasing, functional relationships, spatial arrangements, and detailed architectural and landscape treatments. The degree and character of specificity are functions of the scale and type of solution to be communicated.

The present section will provide examples of design products applied at the city, district, and project scales. Each scale has been organized according to the three categories of design activity previously discussed: *conservation, development focus,* and *development character.* The examples that follow are necessarily limited to "snapshots" of much larger products.

City design

Conservation Preservation of scenic or productive open land in the face of urban growth is a typical conservation issue at the city scale. An example is the city of St. Helena, a small rural town in the heart of northern California's wine country.[2] In St. Helena the major conservation issue was the city's population growth and the consequent consumption of the surrounding vineyards by new development.

On the one hand citizens wanted housing for those who work in the community, but at the same time the only new housing being developed was for relatively wealthy newcomers moving into second homes or retiring to the valley. Those who had recently arrived wanted no growth. The long time residents wanted moderate income housing. The question was one of how to manage this growth and yet preserve the quality of the village in its vineyard setting.

The urban design recommendation was structured in three parts. First, the existing vineyards would remain under the protection of the county agricultural zone which limits development to five acre minimum ranches. Second, to accommodate higher income housing, a hillside development zone (removed from and viewing the vineyards) would be created which would set low density, rural standards for housing, roads, open space, and sanitation systems. Third, the remaining housing demand would be subject to development focus within the already developed residential area of the community (see Figure 13–3).

Development focus In the St. Helena example all the interest groups finally united in favor of slow growth to meet the housing needs of those who work in the community. These individuals and their families would constitute a self-limiting market for new homes. If the city grew at this slow rate it would gain 480 houses by the year 2000 or a population increase of roughly 1,400 residents. Intimately linked to the goal of conserving the vineyards was the question of where this new growth would occur and how much land would be required.

Project design	City design
Malls and plazas	Visual forms survey
Street beautification	Visual image survey
Neighborhood design	Ecological survey
Downtown revitalization	Attitudinal surveys
Public facilities (parks and open spaces)	Landmark surveys
Civic centers	Preservation plan
Industrial parks	Open space plan
Shopping centers	Art facilities plan
Specific highway corridor project	Growth strategy (land use, transportation, growth limits, etc.)
Specific transit corridor design	Urban design plan
Public housing project	Environmental management guidelines
Planned unit development	Others
Others	
	Activities design
System design	Social activities
Street system design	Recreational activities
Highway system design	Festivals, events
Transit system design	Unplanned activities (spontaneous activities)
People mover system design	Promotion and publicities, displays
Pedestrian ways system	Others
Bikeway design	
Signage system	
Public information system	
Others	

Figure 13–2 Urban design program activities in local government that are product-oriented.

The existing streets, water mains, and storm and sanitary sewer trunk lines serve the 600 acres of the presently developed city. Surprisingly, there are over 130 acres of undeveloped land within the boundaries of this built-up area. Deducting 25 percent of that acreage for new streets, the city could accommodate 98 acres of new development which would allow construction of 500 to 600 new homes at 5 to 6 dwellings per acre (the same density as in older sections of the city). In other words, all growth projected between now and the year 2000 could infill the open land within the existing developed area.

While the St. Helena example focuses growth to minimize environmental disruption, a different type of development focus is required to maintain population and economic vitality within declining urban environments. This situation typi-

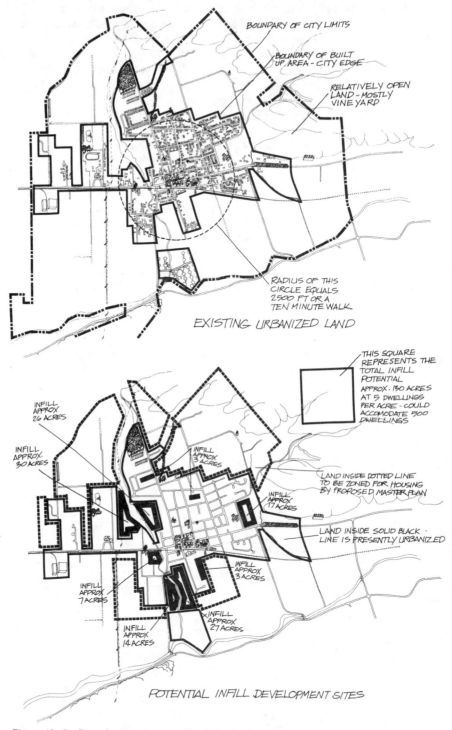

EXISTING URBANIZED LAND

POTENTIAL INFILL DEVELOPMENT SITES

Figure 13–3   Plans for fostering growth within city boundaries,
St. Helena (California) Urban Design Plan.

cally involves strategically located public investment to create incentives for private development and preservation projects. An example is the inner city area of San Antonio, Texas.[3] To bring about inner city revitalization, the city formed a special planning process. Its purpose was to bring flood control and landscape beautification to the San Antonio River which runs through the downtown and to coordinate the potential amenity of the river with other preservation and development opportunities in order to facilitate the revitalization of the inner city (see Figure 13–4).

Unlike those of Dallas or Houston, the San Antonio central business district and inner city area is poor and has limited resources for accomplishing goals for renewal. The limited market for commercial development had been absorbed in scattered suburban sites, while in the inner city useful and in many cases historically important buildings had fallen into disuse. Achieving the desired physical transformation of the inner city required the careful focusing of public and private projects so that these investments could realize maximum efficiency and impact on the surrounding uses. To do this required defining compact functional districts in which different kinds of new development could have maximum economic impact.

For example, on the periphery of the downtown, publicly funded intercept parking areas were proposed to lessen congestion within downtown and to free existing scattered parking lots for new development. Within the resultant framework of vacant sites, access improvements, and river beautification, a number of key projects were targeted to enhance and to serve as catalysts for each of the downtown functional districts—office, civic, retail, and visitor services.

Within the nearby inner city neighborhoods, it was proposed that available federal financial subsidies be concentrated on upgrading the housing environment of the present 16,000 population. This included spot clearance of housing and its replacement with new units as preferred by the displaced households. It also included subsidy for the rehabilitation of existing housing stock. The public investment in river flood control, landscape, and beautification was directed to provide a focus and catalyst for new neighborhood services and unsubsidized housing along the underutilized and vacant land on the river's edge.

Although it is not within the discipline of urban design to evolve social service systems, such systems are nevertheless crucial to the realization of inner city goals for revitalization. To draw residents from other areas of the city, the attractiveness of this inner city area as a place to live depends not only on physical plans but also on an image of high quality education and a sense of safety and security. These aspects, together with coordinated health and social services, were planned parallel to physical improvements to make the area unique in the city and a pilot for upgrading these services elsewhere.

Development character   Without sensitive guidance most new development is at odds with the adjacent character of older buildings and neighborhoods. In the St. Helena example the planning commission had adopted standards for residential streets, sidewalks, and setbacks which were more or less the state-of-the-art of American subdivision planning.

The older sections of St. Helena were laid out as a grid with a strong bias toward accommodating pedestrian and vehicular movements. New subdivision roads, as loops and culs-de-sac, fragment the small city into isolated clusters of homes necessitating frequent automobile trips. The broad streets, deep uniform setbacks, and lack of landscape of new subdivisions contribute to a loss of pedestrian scale and comfort. By contrast, the older streets provide landscaped edges at the curb and on the property line, establishing shadow and visual diversity. Moreover, the houses are varied in setback from the property line, which creates a highly urban character that heightens the contrast between the city and the surrounding open land (see Figure 13–5). Following these principles, a re-

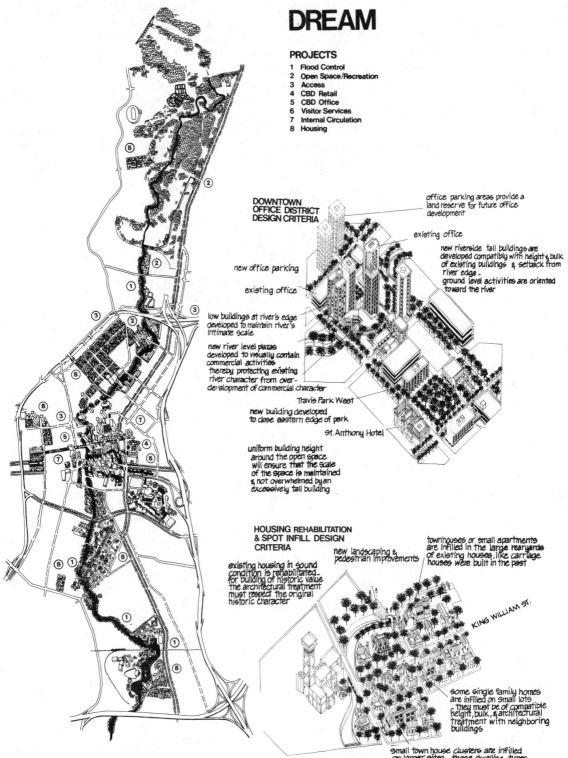

DREAM

PROJECTS
1 Flood Control
2 Open Space/Recreation
3 Access
4 CBD Retail
5 CBD Office
6 Visitor Services
7 Internal Circulation
8 Housing

DOWNTOWN OFFICE DISTRICT DESIGN CRITERIA

office parking areas provide a land reserve for future office development

existing office

new riverside tall buildings are developed compatibly with height & bulk of existing buildings & setback from river edge.
ground level activities are oriented toward the river

new office parking

existing office

low buildings at river's edge developed to maintain river's intimate scale

new river level plazas developed to visually contain commercial activities thereby protecting existing river character from over-development of commercial character

Travis Park West

new building developed to close eastern edge of park

St. Anthony Hotel

uniform building height around the open space will ensure that the scale of the space is maintained & not overwhelmed by an excessively tall building

HOUSING REHABILITATION & SPOT INFILL DESIGN CRITERIA

new landscaping & pedestrian improvements

townhouses or small apartments are infilled in the large rearyards of existing houses, like carriage houses were built in the past

existing housing in sound condition is rehabilitated. for building of historic value the architectural treatment must respect the original historic character

KING WILLIAM ST.

some single family homes are infilled on small lots - they must be of compatible height, bulk, & architectural treatment with neighboring buildings

small town house clusters are infilled on larger sites - these dwelling types are compatible in scale (2-3 stories) with existing buildings & must be made compatible by materials & facade treatment

PIONEER FLOUR MILL

Figure 13–4 Plan for revitalization and conservation strategies, San Antonio River Corridor.

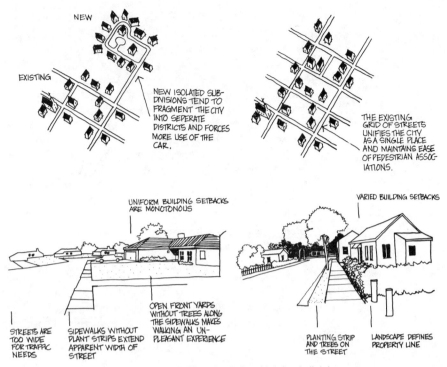

NEW

EXISTING

NEW ISOLATED SUB-DIVISIONS TEND TO FRAGMENT THE CITY INTO SEPERATE DISTRICTS AND FORCES MORE USE OF THE CAR.

THE EXISTING GRID OF STREETS UNIFIES THE CITY AS A SINGLE PLACE AND MAINTAINS EASE OF PEDESTRIAN ASSOC-IATIONS.

UNIFORM BUILDING SETBACKS ARE MONOTONOUS

VARIED BUILDING SETBACKS

STREETS ARE TOO WIDE FOR TRAFFIC NEEDS

SIDEWALKS WITHOUT PLANT STRIPS EXTEND APPARENT WIDTH OF STREET

OPEN FRONT YARDS WITHOUT TREES ALONG THE SIDEWALKS MAKES WALKING AN UN-PLEASANT EXPERIENCE

PLANTING STRIP AND TREES ON THE STREET

LANDSCAPE DEFINES PROPERTY LINE

Figure 13–5   A comparison of new (left) and existing (right) subdivision patterns for the St. Helena (California) Urban Design Plan.

vised set of standards was developed to reflect the historic form and scale of St. Helena.

District design

Conservation   An example of district conservation was developed for the Sacramento capitol area.[4] Within downtown Sacramento, the state of California owns an area of 120 acres, half of which is occupied by existing state office buildings. The present-day character of the land not in state office use is comprised of extensive surface employee parking and the remaining housing stock of a once thriving downtown residential neighborhood. The objective of the urban design investigation was to devise a means to use the new state office building program to restore to downtown the qualities of a good place to work and live—a mixture of office and housing uses that would be compatible with surrounding neighborhoods.

The principle of conservation within the capitol district was directed at the retention of useful and historically interesting buildings which could provide the next generation with economically productive space. The benefits of saving these structures also included the visual enrichment that older buildings can add to the environment.

As part of the urban design plan guidelines were also set for energy conservation. These standards were based on principles of climate responsiveness—a design response to climate that uses sun, breeze, and shade to its greatest advantage. Three principles were articulated. The first set guidelines for building orientation with major exposures to the north and south. The second established guidelines for a building's outer surfaces. An example is the use of exterior porches for circulation as well as southern exposure sun control. The third energy conservation measure addressed the design of open space. This included guidelines for the use of deciduous trees to permit the lower angle of the winter sun to penetrate the leafless trees and warm the interior of a building. The guidelines also called for the extensive use of small courtyards to create comfortable micro climates in close proximity to the workers.

Development focus In the capitol area plan it was recommended that a portion of the state's office building program be located outside the limits of the state owned capitol area. Through the focusing of part of the program elsewhere in the downtown area, additional sites within the capitol area would be made available for new housing and commercial uses. This would reinforce and expand the existing residential character and would create the opportunity for a community of mixed and varied uses in place of a single purpose office district. In addition, the location of state office uses near the downtown retail district would bring additional economic vitality to the business district. Within the capitol area, parking structures for employees and visitors were located in proximity to peripheral arterials. These parking locations provided direct access from the expressway and protected the district's streets from excessive traffic.

Development character Compatibility of buildings within a particular district of the city grows from the wish to reduce the disruptive impact of new buildings inappropriately scaled to their surroundings. Within the capitol district, development site size was used as one criterion for compatible development character. It was recommended that the majority of development sites be one-quarter of a city block in area (160 by 160 feet). This size was found to be suitable for all the contemplated uses—office, parking, and housing. The use of a consistent development site size establishes a scale compatible with existing structures. By using this size of development unit, a program can be built incrementally, over time, with minimum disruptions and dislocations to adjacent uses (see Figure 13–6).

Figure 13–6 Quarter block (below) and single lot (above) infill prototypes for Capitol Area (Sacramento, California) Urban Design Plan.

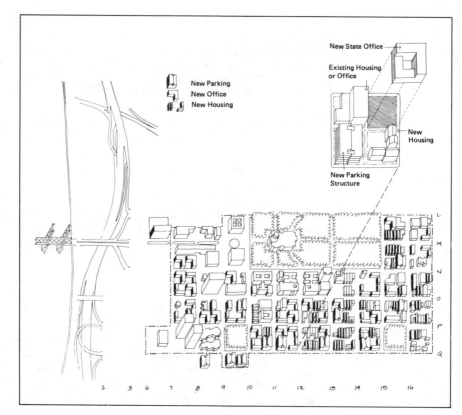

To further reinforce district character, the capitol area plan recommended that the building height of new buildings should relate to the height of existing structures. This principle does not preclude the occasional juxtaposition of contrasting building heights, which can be pleasing, but it does mean that where such contrast occurs it should be gradual and should be tempered by structures of intermediate scale.

With the quarter-block development site, development character was further defined by a mixture of uses that was varied within buildings and blocks. To create the sense of an urban village, the concept of area zoning was consciously eliminated and replaced with small increments of mixed use development. It was recommended that single uses over an entire block be avoided and that identical uses not face each other across streets or at intersections. This mixture of living and working allows the district to be used full-time and avoids the blight of lifelessness after dark.

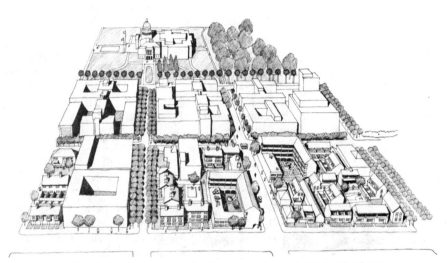

Figure 13–7   Small development sites for different land uses facilitate mixed uses within blocks and over the entire district, as shown here in the Capitol Area (Sacramento, California) Urban Design Plan.

Project design

Conservation   Central to the larger revitalization of San Antonio's inner city was the conservation of the San Antonio River as a natural resource and urban amenity.[5] The river, flowing from north to south, bisects the city and the downtown area. Along most of its route it is hidden by fences and parking lots. Within the downtown area, however, the river was beautifully landscaped in the 1930s by the WPA. Flood protected, this area has restaurants and other public facilities directly adjoining the river's banks. The attractiveness of this area was seen as a model for upgrading the river's neglected segments. To realize this potential, three problems in water management had to be solved.

For example, there is some flood damage every eighteen months, and there have been disastrous floods twice since 1900. As federal insurance programs for new construction require 100 year flood protection, this problem impedes inner city revitalization. Water quantity is another conservation problem as there has been long-term depletion of the river's aquifer and an annual recharge deficit for the past thirty-five years. Finally, water quality is threatened by excessive drawdown from the aquifer which ultimately may cause the river to turn brackish.

The plan proposed that, in addition to the investment subsidized by the federal government for typical Corps of Engineers channel widening, the city add the costs of other treatments which could conserve and enhance the river as a positive amenity. To conserve the existing downtown river landscape as well as other unique natural landscape, bypass channels were proposed which would leave these areas essentially intact. Where conservation was not an issue, Corps of Engineers methods were used to create boating basins or to facilitate other development opportunities along the river's banks. To improve the river's appearance, dams were proposed to raise the water level to a constant width. These same dams would be used to reduce water consumption during droughts by creating retention ponds that could be pumped and filtered to maintain water quality.

Development focus Focusing development at the project scale primarily involves the location of different uses within the project site. This often takes the form of feasibility testing to determine the capacity of the site and the streets to carry the desired program. For example, within downtown Dallas, parking transportation terminals were desired as opportunities to spur directed public and private joint development as well as to reduce vehicular traffic in the downtown.[6] Four candidate sites were identified for the proposed terminals. Selection among these sites was made by evaluating a series of interrelated criteria, including capacity of streets, proximity to downtown, relationship to future transit improvements, and joint development potential. From the evaluation a priority site was selected for detailed project design and feasibility analysis.

For the selected site, two design approaches were evaluated. Each had the same program of uses including transit interchange, parking, retail, and office uses. They differed in the way these uses were located on the site. One approach combined these uses within a single building by means of air rights development. The other combined these uses on separate but adjacent sites. Each was described by its relative advantages and disadvantages in terms of adjacent impacts, phasing, public costs, tax revenue, and investment return to the developer.

Development character At the project scale, development character guidelines are the most detailed. An example of these guidelines was developed for a project to be built within the University Circle area located on the east side of Cleveland.[7] University Circle is the cultural heart of Cleveland and includes Case Western Reserve University, the Institute for Art, and the Severance Symphony Hall. The urban design effort investigated a mixture of residential and commercial uses that would provide a focus for the diverse institutions of the area. Development character for this project was described by plans, diagrams, and sketches. These techniques defined the key elements of the project. They expressed policy agreements made by the advisory committee and served as a basis for economic feasibility testing, city planned unit development approval, and project packaging for detailed architectural design and implementation.

The project was first developed to a level of schematic architectural design that included specific plans and elevations for all uses. From this detailed description, guidelines were abstracted to outline the major design policies (see Figure 13–8). For example, to meet the project's program requirements it was necessary to develop part of the program in tall buildings. To support the objective of creating an identifiable place within the University Circle it was recommended that these tall buildings cluster tightly together. Specifically, the buildings were to be placed no farther apart than their height so that a distant viewer would tend to view them as a single landmark.

To establish a sense of arrival at the University Circle area, it was proposed that two of the tall buildings flank each side of the main avenue bisecting the site to mark a gateway to the area from the north. As nearby existing buildings have deep, landscaped setbacks from the avenue, it was recommended that proposed buildings within the project abut the street and establish a continuous built edge along the sidewalk. The result would be a break in the rhythm of space along the avenue which would further reinforce the project's separate identity within the circle area. The low buildings within the project (retail, parking, and low rise housing) were to be located where visual integration was desired with existing low buildings and housing.

The tall buildings were to be placed in a northern location on the site so that their shadow would fall on streets, with minimal effect on the planned open space environments. Eye level sketch views of the project were used to describe the project's more qualitative aspects such as building materials, landscape treatment, and ground level activity.

Implementation criteria and methods

Making urban design operational requires developing and applying ideas and methods within a framework of criteria and processes that are not yet well formed or widely accepted. Set forth below are design and process criteria that were developed for San Antonio, Texas, on the basis of an urban design agency survey of practices in ten cities.[8]

Each criterion is shown first as part of a checklist making up an ideal urban design process. The criterion is then mentioned in the following paragraph with a summation of the major findings of the design survey findings in the ten cities. This provides at least a rough comparison of the differences between ideal and practice.

Design criteria

Imageable physical concept The design for a city should have clarity of physical image—a physical configuration which identifies the major visual relationships between natural and man-made form and distributes the city's activities in a rational order.

A citywide imageable physical design concept is desirable to guide special area design policy, but it is useless unless accompanied by ways of implementing development controls and by staff to carry on design review and design services.

Comprehensiveness of design The urban design process should be comprehensive. It should be instrumental in integrating the functions of work, housing, transportation, public facilities, and services. The urban design process should also reflect economic, social, and environmental goals.

Comprehensive design provides a useful background for subarea—district and project—design plans. However, the urban design process can operate successfully in a decentralized structure with emphasis on realizable projects in high priority areas.

Design fit: a balance between preservation and development Urban design should include a study of historic areas, new development, and preservation of the man-made and natural environments.

Arbitration of conflicts between preservation and development has traditionally come under the responsibility of appointed commissions. This tends to be shifting toward the use of review bodies specifically trained in design to perform duties of arbitration and interpretation.

Public sector emphasis Urban design should be stressed in publicly controlled functional areas which have the potential for design integration.

Experience in the ten cities surveyed shows that coordinating design activities with other city departments is a perennial problem. For example, if the urban design function is located in the city planning agency, many urban design activities are done independently and in isolation by other departments. Means of pulling this together have not been found.

Process criteria

Goals, policies, and strategies The city's design goals and objectives should be translated into policies and specific strategies for their implementation.

Figure 13–8 Project guidelines for the Mayfield–Euclid Triangle Urban Design Plan, Cleveland, Ohio.

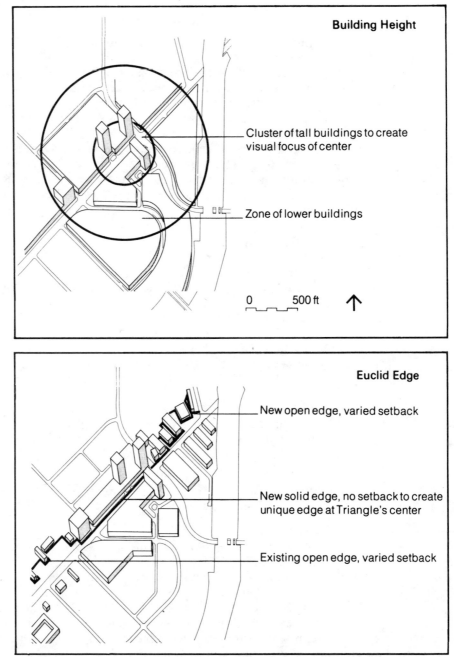

Figure 13–8
(continued).

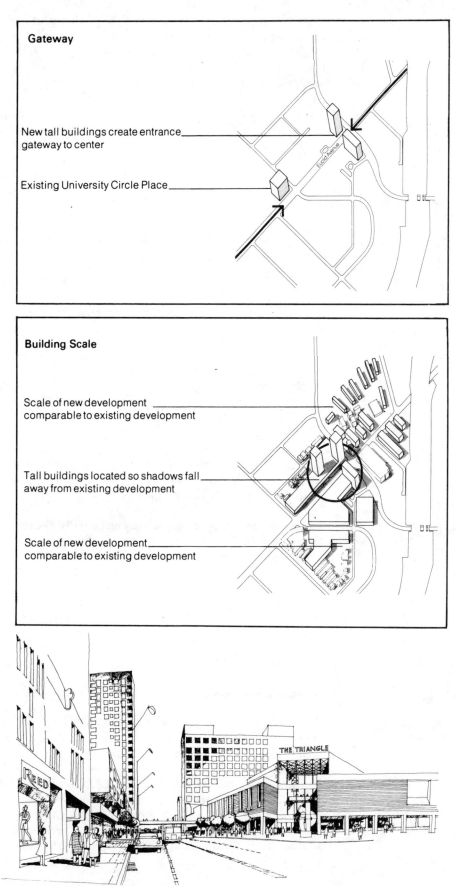

Gateway

New tall buildings create entrance
gateway to center

Existing University Circle Place

Euclid Avenue

Building Scale

Scale of new development
comparable to existing development

Tall buildings located so shadows fall
away from existing development

Scale of new development
comparable to existing development

REED

THE TRIANGLE

Experience in the cities surveyed shows that goals, policies, and strategies need not be developed for all functional or geographic areas of the city at one time, but the more specific the policies and strategies, the more easily they can be translated into controls as part of an effective program: the more that decision makers are involved, the easier it is for controls to be enacted quickly.

Interagency coordination   The planning agencies, action agencies, and city departments involved in public facilities investment, design, and construction should be involved in the development and implementation of design strategies.

New design methods and social–technical change   New design methods emphasize data, quantification, and rigorous analysis to achieve rational solutions. This works well in such stable and limited design situations as the man-in-space program, television by satellite, the designing of a chemical plant, and the long-term evolution of telephone systems. These situations are often under the control of a single organization with objectives fixed at the start. Also, the new systems that emerge are assemblies of existing components or of components whose functions can be settled in advance of the design process.

The real need of our time lies not in methods for limited situations but for intergrating social changes with technical ones. To do this it must be possible to explore the mutual and radical transformation (the creative element of design) of both social organizations and man-made systems. This flexibility is a prerequisite for "technological change."

Source: Abstracted from J. Christopher Jones, *Design Methods: Seeds of Human Futures* (New York: Wiley–Interscience, 1970), pp. 70–71.

Seven of the ten cities reported formal procedures for interagency coordination, but the successful efforts usually had been limited to a specific project area of special concern to several agencies.

Awareness and participation   Active citizen participation and public information programs should be consciously pursued throughout the urban design process.

Citizen participation in setting objectives was strongest at the neighborhood level where there was clear vested interest in the results.

Implementation of action programs and application of controls   As a result of strategy definition, specific action programs should be designated to implement design objectives.

Urban design is of limited usefulness without relative action programs and enforcement of controls.

Development measures

In addition to review and application of design and process criteria as set forth above, implementation requires specific use of development measures, both controls and incentives; these will be set forth in the next two sections of this chapter.

Urban design recommendations can be implemented through a variety of development controls and incentives. Although there are exceptions, the use of controls is especially appropriate in situations of high growth, whereas incentives are used to direct or attract activities in areas of urban decline or where specific public benefits are desired. It should be stressed that all design recommendations are essentially advisory guidelines which, depending on the context, may be translated into a variety of more definitive legal mechanisms.

The range of these measures is broad and covers traditional zoning, several variations of and innovations in zoning, historic preservation, development rights transfer, several kinds of financial aid for developers, civic art support, and other measures that would not have been contemplated in less design-conscious times. Whether the local governing body enacts controls or incentives, or, as is likely to be the case in some cities, a judicious blending of the two, depends on public objectives, the type and scale of the desired impact, the potential of a particular site, and the time and money the government has at its disposal.

Perhaps the most essential component and significant variable of urban design implementation is state law. Enabling powers vary greatly from state to state and cannot be considered as nationally applicable techniques. Similarly, the effectiveness and capacity of local zoning and review functions vary. Finally, implementation mechanisms must reflect local community realities. Often it is the case that the more stringently a guideline is drawn the more difficult it may be to get that guideline enacted. Moreover, the adoption of new guidelines without adequate staff or streamlining of the review process may overburden existing administrative capacity. The selection of appropriate urban design techniques therefore must be weighed against a wide range of local circumstances.

Community interest in a particular environmental quality issue, for example, is essential to ensuring a positive political response. This point deserves emphasis because even within the profession there has always been healthy debate as to whether a particular design technique has achieved the desired result and whether there should be more (or less) guidance of the private marketplace.[9] Despite these differences, it can be agreed that what is applicable to Houston is not necessarily applicable to San Francisco. The purpose here is to describe a range of techniques; it can be inferred that their applicability and success will vary from situation to situation.

Controls

Control techniques vary by degree of specificity and administrative requirements. When individual project review functions are not required, regulatory mechanisms often take the form of uniformly applied controls, most commonly in the form of zoning. Where project reviews are desired to ensure more sensitive compliance to the goals of a particular area, the regulatory mechanism tends to take the form of special controls created for specific districts.

Uniform controls Zoning is the most common form for administering land use and urban design control in America. Its purpose is to predesignate the use and physical character of development within specific geographic areas for a particular administrative jurisdiction. Typically, in a given geographic area regulations specify permitted use, density, maximum building height, bulk, and setbacks. Taken together these constraints define what is frequently called the zoning envelope, an imaginary volume that a building may fill.

Zoning has a number of advantages compared with other techniques. Perhaps its strongest advantage is that rules can be stated simply and require a minimum of discretionary review on the part of the governmental body. Therefore, zoning is relatively inexpensive to administer.

Several important urban design objectives have been achieved under uniform zoning. Notable among them is the accommodation of environmental compatibility by height and bulk controls. For example, these controls were adopted in the San Francisco zoning plan under community pressure because of the disruption of new construction on the existing environmental quality.[10] Height and bulk controls were directed at the following issues. First, significant views to and from the city should not be blocked by new buildings. Second, buildings surrounding plazas and parks should be limited in height to allow the penetration of sunlight. Third, buildings should have uniform façade lines and cornice heights to visually contain the space of larger squares and plazas. Fourth, to emphasize the hill forms of the city and to safeguard views, tall buildings should be located on hilltops while smaller scaled buildings should occur at the bases of the hills. In addition, it should be recognized that buildings with extreme bulk which exceed the prevailing height of existing buildings can visually overwhelm other buildings, open space, and natural land forms, and can block views, disrupting the city's physical character. These concerns were addressed by the establishment of height limits in different geographic areas of the city as well as a range of permissible horizontal dimensions for new construction in each area of the city.

The designer's influence   It is not always understood by those concerned with the visual and sensory relationships between people and their environment, especially by those offended by the design qualities of new development, that city planning departments are rarely responsible for the direct design of anything. City planners in public planning departments are not normally responsible for the design of private or public objects, from buildings, to signs, to parks. Designers working for private or public clients, other than planning departments, design such objects. . . .

The public planner/designer is likely to have most direct influence at the level of city or area design involving the general spatial arrangement of objects over an extended area. There are usually many clients to satisfy. It is also likely that the public planner/designer will have only partial control and that he will be involved with a design that is never complete. Since public planners may influence and regulate whatever is built but rarely design it themselves, the importance of setting a framework for legislation and influence becomes clear, if the public wishes to recognize and deal with urban design issues.

Source: Excerpted from Allan B. Jacobs, *Making City Planning Work* (Chicago: American Society of Planning Officials, 1978), pp. 192–93.

Special district controls   The establishment of special districts is a mechanism that has been used increasingly over the past decade. This technique involves creating a special or overlay district to protect natural or man-made features which are important to the community and are threatened by pressures for new development.

Overlay districts   These are zoning districts in which additional special regulatory standards are superimposed on existing zoning. This takes place without in any way abrogating existing zoning regulations. The use of overlay districts provides a technique for imposing more restrictive standards for a certain area than those specified under basic zoning. Such a technique, for example, might be used for the preservation of views or scenic corridors.[11]

Special zoning districts   These are employed when particularly sensitive protective controls are required for a designated area. The establishment of a special district requires a plan which identifies objectives that have demonstrable value to the city as a whole. Special districts may designate features in specified areas such as land use, as well as landscape, building location, size, and façade treatment. Special districts also require mandatory review of all proposed development. An advisory commission or review board is established as custodian of the planning and design objectives. The power embodied by this board requires state enabling legislation and, where tested, has been sustained judicially.

Landmark preservation and historic districts   These districts are zoning approaches to a community preservation program. By means of landmarks or historic district ordinances, which are typically amendments to the general zoning ordinance, a framework can be established to protect special districts and buildings. With a publicly accepted preservation program very specific ordinances can be adopted for a single site or a district which set forth appropriate regulations. As with the special zoning districts, a commission or board typically administers the program. Once such programs are established, all proposed development actions, including alterations, demolition, and new construction, are reviewed for conformance.[12]

Impact zoning   Impact zoning, as it is sometimes called, evaluates the relationship between a community's capacity for growth and the potential demands on community services created by a proposed development.[13] Impact zoning attempts to assess potential development in terms of minimizing its adverse impact on community service or fiscal systems. This technique or variations of it have been sustained in court as a means to manage municipal growth. The *Ramapo, New York,* case exemplifies a judicially sound growth management plan related to the availability of community services as well as containing urban design criteria to guide the issuance of building permits.[14]

Performance controls   These establish general criteria for assessing the appropriateness of a particular development for a specific area. Unlike broad specifications (uniform zoning) or detailed specifications (district zoning), performance based controls are not directly prohibitive. Rather, they are concerned with establishing minimum requirements to ensure an acceptable level of performance or compatibility. Performance controls tend to fit certain kinds of urban design problems. For example, a sign ordinance might be based on readability of information rather than on the designation of lettering size. Housing quality might be set by performance standards for privacy, sunlight, apartment size, recreation, opportunity, and security.

   Both impact and performance controls are considerably more sophisticated than uniform or district zoning regulations. They have the promise of providing well-defined ground rules while offering flexibility in application. Both, however, have had limited application. Perhaps the reason for this lies in the higher beginning and ongoing administrative costs over those of more traditional techniques. Until these costs are accounted for, the future effectiveness of these controls is unclear.

Designer selection procedures   These procedures are used for public works projects such as schools, parks, and civic centers and are a more direct way of controlling urban design quality at the project scale. Nevertheless, this is a difficult subject to generalize about. Establishing designer selection procedures means formalizing them. This can be done through requesting competitive proposals from qualified designers or through design competitions with cash prizes. Beyond this, there are three methods that have been successfully employed to ensure a high quality of design talent; these are:

1.   The New Haven, Connecticut, method, in which a strong chief executive or executive group, personally committed and highly knowledgeable about design, is in a position of power to select designers
2.   The Columbus, Indiana, method featuring an incentive on behalf of good

design in the form of a bonus, subsidy, or cost underwrite if designers
are selected from an approved list

3. The U.S. State Department Foreign Building Operation method, in which
a blue ribbon panel with binding powers irrevocably selects the
designers.

Incentives

Incentives are based on the use of laws and taxes to encourage individuals and
groups to accomplish their own interests while satisfying the larger public interest. Whereas controls attempt to coerce the right result, incentives seek to create the right result by providing a variety of benefits to the developer. They tend
to fall into two general categories: trade-offs or bonuses, and financial aids.

Trade-offs or bonuses Typically, under the provisions of trade-offs or bonuses, a
developer may choose to accept a design review process in exchange for the
freedom to build more space or to organize a development more effectively than
would be allowed under uniform regulations.

Incentive zoning Such zoning provides floor area bonuses to the developer on
the basis of provision of public amenities. Specifically, floor area, beyond that
permissible under uniform zoning, is allowed in exchange for public amenities.
Amenities usually considered for office districts include public plazas, arcades,
mid-block connections, rooftop observation areas, inclusion of housing, and direct connection to transportation terminals.[15] In the case of housing, allowable
densities may be granted on the basis of the project's accommodation of desired
design amenities such as scale, security, privacy, sunlight, and recreation
space.[16] Each amenity is given a specified number of points and an increase in
floor area or density may be granted on the basis of the set of total points
accumulated.

Development rights transfer This is a technique used to preserve nonreplaceable resources, such as landmarks and unique natural areas, from the pressures
of new development.[17] For example, this technique might involve government
purchase of the unused development potential of landmarks or open spaces and
subsequent sale of them in the form of development rights to be used at another
site. The additional floor area gained by the development rights may be added to
that already allowable under the site's zoning regulations.

The transfer of development rights in this manner removes the preservation
costs from the owner of the property. The process involves a careful balancing
between the preservation of a threatened critical resource and the potential negative impact of an oversized building. In consequence, it is the kind of tool that
requires an urban design plan as well as a case-by-case exercise of discretion.

Planned unit developments The planned unit development process allows a
more flexible placement of buildings than conventional lot-by-lot subdivision
standards. The total site rather than a single lot becomes the unit of regulation.
Densities, therefore, may be calculated for the total site, allowing the clustering
of buildings, the development of useful open space, and a more flexible mixture
of land uses.

Typically, the planned unit development is chosen by developers of large land
areas to minimize infrastructure and development costs and to maximize design
flexibility and marketability. The advantages to the community include preservation of natural open space and a reduction in costs normally associated with
urban sprawl. Approvals must depend on a sensitive design review process
between the developer and the planning review board.[18]

Mixed and joint development   This is a counter response to the single purpose regulations governing most American cities which have given rise to the segregation of uses and people into distinct geographic areas. These regulations have discouraged downtown residential development, preferring to reserve the area for other more intensive uses. Accordingly, many core areas have no functional activity after working hours. The assumption that different uses should be separated has increasingly been called into question.

Broadly defined, mixed and joint development is the use of a particular land area for more than one purpose. For example, a high rise building may combine shopping, housing, office space, and parking. Physically, a project may range from a vertical mixing of interrelated uses (air rights) to an interconnected set of complementary structures extending over a large area. Though there are demonstrable market advantages to the developer, and public benefits as well, such projects are difficult to get under way. Joint development projects are administratively complex and have higher financial risks than do less ambitious single purpose projects. Since they often lack explicit encouragement in the form of public sector assistance, many such developments are not initiated. A number of techniques are currently in use that encourage joint development.[19] Most common is incentive zoning which allows bonuses to a developer for incorporating certain uses within a project.

Private development issues   Our approach to handling private development issues, the small as well as the large, was fairly straightforward. . . . We took the position that, for the kinds of development proposals that had to come to the planning commission for approval, our positive recommendation (if we were prepared to agree to the use at all) would be dependent upon the developer's meeting what we called "urban design terms of reference." These terms amounted to conditions that we felt to be important from a planning standpoint, generally related to function and design, but at times with social overtones as well. . . .

The success of this approach depended on many things, not the least of which was early consultation with developers and their architects. No one wants to change a design once it's completed.

We encouraged developers to see us early so that they would be aware of our concerns before the designs went very far. . . .

Inevitably, the process led to conflicts. The developers, being people, didn't follow "the rules." They never do. They did talk to and influence the mayor and the commissioners. Even when the developers agreed to our conditions, that didn't guarantee that interested citizens agreed or were pleased. Sometimes there were honest differences of opinion. We won some and lost some, although for the most part I think we won more than we lost.

Source: Excerpted from Allan B. Jacobs, *Making City Planning Work* (Chicago: American Society of Planning Officials, 1978), p. 139.

Joint development projects can be associated with publicly planned and funded transportation improvements. The major economic and social impacts of transportation improvements come from land use change, which is typically left to happenstance. Linking land development and urban design with transportation improvements has been largely overlooked as a powerful instrument for promoting urban development and improving financial return to the city.[20]

A promising sign can be seen in the integration of the separate policies of the U.S. Department of Housing and Urban Development and the U.S. Department of Transportation in an activity called *value capture policy*. Authorized by section 104(A) of the Urban Mass Transportation Act of 1974, guidelines have been set to support corridor development which coordinate joint development surrounding a transportation improvement. Such policy can accomplish two goals. First, it can moderate the negative effects of transportation improvements. Second, it can coordinate positive joint development impacts through excess site acquisition where transportation improvements, especially terminals, will be located.

Financial aids   These techniques, either directly or indirectly, offer a private developer financial assistance in order to achieve public benefits.

Tax abatement   This is one technique that may be used in cases where existing tax levels threaten the conservation or redevelopment of a particular property. When this financial aid is used the owner must demonstrate that the current rate of taxation threatens the continued existence of a building.

Tax abatement has been employed to encourage private development of renewal areas without involvement of public funds. Land in renewal areas might be exempted from taxation, or assessed at a reduced rate for a designated period of time and increased gradually until the property pays its appropriate tax share. Exemption from taxes has been used to underwrite restoration costs of historic structures. Such a technique exempts owners of a designated property from the portion of local property taxes that is offset by approved and documented preservation and maintenance expenses.

Scenic or façade easements   These easements prohibit an owner from altering a scenic open space or the exterior appearance of a building. The owner and the owner's successor retain all rights to the use of the property except that of modifying those aspects covered by the easement. A public body or nonprofit organization may acquire a scenic or façade easement which can be deducted from taxable income. When an owner reduces the value of a property by the deducted amount, the value for tax purposes can be deducted accordingly.

Tax increment financing   This is a method of paying for public improvements by an increase in taxes generated by added value to adjoining property or subsequent private development. An example is street beautification, which can serve as a catalyst for new private investment. Under this arrangement, taxes are frozen at the level paid prior to the project area designation. As new private development is stimulated, the tax revenues from the area correspondingly increase. The difference between taxes prior to development and those after is used to pay off the cost of the public improvement. After the debt is paid the full tax revenue reverts to the city tax base.

Land writedowns   Historically, land writedowns have been used in the redevelopment process as an incentive to development. The property is sold to a private developer at a cost below the public cost of land acquisition, clearance, and administration in order to encourage a particular development program. The difference is made up in the taxes generated by the new development over time.

Public infrastructure   This may be used as public sector support for a private development project. Ordinarily, this is in the form of roads and utilities required for the project.

Project components   Project components provided by the public sector have been an incentive to encourage private development. The most common approach has been the provision of parking garages, which creates an amenity for the project that it could not otherwise afford. At the same time, such a facility may satisfy larger district-wide goals for parking. A similar case can be made for a variety of civic-supported uses.

Administrative support   This has been provided, in many instances, by local governments that are willing to become actively involved in the development process. The administrative assistance can range from feasibility studies to demonstrate marketability to the provision of schematic plans and to project packaging, including methods of financing and streamlining the approval process.

Civic art support   This is generally understood as the allocation of 1 percent of the construction cost of public buildings for the inclusion of art such as fountains, sculpture, and murals. It has become a popular mechanism for financing art in new developments and has been enacted into the zoning ordinance in a number of cities. Such an ordinance would be administered by a civic design or art commission which advises on the desirability and suitability of the proposed art.[21] (The relationship of planning and design to the arts is discussed in Chapter 12.)

Management

This section discusses the requirements, location, and operations related to establishing an urban design function in government. The discussion is broadly based on the experience of a number of cities that have developed urban design as part of their administrative responsibilities and should obviously be accommodated to local circumstances.[22]

Requirements

A review of the urban design process, including implementation techniques, suggests five general requirements that pertain to the urban design function within city government. They are listed immediately below.

A commitment on the part of political and administrative leadership to environmental quality   City council members, mayors, county executives, city managers, and others are sensitive to design issues that have a profound effect on the urban environment. They appreciate the value of their city or county in a psychological and aesthetic sense as well as in material terms. They have a sense of balance between the old and the new. A new generation that is more visually and environmentally oriented is coming into positions of political and administrative leadership.

A commitment to and involvement of decision makers in the urban design process   Most urban design situations, even at the project scale, require a lot of time, a great deal of patience, and a respect for the rights of affected parties to be heard. Thus the term *commitment* takes on direct and personal meaning.

Citizen awareness and support of environmental quality issues   A city's history, traditions, geography, and other factors help in gaining public awareness and support. The spectacular vistas of New York, Chicago, San Francisco, and Seattle are hard to compete with, but almost every city has historic associations and certain aspects of environment that can be handled through urban design. Citizen awareness of these community values is a helpful starting point.

The development of enabling legislation and enforceable implementation techniques   This was discussed in the preceding section, Implementation Criteria and Methods.

A commitment to permanent financial support for design activities   Permanent staffing is highly desirable for the urban design process, and a permanent financial commitment is mandatory. The city government has obligations in review of proposals, attendance at meetings, and many other tasks associated with the urban design process which cannot be met only by the regular staff of the planning agency. The public works department, the finance department, and other city departments and agencies are also involved in urban design. The work will fall especially on the planning department, where the city appropriations should most probably be made.

Location

The urban design function can be established within local government in several ways, depending on the nature of governmental structure and the emphasis of local issues. On the basis of existing examples, four locations can be identified as applicable to most governmental organizations: (1) in a planning department; (2) in a public facilities department; (3) as staff to the chief executive; and (4) in a specific location selected to focus on a particular issue. Some governmental organizations have combined certain of these traditionally separate locations into new governmental units. Perhaps the best-known example is the Boston Redevelopment Authority. Under this arrangement urban design was brought together with planning; transportation and engineering were added from the public facilities departments; and the arrangement was further combined with city renewal and operations functions.

A planning department   American practice has ordinarily assigned the governmental activity of urban design to an existing planning agency. Most urban design responsibilities, work, staff, and funding have gravitated to planning departments because, among the various units of government, they have had the point of view most hospitable to and knowledgeable about urban design. This affinity between urban design activities and planning agencies has been embodied in past legislation and institutional arrangements. Because of these similarities there are obvious economies of scale and similar efficiencies in overall office management.

The disadvantage of the planning agency location has been the lack of preemptive power to coordinate activities among other city line agencies. This has been an issue particularly when remoteness has produced difficulties in implementing the design policy.

A public facilities department   Although upgrading the design quality of public facilities (street furniture, lighting, landscaping, graphics, public structures) has always been a primary goal of urban design, it has remained elusive. This can be attributed to the lack of crossover power between planning and public facilities departments. This prevalent condition has suggested the need for an urban design function located within a public facilities department. For example, an urban design function could be organized as staff to a manager of public facilities, thereby providing design services and review to the parks and recreation department, the traffic and transportation department, and the public works department. It is possible that this same staff could also provide design services to normally semiautonomous agencies such as public service boards and transit authorities. The dispersal of design activities in public works agencies would fill an existing gap and would provide access to one of the principal urban design tools for improving environmental quality.

The chief administrator's office   The urban design function has also been organized as a staff function to the chief administrator's office. This allows the greatest leverage for coordinating public projects and setting policy guidelines for other agencies, and would give the chief executive particular advantage in the context of revenue sharing and program budgeting. Urban design would become one of several policy planning staff activities required to give policy guidance for funding allocations. Its special advantage in this location would be its combination with other policy planning staff functions, and thus its greater potential for achieving coordination.

A location focusing on a specific issue   When urban design does not exist as a permanent staff function in a lead agency (and sometimes even when it does) it has often been initiated on an issue-by-issue basis for a specified time period and under contract to the responsible public entity. Under this kind of arrangement, a private consultant or short-term staff might be retained to accomplish the required work. The use of consultants has several advantages. For example, consultants, at a minimum, may be used to temporarily augment an existing staff. A consultant group can also bring certain expertise to a local situation on the basis of past experience with similar issues. A public entity also might engage an outside consultant to deal with politically sensitive issues that might otherwise undermine the credibility of local staff. Additionally, this could provide a fresh, objective viewpoint when local participants were deadlocked.

Operations and activities

The operation of an urban design function within government can be described by the specific responsibilities and staff skills required. The most significant variable in describing this function is the scale at which it operates.

At the city scale the emphasis tends toward areawide consideration of land use and development patterns. General policies are made regarding the separate categories of urban and nonurban land use. At the district and project scales, subjects tend to be specifically related to the unique problems of the particular area under consideration. The nature of staffing, citizen participation, products, and implementation techniques varies according to these scale differences.

For these reasons an urban design function can be most effectively organized around the different concerns of areawide design and special area design. Together these two design functions deal with the full spectrum of urban design from broad to detailed issues. Although their mandates differ slightly, they ideally operate together as a single design resource. It should also be understood that this design resource would be ultimately integrated with the other specialists such as city planners, environmentalists, economists, lawyers, and engineers who make up the larger governmental function of urban planning.

Areawide design   This service would be used to integrate areawide design standards with other parallel planning activities, to coordinate and facilitate areawide public and private development and conservation activities, and to broadly elevate the design quality of public investments. The general responsibilities of areawide design include the following:

1. Organization of a citizen participation process to set areawide goals and provide ongoing guidance to design activities
2. Development of areawide design standards, controls, incentives, and enabling legislation to direct public and private investments in response to areawide goals
3. Design review of public and private plans and projects requiring an areawide framework for decision, as well as the development of standards and procedures to expedite the approvals process
4. Coordination of areawide public and private development to maximize their positive environmental and economic impact
5. Delineation of special districts and projects for more detailed consideration of conservation and development actions.

Citizen participation could relate to an areawide design function in four ways. First, a citizen committee with areawide representation would set goals and policy for conservation, development focus, and development character for all the separate categories of land use. Second, the citizen committee would review and respond to issues which need an areawide context for decision. Third, the committee would initiate public education on urban design issues to ensure awareness and acceptability of design and implementation recommendations. Lastly, the committee would set priorities for selecting special districts and projects for more detailed design consideration.

Staffing for areawide design services would include urban designers with special skills in the broad policy issues of urban as well as nonurban land use, in areawide design controls and incentives, and in the operational requirements of public works and city service departments. In addition to the responsibilities of areawide design, individuals with special expertise in land use categories could provide, as needed, technical support to the special area design staff.

Special area design This service would be used to establish design guidelines for special districts and projects and to enact controls and implementation techniques for conservation and development activities. The general responsibilities of special area design include the following:

1. Organization of a citizen participation process to set special area objectives and to provide ongoing guidance to design activities
2. Development of specific design guidelines, development controls, and incentives required to direct public and private investments in response to special area objectives
3. Design review of public and private projects for conformance to special area design guidelines
4. Coordination of special area public and private developments to maximize their positive environmental and economic impacts
5. Incentive programs including prizes, awards, and competitions to improve the design consciousness and performance of public departments
6. Delineation of special projects for detailed design studies and feasibility analyses
7. Design studies including feasibility testing and development packaging for public and private special area projects.

Citizen participation at the special area scale would consist of individuals with vested interests in the area under consideration. Each special area would have its own advisory committee. These committees would make the initial commitment to initiate a special area design effort as well as guiding and monitoring the work of staff and consultants.

Staffing for special area design would include urban designers with special skills in physical design, rehabilitation, development feasibility testing, project packaging, and the application of implementation techniques. These skills could be supported by consultants or other government staff for dealing with special problems. The urban design staff would function as a single resource that could manage a number of special area problems simultaneously or focus on one at a time as the need arose. A technical advisory committee made up of public and semipublic agencies could be established to better ensure the coordination of their operational concerns with special area design recommendations. Whereas different citizen committees would be established for each special area, the technical advisory committee would provide continuing support and coordination with all special area design activities.

Variations on the governmental management of urban design described above are operating in a number of cities. In particular, one federal act has affected the conduct of planning, design, and development activities in American cities. The National Environmental Policy Act calls for communities to "utilize a systematic interdisciplinary approach which will ensure the integrated use of the natural and social sciences and the environmental design arts in planning and decision making which may have an impact on man's environment." This interdisciplinary approach in which urban design plays a key role holds considerable promise for its future involvement in governmental structure.[23]

Conclusion

It is the intent of this chapter to organize the practice of urban design into a comprehensive and useful overview of the subject. The discussion presented here attempts to establish some boundaries which may aid municipal managers and planners to better understand the interrelationship of urban design and physical development from a process point of view; how urban design can be considered as a product in city, district, and project settings; some of the ways in which design can be implemented; and the major management considerations that impinge on the design process

Urban design services are inextricably linked to the problems of environmental quality brought on by pressures of urban growth and decline. Regardless of the geographic scale or the nature of the design problem, urban design accommodates these pressures by three activities: the determination of what is to be protected, or *conservation;* the determination of where and how development investments are to be located, or *development focus;* and the determination of appropriate physical form and mixture of use, or *development character*.

The complex nature of urban design problems requires a process that stresses learning what to do rather than creating final products. The special products and language of urban design are images which either test design concepts or communicate design agreements. Implementation techniques tend to follow environmental quality problems.

The recommendations in this chapter point to an urban design management approach that takes into account variations in implementation and citizen participation, different geographic scales, and the differing requirements of the urban environment.

The limits of an overview of this kind lie in our continuously changing attitudes toward environmental quality: urban design practice will always be bounded by our collective concern for environmental management.

1 A fourth level, regional urban design, has been omitted. This kind of design is concerned with the open land between already urbanized areas and physically and politically separate but functionally related urban areas with common problems. Regional design is typically administered under federal, state, or metropolitan jurisdiction. Its purpose is to establish public policy for the use of land and for the type and location of the supporting infrastructure of utilities and transportation facilities. Examples include transportation districts and special purpose land zoning such as statewide coastal and agricultural zones. Programs at this scale become urban design issues when they determine the character and location of new settlements and service facilities on open land. These design issues will be covered in Volume 2 of this work.

2 See: Skidmore, Owings & Merrill, *St. Helena, California, Urban Design Study* (San Francisco: Skidmore, Owings & Merrill, 1974).

3 See: Skidmore, Owings & Merrill and Marshall Kaplan, Gans and Kahn, *San Antonio River Corri-*

dor (San Francisco: Skidmore, Owings & Merrill, 1973).

4 See: Skidmore, Owings & Merrill, *Urban Design Element, Capitol Area Plan, Sacramento* (San Francisco: Skidmore, Owings & Merrill, 1977).

5 See: Skidmore, Owings & Merrill and Marshall Kaplan, Gans and Kahn, *San Antonio River Corridor*.

6 See: Arthur D. Little, Inc., et al., *Dallas, Center City Transportation Project* (San Francisco: Arthur D. Little, Inc., 1970).

7 See: Skidmore, Owings & Merrill and Fred Toguchi Associates, *The Mayfield Euclid Triangle: A Residential and Commercial Development Plan for the University Circle* (San Francisco: Skidmore, Owings & Merrill, 1974).

8 John L. Kriken and Irene Perlis Torrey, *Developing Urban Design Mechanisms,* Planning Advisory Service Report no. 296 (Chicago: American Society of Planning Officials, 1973), pp. 3, 13–16. The ten cities surveyed were Washington, D.C.; San Francisco; New York; Montreal; Min-

neapolis; Los Angeles; Dallas; Cincinnati; Boston; and Oakland.

9 Bernard H. Siegan, "Zoning Incentives: Do They Give Us What We Really Want?" *Environmental Comment,* January 1977, p. 4.

10 City of San Francisco, Department of City Planning, *The Urban Design Plan for the Comprehensive Plan of San Francisco* (San Francisco: Department of City Planning, 1971), p. 92.

11 Margot Parke, *View Protection Regulations,* Planning Advisory Service Report no. 213 (Chicago: American Society of Planning Officials, 1966), p. 5.

12 Mavis Bryant, *Zoning for Community Preservation: A Manual for Texans* (Austin: Texas Historical Commission, 1976), p. 45.

13 Roger Wells, "Impact Zoning: Incentive Land Use Management," *Environmental Comment,* January 1977, p. 13.

14 Israel Stollman, "Ramapo: An Editorial & the Ordinance as Amended," in *Management & Control of Growth,* ed. Randall W. Scott, David J. Brower, and Dallas D. Miner, 3 vols. (Washington, D.C.: Urban Land Institute, 1975), vol. 2, pp. 5–13.

15 See: City of San Francisco, Department of City Planning, *San Francisco Downtown Zoning Study* (San Francisco: Department of City Planning, 1966).

16 See: City of New York, Department of City Planning, *Zoning for Housing Quality* (New York: Department of City Planning, 1975).

17 John J. Costonis, *Space Adrift: Saving Urban Landmarks through the Chicago Plan* (Chicago: University of Illinois Press, 1974), p. 32.

18 See: American Society of Planning Officials, *Planned Unit Development Ordinance,* Planning Advisory Service Report no. 291 (Chicago: American Society of Planning Officials, 1973).

19 See: Gladstone Associates, *Mixed Use Developments: New Ways of Land Use,* (Washington, D.C.: Urban Land Institute, 1976).

20 See: Real Estate Research Corporation, *Joint Development: Center City Transportation Project* (Washington, D.C.: U.S. Department of Transportation, 1970).

21 See: Karen E. Hapgood, *Planning and the Arts,* Planning Advisory Service Report no. 313 (Chicago: American Society of Planning Officials, 1975).

22 See: Skidmore, Owings & Merrill, *San Antonio, Urban Design Mechanisms Study* (San Francisco: Skidmore, Owings & Merrill, 1972); Kriken and Torrey, *Developing Urban Design Mechanisms;* and Weiming Lu et al., *The Urban Design Role of Local Government* (Washington, D.C.: National Science Foundation, 1976; available from National Technical Information Service, Springfield, Virginia 22151).

23 See: Andrew F. Euston, Jr., "Urban Environmental Design: An Urban Solution?" *Community Planning Report,* 1 August 1977.

Part four:
Land use
regulation

14

Subdivision regulation and land conversion

Kevin Lynch has made the following statement about the status of regulation— or lack of regulation—of land development in the United States:

Historically, public opinion has favored development almost irrespective of the cost to the environment. Our laws and institutions, many of which evolved during a time when growth was a national ideal, reflect a pro-development bias.[1]

He then pointed to the fact that "processes that allow for sensitive accommodations and balances—that assure protection of critical open spaces and historic buildings, but also assure that essential development needs are met are not yet in effect in most areas."[2]

This chapter deals with the ordinances governing land subdivision. After a brief overview and some discussion of the private and public concerns in subdivision regulation, the chapter takes up the subject of the context of subdivision regulation and discusses such matters as community goals and the planning process, the preparation of subdivision regulations, and the review process. Next, the content of the regulations is discussed in considerable detail. The final section of the chapter is devoted to the new trends in subdivision regulation that are emerging today.

Overview

Land subdivision—the act of splitting a tract of land into separate parcels—is a simple enough proposition. It is an act that has been occurring and has been regulated in this country since its beginnings. The usual purpose of subdividing land is to permit the transfer of the subdivided pieces to someone other than the owner of the original parcel. Most often, subdividing is done for the purpose of permitting development to take place: housing, commercial, or industrial uses; public and private uses. Change is what is contemplated—change from the status of the parcel before it was divided. There are, of course, other purposes for subdividing, for example: transfers of ownership which perpetuate the previous use (farmland sold to another farmer); purchase of additional land by someone who wishes to add to a lot in order to preserve an existing open character; division of land among heirs. But these purposes are minor when the intent of most subdivisions of land is considered.

The chief responsibility for regulating subdivision activity has been delegated to local governments by the states, although certain aspects of this responsibility are now being taken back by the states for various reasons. (See the discussion later in this chapter of new trends in subdivision regulation.)

One of the better, if somewhat optimistic, descriptions of subdivision regulations is contained in *Building the American City,* the report of the National Commission on Urban Problems. This description is given immediately below, as follows:

THE SUBDIVISION REGULATION
While conventional zoning normally applies to individual lots, subdivision regulations govern the process by which those lots are created out of larger tracts.

a. *Regulated subjects*

Site design and relationships: Subdivision regulations typically seek to assure that subdivisions are appropriately related to their surroundings. Commonly, they require that the subdivision be consistent with a comprehensive plan for the area (e.g., by reserving land for proposed highways or parks). Requirements normally assure that utilities (local streets, sewers) tie into those located [on] or planned for adjoining property. Other requirements are intended to assure that the subdivision itself is related to its own site and that it will work effectively. The widths of streets, the length of blocks, the size of lots, and the handling of frontage along major streets, are among commonly regulated subjects.

Allocation of facilities cost—dedications and fees: Subdivision regulations may contain provisions that effectively allocate costs of public facilities between the subdivider and local taxpayers. Commonly, regulations require subdividers to dedicate land for streets and to install, at their own expense, a variety of public facilities to serve the development. These often include streets, sidewalks, storm and sanitary sewers, and street lights. In recent years, more and more subdivision regulations have also been requiring subdividers to dedicate parkland, and sometimes school sites, or to make cash payments in lieu of such dedication. Some regulations go further still, requiring payment of fees to apply toward such major public costs as the construction of sewage disposal plants.

b. *Administration*

Subdivision regulations contemplate a more sophisticated administrative process than do conventional zoning regulations. Instead of prescribing the precise location of future lot lines, for example, subdivision regulations provide more general design standards (based in part on local plans). The local planning commission or governing body then applies these standards, at the time of subdivision, to preliminary and final plats submitted by property owners.[3]

Little mention is made of site planning—and all too often little attention is paid to it—in the subdivision process, either by the public agency reviewing a proposal or by the private developer submitting a proposed subdivision plat. This is indeed unfortunate.

With change in the use of land, new public and private demands are created. The relationship with abutting lands changes—and the neighborhood and the region change. For an understanding of the nature of these changes it is desirable to look at the purpose of subdivision from both the private and public standpoints. If we understand the concerns of both sides we should be able to create better regulations to deal with the process and, consequently, better living environments. Perhaps, then, site planning will in due course become an accepted base for approving or disapproving a subdivision request.

Private concerns in subdivision

When land is sought to provide new opportunities for development or redevelopment, the developer considers a number of factors. These considerations include: the appropriateness of the size and shape of the site for the uses intended (residential, commercial, industrial); site location and proximity to necessary public services (water, sewer, streets, fire protection, schools, parks); natural amenities; ease of development; necessary improvements to render the site usable; local regulations; internal site design; relation to existing or potential uses of abutting properties; establishment of restrictions for development or use of the parcels (covenants); timing and marketability as related to original cost; cost of improvements; and potential sales price relative to the rest of the market. The potential for a successful subdivision depends on all of the above factors, as well as on the quality of the site design itself. The individual factors will vary in importance according to the proposed use. For example, commercial and industrial subdivisions will be dependent on the availability of and access to transportation, while a residential subdivision will be far more affected by proximity to natural amenities and to schools and parks.

Public concerns in subdivision

When subdivision is proposed, the local government having the responsibility for review of the proposal also has a number of factors to consider.

The local government must attempt to ensure that the development proposal is compatible with its surroundings. The reviewing body needs to consider the following: that major streets align with existing or proposed streets adjacent to the property; that utility lines are properly sized to fit the community-wide system; that drainage or other natural hazards will not create problems for abutting properties or for future residents in the subdivision; that improvements are sufficient to serve the proposed uses and are of a quality of construction to minimize future public maintenance costs; that natural amenities are preserved; that the size and shape of the lots and blocks are compatible with the proposed uses and meet zoning or land use restrictions; that the subdivision can be served with necessary public services and facilities; that the timing is such as to be in phase with the community's ability to provide services; that the nature of the site plan is compatible with the neighborhood and community; and that the design of the subdivision creates maximum safety for the future occupants.

This is almost a mirror of the same factors the developer should be concerned about. Why, then, are there differences as to what constitutes a good subdivision ordinance, or what is a proper public concern, or what is a good subdivision design? Why are there so many poorly designed and out of phase subdivisions scattered around the countryside? Why are public facilities so frequently inadequate for the created demand? Why are costs of developing or maintaining streets, parks, and utility systems so high? If local government is controlling the development patterns, why do these problems develop?

There are a number of reasons for these problems, some of which can be listed as follows:

1. The failure of a community to know where and how it wishes to grow and to integrate the subdivision regulations and review process into community-wide goals and policies as part of the comprehensive planning process
2. A lack of understanding on the part of local governments as to how to develop and use a subdivision regulation
3. The failure on the part of local governments to establish adequate procedures for reviewing subdivisions for quality; most local governments merely review what is submitted for technical compliance
4. A lack of knowledge of the natural and man-made resources that should determine the nature of the subdivision
5. A lack of expertise in both preparing and reviewing subdivision proposals
6. A lack of awareness on the part of the local government that it can turn down a subdivision which is unwarranted or unserviceable at a given time—and a consequent hesitancy in saying no
7. Financial institutions which look backward and base mortgage money availability on what has previously been built in an area, with little evaluation of the improved living environments that can be created through better site planning
8. Treatment of the subdivision plat, site planning, and building designs as separate functions.

The context of subdivision regulations

Community goals and the planning process

While in theory a community develops its goals and objectives for future development, expresses these in a guide called a comprehensive plan or a master

Figure 14–1   Public facilities and services that
impinge on and affect a residential subdivision.
The range of services that a household draws on in its
daily living is suggested here. Some are direct
services to property, such as streets and sewer
and water lines; other services are available as needed,
such as playgrounds, police and fire protection,
libraries, and schools.

plan, and then creates tools to implement this plan, this has seldom occurred in the past. The opposite has been the norm. Regulatory tools have largely been created which have been based on models furnished by various professional organizations, examples from other communities, or directions from state agencies. Too often, the writing of the community's development ordinances is treated as an isolated effort. Regulatory tools should be carefully tested against the community's goals and other development ordinances to ensure that they complement and reinforce one another.

This situation is changing. As more citizens and communities begin to question the type of growth that is occurring in their area, how much it is costing, who is paying for it, and how it is affecting the environment—and as housing costs escalate to the point of excluding not only the low income family but the middle income family as well—the need to coordinate the community's planning and control devices is becoming evident to all. A concept is needed of the individual community, what it is striving for, how the pieces relate to each other, and what it wants to preserve and achieve as development occurs. Environmentalists, home builders, planners, architects, financial specialists, political leaders, and the public at large are becoming aware of the shortcomings of the present and past practices. Subdivision regulations cannot effectively accomplish their potential role in upgrading the living environment unless the community develops its other necessary service plans and then measures each subdivision proposal against these plans. As an integral element of the planning process, subdivision approval must include consideration of various elements of the community's policies, plans, and standards. The plans and policies that are necessary in this context are the following:

1. A water and sewer plan for the area which establishes the service area and the size, standards, location, and phasing of treatment facilities and lines to serve the area. This plan should be based on the desired land pattern for future growth, the costs of initial service, and the continued operation costs to the community.

2. A park and open space plan that identifies locations and standards for park and recreation areas to serve future growth, and natural open space areas that are to be preserved.

3. An environmental plan that identifies critical areas that should be protected from development. Such areas include hazardous areas (floodplains, steep slopes, subsurface geological problem areas, slide or avalanche areas, high wind areas); sensitive areas (aquifer recharge areas, historical areas, sensitive vegetation areas, wildlife areas, mineral resource areas); and, areas important to the community's economic base (agricultural lands, forests, recreation areas that contribute to the area's economic health).

4. A street and transportation plan that indicates the location, capacity, and nature of the system including—where appropriate—automobile, public transportation, bicycle, and pedestrian considerations. The effect on existing and abutting land uses is a critical element in the development of this plan as it relates to community development and redevelopment.

5. A school facility plan that identifies standards for school size (enrollment); land area to develop the facility; and location considerations with regard to spacing, streets, and relation to other use areas.

6. Health department standards for control of septic systems, water wells, package sewage treatment plants, and central treatment systems. Areas where wells and septic systems are not permissible should be identified.

7. A fiscal plan that identifies the proportion of costs of public facilities and services that is to be reimbursed from new subdivisions.

8. A capital improvements program that indicates where and when physical improvements are to be made, the size of these improvements, and how

they will be financed. Development regulations other than subdivision controls must exist and must be coordinated. Zoning, environmental, building, or design regulations or guidelines affect and are affected by the site planning that results from the subdivision process.

All of the above items are elements of the planning process that a city or county should develop in creating its comprehensive planning program. Without the coordination of these tools, subdivision regulations are administered in a vacuum; this has led to many of our present deficiences in attempting to create coherent community development.

The preparation of subdivision regulations

In the preparation or revision of a subdivision regulation there are many sources of potential models. Professional and research organizations[4] have contributed models of whole ordinances as well as essential elements thereof which can be used for reference. State planning agencies, councils of governments, municipal leagues, county commissioners' associations, and various university agencies and departments have also furnished such guidelines. Review of the subdivision codes of other governments can also be a source of ideas for dealing with issues of local concern.

Research may include articles from law journals or reports from conferences (such as the annual Southwest Legal Conference) which contribute particular ideas that may be in the forefront of coping with some aspect of subdivision development, site planning, or processing.

Where there is no local staff, other support is required to develop regulations. Lay groups such as planning commissions should seldom attempt to develop regulations on their own. Technical assistance is available from other levels of government, from universities, and from private consultants and should be used to produce the concept and document most appropriate to the individual community.

A crucial consideration is how this information is put together. Developers, realtors, architects, engineers, public staff (if one exists), environmentalists, and representatives of citizen groups active in community development concerns (for example, the League of Women Voters) should all be involved in reviewing the proposed regulations. A task force for such purposes is a desirable approach. This task force can meet frequently and should maintain its enthusiasm. It will know that it has fulfilled its task when a product is adopted.

Initially, a discussion of philosophy as to what is to be achieved with the regulations, how they are to relate to the planning process for the whole community, and how they are to be administered is helpful in bringing all parties together on the task. The planning commission and the political leaders should express their views but need not be actively involved in the initial preparation process. They should be kept informed, and where policy questions are involved they should make decisions, but otherwise they will serve as the review bodies on the product and should become closely involved at that time.

The staff or consultant should become familiar with the concerns and strengths of the existing regulations from the various viewpoints; this includes the viewpoints of the consumer, the builder–developer, public agencies (schools, engineers, utilities, parks, planning, finance, building inspections), environmentalists, lenders, and the planning commission.

The staff or consultant should evaluate existing regulations to see if they are working to achieve the goals of the plans and policies of the community. For example, are the park dedication requirements sufficient in light of current park standards? Is there a need to develop a more efficient way to finance necessary site improvements to hold housing costs to the lowest level possible for the community? Research into what other communities are doing to solve such issues should be fed into the process at this time.

There must be legal evaluation of what the city or town charter requires and what the state statutes require or allow local governments to do. However, if a proposed requirement is not specifically prohibited it is probably worth trying for if the need exists. Local government should not be inhibited by local advisers who say, "I don't think you can do it," or, "It may be unconstitutional." If these advisers cannot produce a specific case in the state, then it is worth pursuing the requirement. However, the regulation must be carefully drafted.

Regulations need to be localized to account for the particular community values, physical characteristics, and climate. Blind adoption of models or of another community's requirements or procedures will lead to problems.

Relationship between zoning and subdivision Newcomers to the field of planning are frequently puzzled by the difference between land subdivision regulations and zoning ordinances. This confusion is shared by many people and leads to the proposal made by some planners and lawyers that both ordinances ought to be combined into a single, consolidated development code.

In general, land subdivision regulations contain rules and standards that are applied to the conversion of farm or vacant land into lots and parcels for urban development. The rules and standards relate to the size and shape of lots and blocks and the width and length of streets. In addition, regulations contain construction standards for streets, curbs and gutters, sewers, water mains, and sidewalks.

In general, zoning ordinances divide a city or county into zones for various classes of land uses (such as residential, commercial, and industrial) and prescribe regulations as to how land or buildings may be used. Moreover, the zoning ordinance specifies spatial relationships between land and the placement of buildings on the land—for example, the size of yards and open space that must surround a building.

Where possible, regulations, standards, procedures, and guidelines of neighboring governmental agencies should be standardized. Time and cost savings as well as improved attitudes can be achieved where a city and a county, or two neighboring communities, can bring their development requirements into conformity. For example, merely standardizing plat submittal requirements or topography intervals in subdivision regulations will provide consistent records and reduce preparation time. Street widths are a major area in which minor differences within a given region are indefensible. Through mutual awareness of requirements on the part of neighboring governments, cooperation and standardization may take place in many areas of subdivision activity to the benefit of everyone concerned.

In the drafting of regulations the following actions should be considered:

1. Be critical. Ask whether each section is accomplishing its intent. How will it improve the product or process and will it provide only that information that is necessary? Is it clear? Is it necessary? Is it subject to abuse, etc.?
2. Provide flexibility. Make it possible for new concepts to be considered as efficiently as possible subject to public acceptance.
3. Build in time limits and due process. Impose time restrictions on administrative reviews, within the staff's ability to respond, to avoid administrative delays. Require that all decisions and conditions be reduced to writing and recorded with the plat to avoid further problems for either the public or the developer.

4. Consider the small developer. Within the context of community goals, recognize that there will be proposals to split land into one, two, or three parcels. The requirements for these actions should be simplified and the process of review streamlined or the cost and time will become prohibitive for small transactions.

5. Develop a companion text of engineering improvement specifications. Except in rural areas, where the subdivision regulations can be greatly simplified and consequently can include the engineering specifications, a separate document is needed which reduces to writing the engineering requirements for streets, drainage areas, water lines, sewer lines, concrete work, bicycle paths, and other improvements. This assures uniform treatment of developers and consistent construction standards for public improvements.

6. Incorporate environmental considerations. Subdivision regulations have given a superficial credence to the physical environment as a basis for the site plan. Rarely were plats denied because they tore up a site. Now, with the emphasis on "designing with nature," people are aware that the earth mover is not the answer. Where possible, local environmental impact statement (EIS) requirements should be incorporated into the subdivision regulations to eliminate duplication, assure consideration at the proper time, and speed up and streamline the review process. Communities have been creating separate ordinances and review boards (required in some states by specific legislation) for environmental impacts. This is redundant and time-consuming. Logically, the EIS should be an integral part of a subdivision plat review. If the planning commission does not consider the environmental, social, and fiscal impacts of a subdivision plat, it cannot execute its task properly.

7. Make use of support documents. It may be necessary in larger communities to develop additional detailed documents that assist a subdivider in achieving the community's goals. These might include a waterfront ordinance, a landscape ordinance, a slope ordinance, or a mobile home supplement. As experience develops with frequently requested types of special cases (mobile home parks, plats along the waterfront, condominium developments), and as consistent applications of standards occur and desired local approaches become clear, they should be recorded and, to save time, should be furnished to prospective developers along with the subdivision code.

8. Provide a checklist that may be used to guide the review as to the adequacy of services necessary to support the development. With this checklist the developer, staff, public, legislative body, and planning commission will all know what is to be considered in the analysis without a search through the code.

Review procedures

In order to achieve sufficient review, a community should establish procedures which assure that the proper agencies and people are aware of requests, have enough time to review them, and have the knowledge to deny them where necessary. Agencies outside local government which usually should be included in the review process are as follows:

1. School districts
2. Local power companies
3. Telephone company
4. Water or sewer districts if the plat is to be served by other than the local government

5. Any other district which the plat incorporates (fire, soil, recreation, library)
6. State highway department, when appropriate
7. City: if a plat is in the country but within a mile (some state laws expand this distance) of a city or town, the plat should be referred for comment (the reverse is also true: cities should keep counties informed)
8. County health department
9. Other agencies, including state departments, that may be required by state law to review local subdivision requests.

Within the local government an internal review process should assure that all concerned agencies review and comment on the proposed plat. In smaller and rural communities this is simple; in larger communities it can become complex. These agencies include, if they exist, the following:

1. Public works/engineer
2. Utilities—water/sewer
3. Parks and recreation
4. Fire protection
5. Planning
6. Finance
7. Transportation (traffic engineer).

Each of these agencies should comment in writing. Many communities find that a regular staff meeting to discuss comments on preliminary requests is essential. The process is educational for the various agencies; it helps each understand why the other's concerns may be critical; in addition, it illuminates points that are arbitrary and could be changed to improve the quality of living for the future occupants.

To achieve the above reviews, an applicant must submit enough copies of the subdivision plat in sufficient time to allow everyone involved in the review process to act. Many smaller communities and counties still attempt to review plats only at their set meetings. This can be unfair to the applicant, the community, and the future occupants. This approval procedure wastes time at the meeting; it frequently results in tabling, or else permits poorly conceived plats to gain approval.

The role of the review agency is to represent the public, future occupants, or owners. Where there is no staff, and where the planning commission or legislative body is the only authority available to review plats, the review should be a two step process: review and discuss at one meeting; adopt or deny at the next. A successful practice in some counties or small towns where there is no staff and where plat requests are becoming frequent is to hire a consultant to review all plats and advise the county or town on the decision. The applicant is charged for the review costs and submits the plat to the consultant. By using the same consultant for review, a consistency of reports is achieved and thus the area's policies can be more easily carried out. In this manner, a rural legislator is not overrun by a high powered presentation by the applicant's lawyer, planner, engineer, or architect.

As separate documents are frequently lost or forgotten, any conditions of approval should be recorded on the plat itself.

During the public review certain simple procedures (such as having an area map on the wall, the plat located on the map, and a copy of the plat also posted) will facilitate the meeting and discussion. Where a staff or consultant reviews the plat written reports should be sent to the review agency before the meeting. If these reports are not received at least two days before the meeting, the item should automatically be tabled. Such a procedure will allow the members sufficient time to review the recommendations, visit the site, and clarify questions with the staff. The staff will also become more concerned with efficiency if they bear the responsibility of the delay.

Consideration of natural and man-made resources

Subdivision ordinances generally require topography, drainage ways, water bodies, existing structures, and roads to be shown as part of subdivision plat submittals. But most communities have no policies on what to do with this information. Drainage areas are allowed to be filled, topography can be drastically altered, vegetation can be removed, and any other feature that interferes with the site plan can be changed. At times, little consideration is given to *off-site* effects (whether bridges or intersections away from but serving the site are adequate; whether conflicts with railroad crossings would become issues; or whether county road maintenance practices would be affected).

Recently, more sophisticated planning programs have realized the significance of the environmental, social, and financial impacts of new subdivisions. In the last ten years this awareness has become widespread. States now require mandatory adoption of subdivision laws by local governments. Environmental impact laws passed by states have been directed toward broadening the concern beyond merely platting lots, blocks, and streets to one of acknowledging the present area conditions and measuring the potential impacts both on and off the site. Plans for plats must now respect the ecological factors of the site and must use these factors as a basis for design. It is necessary to understand the limitations or opportunities with regard to the purpose or nature of the subdivision. Conceivably, the purpose and the site are compatible. If there is a conflict, the purpose should not be altered, nor should a new location be sought. It is the review body's responsibility to see that the site design is compatible with the ecology of the site. Unnecessary future public and private costs can be avoided if this is taken into consideration.

Before the 1940s we lacked the capability of making large changes in the landscape and were forced to do a better job of fitting development to the site. Large scale earth moving equipment has unleashed untold opportunities of destroying natural drainage patterns and, in general, can reshape the environmental character of the site. Large scale systems building methods have encouraged repetitive housing types which require uniform lot sizes and relatively flat topography. These capabilities need not be destructive if the review agencies are sensitive to the impacts and require that before development is approved the effects of such a proposal are fully realized, the problems are identified, and solutions are developed.

The logical point in the development sequence at which to consider the effect on the environment is before a parcel is zoned for uses other than agriculture or open space. Many cities are already arbitrarily zoned for more intense uses. Therefore, the subdivision process should be used to ensure that such concerns are taken into account. A checklist such as that in Figure 14–2 works very well in conjunction with a plat review.

Those persons reviewing and acting on subdivision plats (county or city engineers, planners, lawyers, or other professionals who act as consultants or advisers to the governing body) should not in any way prepare or participate in the procedure in the capacity, formal or informal, of representing the applicant. Unfortunately, in smaller communities (and in some larger ones) this is still a common practice that is highly undesirable and should be avoided. The areas of conflict of interest permeate the entire process.

The need for expertise

When a subdivision is viewed merely as the laying out of lots and blocks the extent of expertise needed is minimal. When a subdivision plat is viewed as a base for future development the degree of sensitivity required in its preparation becomes much greater. Too often the subdivider is simply a marketer of land. The builder is not even on the scene at the time of plat preparation. Minimum development costs, standardization, and conformity to existing community building patterns dominate in such circumstances. Technically, the plat conforms and will usually function when laid out with simple engineering considerations in mind. But the quality of the future development may be marginal. Only the largest developer or the developer of exclusive subdivision developments will consistently put together a total team before platting (using, for example, a land planner, an engineer, an environmentalist, and an architect or a designer). Under the latter conditions a concept of the finished product is thought through before the plat is prepared. Purpose or use and the basic environment are considered inseparable.

On the public review side there is a similar problem. Sometimes the city engineer's office is the only agency that reviews the proposal. The process is intended simply to confirm that the request meets the technical requirements of the code. This is acceptable in cities where the subdivision is an infill of an area. But in new outlying or uncommitted areas, or in large developments where a character can be established, such a minimal review on the public's side is unacceptable. Once a subdivision is created it has a permanent imprint on the area. The initial cost or time spent in preparation or review is relatively insignificant if viewed from the perspective of the expected life of the development.

Saying no

Local governments have believed for years that subdivisions must automatically be approved. The right to subdivide was considered mandatory. This is changing. It is no longer a matter of submitting the plat with lots, blocks, and streets to the right dimensions and assuming approval. Increasingly, adequate water and sewer service must be proved, the critical environmental concerns must be answered, hazardous areas must be avoided, the area must be within a specified service area, and in some cases a demonstration of need must be presented.

The Ramapo, New York, ordinance, which requires a demonstration of minimum facilities and services, was reduced to a numerical formula (for example, sewers, roads, fire protection, drainage, and parks were the values measures) before a subdivision (or a building permit, or zoning on planned unit development) could be approved.[5] This is the most famous application of phasing—of saying no to "premature" proposals.

Petaluma, California, is another highly documented and tested case of a community that has developed a system of saying no to developments which are premature.[6] Petaluma has developed a system of residential control based on three planning documents: the Petaluma general plan, Petaluma Environmental Design Plans, and the housing element of the general plan.

Essentially, in Petaluma there is a limit on the number of building permits that may be approved (500 annually). The plan has been adopted for a five year period. It excludes small subdivisions of four or fewer lots and also excludes single family infill on existing lots.

In Petaluma the evaluation board reviews an application for development and evaluates social, fiscal, and environmental impacts as a total picture. In this way the process of subdivision as a single and isolated step in the development of housing is avoided. The internal site factors and external community factors are considered, as well as the ultimate impact of the application. Annexation, zoning, subdivision, and building design are viewed as a single process.

Other communities have developed similar concepts in an attempt, through incentives or regulation, to discourage or prohibit premature development or development in an unacceptable location. Boulder County, Colorado, has for

Date submitted for review _____

Town of Vail
Environmental review checklist

Project _____   Type of project _____

Owner _____   Legal description _____

An environmental impact report must be made for any activity which may have any negative effect on the environment. Effects include environmental consequences of both primary and secondary nature.

The following questions shall be used as guidelines to decide whether to make a negative declaration or an environmental impact report. (If answer is unknown, cite "unknown.")

1. Could the project significantly change present uses of the project area?
2. Does the project significantly conflict with applicable general plans and the Vail Master Plan?
3. Could the project affect the use of a recreational area, or area of important visual value or preempt a site with potential recreational or open space value?
4. Will any natural or man-made features in the project area which are unique, that is, not found in other parts of the Town, County, or State, be affected?
5. Will the project involve construction of facilities on a slope of 30 percent or greater?
6. Will the project involve construction of facilities in an area of geologic hazards?
7. Will the project involve construction of facilities in an area subject to avalanche?
8. Could the project change existing features or involve construction in any flood plain, natural drainage course, or watercourse?
9. Is the project, as part of a larger project, one of a series of cumulative actions, which, although individually small, may as a whole have significant environmental impact.
10. Does the project involve extensive excavation or fill?
11. Does the project area or the project site serve as a habitat, food source, nesting place, crossing, wintering area, source of water, etc., for wildlife species?
12. Could the project significantly affect rearing areas or habitat of fish species?
13. Are there any rare or endangered plant species in the project area?
14. Could the project change existing features of any of the region's stream frontage or greenbelt areas?
15. Will the project remove substantial amounts of vegetation including ground cover?
16. Could the project result in significant change in the hydrology of the area?
17. Could the project result in the displacement of community residents?
18. Could the project serve to encourage development of presently undeveloped areas or intensify development of already developed areas?
19. Is there appreciable opposition to the project or is it likely to be controversial?
20. Will the project create new or aggravate existing health hazards?
21. Will the project involve the application, use, or disposal of potentially hazardous materials?
22. Could the project generate significant amounts of dust or odor?
23. Could the project generate significant noise?
24. Will the project discharge significant volumes of solid or liquid wastes?
25. Could the project result in damage to soil capability or loss of agricultural land?
26. Could the project significantly affect the potential use, extraction, or conservation of a natural resource?
27. Could the project alter local traffic patterns or cause a significant increase in traffic volume or transit service needs?

Figure 14–2   Environmental review checklist for the town of Vail, Colorado.

28. Additional remarks: _____

_____

_____

_____

Checklist reviewed by _____   Title _____

                     _____   Title _____

For any points answered "yes" or "unknown," the reasons are as follows:

_____

_____

_____

_____

Figure 14–2   (continued).

nine years had a policy of directing urban uses (residential, subdivision, commercial, or industrial) to locate adjacent to, or to annex to, existing urban centers. They have simply said no to scattered requests in the rural areas.

Minneapolis–St. Paul, Minnesota, has gone a step further in that the state legislature has passed a metropolitan area mandatory land planning bill. This bill formalizes the urban service area concept which the Twin Cities had been developing.[7] A city or county in the metropolitan area must adopt a land use plan designating the proposed location, intensity, and extent of land for various uses. The plan must include an "implementation program" to ensure conformity with the metropolitan system plan. Each city or county may also designate an "urbanized area" plan, for a five year period, in which development is permitted. This limits urbanization to urbanized areas in accordance with the plan.

This effort on the part of the Twin Cities is by far the most comprehensive approach to phasing development in an urban and rural area of numerous political jurisdictions. Subdivision controls in this context become part of an integrated whole instead of remaining an isolated independent act in the development process.

A word on coordination

Communities should coordinate all their development policies, codes, and standards. Frequently, the zoning code is not coordinated with the subdivision code. To submit a planned unit development (PUD) and a subdivision plat for the same parcel will require two separate actions and various materials. This defeats the purpose of encouraging better development, increases time delays and costs, and is in fact unnecessary. If we are to continue, as we will in most communities, with pre-regulated standards and a development process which separates zoning, subdivision, and building permits into three actions, then the least we should strive for is to achieve a common goal for all three—and to ensure that each complements and reinforces the other.

In some states and communities subdivision regulations have absorbed the traditional functions of other regulations. Where zoning is an unaccepted or questionable concept of controlling uses or densities, some of the functions are placed in the subdivision code. For example, the model code for cities and counties in Montana bases lot size on health requirements where zoning is nonexistent. In Houston, Texas, which does not have a zoning ordinance, minimum lot sizes, setbacks, and house size are items covered in the subdivision regulations.[8]

The contents of subdivision regulations

There are certain common elements that are included in most codes. As has been previously stated, the content of local codes must be developed with great sensitivity to the particular circumstances of each area. Preferably, the code should be written for the user—the developer—and not for the attorney or planner. The language and intent should be understandable to anyone who uses the documents. Each community has certain formats for regulations which have been used traditionally and will probably prevail for the subdivision code. But the sequence in which the elements are used is a general guide for a pattern to follow in the drafting.

Applicability of regulations

Generally, this section defines what a subdivision is, explains the intent or purpose of a subdivision, and explains when the requirements of the code apply. Definitions sometimes appear here; however, since these are not used or read until a problem or question of interpretation appears, they can logically be relegated to the back of the code where they will not get in the way of the sequence. Definitions should conform to state law.

Review procedures

There are usually three stages of review for subdivision plats in larger communities or active markets: (1) preapplication conference, (2) preliminary plot, and (3) final plat (these stages are discussed below). The process provides adequate opportunity for negotiations and review before a design becomes final and considerable expenditures are made by the applicant. The initial reviews are sought before the applicant has spent very much money on the preparation. As the considerations about subdividing have expanded into environmental concerns, growth policies, land dedications, and capital improvements programs, the process of review has become more complex. Only in rural or in very slow growth areas is it still possible to present a subdivision plat to the legislative body and have it immediately reviewed and approved. Even in rural areas at least a two step process is becoming commonplace.

Preapplication conference   Experience in most communities has shown the wisdom of meeting with potential developers before any design concepts are created. This is the most flexible time in the process and the easiest time to influence the design. Preferably, the discussion is held even prior to the purchase of land. If there is professional staff they are the logical ones to meet with the potential developer. If not, the planning board should fulfill the information role.

The purpose of the preapplication conference is to communicate. The developer provides the community with information as to the overall concept, where the property is located, and what the major uses would be. The spokesman for the community, in turn, should inform the developer of community goals, plans, or policies that might affect the potential development; of off-site considerations; of available data the community has that might affect the site; of whether the property can be served by community facilities and whether there are any outstanding assessments due the city or other developers; of the availability of utilities; and of the general reaction to the subdivision concept.

This preliminary review in larger communities cannot be made at a single meeting. Key representatives of the community should conduct an initial in-

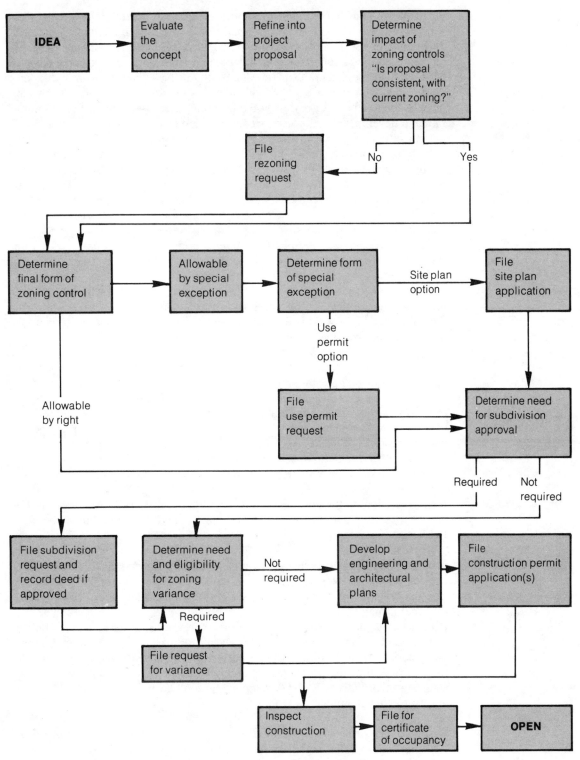

Figure 14–3 Essential steps in the land development process. This generalized
diagram shows the land developer the major steps that must be considered
in planning a project from the original idea to the time when the project
is completed and ready for use.

quiry and should then submit the request to all departments (as well as other agencies such as schools, highway departments, and power companies) that will eventually review a final subdivision proposal. While such a preliminary review may be quick and superficial, and may take no more than a week to ten days to get back to the applicant, it can be valuable in raising a warning or saving expenditures of money on projects that will have difficulty in getting approval. A week or two of investment for review at the beginning can save both parties (community and developer) from needless confrontation later. In smaller or rural communities the review might be completed in one session.

Some cities and counties have instituted an additional step involving the community's legislative body earlier in the process. These communities require the preparation of a "sketch plan"; this essentially requires the same information as a preliminary plat (but to a lesser degree of detail) and is reviewed by both the planning commission and the county commissioners or city council. Thus elected officials can make their feelings known before additional monies are expended. This approach permits the planning commission to review and act on the preliminary plat without the legislative body. The final plat is again reviewed by both bodies.

This approach is more time-consuming but may be desirable where a full staff is not available or the area's policies are not well defined. If there is concern that the legislative body would reverse the staff or planning commission, then the process should provide for an early review.

Preliminary plat   At one time the preliminary subdivision plat served the same purpose as the preapplication conference. However, as costs of land and fees for surveys, engineers, land planners, and architects—as well as community information needs—rose, the flexibility to make major changes in the preliminary plat began to disappear. Major changes after the preparation of a preliminary plat are made with great reluctance, and the idea of the preliminary plat as a concept with a minimum of commitment no longer exists. Therefore, the preapplication or sketch plan stage has become necessary in many areas.

The preliminary plat details the concept worked out in the preapplication conference. Action on the preliminary plat should be a commitment on everyone's part. Approval or conditional approval subject to modifications should be effective for an extended period of time (usually one year).

Because communities are becoming aware of the need to plan for entire neighborhoods and to weigh the total impact of a proposal for external site considerations, developers should be encouraged to bring in, at the preapplication and preliminary plat stage, a concept for all of the land subject to their control. Yet it may be undesirable or impossible for a developer to subdivide the entire acreage of a large parcel at one time; therefore, in order to get a complete concept and at the same time to avoid penalizing the developer, communities allow partial submittals for final plat purposes. This permits the entire concept to be reviewed at the preliminary plat level and the final plat submittals to be staged in accordance with the developer's preference and the market's ability to absorb the development.

Final plat   If a professional staff exists, it is becoming increasingly common for final plats not to be reviewed by the planning commission if the plat as submitted complies with the conditions attached to the preliminary plat. In order to save time and free the planning commission from rubber stamp responsibilities, the final plat can be reviewed by staff and sent directly to the legislative body for their review and acceptance. Only the legislative body can accept streets or other dedications to the public; therefore, this must be the body taking the final action. State law may require the chairman of the planning commission to sign the final plat before recording, but the full commission need not be involved.

Requirements For each review step the process should be explicitly identified. The following should be specified: (1) information to be submitted (contents of the plats, support data, legal documents, and environmental fees); (2) the way in which it should be submitted (number of copies; scale, format, and size of drawings); (3) who will participate in the reviews; and (4) the sequence and time available for the process. At the final plat stage, legal commitments, dedications, financial guarantees, and any other special agreements must be tied down and completed. The signing of the final plat by the legislative body is the last hold a local government has on the platting process. All agreements between the subdivider and the community should be in writing and should be recorded with the plat. When a plat is denied approval the reasons should be stated in writing.

Minor subdivisions For division of land into a relatively few lots (usually a maximum of five), the process and submittals should be streamlined. In some areas *metes and bounds*[9] descriptions of the land are accepted for minor subdivisions where no public dedications are necessary. It should not be necessary for the planning commission to review a minor subdivision. Easements can even be recorded by separate document.

Miscellaneous procedures

If special procedures for site planning are permitted by zoning codes it is necessary to specifically provide for them in the subdivision regulation. Such procedures include, for example: planned unit developments, special development permits, environmental permits, condominium subdivisions, and mobile home developments.

Design standards

The site planning of the subdivision should be of the utmost concern to the reviewing agency. Even today, subdivision platting requirements in many areas are intended to serve merely as a simplified form of legal description for use in official recording and sale of land. In other words, they are used as a means of creating a permanent record of the transaction. Communities that view subdivision in this way, as merely a legal action, are being extremely shortsighted.

The design standards section of a subdivision code gives the community an opportunity to establish community character and upgrade the nature of development. The future residents of the development are not on the scene to speak for themselves, so it becomes imperative that the reviewing agency and staff members attempt to execute that function on their behalf. The goals and policies of the community with regard to the type of development it wishes to encourage and the natural areas it wishes to preserve can be expressed in the design standards. These standards usually include general statements regarding land that is unsuitable for development (for example, such hazardous areas as floodplains and steep slopes) as well as positive statements regarding the types of facilities that the community expects to consider when a basic design is developed.

Design standards provide an opportunity, for example, to assure safe and convenient circulation for automobiles, pedestrians, and bicycles; to minimize conflicts between transportation facilities and abutting land uses; and to ensure adequate park and recreation, water and sewer, and storm drainage facilities. It is in the design standards, too, that the coordination of zoning requirements, floodplain requirements, landscape requirements, and other special area development policies can occur.

Some of the major areas covered by the design standards are discussed immediately below.

Site considerations   Design standards usually begin with regulations concerning the land to be subdivided. Hazardous and sensitive areas are defined and explained in this section (steep or geologically unstable land; subsurface unstable conditions due to mining; primary dunes; floodplains; and any other condition that would endanger the health, life, or property of the future residents, or a critical aspect of the environment). It has become increasingly common for all development to be prohibited by regulation in such areas. Most communities will have escape clauses which will permit applicants who feel they can justify a particular development under certain circumstances to present their plans and concepts to the city engineer; where there is no city engineer the community may choose to submit the proposal to a special consultant for review and approval.

Critical areas   In areas in which development is a problem but not a hazard, limited development can occur under strict controls that identify how and under what conditions development may take place.

These controlled areas are generally termed critical areas. Development in such areas may be discouraged for aesthetic reasons, because of high service costs, for environmental preservation, or for a number of other considerations, none of which can be termed a health or safety threat.

Adjacent problems   Some communities will also have special requirements which are spelled out for subdivisions that border on areas or conditions that might prove to be adverse for future residents: these could include freeways, major arterials, and railroads. Dunes, marshes, and other natural or man-made features that should be given consideration to assure compatibility between the proposed subdivision and the existing or potential abutting uses may also require special treatment.

Streets, roads, and rights-of-way   The general design considerations for streets (alignment with existing roads, intersections, intersection design, arrangement of sidewalks, length or design of culs-de-sac, T and Y intersections, etc.) should be spelled out. Some codes will indicate the dimensions of the cross sections of such facilities in this section. Other codes will place the specific requirements in the form of a chart.

The desirable approach is not to arbitrarily state a total given right-of-way width for a local, secondary, collector, or major arterial street. Preferably, the various elements which compose these types of streets should be identified: for example, the travel lane for a cul-de-sac, a local street, and a higher speed street may be specified as ten feet, eleven feet, and twelve feet, respectively; pedestrian ways may be identified as three feet, four feet, and five feet, for example. It is then up to the applicant to create the type of facility desired for the subdivision.

It may be possible for an applicant to remove all pedestrian ways from along streets and to locate them internally in a block. If this is the case, the street right-of-way width can and should be reduced by the appropriate footage. Or an applicant may choose to prohibit on-street parking in the subdivision; therefore, the applicant should be allowed to remove the parking lane from the local street and provide off-street parking in the subdivision in some manner satisfactory to the reviewing agency. This avoidance of the absolute street dimensions so frequently found in codes, and this provision of a range of designs instead, puts the burden of initiative on the applicant and enhances the opportunities for flexibility in subdivision design, cost savings, and more innovative approaches to site planning. The community and future residents can still be assured that the streets, parking lanes, and pedestrian areas are functional and will serve the need; and the developers are assured that they are not being asked to arbitrarily provide a thirty-four foot street in one area and a twenty-eight foot street in another when all of the same elements are included in each one.

Larger communities will usually have design standards in the subdivision code that are concerned purely with cross section. In smaller communities or rural areas the grading, drainage, and improvement standards for streets may also be included in this section.

Some communities have considered removing the utility easements from under the street pavement to a planting strip alongside the street. This presents difficulties if residents put trees and other improvements in that area. The concept of not having to cut into the streets is a highly desirable one but a very difficult one to implement. In some cities a good answer is the utility easement that runs along rear lot lines.

Alleys and easements   Alleys and easements for utilities and conditions for their acceptance are also specified.

Water bodies   Communities with shorelines, irrigation ditches, or streams should include provisions for maintenance of ditches and ditch rights-of-way and public easements adjacent to the water bodies.

Street naming   If a community is large enough it will have a separate street naming policy and guidelines. Or these may appear as an appendix or within the code itself. Street naming and house numbering should be under the control of the reviewing agency.

Lots and blocks   Width and length standards for blocks and lots prove helpful if a community has developed principles of what it finds acceptable or desirable. Such guidelines can avoid landlocked parcels that prove difficult to assess, impediments to circulation and service, and the need for resubdivision at a later date. Figure 14–4 shows examples of block and lot patterns.

Public sites, reservations, and dedications   Many states and communities throughout the country now are recognizing and accepting the need for parkland and pedestrian and bicycle right-of-way dedications. Street and public utility rights-of-way, of course, have been recognized as normal dedication requirements for many years. School and greenbelt areas are not as widely accepted as legitimate requests except where state or case law specifically authorizes such dedications.

Where there are requests for public land areas above and beyond the area that is directly attributed to the development, or if the development is too small for a park setting, it is desirable to consider some additional requirements. For example, the concept of requiring *either* land dedication *or* cash in lieu thereof is highly desirable. A fee approach is proving much more equitable to everyone unless there is a particular piece of ground desired. Communities should not be forced into accepting parkland dedications in areas where they cannot or do not hope to develop a park, nor should they be forced to accept marginal land for such purposes. In these cases it is most equitable for the community to determine the need generated from various types of development, adopt general standards, and then require a cash contribution in lieu of land for park purposes.

Where land is to be reserved for schools, greenbelts, state highways, or other agencies it is desirable to spell out the conditions under which that land is to be reserved, the period of time for which it is to be reserved, and the interest that is to be paid, and also to state when the price is to be established and when it is to be paid. The price should be set and agreed to before the subdivision is approved.

When communities began accepting cash in lieu of land a fair market value

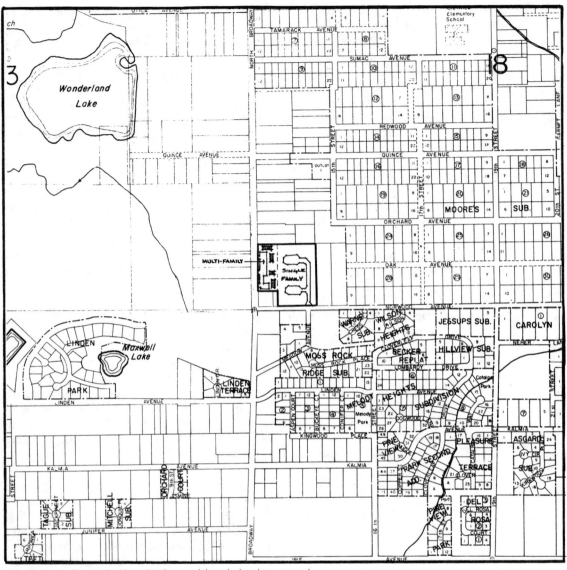

Figure 14–4　Preapplication sketch map (above) showing general
location of proposed subdivision in the center of the mapped area;
preliminary plat (facing page, top) showing lots and contours;
final plat (facing page, bottom) showing land survey identifiers,
precise boundaries, and other information.

was established for the equivalent amount of land that was to have been dedicated. This monetary contribution by the developer may or may not have been sufficient for the community to purchase desirable parkland; in either case, the land value had little relationship to the park needs generated by the development. A far more direct method is to tie the land or cash dedication to the number of people (or number of units) that are expected to be developed in a proposed subdivision. Most park standards include a standard of so many acres per unit of population. It is relatively easy to estimate the number of people per type of unit (single family or multiple family) and per development, relate this to the amount of land the community's park standards require for x number of people, and develop a proportionate cash contribution. This has proved much more desirable than accepting the fair market value of a piece of property in cash or the property itself, as it is directly related to the anticipated number of units and the consequent population that will be generated from a given site. Such a program

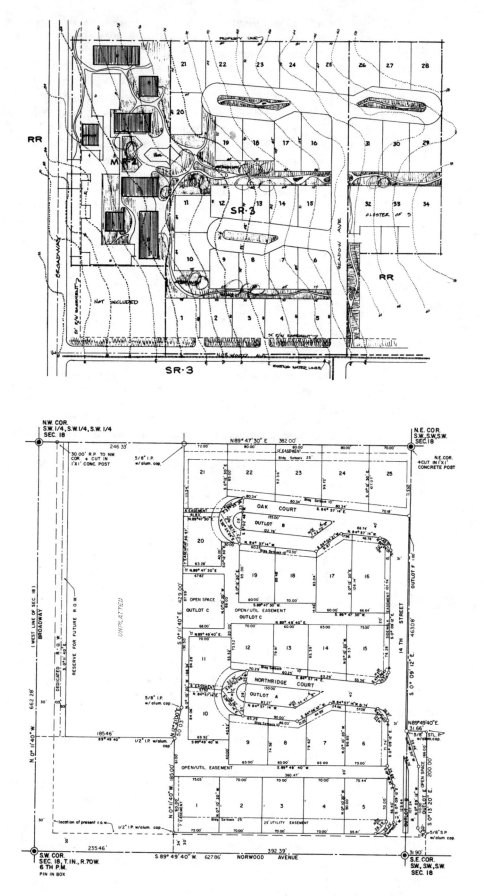

Figure 14–4
(continued).

works most effectively when a community establishes an initial revolving fund which will permit the parks and recreation department to acquire parkland in advance of subdivision activity.

To ensure the development of the parks, a development fee may also be added to the dedication requirement. This practice began when developers objected to the fact that a community required dedication of a piece of property and then, lacking funds, allowed the property to remain undeveloped for many years. Some developers voluntarily attached a $50, $75, or $100 fee to each unit developed within their subdivision and returned this fee to the community for park development purposes in the subdivision. Some communities have now ratified this concept in ordinance form. This permits a community not only to receive dedicated land or purchase it but also to improve the neighborhood park within a specified time. Such an arrangement works to the advantage of the developer who can point to a given timetable for a finished park; to the residents who receive the benefits of having a developed park in their area; and to the community which can reduce the amount of public monies needed for such park developments. The value of the contribution can be increased when the funds can be used to match federal or state park development grants. Where there is a question as to the legality of such practice, it is preferable to attach such requirements at the time of annexation.

Improvements

Smaller communities' engineering specifications for improvements are often contained in the subdivision regulations themselves. In larger communities a separate engineering specification improvement manual is usually prepared, because of the variety and extent of the public improvements necessary in larger communities' standards. The section on improvements may be divided into subsections concerning surface improvements (for example, survey monuments, curbs, gutters, sidewalks, paved streets, alleys, street signs, bridges, culverts, streetlights, and landscaping requirements); utilities (for example, water and sewer lines, storm drains, fire hydrants); and areas where, because of lot and subdivision size, certain of these improvements are not required and individual or private systems may be considered. In a growing number of county regulations solid waste disposal requirements and particular requirements for mobile home parks are also specified. Laws in a number of states now require that a proven water supply and proven sanitation systems must exist, or must have the potential to exist with a guarantee from the subdivider in the form of a monetary commitment.

It is also desirable to recognize private utility improvements such as telephone lines and electric lines, and to make provisions in the improvement requirements that the private companies—if they are providing such facilities—must approve the subdivision before it moves forward. Fire protection and gas systems are also considered. If utility lines are required, communities are increasingly requiring undergrounding of telephone and electric lines. (Frequently, this will be resisted by power companies, who point to the initial cost of undergrounding such facilities. Their accounting procedures do not take into account power outages caused by storms and other natural phenomena which can affect above ground lines. They are basically equipped to put lines overhead and yet, in the light of the total cost of subdividing, the increased cost of going underground is negligible, particularly when compared with the lower maintenance costs and the improved aesthetics and appearance of the subdivision.)

There is usually a catchall clause that identifies and requires other improvements that are not specifically mentioned but are needed because of the peculiarities of the site.

A frequently missing requirement is for final as-built plans. Communities have found that finished plans for improvements, when required, will enable them to keep abreast of what actually was built so that if there are outages or other repairs there will be specific plans from which to work. A registered engineer is required to attest that the working plans as originally planned or amended are what was in fact developed.

More and more, communities are requiring guarantees that the required improvements will be installed. At one time, communities would not permit issuance of building permits until all improvements were in place. Given current building practices this is not feasible in most areas. Therefore, to insure against defaults on the part of the developer, or against financial problems not anticipated by the developer which require the city to come in and build the improvements, financial guarantees are required of the subdivider to assure that all improvements will be installed. Some cities require funds to be placed in escrow in financial institutions. This gives the community the option of calling on funds should the development not proceed as promised. Some communities require performance bonds. However, many communities have found that bonding penalizes the developer and that when problems do occur the community incurs a penalty for trying to collect on the bond. Seldom do bond companies pay off without a fight, and seldom do they pay off entirely on the bond. All of this uses up time, money, and energy. Thus, many communities are using a financial guarantee from the financial institution providing funds for the development. This costs the developer nothing. These financial guarantees should be released only on approval of the public agency.

Environmental impact statements

Environmental impact statements are being required with increasing frequency for proposed subdivisions. Ideally, these can be included within the subdivision process itself; if necessary, the particular requirements of an environmental impact statement should be included in the subdivision code. The approach to the environmental impact statement process; the material to be supplied; and the areas to be covered, such as water, geology, slopes, vegetation, historical features, wildlife, visual impact, community impact, utility systems, public services, land use, housing, circulation system, etc., should be included at this time. Some communities have found that the checklist approach, or the "decision tree," which permits a developer to identify problem areas and only supply detailed information on those areas, is a desirable approach.

Definitions

If definitions have not been covered in earlier sections of the code, they should be included at this time. These should be held to a minimum because throughout the code terms should be explained as they are introduced.

Variances

An administrative section on variances for unusual conditions or for planned unit developments (PUDs) should be included at this point. The submittal requirements for PUDs and for subdivisions should be identical so that there is not a requirement on the part of the developer to provide different information for each. By simplifying the process so that a developer may obtain a PUD and subdivision review at the same time, the community can provide the incentive to encourage a developer to use this route.

Economic hardship should not be a valid consideration for variance. It is the

---

Planned unit development The planned unit development is slightly different [from] cluster, although the basic principle is similar. Both seek a more flexible approach to permit development of large areas as a whole. Clustering usually is limited to residential development, permitting a higher density if the resulting open space is legally permanently open. The advantages of cluster are also characteristic of planned unit development. A further advantage comes from a design freedom which is not possible under single lot–single building consideration.

Planned unit development is a broader concept than cluster. It may apply to commercial and industrial as well as residential development areas. In some cases a mixture of uses—one or more residential types of residence plus commercial—is allowed. A major difference between planned unit development and cluster is that the specific conditions under which the development will be allowed are general in nature for planned unit development, and [are] frequently not applied until actual plans are proposed. In this case, much is left to the discretion of the administrator, the review board, or other controlling authority.

Administrative discretion seems to be one of the larger problems of planned unit development. The real problem is recognition of and a framework for relating planned development and comprehensive planning.

The planned unit development has three major characteristics:

1. Planned unit developments usually involve areas and undertakings of large scale, ranging from campus type developments planned as a whole to new towns.
2. They usually involve a mixture of uses and types. The single use or type falls more into the class of the more usual subdivision.
3. They usually involve stage-by-stage development over a relatively long period of time during which buildings, arrangements, and uses may have to be replanned to meet the changes of requirements, technology, financing, or even concepts.

Source: Excerpted from Joseph De Chiara and Lee Koppelman, *Urban Planning and Design Criteria,* 2nd ed. (New York: Van Nostrand Reinhold, 1975), p. 221.

---

obligation of the purchaser to obtain property at a price that reflects its usability. The practice of pleading hardship has frequently been used to convert a marginal investment into a profit.

Administrative provisions

These are the boiler plate items such as penalty clauses, interpretations of disclaimers, amendment procedures, public hearing procedures, severability clause, variances, and resubdivision procedures. Variances should be very tightly worded so as to avoid abuse.

Appendices

Examples of what is desired in graphic form or standardized wording that can save everyone time in explanation should be included in an appendix or appendices. Some of these items might be the following:

1. Dedication statements for inclusion on the final plat
2. Reservation agreements for public land
3. Owners' signature blocks
4. Engineers' and surveyors' signature blocks
5. Public officials' signature blocks

6. Wording for any improvement or landscaping agreements
7. Financial letters of agreement for installation of improvements and landscaping
8. Street design elements, graphics on cross sections, intersections, cul-de-sac alternative designs, and other rights-of-way "do and don't" examples
9. Acceptable street trees if required
10. Examples of sketch plans, preliminary plats, and final plats.

Design policies expressed in pictures or drawings help bridge the gap between the public's desires and expectations and the developer. Such illustrations should be included in any code.

New trends in subdivision regulation

This chapter has proposed that we use subdivision regulations so as to obtain better site planning. Beginning with an overview of the concerns in subdivision regulation, the chapter goes on to discuss, in detail, the context and the contents of subdivision regulations, with an emphasis on the preparation of regulations. New ways of looking at such regulations are emerging, and some of these have been mentioned earlier in the chapter. A more detailed discussion of these trends is given here.

A common complaint of the building industry is that codes such as subdivision regulations are inflexible. Some groups are asking for new regulations or ways to use our regulations to manage growth. Few are satisfied with past performance. Factors such as these have combined to produce the new trends mentioned above, which are reviewed briefly immediately below.

State involvement

A number of states now mandate that local governments adopt and enforce subdivision regulations. They may either adopt their own set of regulations or use a model drafted by the state.

States are increasingly requiring some form of protection for critical natural areas such as wetlands, shorelands, avalanche areas, geologically unstable areas, and mineral deposits. A major impetus for this approach on the part of the states came from the American Law Institute's *Model Land Development Code*.[10]

States are requiring proof of water and sewer facilities before subdivisions are approved. Previously, large acreage could be subdivided and sold for development for which buyers had to find their own services. Water can be 300 feet down and can be so hard as to be unusable. Colorado, Arizona, New Mexico, and other western states have numerous former ranches that were subdivided and sold to unsuspecting buyers for retirement or second home purposes without water. Many of these developments were of the $1 down and $1 a week variety, in which the buyer would frequently default and the lot could be sold again. Federal and state real estate laws have made considerable headway in stopping such practices. But the scars of rough cut roads in the mountains and high valleys of the West bear witness to these practices. The simple requirement of having to prove an adequate water supply before gaining subdivision approval is a major deterrent to this type of development.

Timing or phasing of development

Counties in particular have begun to use subdivision and zoning approvals as a way of controlling premature development. Approval of requests for premature development is being based on an ability to serve. As density increases, so do service demands. Water, sewer, safety (police and fire), road maintenance, snow removal, school busing, power, and trash removal are some of the demands that increase with population growth. These items are all reflected in budget demands. As this awareness has crept into the thinking of local government officials, so too has a reluctance to approve scattered developments.

Many cities are also aware of this problem and are now measuring the social, environmental, and fiscal impacts of a proposed development before accepting annexation requests. Longmont, Colorado, has employed a systematic approach to weighing the costs of a new subdivision being added to its urbanized area. It has defined in its plan a service area in which the costs to the city are lowest. To amend the Prime Urbanized Area (PUA) in order to make additional areas available for subdivision, the costs of providing water, sewer, electrical, fire protection, schools, parks, and storm drainage services are measured against the revenues generated by the development. The amount of vacant land available in the PUA is also considered, to ascertain that there is a choice available for developers. Obviously, such a system favors those areas in which services already exist or in which topography provides opportunities for low cost expansion of the systems. This is not too different from the controlled growth concept of Ramapo, New York.

Growth paying its own way

Increasingly, communities are attempting to pass the costs of new development back to the new occupants. Water, sewer, parks, streets, drainage, and in some areas school land, are all being required. Off-site improvements that are necessary for a development to occur are also being tried (bridges, major arterial or government cost fees). The concept is one of a corporation, and the newcomer is buying stock in an existing plant. The former popular approach of selling community backed bonds to fund public improvements and then counting on growth to increase the base and thus hold down the rates is being questioned. Existing residents are objecting to the constant raising of user charges. Growth cycles have left some communities with major deficits which have had to be made up when the broader base failed to be realized. Growth on the communities' terms is becoming a more acceptable approach.

When a community follows this concept it must be careful to provide support and, if need be, subsidy for low income housing. Like other concepts, this concept can be abused and used for purposes of exclusion.

Single development control

The idea of continuing development controls in a single code has been discussed for many years. Some communities have taken a step in this direction by codifying with a single set of definitions, hearing procedures, administrative provisions, and processing steps. But they have stopped short of one technique that requires the developer to go through all phases of approval at one time, from zoning (use and density), to subdivision (site plan), to building permit (specific building and development plans for a lot, including landscaping and other site improvements). Planned unit developments are, in fact, this approach. The idea of requiring all developments to go through planned unit development is still not accepted in this country. Predetermined regulations which apply indiscriminately to the land are still the approach used here. But as the incentives increase the planned unit development becomes more and more common. Properly administered, it should achieve the better site planning that we all hope for.

The concepts and ideas expressed in this chapter are intended to help provide for the reasonable control of development in urban and rural areas. Through creative planning and subdivision administration, perhaps, as Edmund Bacon has aptly challenged, our cities will be planned as "an act of will" rather than a "kind of grand accident."[11]

1 Kevin Lynch, *Site Planning,* 2nd ed. (Cambridge, Mass.: The M.I.T. Press, 1971), Preface to the First Edition.

2 Ibid., p. 1.

3 U.S., Congress, House, *Report of the National Commission on Urban Problems to the Congress and to the President of the United States: Building the American City,* H. Doc. 91–34, 91st Cong., 1st sess., 1968, p. 203.

4 These organizations include the following: American Planning Association (APA); American Society of Civil Engineers (ASCE); American Society of Landscape Architects (ASLA); Federal Housing Authority (FHA); International City Management Association (ICMA); National Association of Home Builders: U.S. Department of Housing and Urban Development (HUD); Urban Land Institute.

5 See: Randall W. Scott, David J. Brower, and Dallas D. Miner, eds., *Management & Control of Growth,* 3 vols. (Washington, D.C.: Urban Land Institute, 1975), vol. 2, pp. 7–13.

6 See: ibid., pp. 121–210.

7 See: State of Minnesota, *Metropolitan Land Planning Act,* 1976 New Laws, p. 239; Chapter 127.

8 Scott, Brower, and Miner, eds., *Management & Control of Growth,* vol. 1, p. 225.

9 *Metes and bounds* means *measures and directions.* Beginning at a given starting point, the distance (or measurement) in various directions is given and finally the return to the original point. The key is the accuracy of the original starting point. Trees, rocks, bodies of water, and other movable or moving points were often used. As years went by and the starting point was moved or demolished, the entire description of the parcel of land was lost. Similarly, the measurements might vary, which would lead to additional problems.

10 American Law Institute, *A Model Land Development Code,* complete text, adopted by the American Law Institute, May 21, 1975, with Reporter's Commentary (Philadelphia: American Law Institute, 1976).

11 Edmund N. Bacon, *Design of Cities* (New York: The Viking Press, 1974), p. 31, quoted in U.S., Congress, House, *Building the American City,* p. 495.

Zoning

Zoning—as conceived in the United States in the second decade of this century —is the division of a municipality (or county) into districts for the purpose of regulating the use of private land. These zones are shown on a map. Within each of these districts the text of the zoning ordinance specifies the permitted uses, the bulk of buildings, the required yards, the necessary off-street parking, and other prerequisites to obtaining permission to develop. The principal objective, in its simplest form, was to ensure that commercial and industrial development was segregated from residential areas. Although this concept has been subject to enormous stress over the last five decades, the basic structure of most zoning ordinances today retains the design found in those ancestors of the early 1920s.

This chapter first discusses the history and the legal basis of zoning. Zoning is then discussed in terms of its relationship to comprehensive planning and to subdivision regulations. Next, the chapter covers in detail the basic elements covered by zoning ordinances. Zoning as an administrative process is then discussed; the traditional system is covered first, and then the text turns to more recent innovative techniques, among them planned unit development. The final section of the chapter covers exclusionary zoning: the historic New Jersey cases are reviewed and the implications for current zoning are given. A brief conclusion underscores the changing trends in zoning.

Historical background and legal basis

Zoning had been preceded in the United States by scattered efforts on the part of communities to regulate the use of private land. Ordinances to control height in designated areas had been upheld; however, ordinances to regulate uses in specified blocks of a municipality had been less successful when challenged in the courts. Zoning, however, represented the first effort on the part of the public to regulate, in a comprehensive fashion, all private land. This idea, it is believed, came from the observations made in the early years of this century by a group of New Yorkers of the system employed in some German cities. In any event, New York adopted a zoning ordinance in 1916, and in the next decade comprehensive zoning swept across most of the larger cities and many of the suburbs of this country, aided by the promulgation in 1922 of the Standard State Zoning Enabling Act—a model—by the U.S. Department of Commerce.

Enabling legislation on the part of each state was essential. Zoning is an expression of the police power—the power to regulate activity by private persons for the health, safety, morals, and general welfare of the public; and that power, under our federal system, rests with the state legislatures. Municipalities enjoy no such authority except as it may be delegated to them by the states, either through express provisions in the state constitutions or through the adoption of legislation that "enables" municipalities to regulate the use of private land through zoning. In the 1920s many states adopted such legislation. That did not settle the legal status of zoning; rather, it opened the door to a host of difficult issues that could, under our system, be determined only by the courts.

The threshold question was whether such control over the use of private land, even when authorized by the state legislature, was valid as a constitutional matter. The Fourteenth Amendment to the Constitution provides that no person shall be deprived of his property without due process of law. In the years following the Civil War the U.S. Supreme Court had imbued this clause (originally probably intended to guarantee fair *procedure*) with a substantive content. State laws regulating various aspects of commerce were struck down because the judges believed the laws "went too far"—that is, the laws deprived the complainant of his or her property without due process. So, it was charged, did zoning regulations: no state could authorize a scheme of municipal regulation that prohibited uses of land that had never been regarded as nuisances. Zoning, in short, was said to violate the due process clause.

Figure 15–1   The juxtaposition of housing and steel mills in Bethlehem, Pennsylvania, in this 1930s photograph by Walker Evans, forcefully shows the incompatible uses that zoning can control.
These houses and mills were built long before zoning took effect in American cities.

In the 1920s lawsuits in a number of states attacked zoning on this basis, and, for the most part, they were unsuccessful. State courts, interpreting—as they do—the federal Constitution, generally upheld zoning. But the crucial test remained: what would the U.S. Supreme Court say about zoning and the Fourteenth Amendment? The issue was settled in *Village of Euclid* v. *Ambler Realty Co.*[1] A majority of the Court reversed a federal trial court and held that zoning —in principle—was a valid exercise of delegated police power. It was a very close thing. The Supreme Court took a rare action: it ordered, on its own motion, a rehearing. On reargument the Court benefited from an illuminating amicus brief written by Alfred Bettman, a member of the Cincinnati bar, distinguished for his contributions to the rationale behind zoning in its early days.

It has been said by someone who was close to the Court in those days that the majority decision, as it finally came out, was switched from *no* to *go* by a casual conversation between two justices.[2]

If zoning had barely surmounted its principal legal hurdle, this was the beginning, not the end, of the legal disputes. If zoning was valid in principle, this did not settle the question of whether a *particular* regulation as applied to a *specific* piece of property was valid.

Six years after *Euclid* the U.S. Supreme Court in *Nectow* v. *City of Cambridge*[3] ruled that a regulation which limited a parcel of property to residential use was, under the circumstances, unreasonable—that is, invalid. For more than forty years after *Nectow* the Supreme Court did not touch zoning cases, but more than 10,000 reported zoning cases in the state courts from 1920 through 1970 illustrate the opportunities for dispute long after the principle of a matter is believed to be settled.

Standard zoning and planning enabling acts   For many years the Standard State Zoning Enabling Act prepared by the U.S. Department of Commerce in 1922 and the Standard City Planning Enabling Act prepared by the U.S. Department of Commerce in 1928 reflected with remarkable accuracy the existing state legislation regulating land development in almost all of the 50 states.

The planning act covered six subjects: (1) the organization and power of the plan commission . . . ; (2) the content of the master plan . . . ; (3) provision for adoption by the governing body of a master street plan for the community and the control thereafter of private building in the bed of mapped but unopened streets and of public building in unofficial or unapproved streets; (4) provision for approval . . . of all public improvements; (5) control of private subdivision of land . . . ; (6) provision for the establishment of a region, for the making of a plan for the region and for adoption of the regional plan by any municipality in the region that desired to do so.

The zoning act authorized the classes of local governments specified by the enacting state to control the height, area, bulk, location, and use of buildings and premises. The major characteristic of this model was the authorization given to a local government to divide its territory into zones or districts with uniform regulation throughout the district but with different regulations for each district.

Source: Excerpted from American Law Institute, *A Model Land Development Code,* complete text adopted by the American Law Institute, May 21, 1975, with Reporter's Commentary (Washington, D.C.: American Law Institute, 1976), p. 1.

The fact that zoning law was made at the state level has meant that there has been a significant variation from state to state on just how far a municipality can go in regulating the use of land, a circumstance documented in Norman Williams's monumental five volume work, *American Land Planning Law.*[4]

In addition there have been historical trends in the judicial balancing between the regulatory goals of the municipality and the aspirations of the landowner. In the early decades, possibly down to the early 1950s, more often than not the municipal ordinance, when challenged in its particular application, was struck down. The courts tended to take the side of the property owner. In the following fifteen to twenty years, at least up to 1970, there was a notable swing on the part of the judiciary to a growing sympathy with municipal regulation. It has been only since about 1970 that once again there are signs of increasing judicial suspicion of municipal regulation of private land, but not—as is noted later—for the same property-oriented reasons so apparent in the opinions in the early decades of zoning.

The legal scene in zoning has also been confused by the skill of municipalities in inventing new regulatory devices—schemes of regulation not imagined when the first ordinances were drafted. These have ranged from architectural controls to the mandatory spacing of adult entertainment establishments, and they have embraced a variety of discretionary techniques under which a landowner or developer, instead of knowing precisely what he or she could or could not do, had to negotiate with the municipality every detail of his or her development proposal. Each of these devices was bound to be litigated. It is, indeed, little wonder that zoning disputes continue to crowd the reported decisions.

Relationship to comprehensive planning

Section 3 of the model Standard State Zoning Enabling Act of 1922 provided that the zoning ordinance shall be prepared "in accordance with a comprehensive plan." Zoning enabling acts, when first enacted in most states, contained a similar clause. The notes left by the drafters of the Standard Zoning Enabling Act are not of much help in construing that ambiguous phrase, and for many years it was given little attention by either courts or commentators. This is not surprising in view of the distance in this country historically between zoning regulation and planning. (It was not until 1928, six years after the Standard Zoning Enabling Act, that the U.S. Department of Commerce issued a Standard City Planning Enabling Act.)

By and large, for four decades most municipalities and counties enacted and revised zoning ordinances with little attention to their relationship to a comprehensive planning process, however that phrase might be construed. The adoption of a zoning ordinance was usually preceded by an inventory of the existing use of land which was marked on a map. Boundaries of zoning districts then were drawn on the basis of the recommendations of a consultant, the "gut feelings" of the local decision makers, and the political pressures in the community.

Population projections, transportation policies, and capital improvements programs were hardly of concern to municipal legislators who wished to keep gas stations out of residential areas and apartments out of single family districts. If a plan was thought of, more often than not it consisted of a map of blobs vaguely suggesting how the community should look in twenty-five years. Once drawn, such a "plan" was tacked on a wall and was forgotten while the local plan commission and city council went about the pressing business of acting upon innumerable requests for changes in the zoning map.

The courts were not of much help in bridging the traditional gap between zoning and planning. In the few instances in which a litigant suggested that the state enabling act mandated that the local ordinance be based on a comprehensive plan, the courts held that all that was required was that the ordinance be comprehensive: in short, the ordinance was the plan.

The use of zoning as one tool to implement a series of articulated policies on growth was largely ignored. Of course, zoning was making planning policy of a sort. Each time a zoning change was granted or denied, unconscious policy was being made. Without a conscious planning policy such decisions were, more often than not, bound to be inconsistent, and were often unfair between applicants. The result was an accumulation of ad hoc regulatory decisions that bore little resemblance to serious planning.

There is some evidence that this helter-skelter condition is now changing. For one, state legislatures since about 1970 have begun to put some flesh on the old clause "in accordance with a comprehensive plan." In California, for example, the legislature has specified the content of a comprehensive plan, including open space, transportation policy, and a housing element.[5] Also, a number of states have clearly indicated that comprehensive planning and the zoning ordinance are not the same and that the latter must be based on and be consistent with the planning policies. Thus, in Arizona, the following is indicated:

Each planning agency shall prepare and the legislative body of each municipality shall adopt a comprehensive, long-range general plan for the development of the municipality.[6]

Then, in a separate section, the Arizona statutes provide the following:

All ordinances or regulations adopted under this article shall be consistent with the adopted general and specific plans of the municipality, if any, as adopted under Article 6.[7]

Some states have gone so far as to mandate communities to prepare plans. Florida laws, for example, state that "on or before July 1, 1979, each county and each municipality in this state shall prepare and adopt a comprehensive plan."[8]

And a few states have stated that zoning is permissible only after a planning process has been undertaken. In Kentucky the following prevails:

Cities and counties which are members of a planning unit which has adopted at least the objectives of the land use plan elements may divide the territory within the area of their jurisdiction into zones.[9]

Some courts have also come to see a necessary correlation between planning and zoning, perhaps not so much because the courts view planning as a useful exercise to benefit the community but rather because the bench sees planning as a way of mitigating the unfairness that they have perceived in the zoning process.

One of the most frequently quoted judicial statements is in an opinion of the New York Court of Appeals:

The comprehensive plan is the essence of zoning. Without it there can be no rational allocation of land use. It is the insurance that the public welfare is being served and that zoning does not become nothing more [*sic*] than just a Gallup poll.[10]

More recently an Illinois appellate court made the following observation:

We are constrained to agree that *the failure of Cook County to plan comprehensively* for the use and development of land in its unincorporated areas, and its failure to relate its rezoning decisions to data files and plans of other related county agencies, *weaken the presumption of validity which otherwise would attach to a county zoning ordinance.*[11]

In a famous Oregon case the supreme court of that state observed:

Although we are aware of the analytical distinction between zoning and planning, it is clear that under our statutes the plan adopted by the planning commission and the zoning ordinances enacted by the county governing body are closely related; both are intended to be parts of a single integrated procedure for land use control. The plan embodies policy determinations and guiding principles; the zoning ordinances provide the detailed means of giving effect to those principles.[12]

It is reasonable to predict that with the push from the legislatures and the shove from the courts, more and more local public decision makers will begin to understand the necessary correlation between planning and zoning. This leaves unanswered the question of the relationship between those local plans and regional or statewide interests, a matter treated only briefly in this chapter but developed more intensively in Volume 2.

Relationship to subdivision regulations

It is sometimes said that while zoning generally treats of locational factors—where and how a particular private structure or use may be established—subdivision regulations concern themselves with the provision for and design of public facilities such as streets and sewers, and the layout and division of the site so as to provide protection against flooding and erosion and to ensure consistency with the development of adjacent land with respect to public facilities. Subdivision regulations also have an added purpose: to provide an orderly and simple method for effecting and recording the transfer of title to land.

This is not to say that the line between the function of zoning and that of subdivision controls is always clear. Zoning regulations deal with required lot sizes in various districts and subdivision approval usually involves the design and size of lots. Modern zoning ordinances often require a site plan review of major developments, a practice that is reminiscent of customary subdivision regulations. Some cities have adopted separate plan review ordinances. The increased use in zoning ordinances of the concept of planned unit development—a technique for the grant of development permission that departs from the customary zoning regulations—involves public review of a congeries of standards that combine both traditional zoning controls (use and bulk) and subdivision controls (street design and other public facilities). Indeed, the confusion between zoning regulations and subdivision regulations is illustrated by the risk the developer frequently runs who proposes a planned unit development. The developer may have to proceed on two local administrative tracks: zoning permission and subdivision permission. This confusion will not be resolved until a single local process for development permission is established.

Figure 15–2 Single family house as perceived by the zoning inspector.

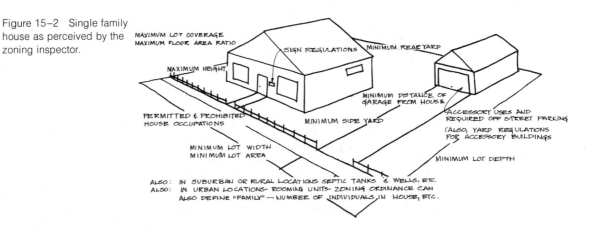

It is illuminating to note that subdivision regulations have encountered far less challenge in the courts than have zoning regulations. In part, this is explained because zoning is concerned with use, and use—more than the design of streets—determines land value for the landowner and most agitates those who live in the neighborhood.

Subdivision regulations have been the basis for one type of municipal regulation that has generated substantial litigation. That is the practice of requiring, as a condition of approval, that the developer–applicant agree to dedicate land for schools or parks or to make payments in lieu of dedication—which payments would be used by the community to provide such public facilities. Most courts have sustained municipal requirements of dedications or payments in lieu. These costs will, of course, be passed on to the buyers by the developer, which suggests to some commentators that those buyers are paying a double tax—that imposed on all residents of the municipality and the special cost imposed on and passed on by their seller.

Basic elements and concepts of zoning

As may be evident from what has been said thus far, a zoning ordinance consists of a text and a map or a series of maps. The text gives the substantive standards applicable to each district on the map and the procedures that govern proposals for changes in both the text and the map. The provisions of the text mean nothing to a landowner unless the landowner knows how his or her land is classified on the map. Only by checking the map can the landowner know which sections of the text of the ordinance are applicable to his or her property.

Land use districts

In light of what has taken place in zoning in the last fifty years, it is worth noting that the first New York City zoning ordinance did not separate multifamily housing from single family housing. In the following decades no feature of zoning has remained so constant as the insulation by law of the single family detached dwelling from other types of housing. There is a multiplicity of reasons for this enduring character. Some of these reasons are related to the impact of greater densities on available public facilities, but the survival of this feature is due to the pervasive belief in this country that the single family detached dwelling deserves a protection from intrusion by other types of dwellings. The wry observation of a New Jersey court twenty years ago is not absent from public attitudes today, namely: "Apartment houses are not necessarily benign."[13]

Most zoning ordinances contain a series of residential zones—as many as a dozen in some cases—based on dwelling type, permitted density, and minimum lot sizes. (A few ordinances even distinguish among single family residential zones by house size, although this practice has come under increasing criticism from courts and commentators.) A variety of residential districts may be created, each distinguished primarily by the required minimum lot size. These lot sizes may go from a minimum of five or ten acre lots in exurban communities to 2,500 square foot lot sizes in older, more crowded cities. There will be a variety of intermediate sizes between these extremes. Minimum frontage and side and rear yards will vary accordingly. Moving up or down the scale, ordinances will also distinguish between types of multifamily zones. In one zone only single family dwelling units and duplexes will be permitted while in the next zone a larger number of dwelling units will be permitted per acre. In the ordinances of larger cities it is not unusual to find a variety of residential zones, from those permitting only a single family detached dwelling on each lot to a district where seventy dwelling units are permitted on each acre. These seemingly simple distinctions among residential districts are often interlarded with more sophisticated regulations such as those which classify residential districts not by residential type but solely by permitted densities.

Among commercial zones the early and simple classifications have also given way to a multiplicity of classifications as public decision makers and their planning consultants or staffs have perceived distinctions among commercial uses in their impact on the public interest. The past twenty years have witnessed such finely drawn distinctions as *neighborhood business, highway-oriented, central business,* and *warehouse-heavy commercial.* No one, by the way, has really solved the bugaboo of many cities—the old linear or strip commercial area, that remnant of the age of the streetcar, which is deteriorating and is packed with vacancies. This is one of the most poignant examples of the limits of zoning: a commercial classification in a zoning ordinance means little unless the market is there.

One of the most striking changes in zoning practice over the past two decades is the attitude toward the relationship between the various zones. The early ordinances generally allowed all uses permitted in the residential districts to be permitted in the commercial zones; and all uses permitted in the commercial zones were permitted in the industrial zones. This cumulative or "pour over" policy reflected the view that zoning was designed to protect the single family house from other uses, and if someone were fool enough to choose to build a house in a business or industrial district that was his own business.

More recently the conviction has grown that there is no "higher" and "lower" classification of uses; each use is entitled to be protected from threats

Figure 15–3 Increasingly, zoning was used after World War II to separate residential, commercial, industrial, and institutional land uses, as can be seen in this postwar residential suburban development.

to its security from the introduction of other uses. (Chambers of Commerce, for example, have concluded that allowing residences to enter industrial zones would not only encourage subdivisions that would make difficult the assembly of land for industrial development, but could also create a potential for complaints that would discourage industrial development.) From this the notion arose that each district was to be exclusive and of equal importance, a conviction that still remains but is already being modified in the face of new living styles and market demands.

Today the following question is being asked: Why, with modern technology, cannot residences, shops, and offices be located in the same building, particularly in the central business districts of our larger cities? And so we are observing the development of "vertical zones" in which, as in the case of Water Tower Place on North Michigan Avenue in Chicago, shops on the ground floor are topped by offices which, in turn, are capped by floors of condominiums. From cumulative zones, to exclusive zones, to mixed use zones—zoning has displayed a capacity to adjust to changes in the market.

Performance standards

The uncertainty and apparent vacillation that have been found in attitudes toward the rightness of segregation and the mixing of uses have reflected two de-

Provisions for site plan review and approval   A. The Planning Board shall approve a preliminary or final site plan unless it makes one or more of the following written findings with respect to the proposed development:

1. The provisions for vehicular loading and unloading and parking, and for vehicular and pedestrian circulation on the site and onto adjacent public streets and ways will create hazards to safety, or will impose a significant burden upon public facilities which could be avoided by modifications in the plan.
2. The bulk, location and height of proposed buildings and structures and the proposed uses thereof will be detrimental or injurious to other private development in the neighborhood or will impose undue burdens on the public facilities, and development of the site is feasible in a manner that will avoid these detrimental and injurious results.
3. The provisions for on-site landscaping do not provide adequate protection to neighboring properties from detrimental features of the development that could be avoided by adequate landscaping.
4. The site plan fails to provide for the soil and drainage problems that development will give rise to and it is feasible to prepare a site plan that will avoid drainage and soil problems.
5. The provisions for exterior lighting create undue hazards to motorists traveling on adjacent public streets or are inadequate for the safety of occupants or users of the site or such provisions will damage the value and diminish the usability of adjacent properties.
6. An applicant for site plan approval in conjunction with a zoning amend-

ment has failed to provide reasonable evidence of his financial capability to complete the development as planned.
7. The proposed development will impose an undue burden upon off-site sewer, water and streets, which conclusion shall be based upon a written report of the Department of Public Works on file with the Planning Board, a copy of which shall be provided the applicant, and the applicant has not submitted a reasonable alternative to relieve such burden.
8. The proposed development will create undue fire safety hazards by not providing adequate access to the site, or to the buildings on the site, for emergency vehicles. Such a conclusion shall be based upon a written report of the Fire Department on file with the Planning Board.
9. In cases where a preliminary plan has been approved, there is a substantial change in the final site plan from the approved preliminary site plan [and] such substantial change will have an adverse effect on public services, adjacent properties, or will not meet the standards provided by this Section VI.

B. All findings by the Planning Board shall be accompanied by written statements that set forth with particularity the precise reasons why the finding was made and how the deficiency could be resolved or that it is incapable of solution consistent with the applicant's objectives. Any finding that does not include such a statement shall not be entitled to a presumption of validity in any appeal from a decision of the Planning Board.

Source: Excerpted from Site Plan Ordinance, Portland, Maine.

velopments. One was an awareness that since the 1920s there had been an improvement in technology that made out-of-date old assumptions on the nuisance qualities of some commercial uses. The other development was a growing sophistication in public control over the external impacts of commercial operations that rendered obsolete old views on the offensive characteristics of some uses. A butcher shop need no longer entice rodents and flies; a paint and varnish factory could, if the owner were willing, operate without excessive odors.

The zoning literature in the 1950s suggested that the permitted uses in "light" and "heavy" industrial zones should no longer be determined by the assumed general characteristics of the particular industry, thereby relegating to the heavy industrial zone a list of necessary pariahs, beginning with *abbatoir* and ending, somewhat redundantly, with *rendering plant*. Instead it was proposed that the industrial zones be classified not by a list of uses but by performance standards: that is, by the ability of an enterprise to meet designated external characteristics. These included standards for noise, particulate matter, vibrations, glare, and fire hazard. The standards were more stringent in the light industrial zone and less severe in the heavy industrial zone. If, for example, the XYZ Paint Corporation were willing to make the investment in afterburners and other equipment designed to cut down noxious odors and particulate matter it could build in the less restrictive industrial area; its more offending competitor would be relegated to the heavy industrial zone. "It's not what you do, it's the way that you do it," became the catchword of industrial performance standards.

This was a sensible idea, but many smaller communities adopted industrial performance standards without realizing that the use of performance standards often required more costly instruments and more sophisticated staff than was available. In recent years the introduction of state and federal regulations over air and water quality has lessened the need for performance standards for industrial uses in municipal ordinances. It has come to be recognized that many offensive characteristics of industrial operations require a regulatory system that goes beyond municipal boundaries because the potential for pollution does not halt at the city's edge.

A spin-off from industrial performance standards has been the attempt in some municipal ordinances to measure the environmental impact of any large scale development and to grant or deny development permission on the basis of that impact. This has been most evident in California where the state environmental protection act has been held by the state supreme court to require an environmental impact assessment for private as well as public projects.[14]

In Minnesota, if neighbors are upset by a rezoning grant by the city council, 500 signatures on a petition are all that is needed to trigger a determination by a state agency on whether the proposed development requires a full scale environmental impact review by the state. In some communities development permission will depend on such arcane measurements as the k factor, a function of slope and soil quality. The growing interest in the use of solar energy as an energy conservation measure will undoubtedly generate new environmental standards in the name of protecting access to solar light.

The tendency of zoning to embrace the latest, and the tendency of the latest to be inserted in the zoning ordinance (for lack of a better place to put it), suggest that this fifty year old legal system is once again about to embark on an uncharted voyage. The environmental trip may be even more perilous than those that preceded it because the environmental standards are so often incapable of quantification and so full—to the lay administrator—of seemingly incomprehensible jargon. After all, it is one thing to have two land appraisers disagree about the dollar impact of a high rise on adjacent single family houses—but what do we make of two limnologists arguing the impact of two parts per billion of carbon tetrachloride on a water supply?

Density and bulk controls

Density and height have been almost as significant a purpose of zoning as use. Indeed, height regulations were established and upheld a decade before comprehensive zoning ordinances became popular. The proposed location of a high rise apartment next to a single family subdivision often caused as much (if not more) of an outcry as would a suggestion that a shopping center go up next door. From the beginning, zoning has segregated by density and height; indeed, in recent years, height controls have achieved even greater importance in the regulatory pantheon because of concern over the restriction upon views of scenic areas. (The voters in San Diego, concerned over the city council's liberality in allowing high rise developments along the ocean, imposed a height ceiling by referendum. The restriction is now in the charter where it cannot be touched by the city council.)

Closely related to density and height are equally traditional regulations over the coverage of land by buildings. This has manifested itself not only in maximum allowable lot coverage but more ubiquitously in requirements for front, side, and rear yards which may be occasion for teasing in the learned journals ("cookie cutter subdivisions") but has a place close to the house buying public's heart that has not diminished in fifty years. While there is talk of "zero lot line" zoning—a concept that proposes to do away with the alleged waste inherent in the required front yard—there is little evidence that such a new style is catching on.

An innovation of the last two decades has been the introduction of floor area ratio (FAR), a method for relating building bulk to lot area while giving the developer or architect some freedom from traditional controls over height and setbacks. If the applicable regulations allow, for example, a FAR of 2.0, a two story building may be constructed covering the entire lot, or a four story building may be built covering one-half the lot area, or any design mix may be proposed as long as the total floor area is not in excess of 200 percent of the total lot area. (The FAR may be subject to yard requirements that affect total lot coverage.)

Parking and off-street loading

All but the most rudimentary zoning ordinances impose minimum requirements for off-street parking and loading. There is not much one can say about off-street loading except that it is a necessary piece of zoning baggage in commercial and industrial zones that does not excite much attention unless overlooked, in which case its omission will result in a nasty traffic problem and, if the offending establishment abuts on a residential zone, will produce vehement protests from neighbors.

Parking requirements are a bit more delicate. Except in the single family districts, where it is assumed the driveway will take care of the overflow from the garage, the issue of how many parking spaces shall be required per dwelling unit can generate disagreement, particularly where the developer is not prepared to spend the money to construct a parking facility or put parking underground. Standards vary, sometimes from as low as one parking space per unit to as high as two and one-half spaces per unit.

Occasionally, ordinances will permit parking areas to be off site within a specified distance, and ordinances may permit required parking to locate in an adjacent and different zoning district where the use itself would not be permitted. Frequently, ordinances will permit a common parking area for two different uses, for example, a store and a church, on the theory that they will be complementary in their employment of the facility. The parking needs of churches are a source of considerable annoyance to neighbors, which may explain, in part, why more and more churches are rebuilding on the outskirts of towns and villages where more land is available and they can, at a more reasonable cost, meet the parking requirements of the local zoning ordinance.

One of the notable twists in zoning policy in recent years has been the turnabout in parking requirements in central business districts. Until the mid-1970s off-street parking was commonly required in downtown buildings; more recent ordinances do not require off-street parking in the central business district, nor, in fact, do they prohibit it. This is a function of the desire to encourage mass transit and the role of the city as an entrepreneur in the operation of parking garages.

Signs

An entire chapter could be written on the history of the effort to regulate signs, and some of it would be quite funny. The tale of the attempt to build a rationale for control over the location of billboards goes from early claims—offered with a straight face—that they were hiding places for fornication and lurking highwaymen to more modern views that they are just downright offensive and therefore may be severely controlled if not eliminated. Billboard regulation also has its serious side. The political and economic forces behind the billboard industry are not inconsequential. Serious restrictions can affect some jobs, and attempts to regulate billboards too severely may threaten long-standing political–commercial relationships. Suggestions for regulating billboards have run from total outlawing, to mandatory clustering, to mandatory spacing. One may find almost anything one wishes to find in the zoning regulations for signs across the country.

Billboards are not, of course, the only issue regarding signs. Business signs are often a necessary service to the potential customer, and a well-designed business sign may not only serve commerce but may also improve the ambience of a commercial area. Zoning ordinances do distinguish between business and advertising signs. Most ordinances deal with the size, height, and location on the building of signs, and many ordinances regulate or prohibit flashing and moving signs. Few if any ordinances try to control the message on signs other than in residential neighborhoods where severe restrictions generally limit signs to small sizes intended to advertise the sale of a house or, when permitted, a professional office.

Signs are the most frequent object of zoning provisions that are designed to gradually eliminate (amortize) nonconforming uses, a subject discussed later.

Occasionally, sign regulation is treated separately from the zoning ordinance.

Accessory uses and home occupations

A house in a single family residential district is a principal use; a garage on the same lot would be an accessory use. An industrial plant in a manufacturing district is a principal use; the dwelling of its caretaker or security guard would be an accessory use. These are examples of accessory uses, but in some ordinances swimming pools, horse barns, and a variety of uses long identified as tributary to the principal use are permitted in the same district as the principal use. Probably the most significant purpose of the term *accessory use* is to make clear the fact that it would not be permitted in the district without the principal use to which it is an appendage. In some zoning ordinances it is forbidden to build a garage until the residence is constructed, apparently because of a concern that someone might build a garage and decide to convert it to a house rather than building the dwelling itself.

A good deal of zoning lore has grown up around home occupations. They are an exception to the protection from commercial intrusion into the single family residential district, and the concept goes back to the earliest days of zoning. Undoubtedly, when zoning was first introduced it was recognized that many residential neighborhoods were larded with piano teachers, insurance salesmen operating out of their houses, and a hairdresser or two. It was concluded that as long as the establishment still looked like a house and the occupation remained modest in scope there was little threat to the residential character of the neighborhood. Also, the small income generated by a home occupation might be the only way to keep the house from having to be sold to someone who would try to convert it into a duplex or a boardinghouse.

Thus, the notion of limited commercial uses known as home occupations came to be accepted, and each municipality had heated debate over where to draw the line. Should the occupant be permitted or forbidden to have an employee who was not a member of the family? Or to operate any equipment not customarily found in a house? Or to advertise in the newspapers? Zoning ordinances impose a variety of regulations on "home occupations."

In an age when zoning ordinances often read like the more abstruse sections of the Internal Revenue Code, one can always turn to the definitions section and find a paragraph on "home occupations," a comforting reminder of the good old days.

Nonconformities

The early proponents of zoning were troubled by one inevitable consequence of laying a rational zoning map down on a community that was already substantially developed. The zoning districts threatened to look like Joseph's coat, as there were preexisting uses and structures within districts that did not conform to the new regulations. What should be done with them? They could be condemned and torn down—an alternative authorized in Minnesota but rarely used because of the obvious expense and some doubts as to whether such a taking would meet the "public purpose" test. They could be allowed to carry on as though there were no zoning—a sort of grandfather clause. This seemed distasteful because their expansion or increase in intensity would threaten the stability of the neighborhood that the ordinance was designed to protect.

The logical compromise was to allow these nonconforming uses and structures to remain but to circumscribe them with restrictions on expansion, to prohibit change to another nonconforming purpose and, if they were abandoned, to prevent their reopening, or should they by chance be substantially destroyed, to prevent their reconstruction or reuse except in a manner and for a purpose permitted in the district in which they were located. (This solution gave the nonconformity a certain element of monopoly, at least in a limited market—a point advanced by the opponents of zoning in one early lawsuit.)[15] The theory was that the nonconformity, hedged in as it was by restrictions, would eventually disappear. There are probably few if any reliable statistics to demonstrate that this has been the fate of nonconforming uses and other nonconformities. It is just as likely that existing nonconformities have been the excuse offered by those seeking to introduce similar developments in a neighborhood.

There is one serious legal aspect to nonconformities. The boundary lines of zoning districts must take care not to create too many nonconformities. If, for example, 70 percent of the dwellings in a single family district turn out to be duplexes, a property owner who wishes to convert his or her house into a duplex may successfully challenge the single family classification. Each time a comprehensive amendment is made to a zoning ordinance which involves a complete rewriting of the text and a redraw of district boundaries, the problem of the creation of new or additional nonconformities will arise. Substantial pressures will be exerted on the city council to leave the map as it has been; if the council does not, court challenges will undoubtedly follow.

It should be added here that a rezoning of vacant land to a more restrictive classification is not the same as the creation of a nonconforming use or other nonconformity. The practice of down-zoning has been widely followed in recent years by municipalities in an effort to correct years of overzoning for commercial or multiple family use. Parenthetically, it should be noted that there is a widespread and misplaced belief by lay persons, as well as by some lawyers who should know better, that once a vacant parcel is given a zoning classification it can never be reclassified to impose greater restrictions on development. There is no vested right in the continued enjoyment of a zoning classification unless the developer has undertaken actual improvement and often only after he or she has received a building permit.

The failure of nonconformities to disappear has led some communities to insert provisions in their ordinances to provide for the gradual amortization of nonconforming uses without compensation. For example, all nonconforming signs might be required to be removed in two or three years, all nonconforming junk yards or gas stations in four or five years, and all nonresidential buildings nonconforming because of bulk within one or two decades. Sometimes the time period is staggered depending on the assessed value of the structure. If the nonconformity is a use in an otherwise conforming building (such as a barbershop in a duplex building), the time span may be short.

Amortization has received a mixed reception in the courts, but generally this type of regulation has been sustained, particularly where the use is not very popular and the investment is not great. More often the problem with amortization provisions is that they have not been enforced; they remain unnoticed on the books—a testament to the enthusiasm of the drafters and a reminder of the reluctance of the administrators.

One final word about nonconformities is that they come in various shapes and sizes. Too often, it is customary to refer to this feature of zoning as *nonconforming uses*. There are in fact three types of nonconformities. There are nonconforming *uses* such as a liquor store in a three story walk-up located in a zone classified for apartments. There are nonconforming *structures* such as the single family house in a single family district which intrudes into the yard space that would be required if the house were to be built today. Finally, there is the nonconforming *lot,* that lot subdivided before the ordinance was adopted that has a smaller area than would now be required under the regulations applicable in the zoning district in which it is located. This last nonconformity is one of the most troublesome; the law generally requires that the owner of such a "substandard" recorded lot be permitted to build on it unless he or she happens to own an adjoining vacant lot or unless he or she created the nonconformity by conveying a part of the lot to a neighbor after the ordinance became effective.

Aesthetics

In the context of zoning regulations, *aesthetics* has usually meant controls over architectural design, the external appearance or shape of a building. No such purpose or objective was included in the purposes section of the early state enabling legislation at a time when such phrases as "avoidance of congestion in the streets" and "preservation of light and air" were representative of the public goals zoning was intended to advance. Except in such famous historical areas as the French Quarter in New Orleans and Beacon Hill in Boston, few cities sought to use the police power to impose design controls. *Aesthetics* was often a pejorative charge against various zoning regulations when a landowner wanted to protest a restriction and was hard put to find some other basis for attacking the offending regulation. To try to sustain a zoning regulation solely on the basis of aesthetics would have been a bold venture. Few courts in the early decades of zoning would have subscribed to Chief Judge Pound's dictum: "Beauty may not be queen but she is not an outcast beyond the pale of protection or respect. She may at least shelter herself under the wing of safety, morality or decency."[16] For the most part, the courts in the early and middle epochs of zoning developed a common response to such allegations: the fact that there might be aesthetic considerations behind the regulation did not render it invalid if there were other less dubious public purposes that would be furthered by the regulation.

For many years everyone concerned with defending zoning shied away from aesthetic considerations which is why, for example, a variety of implausible fictions were concocted to justify the severe regulation of billboards when everyone knew the real motive was that they were regarded as aesthetically distasteful.

Only in the past decade have some courts ventured to justify regulation solely on the basis of aesthetics. In one delightful case the New York Court of Appeals held that an ordinance prohibiting the hanging of washing in front yards was a valid regulation and based its decision on the conviction that the ordinance did no more than regulate that which "offends the sensibilities of the average man."[17]

Courts in other states have upheld architectural review boards which prohibited A-frame houses in a subdivision of ranch style houses and which subjected housing projects to review for exterior colors and roof styles. Even where there is no clear authority for such architectural review such regulations flourish, and for a very good reason: only the most obstreperous of builders or landowners want to spend the time and money to litigate an issue of design. If the municipality stands firm the applicant will usually accede to the design requirements even though the applicant suspects there is no lawful basis for the regulation. That is known as municipal leverage.

Architectural controls are widespread even among suburbs not known for their sensitivity to imaginative design. The same ordinance that mandates that all shops in the business district look like Tudor England may also require that every house in a residential block vary in some aspect of its design from other houses in the same block. These "look-alike" and "no-look-alike" ordinances may come in for their knocks from commentators, but they flourish.

A more serious aspect of aesthetics arises in our larger cities where nostalgia and a desire to preserve some evidence of our past have spread west across the Alleghenies and north up the Mississippi. No longer are efforts to protect a physical record of our urban past limited to late eighteenth century enclaves. Today, early twentieth century areas of Rochester, New York, and late nineteenth century blocks in Chicago are designated as subject to architectural review, which serves to remind us that time alone may turn the ordinary into the special, particularly if we have bulldozed most of the remnants of those earlier eras.

These special architectural districts are usually under the domain of a special review board which operates independently of the local planning commission. These boards are often (and with reason) made up of residents of the special area, which leads some developers to protest that the judge is also the prosecutor. It might be more equitable to treat such boards as advocates for a point of view and to provide that the plan commission or the city council finally balance the competing interests of developer and historical area protagonists.

Open space preservation

The desire to provide for and protect open space remains an abiding American dream, even in the closing years of the twentieth century. The United States was the first country to create large national and public parks that were not the private domain of princes of wealth or birth. Its major cities contain magnificent open areas that are testimonials to the ability of a capitalist democracy in the late nineteenth century to put amenity above profit—at least on occasion. And this interest—not solely sentimental—is evident in the struggle during the past twenty years to merge this regard for open space into a system of land use regulation when increasing land costs and greater municipal budgetary constraints have made the outright purchase of open land by the public more difficult.

Zoning was again called upon, and, again, the record is mixed.

During the 1950s a number of state courts upheld large lot zoning when persuaded that such regulations helped to preserve open space, without bothering to ask: Open space for whom? It went unnoticed that advocates of private open space often bitterly resisted proposals for regional parks out of a concern that outsiders would invade their exurban acres.

There was also the difficult task of articulating the purpose of preserving open space. Was the objective to protect prime agricultural land, to conserve sensitive ecologic areas, or to guide development in a more rational manner? Sometimes it became apparent that the police power was being stretched too far and the only lawful alternative was to condemn and pay for easements or the full fee title. And this has been done, in Suffolk County, New York, to protect the rich potato fields from being subdivided, or along the Delaware River to preserve magnificent scenic views. We occasionally need reminding that the police power—regulation—needs to be shored up with another sovereign power—the power to condemn.

It should be noted that many communities have strict regulations on development in floodplains, and in some communities there are severe controls over filling of marshlands and swamplands. Generally, recent court opinions have viewed such efforts with sympathy.[18]

Administration

After all the excitement has died down over an innovative substantive land use regulation, the heart of zoning boils down to how the local decision is made: How fair is the *process* by which permission to develop is granted or denied? For zoning is an administrative process which is unique, even given the vast proliferation of administrative agencies at all levels of government. The hallmark of zoning is the opportunity for individuals to petition for relief—to seek a change—from the general comprehensive zoning plan.

This has to be so, when the inevitability of change in the use of land is considered. Cornfields are proposed for residential subdivisions; old brownstones are sought to be demolished to make room for high rises; and a shopping center may soon be proposed on land zoned for industrial use. From the early decades of this century until today, American zoning ordinances have recognized the dynamics of land use. In response, zoning ordinances authorize, if not invite, in a manner and to an extent foreign to other municipal regulations, individual petitions for relief. There is no other system of municipal law in which the right to request a new set of rules for an individual is so dominant a feature. No building code permits a building owner to petition for relief from a requirement that all elevators have emergency brakes; no health code allows a restaurant owner to be exempt from minimum standards of cleanliness; no traffic code invites a driver to be given a "variance" to drive fifty miles an hour in a thirty-five miles an hour zone. Zoning, on the contrary, anticipates such petitions.

In addition, zoning, as an administrative process, is distributed among a multitude of local jurisdictions. Each municipality or county, within the broad limits established in the state enabling acts, fashions its own standards. In this way, zoning is in contrast to the laws that govern public utilities, or the laws that regulate the sale of securities which are statewide or embrace the entire nation. Finally, within each local jurisdiction there will be more than one agency empowered to make or influence decisions: namely, the plan commission, the board of adjustment and the city council or other local legislative body.

This disparate system, as might be expected, has come in for substantial criticism—for its casual practices and lack of a consistent administrative ethos. There is some recent evidence, however, that courts and state legislatures are seeking ways to eliminate the frequent chaos that was to be expected from such a fractured administrative process.

The traditional system

The agencies Historically, the responsibility for considering requests for changes in the applicable zoning rules was divided among three agencies: the municipal legislature, the plan commission, and the board of appeals (in some jurisdictions known as the board of adjustment). In some states a zoning commission is charged with preparing, for the consideration of the local legislature, an original zoning ordinance, and in most jurisdictions the issuance of building permits where a development meets applicable zoning laws and other municipal regulations rests with the building department. In neither of these cases is either agency directly involved in responses to requests for changes in the rules.

The local legislature The local general legislature—in all but a few jurisdictions such as Connecticut—is the agency responsible for the enactment of an amendment to the text or the map of the zoning ordinance.

The plan commission The usual role of the plan commission, under the zoning ordinance, is to hold a public hearing mandated by the state enabling act on the requested amendment, the planned unit development, or the conditional use and to make a recommendation to the local legislature, which may or may not follow the plan commission's recommendation.

The board of appeals The board of appeals, usually consisting of either five or seven persons appointed by the mayor or city council, customarily has two functions: to grant variances from the otherwise applicable rules in cases of hardship, and to hear appeals from interpretations of the ordinance in cases where, for example, the official responsible for issuing permits has denied a permit because, in his or her opinion, the proposed development is in violation of a zoning regulation.

The various kinds of changes The various kinds of changes that can be made to the zoning ordinance include: amendments, variances, and conditional uses. These are discussed immediately below.

Amendments The traditional dogma concerning amendments is that they are to be granted only where there is a showing that the amendment would be in the public interest. This is probably the source of another pervasive rule: that "spot zoning"—the granting of a rezoning that would single out a small parcel for a classification different from that of surrounding property—is invalid. In a few jurisdictions, notably Maryland, the courts have developed what is commonly known as the *change or mistake* rule. No map amendment is valid unless it can be shown that circumstances have changed in the area since the original zoning or that a mistake was made when the land was first classified.

The amendment process has had one particularly troublesome aspect in some jurisdictions. This is what is known as *conditional* or *contract* zoning. The difficulty comes about because the applicant for a rezoning often claims that if he or she is granted a map amendment to, for example, a B–3 business district from an R–1 residential district, he or she will undertake a specific use. The catch is that, although there is no objection to the particular development the applicant proposes in the B–3 business district, there are thirty-seven other permitted uses in that district, and the city council or plan commission would not be happy if some of these other uses should become established. (The same type of problem arises when an applicant makes representations about amenities he or she intends to provide that are not required by the ordinance. Too often the development, when completed, is missing those items.) Faced with this recurring problem, some municipalities have responded by trying to bind the developer, as a part of the rezoning or amendment process, to a promise to do precisely what the developer has stated he or she will do.

The consequence is that although the zoning map appears to show that land is classified in a particular way and hence is subject only to the regulations in the text which are applicable in that district, there is a document—not a part of the zoning ordinance—that further restricts the use of the parcel. This additional restriction may take the form of a covenant in a deed, or it may be a resolution of the city council to which the applicant files a written consent, or it may be a written agreement between the municipality and the developer. Such arrangements have had mixed responses from the courts. In New York, for example, they appear to be permitted, but in Illinois the courts have for the most part regarded them as unlawful.

It should not be forgotten that in most instances in any hearing which involves a requested amendment to the zoning map the real conflict is between the applicant and the neighbors, even though, if the dispute ends up in court, it may appear that the dispute is between the applicant and the municipality.

Variances Those lawyers who first conceived and gave birth to zoning were properly concerned about the difficulties of drawing general rules over land use that would end up being applicable to innumerable pieces of property. There would be cases, for example, where a general requirement that all side yards be three feet wide would work a hardship because one or two lots might have a shape that was not consistent with the standard pattern. Therefore, the variance was included in the original zoning concept as a device to alleviate unfairness in particular cases. Permission could be granted to depart from the standard rules. In most states the legislature did not establish much in the way of guidelines for the local administrators. "Particular difficulties" and "unnecessary hardship" were generally the only standards. As might be expected, variances became a way of relaxing zoning regulations in a wholesale fashion.

The liberal practice that ensued caused some municipal councils to prohibit the grant of use variances if they could do so under the state enabling act. The prevailing attitudes of the boards of appeals toward variances have been the subject of unending criticism on the part of those who see the practice as a cross to be borne by responsible city planning, and of ongoing support from those who view the variance as a protection for the small landowner against the alleged arrogance of the technocrats.

Conditional uses Amendments and variances seemed sufficient in the first decades of zoning to take care of the need for changes in zoning regulations. Development was fairly simple in the 1920s, little development occurred during the 1930s, and during World War II zoning was generally irrelevant. With the burst of growth in the 1950s a peculiar problem became apparent: there were some uses that clearly were necessary within residential districts but for which careful scrutiny was required to ensure that they did not offend too greatly the character of the residential area. Such uses might include an electric substation, a water tower, or a heliport. Neither the amendment nor the variance process seemed to fit. Therefore, the *conditional use* or *special use* was proposed as a category that was acknowledged to be necessary but that should have a degree of review to ensure that the design and location did not impinge too greatly upon the predominant uses in the neighborhood.

If a request for a special or conditional use was made, the plan commission (or the board of appeals) would negotiate with the applicant on various aspects of the proposed development. This was the first glimpse of a notion of licensing in zoning—of bargaining between applicant and local government. In recent years the concept of the conditional use has been greatly expanded to embrace many uses, such as gas stations, trailer parks, and halfway houses, that are believed to present problems.

More recent administrative techniques

Zoning as a legal system is like the god Janus: it looks both backward and forward. The same ordinance that contains provisions for variances that date back to 1924 will have a variety of novel administrative techniques conceived only last year. Some of these are discussed below.

The zoning administrator   A very few cities, such as Los Angeles, have had an office of zoning administrator for many years. More recently this position has been created in many of the other larger cities. The office is intended to consolidate in one staff the multifaceted administration of zoning. The zoning administrator may process building permits, insofar as they involve zoning; may serve as staff to the board of appeals; and may be responsible for the publication and serving of the innumerable notices that are required at so many steps in the zoning process. In some cities, where the law permits, the zoning administrator may also be authorized to grant minor variances that are believed to be too insignificant to place on the agenda of the board of appeals. The office is one more effort to bring professionalism and rationality into the process.

The zoning hearing examiner   In a few cities the zoning system is beginning to adopt a device long employed by many state and federal administrative agencies: the employment of a qualified person to hold a hearing on a request for a change, take evidence, make findings of fact, and recommend a decision to the local legislature. The office of hearing examiner has been established in such disparate places as Seattle and surrounding King County, Washington, in Indianapolis, and in Montgomery County, Maryland. The hearing examiner relieves the plan commission of the tedium of innumerable hearings, and the office greatly improves the conduct of the hearings and the quality of the findings. In places where it has been tried, the use of the hearing examiner has been well received and has not, contrary to fears in some cities, resulted in a "zoning czar."

The neighborhood zoning authority   The neighborhood has received considerable attention these past ten years from sociologists, political scientists, and other students of our urban areas. It is not surprising that those who live in the neighborhoods of our larger cities have perceived zoning as one of the few municipal policies which they could understand and influence. Very often the origin of a neighborhood organization is a zoning dispute. In the offices of many urban planning departments there is a large map of the city divided into named communities or neighborhoods. The relationship between neighborhood organizations and city hall varies from warm intimacy ("We make the telephone call and run down to city hall to answer it") to downright mutual suspicion ("The neighborhoods are a pain in the neck").

Little has been done to date to delegate actual decision making in zoning to neighborhood organizations, although in Minneapolis no apartment building with more than ten units may be built without a hearing before a neighborhood organization, and in numerous cities it is the administrative practice to refer an application for a rezoning to a community group. In Chicago an ordinance submitted by an independent alderman proposed to create zoning boards in each ward that would have the initial but not final decision on rezoning requests.

It is probable that the next decade will see the evolution of a more formal neighborhood participation in the zoning process. Zoning may not be very important in the central business districts of our larger cities, where little will stand in the way of any development, but to the residents of many neighborhoods zoning as a shield against unwanted development is regarded with the same importance as it is in many suburbs.

Innovative substantive regulations

The name of the zoning game, as was suggested earlier, is the opportunity for change, but in the early and middle years of zoning the text of the ordinance gave the appearance, at least, of rigid and inflexible districts with each use assigned to its proper place. It has only been since the later 1960s and the 1970s that the texts of many zoning ordinances have explicitly acknowledged that the municipality was prepared to bargain on the terms of permissible development. The most pervasive device to introduce outspoken flexibility has been the planned unit development, commonly known as the PUD.

Planned unit development

There are probably as many ways to define the PUD as there are drafters of PUD sections of a zoning ordinance. It may be spoken of as a way to adjust development to the particular conditions of the land or a method to ensure that there will be better design and more open space. In terms of the zoning ordinance, PUD provisions in the text provide an opportunity to develop land in a manner that does not fit into all use, bulk, and open space requirements of any of the standard zoning districts. A residential PUD—and most PUDs have involved predominantly residential development—may mix single family detached houses with town houses and possibly a high rise apartment building. Such a mix might not meet the customary standards of height, yards, or dwelling type in any district.

In most but not all cases, the PUD represents an alternative available—if granted—at the option of the developer: he or she can build in conformity with the existing regulations, can ask for an amendment to obtain a rezoning to achieve greater density, or can apply for a PUD. Generally, the provisions for a PUD will have to hold some attractions for the developer; otherwise the developer may find unpalatable the long and tortuous process of securing permission for a PUD. Such incentives might include the opportunity to obtain a few more dwelling units than would be allowable in the underlying zoning, or an opportunity to include some small retail uses in the residential development, or no more than a chance to design a development without being constrained by the rigid yard requirements prevalent in most residential zones.

It is in the nature of most PUDs to result in more common open space than would be found in standard residential developments because clustering of dwelling units, a hallmark of a PUD, leads to substantial areas not appurtenant, so to speak, to any particular dwelling unit. This requires some device to maintain the open space (which may include a recreation building for the residents), and this need usually results in the establishment by the developer of an association of the residents which assesses each resident his or her share of the cost of management of the common areas. In some municipalities the city reserves the right to enter the premises if the open space is badly kept up in order to maintain the premises and to assess each owner for the cost of municipal maintenance.

Most PUD ordinances are short on substantive standards to guide the plan commission and the council when they are considering whether to grant permission for a PUD. The ordinance will probably set forth maximum permitted densities, height and ground coverage, and permitted dwelling types. In the end, however, the decision to grant or deny a PUD is discretionary and the applicant cannot avoid the risk that a member of the commission or council may vote against the applicant's proposal simply because he or she does not like the applicant's design. Were the standards more specific, the PUD would become just another district with a series of rigid standards, and the flexibility the PUD concept was designed to introduce would disappear.

Figure 15–4   A continual and largely unresolved problem is to design good imaginative housing at low cost. Clusters of prefabs, such as Paul Rudolph's Oriental Masonic Gardens Housing Project in New Haven, Connecticut, are part of the answer.

It is feasible, however, to spell out in greater detail than has often been the case the procedural rules for processing a PUD so that both the applicant and the neighbors know the ground rules. Because delay in processing is a ubiquitous problem, some ordinances specify time frames at each step within which the commission or council must make decisions, and in such instances the ordinance will provide for presumptions of approval or disapproval if a decision is not reached within the specified time. Some ordinances, more conscientiously than others, set forth what rights are vested at each stage so that the developer knows that a decision once made will not be capriciously revoked. A few ordinances require a full written disclosure of the reasons why a particular PUD was authorized or turned down.

PUD represents a healthy departure from the old, seemingly more rigid zoning system, and PUD permits more adaptability by local ordinances to changes in the housing market. But it is necessary to remember that one person's rigidity is another person's certainty and the very flexibility of PUD requires a high degree of sophistication and a sense of fairness that has not always been present in zoning administration.

Transfer of development rights

In the early 1960s a New York developer, David Lloyd, suggested that if a community did not want development in a particular area, the community should permit the landowner to sell his or her development rights to someone who owned land in an area where the community wanted to encourage development. Lloyd's idea was largely ignored, and it was not until a decade later that a law professor, John Costonis, struggling to find a system to preserve landmarks in Chicago where there were no public funds to buy them, picked up Lloyd's idea and rationalized it. Through Costonis's articles and books, the concept of transfer of development rights (TDR) became a cause of debate among planners and others involved in land use regulation.[19]

Basically, TDR offers a person whose right to develop is restricted an opportunity to sell those rights to the owner of land in an area where the local government is prepared to allow development. TDR may be used to protect a landmark such as Grand Central Station in New York City by forbidding the demolition of the station but permitting the sale of many thousands of square feet of buildable floor space to one or more owners of land in a designated area.[20]

In New Jersey it has been proposed that the TDR concept be used to preserve open space in prime agricultural or ecologically sensitive areas by allowing landowners in those sections of the state to sell development rights to landowners in other areas where development is deemed appropriate. Of course, owners in the ''transferee area'' must have a market for this additional space, which means that the zoning cannot be so generous to start with that these owners have no incentive to purchase the rights. If there are no buyers, TDR will remain an academic exercise, appealing in learned journals but of little value in the marketplace.

At the very least, TDR must be accompanied by severe down-zoning—cutting back of allowable densities or floor area ratios from those that have prevailed in most jurisdictions for so many years. TDR has not been widely adopted, but it suggests one method for introducing quantitative controls into zoning, a step that is necessary and is probably inevitable as well.

Special districts

With the exception of historic districts, zoning has traditionally treated all zoning classifications as fungible by permitted use, bulk, and yard requirements. By that it is meant that it was assumed that every one of the many areas of the city that was zoned, for example, R–1, R–3, or M–1, was similar to every other similarly zoned district. In fact, many neighborhoods in our larger cities have characteristics that are unique or problems that are special but such would not be apparent from a study of the text of the zoning ordinance; every R–2 district was assumed to be similar, if the zoning ordinance was to be believed. There was another difficulty, caused by the traditional division of the municipality by the trilogy of residential, commercial, and industrial. Such classification did not adequately deal with the problems raised by large institutional uses such as hospitals and universities.

Therefore, the special district was conceived. In many cities hospital zones or university zones were created either as overlay districts, put down on top of the basic zoning districts, or as regular zoning districts. In these special zones provision was made for the needs of the institutional use, and an attempt was made to anticipate its impact on the neighborhood. The goal was to try to avoid the constant bickering between the institution and its neighbors occasioned by repeated requests for changes in the traditional zoning regulations.

The other reason for the creation of special districts is more exotic. Zoning ordinances in a few cities have begun to single out specific areas for special treatment, because an area perceived that it was threatened by a particular market force, because the rest of the community wished to contain an offensive development, or because a neighborhood believed special treatment under the zoning ordinance would preserve a particular character.

The most notorious special district is the Adult Entertainment Zone in Boston, a dubious attempt to contain commercial sex. The so-called Boston Combat Zone purports to restrict pornography to a designated area, in contrast to the Detroit method that seeks to scatter these uses by the old technique of imposing minimum distances between each such use. New York City has raised the special district to an art. New York has special districts for almost any purpose: for example, the Clinton area, which protects a moderate income neighborhood from the threat of commercial encroachment; or the Little Italy district, which, by special use and bulk controls, hopes to preserve an ethnic area; or the Greenwich Street district, which sought to induce developers to provide off-site public facilities or amenities.

Figure 15–5   These drawings of San Francisco show
that a tall building at the top of a hill (left)
allows for an unobstructed view down the street and beyond,
while a tall building on the slope severely restricts
the view from above.

Special districts are probably the wave of the future in big city zoning. The system may impose intolerable administrative burdens on the staff, and the concept may not be everything that special district advocates believe it is, but, as with many schemes, what is *believed* to be important may be more significant than what actually takes place. And special zoning districts do provide a sense of place to the residents that was absent from most zoning policy, at least in the big cities. The technique also acknowledges that in our larger cities it is not feasible to construct a land use regulatory system that ignores the social and economic diversities of the multitudinous residential and commercial areas.

Exclusionary zoning

Twenty years ago almost no one saw zoning regulations as a device that operated to keep persons with low and moderate incomes out of a municipality.

Today many suburbs are being charged with using the zoning and subdivision ordinances, consciously or unconsciously, for just that purpose.

It is probable that the change was due in part to the escalation in housing and land costs, and the growing sensitivity in the late 1950s and the 1960s to a variety of discriminatory practices against minority groups. Some persons and organizations suddenly discovered zoning as another significant occasion for discrimination on the basis of race or economic class. The potential had been evident for many years in such not uncommon practices as minimum large lot or minimum house size requirements, or exceptionally severe subdivision standards, or a total prohibition against mobile homes. Zoning in suburban areas was discovered as a source of social injustice.

Inclusionary zoning Many scholars and critics have noted the negative effects of zoning on the economic feasibility of low and moderate income housing. In response to this problem a number of local governments include language in zoning ordinances that requires a private developer to provide a certain number or ratio of low and moderate income housing units within a proposed development.

Fairfax County, Virginia, requires that developments of fifteen multifamily units or more contain not less than 6 percent low income dwelling units and not less than an additional 9 percent of dwelling units for moderate income families. The ordinance provides a density bonus whereby one additional conventional unit will be allowed for every two low or moderate income units, provided that the density increase does not exceed 20 percent.

In Montgomery County, Maryland, all developments of fifty or more dwelling units are required to have not less than

15 percent moderately priced units. This requirement is increased to 20 percent for special planned-neighborhood or new town zones. A density bonus similar to the one in Fairfax County is also used. In addition, other incentives are provided to a developer by reducing yard and parking requirements and permitting increased height limits. In addition, duplexes and town houses are permitted in single family districts.

Los Angeles requires that all multifamily, condominium, and cooperative developments of five units or more contain not less than 6 percent low income units and not less than an additional 9 percent moderate income units. However, no further incentives or density bonuses are provided.

Source: Abstracted from Herbert M. Franklin, David Falk, and Arthur J. Levin, *In-Zoning: A Guide for Policy Makers on Inclusionary Land Use Programs* (Washington, D.C.: Potomac Institute, 1974), pp. 140–41.

The first judicial articulation of this concern was in 1962 by Justice Frederick Hall of the New Jersey Supreme Court in his dissent in *Vickers* v. *Township of Gloucester*.[21] In that case the zoning ordinance excluded mobile homes from the entire township. A majority of the New Jersey court held that a municipality could legally so zone. Judge Hall struck a note that forecast a debate that still goes on today and probably will continue.

Certainly general welfare does not automatically mean whatever the municipality says it does, regardless of who is hurt and how much. . . . [T]he . . . general welfare transcends the artificial limits of political subdivisions and cannot embrace merely narrow local desires.[22]

Since the *Vickers* dissent, the top courts of Pennsylvania[23] and New York[24] have said that regional housing needs are an important consideration in determining the validity of suburban zoning ordinances, and even the California Supreme Court, a bench with a tradition of sympathy to municipal land use regulations, has sent back to the trial court an alleged restrictive zoning system in the city of Livermore for a determination whether or not the zoning scheme has an adverse impact on housing in the city and in the region of which Livermore is a part.[25]

The most widely reported case, however, was the decision in 1975 of the New Jersey Supreme Court in *Southern Burlington County NAACP* v. *Township of Mount Laurel,*[26] and it was fitting and to be expected that the opinion was written by Justice Hall, shortly before he retired from the court.

In that opinion the court held that the whole scheme of the Mount Laurel zoning ordinance operated to exclude the poor, the young, the old, and minorities, and was invalid under the New Jersey constitution. Even more significantly, the court said that its decision was intended to apply to all "developing communities" in New Jersey and that Mount Laurel should redraft its ordinance in a manner that would correct those aspects the court regarded as exclusionary.

Of course, the *Mount Laurel* decision does not settle the matter, even in New Jersey. In more recent lawsuits arguments are arising over whether a particular township is a "developing" community, and other New Jersey municipalities are insisting that their ordinances do not operate to exclude in the manner of Mount Laurel.[27] The New Jersey legislature has not undertaken to implement the *Mount Laurel* decision with any revisions to the zoning enabling legislation,

---

Zoning—from the neighborhood point of view Dealing with zoning ordinances is very trying. It affects everybody over a wide area. It affects the value of their property, which is what people consider the last bastion of their rights. Usually rezoning takes a lot of time and causes friction and a lot of trouble. Many neighborhood plans involve zoning trouble; in fact, many times zoning is what neighborhoods want. Neighborhoods want us to pay attention to getting the zoning fixed up so that apartments cannot come in. Then they want us to get the traffic off the streets, and they would also, incidentally, like to have the dogs stop barking.

Source: Excerpted from Ernest Bonner, "Portland: The Problems and Promise of Growth," in *Personality, Politics, and Planning: How City Planners Work*, ed. Anthony James Catanese and W. Paul Farmer (Beverly Hills, Calif.: Sage Publications, 1978), p. 147.

---

and the governor of New Jersey decided not to put into effect guidelines prepared by the state department of community affairs for low and moderate income housing allocations for all New Jersey counties. Guidelines of a sort were released in May 1978, but there were no discernible results as of 1979.

It is very difficult for courts to oversee abuses in a system as fractionated as municipal zoning, particularly where the system involves the use of land with its innumerable variations in circumstances. Nevertheless, these few state courts are compelling the municipalities in those states to rethink their traditional assumptions about their responsibility—or lack of responsibility—to those who live in their region but outside their municipal boundaries. We have not heard the last of this issue in the state courts. We probably have, however, heard the last of exclusionary zoning in the federal courts.

In the 1950s and 1960s school desegregation and legislative reapportionment were viewed by many organizations as necessary reforms to be achieved through the federal courts. In the early 1970s the land use practices of suburban communities came to be regarded by some advocates as a similar cause of social and economic discrimination. And to some organizations and lawyers it seemed logical that the attack on exclusionary zoning should also be mounted in the federal rather than the state courts. From their point of view the results of this choice have been disastrous, and, from the view of any student of zoning, they have been predictable.

Between 1928 and 1974 the U.S. Supreme Court refused to hear a single zoning case. During the same period more than 10,000 reported zoning decisions were handed down, nearly all of them by state courts. Then, in the early years of the 1970s, zoning cases began to appear in the federal courts, most of them charging that local zoning regulations were exclusionary and in violation of one or more provisions of the federal Constitution.

Between 1974 and 1977 the U.S. Supreme Court decided four cases which involved allegations of exclusion. In one case the Court narrowly limited the parties who had standing to complain about local zoning regulations,[28] and in the other three cases the Court upheld the municipality. In one the complaint was that the definition of *family* operated to exclude persons not related by blood or marriage from living together, but the Court, in an opinion written by Justice Douglas, upheld the definition.[29] In the second case a provision of municipal charter that required a referendum on every zoning change was held not to violate the Fourteenth Amendment.[30] In the third a refusal to rezone to permit a racially mixed housing project was upheld against constitutional attack because there was no proof that the municipal decision makers were motivated by racial bias.[31]

Lower federal courts have been no more sympathetic to critics of alleged municipal exclusion. They have appeared to hold that unless race is an issue and unless the persons injured are residents of the municipality, there is no basis for invalidating the municipal regulations under the federal constitution.[32] The contrast in these federal decisions with the rationales in the state court opinions could not be more striking.

In 1976, Justice William Brennan of the United States Supreme Court cautioned members of the New Jersey bar in the following words:

I suggest to the bar that although in the past it might have been safe for counsel to raise only federal constitutional issues in state courts, plainly it would be most unwise these days not also to raise state constitutional questions.[33]

The significance of these messages stems from two features of our federal system. First, the supreme court of the state is the final arbiter of that state's constitution; its opinion on the meaning of its state constitution cannot be reviewed by the U.S. Supreme Court, a constitutional imperative well understood by Justice Hall when he based the *Mount Laurel* decision solely on the New Jersey constitution. Second, where there are provisions in a state constitution that are counterparts to provisions in the federal Constitution (such as the due process and equal protection clauses), the state court is not bound by opinions of the U.S. Supreme Court which interpret that provision in identical circumstances. The California Supreme Court made the following statement in a criminal case:

We declare that [the decision to the contrary of the U.S. Supreme Court] is not persuasive authority in any state prosecution in California. . . . We pause to reaffirm the independent nature of the California Constitution and our responsibility to separately define and protect the rights of California citizens despite conflicting decisions of the United States Supreme Court interpreting the federal Constitution.[34]

It may be expected that, to the extent that there is an ongoing resort to the courts in disputes concerning exclusionary zoning, the selected forum from now on will be the state courts, not the federal judiciary.

This chapter should not end without an acknowledgment that some suburban communities are, on their own initiative, seeking ways of encouraging moderate and low income housing within their boundaries; that a few state governments are making efforts to pressure communities to relax their rigid standards;

and that some metropolitan areas are trying to obtain intermunicipal compacts to allocate shares of low and moderate income housing among the constituent municipalities. In one instance a New Jersey municipality, under that state's liberal variance authority, employed the variance technique to permit subsidized housing where it probably would not have authorized the same increase in density for market housing.

Occasionally, a community will adopt a policy of granting permission for additional dwelling units if the developer includes some subsidized units. Fairfax County, Virginia, tried unsuccessfully to compel a percentage of subsidized housing in any development involving more than fifty dwelling units, but the Virginia Supreme Court invalidated the provision.[35]

There has been little activity on the part of the executive or legislative branches of state government to stimulate communities to revise their land use ordinances to provide greater opportunities for lower cost housing. Massachusetts has a so-called anti-snob zoning act under which a developer whose proposal for subsidized housing is turned down by the locality can take an appeal to a state administrative agency which may, subject to the guidelines set by the state law, compel the issuance of development permission. The Pennsylvania department of community affairs has refused a request from an affluent Pittsburgh suburb for funds for open space acquisition on the grounds that the municipality's zoning ordinance is exclusionary. The authority of the department to base a denial of funds on those grounds is now before the Pennsylvania Supreme Court.

The California legislature has mandated that municipalities must prepare comprehensive plans and that those plans must include a housing element. The state department responsible for administering the legislation has issued tentative guidelines which speak of the need for local housing plans to take into consideration the housing needs of the region.

A few metropolitan areas have tried to arrange fair share proposals. The Dayton, Ohio, plan has been widely publicized—but the cutoff of most federal funds for subsidized housing has not permitted an adequate test of the effectiveness of such voluntary pacts. Some regional planning agencies which have the authority under the A-95 program to review municipal requests for funds under numerous federal programs have begun to question the appropriateness of such requests, for example, for open space or sewer improvements if the municipal applicant is dragging its feet on the question of low and moderate income housing.

A concluding observation is that although zoning practices do contribute to the difficulties of locating reasonably priced housing near jobs in many suburbs, escalating land costs, high interest rates, local real estate tax policies, and federal housing policy—or lack of it—all contribute to this serious crisis.

Conclusion

Zoning has been discussed in this chapter from the standpoint of its history, legal basis, planning context, basic elements, and administration. The importance of the legal context has been emphasized, along with the relationship of zoning to both comprehensive planning and subdivision regulations. The section on basic elements includes land use districts, performance standards, density and bulk controls, parking, signs, accessory uses, nonconformities, and aesthetic considerations. The last sections of the chapter are concerned with administration—both traditional and innovative—and with innovative regulations and, finally, with the subject of exclusionary zoning and its implications for the future.

One subject that is not taken up here is that of local land use controls and state and regional planning. This will be discussed extensively in Volume 2.

At this point a historical comment seems appropriate. For the first forty years of zoning the locus of power was in each municipality or county, and it was assumed that no municipality had to pay much heed to the impact of its land use policies on other communities. As has been observed above, this appears to be changing, not only because some courts are calling for regional considerations but also because the environmental era has generated an awareness that many practices which damage the ecology cannot be dealt with by each municipality. (State environmental regulations, however, rarely related directly to housing policies.) Finally, it is worth noting that for the first time since 1922 there is a model land development code, published by the American Law Institute in 1976.[36] Article 7 of that model clearly provides for a sharing of responsibility between municipalities and the state over the implementation of land use policy. Perhaps that model will have the same influence on state policy that was enjoyed by its ancestor in 1922.

1 *Village of Euclid* v. *Ambler Realty Co.*, 272 U.S. 365 (1926).

2 One account states that a majority of the Court had initially voted to sustain the district court which had invalidated zoning: "Justice Sutherland, for instance, was writing an opinion for the majority in *Village of Euclid* v. *Ambler Realty Co.*, holding the zoning ordinance unconstitutional, when talks with his dissenting brethren (principally Stone, I believe) shook his convictions and led him to request a reargument, after which he changed his mind and the ordinance was upheld." McCormack, *A Law Clerk's Recollections*, 46 COLUM. L. REV. 710, 712 (1946).

3 *Nectow* v. *City of Cambridge*, 277 U.S. 183 (1928).

4 1 N. Williams, Jr., AMERICAN LAND PLANNING LAW, Ch. 6 (1974).

5 CAL. CODE ANN., Government Code, Title 7, Art. 5, § 65300.

6 ARIZ. REV. STAT. ANN. § 9–461.05 (Supp. 1975).

7 *Id.* § 9–462.01 E.

8 Fla. Session Laws, Ch. 75–257, § 4(2) (West. 1975).

9 KEN. REV. STAT., Ch. 100, § 100.201 (1971).

10 *Udell* v. *Haas*, 21 N.Y.2d 463, 469, 288 N.Y.S.2d 888, 893, 894 (1968).

11 *Forestview Homeowners Ass'n., Inc.*, v. *County of Cook*, 18 Ill. App. 3d 230, 243, 309 N.E.2d 763, 773 (1974). (Emphasis added.)

12 *Fasano* v. *Board of County Commissioners of Washington County*, 264 Ore. 574, 582, 507 P.2d 23, 27 (1973).

13 *Fanale* v. *Borough of Hasbrouk Heights*, 26 N.J. 320, 325, 139 A.2d 749, 952 (1958).

14 *Friends of Mammoth* v. *Board of Supervisors of Mono County*, 104 CAL. RPTR. 16, 500 P.2d 1360 (1972).

15 *City of Aurora* v. *Burns*, 319 Ill. 84, 149 N.E. 784 (1925).

16 *Perlmutter* v. *Greene*, 259 N.Y. 327, 332, 182 N.E. 5, 6 (1932).

17 *People* v. *Stover*, 12 N.Y.2d 462, 191 N.E.2d 272 (1963).

18 *Just* v. *Marinette County*, 56 Wis.2d 7, 201 N.W.2d 761 (1972); *Turnpike Realty Co., Inc.* v. *Town of Dedham*, 362 Mass. 221, 284 N.E.2d 891 (1972).

19 Costonis, *The Chicago Plan: Incentive Zoning and the Preservation of Urban Landmarks*, 85 HARV. L. REV. 574 (1972); Costonis, *Development Rights Transfer: An Exploratory Essay*, 83 YALE L.J. 75 (1973).

20 *Penn Central Transportation Co.* v. *City of New York*, 98 Sup. Ct. 2646 (1978).

21 *Vickers* v. *Township of Gloucester*, 37 N.J. 232, 181 A.2d 129 (1962).

22 *Id.* at 243 and 145.

23 *National Land & Investment Co.* v. *Kohn*, 419 Pa. 504, 215 A.2d 597 (1965); *Appeal of Kit-Mar Builders, Inc.*, 439 Pa. 466, 268 A.2d 756 (1970).

24 *Berenson* v. *Town of New Castle*, 38 N.Y. 2d 102, 378 N.Y.S.2d 672 (1975).

25 *Associated Homebuilders of the Greater Eastbay, Inc.* v. *City of Livermore*, S.F. 23222, Supreme Court of California, December 17, 1976.

26 *Southern Burlington County NAACP* v. *Township of Mount Laurel*, 67 N.J. 161, 336 A.2d 713 (1975).

27 *Pascack Association, Ltd.* v. *Mayor & Council of Washington Township*, 379 A.2d (1977).

28 *Warth* v. *Seldin*, 422 U.S. 490 (1975).

29 *Village of Belle Terre* v. *Boraas*, 416 U.S. 1 (1974).

30 *City of Eastlake* v. *Forest City Enterprises*, 96 S. Ct. 2358 (1976).

31 *Village of Arlington Heights* v. *Metropolitan Housing Development Corp.*, 429 U.S. 252 (1977).

32 *Kennedy Park Homes Ass'n* v. *City of Lackawanna*, 436 F.2d 108 (2d Cir. 1970), *cert. den.* 401 U.S. 1010 (1971); *Southern Alameda Spanish Speaking Organization* v. *City of Union City*, 424 F.2d 291 (9th Cir., 1970); *United States* V. *City of Black Jack*, 508 F.2d 1179 (8th Cir., 1974). *Cf. Construction Industry Ass'n of Sonoma County* v. *City of Petaluma*, 522 F.2d 897 (9th Cir., 1975), *cert. den.* 424 U.S. 934 (1976).

33 Brennan, *Developments in Constitutional Law*, 99 N.J.L.J. 473 (June 3, 1976).

34 *People* v. *Disbrow*, 127 CAL. RPTR. 360, 545 P.2d 272 (1976).

35 *Board of County Supervisors of Fairfax County* v. *DeGroff Enterprise*, 214 Va. 235, 198 S.E.2d 600 (1973).

36 American Law Institute, A MODEL LAND DEVELOPMENT CODE (1976).

Planning portfolio

A different and more visual perspective of planning can be gained through photos that show what happened in areas and cities as diverse as New York, Cincinnati, Kalamazoo, and Toronto.

The pictures in this portfolio, mostly taken in the 1960s and early 1970s, make up, with the text narration, a visual/verbal story of planning in the United States in the last generation. The emphasis is environmental and physical.

The urban planning shown here encompasses cities and their suburbs.

Although the areas and cities are metropolitan, ranging in scale from Kalamazoo to New York, most of the points illustrated will apply to communities outside metropolitan areas as well.

The first half of this portfolio is historical, showing primarily changes in transportation and housing development, the pioneering work a half century ago in the planning of Radburn, New Jersey, and the movement of economic enterprises to the suburbs. The second half of the portfolio builds on this to show the positive effects of planning at work, especially in zoning, transportation, economic development, and housing.

Apartment building next to railroad station in Great Neck, Long Island.

Jumble of land uses
on the outskirts of
Paterson, New Jersey.

The portfolio concludes with a Canadian city, Toronto, where a very high level has been achieved in coordinating transportation and land development planning.

Four themes are woven into this portfolio:

1. Housing: where people live
2. Activities: the things people do outside their homes, especially jobs, shopping, and recreation
3. Transportation: how people move from one place to another; transportation plays a key role in determining where development takes place and in making jobs and other activities possible.
4. Natural environment: open land preserved for passive and active outdoor recreation and for ecology.

The early years   Rail was still the dominant mode of transportation from 1900 to 1930, and development in

urban areas was highly concentrated— in the cities and around the rail stations of the early suburbs. These suburbs were strung out along the rail lines like so many beads on a string, and most roads still paralleled the radial rail lines, leaving a good deal of land open between the tracks.

This pattern led to high densities in the built-up areas, with everyone wanting to be as close to his or her job or the station as possible. There was a considerable jumble of homes, industries, and commerce.

Zoning, the planners' basic tool, was addressed to these conditions:
(1) assuring circulation of light and air;
(2) controlling lot coverage, height, and distance between buildings; and
(3) providing separate zones for industry, commerce, and housing.

Radburn: the pioneering new town   From the start planners sought to create an attractive and satisfying as well as a livable environment. Radburn, in Fairlawn, New Jersey (about twenty-five miles from Manhattan), was one of the most ambitious and durable of these efforts. It was and is in many ways even more relevant to our present problems than it was at the time it was conceived.

The original concept called for a town of 30,000 with commerce, industries, schools, and recreational areas as well as a variety of housing types. Building began in the late 1920s, but development was cut short by the Depression in the early 1930s after homes for only 3,000 people (866 dwelling units) and

the commercial section had been completed on a 149 acre tract.

Of the 866 homes completed, about half are single family; the rest are duplexes, town houses, and apartments.

The density of the built-up areas was quite in keeping with the times. The single family homes are on 40 or 45 by 100 foot lots, an average of ten homes to the acre.

What sets Radburn off from the conventional subdivision is the variety of housing types it offers and their arrangement: (1) all houses are "turned around"

Portion of Radburn showing culs-de-sac and open space.

Interior view of Radburn with town houses and pedestrian paths.

Highway built in the 1930s penetrating remote areas of farms and woodland.
Such roads helped generate postwar commuting and suburban growth.

The Ackerman farmhouse,
built in 1883.

Bulldozer knocks down a stand of trees. The Ackerman farmhouse followed moments later.

Portion of subdivision built on Ackerman site. Although the new homes were middle income in price level, half of the new homeowners held blue collar jobs.

so that they front on landscaped pedestrian paths rather than on the street; (2) cars and pedestrians are separated, with the footpaths passing beneath the main roads, so that it is possible to move from home to stores to school without crossing a major traffic artery; (3) the high density leaves about half of the 149 acre tract available for other uses—commercial center, community center, school, playing fields, and tennis courts, and, what is most important of all, large areas of open parkland.

Radburn has stood the test of time. On its fiftieth anniversary (as noted by Mildred Jailer in *Planning* for May 1979) about 15 percent of the original residents still lived there together with "a

Tenements in New York. During the 1940s this block changed from Italian to Puerto Rican.

Frederick Douglass Houses, a publicly assisted development in New York.

Development near Milford, Connecticut: shopping center and movie house in left center, four factories to right and upper right, and two motels in foreground.

large number of second- and third-generation Radburnites."

The 1930s During the Depression years of the 1930s public works took the place of housing and other private development. The first "superhighways" (now generally termed expressways or interstates) were built. These highways were used mostly for long distance travel, and their full effects were not felt until the suburban boom of the 1950s.

The new suburbia The 1950s was a period of enormous growth in urban areas; all of the net gain in these areas was registered in the suburbs. The suburban building boom was fueled by: pressures built up during fifteen years of depression and war; large scale mass produced developments that cut the cost of each house; government guaranteed mortgages; easy credit for cars; and a prosperous economy.

Three photos show a sequence that was repeated for thousands of subdivisions across the country. The farmhouse was built by John Terhune Ackerman in 1883 in Waldwick, New Jersey (twenty miles from New York City), on 300 acres of open and wooded land which Terhune's family had farmed since the

Revolution. The subdivision that took its place provided a high standard of housing for hundreds of families—mostly young, white, middle income—who substantially improved their standard of living.

Those left behind As middle income families moved to the suburbs, many of the homes they left behind were taken over by poorer families moving up from the slums, and a new wave of migrants moved into the slums. Although diverse in origin, the migrants had in common a rural background which provided them with few urban skills, especially white collar skills at a time when employment was shifting heavily toward office jobs.

Slum clearance and redevelopment with public housing disrupted not only the traditional fabric of the cities but also the natural rhythms and disciplines of life that a more human scale had fostered. Few of the new public housing projects were juxtaposed with middle income housing. Built on the site of the slums they replaced, most of the new projects were in ghetto neighborhoods which cut the poor off from the mainstream of city life.

Business moves to the suburbs
Factories usually were the first large

Two way commutation on the Long Island Expressway in 1960.

enterprises to move—usually to suburban locations. Retail stores and office buildings followed as shopping centers and expressways were built in the 1950s and 1960s. Factories needed space for horizontal, continuous flow layouts; retailing followed its markets; and office employers wanted to be close to their work forces.

The development shown on the previous page (Milford, Connecticut) followed the opening of a major expressway interchange about halfway between Bridgeport and New Haven.

By the late 1950s highways were crowded in both directions during rush hours. The phenomena of reverse community and cross country commuting established new traffic patterns as employment was dispersed.

Progression from relatively small lots to large lots in Washington Township, New Jersey, 1960 to 1965. Photos show houses of identical construction on one-fifth acre lots, (right), and half acre and one acre lots (facing page). All houses were built by the same developer on contiguous tracts of land.

The suburban pattern of development   Between 1950 and 1960 subdivisions changed from sprawl at relatively high densities to spread at very low densities.

The communities that were almost completely built up in the wave of development during the 1950s could do little to help themselves out of a bind of soaring school costs to meet a soaring birthrate and a fixed revenue base tied to the local property tax. Those farther out with a good share of their land still open could and did take steps to protect themselves. Their means was defensive zoning: raise minimum lot sizes to hold down the number of houses and at the same time seek to attract commerce and industry, which pay taxes but send no children to school.

Thus, a 1962 survey of the zoning ordinances governing the developable land still open in the tri-state New York urban region showed that two-thirds of this land was zoned for minimum residential lot sizes of one-half acre or more; nearly one-half of the total was zoned for one

Aerial view of a Columbia neighborhood, and a view of open space at the neighborhood level, in Columbia.

acre lots or more. In the early 1950s when the Levittown-like suburbs were being built, the average lot size in the region had been 6,000 square feet, or one-seventh of an acre.

Three big problems were posed by large lot zoning: (1) it ate up open land at an unprecedented rate; (2) it spread homes ever farther from jobs at densities which could not support public transportation; (3) it sharply raised the cost of housing.

Changes in planning methods The preceding sections of this portfolio have

sketched in planning and land development trends up to the mid-1960s. Two major trends (and problems) were declining cities and increasingly spread out suburbs.

The balance of this portfolio will review cluster zoning and planned unit development—two significant methods for more economical and effective residential land use—and approaches to city revitalization in Kalamazoo, Cincinnati, and several other cities.

Cluster zoning is a planning tool intended to reduce spread and gain

Kalamazoo Mall shortly
after its opening in 1959.

greater amenity without appreciably changing overall density of the total area.

Planned unit development (PUD) is a more extensive alternative to scatter and spread. PUD extends the clustering principle to the point where almost any city or town (at least in the tri-state New York region) may waive its conventional zoning in favor of a development plan patterned specifically to the characteristics of a large site—normally 100 acres or more. Under PUD the plan may cluster single family homes, town houses, and apartments along with community facilities, commerce, and industry in any pattern that is felt to be the most efficient and the best suited to preserve the natural landscape.

In Columbia, Maryland, the PUD principle expanded to new town dimensions has now come close to full realization. Columbia has about one-third of its goal of 110,000 people on twenty square miles of rolling land between Washington and Baltimore.

The basic development unit in Columbia is the neighborhood of 2,000 to 5,000 people with an elementary school, a swimming pool, and a community building. Each neighborhood offers a variety of housing types ranging from single family suburban-like homes on lots up to a quarter of an acre, through two story and three story town house clusters, to middle rise apartments.

The next step is the village, designed to serve three to five neighborhoods ringed around it, or up to 15,000 people. Each village has a middle school and a high school and a range of activities such as would be expected in a well-equipped local center: professional offices, a supermarket, and a number of specialty shops and services.

The villages in turn are grouped around the third step in the hierarchy, Columbia Downtown, the central business district.

By clustering its homes and facilities Columbia can provide a good deal of open space for play and relaxation at every level—block, neighborhood, and village—and large wooded areas and lakes for the whole community.

Revitalization of cities   The exuberant growth that characterized metropolitan areas in the 1950s and 1960s has leveled off in many parts of the country. There are fewer economic resources (factories, stores, office buildings, hotels, etc.) to distribute than had been projected, and it is unlikely that any large proportion of these can be located in the suburbs or even in new towns without seriously jeopardizing the

The multipurpose Kalamazoo Center—outside view and atrium–lobby (facing page).

promising but still precarious comeback which many of the troubled cities have been making. Consequently, there is renewed interest in older cities—not only major central cities such as New York and Chicago but also smaller centers.

Throughout history the strength of the cities has depended on the magnetism of the activities they offered. Downtown was the place for the action—the greatest variety of jobs and proximity to a wide choice of other attractions: museums, concerts, nightclubs, college classes, sporting events, libraries, department stores, and specialty shops.

For planners seeking to revive cities the first order of business has been to try to restore the magnetism of their downtowns—to create a setting there that will pull the activities back together. It has been a battle against predominant trends, but one which has begun to pay off in a large number of places.

In Kalamazoo, Michigan, the first outdoor pedestrian mall in the country (built in 1959) changed the image of a declining small central city and served as a catalyst for overall revival.

The mall was the major force in the

construction of a new library and a new art center and museum, in expanding the city auditorium, in expanding the Upjohn Company's downtown headquarters, and in attracting major capital from outside (Inland Steel) to help build the Kalamazoo Center with office space, a convention center, a 288 room hotel, and restaurants and other facilities.

In Minneapolis a mall also turned out to be a new image builder. In addition to ample space for pedestrians and a lot of street furniture and plantings, Nicollet Mall has a serpentine transitway for buses down its center. Skywalks radiating from the IDS Building provide a network for pedestrian access to most of the central area (see Chapter 8).

Senior citizens ride free except during rush hours. These free rides are seen as an important contribution to the stability of the neighborhoods of heavily treed and immaculately kept small homes in the city's famous Lake District, now populated mostly by older families.

Cincinnati began its economic revival with the plan drawn up in 1964 to strengthen its downtown and link it to revitalized residential neighborhoods. The first step was clearing the area around Fountain Square. A skywalk system in the downtown area serves Fountain Square, the convention center, major hotels, major department stores, and other stores and facilities.

Cincinnati's most magnetic landmarks are outside the downtown, where planners sought to recycle old structures as catalysts to revitalization of blighted neighborhoods. By reinforcing already attractive facilities and adding a full mix of local services, their aim was to create a number of new town centers that would spark the rehabilitation of

housing and other improvements throughout the larger area.

For example, the Findlay Market, a historic meat and produce center, was rebuilt around its original cast iron frame. Across the street a new social services and recreation center was built, consisting of four buildings ranged around an interior court.

During the 1950s and 1960s the cure prescribed for blighted neighborhoods was to level everything and start all over again, often in the most seriously

Nicollet Mall in
Minneapolis; note bus
in background.

Crystal Court in the IDS
Building, Minneapolis—a
sky-lighted interior space
with stores and restaurants;
at the mezzanine level four
skywalks connect with
twelve downtown blocks.

Fountain Square, Cincinnati, as seen from the skywalk. A large open space surrounded by office buildings—several of them new—attracted by the square

HUB Services Center, Cincinnati, showing the neighborhood services brought together (along with a library).

Part of the audience at
the annual convention of
the Roseville Coalition,
a neighborhood
association in Newark.

affected neighborhoods, with public
housing. Today the emphasis is on
public participation and rehabilitation.

Several years before neighborhood
preservation programs were started in
Jersey City, New Jersey, a concerted
effort by the Van Nostrand Street Block
Association had already made
important progress toward turning that
block around. Whenever a house on the
block became vacant the association
had seen to it that it was carefully
boarded up and protected, and then
had sought a new owner who would
agree to live up to the high standards
that the association had set for itself.
Meanwhile, with the aid of the association, most of the homeowners on the
block had managed to obtain loans to
fix up their properties.

Under the neighborhood preservation
program in Jersey City, city officials
and the block association have worked

closely together, with a committee of
the block association now taking an official role for screening prospective new
homeowners.

Transportation: the key element   The
location of cities, historically, has
usually been determined by transport—
the confluence of navigable rivers; the
presence of a large, navigable
harbor, later, the railroads; today, the
interstate highways.

In Passaic, New Jersey, the train
stopped running down the middle of
Main Avenue in the mid-1960s, and the
tracks were removed in the early 1970s.
So long as the tracks split the street
there was little planners could do to
improve its amenity and thus its prospects as a commercial center. But with
the tracks slated to go they drew up
plans which filled the center of the
street with a landscaped parking area
for cars (parking would be at a

Rehabilitation of a house in the Roseville area of Newark.

premium if business picked up), added new street furniture and sculpture, and inserted a number of miniparks for rest and relaxation.

As the nation became more energy conscious and public transportation-oriented in the last half of the 1970s, reserved expressway lanes were designated in the New York, Washington, D.C., Atlanta, Chicago, and San Francisco areas. During rush hours these lanes can only be used by buses and four person car pools. These lanes are improving commuting time and thus are persuading commuters to get out of their one person cars for the journey to work.

In Toronto planning has achieved extraordinary results with the blending of zoning, a subway built in the 1950s and extended in the 1970s, the civic center, and the effective preservation and rehabilitation of older sections of the city.

The catalyst that transformed Toronto from a dowdy city to one of the showplaces of the world was the construction of its subway system in the mid-1950s. Hand in hand with that went a far-reaching city (and ultimately metropolitan) plan which keyed density to transportation and decreed by special district zoning that all major new facilities must be clustered at the points of access (that is, around subway stations). This assured a number of high points (literally) of varied activity, all linked to the downtown.

The subway system has been meshed

These houses in Jersey City were restored with the help of Community Development Block Grant funds under the city's neighborhood preservation program.

Publicly assisted housing in a predominantly brownstone section of Jersey City. Built with the active participation of the city's Puerto Rican Association, which chose, and worked closely with, the architect.

with the rest of the transit system. By 1975 a total of 96 of the 109 bus and trolley routes that spanned the metropolitan area made 131 subway connections.

The government of Toronto has taken many diversified steps to preserve amenity and maintain housing for all income levels. Careful combining of controls and incentives is reflected in:

the large landscaped areas around apartment buildings; underground car parking to serve apartment buildings; public walkways, similar to arcades, to open up long blocks; and high rise buildings with mixed uses (for example, the Colonnades with speciality shops and restaurants on the first two floors, three floors of offices, and ten floors of apartments).

Railroad tracks down the center of Main Avenue in Passaic, in the early 1960s.

Minipark in Passaic.

Three lanes reserved for buses and four person car pools on a highway feeding into San Francisco.

The Toronto subway runs north and south through the heart of the city. Yonge Street is the city's main commercial street; the Bloor/Danforth intersecting line links heavily settled residential areas.

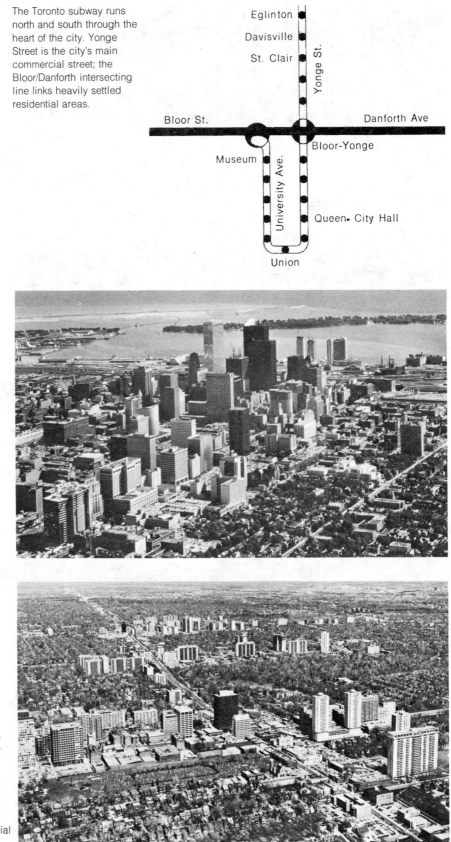

Zoning is clearly evident in the top photo of Bloor Street in Toronto facing south toward the harbor with the massing of the commercial district that is one block on each side of the subway. In the opposite direction on Bloor Street, four subway stops are shown by the concentrations of tall buildings that have been carefully developed with other kinds of residential and commercial buildings.

The Yorkville section of Toronto where zoning protects old buildings and encourages development of small shops and other specific uses.

Housing built in Toronto in 1913—260 units for worker families. Built by a foundation as model housing and used that way until 1974 when the city bought the properties for $7 million.

Part five: Social and economic development

16

Maintenance and renewal of central cities

The usual perception of the central city is of an older place which serves as an industrial and commercial center, such as Boston, New York, Baltimore, Cleveland, and Milwaukee. Often such cities have roots going back to the eighteenth century, serve as manufacturing and commercial centers, provide significant port and docking facilities, and have highly concentrated central business districts.

Many of the central cities in other parts of the country, however, are substantially different. Places such as Dallas, Phoenix, Los Angeles, and Denver have different economic orientations and are heavily dependent on the automobile.

It is the purpose of this chapter to survey major issues in the maintenance and renewal of central cities, particularly the older cities in the northeastern and midwestern parts of the United States. The discussion remains within the context of the public planning agency. Initially, the chapter reviews the following issues: the conservation of public and private facilities; investment in infrastructure; and the issues of immigration and ethnic diversity. The economy of the central business district is then reviewed, with special reference to its industrial and retail trade and merchandising bases. This is followed by a discussion of central city finance. A major section of the chapter then deals with the impact of citywide policies and programs under four sections: urban redevelopment, urban renewal, Model Cities, and Community Development Block Grants. The final section discusses and evaluates planning strategies and also discusses available resources and certain creative initiatives that have been taken.

The conservation of public and private facilities

The disparity in age of the physical stock provides an important contrast between central cities and outlying suburbs in a number of metropolitan areas. This is the case far more frequently in the Northeast and the Midwest than it is in the West and South. In housing stock, for example, age disparities among central cities and between cities and suburbs can be seen in Table 16–1.

It is difficult to draw conclusions solely on the basis of age. As shown in Table 16–1, the housing stock in central cities tends to be much older than that of the surrounding suburban areas. For example, in the city of Baltimore 60 percent of all housing units were built before 1939 whereas in suburban Baltimore County only 19.1 percent of the housing was built before 1939.

But age cannot be equated automatically with quality. In many European cities the housing stock is much older than that found in the United States. Many of the more fashionable sections of Paris, Amsterdam, and London are more than 200 or 300 years old. Similar comparisons can be made within the United States where some of the more desirable residential locations are found in older parts of cities, for example: Georgetown in Washington, D.C., Pacific Heights in San Francisco, and Greenwich Village in Manhattan. In spite of age the dwellings in these areas are among the most fashionable and expensive places in which to live.

Table 16-1 Age of housing stock by regions,
cities, and suburban areas.

Region, city, suburbs	% of housing stock built during			
	1960–70	1950–59	1940–49	Pre-1940
Northeast	11.4	11.5	8.9	68.2
Boston	9.2	5.9	7.7	77.2
Suburbs	14.1	13.9	8.1	63.8
New York	13.6	12.3	12.1	82.1
Suburbs	34.2	4.5	17.4	43.9
Philadelphia	10.4	11.0	9.0	69.4
Suburbs	24.9	27.0	10.9	37.3
Baltimore	10.2	15.2	14.7	60.0
Suburbs	30.2	34.1	16.7	19.1
Washington, D.C.	15.7	16.4	20.9	47.0
Suburbs	46.8	27.6	14.7	10.9
North Central	14.3	13.8	9.1	62.8
Chicago	10.5	11.4	11.5	66.6
Suburbs	33.1	31.1	9.9	25.9
St. Louis	6.5	8.7	11.1	73.8
Suburbs	22.7	20.6	9.7	20.7
South	25.0	27.0	17.7	30.3
Atlanta	26.7	24.7	18.3	30.3
Suburbs	50.5	28.2	10.8	11.0
Dallas	33.7	30.6	16.8	18.1
Suburbs	49.7	30.1	11.4	8.7
West	25.0	24.9	12.7	37.4
Phoenix	35.8	38.7	14.4	11.2
Suburbs	58.6	25.5	8.7	7.1
Los Angeles	22.5	25.8	19.5	32.2
Suburbs	25.2	35.0	19.5	20.2

Source: U.S., Department of Commerce, Bureau of the Census, *1970 Census of Population* (Washington, D.C.: Government Printing Office, 1973); U.S., Department of Commerce, Bureau of the Census, *1970 Census of Housing: Components of Inventory Change* (Washington, D.C.: Government Printing Office, 1973).

Our housing stock and public buildings have extremely long lives—a condition that is self-evident when one observes the physical capital of an American city. It is not uncommon to see habitable and usable buildings which are close to—or more than—100 years old. Buildings have an extremely long and useful life by virtue of their slow rate of physical depreciation. Furthermore, whether residential, commercial, or industrial, buildings are expensive to construct. No city is so rich that it can easily discard its physical plant.

While the long life of buildings is desirable from an economic point of view, the extreme long life of buildings may have certain negative effects. For example, buildings that become obsolete often remain standing because it may not be economically feasible to remove them and construct new buildings. Obvious examples of negative implications of building longevity are the slums in some of our major cities, which remain standing although they provide substandard housing. Of all occupied housing units in the United States in 1970, 5.5 percent lacked some or all plumbing facilities; of those housing units built prior to 1939, 14.6 percent lacked some or all plumbing facilities.[1] Although such old buildings may appear to be past their useful lives as shelter, they often remain standing and in use.

Obsolescence may also take its toll on the physical stock. Although buildings may remain in excellent working condition, they, like other assets, may become obsolete. A building usually becomes obsolete because of technological change,

change in style and taste, or change in economic circumstances. The impact of technological change is clearly evident in the context of industrial and commercial buildings. There have been dramatic changes in technology over the past three decades which have altered methods of production and distribution. Loft buildings, common to many older industrial districts, are now inadequate for modern continuous processes, which require single story plants such as those found in a typical suburban industrial development.

A similar technological change has occurred in retailing. The new suburban shopping center, often a mall containing several department stores and scores of variety shops, is different in kind from the traditional downtown area. Direct adaptation to the automobile has enhanced the suburban shopping center. On the other hand, congestion and lack of parking space have adversely affected the downtown areas of central cities.

Figure 16–1 Even structurally sound housing will be abandoned when social and economic factors produce deleterious effects.

Infrastructure investment

What tends to distinguish urban areas from rural areas is really the amount of investment in the infrastructure that the urban area has received. Central cities, which are the most heavily urbanized portions of the metropolitan area, contain the most intensive capital investment in the infrastructure. Infrastructure is a term used to encompass the kinds of supporting facilities which enable the city to operate: streets, sidewalks, water lines, sewers, roads, public transportation arteries, schools, hospitals, cultural facilities, churches, and various other institutions and facilities. This infrastructure is much more concentrated, expensive, and complex in central cities than in suburban areas. This tremendous investment in central city infrastructure is not only expensive to establish; it is also difficult to replace.

One of the major challenges to the planning agency lies in helping both public and private organizations seek ways to conserve buildings and facilities that still have economic and social value. This involves bringing together diverse groups that have an interest and an economic stake in factories, warehouses, railroad stations, bus stations, transportation lines, apartment buildings, and other resources to ascertain what measures are possible.

This infrastructure will age and will depreciate. It will require constant maintenance and occasional rebuilding. The financial burden of maintaining and restoring this tremendous infrastructure falls on the central city, although, in fact, many urban facilities such as stadiums, parks, zoos, public transportation, churches, and cultural facilities are used by the entire metropolitan area. And the investment, which is too costly to be duplicated in the suburban areas, is frequently too costly to be maintained solely through the resources of the central city.

Obviously, the physical capital of the central cities must be adequately maintained if the quality of services offered by it is to remain high. Aging can be countered by adequate maintenance. With regular maintenance, the housing stock, public buildings, private commercial buildings, and religious and cultural buildings can be kept in use.

The burden of maintenance of the physical stock, which is a metropolitan resource, falls heavily on the central cities. But many suburban communities built largely after World War II are now beginning to feel some of these same pressures on their physical stock. The older suburban housing, much of it built in the 1920s, is now in need of similar maintenance or replacement. The same is true of the aging suburban infrastructure.

Between 1960 and 1970 over 10 percent of the nation's housing stock had been removed: 6.5 percent had been lost by demolition, and 4 percent by other means.[2]

Figure 16–2   Expenditures by residential property owners for maintenance, repairs, and construction improvements for selected years, 1966–77.

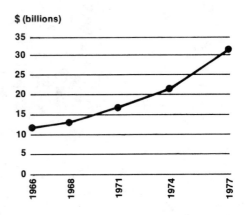

There is considerable activity within the cities' stock of physical capital. Buildings are removed and new ones are constructed. In addition, there is a constant process of upgrading the deteriorating stock. Although the physical capital within central cities is old, it is serviceable not only currently but also for the foreseeable future. The lifeblood, then, of the physical stock of our cities is the constant infusion of funds for maintenance and rehabilitation.

Figure 16–2 shows the amount spent by homeowners for home improvements to keep the housing stock liveable and habitable. Comparable expenditures are also made by private businesses for the maintenance of their stores, offices and factories.

Immigration and demographics[3]

The central city has traditionally been the port of entry for the nation's immigrants. Waves of European and Asian immigration in the nineteenth and early twentieth centuries, and the more recent rural to urban migration, have populated the central cities.

Traditionally, the immigrants from Europe arrived in New York, Boston, and other seaports along the Atlantic. Many of these immigrants began their new life within these cities. Today the European immigration to the United States is a fraction of what it was at the turn of the century. However, some 120,000 immigrants, on the average, still enter the United States legally each year. Their traditional staging area is more than likely to be the central cities.

In the nineteenth and early twentieth centuries there were severe housing shortages in the cities receiving large numbers of immigrants. To accommodate these immigrants tenements were erected. By today's standards the tenements created prior to 1900 were abominable, lacking sufficient ventilation, sanitary facilities, and space. Instant slums were created within New York City. Reformers such as Jacob Riis were instrumental in having the housing codes amended, so that the conditions under which tenements could be built were considerably improved after 1901. The "New Law" tenements, which were an improvement over the existing tenement buildings, contained more in the way of light, heat, ventilation, and sanitary facilities.

Figure 16-3 Population movement today is much more than rural to urban migration.

A comparable situation existed on the West Coast for Asian immigrants. Before the turn of the century thousands of immigrants from China were brought to the United States to work on the railroads. They settled in San Francisco, Seattle, and southern California. Today the Chinatowns within these cities still serve as the ports of entry for Asian immigrants.

The rural to urban migration has been taking place since the turn of the century. Although it has not been on the scale of the European immigration, it has nevertheless been significant. In 1900, 59.5 percent of the population of the United States lived in rural areas. Since that time the farm population has been steadily shrinking, so that today a mere 4.1 percent of the population actually lives and works on farms in the United States, and what we consider the rural population has shrunk to less than one-third of the population.

One sizable wave of rural to urban migration has been that of blacks from the rural south into urban areas. During the first half of this century this migration was largely to urban areas in the North. However, since the 1960s there has been considerable migration to the major cities in the South, such as Atlanta, Houston, Dallas, New Orleans, and Little Rock. By 1970 the black population of the country was overwhelmingly urban and central city.

Since the late 1940s there have also been waves of Hispanic immigrants into this country. One of the larger ones has been the migration from Puerto Rico to the eastern United States. In New York City as of 1970 more than a half million Puerto Ricans had located in Manhattan, the Bronx, and other parts of the city. Other cities with large Hispanic groups (largely from Puerto Rico) include Philadelphia, Boston, and Chicago. There is also a continued migration from Mexico and Central America. Within the western United States, Hispanics, mostly Mexican, form the largest ethnic minority group.

The in-migration of ethnic groups to the central cities, combined with the migration to the suburbs of more affluent city dwellers, has had a significant impact on the composition of the larger cities. For example, before World War II the ethnic minority composition of the ten largest cities in the United States was an average of 9.8 percent. The 1970 census indicated that this had increased to 37 percent.

By the 1960s and 1970s the central cities had become the homes of the nation's disadvantaged minority groups. One authority has described the factors that cause the poor to be concentrated in the central cities in the following words:

It is necessary to address the elementary question of why the poor [have tended] to concentrate in the central cities rather than in the suburbs. A number of answers have been suggested in this controversial area. It has been held that the rural poor [have been] attracted to urban areas in the hope of improving their lot through better education and job opportunities. . . . The availability of housing and acculturation opportunities [have also attracted] them to the cities. (Acculturation is usually defined as the process whereby newcomers learn how to live and function in a strange environment—in this case, an urban environment.) . . . Since the core of the central city is likely to be very old, many of its buildings are outmoded. Yet the durability of buildings, the complexities of assembling land, and the cost of clearing land have made it difficult to tear down and replace old facilities in most central cities. Some of these old facilities are the only ones in which the urban poor can afford to live, and for this reason the older neighborhoods [have been] the points of entry for many of the poor and members of minority groups migrating to the city.[4]

Ethnicity

Many areas of the central cities have traditionally been identified with various ethnic groups of European, Asian, Hispanic, and Afro-American background. The neighborhoods take on the flavor of these groups and their institutions.

There are examples of ethnic neighborhoods in every major city in the United States. Many of the former European ethnic communities have undergone out-migration during the past several decades to the extent that they have ceased to exist, but in many cities European ethnic communities are still solidly entrenched. These communities take pride in both their existence as an identifiable community and their ethnic roots.

The various ethnic enclaves exist, however, in the context of an overall city. There is always a question of how provincial and inward looking a particular community ought to be in its relationship to the city as a whole. This issue is particularly sensitive in many European ethnic communities in major industrial cities.

Some racial conflict has resulted from the interaction between ethnic communities of European background and disadvantaged minority communities which may be close by. Conflicts of racial transition which have arisen when black or Hispanic families have begun to move into some ethnic neighborhoods have caused tremendous friction, sometimes leading to violent confrontations.

A problem occurs in trying to determine whether the natural cohesion and inward looking characteristics of certain ethnic communities actually result in exclusion and racial discrimination. Discrimination based on race is against the law. In their desire to keep their identity and to keep their own community intact, ethnic communities may run the risk of discrimination against other people who have a right to live within the community.

Policies for quality of life The citizen forms a set of expectations of his or her city government that is in the nature of a contract. He or she furnishes or delivers citizenship, taxes, law-abiding behavior, and the vote. In return he or she expects well maintained streets, psychologically secure neighborhoods, public safety both inside and outside the home, and many other satisfiers of needs.

Satisfying these needs—which step up psychologically from basic existence needs to growth needs—is a major part of the quality of life.

To manage a city toward the goal of better quality of life, several policies are relevant. First, a joint problem-solving approach should be used among administrative, political, and citizen systems to establish the minimum level of satisfaction of existence needs for all citizens. Such needs will include nutrition, sanitation, housing, and public safety.

Second, a "negotiative policy process" should be established to determine higher levels of existence needs for citizens. Many of these are physical amenities such as smooth flow of automobile traffic, well maintained streets, etc. At this point the best possible understanding is needed between citizens and their city government about what is to be provided, what it will cost, and what the trade-offs are.

Third, "Cities which truly aspire to deal with quality of life will have to find new ways to assist citizens in meeting their needs for positive human relationships." Success in this area can be seen in physically and psychologically supportive neighborhoods, good communication in every major sense of the word, and local government processes which stimulate and sustain citizen participation.

The fourth policy is the broad area of intellectual, aesthetic, and emotional growth. "The opportunity to develop one's self to full potential would seem to be important in a humanistic society."

Finally, in viewing quality of life, consideration should be given to citizen needs for power, novelty, excitement, and achievement.

Source: Abstracted and partly excerpted from William B. Eddy, "Managing for Quality of Life," paper presented at the Conference on Managing Mature Cities, sponsored by the city of Cincinnati and the Charles F. Kettering Foundation, Cincinnati, Ohio, 9–10 June 1977.

Today there is a greater appreciation than in the past for cultural diversity in American life. Although most Americans are proud of their common history and heritage, it is true that every American is in some way an ethnic and an immigrant. Most people are proud of their heritage. Every ethnic community brings a particular flavor, vitality, and strength to the city. These often are not recognized for what they are—strong elements which reinforce the entire fabric of the central city. One issue faced by planners in dealing with the ethnic communities in the central cities is how to preserve the distinctive features of the community's heritage and yet assure that true freedom of residential choice and the availability of public services are available to all citizens of the community and not just to particular neighborhoods.

The economy of the central business district[5]

The central cities in metropolitan areas have economic functions which are quite distinctive, especially in the central business districts. The central business district is generally characterized in terms of concentrated land use: high rise office buildings, theaters and movie houses, specialty shops, large department stores, and the hub of the transportation network. On the edges and spreading out from the central business district will be found the apartment buildings and the large and small industries that provide diversified employment for thousands of people. In addition, hundreds of small enterprises are found that service the larger enterprises that make up the central business district.

The central city, especially the central business district, offers unusual advantages because of this density and concentration. These advantages include the following:

1. Small businesses and industries are much more easily serviced by a variety of support enterprises. Although some of these businesses are competitive, they are all highly interdependent.
2. Concentrated office space is provided for "confrontation industries," occupations and professions that depend on frequent, even daily, face-to-face contact for the conduct of business.
3. Large department stores and small specialty shops provide the opportunity for specialized and comparative shopping. This is a function that even the larger regional shopping centers have not been able to duplicate. (For a discussion of regional shopping centers see Chapter 9.)

It should be stressed that these economic advantages of concentration are often overlooked in the more generalized discussions of the cultural advantages of museums, theaters, libraries, and other educational and cultural facilities. The economic significance of three traditional features of the central business district—office buildings, hotels, and retail trade—is discussed below.

Office buildings

The central cities have several functions which have not been decentralized to the suburbs. The largest concentration of office buildings in the metropolitan area is still generally found within the central city. In some downtown areas the rise in office building construction since World War II has been spectacular.

The office function of the downtowns has been enhanced by the building of rapid transit facilities in such cities as San Francisco, Oakland, Washington, D.C., Baltimore, and Philadelphia. The percent of increase over the decade of the 1970s, as measured in square feet, ranged from 33 percent in Chicago to 90 percent in Houston and 100 percent in St. Louis.[6]

Hotels

The status of hotels in the central city seemed mixed at the end of the 1970s. There has been significant and visible building in many of the major cities across the United States. San Francisco and Atlanta are conspicuous examples of places in which hotel rooms were built in the 1970s. However, much of the new hotel space may be at the expense of older hotels in central cities, since the number of hotels rooms in central cities has been decreasing.

Retailing

Retail functions in downtown areas of central cities have not kept pace with office building construction and general employment. During the 1960s and 1970s the proportion of retail trade in downtowns declined constantly. This was a function not only of population decline in central cities but also of the movement of upper and middle income families to the suburbs. The remaining population, heavily minority and heavily poor, have not been able to afford the large amounts of money required to maintain shopping at the former level. Competition of outlying shopping centers has also been an important ingredient in the reduction in retail sales in central cities.

The magnitude of this shift is indicated in the following description:

Huge shopping centers are established on the periphery; downtown department stores open suburban branches; food stores are quick to tap the growing market; and discount houses emerge to offer a new form of competition to the merchandising traditionalists. Convenient to the suburban housewife and equipped with ample parking facilities, the new centers lure shoppers away not only from the downtown stores but also from the business districts of outlying neighborhoods and the older suburban communities. These latter concentrations are especially vulnerable, since they have neither the amenities of the new shopping centers nor the wide selection of merchandise of the central business district.[7]

Policy options for public and private infrastructure Neighborhoods should be the "building blocks of cities." In planning for urban infrastructure, cities have quite a few tools for influencing and directly affecting policies of other governments. Examples include: (1) marketing excess capacity (water and sewer service, for example) to the suburbs; (2) changing federal matching funds formulas to encourage improvement of inner city capital stock; (3) working with state municipal leagues and other state and national organizations to change state and federal laws; (4) working for state–local and regional–local tax sharing; (5) working with the state on public transportation financing (in Michigan, for example, 1 percent of the state sales tax is earmarked for local transit);

(6) working with the state for state-imposed limits on certain types of urban growth; (7) encouraging urban homesteading; and (8) continually reviewing federal and state policies, particularly grant programs, for unintended or unrecognized adverse side effects.

Overall, cities need to develop a "foreign policy" to monitor, evaluate, and change state and federal policies and programs.

Source: Abstracted from Mark J. Kasoff, "Public and Private Infrastructures in Mature Cities," paper presented at the Conference on Managing Mature Cities, sponsored by the city of Cincinnati and the Charles F. Kettering Foundation, Cincinnati, Ohio, 9–10 June 1977.

Despite the significance of this shift, the central business district still retains a basic retail strength in large department stores and specialty shops. The strength of central business district retailing is derived primarily from people who are there for purposes other than shopping—that is, people who work in the central area; those who are in the central area for medical or dental services; persons who are downtown for business, financial, or legal matters; and tourists and out-of-town visitors attending conventions or sports events.[8]

The obsolescence of industrial sites

The industrial areas of our central cities have not fared as well as have the central business districts. A significant amount of industry has left the central cities primarily because of obsolescence of industrial sites and deterioration of the industrial infrastructure. Two significant reasons are the changes in methods of transporting goods and the changes in technology which have rendered the old plants obsolete.

Traditionally, the location of industry within the central cities was tied to the railroads, and, until well into the twentieth century, the primary method of shipping goods was by rail. Industrial areas in the central cities were inevitably linked to rail traffic.

Inner city industrial districts began to become obsolete when the motor driven truck was developed in the early 1900s. This was accentuated by the development of a network of good roads and highways in the United States after World War I. At that point industrial development was no longer closely tied to railroads, and industry could look to other sites, primarily along the highways.

Gentrification   *Gentrification,* a term taken from the movements of social classes in and around London, is a trend that has been noted during the 1970s in large central cities in the United States, especially in the Northeast and the Midwest. Several reasons can be assigned to this trend.

First, cities increasingly are drawing highly skilled professionals who deal in information in all of its ramifications: banking, law, finance, publishing, radio–television, advertising, etc. The long-term national shift in employment from manufacturing to service employment has been magnified in the cities.

Second, the rapidly rising cost of housing in suburban areas makes central city real estate much more competitive.

Third, there is recognition of quality, or personal value, factors, including: a preference for the cultural strengths of the central city compared to the life-style offered in the suburbs; a willingness to accept, as a trade-off, the noise, pollution, congestion, and other drawbacks of the central city in return for many advantages; and an appreciation of both the aesthetic and structural values of central

city housing that was largely built prior to the 1930s.

Fourth, the generally smaller housing units—both apartments and row houses—characteristic of larger central cities are adequate because families are smaller.

Finally, the persons moving into these rehabilitated housing units are young, well educated, and affluent.

These changes, however, come at a price.

First, the extensive renovations and improvements to residential and commercial properties inevitably raise rents and property values. This drives the poor and working class persons formerly in those areas to other locations.

Second, this movement, which has been noted in London, Paris, and Washington, D.C., brings urban tension, including racial unrest.

Source: Abstracted from Blake Fleetwood, "The New Elite and an Urban Renaissance," *The New York Times Magazine,* 14 January 1979, pp. 17 ff.

Once the Interstate Highway System and supporting state roads were in place, the nation had a transportation system that was more intricate than the railroad system and that covered more territory than did the railroads. Trucks could be used to deliver most goods, for both long and short hauls, between and within the metropolitan areas. The new industrial locations became those sites which had access to the new highway network.

The older industrial areas located within the central cities were served by a series of streets which were not built for heavy truck traffic. The garment district in New York, for example, where trucks still attempt to navigate in, out, and through the narrow streets, testifies to the difficulty of serving manufacturing and distribution functions in older central city industrial areas. The truck also made many of the older industrial sites obsolete because they could not accommodate the parking, turning, and other functions required by truck shipment.

Three factors, then, hastened the exodus of industry from central cities. The first was the development of the Interstate Highway System, which made it possible for industrial plants to be located almost anywhere in the United States. With goods that could be shipped by truck, and employees who could commute by automobile from distances of sixty to seventy miles, a factory had almost unlimited locational possibilities. The preferred location has been along the Interstate Highway System, preferably near an interchange.

The second factor was the development of continuous flow automation processes, common to many industries, which require a large floor area in a single story plant. The multistory loft buildings common to older industrial areas in central cities are obsolete for most modern industrial processes.

The third factor is space for employee parking. Public transportation is often inadequate or nonexistent, and workers therefore depend on their cars. Land for parking is mandatory. Older industrial sites in central areas cannot compete with the modern industrial facility that provides generous off-street parking.

Central city finance

The financial difficulties of New York City in the 1970s are a vivid reminder of the revenue problems of local government finance. The fiscal question facing cities therefore is not whether the budget will be balanced (the budget must be balanced) but at what level public services can be provided and public facilities maintained.

Under these circumstances, where revenues do not match the rate of increase in the price level of goods and services (usually the rate of inflation), the level of public services must be dropped to balance the budget. This can be done in either of two ways: ordinary public services can be cut back; or normal maintenance, such as street cleaning and repair, maintenance of public buildings, and maintenance of other facilities, can be curtailed. In either case the residents of the city bear the consequences. If public services are curtailed the quality of life for residents of the city is reduced. This is especially true for low income residents who have little recourse in the private market for additional education and health services. If public maintenance is curtailed the massive investment in the infrastructure will deteriorate to the detriment of the entire metropolitan area.

The property tax

The traditional source of financing the bulk of city expenditures has been the property tax, an ad valorem tax on real estate within the boundaries of the city. Property taxation has been left almost exclusively to the cities as their primary means of revenue generation. Effective tax rates in cities of 50,000 or more for single family residences at the beginning of the 1970s ranged from 0.1 to 6.4 percent of the sales price.[9] The city can add to its tax base by having privately owned residential, commercial, or industrial property built within its boundaries. This is why most cities are anxious to obtain new industry, office buildings, or high value residential real estate.

A problem faced by many older central cities is that the tax base is shrinking. The amount of taxable property either has been decreasing (in terms of constant dollars) or has not been increasing at a rate sufficient to maintain a given level of services. Some cities in the United States have actually had a decrease in their tax base.

One reason for this shrinking tax base has been population loss. For example, Chicago lost 295,273 in population between 1970 and 1976, a drop of 8.8 percent. In Cleveland the numerical population loss (125,236) was much smaller than in Chicago but the drop was 17 percent.[10] Loss of population can have a disastrous effect on the tax base if it leads to housing abandonment. A loss of business and residences will mean a loss in the value of taxable property.

Cooperative approaches to urban services Revitalization of local government and the physical, social, and economic systems it supports demands building greater capacity into neighborhoods. Such rebuilding can best be done through the following four approaches.

A neighborhood multility is a corporate or cooperative organization for providing interlocking tools to meet basic requirements for food, energy, shelter, water, air, and waste management.

The neighborhood mutual involves decoding community information from hospitals, the police department, schools, and other sources to define underlying problems, and then developing action options that are neighborhood-based and supported. In Evanston, Illinois, for example, the Learning Exchange is an organization of 40,000 members who can teach at low cost on any of 6,000 topics. The system provides an extraordinarily wide range of educational choices. Any member can phone a central information center and get a reference to possible teachers.

The work of the South Shore National Bank in Chicago to invest in a deteriorating neighborhood is a good example of organic banking. Through its Development Center, the bank works continuously to seek out investments in the neighborhood that will stimulate housing and commercial renewal. The bank looks not only at conventional investment and credit but also at the capacities and objectives of the people in South Shore.

"Neighborhood governance is the fourth dimension of building neighborhood vitality." There are many forms of such governance, but neighborhood forums provide one of the best ways for citizens to express their concerns and interests to local government and to other bureaucracies as well.

Source: Abstracted from Stanley J. Hallett, "Low-cost Options: Explorations in Alternative Urban Constitutions, Policies and Practices," paper presented at the conference on Managing Mature Cities sponsored by the city of Cincinnati and the Charles F. Kettering Foundation, Cincinnati, Ohio, 9–10 June 1977.

In assessing commercial property most appraisers use the income approach. When business decreases there is a slackening in the demand for industrial and commercial space, which usually means that rents will fall. As rents fall so will the valuation of commercial property, since such property is usually valued on an income basis. When this happens the amount of the assessments for commercial and industrial property decreases.

Most residential property is assessed on the basis of its comparable market (sales) value. In some sections of some central cities the problems of abandonment and deteriorating conditions are so severe and the environment has become so poor that the desirability of the area as a place to live has been adversely affected. This has had the effect of reducing the market value for individual houses; the result is a decreasing amount of taxable residential property within the city.

In addition to the lowering of values of residential properties and the loss of income as business and industry move to the suburbs, other erosions of the property tax base can come about through the increase in tax exempt properties such as universities, hospitals, and other nonprofit institutions.

Sales and income taxes

The property tax has been the traditional and accepted method of financing local government. Central cities with declining property tax bases face the fact that other taxes are difficult to enact.

The local sales tax is in use in about half the states and is a possible revenue source, but it presents serious problems in correlation with neighboring jurisdictions. The principal objection, however, is the inherent limitation of regressiveness—that is, as proportion of income the tax falls more heavily on the poor, who, of necessity, must spend a higher proportion of their income on food, clothing, and housing.

The local income tax is another significant revenue source; it existed in the local governments of nine states and the District of Columbia as of 1972. Thirteen of the forty-eight largest cities in the United States had this tax in 1972. Like the sales tax, however, it is exceedingly complex and difficult to administer, although it brings a significant amount of revenue.

Attempts to enact a municipal income tax usually meet with fierce opposition. The opposition is particularly vehement from commuters, who usually have allies within state legislatures.

Categorical aid programs

Although in recent years there has been a tendency on the part of the federal government to reduce categorical aid programs (that is, federal monies for separate, specific programs) in favor of block grants, several important categorical aid programs benefit cities.

The Urban Mass Transportation Administration (UMTA) provides grants to city transport systems for both capital acquisitions and operating expenses. Over the years these grants have been increased, so that today a significant portion of local transportation is paid for with federal funds. UMTA will provide up to 80 percent of the capital costs for rolling stock and other expenses. In addition, federal operating subsidies may account for as much as one-third of the operating costs.

There are other federal programs that also provide fiscal support and relief to the central cities. These are special education programs, funded by the Elementary and Secondary Education Assistance Act, that provide central city school districts with education programs aimed at disadvantaged students.

Other categorical programs which aid cities include those undertaken by the Economic Development Administration and the Environmental Protection Agency (water and sewer facilities grants), but the categorical programs have been small compared with federal assistance to cities under what is known as general revenue sharing.

Revenue sharing

In 1964 a revenue sharing plan was outlined by Walter W. Heller and Joseph A. Pechman. Under this plan the receipts of the federal government from the federal income tax were to be unconditionally shared with state and local governments. The plan was proposed because problems had been arising with regard to state–local finances, since state–local tax revenues are slower in responding to changes in national income. Revenue sharing was intended as an addition to, rather than a substitute for, federal categorical grants.

In October 1972 the State and Local Fiscal Assistance Act of 1972, or general revenue sharing, became law. Initially, the law provided unconditional grants of $30.2 billion for five years, one-third going to state governments and two-thirds going to general purpose local governments. Two separate formulas which form what Maxwell and Aronson have called "a dualism without parallel in any other federal fiscal measure"[11] are used as criteria for grant allocation. The Senate formula, used for allocations to thirty-one states, consists of three criteria: population; per capita income; and tax effort, or the ratio of total state and local tax revenue to personal income of the residents of the state. The House formula, used for allocations to nineteen states and the District of Columbia, consists of five criteria: population; per capita income; urbanized population; tax effort; and 15 percent of revenue from personal income taxation. The thirty-one/nineteen breakdown is not fixed by law; use of either formula depends on which one gives a state a more favorable allocation. The original revenue sharing program expired 31 December 1976; it was extended by Congress until late 1980.[12]

According to one study,[13] local jurisdictions have used 57.5 percent of revenue sharing funds for "new" purposes and 42.5 percent for substitution. Substitution includes using the funds for reducing present taxes, stabilizing taxes, or avoiding borrowing. State governments used 35.7 percent for "new" purposes and 64.3 percent for substitution. During the period 1974–75, for the United States as a whole, revenue sharing receipts were 2.6 percent of state total tax revenue and 6.8 percent of local total tax revenue. However, revenue sharing receipts were 34.7 percent of the total increase in state tax revenue during 1974–75 across the United States. Similarly, revenue sharing receipts accounted for 87.2 percent of increase in local tax revenue during 1974–75. As a percent of total tax revenue in each state, revenue sharing receipts ranged from 1.3 percent in Alaska to 5.4 percent in Mississippi. With regard to local tax revenues, revenue sharing receipts ranged from 4.1 percent in New Jersey to 26 percent in Mississippi.[14]

An evaluation of central city finance

Many of the fiscal problems of metropolitan areas are a part of the fiscal plight of the central cities. By the 1970s about one-half of the nation's poor lived in metropolitan areas, and of those persons about twice as many lived in central cities as in the suburbs. The special conditions of the poor, and of others in the central cities, put special pressures on the municipal government for services, especially for education, welfare, and health—the most expensive services to provide. This in turn puts pressure on local revenue sources which are not as responsive (especially the property tax) as are many of the revenue sources for state and federal governments.

Werner Hirsch has noted that the residents of America's central cities made heavy demands on city budgets in the 1970s and these demands were intensified not only by congestion but also by the expectations spawned by the various federal programs of the 1960s. The revenue sources of central cities are not, in the language of the economist, sufficiently elastic to respond to these demands— that is, the revenue from these types of sources tends to rise at a slower rate than the rise in aggregate income. The low income elasticity of tax revenues forces central cities, and many of the older suburbs as well, to turn to greater reliance on state and federal grants.[15]

This disparity led to the interest in revenue sharing and the Community Development Block Grant (CDBG) program which came to the fore in the early and mid-1970s. These revenue sources helped overcome the poor match between municipal resources and the demands for municipal services that are heavily oriented toward the broad spectrum of health, education, and welfare. (These financial issues are covered in greater detail in Chapter 5.)

The impact of citywide programs and policies

Almost all of our older central cities, as this chapter has indicated, face chronic financial problems that are exacerbated by the correlative conditions of the increased costs of slums, poverty, crime, and a revenue structure based on a deteriorating tax base. Efforts to correct these conditions, which have depended largely on federal grants, have been going on for a generation. The federal Housing Act of 1949 is usually considered the starting point of major large scale urban redevelopment in this country. Not only was money made available for massive clearance and redevelopment of central city areas, but the stage was also set for political and public acceptance of these programs. The Housing Act of 1954 made the highly significant addition of urban renewal. In addition to land clearance and redevelopment, the ideas, concepts, and, subsequently, the programs, were provided for rehabilitation and conservation. This three part approach—clearance, rehabilitation, and conservation—has carried forward to the present time.

The three Rs of planning The three Rs of planning in the mature city are reorientation, replanning, and reimplementation.

Reorientation means, for example, that instead of planning for 10,000 more people we plan for 10,000 fewer people. General goals and objectives are about the same, but the issues, alternatives, and strategies are different. Some of the practical applications in Dayton include extensive citizen participation, extensive use of priority board need statements, a fragmented planning and development process, and a management by objectives program.

Replanning has been done for major elements, including neighborhood planning process, city commission issue and policy sessions, land use planning that emphasizes the management of change, transportation planning that emphasizes what we have rather than system extensions, urban design for the central business district that emphasizes the human scale, economic development emphasizing the service sector, and capital programming.

Reimplementation efforts are [directed toward making] the city of Dayton . . . a viable urban community. Such efforts include the development of historic districts, the development of environmental quality districts, promotion of living within the city, and public–private development and redevelopment partnerships in such activities as urban renewal, neighborhood initiative programs, business district initiative programs, and management of changing land uses.

Source: Anthony B. Char, Director, Department of Planning, and George Farmer, Senior Planner, Department of Planning, City of Dayton, Ohio, remarks made at the APA National Conference, Miami Beach, Florida, 3 March 1979.

Further landmark federal legislation was enacted in 1966 with the Demonstration Cities and Metropolitan Development Act. This act provided for the Model Cities program, which enabled neighborhoods or other small designated areas of cities to (within statutory limits) set up their own programs for conservation and rehabilitation. Even though Model Cities as a federal program later was eliminated, it was highly significant in providing the groundwork for citizen participation—a concept that has been carried forward to the present time.

Finally, in 1974 Congress passed the Housing and Community Development Act, which abolished categorical grants-in-aid and replaced them with a block grant system. One of the most significant features of Community Development is to encourage a federal approach to local planning on a more integrated scale. (See Chapter 2 for a brief description in a historical context of these federal acts.)

These federal programs have set in motion the expansion of city planning, training, and practice; the growth of many kinds of federal grant programs aimed generally at the reconstruction and preservation of cities; and the emergence of citizen participation in a framework outside conventional citizen boards, commissions, and advisory committees. The effects of these programs and some of their implications for local government planning are set forth in the following sections, covering urban redevelopment, urban renewal, Model Cities, and the Community Development Block Grant program.

Urban redevelopment

Urban redevelopment as the natural process whereby cities continually renew themselves through private and public investment must be differentiated from the federal urban renewal program. Urban redevelopment in the generic sense can be considered a process whereby the physical face and form of the city change naturally because of economic decisions, or political or administrative action, or in the aftermath of a natural disaster. (The urban renewal program, on the other hand, attempts to change the development pattern of the city, usually in designated areas, through governmental intervention, including federal subsidies, local government land clearance and assembly, and resale of land for specified purposes.)

The stock of buildings slowly deteriorates because of wear and tear and obsolescence. At some point it may become economical to demolish an old structure and put the land to a more productive use. In most instances a decision to replace one land use with another is predicated on the new investment's producing a higher rate of return than that of the existing one. The concept used by appraisers is that the highest and best use maximizes the economic return to the landowner. The operation of this concept is frequently evident in downtown commercial reuse of land. Because of high land values in downtown locations the highest and best use of land may often be intensive commercial development such as high rise office buildings or hotels.

In many instances market incentives are sufficient to initiate demolition and reuse or rehabilitation of old buildings. If the rate of return in an alternative use is higher than the current return, the business decision would be to rebuild or rehabilitate. This situation tends to make economic sense when the current market value of the existing structure is low and the imputed value of the site is high, and where the anticipated reuse promises a greater return. For example, an old and obsolete building located at a desirable downtown intersection may be worth far less than the site. The economic decision to demolish and rebuild would be an easy one. But one might consider another case, where the building is not quite obsolete but the site is not being put to its optimum use. A decision to demolish and rebuild may not be as easy in this case because the current land use represents substantial value. Return from a new land use must be high enough to compensate for the destruction of value in the former use.

Aside from economic forces, the renewal process occurs in response to local government decisions. Local governments need real property for offices, schools, parks, hospitals, roads, and other public facilities. The decisions are not always based on purely market considerations, nor are they always based on highest and best use criteria. The city council may not be able to selectively choose properties on the basis of price, as in the case of right-of-way acquisitions or hospital and school expansions. There are many factors that a public body must consider in deciding on use and reuse of land for public purposes, and highest and best use, in the traditional economic sense, is only one criterion among several.

Cities often change dramatically as the result of natural disasters, such as floods, earthquakes, and fires. The great Chicago fire and the San Francisco earthquake left large portions of these cities devastated. The rebuilding which followed did much to change the character of neighborhoods.

More recently, the riots of the 1960s in many large central cities devastated extensive areas. Although the devastation was not on the scale of the Chicago

Figure 16–4   Before (top) and after (bottom) views of the conversion
of the abandoned plant of the American Machine and Foundry Company
to the Lutheran Medical Center in Brooklyn, New York. The facility
includes more than 500 hospital beds.

fire or the San Francisco earthquake, they still altered the characteristics of many neighborhoods.

An important market factor, if land is to be reused, is that the property to be rehabilitated or removed must usually be of low current value with a significant differential in the economic return between the existing and alternative uses of the property. If the structure, has significant current value, then the value of the land in an alternative use may not have a differential that is large enough to warrant the demolition of the old property. This is frequently encountered in residential land uses. Even older deteriorated apartment buildings and single family houses have current values which are too high to make demolition and rebuilding feasible, given the existing return.

Another impediment to land reuse is the difficulty of assembling individual sites into large parcels. When individuals hold out for higher prices, this difficulty is compounded.

Land use management and economic reality What land management strategies are open to us as we thin out and [as] holes open up in the city? . . . We could try to guide depopulation into some kind of a checkerboard pattern, clustering both those persons who remain and those places emptying out. Or we could try to thin out residential density—encourage larger lots.

The checkerboard pattern strategy of trying to keep the remaining population tightly clustered comes to mind easily because of military analogies—regrouping after losses, consolidating a position. . . . One obvious advantage of using a checkerboard strategy is to maintain efficiency in the delivery of public services. . . . Under depopulation, checkerboard style, we could [achieve] greater physical separation between communities and help them establish greater physical identity which could lead to greater community identity.

We don't really have to economize on space for its own sake, so we are free to thin out, here and there, down to suburban densities. In those central cities that depopulate down to [for example] two-thirds to three-quarters of their peak populations we could accommodate more than one-half of the households on quarter-acre lots. The arithmetic is convincing. . . . There is one clear and powerful advantage [to] opening up the housing pattern by thinning: most families prefer smaller private spaces to larger public spaces. There are fewer spillovers of noise, and smells of burning things, and whatever else bothers people living too close together. Privacy is much greater.

Source: Excerpted from Wilbur Thompson, untitled paper presented at the Conference on Managing Mature Cities, sponsored by the city of Cincinnati and the Charles F. Kettering Foundation, Cincinnati, Ohio, 9–10 June 1977.

A problem continually faced by the older central cities is how to both prevent and eradicate slums and blight in residential, commercial, and industrial sections of the city in the absence of private economic incentives. Private market incentives have frequently proved inadequate to cope with neighborhood blight in the central cities, especially in low income neighborhoods. There are exceptions of course, such as Old Town in Chicago, Georgetown in Washington, D.C., Greenwich Village in New York City, and Pacific Heights in San Francisco (as mentioned earlier), where widespread private rehabilitation has occurred—but these areas, again, are exceptions.

Urban renewal

The federal urban renewal program, which lasted from 1949 to 1974, was an attempt to use federal subsidies to overcome the economic difficulties involved in renewing deteriorated portions of central cities. The purpose of Title I of the Housing Act of 1949 was to clear slum areas and rebuild with new housing. Over the years the program evolved into one of land clearance and land assembly for moderate and high income housing, downtown redevelopment, and industrial area renewal, in addition to its original purpose of providing new housing for the poor.

The mechanics of the urban renewal program were fairly simple. First, a community had to devise a workable program for community improvement which indicated that it had appropriate zoning, housing, and building codes and mechanisms for citizen participation. On the acceptance of the workable program, the U.S. Department of Housing and Urban Development (HUD)—or predecessor federal agency—would certify the community's eligibility for certain loans and grants. The city would then set up a local public agency (LPA) (such as an urban renewal agency) to administer its program. The LPA would submit redevelopment plans to HUD; if these were approved HUD would lend money to the LPA to carry out the program.

The program itself would consist of land acquisition, relocation of residents in the project area, site clearance, site preparation, and site disposition to a private or public developer for reuse. The sale proceeds would be deducted from the total project cost and the net project cost would be shared by HUD and the LPA. The LPA would be required to pay only 25 percent of the net project cost —the difference being the land writedown, or subsidy. The size of the land writedown was significant enough so that many projects which would not have been feasible as private ventures (on the basis of before and after rates of return) were in fact undertaken.

Evaluation of the program   By 1974, when the urban renewal program was formally halted, 2,107 projects had been approved by HUD. Approximately 43 percent had been completed, and the remainder were in various stages of completion. The urban renewal program had completely changed the face and character of many city neighborhoods and downtown areas. Dramatic changes had occurred in many cities such as San Francisco, Baltimore, and Hartford. Many slum neighborhoods had been completely eradicated and many others rehabilitated. New commercial and residential projects had been used to anchor declining central business districts. Older industrial areas had been refurbished and modernized. Many universities and hospitals had used the program to provide land for expansion and to upgrade their immediate environs. Across the nation many cities could point to impressive redevelopment projects in areas which had once been slums.

In spite of the numerous successes of the federal urban renewal program, the program was terminated by Congress with passage of the Housing and Community Development Act of 1974. Offsetting the successes of the program were many examples in which the program had not worked out as Congress had originally intended. Slum clearance in itself had not worked to cure the underlying problems causing urban decay.

The federal urban renewal program did not adequately serve the needs of the poor as had been originally intended. Although many slum buildings were eliminated, they were often not replaced with low income housing. When the program was enacted it was anticipated that a vigorous public housing program would accompany it. The Housing Act of 1949 had authorized 800,000 units of public housing to be built by 1955. New public housing was to provide housing for most of those being displaced. But the public housing construction did not approach keeping pace with the demolitions. By 1955 less than 250,000 units had been built. There were serious problems in relocating those who had been displaced. The poor were often shifted from one slum area to another, and new slums were often created in the process.

Congress became uneasy when it was evident that the underlying problems were not addressed by clearance alone. In 1954 the law was amended to place greater emphasis on rehabilitation and conservation and to allow nonresidential use of urban renewal funds. By 1961 as much as 30 percent of urban renewal activity could be for nonresidential uses.

It would be safe to say that urban renewal has about as many supporters as it has detractors. One can point to many positive activities that never would have occurred had it not been for the program. Yet the program has been criticized as being inefficient, wasteful, and ineffective in dealing with the original purpose— that of providing decent housing for the poor. These arguments continue as the cities continue to face the same problems that they had when urban renewal was originally introduced—deteriorating residential and industrial areas, obsolete downtowns, shrinking tax bases, competition from the suburbs, and expanding requirements for public services.

Lessons learned from the process Now that the federal urban renewal program is history, what lessons can we point out that were learned from the process? This is especially cogent since the central cities still face what appear to be the same difficult issues of redevelopment and conservation. A quarter of a century later blight and other types of physical deterioration are evident, as well as a myriad of social and economic problems. If we examine what has been accomplished and recognize what yet remains to be done, we might sum up the essense of the lessons learned from the urban renewal experience in the following six statements.

First of all, positive and thoughtful planning to eliminate blight and support rehabilitation and conservation can in itself have a stabilizing effect. The awareness on the part of property owners and residents that the city is concerned and prepared to act could frequently eliminate the uncertainty that would often lead to neglect and deterioration.

Second, there are limits to what can be accomplished solely by slum clearance and rebuilding. Such activities often produce an improved environment by eliminating the worst of the housing stock and replacing it with decent housing. The appearance of neighborhoods may be greatly improved, the tax base enhanced, and housing opportunities for those fortunate enough to live there greatly upgraded. But much of the good can be undone if slum areas spontaneously form elsewhere and no fundamental improvement is made in the lives of those who are displaced. The blight and misery will reappear, possibly to be the subject of a future slum clearance project on the other side of town.

Third, the dislocation and displacement of people as a result of renewal and rehabilitation programs cannot be ignored or treated lightly. Whether the dislocation is the direct result of a government program or the indirect result of government supported programs or of independent private efforts, it is the burden of the city to take positive steps to assure adequate housing for those dislocated. It has taken time, plus litigation, for this lesson to sink in. But to pretend that this is not a problem or that it is someone else's responsibility is to sweep the dirt under the carpet.

Fourth, public subsidies are not a replacement for a healthy economic base and for well-planned commercial and industrial development. By no means does this imply that economic development can be reduced to a growth/no growth simplism. Although there are rare exceptions, the underlying generalization is that economic strength comes from the private sector—its employment, its capital investment, and the taxes it pays.

Fifth, community involvement in the planning for redevelopment can be positive and productive. There was considerable experimentation, often amid controversy, over the best form of neighborhood and citizen involvement in urban renewal. What emerged was the formal requirement for project action committees, composed of residents, to work with the local agency. On the balance the citizen input, which could take a variety of forms, proved to be a stabilizing and positive factor.

Sixth, code enforcement administration can be a valuable tool in conservation. The workable program required that cities develop building and housing codes to qualify for urban renewal. Few cities had housing codes prior to 1954 when the requirement was imposed. Today, innovative and flexible methods of code enforcement are continuously evolving.

The above are among some of the important lessons learned from the twenty-five years of the federal urban renewal program. To the extent that they have been learned by planners and policymakers, they will help in guiding urban redevelopment and conservation efforts in the future, regardless of whether federal or local programs are used.

Cutback planning All this has crucial implications for planning. In the future, cities will have to plan for stability and decline, and the growth-planning of the past will have to be replaced by what I call cutback planning. Like other city decision-makers, planners will have to learn how to plan for reduced and declining capital and operating expenditures, and to figure out how to develop a viable and functioning city under conditions of decline.

The goals, concepts, indicators, and methods of cutback planning remain to be invented, but it is clearly high time to invent them. The first step is to begin to identify—as much as possible empirically—the various consequences of stasis and decline, and to determine both the costs and benefits for the various groups and aggregates in the city. The most important issue in cutback planning is, of course, who should bear the major costs, financial and otherwise.

Source: Excerpted from Herbert J. Gans, "Planning for Declining and Poor Cities," *Journal of the American Institute of Planners* 41 (September 1975): 305.

Model Cities

The Model Cities program was an outgrowth of the Demonstration Cities and Metropolitan Development Act of 1966. The purpose of the act was to produce a program through which physical and social activities could be coordinated to provide more effective aid to low income people in the central cities. The program sought to enlist the interest and energies of the people who lived in low income areas and use them to the extent feasible in administering programs of social service.

The program, which became known as Model Cities, employed a two stage process: the planning of coordinated activities, and the program execution. City demonstration agencies (CDAs) were formed to work with the disparate local public and private organizations to carry out the program. In many ways the CDAs were independent of the local political structure. CDAs were funded by HUD directly with little liaison with the local government; this frequently caused considerable friction with local elected political leaders.

For the action or second stage of the program HUD would finance programs with direct grants or would provide seed money to activate and institute other federal programs. Under Model Cities, a great variety of activities were undertaken, since the program provided the flexibility. Nearly half of the programs were in education, housing, and health.

The Housing and Community Development Act of 1974 ended the Model Cities program by placing it within the Community Development program. Throughout its brief existence, Model Cities had been controversial. There were many charges to the effect that the program was wasteful and inefficient. It was unpopular with elected officials because they had little control over it. And, in the end, the Model Cities effort had little effect on alleviating the problems faced by low income people living in the central cities: slums and blight, lack of adequate opportunities, and racial and ethnic discrimination.

In spite of the controversy surrounding Model Cities, however, the program did in fact bequeath a positive legacy. First, it provided opportunities for many central city residents to participate in program administration. Many who might never have had the opportunity were given administrative and policymaking experience. Second, it supported a number of viable community development enterprises, many of which are still in existence. Third, it established the fact that local citizen input can be positive and valuable in the attempt to fight blight and poverty.

Another important contribution of Model Cities was the acceptance—even to the point of institutionalization—of neighborhood input into the planning and resource allocation process. Low income neighborhoods finally had a structure which could sustain their efforts to communicate their positions and ideas on issues which affected their welfare.

Before the advent of Model Cities, lower income neighborhoods did not have the kinds of stable social organizations that could express their interests and represent them on such matters as local economic development, public services delivery systems, physical redevelopment, and social services. Traditional neighborhood social clubs, church groups, and political organizations, while influential, were not prepared for such a range of activities. The Model Cities program sponsored community based organizations that filled a definite need.

And, in fact, the impact of the program went beyond the low income Model Cities neighborhoods. Residents of moderate and middle income neighborhoods could observe the recognition afforded to the Model Cities neighborhoods by city hall. It is probably no coincidence that stable neighborhood based organizations are now common in most cities.

Local governments have now had experience with active citizen participation in local programs that extends back to the late 1960s. Although the strongest roots of this movement go back to Model Cities, such participation is now routinely accepted as integral to the administration of most programs.

Community Development Block Grants

By 1974 the direct assistance to cities from HUD consisted of several categorical programs, each targeted toward a specific phase of urban development. The Housing and Community Development Act of 1974 consolidated most of the categorical programs and replaced them with the Community Development Block Grant (CDBG) program. The former categorical programs such as urban renewal, Model Cities, water and sewer grants, and urban beautification were subsumed under the new program. Instead of receiving aid for particular programs, the cities received a lump sum which could be used in a variety of urban development activities.

Eligible recipients of CDBG funds are cities with populations of more than 50,000 and urban counties with populations of more than 200,000. Certain smaller cities that had previously participated in HUD programs were continued under a hold harmless provision. One very important distinction between Community Development Block Grants and the earlier programs that it supplemented is that CDBG is an entitlement grant which does not require the elaborate justification that the categorical programs required. Money is given to eligible recipients on the basis of an entitlement formula. Some restrictions are placed on the use of the funds, but the recipients have far more latitude in determining the mix of programs than was the case under the categorical programs.

The funds authorized by Congress for the program are distributed on the basis of a formula which considers population, housing condition, and poverty, with poverty given extra weight. In 1977 the formula was amended to give cities the option of using the original formula or an alternative formula which includes age of housing as a variable. The latter formula is more advantageous to older cities in the Northeast and Midwest. The original formula was heavily criticized as favoring the cities in the Sunbelt, or the South and West. Under the dual formula system the cities can select the more favorable calculation. The differences between the amounts under the alternative formulas can be significant. For example, the differences between the formula entitlements for Philadelphia was approximately $33 million for fiscal year 1980.

Objectives and requirements The Community Development Block Grant program has the following eight objectives:

1. Elimination of slums and blight
2. Elimination of conditions which are detrimental to health, safety, and the public welfare
3. Conservation and expansion of the nation's housing stock to provide a decent home and suitable living environment to every family
4. Expansion and improvement of the quantity and quality of community services
5. A more rational use of land and other resources
6. Reduction of the isolation of income groups through spatial deconcentration of housing opportunities for persons of lower income
7. Restoration and preservation of properties of special value
8. Expansion of economic opportunity, principally for low and moderate income persons.

These objectives encompass those of the urban renewal and Model Cities programs. Slum and blight eradication, housing conservation, and historical preservation were all purposes of urban renewal. Improvement of community services and expansion of economic opportunities have roots in Model Cities. In addition, the CDBG program has an expressed mandate for affirmative action in pursuit of the goals of the 1968 Fair Housing Law.

Congress intended the CDBG program to address a variety of urban situations—from physical renewal to community services. However, there are some conditions attached to receipt of a Community Development Block Grant. First, most of the money is to go for activities which benefit low and moderate income families. It is not intended to be spread throughout a city and used in areas which are clearly not low or moderate income; however, economic development activities that occur in nonresidential areas are eligible.

All recipients must prepare a housing assistance plan (HAP), which has the following four essential parts:

1. A statement of housing conditions in the community, indicating the portion of substandard housing
2. A statement of housing needs by age and race
3. A statement of the community's goals for the immediate future for providing housing assistance, based on the existing housing conditions and the demonstrated needs
4. A statement showing where in the city or county the assisted housing will be provided.

In estimating housing needs the recipient must determine not only the needs of its present residents but also the housing assistance needs of those who can reasonably be expected to reside in the community. This provision in the HAP relates to the sixth goal of the CDBG program—reduction of the concentration of persons of lower income. It also assists in the implementation of the Fair Housing Law to provide expanded housing opportunities to minority groups, many of whom need housing assistance. Cities must make good faith efforts to implement the requirements of the housing assistance plans, including the expected-to-reside portion. Failure to make good faith efforts to provide low and moderate income housing may be grounds for denial of participation in the CDBG program.

One further point of interest in the operation of the CDBG program is that, although great latitude is given each recipient in determining the specific projects, the money must be spent for Community Development activities. The money must not be used as a substitute for or augmentation of the city's regular operations. It cannot be used to pay for ordinary and normal services, such as police and fire protection and other routine municipal functions. And it was not intended to relieve the property tax burden on any city.

Figure 16–5   Courthouse Square, Dayton, Ohio. Work was almost finished in mid-1979 for redevelopment of the entire block to encompass the restoration and rehabilitation of the Montgomery County courthouse, built in 1850, and the construction of an open plaza, two major office buildings, two underground restaurants, and a major department store.

Urban Development Action Grants   The Housing and Community Development Act of 1977 created the Urban Development Action Grant (UDAG) to aid cities that demonstrate economic and physical distress. The initial congressional appropriation was $400 million annually for fiscal years 1978, 1979, and 1980. UDAG eligibility is calculated by a formula that measures distress factors such as population decline, unemployment, poverty, age of housing stock, and job decline. Cities are rated by an index composed of these distress indicators.

Urban Development Action Grants are meant to provide an incentive for private economic development efforts. The public money is intended to be catalytic in nature rather than to provide the primary financing of a project. UDAG funds should be leveraged with private capital to create the total investment package. For example, UDAG funds might be used to purchase property in an older industrial district for which there were existing tenants. Or it could be used to provide utilities or land improvements for the purpose of attracting businesses to the area. A UDAG might be for a downtown project that creates jobs, such as a hotel or a convention center.

Cities must compete for UDAGs. Mere eligibility based on distress factors does not entitle a city to a grant. A successful grant application must demonstrate: (1) that the project is economically feasible and viable; (2) that there is a commitment of private investment and that the grant funds will be augmented; and (3) that the city has demonstrated results in providing equal opportunity in employment and housing.

Where planning gets done Another characteristic of our approach is the focus on helping make decisions today that create a future tomorrow. We are not really interested in predicting the future. We are interested in making the future. . . .

Another characteristic of our Kansas City environment is that it is driven by the private sector. *We can help the private sector get things done, but the private*

sector is really making decisions that affect the form, function, physical character, and life within the city.

Source: Excerpted from Joseph E. Vitt, Jr., "Kansas City: Problems and Successes of Downtown Development," in *Personality, Politics, and Planning: How City Planners Work*, ed. Anthony James Catanese and W. Paul Farmer (Beverly Hills, Calif.: Sage Publications, 1978), pp. 107, 109.

The competitive nature of the UDAG program distinguishes it from previous urban renewal efforts at economic development. Also, UDAG offers little in the way of a direct subsidy for economic development projects. Projects have to prove their viability and stand on their own, as UDAG is the catalyst and not the crutch. This insistence on economic viability is certainly one of the lessons learned from urban renewal.

Planning strategies for conservation and redevelopment

The climate of planning in central cities has shifted since the 1950s and 1960s. Those decades which produced substantial change were essentially decades of urban growth. Metropolitan areas were growing, even though the central cities were declining in population. Cities seemed confident that the root of their problems was the maldistribution of urban growth—that the suburbs were growing at the city's expense. Therefore, the solution seemed obvious: that of capturing a fair share of the suburban growth. Downtown could be made more competitive with the outlying shopping centers. Incentives could be offered to industry to remain in, or to be attracted to, the city. Middle and upper income housing could be built to attract a middle class return to the cities. These were essentially the planning policies of growth, predicated in part on the assumption that growth in the metropolitan area was inevitable.

By the late 1970s it was realized that the issues were not so simple. The areas with the worst urban distress, the metropolitan areas, were no longer experiencing growth. Between 1970 and 1974 one quarter of all metropolitan areas declined in population. Not only had central cities lost population; many suburbs had also lost population. The decline was most noticeable and critical in the East and Midwest, but the tendency was not restricted.

The underlying causes of the decline were a drastic fall in the birthrate from the post–World War II levels; the lack of appreciable foreign immigration; and the secular shift from the Frostbelt to the Sunbelt. Demographers feel that these trends will not soon be reversed.

The result of these cumulative demographic shifts is that the strategy to capture metropolitan growth is no longer viable for most central cities. The realities are that there is not much net growth to capture and that there is severe competition for what little growth there is. It is true that some standard metropolitan statistical areas (SMSAs) in the Sunbelt (such as Houston and Phoenix) are projected to continue to grow in the 1980s, but this growth is irrelevant to such areas as Detroit and Boston, where the SMSAs are losing population.

The plans and realities of planning
We were impressed by the inherent optimism in each of these people. . . . This optimism was not typified as the crusading zealot but as the operational pragmatist. They tended to pooh-pooh planning theory that was promulgated by cynical intellects and profess an optimistic pragmatism based on the need to bring complex problems down to a human level. . . . This means to us that the planning profession must be quite healthy, peopled by optimists, and

concerned with an indigenous approach to making the quality of life better for people living in large cities. This is not always well understood.

Source: Excerpted from Anthony James Catanese, "Learning by Comparison: Lessons from Experiences," in *Personality, Politics, and Planning: How City Planners Work,* ed. Anthony James Catanese and W. Paul Farmer (Beverly Hills, Calif.: Sage Publications, 1978), p. 206.

The impacts of the no growth local economy are being felt in central cities. There is, first of all, the population decline already mentioned. There is the loss in aggregate purchasing power brought about by loss in population and exacerbated by the shift in population that has produced an increasing low income population. The reduction in aggregate purchasing power has meant a reduction in the demand for commercial and retail space. The reduction in the demand for retail space is one of the harshest realities faced by urban planners today. The desire to redevelop and revitalize downtown and outlying neighborhood shopping districts is tempered by the realization that there may not be the local purchasing power to bring these older districts back to their former status.

The no growth climate and a host of market factors merely serve to frame the issues. In themselves they do not provide the kind of guidance that planners need to deal with the tasks of meeting the current needs of the city. What resources are available for the purposes of conservation and development?

Available resources and the planning horizon

At any one time the resources available to a city for community conservation and redevelopment seem small in comparison with the tasks that remain. But the city has many functions requiring the judicious allocation of scarce funds.

First, the daily needs must be met. Routine services must be kept at an acceptable level. It is difficult to eliminate or curtail services, and often it is impossible to pass the costs on to other levels of government or to other governmental jurisdictions.

Next, there is the maintenance of the enormous investment in public infrastructure. Deferring maintenance is self-defeating in the long run because elements of the infrastructure will deteriorate and break down—a condition no one desires. Unfortunately, even though city populations have been declining it has not meant a corresponding reduction in the costs of municipal government. For example, the costs of establishing and maintaining a water system are largely fixed. The system cannot easily be cut back if population declines. In fact, if there are fewer people to pay for the fixed costs there may be a corresponding rise in fixed costs per capita.[16]

The funds available for conservation and redevelopment tend to be residual after the vital operating and maintenance, health, and social services are met. Under stable or declining conditions these resources become scarce and precious. However there is federal assistance: Community Development Block Grants, Urban Development Action Grants, revenue sharing, and urban mass transportation assistance.

The nature of federal assistance to cities almost mandates that conservation become the main tool of cities in upgrading their physical environments. There are no more funds for large scale renewal or clearance projects. The CDBG money comes in increments and is spread over a variety of programs and projects. But the CDBG money does come regularly, and with only a small administrative burden attached.

One likely impact of the pattern of the receipt of funds in annual payments is that it is apt to dictate a pattern of incremental activities. Rather than preparing large "Burnham type plans," as in the days of urban renewal, planners will tend to "take a little at a time." This may not necessarily be a bad way of approaching conservation and redevelopment, considering the complexities of the task.

The combination of local, state, and federal funds does provide resources for a city's conservation and redevelopment. Whether such funds are adequate may be a matter of dispute among local, state, and federal administrators. A problem in determining the adequacy of resources for conservation and redevelopment at any given time is the apparent imbalance between the funds available and the tasks at hand. For example, $1 million is a sizable sum, although it is probably not enough to rehabilitate all of the houses on only one typical city block.

In a large central city, with hundreds of blocks in need of rehabilitation, with deteriorated shopping and industrial districts in need of modernization and refurbishing, and with abandoned and vacant properties in need of attention, the immediate price tag for the total job would appear astronomical. Therefore, from an immediate perspective no amount of available money would seem sufficient.

This calls for a much longer planning scheme for conservation and redevelopment activities. Since the total physical needs cannot possibly be met in the short run, the time frame should be lengthened to what is realistic. After all, it took three decades of decay and abuse for central cities to be reduced to their present state, and there is no reason, given demographic and market realities, to believe that the problems will be completely solved in substantially less time.

However, the political time horizon of elected officials (mayors, city councils) is usually shorter—more in the nature of four years, when they must face reelection. It is not easy to sell the practicality of long-range plans—but neither is the task of city redevelopment an easy one.

From the early days of the urban renewal program cities began to classify and designate neighborhoods for redevelopment or conservation. At times explicit priorities were given in redevelopment plans, but usually it was assumed that all redevelopment areas would be worked on in the short run—whether this was possible or not.

With CDBG annual funding, which in any one year is small in comparison with the total amount needed, effective planning requires a realistic long-term plan for orderly assistance to neighborhoods. This will require continuation of the practice of inventorying and classifying neighborhoods. Then, realistic timetables for their assistance should be set up, taking the following into consideration: level of need, viability, money required, and timing of assistance. Although this may seem elementary, it is not without some practical drawbacks.

First, the designation and classification of areas of a city can have a negative side effect. When a neighborhood is designated as blighted, no matter what it is called, it may be taken as a signal by property owners, businesses, and local lenders to disinvest. The nomenclature and method of communication are serious matters because the subject is so sensitive. The recent experience of the city of St. Louis in classifying and designating neighborhoods by condition and program treatment is an interesting case in point. When this was under consideration in St. Louis it was quite controversial.[17] Thus, most cities have refrained from neighborhood classification, as the political results are controversial. However, effective planning requires *some* official recognition of relative needs and differences among neighborhoods, in order to effectively allocate scarce public funds.

Four steps toward neighborhood identity To make the metropolitan area understandable and less [forbidding] we require that it be broken down into manageable parts, to a size a child can perceive and feel safe in. Such is the role of the neighborhood. . . .

We have found four major characteristics that we think are essential in creating a sense of identity in the neighborhood. First, like a child, a neighborhood needs a name. The requirement is for place recognition so that a community can be referred to and endowed with pride and respect. . . . Second, in trying to establish these essentials of identity, we tried to create a number of clearly defined boundaries. When one enters an area, one should know and feel that [one] is inside that area. When one leaves, one should know that [one] is leaving. . . . Third, there is a need for a

central place within a neighborhood. This could be a location where people naturally gather; a building where meetings can be held; a park where children can drift in and find companionship; or a plaza or village center where food can be purchased or people can sit, meet, read, or simply stare at one another. . . . Finally, in trying to create a sense of identity, there need to be organizations and recognized leaders. Organizations become important for sharing interests and concerns; they are a way for a person to relate to others.

Source: Excerpted from Leon S. Eplan, "Planning, Budgeting, and Neighborhoods," in *Personality, Politics, and Planning: How City Planners Work*, ed. Anthony James Catanese and W. Paul Farmer (Beverly Hills, Calif.: Sage Publications, 1978), pp. 41–42.

Developing a realistic timetable may mean that some neighborhoods may have to wait several years for an appreciable infusion of redevelopment and conservation money. Although this may make sense from a fiscal point of view, it may be considered a policy of neglect by those neighborhoods. There is likely to be pressure from those neighborhoods scheduled for redevelopment or conservation at some time in the future, but we are practicing in a time when many difficult choices must be made.

Creative local initiatives

Some cities have responded to their conservation and redevelopment needs by devising creative approaches to financing investments. The crucial ingredient is the ability to obtain limited public money through using the existing financial markets and local financial institutions. *Leverage,* which in this sense may be called a term for using someone else's money, is what businessmen use every day. Using as little as possible of one's own money (the more debt, the better) to finance large ventures is looked upon as business acumen. The technique of using scarce public funds to leverage private capital has several potential applications to urban conservation and redevelopment. The flexibility of the CDBG program offers unique opportunities for such creativity. The following are examples of creative leverage with public money.

In 1977 the city of Chicago issued a $100 million bond issue and used the proceeds to make mortgage loans for home purchases in the city. The mortgage rate has tended to be two percentage points lower than comparable mortgage rates from private lending institutions because of the city's ability to borrow money at a preferential interest rate reflecting the nontaxable status of its bonds. Mortgage payments will be used to retire the bonds. The mortgage loans are processed and serviced by a local savings and loan company for a fee. There is no reason why this idea could not be used for targeted neighborhoods undergoing rehabilitation. It should be pointed out, however, that the effect of such subsidies on the cost of borrowing other monies is yet to be seen.

CDBG funds can be used to guarantee loans issued by commercial banks. This takes the risk out of making such loans on the part of the lender. The risk reduction should have two positive effects. First, it should make more money available for homeowner repairs and renovations. Second, it should result in better terms to borrowers—lower interest rates and longer time for repayment. By guaranteeing loans rather than direct lending, a relatively small amount of money can generate a large number of loans.

Some states allow tax increment financing, which allows the tax rate on property to be frozen at a low level prior to redevelopment. After redevelopment the property is taxed at the full market rate, but the incremental tax brought about by the new investment does not go into general revenue. Instead, the tax increment can be used to guarantee bond payments the proceeds of which may have been used to clear and upgrade the site for the development. There are many illustrations of successful projects financed by tax increment financing, especially in California.

It would appear that use of the capital markets and local financial institutions is a resource awaiting skillful and imaginative application to finance some kinds of urban redevelopment and conservation activities. It is not being mentioned here as a panacea but as one more avenue to be explored in urban conservation and redevelopment.

Conclusion

Since the end of World War II the nation's central cities have entered a phase of their maturity which has affected the manner of planning conservation and redevelopment activities. Important dimensions of the mature central city are: a lower population that is more heavily minority and low income; some thinning out in terms of lower densities; fewer industrial and distribution jobs; a stable or increasing number of white collar jobs downtown; an aging physical infrastructure requiring substantial maintenance; and a local tax base struggling to hold its own in a time of nongrowth. All of these factors are interrelated in ways that affect the ability of the mature central city to conserve and redevelop itself.

Planners involved with the conservation and redevelopment processes in central cities need to be aware of and knowledgeable about the intricate and complex web of interdependencies that both support and restrain the possible range of options. Factors within the city which are interdependent—such as population, level of income, condition of the housing stock, viability of local businesses, and strength of the tax base—determine in large measure what activities are appropriate and possible. External factors, such as the state of the metropolitan area economy, population trends, and the policies of assistance of the federal government, tend to restrain what is possible and influence what is feasible.

The ability of mature central cities to conserve and improve their physical stock of private houses, apartment buildings, industrial and commercial structures, and public facilities depends on the willingness of the private sector to invest, the ability of the city to effectively plan and administer programs for conservation and redevelopment, and the level of federal assistance in the various programs.

The termination of the urban renewal program mandated a reassessment of large scale redevelopment and slum clearance programs. The characteristics of the Community Development Block Grant program tend to make conservation, rather than large clearance projects, a more viable strategy for mature central cities.

1 U.S., Department of Commerce, Bureau of the Census, *1970 Census of Housing: Structural Characteristics of the Housing Inventory* (Washington, D.C.: Government Printing Office, 1973).

2 U.S., Department of Commerce, Bureau of the Census, *1970 Census of Housing: Components of Inventory Change* (Washington, D.C.: Government Printing Office, 1973).

3 Much of the information in this section comes from: U.S., Department of Commerce, Bureau of the Census, *1970 Census of Population: Detailed Characteristics, U.S. Summary* (Washington, D.C.: Government Printing Office, 1973); see also: *Thirteenth Census of the United States* (Washington D.C.: Government Printing Office, 1910).

4 Werner Z. Hirsch, "Metropolitan Problems," in *Management Policies in Local Government Finance,* ed. J. Richard Aronson and Eli Schwartz (Washington, D.C.: International City Management Association, 1975), p. 190.

5 This discussion is based in part on: John C. Bollens and Henry J. Schmandt, *The Metropolis: Its People, Politics, and Economic Life,* 3rd ed. (New York: Harper & Row, Publishers, 1975), p. 102.

6 U.S., Department of Commerce, Bureau of the Census, *1972 Census of Retail Trade: Major Retail Center Statistics* (Washington, D.C.: Government Printing Office, 1974).

7 Bollens and Schmandt, *The Metropolis,* p. 99.

8 Ibid., pp. 102–3.

9 U.S., Department of Commerce, Bureau of the Census, *1972 Census of Governments,* vol. 2: *Taxable Property Values and Assessment–Sales Price Ratios* (Washington, D.C.: Government Printing Office, 1973).

10 U.S., Department of Commerce, Bureau of the Census, *County and City Data Book, 1972* (Washington, D.C.: Government Printing Office, 1973).

11 James M. Maxwell and J. Richard Aronson, *Financing State and Local Governments,* 3rd ed. (Washington, D.C.: Brookings Institution, 1977), p. 73.

12 Ibid., pp. 71–74.

13 Richard P. Nathan, Allen D. Manvel, Susannah E. Calkins, and associates, *Monitoring Revenue Sharing* (Washington, D.C.: Brookings Institution, 1975), cited in ibid. p. 74.

14 U.S., Advisory Commission on Intergovernmental Relations, *Significant Features of Fiscal Federalism: 1976–77 Edition,* vol. 2: *Revenue and Debt* (Washington, D.C.: U.S. Advisory Commission on Intergovernmental Relations, 1977), p. 57.

15 Hirsch, "Metropolitan Problems," pp. 190–91, 196–97.

16 For a discussion of these and correlative issues on older central cities, see the compendium of essays prepared for: U.S., Congress, House, Committee on Banking, Finance, and Public Affairs, Subcommittee on the City, *How Cities Can Grow Old Gracefully* (Washington, D.C.: Government Printing Office, 1977).

17 See: S. Jerome Pratter, "Strategies for City Investment," in *How Cities Can Grow Old Gracefully,* pp. 79–90.

17 Planning for diverse human needs

Social planning—to be effective—must be an integral part of all physical, economic, and fiscal planning. The social planner should be an interpreter: he or she must understand the goals and limitations of physical, economic, and fiscal plans in order to articulate the elements of each in achieving an integrated and workable plan. At the same time the social planner must be able to interpret the highly technical elements of the physical, economic, and fiscal plans to the community, and also to articulate the community's needs to the planners. The roles of goal definition, needs analysis, development of action steps, and implementation—in the setting of the community—are at the heart of the social planning process.

Social planning by its very nature incorporates the elements of physical, economic, and fiscal planning into a broader planning context that is responsive to the needs and the demands of the community. Too often social planning is oversimplified and is defined as "planning for social services." While planning for social services is an important element of social planning, effective social planning is much more than planning for recreation, education, and job training.

Social planning is, increasingly, being defined as a profession—or as one component of the planning profession. The social planner is often someone trained in physical or economic planning, public administration, or social work, who is also socially sensitive and is thus able to perform the important function, mentioned above, of articulating the needs of the community.

Often, the social planner is a local official in another capacity. As the planning director or city manager, he or she understands the concept of social planning well enough to integrate goals and objectives which complement each other and include the requisite physical, economic, and fiscal elements. He or she can do this in a number of ways, all of them difficult, and the ultimate result of such a process will be a socially responsive plan. Local officials who work in this capacity, then, can be defined as socially responsive planners. They fulfill this definition by training, by vocation, or simply by meeting the demands of an increasingly active citizenry.

The causes and effects of social problems have always been the concern of organized society, but the concept of specifically addressing social planning through organized institutions is relatively recent. Current definitions of social planning range from generalizations such as "thinking about the problems of society" to such narrow descriptions as "time-phased programming."[1]

For purposes of this discussion, planning is defined as "a method of determining policy under which developments may take place in a balanced, orderly fashion in the best interests of the people in a given area."[2] This definition supports the position that distinctions among social, economic, and physical planning are largely artificial since one cannot be effective without the others. The consequences of economic planning are invariably social in nature, and economic and physical planning performed without consideration of social impacts can easily damage vulnerable groups located in urban settings.

While it is possible to pinpoint the need for social planning, it is rather difficult to delineate its terrain. Public policies are defined as overt actions of government or agencies which operate in the public sector. Social policies are often defined within the context of public policies that are directly responsive to human needs. Such a dual definition, however, tends to distort rather than to clarify, because few, if any, public policies have no social consequences. Choices are continuously made simply through the allocation of funds for government programs. These choices, whether implicit or explicit, often have far-reaching social consequences.

A brief history of social planning

The beginnings of social planning in the United States can be traced to the early social programs of the nineteenth century. Early social planning was the province of the churches. By the mid-nineteenth century local and state governments had become involved in educational planning.[3] The concept of the social responsibility to provide relief for the poor was furthered by the emergence in the mid-nineteenth century of the Charity Organization Society and the settlement house movement.[4] The Charity Organization Society's concern was to avoid duplication of services, while the settlement house movement wished to affect the political process as a means of changing public policies. Emerging patterns in the development of present-day social planning reflect the efforts of both groups.

The growth of the social welfare profession and the development of specialized social service agencies in the early twentieth century were the result of an increasing interest in social reform. They were also evidence of the early realization that physical and economic planning were insufficient to provide for the individual's needs.

This movement for social reform and the institutions it engendered took place at the local level only. The federal government was as yet involved only in a few social planning areas: military medicine, merchant marine hospitals, public health programs in environmental sanitation, military pensions, and old soldiers' homes.[5] It was not until the Depression of the 1930s that the federal government began to be involved officially in social planning, with the creation, by President Roosevelt, of the advisory National Planning Board.[6]

Several historical points are relevant to an understanding of contemporary social planning. First, social planning was not undertaken only to address the needs of the poor but also to address the needs of all levels of society, including the military. Yet social welfare (and consequently social planning) was often narrowly defined solely as the provision of services for the disadvantaged. This is still an important element of social planning, and it is referred to as social service planning or social welfare planning, but it is only one specialized aspect of total social planning.

The second historical point is that social planning was initiated and carried out almost entirely at the local level until the 1930s. Today a major part of the responsibility for social planning still rests with municipalities. The federal government has yet to enact a comprehensive national policy, although a number of federal programs address social needs. It may be that in a society as diverse as that of the United States a truly comprehensive urban policy is not possible. Therefore, the best that might be feasible would be a reaffirmation on the part of the federal government that it will give the needs of cities high priority when it creates its major domestic and international policies.

The third point is that, historically, social planning in this country has displayed a strong reactive element which has stood in the way of comprehensive long-range planning. Most social planning has responded only to immediate and pressing problems: the plight of immigrants in the nineteenth century; the problem of increasing urban slums; the plight of unemployed millions during the Depression; and the plight of the nation's cities as reflected by the urban riots of

The village and the jungle In most American cities there are two major types of low-rent neighborhoods: the areas of first or second settlement for urban migrants; and the areas that attract the criminal, the mentally ill, the socially rejected, and those who for one reason or another have given up the attempt to cope with life.

The former kind of area, typically, is one in which European immigrants—and more recently Negro and Puerto Rican ones—try to adapt their nonurban institutions and cultures to the urban milieu. Thus it may be called an *urban village.* Often it is described in ethnic terms: Little Italy, The Ghetto, or Black Belt. The second kind of area is populated largely by single men, pathological families, people in hiding from themselves or society, and individuals who provide the more disreputable of illegal-but-demanded services to the rest of the community. In such an area, life is comparatively more transient, depressed if not brutal, and it might be called an *urban jungle.* It is usually described as Skid Row, Tenderloin, the red-light district, or even the Jungle.

Source: Excerpted from Herbert J. Gans, *The Urban Villagers: Group and Class in the Life of Italian-Americans* (New York: The Free Press of Glencoe, 1962), p. 4.

---

the 1960s. In this respect social planning differs little from economic or fiscal planning in our society. Long-range measures are easy to articulate but difficult to enforce. A society based on private enterprise will resist public sector dominance except in a time of emergency.

The above brief historical background requires some discussion of the context of social planning. This follows immediately below. Next, the chapter takes up the subject of the relationship of the government to the community in the area of social services. Identifying the client and the client's needs is next discussed; after this, attention is given to ways in which values are determined and preferences are established in social planning. Comprehensive planning is then described briefly. Finally, the following are set forth as the elements of social planning: task definition, policy development, policy implementation, and evaluation. An evaluative conclusion emphasizes the importance of social planning at the local government level.

The context of social planning

While there is little consensus on the precise definition and scope of social planning,[7] many would agree on the following definition: social planning is the process by means of which planners define society's goals and translate them into effective plans and programs.

The debate centers around the scope of social planning. Some define it strictly as planning for social services with the less privileged in society being those who primarily benefit from such planning. Others define it as a separate component in planning that is not encompassed by physical, economic, and fiscal planning. Still others see it as the use of all elements of planning to bring about desirable social change. These diverse points of view have one element in common: social planners must define society's goals and translate them into effective plans and programs. Social goals are seldom defined for the planner, and he or she in practice often encounters conflicting goals which must be reconciled for the sake of an effective plan.

Local governments often make the task of the socially responsive planner more difficult by separating physical planning (performed by local departments of development and planning and local departments of public works) from social planning (performed by human services agencies). Even in cities such as those in Santa Clara County, California, where social planning is an officially mandated element in the city plan, the process is designated as *human resource planning* and is carried out by such diverse entities as an ad hoc study group (in the city of Campbell) or a human relations commission (in the city of Hayward).[8]

Few cities have emulated Pasadena, with its planning team composed of representatives from the city manager's office, the advance planning department, the school district, United Way, and the community service commission.[9] This group is working concurrently to revise Pasadena's general city plan and to develop a social element by integrating all aspects of the plan.

Goals and social planning

The socially responsive planner should begin by identifying social goals. General goals—reflecting societal values—are easily agreed on. It is difficult to oppose such goals as better housing or universal education. The socially responsive planner needs to provide specific definitions of these goals with explicit statements of what will replace unsatisfactory conditions.[10] Reaching consensus

---

Working class perception of middle class life   My limited observations suggest that, on the whole, the advantages of working-class subculture do outweigh the disadvantages. The latter are real, and ought to be removed, but they are not overwhelming. Thus, given our present knowledge, there is no justification for planning and caretaking programs which try to do away with the working-class subculture. John Seeley has suggested why it should not be done away with in his description of a Polish working-class group with whom he once lived:

"No society I have lived in before or since seemed to me to present so many of its members . . . so many possibilities and actualities of fulfillment of a number at least of basic human demands: for an outlet for aggressiveness, for adventure, for a sense of effectiveness, for deep feelings of belonging without undue sacrifice of uniqueness or identity, for sex satisfaction, for strong if not fierce loyalties, for a sense of inde-

pendence from the pervasive omnicompetent, omniscient authority-in-general which at that time still overwhelmed to a greater degree the middle-class child. . . . These things had their prices, of course—not all values can be simultaneously maximized. But few of the inhabitants whom I reciprocally took 'slumming' into middle-class life understood it or, where they did, were at all envious of it. And, be it asserted, this was not a matter of 'ignorance' or incapacity to 'appreciate finer things,' but an inability to see one moderately coherent and sense-making satisfaction-system which they didn't know as preferable to the quite coherent and sense-making satisfaction-system they did know."

Source: Excerpted from Herbert J. Gans, *The Urban Villagers: Group and Class in the Life of Italian-Americans* (New York: The Free Press of Glencoe, 1962), p. 267. Seeley quotation from John R. Seeley, "The Slum: Its Nature, Use and Users," *Journal of the American Institute of Planners* 25 (1959), p. 10.

---

on specific goals, however, is not an easy task. Vague and ambitious goals make planning difficult and evaluation almost impossible. While a degree of vagueness has come to be accepted in social planning, in contrast to physical planning where specific goals must be set forth so that detailed specifications for the engineer and the architect can be drawn up, it is just as dangerous to have vague social plans as it is to have vague physical plans.

The socially responsive planner may find that the general welfare, and also employment growth, are goals on which the community can agree, but it is only when these goals are defined in *specific* terms that planning can begin, that resources can be allocated, and that effectiveness can be measured. Being specific also enables planners to realize that there are different perceptions of what constitutes the common good and the means by which it is served.[11] In a sense all planning may be seen as a process of resource allocation,[12] but with the increasing costs of social services, social planning assumes greater importance.

The difficulty of resource allocation in the social planning process is emphasized by the problem of determining values. Communities differ in the delicate balance between individual and community rights, in the role to be played by government, and in the allocation of individual and community resources. Most communities seem to agree that the aim of social policies and programs is to achieve a quality of life acceptable to the community as a whole. Although the concept of quality of life is nebulous in the contexts of social accounting, performance evaluation, and national goal setting,[13] communities generally find it relatively easy to agree on the ends of social policies. The difficulty comes in defining the means.[14] Too often a grave disparity exists between the stated ends of social policies and the ends achieved.

Policies and social planning

The reasons for the disparity between stated goals (as articulated in political rhetoric and preambles to laws) and the policies which implement these goals are many.

Social policies are often reactions to problems rather than dynamic actions. This is caused partly by the frequent changes in the composition of policymaking bodies, and also by the fact that it is difficult to implement social policies that affect the individual directly and personally.

The key to formulating effective social policies lies in integrating three factors: social needs, political feasibility, and value preferences. This was amply demonstrated by both the Office of Economic Opportunity and the Model Cities policy initiatives.[15] Social needs can be determined in a variety of ways, since sociological and economic measures exist to measure change and variation from stated social norms. Political feasibility is most often tested early in the drafting stage of policy, since policymakers frequently refrain from implementing initiatives that are politically unacceptable. Perhaps the most difficult to determine—and most cursorily addressed—is value preferences, which permeate all decisions of the social planner.

Identifying and defining social values

The socially responsive planner has to identify and define social values with skill if a plan is to be effective. A plan which goes counter to the values of those who are to benefit is doomed to failure. For example, the bilingual education legislation that has been passed in twenty-one states runs counter to the "melting pot" values of a monolingual country of immigrants, has been difficult to implement in local schools, and has largely failed to educate children who speak a native tongue other than English.

The socially responsive planner should seek ways to mobilize community groups. He or she should either work with a community organizer or assist diverse groups in pursuing common goals. The socially responsive planner should help identify and define goals which will induce groups to organize around common interests. And when groups have varying interests, effective planning helps define common ends that are not antithetical to diverse particular interests. In fact, *the common good* is defined as the interaction of these particular interests in relation to overall social policy.

For socially responsive planning to be effective in the United States, it must value both individual liberty and community needs. Americans are skeptical about the ability of large bureaucracies and corporate structures to solve social ills. They often feel that the growth and development of human identity and a sense of community are shunted aside in large scale planning.

To be effective, then, social planning must maximize individual participation in decision making. When people have a say in what happens, they are more committed to acting on the outcome. These citizens know what the issues are. It is the responsibility of the social planner to involve individuals and groups in the community's accountability structure. The planner should involve the largest possible numbers of persons and groups in efforts aimed at the common welfare of the community. Social planning is meaningless without social change, and social change requires the development of means for intervention.

Strategies of intervention

Six strategies of intervention for social change have been identified by Martin Rein. These are given below with the phrase *the individual* substituted here for Rein's references to *the poor,* as the general welfare is the legitimate goal of *all* social policies.

1. Amenities: the provision of those services which enrich or strengthen the quality of life; the normal services humanity needs to survive in a changing society
2. Investment in human capacity: the improvement of the economic capabilities of the individual by the provision of schooling, job training, job opportunities, and job information
3. Transfers: the redistribution of income of one population to another (young to old, rich to poor); a guaranteed annual income
4. Rehabilitation: the changing of people involving the use of psychological and sociopsychological approaches
5. Participation: the provision of programs which promote social inclusion, providing the individual with a stake in society
6. Aggregative and selective economic measures: aggregative measures are those that filter down to the individual—the benefits of economic growth resulting from tax cuts, capital depletion allowances, and other incentives to stimulate production; selective measures are those that "bubble up" the individual into the economic mainstream by creating jobs for the underskilled, establishing a minimum wage, etc.[16]

This list is not exhaustive, but it establishes two facts. First, to intervene effectively in the policy process, the social planner needs to define and develop specific strategies of intervention that are relevant to political and economic realities. Second, and perhaps more important, to implement any strategy, definite—and often conflicting—value choices must be made.

For example, we believe in the dignity of the individual, and most of us would agree that a person's ability to work fosters dignity; therefore, it can be argued that a society which is economically stable should foster individual dignity for its citizens. However, the Nobel prizewinner and economist Paul Samuelson tells us that goals of high level employment and high economic stability conflict in a free market society.[17]

Another example is that while American society has traditionally agreed on the importance of education and of giving individuals the opportunity to better themselves, education for individual choice is often apparently contradictory to the needs of society. For example, an individual may wish to study law while his or her community is in dire need of doctors; or a college graduate may abandon his or her small rural community to go to a large city, thereby contributing to a drain of talent from the small community. The conflict between the individual's rights and society's needs is indeed always present.

The community and its functioning

An American community is a plurality of communities and subcommunities. These need to be stratified to reflect common values and goals. The stratification of function, authority, and responsibility should be accepted and indeed fostered by planners.

Stratification by function and authority necessitates the dispersion, distribution, or decentralization of function and authority to diverse groups, each of which possesses a measure of authority that is based on its unique function in the community. This decentralization helps protect individual freedom against the incursions of community demands.

Both the stratification of groups and the delegation of function and authority promote autonomy. Each group must be endowed with the greatest possible autonomy consistent with its functions in the community. Diminishing the exercise of autonomy and free will leads to the loss of a sense of participation and control over community and individual destiny.[18]

The role of tradition

Autonomy and decentralization are embedded in the culture and traditions of the United States. The Latin *traditio* can be translated as ''giving over by means of words.'' Tradition, then, involves personal communication which emerges from community discussion and consensus, encourages social interaction, and leads to coalitions of like-minded persons.

Personal communication takes place best in small, local units of association.

Figure 17–1 This building mural in a Hispanic section of Chicago symbolizes the importance of localism, the family, and the neighborhood as primary forms of association.

This *localism* emphasizes family and neighborhood as the primary forms of association. This sense of place—of having somewhere to anchor oneself—insulates the person and the community against various forms of estrangement and alienation. It offers a sense of roots.

The role of the city planner

Yet in order to respond to diverse client interests today's socially responsive city planner must be concerned with physical, economic, and social planning.[19] This calls for comprehensive planning, which makes citizen participation more difficult to achieve. To address this variety of interests, the socially responsive planner needs to go beyond the traditional concern of the planning profession with the physical environment, a concern which, according to Davidoff and Reiner, has "warped the profession's ability to see physical structures and lands as servants to those who use them," and proceed to a concern with the total social and economic environment.[20]

Professional planners do not share a history of responsiveness to social concerns. Traditionally, the typical planner has been concerned with the physical plan, that is, with the facilities, rather than with the social programs to be instituted in these facilities once they are built. The planner has looked at the size, location, and design of a school rather than at its curriculum. It is rare when a planner's responsiveness encompasses a dialogue involving the architect, the school board, and the community.

The socially responsive planner, on the other hand, understands the physical planning and the curriculum planning, as well as the correlative group dynamics, well enough to translate the elements and help to achieve an integrated physical and economic plan that incorporates relevant social goals and objectives. For example, when one large hospital in a large city built its maternity facility, the architects talked to the administrators and, to some extent, to the nursing supervisors. They did not, however, talk directly to the clients—the patients—or, for that matter, to floor nurses. As a result, the "rooming-in" section (where mothers had twenty-four hour access to babies) was an architectural failure. Physically it consisted of three adjoining rooms—a semiprivate room attached to a nursery attached to a semiprivate room. The nursery had doors leading to each semiprivate room and the hall; it could hold four babies. The nurse had no telephone there, however, because the architects did not understand the rooming-in concept. Thus, after the unit was operational extensive reworking was required to install telephone cables to the nursery. In addition, the rooms had no adjacent bathroom. A common bathroom was located across the hall. The result was uncomfortable first days and general confusion for postnatal maternal care.

Social purpose and physical planning

Often, even with the best intentions, it is difficult to integrate social purpose into physical planning. The city of Chicago, for example, through its building code, encourages builders to provide open space surrounding high rise development. Accordingly, a number of buildings feature public open spaces, but some of these areas, like the large public plaza by the civic center, serve as little more than handsome settings for a large piece of sculpture, while others, like the First National Bank Plaza, are a hive of activity (Figure 17–2). A poll of citizens strolling in these plazas revealed that it was the physical layout that determined use. The civic center plaza with its handsome Picasso sculpture is a large empty space with few benches and fewer trees. It is usually deserted, and thus it is an intimidating place in which to linger. The First National Bank Plaza features a series of intimate spaces: benches and steps sheltered from the sun and

Figure 17–2 The formality and lack of use of Daley Plaza, by the civic center, contrast strikingly with the varied activities at the First National Bank Plaza. Both plazas are in Chicago, just two blocks apart in the heart of the central business district.

wind; a central fountain; and a number of entrances to building spaces surrounding the plaza, which make the plaza a natural passageway as well as a pleasant resting place.

This integration of social function into a physical plan can result in a planning process that addresses social as well as physical needs. However, the city planner should not assume that the physical and social planning processes are identical or even easily integrated. Nor can the planner assume that the technology of physical planning can be easily applied to social planning.

Many American cities have built pedestrian malls to renew deteriorating downtown areas, under the assumption that a beautiful physical setting filled with plants and fountains would solve such problems as crime, a deteriorating economic base, or even a changing life-style. Obviously they have not, and many downtown malls built in the 1960s have been the setting for continued erosion of the central business district in the 1970s.

In the same way school boards faced with vandalism, absenteeism, and decreasing numbers of students finishing high school have sought to address the demands of angry parents by building shiny glass and steel schools which stand as air-conditioned monuments to lower reading scores and higher absenteeism, while old red brick buildings with inadequate heating systems in less troubled districts continue to graduate merit scholarship winners. The bricks and mortar approach to solving social problems is dangerous because it wastes scarce resources, raises community expectations, and results in disillusionment and alienation.

The planner may not have sufficient expertise to fulfill the roles of the physical, social, and economic planner, but he or she is responsible for ensuring that a comprehensive planning process incorporates social, economic, and physical goals before resources are allocated.

Identifying the client

The problem of consensus

Perhaps the most important step in achieving effective planning is identifying the client. This step may appear deceptively simple to the physical planner who can easily identify the city council, county board, school board, or hospital commission as the agency that contracts for his or her services. However, increasing citizen participation has made the client more difficult to define for the social planner. For the socially responsive planner, the definition of the client is an intricate process which, if not carried out adequately, can result in ineffective planning and less than acceptable programs.

A consensus seems to be forming to the effect that the entire population—not merely the poor or various interest groups—is the ultimate client of the social planner. For the present, however, pressing social needs give priority to the poor.[21]

This focus on the poor by planners considered socially responsive is counterproductive. As has been pointed out, effective planning cannot take place without consensus. If the planner designs policies and programs to address solely the needs of the poor, it is far more difficult to reach consensus and to obtain the resources needed for effective programs. The poor do represent a needy minority in American society. Yet few policies and programs addressed solely to the needs of minorities have become successfully established in American society. The largest social welfare program in the United States—social security—was not established until the middle class joined the poor on the breadlines.

The above is not intended to suggest that the varied needs of different groups in our society demand different programs; it is intended, rather, to suggest that effective social programs are better designed and much more quickly and successfully implemented when they address the overall interests of the society.

The diversity of client needs

In a sense, today's socially responsive planners should be as concerned about the persistence of separate but equal programs as educators have been about separate but equal facilities since *Brown* v. *Board of Education* in 1954.[22] Programs and facilities designed exclusively for the poor often fail to receive adequate support and to fulfill client needs. One can consider the service at most health clinics in poor communities—where an expectant mother is often shuttled among several facilities in order to get prenatal care for herself and infant care for her sick children. One can also contrast public housing developments in bleak, crime-ridden surroundings with modern apartment buildings in attractive neighborhoods under a rent supplement program. Isolation results in discrimination; this can be seen in the contrast between the massive Cabrini–Green housing complex on Chicago's North Side (Figure 17–3) and the scattered site housing in the Hyde Park community surrounding the University of Chicago. The first is unsightly and riddled with crime, while the second is impossible to distinguish from its neighbors.

While planning may start with an empirical exploration of value preferences, different groups in the population hold different views on the objectives of a specific plan. A satisfactory consensus will not occur until bargaining has maximized the gains and minimized the losses for each group. Perhaps the most vivid illustration of this is the urban renewal programs of the 1960s. Although urban renewal brought an immediate benefit to the community as a whole by bringing valuable property into the tax rolls, it destroyed entire neighborhoods and contributed to a loss of roots for those whose communities were demolished. Since the homeless were often crowded into other less well established communities, neither the needs of the immediate community nor the ultimate needs of the community as a whole were met.

Determining values and establishing preferences

The socially responsive planner should pay systematic attention to determining values and establishing preferences. The planner may do this by employing a combination of the following techniques: market analyses; public opinion polls; anthropological surveys; public hearings; interviews with community leaders; press content analyses; and studies of laws, administrative behavior, and budgets.[23]

Each method offers a means of assessing needs, and each has its limitations. No single method should be used exclusively. Market analysis is a highly technical tool which is better used to determine product preference than to assess attitudes and values. Public opinion polls often reflect an idealized solution rather than an analysis within the reality of fiscal constraints. Anthropological surveys are highly refined tools, but they must be developed and conducted by professionals and thus they require costly time and labor. Public hearings are most often used and are often mandated by federal regulation, but they can have severe limitations. Interviews with community leaders offer insight into community sentiment only if those identified as leaders by the planner are truly representative of the community, which is not necessarily the case. Press content analysis may reveal little more than the preferences of editors and publishers or of the power structure whose views they share. Studies of laws, administrative behavior, and budgets provide an excellent context of reality in which to analyze the findings resulting from employing the other methods.

Whatever methods are used, it is important to remember that the socially responsive planner is not seeking *the* answer—*the* solution—to a social problem.[24] Rather, the planner is developing a process for making choices that reflect and incorporate a series of value judgments.

All of the methods that can be used to identify client needs are dependent on involving the community through a group process that, in turn, involves local people in identifying salient goals and objectives. If this is successfully done the local community will identify the values and issues involved, and those who

Figure 17–3   Cabrini–Green housing complex, Chicago.

have a stake in the issue will be given an opportunity to participate in making resource allocations.[25]

The role of public hearings

The public hearing provides an opportunity for neighborhood residents to comment on proposed policies and programs, and it can serve to identify interests that the planner may have missed. It should be borne in mind, however, that the public hearing should not be relied on as an exclusive method of determining community involvement. At public hearings on the proposed downtown subway in Chicago, alternative plans were carefully presented by competent engineering consultants. However, community people attending wanted to discuss jobs which would be generated regardless of the plan chosen, and the local American Institute of Architects chapter wanted to present alternative plans that would preserve the current elevated structure. There was little discussion of the plans presented to the audience, and they did not understand the costs and benefits of each alternative.

Long before a proposal is prepared for a public hearing, the planner should involve the relevant community in the planning process. This will help ensure that the hearing is a public discussion by informed citizens concerning relevant issues.

Community involvement

For the planner, community involvement is an essential component of a broader process in which the probable effects of social actions are determined. Feedback and evaluation are an integral part of each component of the planning process. Feedback is part of the process of adapting plans and programs to environmental signals.[26] To be effective, however, feedback (including formal report-

Figure 17-4 Public housing does not have to be isolated, segregated, and overwhelming in scale. These views of Trumbull Park, Chicago, were taken (top to bottom) in 1941, 1951, and 1974.

ing, informal communication, auditing, evaluation, and research) needs to be built into every phase of the task.[27]

Social impact analysis

Social impact analysis, an expansion of the environmental impact analysis methodology developed in the 1970s, is being required increasingly for the funding of projects which will seriously affect the physical, and thus the social, environment of a neighborhood. Such analysis helps to determine how a community will be changed by proposed development or by expansion of existing facilities (see Figure 17–6). The methodology includes: collecting baseline data for the physical, social, and economic characteristics of a neighborhood; identifying the physical and social changes that will occur with the development; evaluating the significance of the changes; and, also, identifying any negative impacts occasioned by the changes and developing strategies to lessen their effects.[28]

Figure 17–5   This hallway in a public housing development had been planned as a multiuse space for a nursery, playroom, laundry, and social center. This 1969 view shows the reality—space that was unused and shunned by residents who feared for their physical safety. The doors lead to the unused laundry rooms. Social planning in relation to physical planning has advanced significantly in recent years because of the experience gained in this and other housing developments in the United States.

Social impact analysis carried out in conjunction with public hearings, public opinion polls, and citizen surveys can offer a valuable tool to the planner. Social impact analysis, however, while it may be sufficient to fulfill federal government funding requirements, is too much affected by value judgments to provide an accurate *single* measure for the socially responsive planner.

It is difficult to determine precisely what impacts new social policies and programs have on people. One can measure, for example, the rise of reading scores after the institution of new curricula in an elementary school system, but it is more difficult to measure what impact improved reading scores will have on the overall educational achievement and societal adaptation of the students. One can measure the frequency of the use of a health care facility in the community, but it is a more intricate task to measure the actual improvement in individual health. Yet to plan responsively and effectively, the planner needs to help design systems that do both.

The task becomes infinitely more difficult when the planner is measuring the effect of desirable—but disruptive—public works projects. A new expressway may facilitate shipping for a languishing inner city industrial site, and it may relieve traffic flow which eases the trip to work for many city residents, but it will also disrupt neighborhoods, bring increased pollution, and generate increased automobile congestion.[29] The planner, then, needs to design evaluation systems that can effectively monitor the project before, during, and after its execution, so that evaluation actually affects the design.

Comprehensive planning

The comprehensive plan, when the city or county has one, provides the overall framework for social planning. Planners agree that planning is a process, that the comprehensive plan should not be regarded as a monolith within which policies and programs must conform, and that no comprehensive plan is truly comprehensive in the sense of being complete.[30] Nevertheless, the comprehensive plan is valuable to the socially responsive planner because it provides a well-tested and workable process for establishing priorities and programs.

The physical planner has the luxury of seeing some of his or her work literally "set in concrete," but no comprehensive plan—such as Daniel Burnham's visionary plan for the city of Chicago—is ever complete. The Burnham plan did set the stage for urban growth by establishing priorities for development and by providing community guidelines to preserve green space, provide for traffic flow, and encourage the growth of neighborhoods.[31] A comprehensive social plan can do no more and, indeed, should do no less.

The planning function may be broken down into two phases. The first phase includes defining objectives, establishing priorities, and identifying resources. The second phase is the specific management of those resources, including the development of guidelines and regulations and the design and implementation of service delivery systems.[32] Although the local government manager must make provisions for effectively carrying out each phase, it may well be that two different persons or agencies—one specializing in planning and the other in administration—may be required to adequately supervise each phase. To provide continuity, both phases must be integral parts of the social plan, and there must be constant coordination and feedback because, when formulation is separated from implementation, the planning may be disjointed and ineffective.

Each step in the planning process contains contradictions which become more evident as the plan becomes more specific. Defining goals in general terms is easier than defining objectives, which may conflict with each other. For example, when the predominantly Puerto Rican community in Chicago's Humbolt Park rioted over alleged inadequacies of education in the local public high school, city officials agreed with the community's demands for higher quality education. Members of the school board disagreed on whether this would best be done by building a new school or by offering special educational programs. Those who agreed that new educational programs were needed disagreed on what these programs should be. The board echoed the confusion in the community and at the same time added to it. When a handsome high school was built and named for the popular Puerto Rican hero Roberto Clemente, its excellent recreational facilities, which had been designed to serve the community, were promptly closed at three in the afternoon, because the school board would not allocate funds for what was essentially community recreation. This was a function of the Chicago Park District, which had not been involved in the planning of the new school. No funds had been allocated for operation of the school's gym-

The checklist for social impact identification provides a systematic way of recording the effects of project proposals on people living in the immediate area, residents of the site, people working at the site, and other users with respect to social well-being.

Components and factors of social well-being	Project and surrounding area effects			Effects under[1]		Nature of effect and subgroup affected
	Yes	Uncertain	No	Worst conditions	Best conditions	
Material well-being						
Income and wealth						
Employment opportunities						
Protection of property from crime or fire						
Opportunities for shopping						
Mobility						
Discretionary time						
Physical well-being						
Health						
Protection of life						
Soundness, adequacy, affordability, and availability of shelter						
Other aspects of physical well-being						
Psychological well-being						
Social participation						
Sense of security						
Recreational experience						
Mental health						
Neighborhood cohesion						
Livability of the neighborhood						
Other aspects of psychological well-being						
Intellectual well-being						
Educational experience						
Other areas of community concern						
Racial integration in:						
the immediate vicinity of the project						
the project site						
other parts of the county						
Economic integration in:						
the immediate vicinity of the project						
the project site						
other parts of the county						
Age integration in:						
the immediate vicinity of the project						
the project site						
other parts of the county						
Life-styles of:						
the people living in the immediate vicinity of the project						

Figure 17–6   Checklist for social impact identification with measures of impact and significance.

Components and factors of social well-being	Project and surrounding area effects			Effects under[1]		Nature of effect and subgroup affected
	Yes	Uncertain	No	Worst conditions	Best conditions	
the residents of the site						
the employees						
users						
other county citizens						
Attainment of any public goals or standards dealing with:						
employment						
transportation						
health						
housing						
crime						
fire						
mental health						
recreation						
education						
libraries						
Socially vulnerable groups (in any of the subject areas listed previously)						
Other areas of community concern (specify)						

The measures of impact and significance provide analytical backup and correspond to the components and factors of social well-being that make up the checklist. A threshold of significant change for any measure is shown by designating upper and lower boundaries of absolute change (such as change in number unemployed) or relative change (such as change in percent of unemployed) which are acceptable. Such thresholds may be based on standards, goals, or rules of thumb. Because of the length of this list only the first page has been reproduced here.

Impact area	Possible impact measure(s)	Direc- tion[2]	Threshold of significant change	Federal, state, and county standards	County and community goals	Rules of thumb
Material well-being						
Income	Change in median income	+				
Adequacy of income	Change in no. and percent of house- holds below the minimum cost of living (for that size household)	−				
Wealth	Percent change in the value of real estate	+				
Availability of jobs	Change in no. of long-term jobs	+				

Figure 17–6   (continued; concluded next page).

Impact area	Possible impact measure(s)	Direction[2]	Threshold of significant change	Federal, state, and county standards	County and community goals	Rules of thumb
	Change in no. of short-term jobs	+				
	Change in no. or percent unemployed	–				
Quality of jobs	Change in no. and percent of people underemployed	–				
	Change in no. and percent of people who are satisfied with their jobs	+				
Experience with property crimes	Amount and percent change in value of property stolen yearly	–				
Experience with property losses from fire	Amount and percent change in value of property lost each year from fires	–				

1 Indicate possible magnitude and direction under the worst and the best sets of conditions: + + very beneficial impact, + beneficial impact, 0 unknown or neutral, – adverse impact, – – very adverse impact.

2 Direction refers to whether an increase in the impact measure is beneficial (+) or adverse (–).

Figure 17–6   (concluded).

nasium after school hours. And long after the entire physical plan was operational, the validity of the special educational programs was still being debated by the school board and the community.

The elements of social planning

The social plan has been defined classically as consisting of four basic elements: task definition, policy development, programming and reporting, and feedback and evaluation.[33] A variation of this classification will be used in the following sections of this chapter, covering task definition, policy development, policy implementation, and evaluation.

Task definition

In the defining of the task, the value preferences of society as a whole as well as those of the target community need to be taken into account. In an age of technology, there is a temptation to leave the identification and solution of social problems either to the social scientist or to the technocrat who designs policies and programs with little, if any, attention to social values. Although technology can be used to help fashion the complex solutions to social problems, even basic social research is permeated with value preferences.[34] For example, technology can be applied in the selection of housing sites by compiling data on soil testing, determining floodplains, or even charting demographic growth; and engineering technology can provide for the inexpensive mass production of housing. But as the failure of Operation Breakthrough, the 1969 federal government proposal to mass produce inexpensive housing, illustrated, housing choices reflect a complexity of value preferences. Modern technology can help solve the housing crisis only in conjunction with social and political considerations.

Once the task has been defined, the planner needs to formulate policies that will develop the solution to the problem. Policies are standing plans which act as guides to decision making.[35] Since policy formulation is the result of task definition, it cannot be done independently of the political system. Ideally, the planner interacts with the policymakers and the community in addressing the defined task.[36]

Policy development

The first step in developing social policy is to focus on the community and its service network, and then to define the existing system in light of policy alternatives. The planner must look to the system as a whole, since alteration of any part of it will affect other areas. It should be remembered that individuals and their problems do not necessarily align themselves with existing agency programs. For example, the creation of a meals on wheels program may encourage the elderly to live at home and postpone or dispense with institutional care. This, in turn, may require the provision of other services, such as health care or the adaptation of a transportation network to facilitate accessibility to these services. The planner should look at the components of the problem and the ways in which these components fit (or do not fit) together. It is then possible to determine the role which individual agencies will play in meeting needs.

In addition to formulating policy, the planner needs to assure that the community—particularly the target population—has access to integrated services. Once policies have been fully developed in conjunction with the task and in the context of the community and the network of services available, the plan should be translated into specific programs with appropriate goals, timetables, and financing.

For example, communities increasingly define public transportation as a public service worthy of local government subsidy. Public transportation is a labor-intensive industry requiring large capital outlays. Transportation officials readily agree that if the service is provided only at the rush hour along well-traveled routes it would generate profits. On the other hand, in order to provide community access to jobs and services, many unprofitable routes must be run at all times—and no route runs profitably during the late night hours. For a sizable segment of the community, however, it is the off-peak hour service that provides access to badly needed jobs. To argue that off-peak service is cost-effective on the basis of artificial tortured data on wages earned by those riding is an exercise in futility. In fact, such routes are costly but they reflect a value choice which holds that mobility and access to employment for all its residents is prized by the community.

Policy implementation

Policy implementation is the interpretation and translation of social planning into specific actions and programs. In identifying and defining the policy issues for programming choices, the planner needs to choose levels and kinds of services among public and private agencies; assign responsibility to relevant government agencies; and recommend appropriate levels of government to finance the various parts of the program. In implementing the plan, the planner needs to coordinate policy and programs so that one reflects the other with respect to the resources available in the community and the governmental and political processs. For example, in developing a housing plan for a specific neighborhood, the planner will have to coordinate the actual physical planning of housing with social considerations contributing to community development. This coordination will determine the placement and density of housing, the placement of community facilities, and the provision of open space.

Failure to coordinate all elements of the plan produces physical planning which does not meet community needs. For example, a consulting firm was developing a plan to meet the housing needs of a predominantly low income neighborhood in a small city in Illinois. The planners proposed an ambitious and handsome development of town houses and apartments to be designed by one of the area's leading architects. City officials, showing unusual social awareness and sensitivity, commissioned a separate survey of neighborhood residents and learned that not only were the majority senior citizens but also over 80 percent owned their own homes free of mortgages. These people understandably had no desire to assume the responsibility of moving and assuming mortgage payments. Furthermore, the majority of residents were largely satisfied with their present housing and wanted available funds to be spent for renovation of individual homes. Plans for the ambitious town house development were permanently shelved.

Appropriate government agencies, as well as the community at large, should be included in the decision-making process. Experts including engineers, architects, real estate developers, and social agency professionals should be assigned roles in such a way that they contribute to the final decision and that no one group arbitrarily predetermines or dominates the outcome.

Evaluation

Evaluation criteria need to be built into every phase of social planning to justify program needs. Newer technical schemes, notably decision theory, can be used to handle uncertainties, and value preferences can be incorporated into such decisions.[37]

All too often those in charge of social service agencies, struggling with inadequate budgets, feel little but frustration when public works and community development agencies receive a seemingly disproportionate amount of fiscal resources. However, these agencies can offer hard evidence—often in the construction of actual projects—to justify their expenditures. The social service agency, instead of establishing definite goals and evaluation criteria for measuring success in meeting these goals, merely points to a general improvement in the quality of life.

While physical planners document their progress with pictures of water filtration plants, schools, and auditoriums, social planners share photographs of smiling young children or blissful senior citizens sitting on a park bench. Some staffs of social agencies resolutely refuse to establish specific evaluation mechanisms and accuse city councils and state legislatures of not caring for the poor. Although the effects of social planning cannot be measured as easily as miles of poured concrete, the social planner must be similarly careful in accounting for funds expended and in evaluating the effects of programs financed.

Conclusion

Effective planning is essential if communities are to make the greatest use of limited resources. For planning to be effective, it must address the needs of both the individual and society. Thus, effective city planning must embody physical, economic, and social planning. Indeed, public officials find it difficult, if not impossible, to differentiate between determining the physical location of industrial parks, providing economic incentives for industries to locate in those parks, and training an adequate labor force. The results of such industrial locations cut across physical, economic, and social lines. They include increasing claims on water and energy resources and resultant environmental effects, an increased property tax base, jobs, and added income for community residents.

Although local officials may assign responsibility for physical, economic, and social planning to different agencies, the work of these agencies needs to be carefully integrated for maximum effectiveness. This does not mean that every physical planner should become a social planner, or that the socially responsive planner must be able to interpret engineering specifications. It does mean that dialogue must be established and maintained and that each professional must understand the opportunities and possibilities as well as the limits and constraints of the planning process.

Furthermore, in the society of the 1980s this integration of physical, economic, and social planning needs to be done by local governments. While planners may support the need for a national urban policy, the reality is that such a policy cannot exist unless it is so general as to need individual interpretation by each community to translate it into defined tasks, specific policies, and workable programs.

It may well be that the way things are is the way things should be. Individuals in American society resist planning by the federal government. Thus, integrated planning for the welfare of the community as a whole rests with local government. The federal government formulates policy and programs with guidelines to provide funding. It is up to the individual community to choose among these programs according to its needs.

While the local government is the appropriate entity for determining local need, local government resources for social services and programs are limited. It is local government which should identify all resources in federal, state, and local government and in the private sector for meeting those needs and which should assume leadership in the formulation of social policy. This is not to say that local government must actually deliver all of the services. A community can fulfill its responsibility to its residents simply by ensuring that adequate services are being provided.

The integration of social, economic, and physical planning should result in nonservice solutions to many social problems. For example, more industrial jobs in a community should diminish the number of unemployed dependents on social services; physical planning which preserves community stability could result in reduced demand for mental health services such as family counseling; and zoning for residential and commercial locations can result in a community that has street traffic in both daytime and evening hours, which could reduce street crime.

As has been emphasized above, the local government should assume responsibility for identifying the needs of its citizens and integrating social, economic, and physical planning to enhance the quality of life and minimize social problems. It should define tasks and develop policies that will ensure adequate provision of social services by the appropriate agencies. Obviously, the capacity for social service delivery differs from one municipality to another, but all cities and counties have the responsibility for assuring that such services are delivered.

The mistake many local governments make is that of isolating social planning in a separate department and defining its work as the traditional social welfare function of providing services to the poor. Although a large municipal government may assign physical planning to a department of development and planning and social planning to a department of human resources, in reality physical planning is integrated into all other functions—in agencies such as the zoning board and the planning commission, and even into the design of schools for the school board, clinics for the board of health, and rapid transit for the transportation department. For social planning to be truly responsive and effective, it is essential that it be integrated with other planning operations and institutionalized in a manner that ensures its status as an integral part of every local government policy and program.

1   Alfred J. Kahn, *Theory and Practice of Social Planning* (New York: Russell Sage Foundation, 1969), p. 1.
2   Joseph H. Bunzel, "Planning for Aging," *Journal of the American Geriatrics Society* no. 9 (January 1961): 32.
3   Cf. Alice Tyler, *Freedom's Ferment* (New York: Books for Libraries, Inc., 1944); and Robert H. Bremner, *From the Depths: The Discovery of Poverty in the United States* (New York: New York University Press, 1956).
4   Ralph E. Pumphrey, "Social Welfare in the United States," in *Encyclopedia of Social Work*, ed., Harry L. Lurie, 1965 ed., vol. 15, p. 25.
5   Ida Merriam, *Social Welfare Expenditure under Public Programs in the United States (1929–1966)*, U.S. Social Security Administration, Office of Research and Statistics, Research Report no. 25 (Washington, D.C.: Government Printing Office, 1968).
6   George Saule, *Planning U.S.A.* (New York: The Viking Press, 1967), pp. 109–15.
7   For useful definitions and analyses, see: Michael P. Brooks, *Social Planning and City Planning*, Planning Advisory Service Report no. 261 (Chicago: American Society of Planning Officials, 1970); Joseph S. Himes, *Social Planning in America: A Dynamic Interpretation* (Garden City, N.Y.: Doubleday & Company, 1954); Kahn, *Theory and Practice of Social Planning;* and Robert Morris and Robert A. Binstock, *Feasible Planning for Social Change* (New York: Columbia University Press, 1966).
8   League of California Cities, *Social Element Planning in California* (Los Angeles: League of California Cities, 1977), p. 35.
9   Ibid.
10 Morris and Binstock, *Feasible Planning for Social Change*, p. 89.
11 Neil Gilbert and Harry Specht, *Dimensions of Social Welfare Policy* (Englewood Cliffs, N.J.: Prentice-Hall, 1974), pp. 5–6.
12 Kahn, *Theory and Practice of Social Planning*, p. 9.
13 Kurt Finsterbusch and C. P. Wolf, *Methodology of Social Impact Assessment* (Stroudsburg, Pa.: Dowden, Hutchinson, and Ross, 1977) p. 182.
14 See: William B. Eddy, "Managing for Quality of Life," paper presented at the Conference on Managing Mature Cities, sponsored by the Charles F. Kettering Foundation and the city of Cincinnati, Cincinnati, Ohio, 9–10 June 1977. Eddy proposes a psychological contract between the citizen and his or her city government to help provide realistic expectations in determining both ends and means of policies affecting the quality of life; he also suggests ways of ascertaining citizen needs and briefly discusses management strategies for implementation.
15 For a complete discussion of the interplay of these and other factors, see: J. David Greenstone and Paul Peterson, *Race and Authority in Urban Politics: Community Participation and the War on Poverty* (New York: Russell Sage Foundation, 1973).
16 Martin Rein, *Social Policy: Issues of Choice and Change* (New York: Random House, 1970), pp. 23–25.

17 See: Paul Samuelson, *Economics*, 10th ed. (New York: McGraw-Hill Book Company, 1976).
18 Bruno Manno, "Subsidiary and Pluralism: A Social Philosophical Perspective," paper presented at the University of Notre Dame, Notre Dame, Indiana, 1 June 1977.
19 Paul Davidoff and Thomas A. Reiner, "A Choice Theory of Planning," *Journal of the American Institute of Planners* 28 (May 1962): 103–4.
20 Ibid.
21 Bernard J. Frieden, "The Changing Prospects for Social Planning," *Journal of the American Institute of Planners* 33 (September 1967): 323.
22 *Brown v. Board of Education*, 347 U.S. 483 (1954).
23 Davidoff and Reiner, "A Choice Theory of Planning": 111.
24 Kahn, *Theory and Practice of Social Planning*, p. 114.
25 Ibid., p. 116.
26 Raymond A. Bauer, "Detection and Anticipation of Impact: The Nature of the Task," in *Social Indicators*, ed. Raymond A. Bauer (Cambridge, Mass.: The M.I.T. Press, 1966), p. 56.
27 Kahn, *Theory and Practice of Social Planning*, p. 323.
28 For an excellent discussion of social impact analysis, see: Kathleen Christensen, *Social Impacts of Land Development: An Initial Approach for Estimating Impacts on Neighborhood Usage and Perception* (Washington, D.C.: The Urban Institute, 1976).
29 For an excellent analysis of the conflicting effects on public works projects, see: Robert A. Caro, *The Power Broker: Robert Moses and the Fall of New York* (New York: Random House, Inc., 1975).
30 Alan A. Altshuler, *The City Planning Process: A Political Analysis* (Ithaca, N.Y.: Cornell University Press, 1965), pp. 300–310.
31 See: Daniel Burnham and Edward H. Bennett, *Plan of Chicago* (Chicago: Prepared under the direction of the Commercial Club, 1906–9).
32 Robert M. Moroney, "Needs Assessment for Human Services," in *Managing Human Services*, ed. Wayne F. Anderson, Bernard J. Frieden, and Michael J. Murphy (Washington, D.C.: International City Management Association, 1977), p. 130.
33 Kahn, *Theory and Practice of Social Planning*, p. 323.
34 Gunnar Myrdal, *Value in Social Theory* (New York: Harper & Brothers, Publishers, 1958), pp. 260–62.
35 Preston P. LeBreton and Dale A. Henning, *Planning Theory* (Englewood Cliffs, N.J.: Prentice-Hall, Inc., 1961), p. 9.
36 The seminal work on policy formulation in social planning is Kahn, *Theory and Practice of Social Planning*.
37 For discussion of these techniques, see: Ralph L. Keeney and Howard Raiffa, *Decisions with Multiple Objectives: Preferences and Value Tradeoffs* (New York: John Wiley & Sons, Inc., 1976); and Ernest E. House, "Justice in Evaluation," *Evaluation Studies: Review Annual*, vol. 1, ed. Gene V. Glass (Beverly Hills, Calif.: Sage Publications, 1976).

18

Social planning and policy development

This chapter is divided into three main sections. The first outlines and analyzes the basic framework of social planning. It offers a functional division of various levels of decision making, and then outlines technological, organizational, and financial factors influencing the most pertinent components. It concludes with a description of the needs dimension of this framework. The second section offers a summary breakdown of the methodological approaches to social services planning. The third section brings the preceding discussion into practical focus by noting the managerial specifics molding the operational role of local governments in human services planning. There is also a concluding section which discusses some issues and problems, as well as roles and functions, and also discusses equity and justice in the delivery of human services.[1]

Throughout the discussion the chapter will be guided by three major themes, and it is as well to make these explicit at the outset. The first theme is that social planning in the contemporary world is far more demanding than physical planning. This is not because physical planning is more susceptible to quantification (although this provides part of the explanation) but rather because most physical planning has been naive. It has been largely preoccupied with capital investment decisions and their associated locational sites and buildings. There has been a general failure to address the host of concerns about who uses such facilities and under what auspices. The planning of school, library, park, and hospital dominated health systems has suffered from this limited vision. Those who dismiss social services planning as ''soft'' and opt for the more certain world of physical planning do themselves and their communities a major disservice. The operating problems of communication, funding, programming, and management need to be an integral part of initial planning decisions.

The second major theme is that planning, for either services or buildings, is comprised of two principal interrelated dimensions. It is both a thinking process and a sociopolitical process. While this factor has been overlooked in physical planning efforts of the past, the growth of social concerns during and since the 1960s indicates that the participatory nature of public policy decision making cannot be overlooked. The arena for social services delivery is crowded, competitive, and not always logical. Those entering it have to be prepared to deal with a difficult and often bewildering environment. Citizen participation in planning is not only an expression of democratic ideology; it is also a necessity for coping with the swirl of private interests associated with social services.

The third basic theme of the chapter is that human services planning must take into account all structural and process elements of service delivery. Social services planning is concerned with competing theories of service delivery, differing criteria for resource allocation, differing concepts of types of service to be offered, complex institutional and cultural frameworks, and the attendant diffused distribution of power and resources. Beyond this, social services planning requires specific recognition of tasks, roles, and skills among those delivering service. Finally, many human services systems have developed complex financing mechanisms that have to be taken into account by key decision makers and their staffs.

The framework of social planning

Given the background of social planning, contemporary local government administrators are faced with a decision-making arena of high complexity characterized by a series of problems. From the point of view of the recipient, too, the delivery of human services poses an incredible array of activities, organizations, and financial burdens with no special guarantees of quality. The recipient sees a host of problems associated with the availability of and/or access to appropriate services (including eligibility, cultural, and knowledge barriers). He or she may find that needs cannot be fulfilled by a single individual or agency because specialization has subdivided the recipient's problem into several professional jurisdictions or areas of organizational responsibility. Seeking assistance may require an organizational road map that few have the skill or knowledge to draw. Obtaining services from a multiplicity of agencies or professionals may result in conflicting advice or counterproductive treatment. Where a sequence of services is indicated, consumers often find that they are left to their own devices as to a future course of action.

These factors present problems that the decision maker who is planning human services provision must face. Further, as local government managers are well aware, the task is compounded by problems of method, definitions, goals, and measurement. The definition of social planning itself has long been a morass of confusion. Some have distinguished *societal* planning (which would approach social planning in a manner similar to the land use comprehensive master plan) from *social services* planning (which focuses only on the planning of services). Some have seen social planning as different from physical planning because citizen participation has been involved (as though citizen participation were not necessary in physical planning). Another view suggests that social planning should be concerned primarily with racial or economic justice. The present discussion focuses on the planning of social services, although this can never be undertaken in a vacuum separate and distinct from the social and economic conditions which give rise to the demand for such services.

In this context, the following section describes two frameworks within which the tasks of human services planning can be viewed and understood. The first framework presents a functional description of the *levels* and *types of decisions* that must be made in planning for human services delivery. It introduces four levels of decision making, then presents a detailed analysis of technological, organizational, and financing factors influencing the important third level of decision making. The second approach is that of a needs framework within which the *goals* of social services planning may be viewed systematically by the decision maker.

A functional framework

Concept of the four levels of planning decisions   Figure 18–1 suggests the outline of a functional framework for human services planning. It proceeds through a series of decision levels showing the planning dimensions involved in each. It represents an effort to provide a general statement regarding the elements involved in planning any community service—from the traditional services of water supply and transportation to newer programs such as halfway houses for alcoholics or special projects for children with learning disabilities. The first level deals with the vital value aspects of human services planning. The second level addresses the question of the types of services to be supplied and the allocations among services. The third level is, as Figure 18–1 indicates, the most complex level of decision making and the most pertinent for purposes of this discussion. Technological, financial, and organizational factors all intrude at this point as the method of delivering goods and services is considered. Finally, fourth level decisions concern the design of the specific delivery unit and service setting. A discussion of each of these levels follows. Because much of the critical area of management decision focuses on the third level, that level will be examined in greater detail.

Level One The first level might appear to be more theoretical than practical at first glance. It asks the question that is fundamental in any political economy: Who gets what?[2] It determines what services are to be provided and whether they are to be provided by private enterprise or by government. How such decisions are made is extremely complex and involves more than just the issue of whether private enterprise makes a profit (thereby, some would argue, presumably dictating that government refrain from involvement).

Such decisions are not, however, necessarily beyond the scope of the local planner, particularly in human services planning. Local government planners frequently face the necessity of determining whether the community is better served by private or by public sponsorship of a particular service. Most local health systems, for example, involve public agencies, nonprofit private agencies, and proprietary firms. One entire segment of the health system—nursing homes—is dominated by private, profit making firms in many sections of the country.[3]

Thus, the basis for making such decisions is far from clear-cut and planners will recognize that it depends on the traditions, values, and existing institutions of the community. Even economic efficiency is not a completely dependable criterion. In this field, the conventional wisdom that private organizations are more efficient than public ones does not necessarily hold. Many such decisions are made at the legislative level or are based on certain predispositions in the federal executive branch. For example, both the Partnership for Health Act of 1966 and the Health Planning Act of 1974 tend to favor private, nonprofit agencies for local health planning rather than public agencies. This is so in spite of the resultant problems of integration and local sanction that such agencies have experienced. On the other hand, federal acts and agencies tend to favor public agencies in such areas as education and manpower training.[4]

One finds a multitude of variations at the local level. For example, cities such as Jacksonville, Florida, and Cincinnati, Ohio, have a long history of municipal sponsorship of local primary health care clinics.[5] In other communities this function has been the exclusive province of private physicians or community hospitals. Emergency health services are provided by city government in Boston but by private funeral parlors in the South and Midwest.[6] Home care in one region of Upstate New York is provided by both county government and nonprofit organizations. In some instances this is characterized by cooperation, in others by competition.[7]

Criteria for such decisions depend heavily on the goals of the individual community. Two extreme models have been developed to highlight the range of possibilities. The first is a monopolistic one which envisions a service network controlled by a central planning and management authority. Each agency in the system performs its subunit tasks in concert with all other agencies. This is a highly interdependent model with centralized authority and decision making; it would feature strong emphasis on public organizations delivering services. The second model might be characterized as a free enterprise, free market model. Here service providers would be private autonomous agencies competing for clientele, with policies and programs determined by the unseen hand of the market. Neither model is likely to be found in pure form in any community. But the dominant values and traditional roles of the community will play a large part in determining which model local officials lean toward in their planning decisions.[8]

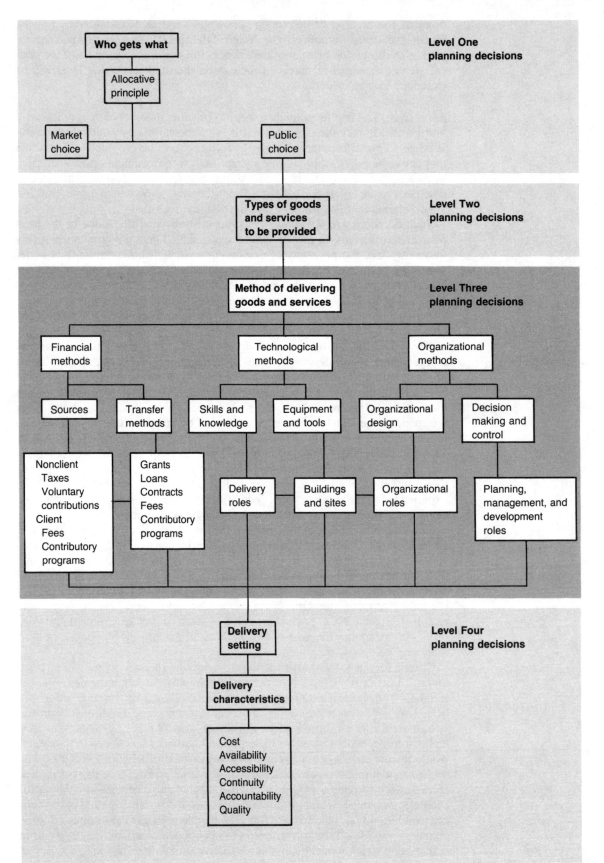

Level Two   At the second level of decision making lie the questions of the types of services to be supplied and the allocations among services. Decisions such as how resources should be allocated toward education as opposed to health, or mental health versus manpower training, or recreation versus child care programs become key issues for local government managers. In addition, this level is the locus of decisions regarding who should be eligible for services and the design of the various components of the service package on the basis of concepts of need. Once again, such decisions are frequently made at the legislative level, but, as has been pointed out, they are being left increasingly to local governments.

Of key importance at this level is the issue of universality versus selectivity.[9] In other words, should a service be provided to the entire population as a matter of right (such as public education in the United States) or should some services be provided only to a select group of people (such as the mentally retarded or the poor)? Gilbert and Specht, in their *Dimensions of Social Welfare Policy,* have indeed suggested that there is a "continuum of need" which further articulates the issue of universality versus selectivity. They suggest four illustrative classifications of need, ranging from the most universal to the most selective, as follows:

1. Attributed need—services are provided to all members of the community on the assumption of a common need (e.g., health care in Great Britain and public education in the United States are viewed in this light). Such determinations of common need are based primarily on the values of the community involved—be it national or local.
2. Compensatory need—services are provided to compensate people who have suffered unmerited hardship at the hands of the community (e.g., those displaced by urban renewal); who have made some special contribution to the community (veterans' benefits are the prime example of this); or who have contributed in advance for perceived future needs (e.g., unemployment compensation, social security payments, and other forms of prepayment insurance).
3. Diagnostic differentiation—services are provided on the basis of professional diagnoses of individual cases. Many health and mental health problems are seen in this light, particularly those that focus on acute care. While the concepts of attributed need and compensatory need are strongly rooted in the values and culture of the community, the criteria for diagnostic differentiation are purely technical.
4. Means tested need—services are provided to those unable to purchase goods or services for themselves. This is the most selective end of the continuum and is based on economic criteria of eligibility. This has been a relatively prevalent way of defining need in the United States and can be found in welfare, health, public housing, legal aid, and food distribution programs.[10]

In addition to the concepts of how social services are demanded, the ways in which the producers define their skills and organize their resources for service delivery also affect decision making at this second level. While the technology of service delivery is discussed in greater detail below, the historical evolution of some skills (and the resulting professional or trade associations this has produced) is an important determinant of the nature, scope, and organization of services. For example, because of ideological and professional differences, mental health services have grown up operationally separate from general health services, and the mental health profession has come to be defined according to a completely different set of ideals.[11]

In local communities there is a great deal of variation at this level of decision making. The field of alcoholism, for example, is characterized by the operation

Figure 18–1   A functional framework for human services planning. Planning dimensions and considerations are illustrated for each of the four decision levels. See text for further discussion.

of two distinct treatment modalities. On one hand, community hospitals rely to a great degree on physician professionals; on the other hand, private groups such as Alcoholics Anonymous depend exclusively on nonprofessionals in the treatment of alcoholism. Mental health services rely increasingly on paraprofessional providers, while health systems function with rigidly hierarchical professional roles.

From the point of view of local human services planning, this second level of decision making is the key frontier in determining the nature and quality of the services network. Needs assessment surveys, a full understanding of existing community resources, analyses of local and external forces shaping the community environment, and the development of consumer and provider participation are the crucial elements at this level. As Figure 18–1 indicates, subsequent plateaus are increasingly technical in nature and are shaped conclusively by decisions at this level.

Level Three At the third decision level one begins to encounter the full range of complexity in human services planning. Figure 18–1 shows three key areas which are involved at this point: technological factors, organizational factors, and financing factors. This level is of sufficient importance to warrant a separate and detailed analysis later in this discussion (see below, following the characterization of Level Four).

Level Four Decisions concerning the design of the specific delivery unit and service setting constitute the final level of planning decisions. These include such elements as the location and quality of land sites; the design, financing, and construction of buildings; the staffing arrangements and positions (including the relationships between practitioners, paraprofessionals, administrators, supervisors, planners, board members, and supporting clerical and maintenance positions); and specific budgetary allocations.

Many of the planning concerns at Level Four are typical of traditional city planning views of the design of public services. One further complication arises in human services planning, however, which has an important impact on this fourth level of planning. Settings in which services are actually delivered may be quite varied and separate from the offices of a human services agency. Guidelines for health systems plans, for example, specify the following six types of support settings for the delivery of health services: home; mobile; ambulatory; short stay (i.e., acute care); long stay; and freestanding.[12] In addition, human services are rendered in factories, offices, store fronts, and many other locations. Thus, for some services the location of the agency may be nothing more than the place where the provider has a desk and maintains supplies, materials, and client records.

The third level of planning decision: a detailed analysis Having outlined the implications of a four level functional framework of planning decisions for human services, we can now return to the crucial third level and examine it in detail. The following analysis therefore takes a look, in turn, at technological, organizational, and financing factors operative at this level.

Technological factors As used in the present discussion, *technological factors* refers to the ways in which service is to be delivered. These may vary significantly and are thus one source of complication and confusion in services planning. In the delivery of water to a community, for example, there is a combination of human skill and capital equipment which comprises what an economist would call the *production function*. In systemic terms, water as found in its natural state is fed into a system of purifying treatment plants, storage facilities, and pumping equipment to prepare it for delivery to the consumer. There is then developed a distribution network (in this case pipes) which conveys the purified water to the consumer at the point of use. Civil engineers and skilled technicians are required to design and build the service system and to monitor its functioning and the quality of its product.

The delivery of human services requires the same conceptual approach. Some are more labor intensive (requiring relatively greater input of human skill) and some are more capital intensive (requiring equipment, machinery, etc.). For human services the production function can be extremely complex and sophisticated since the goal of any particular service may be an adjustment in client behavior. Much more is known about the technology of water supply than is known about the *technology of behavior.*[13] Thus, the goals of a municipal human services program are much more difficult to derive, measure, and evaluate than are the goals of a municipal sanitation program. The human services production function does not in every case provide the appropriate direction, therefore, toward the provision of the optimal type of treatment.

For this reason the technology of human services delivery is constantly changing and evolving. One prime example of this is the mental health field. At the close of World War II, mental illness was seen as entirely analogous to physical illness; that is, it required treatment by a physician specialist trained in psychoanalysis who sought to effect a "cure." Patients were hospitalized and care was administered in a centralized location. Unfortunately, hospitalization often led to no treatment at all, high levels of institutional dependence, and the isolation of patients from their communities and daily lives. In the 1950s two major changes in "technology" dramatically altered the mental health field. One was the advent of mood-altering drugs (i.e., a physical agent) and the second was the idea of community mental health, which encouraged the return of patients to a community environment as soon as possible (i.e., a change in the use of human skills). Group and *milieu* therapy emerged along with community mental health centers, halfway houses, sheltered workshops, and other rehabilitative services. The result was the complete transformation of the technology of mental health.[14] In the transformation, the governments of local communities have taken on significant new responsibilities.

Similar changes in technology can be documented in a human service traditionally provided by local government—public education. The old image of the classroom and the traditional roles of teacher and pupil reflected a very simple technology. The teacher's skills were the result of a prescribed training program, and very simple physical agents or tools were employed—books, paper, pencils, etc. But the classroom of today only slightly resembles that outdated image. The technology of education has significantly expanded. New learning theories have produced not only new methods of teaching but a whole new range of physical tools as well. Television, films, audio cassettes, computer "teaching machines," and computerized libraries are but a few of the highly sophisticated physical agents found in today's schools.[15]

Variability of technology may occur even within the same service. A neighborhood clinic offering primary health care may range from the application of purely human skills (e.g., health education or family planning, nutrition, child care counseling) to the application of a number of physical agents (e.g., drugs, X rays, minor surgery). When one thinks of a full-scale modern teaching hospital, the technology employed is immediately perceived to be significantly advanced in both human skills (i.e., highly sophisticated practitioners in a wide range of specialties) and complex physical agents (e.g., linear accelerators, cobalt machines, dialyzers).

Thus, human services run a gamut from very simple technologies to the most complex. This places an added burden on the human services planner. He or she cannot possibly be knowledgeable in all of the many areas of technology and in their changing characters. The planner, then, is highly dependent on the collaborative advice and counsel of the specialist providers. City planners who followed traditional paths of training in engineering and architecture have sometimes found themselves with a technical capacity to function in many fields of municipal public works. This is clearly not the case with human services planners.

Organizational factors: what they are Flowing from planning decisions that are influenced by the technology of a service are decisions that relate to the organizational arrangements which will provide for the most effective delivery. Some of these concerns are traditional and well recognized. Others emerge from the ever-changing nature of the technology of services. Still others stem from the increasing concern of consumer groups with issues of quality assurance and responsiveness of providers.

It is sometimes difficult to think of organizations as being planned or designed in the same way that one would design a building or a water system. Most organizations begin very simply and on a very small scale and then grow and change over time. However, this growing and changing needs to take place in a planned fashion if an organization is going to effectively accomplish its goal and properly maintain itself. Moreover, some organizations of significant size do come into being de novo as part of a deliberate planning process, particularly in government programs and human services systems. In the 1960s Model Cities and poverty agencies were designed and brought into being. Entire new organizations and systems of organizations were created in the 1970s through such congressional actions as the Health Planning and Development Act, Title XX of the Social Security Act, the Older Americans Act, and other legislation.

At the very bottom, decisions have to be made concerning the ways in which the various tasks of an organization will be divided and how they will be coordinated and controlled. Beyond this, students of organizations have developed a host of additional design variables which influence the functioning of an organization. From this a new literature has begun to emerge that is expressly addressed to the task of organizational design.

Galbraith provides one such text, and in his book there is an excellent diagram of the variables involved in the process.[16] This diagram is shown in Figure 18–2. Galbraith traces the history of concern with various elements that have been exemplified by the various "schools" of thought in organization theory. The first such school is the classical school, whose major focus was on the key issues of task and structure. Significant attention was given to the "vertical" design issues of authority and hierarchy.

Even more important became the questions of departmentalization,[17] and these issues are still crucial in human services planning. They revolve around the questions of geography, function, specialization, and clientele. These are discussed immediately below.

Organizational factors: geography One area in which the planning of human services has been significantly deficient has been in the field of location theory and analysis. For private industry, it is currently possible to analyze with some precision the best location for production facilities, the appropriate size of market area, and the most effective means for distributing satellite facilities.[18] In the human services, however, this analysis is replaced by what can only be described as largely guesswork. One frequently hears of a need for developing uniform service areas, but there are as yet few, if any, objective criteria for designing such areas. A typical approach is described by Chu and Trotter in their analysis of the federal government's community mental health center program. In deciding on the service (catchment) area size for a community mental health center, the federal planners intuitively "felt" that a population of fewer than 75,000 individuals was insufficient to justify or support the staff and services being planned in such centers. At the other extreme, it was felt that a population service area much larger than 250,000 would be too large, exceeding the image of a local community service. This, unhappily, was the extent of the analysis for what is recognized in private industry as a key analytical concept in service delivery.[19]

Organizational factors: function The delivery of human services can also be viewed in terms of functions which organizational arrangements can serve to highlight. There is a substantial literature in this field, but the following are essentially the key functions in social services: *maintenance, service, intake and referral, outreach, treatment, follow-through, record keeping,* and *evaluation.*[20] Human services vary considerably along this dimension both between organizations and within organizations. Some human services organizations perform all eight of the listed functions; others perform only a few. Some localities, for example, have developed centralized intake and referral organizations (such as Chattanooga's neighborhood service centers)[21] which primarily serve to link the client to other appropriate organizations for treatment. Some health services have devised separate organizations for centralized record keeping or maintenance.

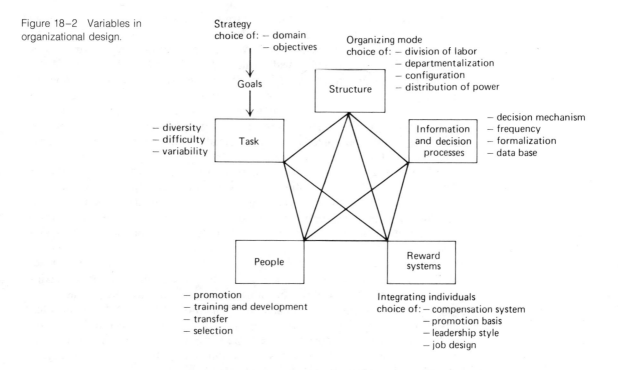

Figure 18–2 Variables in organizational design.

The fragmentation of these functions into separate organizational units has been the focus of much concern. For many services, follow-through, for example, is nonexistent because no single organization sees this process as its responsibility. Where this occurs, the real outcomes of services can never be known or evaluated. Separating the record keeping function from treatment may result in errors arising from inappropriate or inaccurate information. Recent efforts at services integration and the employment of such techniques as case management and client advocacy functions have attempted to focus on this problem.[22]

Organizational factors: specialization Organizations form around professional specialties quite naturally. This process is most evident in medicine and health but can also be seen in other areas of social welfare. A group of individuals with a common professional interest in a given problem or area of need come together for closer communication and to refine and further develop their skills and interests. Presumably, such activity also yields better service to the client. That it may result in too narrow a view of client problems and treatment is one negative dimension of such arrangements. Needed supporting functions are often overlooked by specialist organizations so that continuity of service is sacrificed for the higher sophistication of the specialist. Thus, the factor of specialization places unique demands on an organization for close linkages with other agencies that are able to provide the necessary additional dimensions of a comprehensive treatment program.

Organizational factors: clientele   Since the beginnings of charitable organizations, social services have developed organizationally around specific clients (e.g., retarded children, juvenile offenders, the elderly, unwed mothers, the blind, the handicapped, drug abusers, alcoholics). Since the 1960s organizations have developed which include among their specific client groups minorities and other uniquely disadvantaged groups. Many such organizations perform a full array of functions (in many varied geographical settings); others (such as client advocates) serve only in a limited fashion.

As noted, these factors constitute the traditional ways in which organizations have developed in human services delivery. They have guided agencies in their internal management decisions and have also served to elucidate organization development on a community-wide scale. A key difficulty is that none of these factors provides any certain criteria for choice. As was pointed out as long ago as 1948, these factors often conflict with each other and result in a lack of theoretical or rational guides as to which should prevail.[23] Particularly difficult in human services delivery has been the development of organizations around specific functions or specialized areas, which leads to fragmentation, lack of continuity, and lack of accountability.

Following the classicists, the human relations school, as a result of studies in the 1930s, focused more attention on the people of an organization and the problems of integrating individual needs with organizational goals. Thus training, job development, job designs, promotion policies, and the arrangement of rewards and statuses can be seen to be important added factors in organizational design.[24]

With the introduction of computers and the work of scholars at Carnegie–Mellon University, greater attention was given to the nature of decision making in organizations and the flows of information necessary to enhance such programs. From this came the application of operations research techniques and the development of mathematical modeling of organizational processes. Formalized management information systems are now part of the management of many organizations and are expressly instrumental in the design of new organizations or the modifications of existing entities.[25]

Contemporary views have introduced additional factors. The research of Laurence and Lorsch for example suggests close association among differentiations of tasks, predictability of tasks, and mechanisms for integration.[26] The work of Forrester has provided considerable stimulus to the current thinking of human services planners.[27] His industrial systems model examines the implications of tracing various flows (e.g., materiel, orders, money, people, information) through an organization as a means of finding more effective arrangements of roles, tasks, and functions. Examples of the impact of such an approach can be seen in current integration efforts based on a client "pathway" analysis which traces the route of a client through a human services system while observing all who come into contact with the client and the functions and roles they perform. At a deeper level, the support activities necessary to maintain those with primary client contact are analyzed, leading to essential control functions such as administration, planning, and development.[28]

Organizational factors: other approaches   Other contemporary approaches to organizational design include concern for communications processes,[29] environmental uncertainty and its impact on organizational structure,[30] complexity,[31] and the effects of implementing organizational change.[32] Of particular interest to human services planners has been increased attention to the problems of interorganizational relations.[33] Very often, human services planners are concerned with the planning of systems of organizations rather than a single entity.

Approaches with broader political implications are also noteworthy. A key approach to organizational design involves greater consumer control of provider organizations. This concept is reflected in the fact that consumer representation has been established by statute in many of the federal categorical grant-in-aid programs and in the federal provisions for local planning.[34] The basic idea behind this approach is that, with consumers serving in the key policy oversight role, greater accountability can be realized. Evidence that this is in fact so is not yet conclusive, but consumer representation on policy boards of human services agencies is clearly increasing and can be viewed as a major element in organizational design.[35]

Still other approaches include developing review and comment powers for centralized local planning agencies which would guide the flow of public funds to service agencies; dispensing governmental aid contractually to private agencies with specific accountability measures included; granting more powers to local general purpose governments; and awarding federal grants for implementation of experiments in services integration and capacity building.[36]

Financing factors: appropriation to delivery   The intricate web of human services delivery involves even greater complexity when one examines the factors involved in the financing mechanisms currently in use. From the simple days of charitable donations, the human services field has evolved into a sector of the national economy of major importance. In the mid-1970s estimates indicated that more than 25 percent of the gross national product (GNP) was spent in the human services field, exclusive of fee-for-service payments. Eleven percent of the GNP was spent on direct services (excluding insurance and pension programs) and about 90 percent of these expenditures came from government.[37] The pathways through which these funds move from legislative appropriation (or from charitable gifts) to the actual point of service delivery can be tortuous and complex.

Gilbert and Specht have suggested that this subject can be broken down into two parts: the sources of funding and the transfer arrangements directing funds to the point of service delivery.[38] Figure 18–1 again reflects this analytical distinction. This twofold division will be adopted in the following discussion.

Financing factors: sources of funding   Funding sources for human services can be summarized in terms of two general points of origin. Funding can be derived from the *clients* themselves or from *nonclient sources*. A traditional mechanism in the health and mental health fields is the fee-for-service practice, in which the provider directly bills the client for services rendered. This method of funding places the provider in the same position as any private entrepreneur in a market economy (although some providers charging on a fee-for-service basis may be nonprofit or even public). Fees are structured to meet all costs incurred in providing the facilities, equipment, and staff necessary. This, of course, is the simplest funding form. Increasingly, however, it is the least satisfactory. In many instances rapidly escalating costs (particularly in the health and mental health fields) mean that the service is available only to more affluent clients.

Funding through third party payers has become more prevalent since World War II. This mechanism operates through a prepayment scheme. It is best exemplified by medical insurance, social security, and membership in health maintenance organizations. These contributory programs operate in the form of insurance for the individual consumer but, in the last analysis, it is a consumer-derived payment. In the health field in recent years approximately two-thirds of health expenditures have been derived from consumers and about 40 percent of this is covered by health insurance.[39]

Nonclient sources of funding include funds derived from charitable gifts and from public taxes. In the later 1970s gifts accounted for about 10 percent of nonclient funding; about 90 percent came from governmental sources.[40]

Financing factors: transfer arrangements   Public funds are applied to human needs in a variety of ways. In the simplest method, local government units directly appropriate funds from the tax base, which are then applied by a city or county operating department. Such funding is part of the normal local government budgeting function and need not be discussed in detail here. Funding for local services from state or federal sources, however, requires some arrangement which can direct the funds to the point of service delivery. Four such transfer arrangements have developed over the years:

1. Grants-in-aid: grants provide the most common method of transferring funds from one level of government to another. Under housing and urban renewal programs, grants were often made directly from the federal government to the local unit. In social services, however, the traditional procedure has been for the federal government to make grants to state governments which, in turn, make grants to either local governments or local private providers. (In some programs grants have been made directly to a local private agency by the federal government, particularly for research or experimental efforts.)
2. Loans: funds are advanced as a loan for the development of human services. Use of this method of transfer is most prominent in housing and urban renewal programs, particularly in governmental underwriting of private housing mortgages.
3. Contracts for service: governmental units may enter into contracts with private providers for the delivery of services. This is a feature of public welfare under Title XX of the Social Security Act which permits state governments to enter into such contracts. It has also been used in Community Action and Model Cities programs.
4. Third party payments: the Medicare and Medicaid programs have established the federal government as a major third party payer. This method of transferring federal tax revenues to local providers preserves the fee-for-service system by reimbursing health providers on the basis of standard bills for services.

These transfer methods of nonclient funds clearly may have significant impact on the stability, size, and operating characteristics of social welfare organizations. They may also pose significant planning problems where numerous combinations of funding sources and transfer arrangements coexist for a single provider as well as for the entire local human services network.

A *needs framework*

Having taken a look at the functional framework of social planning, we can now move on to a look at the needs framework. The human services system reflects a bewildering array of organizations, professions, and services. At first glance, any systematic generalizations about such diversity seem nearly impossible.

Many managers will agree, however, that it is important in developing the human services planning framework to assemble some organizing principles to describe and systematically view the total network. A variety of ways have been devised to do this. Two of the most promising—the concept of human need and the *UWASIS* approach—are presented below.

The concept of human need The concept of human need is derived from such theoretical formulations as Maslow's hierarchy of needs as well as from the more developmental concepts of personality growth exemplified by the work of Erikson.[41] The Maslow hierarchy begins with fundamental physiological and survival needs and builds on a pyramid to more sophisticated human demands for love, esteem, and self-actualization. Such needs may be partially satisfied in a variety of social services oriented toward increasing independence, averting isolation, and providing opportunities for human expression.

Erikson, on the other hand, is a leading figure in a school of psychology which sees human needs in a developmental light. This view may be instrumental in clarifying the role of a number of human services geared to very specific target populations. Erikson identifies eight identity crises in the maturing process of the human life cycle. A number of human services can be identified that serve people as they pass through these eight critical points in their lives. Four stages of childhood are viewed as influential to later development, and many service providers concentrate on serving children in these crucial years. A number of specialized providers focus on people undergoing the stresses of subsequent life transitions as well, such as adolescence, marriage, retirement, and aging.

Many people argue that history suggests that people undergoing these transitions do not require special agencies and services. Indeed, this argument will undoubtedly arise in appropriations debates in city and county councils for some time to come. But the rise of social services suggests that the advent of urbanization and industrialization has induced changes in the social structure of such a nature that many of the formerly supporting institutions (e.g., the family or the church) are no longer adequate to deal with the stresses and frustrations of contemporary life. In addition, many human needs may now be better met by trained specialists who are able to provide more sophisticated help, thereby permitting more satisfying levels of social functioning.

Whatever the arguments pro and con, the needs framework of the developmental psychologists can serve as an organizing principle by which social services may be classified and understood. An example of the use of such a framework by the city of Cambridge, Massachusetts, illustrates an application of this model to human services planning in local governments. In conjunction with the social planning component of its community renewal program, the city developed a matrix which correlated six life stages (which are generally age-defined) with six basic areas important to individual health and welfare. The life stages were: child, 0–6 years; child, 6–12 years; teen; adult; elderly; and family. Health and welfare needs were allocated according to the following divisions: education, recreation, employment, physical health, mental health, and fiscal health. Each cell of the matrix was then used to list the kind of needs, in line with the established divisions, appropriate to the various life stages. These listings, when coupled with relevant demographic data, were employed by the city to provide estimates of need for services among each group, and to predict related changes in the levels of need. The two dimensional needs framework used by Cambridge can be expanded to various scales of geographic organization, including neighborhood, community, regional, and/or national scales.

The UWASIS approach A second approach to classifying human services providers was developed by the United Way of America—the United Way of America Services Identification System (*UWASIS*).[42] This system, first developed in 1972 and revised in 1976, was based on the identification of six major goals of social functioning which represent the basic organizing principle of the system. From this, a series of service system objectives to meet the goals could be derived. "Clusters" of service programs designed to fulfill the objectives were then specified.

The published version of the original *UWASIS* included a chart which listed the six goals and, under each, the various objectives and specific programs which applied to them. Although the chart as such does not appear in *UWASIS II,* the 1976 revision, an example from the chart highlights the system's general-to-specific organizing principle and its potential value to key decision makers in local governments. For example, the *UWASIS* goal that is defined as "optimal personal and social adjustment and development" is itself divided into three areas representing different objectives intended, as discussed above, to help the general goal. One objective—an individual and family life services system—is comprised of services devoted to family preservation and strengthening, family substitution, crisis intervention and protection, and support to individuals and families. The specific programs listed for the family preservation and strengthening aspect include counseling, homemaker services, and family growth control and planning assistance.[43]

Although the specifics of this system will not, of course, be susceptible to direct application in all cases, it represents an approach to the definition and classification of human services which all local officials can use as a foundation for planning and decision-making processes in their own communities. *UWASIS* is designed, in fact, to be a flexible tool which can be tailored to the individual requirements of local needs. As the human services encompass an ever broader spectrum of concerns and as the human services aspects of traditional local functions become more widely recognized, *UWASIS* also provides a means for relating some of the traditional public services to the "newer" human services.

Community surveys provide the most direct and accurate measures of human needs. Such needs assessment studies are increasingly being carried out by local governments and involve mail, telephone, or direct interviews with a representative sample of community residents, coupled with data from local service providers, local clergy, and local civic leaders. Many technical guides for such community studies have recently been developed.[44] In addition, the past few years have seen many such studies published. In short, considerable technical experience in needs assessment has developed in the 1970s, and planners should make full use of this experience for the benefit of their own communities.[45]

Methodological approaches to social services planning

An overview: the political and the managerial approaches

Until recent years, self-consciousness about the methods of social services planning has been notably absent. Since the turn of the century two major strains may be identified: political methods and managerial methods. The first originated in the reform spirit which conceived of solutions to social problems in political terms. These nineteenth century traditions can still be found in the work of the followers of the late Saul Alinsky.[46] Social problems in their view represent a conflict between the haves and the have-nots, and social action is largely a struggle for power and resources. Virtually no structured analysis was undertaken since adherents to this view believed that the ideology "explained" the origin of social problems.[47]

The managerial orientation, on the other hand, has its roots in the nineteenth century charity organization societies and the more recent health and welfare councils, community chests, and United Way organizations. People's needs had to be met with scarce resources and, therefore, budgeting, merit systems, and efficiency techniques were applied to ensure that those needs were met no more lavishly than necessary. Few substantive analyses of the nature or causes of need were undertaken.

Contrasting these methodologies of social planning with those of city planning points out their respective values. City planning developed as a profession with an apolitical bias. Government was used as an institutional base, but the rules of urban development were structured so that political processes intervened only minimally. From 1950 to 1967 the focus of city planning was on the adaptation of the social sciences to a better understanding of the complexities of urbanization.[48] City planners saw their role in society as that of deriving the optimal rational choice for action. If the political system rejected their prescriptions, they blamed it on the hidden, unknowable forces of "politics." In retrospect, the political perspectives of social planning could well have made city planning more effective, just as the scientific perspectives of city planning could probably have improved social planning.

In the 1970s, city planners became much more well versed in the intricacies of political processes, and social planners came to accept the fact that social problems and human needs require more complex treatment than simply getting the right committee together or conducting demonstrations in front of city hall. Both groups have come to realize what Webber pointed out some years ago—there is unity between research and action.[49]

An illustration of the orientation of social planning may be noted in a concept of developmental process which was part of the evolution of city planning method. Four stages of methods development can be identified:

1. The practice or craft perspective: practitioners agree upon very simple goals and rely upon experiential judgment
2. The cognitive, or scientific, perspective: scientific methods are used in an attempt to develop greater understanding, more reliable generalizations, and more certain outcomes from intervention
3. The policy development perspective: the complexities of the value framework become the focus for increased understanding and enlightened social action
4. The policy analysis and program evaluation perspective: the approaches of the cognitive and the policy development perspectives are combined to form the basis for a "sophisticated search for a combination of analysis, design, and process knowledge."[50]

For city planning, these stages evolved slowly, providing opportunities for the growth and maturation of each perspective. Social services planning has not had the same germination of methodological focus. It remained much longer in the "craft" stage of development and then, focusing on values and process, bypassed the cognitive stage. The profession that might have pursued more advanced cognitive development—social work—turned its attention to psychoanalytic methods and working with individuals. Those in "community work" among social workers quickly became (and have remained) a small minority.

Thus, human services planning draws its practitioners from a variety of training and methodological orientations. Emergence from the craft stage began to occur in this field around 1970. With conservatism and scarcity came increased demands for accountability and evaluation of effectiveness. Burgeoning welfare case loads, rising unemployment, increasing complexity and bureaucratization of health care, shifting technologies in mental health, and other factors placed tremendous burdens on human services planners to demonstrate capabilities more focused on the substance of social problems.

In sum, human services planning of the later 1970s may be characterized as weak in the substantive understanding of human need and social problems. Its strengths may be found in skills related to those social action processes which involve both consensus and conflict strategies, and in the appreciation of community values and their role in shaping and forming the need for human services. Because of this combination of strengths and weaknesses, planning in human services tends to be incremental, remedial, and short term.

In light of the above overview, it is now possible to identify the methodological approaches currently being developed in human services planning with the appropriate understanding of their tentative and underdeveloped nature. In the discussion that follows, four key strains of methods development are described. The full range of activity and research cannot be adequately covered within the scope of this chapter but the major highlights and applications of each are provided. The four strains are: management and social control methods; social science methods; systems theory methods; and futures forecasting methods.

Management and social controls

The 1970s have seen a confluence of a number of strands of thought that first appeared in the 1950s and evolved into a variety of applications in the 1960s. The origins can be found in group dynamics research and in the study of industrial human relations.[51] These themes, combined with the discipline of scientific management,[52] produced in the 1970s a highly sophisticated view of social control mechanisms for formal organizations. These views have found their way into human services planning for a variety of reasons, accountability and evaluation of the effectiveness of service providers being the most notable. The following are typical areas in which managerial viewpoints and philosophies have become a part of social services planning.

Human services management information systems Essential to any planning effort is the availability of adequate information related to the problems at hand. The lack of appropriate data for planning has been a long-standing problem in the provision of social services. The availability of computer technology has done much to ease this problem. Local areas are increasingly developing standardized management information systems (MISs) as a foundation for local planning efforts. One such effort is found in the Chattanooga Human Services Delivery System, the centralized data bank of which contains information about available service programs as well as uniform client records.[53]

The key problem in developing such systems lies in determining the exact nature of the data to be collected. While many studies describing the design of urban services data banks make them appear to be very precise and workable, the actual selection of variables to be included requires a sophisticated understanding of contemporary social theory. The operationalization of such theories into meaningful and appropriate social indicators requires considerable skill and creativity. The task includes decisions about whether to maintain information about resources, processes, or outcomes. Desirable knowledge is often not easily measured or observed, and "proxy" variables have to be devised and substituted. In addition, many technical problems of data accuracy and reliability abound.[54] Finally, there is the major problem of what to do with the deluge of information when it reaches the decision maker's already crowded desk. Notwithstanding the difficulties, many managers have found that the task of developing a useful body of information that can provide the means to monitor and evaluate the delivery of social services is an initial step in developing a truly effective planning process.[55]

Merging of planning and budgeting Development of the planning-programming-budgeting system of management (PPBS) has had an increasingly important influence on human services planning. While some consider PPBS a fad of the Johnson administration, many of its key principles were, in fact, enunciated at the time that Franklin Roosevelt was President.[56] While many have suggested that this method is on the wane, in fact the use of the key ideas of PPBS is actually on the rise in contemporary human services planning.

One of these key ideas is the preparation of budgets in terms of performance goals, or outputs, rather than in terms of inputs (as most municipal budgets traditionally have been prepared). The adoption of goal-oriented budgeting necessarily requires a higher level of precision in planning: the budget is thought of in terms of activities, programs, and services rather than salaries, equipment, and supplies. Greater attention is also given to the process by which priorities are developed. The techniques of cost-effectiveness determination make explicit the differences in efficacy of alternative programs seeking the same objective. The most recent terminology, *zero-based budgeting,* is in many respects an extension of these same concepts. Its focus on individual program justification carries forward the basic idea of cost-effectiveness studies.

The application of such methods to planning social services has encountered considerable difficulty. Measuring the qualitative effects of complex service delivery networks in quantitative terms is more often than not unsatisfactory.[57] Used with understanding of its limitations and application, PPBS can be an effective method of planning for human services by local governments. Its key advantage lies in its emphasis on monitoring and evaluating the actual effectiveness of service delivery.

Management by objectives Management by objectives (MBO) represents a refinement of PPBS which retains many of the latter's key ideas. One of the difficulties of PPBS is that it tends to centralize decision-making responsibilities in a single office or individual. MBO, although it takes the same goal-oriented approach to the budgeting process, explicitly provides mechanisms which make broader-based decision making available. The principal idea of MBO is that goals and objectives are prepared by the people who will be responsible for carrying them out. In theory, this not only allows for those with the greater expertise to design the objectives and related programs but also makes for greater commitment on the part of those who will be expected to carry out those objectives. Thus, central decision makers can focus more on the standards and guidelines for budget preparation, on the problems of overall resource allocation, and on the monitoring and evaluation function. Program administrators jointly plan and negotiate their own objectives and then carry them out. The other key idea of MBO is an explicit effort to structure programs hierarchically so that problems in service delivery can be identified and directly approached at the appropriate level.

Other major ideas involved in MBO may be summarized as follows: operational objectives with clearly defined performance measures; explicit priorities, including the justification for abandoning or deferring activities; and specific targets and timetables, not only for ultimate program outcomes but also for each step along the way.[58] Advocates of MBO also argue that organizational structure should follow program strategy, an idea derived from Warren Bennis's concept of "organic" organizations built around impermanent task forces.[59]

Integration techniques From the fields of both community organization and business management have come a number of approaches that attempt to overcome the fragmentation and diffusion of the human services delivery system. These are primarily aimed at the integration and coordination of programs, services, and systems.

The sophistication of such efforts is varied and has not been effective in all cases. The root of the problem has been stated succinctly by Chester Barnard in his *Functions of the Executive:* "Cooperation has no reason for being except as it can do what the individual cannot do."[60] In short, services integration techniques have yet to produce the leverage which stimulates the motivation and desire for cooperative action at all levels. The range of methods runs a full gamut from complete government reorganization to selective and incremental cooperative arrangements on a limited and highly focused basis. Many current integrative techniques have been borrowed from private industry where corporate expansion and diversification have created some of the same problems faced by the human services delivery system. Some, however, are unique to human services agencies. Industry, for example, does not have to face the problem of integrating completely autonomous units as social services planning frequently does. Human services integration generally requires substantially greater sensitivity to reward and incentive systems for effectiveness.

Community organization and organization development   Techniques of social change have been a major focus of two separate disciplines: community organization and organization development. Both attempt to devise specific methods of intervention in social networks in order to foster higher levels of cohesion and effectiveness. Whether these methods are part of already structured formal organizations, newly emerging citizens groups, or ad hoc, interdisciplinary task forces, their proponents attempt to establish a base for cooperative effort toward social change. Drawing significantly on group dynamics, these methods place heavy emphasis on behavioral approaches to change. One common technique derives from Lewin's *field theory,* in which the *change agent,* together with the client group, analyzes the forces available in support of, and resistant to, change. Such techniques stress awareness of the need for change and the levels of change, methods for developing the goals of change, and the overcoming of resistance to change.[61]

These techniques clearly require trained and experienced change agents, but many managers have found that the importance of the techniques to the planning of human services cannot be overemphasized. For many communities the human services delivery system has become so complex that major efforts are needed to bring it under effective control. The achievement of such control requires skill in planned social change; its implementation will significantly affect the existing patterns of rewards, statuses, and roles.[62]

Social science

It is beyond the scope of this chapter to review fully the social science theory and methods that are relevant to human services planning. In many respects the social sciences enrich and enlighten human services planning even more than they do physical city planning. This, however, would be difficult to discern from a glance at many human services planning efforts. There is little question that one of the major needs for improvement in human services planning is a more conscious application of social science methodology. Let us therefore take a look at some familiar and less familiar social science techniques.

The use of the social survey began—at least in the United States: there are European antecedents—in 1905 with the Pittsburgh Survey. This tool is now a common technique found in virtually all human services planning efforts. Interview programs among households, service providers, and clients are frequent tools for data collection. They form the basis for needs assessments as well as for evaluation of how well needs are being met by the providers of the community.[63]

Other applications of social science techniques, however, are more often implicit. The assumptions about utilization behavior (or help-seeking behavior) and problem behavior are firmly grounded in contemporary knowledge of psychology and other behavioral sciences.[64] Such assumptions are rarely stated explicitly and the human services planner is hard pressed to keep up with the latest theoretical developments in these disciplines.

Some of the analytical tools common to city planning should perhaps be applied more consciously to social services planning, demography being a particularly apt example. Changing birthrates, longer life spans, increased mobility, changing life-styles, and alterations in family composition all have a significant impact on the demand for human services, and the application of advanced techniques of population analysis and forecasting could play a significant role in determining the implications of these issues. This has been recognized in the health and mental health fields but is seldom applied in other areas of human services planning. Forecasts of economic and social conditions in a community have also been long overlooked. The need for greater cooperation between the human services planners and the city planners of any given locality is clearly evident. This situation poses a particular challenge for administrators.

Figure 18–3 The symbol versus reality. Symbols are only a tool for helping to measure reality.

The mathematical techniques of the social sciences are increasingly being employed in social planning. Such techniques as multiple regression, factor analysis, discriminant analysis, and path analysis are slowly finding their ways into more inventive planning efforts. These mathematical modeling techniques have been most helpful in understanding the complexities of service delivery and designing more effective modes of operation.

The use of social indicators has also become prevalent in human services planning, particularly in the development of data banks and information systems, noted above. Such indicators are now required elements in the preparation of federally aided comprehensive health plans. Numerous problems are involved, however. In many circumstances only so-called input indicators are available (e.g., numbers of hospital beds, physicians, or schoolteachers; pupil–teacher ratios). Such indicators can reveal very little about the effectiveness of programs or the quality of life in the community. Thus, the major goal is to develop output, or goal, indicators. The data for such indicators, however, are much harder to define and much more difficult to measure. Indicators of agency or program effectiveness (referred to as process indicators) are also useful but are equally difficult to develop. Thus, while there is a growing literature of social indicator potentials, there is relatively limited application.[65]

Systems theory

Systems theory has become increasingly prominent in human services planning. Its appeal lies in its "commonsense" character, its seeming simplicity (in spite of frequent intricate computer modeling), and its reduction of complex phenomena into simple, manageable parts.[66]

In elementary terms, a system is comprised of discrete sets of activities which are closely linked together. These linked subsystems exist in an environment that is constantly making demands on the system: in the language of systems theory, these demands are a part of the system's inputs. The linked subsystems deal with the inputs in various ways and transform them into system outputs which are consumed in the environment. This process culminates in evaluation and feedback which may result in changes in the demands on the system from the environment.

This has proven an attractive metaphor in attempting to understand human services systems. Systems models can be developed from a number of points of view. One of the more promising perspectives is the conceptualization of a system along the "client pathway," but other flows—of communication, data, or personnel, for example—can be used with equal effect, depending on the purposes of the analysis. Such views permit a close examination of each subsystem, its linkages, and its support requirements.

Systems analysis is an excellent method for quickly comprehending complexity. It has its limitations, however, as a planning methodology. It assumes a high level of stability in linkages between subsystems and implies an assumption of no technological change. There is disagreement over the question of whether systems theory allows for any significant change. However, the systems depiction of human services networks is proving to be of significant practical value, notwithstanding its theoretical limitations.

Futures forecasting

A final perspective on human services planning methodology lies in the area of futures forecasting. The techniques suggested here have not been extensively used in this context. They are mentioned only because they are gaining prominence in other areas of planning and could easily be adapted for social planning purposes.[67]

One such technique is the Delphi method of forecasting. This involves independent consultation with experts in the various aspects of human services delivery with the purpose of developing a list of likely technological changes in human services delivery and estimates of dates for the probable development of such changes.

Another closely related technique is technology assessment, which involves efforts to trace out the effects of a given technological improvement.[68] It is usually thought of in terms of physical technology (such as the impact of automobiles or television on American society) but can also be applied in human services planning. A thorough assessment of drug therapy and its impact at all levels of the community may have revealed many of the problems now being experienced as state and local governments attempt to deinstitutionalize patients and put them under the care of local community services.

Futures forecasting proper is still another approach to developing innovative and creative concepts in human services planning. The method, as implied by its title, is the preparation of "future scenarios" around a specific set of assumptions. Alternative future scenarios permit planners to trace various possibilities as a basis for decision making. One scenario may well represent a "do nothing" or "drift" situation; others may make an attempt to play out the consequences of specified policy alternatives.[69]

As suggested, these techniques have not been widely adopted in human services planning but their potential use seems highly promising.

The role of local government in human services planning

In light of the foregoing description of a framework for human services planning and the brief inventory of its methodology, it is now possible to discuss the potential dimensions of human services planning in local government. Needless to say, there are numerous possibilities and the potential mix of roles, responsibilities, and decision-making arrangements is infinite. In any given community, these will depend very much on the staff resources of the local government and the private service providers, historical patterns of service development, community values, and established patterns of communication. In the discussion below no prescribed role or combinations of roles are set forth as most desirable. Local factors will be such that the relationship between the local government and already existing service providers must be negotiated on a continuing basis.

Generally, the planning role of the local government will bear a close relationship to the kind of service delivery role that the local government assumes. In other words, the more the local government is involved in the provider role, the more demanding and comprehensive will be the planning roles. In addition, any determination of the planning role of local government in the social services field is contingent on at least two factors: how the community perceives its local government's planning role in general, and the strength of planning resources already available. Finally, as will be suggested below, the distribution of power among the service providers will be an important determinant of the local government planning role.

Potential local government service delivery roles

The New England Municipal Center has suggested that local governments may potentially play five roles in the delivery of human services. For the purposes of this discussion, these roles are summarized as follows:

1. Provider role: the local government directly provides service. Examples of this are numerous and well known—municipal hospitals, schools, recreation programs, etc.
2. Regulator role: the local government oversees and regulates other agencies that directly provide services. Examples of this include county governments and councils of governments (COGs) which, under authorization by OMB Circular no. A-95, are given review and comment functions respecting any service provider that operates with federal funds. Similar arrangements are also found in comprehensive health planning.
3. Funder role: the local government, using its own funds (sometimes from federal revenue sharing or Community Development Block Grants, both of which authorize funding for social services), enters into contracts with service providers. Local government may exercise a performance control

over such contracts through contract monitoring and evaluation, including the power to withhold payment, exact penalties, or terminate for any failure of service.

4. Capacity builder role: the local government provides advice, consultation, and technical assistance to build up the planning, management, and coordination capacities of other agencies. Local government might, for example, use its tax or grant funds to assist a local citizens' council in mental health planning or to build a network of emergency services.

5. Facilitator/coordinator role: the local government may focus on providing the mechanisms by which local service providers, client groups, and others may come together and negotiate goals, policies, programs, and activities.[70]

These roles are by no means exhaustive. Many experienced local officials are familiar with the "passive contributor" role in which a local government is asked to contribute matching funds to a federally financed service, but is given no voice in the nature or policies of that service. The focus in this discussion, however, is on active local government participation as illustrated by the five roles outlined above.

Combinations of these roles represent the most common situation. With the fragmented development of social services, local governments might be simultaneously providers, regulators, and funders of social services. They may also be invited to take on capacity building or facilitating roles in still other service delivery systems. Many cities, for example, have a dual health system with parallel public and private facilities. In other localities, mental health services may also be provided under a dual system. Some services are shifting in their control configuration, with the responsibilities of local government changing correspondingly. Some states, for example, now require that public education opportunities be made available to children with learning disabilities.[71] This means that local governments are required to provide special educational and psychological counseling services formerly offered by private agencies.

In short, the five service roles described above are useful analytical categories, but most local and county governmental units are heavily involved in several of these roles.

Relation of human services planning roles to delivery roles

Each of the roles described above reflects a different degree of "activism" on the part of local governments in the provision of human services. Each has a corresponding degree of planning responsibility associated with it. These variations in planning requirements are spelled out in Figure 18–4, which relates the planning levels depicted in Figure 18–1 to the five service roles described above. As Figure 18–4 suggests, the direct provider role requires a full range of planning responsibility from the broadest policy level to the specific design of delivery settings. Consequently, the direct provider role places the greatest demands on local government planning capabilities.

The regulator and funder roles are somewhat less rigorous. They require the following:

1. The capability to provide guides and standards at the highest level of policy development
2. An understanding of the needs of the community and how such needs are being met
3. The ability to develop a vision of what the ideal mix of services should be in the community

**Local government
service delivery role**

Local government planning responsibilities	Direct provider	Regulator	Funder	Capacity builder	Facilitator/ coordinator
Level One					
Basic goal and policy development	+	+	+	+	+
Development of priorities	+	+	+	(o)	(o)
Monitoring and evaluation	+	+	+	(o)	(o)
Level Two					
Needs assessment	+	+	+	o	o
Inventory of service providers	+	+	+	o	o
Design of services mix	+	+	+	o	o
Development of eligibility standards	+	+	+	o	o
Development of technical and operating standards	+	+	+	o	o
Level Three					
Service area delineations	+	+	+	o	o
Planning of service technology	+	(o)	(o)	–	–
Planning of organization, coordination, and management arrangements	+	(o)	(o)	–	–
Planning of funding arrangements	+	o	(o)	–	–
Level Four					
Site location and site planning	+	(−)	(−)	–	–
Building and facility planning	+	(−)	(−)	–	–
Staffing and program planning	+	(−)	(−)	–	–
Special setting design planning	+	(−)	(−)	–	–

+ = local government responsibility
o = may be carried out by local government or others
(o) (−) = carried out by others with local government review
− = carried out by others

Figure 18–4   The extent of local government responsibility for various aspects of planning decisions is related to the local government service delivery role.

4. The capacity to develop priorities
5. The capability to develop criteria for decision making in the regulation and funding of services that can be applied continuously and that have the capacity for evaluating and monitoring performance.

Stated in another fashion, local governments in regulator and funder roles must have a comprehensive planning and policy development capacity. Those which are direct service providers need that same capacity plus the added ability to plan specific projects and programs.

The capacity builder and facilitator/coordinator roles are less active, placing fewer demands on local government. While local government should be directly involved in basic goal and policy development, these roles would also be compatible with the location of a general comprehensive planning capacity in other agencies (such as a health and welfare council or United Way organization). With a local government in either a capacity builder or facilitator/coordinator role, specific project and program planning may be carried out directly by the private service provider.

Combination roles: dominant patterns
in local government planning

As has been suggested, it is unlikely that local government at the municipal or county level will be playing only one of the five defined roles. This variability can best be seen by using the example of a hypothetical urban community in the northeastern part of the United States. Figure 18–5 suggests the typical dominant provider roles that one might have found in such a community in the 1970s. This is charted in Figure 18–5 in relation to the six goals for social welfare services set up in the original *UWASIS* classification scheme discussed earlier. Of four possible service deliverers—local government, state government, federal government, and the private sector—the figure indicates the group most likely to actually deliver services in such a community (as opposed to funding, coordinating, or planning services). The resulting pattern suggests the difficulty of generalizing about local government roles.

Under Goal One—adequate income and economic opportunity—the federal and state governments dominate (although county governments might serve as agents of state government in providing such services). Local governments share in the delivery of special needs in manpower development (often a legacy from the War on Poverty or Model Cities programs), but social insurance, financial aid, and consumer protection services are largely in the hands of higher levels of government. This is not to suggest that such a pattern is static. Many localities particularly hard hit by economic distress have used federal revenue sharing, community development, and antipoverty funds to develop locally sponsored training and consumer programs.

In contrast, Goal Two—optimal environmental conditions and provision of basic material needs—finds local government playing a dominant role. This is not surprising since the traditional services of protection, transportation, utilities, housing, and urban renewal are represented here. While state and federal governments and some private agencies share in delivery (and other) roles, local government is still the dominant force in meeting this goal.

Goal Three—optimal health—presents a very mixed picture. Local government shares responsibilities with others to a large extent and the dominant service provider emerges in the form of private organizations. Public health services (i.e., sanitation, immunization, screening, and prevention programs) are most commonly associated with local government. The delivery of medical care may be found in local government institutions (e.g., city or county hospitals, neighborhood clinics), but such care traditionally has been limited to those unable to purchase normal private services. In addition, local governments have had very little role in mental health, retardation, and rehabilitation services. This is an area where local government influence is very much on the rise, however. Efforts to reduce the costs of health care and rationalize the proliferation of capital-intensive acute care facilities have created a major interest in comprehensive health planning. The deinstitutionalization of patients in state mental hospitals has placed a new burden on local governments to provide community based services and facilities. State laws have increasingly mandated the education of the retarded in normal school settings; the responsibility for this has fallen upon the local school system coming into the 1980s. This third goal, then, is in a state of transition: local governments can be expected to play an important and dominant role in the future in the provision of optimal health.

Goal Four—adequate knowledge and skills—has been a key responsibility of local government since the beginning of the public school movement in the United States in the early nineteenth century. Local government is still the dominant provider in this area. Traditionally, the federal government has taken almost no part in the actual provision of education, although it has provided financial assistance at all levels of learning, particularly since the 1960s.

Goal One

Adequate income and economic opportunity

	L	S	F	P
Manpower development services		+	+	
Special services for handicapped and disadvantaged	⊞	+	+	+
Social insurance services		+	+	
Financial aid services		+	+	
Consumer protection services		+	+	

Goal Two

Optimal environmental conditions and provision of basic material needs

	L	S	F	P
Food and nutrition services	⊞	+	+	+
Clothing and apparel services				+
Housing and urban renewal services	⊞		+	+
Transportation services	⊞	+	+	
Public protection services	⊞	+	+	
Environmental protection services	⊞	+	+	

Goal Three

Optimal health

	L	S	F	P
Health maintenance and care services	⊞	+		+
Mental health services		+	+	+
Mental retardation services	⊞	+		+
Rehabilitation services		+		+

Goal Four

Adequate knowledge and skills

	L	S	F	P
Preschool services				+
Elementary and secondary services	⊞			
Higher education services			+	+
Informal education services	⊞			+
Special education services	⊞	+		+

Goal Five

Optimal personal and social adjustment and development

	L	S	F	P
Family strengthening services				+
Family substitute services		+		+
Other supportive services				+
Recreational services	⊞	+	+	+
Intergroup relations services	⊞			+
Cultural and arts services				+

Goal Six

Adequately organized social instrumentalities

	L	S	F	P
Community planning services	⊞			+
Community organization services				+
Human services funding services	⊞	+	+	+
Economic development services	⊞	+		
Communications and information services	⊞			+
Equal opportunity promotion	⊞	+	+	+

L = Local government
S = State government
F = Federal government
P = Private (profit and nonprofit)

Figure 18–5 Typical providers of certain services, shown according to *UWASIS* goal classifications. The areas most often handled by local government are indicated by the boxed-in crosses. See text for further discussion.

In the area of Goal Five—optimal personal and social adjustment and development—local government has assumed a minimal role except in recreation. This has also been true of state and federal government roles in these areas with some exceptions. Again, this traditional pattern is changing, particularly in regard to family support and group relations services that are linked to the mental health field.

One exception to the above should be noted—the role of local government in dealing with relationships among racial and ethnic groups. In some communities, court-ordered busing programs to achieve integration in the schools have brought this problem to prominence. But increasingly, all local government units must face up to such problems. Many communities unaffected thus far will find themselves, in the near future, with major responsibilities for the advancement of more harmonious racial and ethnic relations.

Finally, Figure 18–5 depicts local government as being very heavily involved in Goal Six—adequately organized social instrumentalities. Local government itself is one of the primary social instrumentalities that ensures the quality of life and the provision of needed services. Many of the services under this goal have shared responsibility, but the key role of local government in general cannot be overlooked. And, of course, one of the major thrusts of the New Federalism of the early 1970s was the further enhancement of the role of local government in the planning, development, and delivery of human services.

The variable pattern which has just been outlined highlights the complexity of the human services planning task in all of its principal dimensions. The total range of factors involved in planning—the richness and diversity of methodology, the variability of roles, and the shared responsibilities with other levels of government and private providers—offers a view of human services planning that should prove useful in assisting managers as they adapt to the changing patterns of local government involvement.

Conclusion: issues and problems in human services planning

This chapter has explored the terrain of human services planning in most of its myriad dimensions. It has presented a framework of social planning; the methodological approaches to social services planning; and, in the discussion just concluded, the role of local government in human services planning.

In the course of the analysis, a fuller range of planning responsibility has been suggested for all public services. The mandates of the New Federalism of the 1970s and the effort to return power to state and local governments signify the increased planning responsibilities at the community level.

Decisions affecting whether public or private agencies shall deliver services, the types of services to be delivered, and the allocations of resources have been assumed in the past by the federal government, local government having had no voice in these decisions in many years. In addition, local planners have usually faced only limited technical modes of service delivery and simple means of financing (frequently severely constrained by law). Planning responsibilities are being returned to local government at a time when the technology of service delivery is rapidly changing and mechanisms of finance are diverse and complicated. It is only recently that local planners have assumed the responsibility for the design of new service organizations from their inception.

Developing a base of understanding of the wide range of human needs was never considered a major practical concern, especially where the family and the church were the institutions that individuals looked to in times of stress. The breakdown of family units, the search for secular roles by religious bodies, and the increase of knowledge and professionalization in the "helping" services are

forces which have placed the human services provider near center stage for almost all income, ethnic, and religious groups. Local government is thus taking
on rapidly multiplying roles to fill the gaps left by other institutions.

This new climate in social welfare brings local government face-to-face with
many issues for the future. The most prominent and immediate difficulties are
fivefold and include: the need to integrate methodological development; the lack
of agreement on objectives and priorities; increasing problems of coordinating
planning; roles and functions in human services planning; and equity and justice
in the delivery of human services.

The need to integrate methodological development

Human services planning, more than any other form of planning, is truly multidisciplinary. The biological sciences, the behavioral sciences, the social sciences, and the management sciences all underlie the planner's needed skills.
High levels of specialization make the planner very dependent on the service
provider. Yet too great a reliance on the specialist overlooks the very great
range of self-interest that the specialist may exert in any given planning situation. Means for accountability and for reflecting the legitimate interests of clients, funders, and others must be sought. While participation opportunities can
to some degree help, providers still enjoy a higher level of power and status
because of their expertise and skill. In the face of this, the planner has looked to
the management sciences for methodological assistance, thereby uncovering
again the traditional conflict between expertise and organizational hierarchy
noted frequently in the literature of organizational studies.[72]

This multidisciplinary character is a likely instrumental cause in the failure to
develop a unified methodology of human services planning. Yet this lack of
methodology will continue to offer difficulty until the problem is more promi-
nently identified and dealt with. Previous work in utilization and systems theory
models is perhaps an appropriate beginning point in this search for higher levels
of skill in planning. In addition, more attention to methods of futures forecasting, scenario development, and impact and assessment techniques should prove
beneficial.

The lack of agreement on objectives and priorities

Human services delivery is a highly pluralistic arena. Power and authority are
diffuse, interest groups abound, and the competition for resources is high. For
many communities it is extremely difficult to find agreement on the basic goals
of the human services system. For the general public it is an arena of confusion,
costliness, and ineffectiveness.

Most goals center around vague concerns with adequate social functioning,
optimum independence, and good health. Yet the means to achieve these is seldom clear-cut. Indeed, the ways to observe and measure whether the goals are
being achieved by any means are not always available. Since goals are essentially statements of values, they are continually subject to change and adjustment. Goals often conflict with each other. Changing techniques of service delivery or funding create changes in goals and priorities. This turbulence in a very
complicated arena is most disconcerting for the planner who faces demands for
high levels of perceptiveness and adaptability as well as for effective means of
communicating the potential effects of turbulence on policies and plans. So long
as the system remains pluralistic and the participants retain high levels of autonomy, this turmoil of values, goals, and priorities will remain a prominent characteristic of human services planning.

Increasing problems of coordinating planning

The last few years have seen planning institutionalized in a variety of settings—largely aided and abetted by federal statutes or guidelines. Planning for human services has, as a result, become almost as disjointed as the delivery system itself. Planning agencies have arisen around a variety of functional service areas at numerous geographical levels. Some planning agencies are private, others public; some are local, others regional; some are intended to be "comprehensive," others are focused on a particular service.

As these substate planning units proliferate, the human services planning scene becomes as pluralistic as that of the providers. There have even been examples of planning agencies that were competing on the same turf in the same community. (Prior to the Health Planning Act, for example, Philadelphia had two competing health planning agencies.) Increasing attention will clearly have to be given in the near future to coordinating and integrating the planning function.

Roles and functions in human services planning

Another issue of importance in human services planning has been alluded to indirectly. It is a problem that touches on virtually all other problems in the field—the relative roles and statuses of various actors in the human services arena. What should be our expectations of citizens, elected officials, professional service providers, administrators, planners, and others involved in human services policymaking? How does the planning process stimulate a delivery system that is responsive to needs, is accountable, and is comprehensive? How can the participation of all these actors be assured, especially where expectations have been changing drastically in the last few years? These questions of roles and functions in human services planning will continue to be a key issue in the coming years.

Equity and justice in the delivery of human services

A final, and extremely important, issue that will continually press upon human services planners is that of assuring equal access to services of high quality for all members of our society, regardless of race, religion, ethnic background, or sex. The presence of dual systems in such service areas as health and mental health (one for the mainstream of American society, another for the poor or minorities) poses grave issues of distributive justice in our overall concern for national social welfare. These issues are particularly difficult at the local level where fears and prejudices are most sharply felt. Human services planning is inextricably linked to this core issue of our society.

This list highlights only the most important issues that face social services planning in the coming years. Others include problems already referred to: evaluation and accountability, cost containment and cost-effectiveness, and the effects of new roles. These would include those of the paraprofessional, the advocate, and the case manager.

With this array of complexities, ambiguities, quandaries, and competitive dimensions, one might well ask why local government should become involved. There is no single answer for every local unit. The trend, however, is that fewer and fewer localities have the luxury of making such a decision independently. The answer is increasingly being forced both from above (the New Federalism and new state legislation) and from below (neighborhoods and other local organizations continue to turn to city hall to assume responsibility for all aspects of the quality of life). In many respects local government is being viewed as a last resort in the pursuit of rationalizing a system that is, by and large, not of its own making. Ironically, this is occurring in areas of responsibility which were taken away from the local governments many years ago for reasons of lack of professionalism, favoritism, parochialism, and other shortcomings.

Thus, human services have come full cycle and are increasingly again a responsibility of local government. This time there will probably be considerably more interest and help on the part of state and national government. Private providers will increasingly look to city hall for funding and sanction. But the times are quite different from those of the last century. The contemporary American community has an entirely new array of needs and a completely new array of providers attempting to meet those needs. City hall is being asked to perform tasks that federal and state governments could not previously handle themselves.

But this is also the promise and hope of the future in human services planning. The return of planning and decision making to the local level can do much to overcome the abstract quality and large gaps of understanding and insensitivity that come from a planning process too highly centralized. The transfer of decision-making power casts an extremely large shadow of responsibility on local government. But only at the local level can the ordinary citizen really sense that he or she is a vital part of the process and has the power to effectuate change that can meaningfully improve the quality of life.

1   This chapter is excerpted from: Richard S. Bolan, "Social Planning and Policy Development in Local Government," in *Managing Human Services,* ed. Wayne F. Anderson, Bernard J. Frieden, and Michael J. Murphy (Washington, D.C.: International City Management Association, 1977), pp. 85–127. Some new material has been added.

2   Neil Gilbert and Harry Specht, *Dimensions of Social Welfare Policy* (Englewood Cliffs, N.J.: Prentice-Hall, Inc., 1974), pp. 28–33.

3   Some problems associated with this were highlighted in a series of articles dealing with New York's nursing homes. See: John L. Hess, "Care of Aged Poor a Growing Scandal," *New York Times,* 7 October 1974.

4   As of September 1976, 174 Health Systems Agencies (of 196 organized under the Health Planning and Resources Development Act) were private, nonprofit corporations; 18 were regional governmental planning bodies; and 4 were units of local government. See: *Health Resources News* 4 (December 1976): 2.

5   Ronald L. Nuttall and Richard S. Bolan, "The Success of Health Plan Implementation: A Test of the Theory," report prepared for U.S. Department of Health, Education, and Welfare, Health Resources Administration, Division of Comprehensive Health Planning, 1976, vol. 1, Chapter 5.

6   Ibid., Chapter 2.

7   Ibid., Chapter 4.

8   Robert Alford, *Health Care Politics* (Chicago: University of Chicago Press, 1975), Chapter 1.

9   Alfred Kahn, *Theory and Practice of Social Planning* (New York: Russell Sage Foundation, 1969), pp. 201–4. See also the discussion of different models of social policy in: Richard Titmuss, *Social Policy* (London: George Allen & Unwin, 1974), Chapter 2; and Gilbert and Specht, *Dimensions of Social Welfare Policy,* pp. 56–59.

10 Gilbert and Specht, *Dimensions of Social Welfare Policy,* pp. 66–76.

11 Alfred Kahn, *Studies in Policy and Planning* (New York: Russell Sage Foundation, 1969), Chapter 6.

12 U.S., Department of Health, Education, and Welfare, Bureau of Health Planning and Resources Development, "Draft Guidelines Concerning the Development of Health Systems and Annual Implementation Plans," memorandum, 18 June 1976, pp. 11–12.

13 B. F. Skinner, *Beyond Freedom and Dignity* (New York: Alfred A. Knopf, 1972), Chapter 1.

14 Kahn, *Studies in Policy and Planning,* Chapter 6.

15 K. Patricia Cross, *Accent on Learning* (San Francisco: Jossey-Bass, 1976), Chapters 3 and 4.

16 Jay Galbraith, *Organization Design* (Reading, Mass.: Addison-Wesley Publishing Co., 1977), p. 31. For other works expressly devoted to organizational design, see: Ralph Kilmann, Louis Pondy, and Dennis Slevin, eds., *The Management of Organization Design: Strategies and Implementation,* 2 vols. (New York: North Holland, 1976); Arlyn J. Melcher, *Structure and Process of Organizations: A System Approach* (Englewood Cliffs, N.J.: Prentice-Hall, Inc., 1976); and Jay Galbraith, *Designing Complex Organizations* (Reading, Mass.: Addison-Wesley Publishing Co., 1973). Earlier works related to the design of organizations include: Rensis Likert, *New Patterns of Management* (New York: McGraw-Hill Book Company, 1961); and A. Chandler, *Strategy and Structure* (Garden City, N.Y.: Anchor Books, 1966).

17 Luther Gulick, "Notes on a Theory of Organization," in *Papers on the Science of Administration,* ed. Luther Gulick and Lyndall Urwick (New York: Columbia University, Institute of Public Administration, 1937), pp. 1–45.

18 For a general coverage of the field of location analysis, see: Walter Isard, *Introduction to Regional Science* (Englewood Cliffs, N.J.: Prentice-Hall, Inc., 1975).

19 Franklin D. Chu and Sharland Trotter, *The Madness Establishment* (New York: Grossman Publishers, 1974), pp. 73–83.

20 Joan Wright and William Burmeister, *Introduction to Human Services* (Columbus, Ohio: Grid, 1973), pp. 21–23.

21 Tennessee Municipal League, *Chattanooga Human Services Delivery System* (Nashville: Tennessee Municipal League, 1975).

22 The Research Group, Inc., and Marshall Kaplan, Gans and Kahn, "Integration of Human Services in HEW: An Evaluation of Services Integration Projects," report prepared for U.S. Department of Health, Education, and Welfare, August 1972, pp. 110–13.

23 Herbert A. Simon, *Administrative Behavior,* 2nd ed. (New York: The Free Press, 1957), Chapter 2.

24 The impetus for the human relations school is found in F. J. Roethlisberger and W. J. Dickson, *Management and the Worker* (Cambridge, Mass.: Harvard University Press, 1939). More recent works of this school would include: Chris Argyris, *Integrating the Individual and the Organization* (New York: John Wiley & Sons, Inc., 1964); and D. Katz and R. Kahn, *The Social Psychology of Organizations* (New York: John Wiley & Sons, Inc., 1966).

25 See: Simon, *Administrative Behavior;* R. Cyert and J. March, *The Behavioral Theory of the Firm* (Englewood Cliffs, N.J.: Prentice-Hall, Inc., 1963); Herbert Simon, *The Shape of Automation for Men and Management* (New York: Harper Torchbooks, 1965); Robert Thierauf and Robert Klekamp, *Decision Making through Operations Research,* 2nd ed. (New York: John Wiley & Sons, Inc., 1975); and Russell Ackoff and Patrick Rivett, *Manager's Guide to Operations Research* (New York: John Wiley & Sons, Inc., 1963).

26 Paul R. Lawrence and Jay W. Lorsch, *Organization and Development* (Homewood, Ill.: Richard D. Irwin, Inc., 1969).

27 J. W. Forrester, *Industrial Dynamics* (Cambridge, Mass.: The M.I.T. Press, 1961).

28 For two case studies which provide excellent examples of the concept of client pathway, see: Stephen D. Mittenthal, *Human Services Development Programs in Sixteen Allied Services (SITO) Projects* (Wellesley, Mass.: Human Ecology Institute, 1975), Appendices B and M.

29 See: Jerald Hage, *Communication and Organization Control: Cybernetics in Health and Welfare Settings* (New York: John Wiley & Sons, Inc., 1974); and Wendell L. French and Cecil H. Bell, Jr., *Organization Development: Behavioral Science Interventions for Organization Improvement* (Englewood Cliffs, N.J.: Prentice-Hall, Inc., 1973).

30 F. E. Emery and E. L. Trist, "The Causal Texture of Organizational Environments," *Human Relations* 18 (1965): 21–32.

31 See: Hage, *Communication and Organization Control;* and Jerald Hage and Michael Aiken, *Social Change in Complex Organizations* (New York: Random House, 1970).

32 See: Gerald Zaltman and Robert Duncan, *Strategies for Planned Change* (New York: John Wiley & Sons, Inc., 1977); Roland Warren, *Social Change and Human Purpose* (Chicago: Rand McNally and Company, 1977), Chapter 6; and Hage and Aiken, *Social Change in Complex Organizations.*

33 See: Edward Lehman, *Coordinating Health Care: Explorations in Inter-Organizational Relationships* (Beverly Hills, Calif.: Sage Publications, 1975); Kilmann, Pondy, and Slevin, eds., *Management of Organization Design,* vol. 2, Chapters 10

and 11; Sol Levin and Paul White "Exchange as a Conceptual Framework for the Study of Interorganizational Relationships," *Administrative Science Quarterly* 5 (March 1961): 583–601; Michael Aiken and Jerald Hage, "Organization Interdependence and Intraorganizational Structure," *American Sociological Review* 33 (1968): 912–30; Roland Warren, "The Interorganizational Field as a Focus for Investigation," *Administrative Science Quarterly* 12 (1967), pp. 397–419.

34 See, for example: Public Law 93–641, Sec. 1512 (3)(C)(i)—the Health Planning and Resources Development Act (1974).

35 For a statement of the rationale for this, see: Orion F. White, Jr., "The Dialectical Organization: An Alternative to Bureaucracy," *Public Administration Review* 29 (January/February 1969): 32–42.

36 Sidney Gardner, "Services Integration in HEW: An Initial Report," report prepared for the U.S. Department of Health, Education, and Welfare, February 1971; U.S., Department of Health, Education, and Welfare, "Services Integration—Next Steps," by Elliot L. Richardson, memorandum, 1 June 1971, both cited in Douglas Henton, "The Feasibility of Services Integration," evaluation report prepared for the U.S. Department of Health, Education, and Welfare's Interagency Services Integration Research and Development Task Force, Berkeley, Calif., March 1975, pp. 5–8.

37 Estimates derived from: U.S., Department of Commerce, Bureau of the Census, *Statistical Abstract of the United States: 1975* (Washington, D.C.: Government Printing Office, 1975).

38 Gilbert and Specht, *Dimensions of Social Welfare Policy,* Chapters 6 and 7.

39 U.S., Bureau of the Census, *Statistical Abstract: 1975.*

40 Ibid. Estimates derived by author.

41 Abraham H. Maslow, *Motivation and Personality* (New York: Harper & Row, Publishers, 1954), Chapter 5; and Erik H. Erikson, *Identity, Youth and Crisis* (New York: W. W. Norton & Company, 1968).

42 United Way of America, *UWASIS II: A Taxonomy of Social Goals and Human Services Programs,* 2nd ed. (Alexandria, Va.: United Way of America, 1976). The first edition is: United Way of America, *UWASIS: United Way of America, Services Identification System* (Alexandria, Va.: United Way of America, 1972). A chart was published in 1976 as a backup for *UWASIS II* showing eight goals with their objectives and specific programs. The eight goals for *UWASIS II* are to obtain, through organized action, the following: optimal income security and economic opportunity; optimal health; optimal provision of basic material needs; optimal opportunity for the acquisition of knowledge and skills; optimal environmental quality; optimal individual and collective safety; optimal social functioning; and optimal assurance of the support and effectiveness of services.

43 United Way of America, *UWASIS,* Appendix A.

44 For a general discussion of needs assessment concepts, approaches, and methods, see: Robert M. Moroney, "Needs Assessment for Human Services," in *Managing Human Services,* ed. Anderson, Frieden, and Murphy, Chapter 5. Technical guides are also available from the League of California Cities and from the New England Municipal Center.

45 Two different types of needs assessment studies are found in two recent projects of the Boston College Graduate School of Social Work, *Human Services Needs Assessment,* Lexington, Mass., 1978, and *Human Services Inventory: Planning, Coordination, and Cooperation,* Malden, Mass., 1975.

46 See: Saul D. Alinsky, *Reveille for Radicals* (Chicago: University of Chicago Press, 1946). See also Harry Specht, "Disruptive Tactics," in *Readings in Community Organization Practice,* ed. R. M. Kramer and Harry Specht, 2nd ed. (Englewood Cliffs, N.J.: Prentice-Hall, Inc., 1975), pp. 336–48.

47 See: Amitai Etzioni, *Social Problems* (Englewood Cliffs, N.J.: Prentice-Hall, Inc., 1976), pp. 9–15.

48 See: Lawrence D. Mann, "Social Science Advances and Planning Applications: 1900–1965," *Journal of the American Institute of Planners* 38 (November 1972): 346–58.

49 Melvin M. Webber, "The Roles of Intelligence Systems in Urban Planning," *Journal of the American Institute of Planners* 31 (November 1965): 289–96.

50 Michael Tietz, "Toward a Responsive Planning Methodology," in *Planning in America: Learning from Turbulence,* ed. D. R. Godschalk (Washington, D.C.: American Institute of Planners, 1974), pp. 86–110.

51 See: Roethlisberger and Dickson, *Management and the Worker;* Kurt Lewin, "Group Decision and Social Change," in *Readings in Social Psychology,* ed. G. E. Swanson et al. (New York: Holt, Rinehart & Winston, 1952); and Simon, *Administrative Behavior.*

52 The "birth" of scientific management is generally regarded as being represented by F. W. Taylor, *The Principles of Scientific Management* (New York: Harper & Brothers, Publishers, 1911).

53 Mittenthal, *Human Services Development Programs,* Appendix C.

54 Demetrius J. Plessas and Ricca Fein, "An Evaluation of Social Indicators," *Journal of the American Institute of Planners* 38 (January 1972): 43–51.

55 For a discussion of computer applications in local government, and of information and record keeping generally, see: Shimon Awerbuch, Robert J. Hoffman, and William A. Wallace, "Computer Applications in Public Works," in *Urban Public Works Administration,* ed. William E. Korbitz (Washington, D.C.: International City Management Association, 1976), pp. 53–85.

56 Allan Schick, "The Road to PPB: The Stages of Budget Reform," *Public Administration Review* 26 (December 1966): 243–58.

57 Elizabeth B. Drew, "HEW Grapples with PPBS," *The Public Interest* 8 (Summer 1967): 9–24.

58 Peter Drucker, "What Results Should You Expect? A Users' Guide to MBO." *Public Administration Review* 36 (January/February 1976): 12–19.

59 Warren G. Bennis and Philip E. Slater, *The Temporary Society* (New York: Harper Colophon Books, 1968).

60 Chester Barnard, *The Functions of the Executive* (Cambridge, Mass.: Harvard University Press, 1938), Chapter 3.

61 See: Ronald Lippit, Jeanne Watson, and Bruce Westley, *The Dynamics of Planned Change* (New York: Harcourt, Brace and World, 1958), Chapters 5 and 6; French and Bell, *Organization Development,* Chapters 9 and 10; and Zaltman and Duncan, *Strategies for Planned Change.*

62 Robert R. Mayer, *Social Planning and Social Change* (Englewood Cliffs, N.J.: Prentice-Hall, Inc., 1972).

63 Discussion of various forms of survey research can be found in Ray Eldon Hiebert "Research and the Public Relations Process," in *Public Relations in Local Government,* ed. William H. Gilbert (Washington, D.C.: International City Management Association, 1975), pp. 26–40.

64 For a review of utilization studies, see: Nancy W. Veeder, "Health Services Utilization Models for Human Services Planning," *Journal of the American Institute of Planners* 41 (March 1975): 101–9.

65 Plessas and Fein, "Evaluation of Social Indicators."

66 Jack Lapatra, *Applying the Systems Approach to Urban Development* (Stroudsburg, Pa.: Dowden, Hutchinson and Ross, 1973), Chapter 1.

67 For a good introductory discussion of this method, see: Stuart Sandow, "The Pedagogy of Planning: Defining Sufficient Futures," *Futures* 3 (December 1971): 324–37.

68 For a basic description of technology assessment, see Martin V. Jones, "The Methodology of Technology Assessment," *The Futurist* (February 1972): 19–26.

69 See Sandow, "Pedagogy of Planning." Examples of the use of future scenarios may be found in: Energy Policy Project of the Ford Foundation, *A Time to Choose: America's Energy Future* (Cambridge, Mass.: Ballinger Publishing Company, 1974); and Alfred Heller, ed., *The California Tomorrow Plan* (Los Altos, Calif.: William Kaufman, 1971).

70 New England Municipal Center, *Opportunities for Municipal Participation in Human Services* (Durham, N.H.: New England Municipal Center, 1975).

71 One example of such a law is found in General Court of Massachusetts, *Acts of 1972,* Chapter 766.

72 Amitai Etzioni, *Modern Organization* (Englewood Cliffs, N.J.: Prentice-Hall, Inc., 1964), Chapter 8.

19 Citizen participation in planning

The involvement of citizens in the governing of society is the subject of history itself. For the most part the demand for greater citizen control has been the central issue—too often expressed in wars and revolutions—and has resulted in levels of involvement from dictatorships to democracies. Within the governmental system of the United States, the level and the effectiveness of citizen participation have varied both in kind of involvement and in degree of control. The Constitution, in providing for a representational form of government, allows varying interpretations of the degree of citizen control. This representational form of government is the predominant form throughout state and local government.

This chapter begins by discussing the background and development of citizen participation in urban planning. Subjects included in this discussion are the social context of participation, the desire to participate, the value of participation, the federal background, and two developments which helped shape the nature of citizen participation: the Alinsky organizations and advocacy planning. Various approaches and mechanisms employed for citizen participation are the subject of the next section, which also analyzes the respective roles in the planning process of the citizen, the planner, and the public official—and the relationships among them. The chapter then moves on to the problems of participation: the costs and benefits; the issue of power and control; and the issues—philosophical, psychological, and political—that present the planner with a series of dilemmas. The chapter ends with an evaluative conclusion that stresses the societal values underlying citizen participation.

The evolution of citizen participation in local planning

The social context

In the early 1900s the emphasis of citizen involvement in government in the United States was on increasing citizen control over the legislature. The current demand for increased citizen participation at the local level developed out of far more recent events and circumstances. The social context of poverty and racial discrimination in the early 1960s; the federal government's response during the mid-1960s and late 1960s; the attempts of middle class neighborhoods to improve services through citizen participation; and the many years of trying to achieve meaningful citizen participation in city planning are all important antecedents. They have all contributed significantly to the form, content, and method of current participation practices.

Another factor that has increased the demand for citizen based solutions to nationally pervasive urban problems has been the ineffectiveness of urban government. City government links with individual neighborhoods were weakened or severed with the rise of centrally controlled professional bureaucracies; the latter situation reduced the effectiveness and quality of neighborhood services and engendered citizen mistrust. In addition, the combined effects of racial conflict and poverty drew attention dramatically to the inadequacies of centralized urban government.

The influx of poor and minority populations into many inner cities both revealed and exacerbated the problems of centralized urban government. When urban government failed to respond adequately to complaints of poor services, the white middle class could grumble, pay for alternative services privately, or move to the suburbs. But low income black residents of inner city neighborhoods could neither alter nor avoid the city's failure to deliver the whole array of urgently needed services. Furthermore, the provider of services, in the eyes of many black residents of inner city neighborhoods—the police officer, firefighter, social worker, or teacher—was not only a representative of a poorly functioning, distant, impersonal bureaucracy but was also the executor of policy and the front line soldier of an oppressive white bureaucracy. This deliverer of services was perceived as the immediate, visible enemy. Caught between the inability of city hall to live up to black needs and the "ingratitude" and, at times, active hostility of their clients, the deliverers of services began to view the black neighborhood with suspicion and fear. Here, then, in the black inner city neighborhoods, in a climate of unhappiness, frustration, and mutual suspicion, the negative causes of future demands for neighborhood power were spawned and nurtured.

As conditions continued to deteriorate, and after the futility of riots and self-destructive attempts became apparent, the hostility began to be superseded by a feeling of black pride expressed in demands that black people should solve black people's problems in black neighborhoods; that the planning and delivery of services in black neighborhoods should be managed and controlled by the people of those neighborhoods; and that the separateness of black neighborhoods should be maintained and enhanced for the purpose of evolving a strong, proud, black subculture on the American scene.

At the same time, support for self-governance developed and gained support in middle class white neighborhoods, with the objective of general improvement of social and physical services. In these neighborhoods citizen control frequently took the form of contracting privately for services such as garbage collection, park facilities, and, occasionally, police protection. Thus, two vastly different sets of social conditions resulted in a growing acceptance of and demand for increased citizen participation through neighborhood governmental decentralization.

It should be emphasized that the citizen participation of the 1960s and 1970s developed its frequently strident form of urgency and its attempts at comprehensiveness of control because it arose not from a philosophical belief in democracy, nor a belief in the duty of citizens to participate, but rather from basic, unfulfilled needs—both physical and social. In other contexts these conditions have produced revolutions; in the United States, because of both its constitutional provisions for change and the identification by a portion of its middle class intellectuals of the good of society with the needs and aspirations of the poor, the demand for citizen participation took the form of political and social pressure for increased citizen control.

The desire to participate

Citizen participation is most often stimulated by existing social problems coupled with a lack of confidence in official solutions—and it varies with economic and social conditions. When citizens feel that officials are making decisions similar to those that they themselves would make, or that these decisions necessitate special knowledge that the official has and the citizens do not have, or when they feel that the decision is economically sound, they are not likely to actively participate in government. It is when these criteria of government performance are not being met that citizens lose confidence in government officials and the demand for active participation arises. However, the move toward citizen participation varies with economic class lines.

For residents of slums—the "frustration zones" of our cities—the social problems are acute and immediate. Solution of these problems by participation in a planning process is seen as long range and irrelevant to day-to-day needs. Also, residents of depressed neighborhoods are often suspicious of the professionals with whom they must work in any participatory process. These citizens fear that, as representatives of government agencies, such professionals do not actually intend to solve problems but are there only to pacify the residents and to stifle their just complaints. Thus, while there is a desire for the solution of problems, constructive citizen participation in poverty areas needs to be developed by planners and local governments.

Who plans your neighborhood? There will be an emphasis on neighborhoods and the whole relationship to the comprehensive plan. . . . It starts with a map that shows *your* house, on *your* lot, on *your* street. That is where we start. It does not start with a rap about a bar chart that shows the various uses of energy. It does not start with a map of a regional transportational system. It does not start with a discussion about how we control the use of land. It starts with your house, your lot, and your street. When we get there, then we can begin to get people interested. That is where they are interested, and sometimes we can get them to take as wide a vantage point as their whole neighborhood. Sometimes,

among those people that are interested in their whole neighborhood, there will be a few who might even be interested in how their neighborhood fits in with all the other neighborhoods in the city. But we will not get them there without taking them from the beginning. If anything has been brought home to me, again and again, it is to start where the people are, not where we want them to be.

Source: Excerpted from Ernest Bonner, "Portland: The Problems and Promise of Growth," in *Personality, Politics, and Planning: How City Planners Work,* ed. Anthony James Catanese and W. Paul Farmer (Beverly Hills, Calif.: Sage Publications, 1978), pp. 152–53.

In less depressed neighborhoods there is an existing demand for citizen participation as an attempt to solve local problems. There is a rudimentary knowledge of planning and government which, when combined with a lack of confidence in existing authority's ability to satisfactorily solve local problems, gives rise to various forms of citizen participation. These citizens may go so far as to justify their participation as an interest in the quality of life in general. In reality, however, their interests are often primarily limited to solution of their own specific problems. Interest in groups dealing with general problems, as measured by meeting attendance and time volunteered, has been shown to be much lower than interest in personal, local problems.

Participation in citywide or general-issue-oriented groups is most likely to be found in upper economic group citizens and in long-term city residents. This is understandable, as these are the citizens with the greatest amount of leisure time to spend in group activities; they are also the citizens who are most likely to be not only aware of, but also socially acquainted with, the existing government officials. This contact increases the chances of their successful participation in government.

Thus, citizen participation occurs when there is a meeting of several factors: existing social problems; dissatisfaction with the solutions of local authorities; at least a minimum of affluence to provide the leisure time for planning for future solutions; and knowledge of government and planning. In the poorest neighborhoods this combination of factors occurs through the intervention of middle and upper economic class professionals who provide the tools for dealing with local problems. In more affluent neighborhoods the ingredients necessary for citizen participation are already there.

The value of participation

One of the societal values of citizen participation is that it allows each citizen the right to influence governmental decision making. Citizen participation is viewed as revitalizing democratic practice in general by giving opportunities for local self-government to the "average" citizen—an urban return to grass roots.

Encounter, action, impact The city is where the action is. It is the first line of government for most people. They feel their problems and frustrations where they live and work, and it is in their communities where people state their expectations and lodge their complaints. It is possible to do planning in cities within a context of specific faces and names as well as of places and things. It is possible to relate abstract policies and plans and programs to tangible experiences. . . .

Even if city planners rarely design or

build anything directly or operate a program, they can, working at the city level, have an impact on the environment. They can help a community decide what it wants to be and then help [it] to achieve that future. They can see their successes and their failures, even those successes that are represented by something that did not happen.

Source: Excerpted from Allan B. Jacobs, *Making City Planning Work* (Chicago: American Society of Planning Officials, 1978), p. 316.

Another societal value of citizen participation is that it can help maintain the stability of society. Varying degrees of citizen control are proposed for implementing this value. The most conservative approach views citizen participation as strictly supportive of existing government officials, their representatives, and their programs; in this approach citizens' groups have no innovative or decision making functions. Thus, a limited form of citizen participation is encouraged as supportive of the system. Others have suggested that citizens should be encouraged to participate but only in a traditional political structure such as a ward format. Citizen participation in this case would be limited to advising and generally supporting their ward politician. This would give citizens access to the power of the political structure.

A more independent form of citizen participation that gives actual decision-making power to citizens is also viewed as contributing to the stability of urban society. It is argued that when citizens have been actively involved in the decision-making process they are more aware of the possible problems and are more willing to live with the consequences than they are when decisions are imposed from the outside. Thus, through active participation, citizens are educated to political realities, become more aware of problems, and tend less toward explosive solutions.

Yet another societal value of citizen participation is that it guards the public interest. As government grows more complex, active citizen participation is necessary to ensure that the bureaucracies are responsive to the public and to combat special interest groups. Citizens' groups are characterized as watchdogs of society and are seen as filling the role of general ombudsman.

A final societal value of citizen participation is its capacity to reduce the alienation of the individual. Maintaining the complex organization of modern society requires that individuals have a clear understanding of their roles and their importance. A lack of such understanding and its accompanying feeling of political helplessness, combined with a general distrust of power, is the personal situation known as alienation. Participation in the governmental decision-making process can have the psychological benefits of increasing the individual's confidence in his ability to control his own life and environment. Thus, citizen participation in governing has been seen as a positive force for reducing or eliminating alienation.

Federal antecedents

Direct citizen participation has been supported increasingly over the last three decades by federal legislation. The specific subjects of the legislation have generally encouraged citizen participation and have also responded to popular movements such as civil rights and ecology. The federal Administrative Procedures Act of 1946, in setting minimum standards for openness in decision-making procedures, gave official sanction to the citizens' right to greater access to the decision-making processes in federal agencies. The Freedom of Information Act of 1966 and the National Environmental Policy Act of 1970, in addition to providing for administrative accountability to the citizen, made this open access to information legally enforceable by individual citizens.

Programs most active in mobilizing new forms of citizen participation were urban renewal, Community Action, and Model Cities. In the extensive urban renewal programs of the 1960s citizen participation played an increasingly important role, culminating in federal regulations requiring Citizen Conservation Councils in urban renewal areas. This requirement brought about the passage of state laws enabling cities to set up such citizen advisory councils and thus elevated the concept of direct citizen participation to a new legal status. The Community Action program viewed increased power and influence of the poor as a necessary component in the War on Poverty and eventually required that at least one-third of each Community Action board be representative of the poor. Although citizen participation in these federal programs took place on a citywide basis, the citizen leadership that developed in these programs was an important factor in the success of the U.S. Office of Economic Opportunity's (OEO's) own, later, neighborhood representation program.[1]

The Model Cities program continued to require the participation of neighborhood residents in policy formulation, planning, and program implementation. This program, with its strong neighborhood focus, gave further impetus to the demand for citizen participation on a neighborhood basis. It produced a large number of new neighborhood organizations that reinforced and expanded neighborhood leadership structures established earlier by urban renewal and OEO programs. Where, under urban renewal, legal status was added to the concept of local citizen controls through the creation of Citizen Conservation Councils by means of state enabling legislation, under Model Cities the prestige of financial power was added. Federal money for model neighborhoods was forthcoming only when the central city bureaucracy successfully coordinated the model programs with the appropriate neighborhood organizations.[2]

In addition to the federal government, administrators of these programs began actively to support citizen participation. Recommendations were published calling for the establishment of neighborhood subunits in large cities, as suggested in 1967 by the U.S. Advisory Commission on Intergovernmental Relations, and calling on large city governments to decentralize neighborhood services, as suggested by the 1968 report of the National Commission on Urban Problems. While this seeming change in urban administrators' attitudes may well be attributed to an attempt to prevent more violent forms of citizen action rather than to a commitment to citizen participation in principle, it was a contributing factor in the development of direct citizen participation.

The origins of citizen participation in urban planning

Until the mid-1960s urban planning was primarily a function of central city government. The entire city was the focus of planning activity. While citizen participation in planning has been advocated since the 1920s, such participation was usually limited to the appointment of citizens to various commissions, committees, and study groups. While the neighborhoods have been the traditional units of city planning, the planning of and for these neighborhood units was usually done at city hall by professional planners. As has been mentioned, the combining of planning on a neighborhood basis with neighborhood participation in such planning was a product and outgrowth of the urban crisis of the 1960s and was part of the general trend toward neighborhood decentralization of city services. Again, as mentioned earlier, the programs established by federal legislation, such as Model Cities and the OEO programs, and some later urban renewal programs, required neighborhood participation in the planning for target neighborhoods. This requirement had several far-reaching effects on the movement toward decentralization of the planning function: it made neighborhood residents and their leaders familiar with the concepts and processes of urban planning; it opened a dialogue and a bargaining–negotiations process between the neighborhood and the central city administration; and it balanced the traditional focus of citywide, comprehensive planning with a new focus and emphasis on small scale, local-oriented, incremental planning. The requirement for neighborhood participation also made the professional planner sensitive to the needs of the people whose problems were immediate and in need of prompt solutions. Thus, urban planning grew from an almost theoretical, central city government profession to an application of professional training to specific problems involving real people who not only demanded to be heard and understood, but who also had a growing desire to participate in the solutions. The many approaches and techniques that have been developed within this context are discussed in detail later in this chapter.

Other approaches

Two other important developments shaped the context and nature of citizen participation. One was completely outside of the planning community and the other suggested a new planning focus outside of government.

Alinsky organizations The first development grew out of Saul Alinsky's work as a criminologist in the Illinois prison system. His first project as a community organizer was in a Chicago slum, where he founded the Back of the Yards organization. Alinsky emerged as a national figure with his establishment of The Woodlawn Organization (TWO) in the 1960s and his organization of similar groups in Rochester, New York. In 1968 Alinsky formed the Industrial Areas Foundation (IAF) to train organizers.[3]

An Alinsky organization is formed when an invitation is received from a neighborhood accompanied by a guarantee of funding, frequently by a church based group. After this, a paid organizer enters the community. This professional organizer is the key to the Alinsky organization. It is the organizer's job to identify problems, develop citizen awareness of them, and generate action. Identification and recruitment of local leaders is essential to the Alinsky organization. Local residents with leadership qualities of intelligence, articulateness, and the ability to get along with others are recruited if they are already in local leadership positions, and, if they are not, they are trained for leadership.

An Alinsky organization's members are not individual residents but are other local organizations that participate by sending delegates to meetings of the community organization. In cases where there are no local organizations, creating them becomes the first task of the organizer. Typically, block clubs and church groups make up the largest percentage of local organizations joining the Alinsky umbrella organization, although some social service and education-oriented groups are also represented. Thus, the Alinsky organization brings together disparate groups within the community and, through the resulting cooperation of a large number of community residents on specific issues, increases the community residents' participation and their power to effect change.

Congresses or conventions are held annually to which member organizations send delegates. One authority describes these congresses in the following words:

The congress has constitutionally authorized powers. It has the authority to amend the constitution, accept new member organizations, adopt the budget, elect officers, receive reports, and authorize programs. . . . The congress performs other tasks vital to the maintenance and enhancement of the organization. It generates enthusiasm, gives recognition to the activists, and informs the public of the organization's activities. Many of its tasks are symbolic and serve to increase the degree of cohesion within the organization.[4]

The annual congress also elects the officers for the following year.

The senate meets monthly, establishes committees, and appoints committee chairmen. It also gives final approval to policy matters. In the senate meetings, reports of the various standing committees are presented, often followed by direct and frequently dramatic action, as in the case where a man reported police harassment and the local police–community relations board was called directly from the senate meeting to answer charges. The role of the executive board is not clearly defined, being to some extent a parallel of the senate's role, although the executive board frequently operates with greater confidentiality. In addition to the constitutionally defined structures, there are income producing programs such as day care centers, job training, housing construction, and the publishing of local newspapers.

Basic to Alinsky's approach is the belief that power is the basis for successfully negotiating for economic or political gains. He believes that the power that community organizations have is the power to disrupt normal activity, and this is the tool Alinsky organizers use—social protest. Protest tactics include pickets, boycotts, marches, rent strikes, harassment of local officials, and unannounced attendance at public meetings or at officials' offices—or, at times, their homes. The type of protest is matched to the type of issue.

Alinsky organizations also mediate between the community and outside forces involved in an issue, clarifying the residents' demands and establishing contacts within the city bureaucracies.

Alinsky organizations arise and are effective primarily in social environments where there are pressing social problems, where the residents feel powerless to effect change themselves, and where there is an existing institution to provide funds.

Advocacy planning   A different approach to citizen participation which focuses on the planner's role is advocacy planning, first articulated in the planning community by Paul Davidoff.[5] Advocacy planning assumes that there is no overall, common, and identifiable public interest to be served but rather a wide variety of client groups with diverse and sometimes opposing goals and interests. Planners, according to this view, should be cognizant of this reality and should, therefore, serve a given client group's interests and should do so openly, as lawyers serve their clients' interests. It is the planner's job not only to develop the plans for a particular project but also to speak for the interests of the group or individuals affected by these plans. In this way the citizen is included not only by being heard but also by having professional representation to the government agencies with the decision-making power.

In fact, private institutions and businesses have frequently hired private planners as advocates to develop plans and to maintain local government contacts. More recently, professional planners have instituted volunteer programs to aid community groups. These cases are relatively straightforward. However, a position of "advocate planner" for a planner who is employed by a local government agency becomes more complicated. For whom is he or she an advocate? For the groups affected by his or her plan, or for the interests of the city government officials? While in theory these two groups might have the same interests, in fact, they frequently do not. Thus, the concept of advocacy, while clear in definition, is relatively unclear in practice.[6]

An extremely influential work that articulates various approaches to citizen participation is Sherry R. Arnstein's framework for analyzing citizen participation, the Ladder of Citizen Participation[7] (Figure 19–1). Arnstein defines citizen participation in terms of the amount of actual control citizens have over policy decisions. Participation is divided into three categories, ranging from no control

Figure 19–1 The Ladder of Citizen Participation.

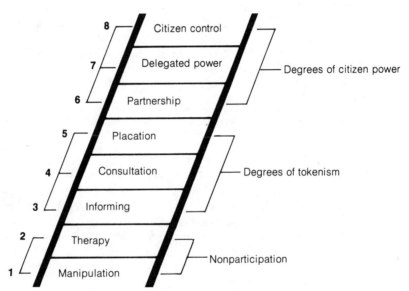

to complete citizen control. These categories are *nonparticipation, tokenism,* and *citizen power.* Types of citizen involvement are then labeled and grouped under the appropriate categories. Thus, *manipulation,* a type of citizen involvement which includes placing citizens on advisory panels, is a form of nonparticipation. *Therapy,* drawing attention away from basic economic causes of local problems and centering it on changing the individual's reaction to the problem, is another form of nonparticipation. *Informing* citizens of decisions already made which affect them, *consulting* citizens by holding public hearings or attitude surveys, or *placating* them by appointments to boards in an advisory capacity, with no delegation of authority, are degrees of tokenism. *Partnership,* in which authority is shared by citizens and officials, and *delegated power,* in which citizens actually have final project approval over a plan or some aspect of a plan, and actual *citizen control* over decision making are at the top of the ladder under the category of citizen power.

Arnstein believes that without actual redistribution of power citizen participation is an "empty ritual" and is basically a frustrating process. In order to bring about significant social reform, citizens must engage in activities high on the ladder of participation. The degree of citizen participation that actually occurs will be the result of how much the citizens really want control and the willingness of the involved agencies to share control. Obviously, some agreement between the two must be reached for change to occur.

The Ladder of Citizen Participation can be an effective guide for citizens in choosing their activities and in deciding whether to accept the roles offered to them by the agencies whose control they are attempting to share. This framework also provides a useful concept for assessing the various forms of participation.

Examples of citizen participation

At present citizens participate in government in several different ways. Local governments have provided various forms intended to increase citizen participation, such as field offices, multiservice centers, little city halls, and outreach programs.

Citizen participation in local planning occurs through the formation of citizen advisory and planning committees, special purpose planning groups, and even legally based citizen planning and zoning organizations. Over the last two decades citizen participation was given impetus and prominence by the federal programs discussed earlier in the chapter. The most recent requirements for citizen participation under the block grant programs are not as stringent as those under earlier federal programs and can even be viewed as lessening federal support for citizen participation.

Local government approaches

Several different approaches to citizen participation, ranging from traditional forms such as field offices to multiservice centers, neighborhood city halls, and outreach programs, have been instituted in different parts of the country. A major factor in the success of these approaches has been the degree of their coordination with the central city or county authorities. As institutions and techniques for implementing citizen participation are being developed and improved, elected officials and other government authorities are beginning to view citizen participation as a positive contribution to the administration of neighborhood programs.

Field offices   The traditional institutions for implementing citizen participation are those that locate field offices in neighborhoods to provide regular municipal services such as building and safety engineering, street maintenance, sanitation, and planning. There are several cities using this approach.[8] Los Angeles has eleven branch city halls, two of which provide all the services available at the main city hall. An integral part of this approach in Los Angeles is that the fifteen council members are considered "citizen advocates," most of them having district offices. San Antonio maintains three area service centers providing public works and building inspection functions. Unlike Los Angeles, in San Antonio area engineers in charge of the centers are given decision-making authority and can institute work programs in accordance with their neighborhoods' needs. Kansas City has two city hall annexes. Although they do not handle a significant amount of business, the city council justifies their continued existence on the basis of citizen satisfaction. Thus, the main benefit of the traditional approach to citizen participation, the field office, is that the city hall staff is aware of each neighborhood's particular needs and can develop individual programs geared to those needs.

Multiservice centers Another approach, the multiservice center, provides social welfare and recreation opportunities for the neighborhood in which it is located. Unlike the functions of the field offices, none, or very few, of the city hall functions are handled in multiservice centers. Chicago and Norfolk are two cities with multiservice center programs. Chicago has the most extensive program, with nine large urban progress centers, six outposts, and five small multiservice centers. The larger centers typically provide employment services, legal aid, vocational training, youth programs, and a mayor's complaint desk, while the smaller store front centers coordinate and direct programs scattered among different blocks throughout each neighborhood.

Norfolk has one large multiservice center which provides primarily recreational activities but also has a medical clinic, a mental health center, a social service office, a juvenile probation office, an employment agency, a business league, legal aid, and senior citizen services. There is no regular ombudsman or citizen advocate and municipal complaints are not emphasized. Thus, multiservice centers can provide the very basic services needed particularly in poor neighborhoods. Their location in the neighborhoods gives easier access to those services to the residents and, particularly in the cases of recreational and youth activities, provides services essential to maintaining a stable neighborhood.

Little city halls A third approach, neighborhood or little city halls, provides for quick communication between neighborhood residents and the central city hall.[9] This approach had its beginnings in the late 1960s as an attempt to prevent urban violence by increasing communication between neighborhood residents and city hall authorities. Little city halls are also designed to improve the effectiveness of services by the follow-up of center managers who serve as ombudsmen.

New York, Atlanta, and Houston have neighborhood city hall programs of this type. Houston has mobile units serving as little city halls which are moved between neighborhoods as they are needed, in addition to permanent neighborhood city halls. The main function of the Houston staff is to follow up on complaints and to dispense information, although they also accept job applications and collect taxes and license fees. Both Atlanta's and Houston's neighborhood city halls are in poor neighborhoods.

New York City has six store front neighborhood city halls and three mobile units. In addition, New York City has an urban task force composed of citizen volunteers and chairmen appointed by the mayor. The task force works with the neighborhood city halls to dispense information, offer agency referrals, and help residents resolve their problems in dealing with city departments. The urban task force is directed by the Office of Neighborhood Government, established expressly for that purpose.

Another type of neighborhood city hall can be seen in Baltimore's three store front "mayor's stations." In addition to information, these centers deal with city complaints and provide employment services, welfare assistance, and other social services. Columbus, Ohio, has mini-city halls created to house the community relations department and the youth opportunity office. Since the space was needed, it was decided to locate those offices in a poverty area and use it as a base for developing a city services center.

Boston has fourteen little city halls located in store fronts, trailers, and old municipal buildings throughout the city. These centers deal with complaints and information, voter registration, parking permits, social security assistance, and other services. The staff members are actively involved in providing assistance to local communities and in acting as citizen advocates on behalf of the residents.

Outreach programs Another approach to local citizen participation is the outreach program. San Francisco has established a Mayor's Office of Outreach, with two aides who serve as ombudsmen handling citizen complaints and neigh-borhood problems. There are no neighborhood city halls, but there is one state service center and there are federally funded health and community action cen-ters in poverty areas.

When viewed in terms of Arnstein's Ladder of Citizen Participation, all of these approaches are in the category of tokenism. They are primarily concerned with improving services to the residents by better communication and local ser-vice centers. However, they do not involve granting any decision-making power to citizens.

Organizational approaches

Types of citizen advisory organizations   A traditional form of citizen participation in planning is the citizen advisory organization. These include citizen advisory committees; citizen planning committees; community-wide housing and plan-ning councils; special purpose planning groups; and intercommunity, regional, and national organizations. The citywide groups are usually appointed by the elected authorities and are semiofficial organizations, while the special purpose groups are frequently self-organized on a neighborhood level.

Citizen advisory committees are often established to encourage citizen partic-ipation, particularly in urban renewal activities. As their name suggests, they have no authority other than for presenting or discussing government policies and programs.

Citizen planning committees study issues and develop plans much as the city planning commission does and occasionally will have elected officials or depart-ment officials as members. However, their powers are only advisory. These committees, because they are composed of residents from many neighborhoods and different professions, bring in opinions and recommendations and are an attempt to create a bridge between the official planning agencies and the people for whom they plan. In recent years such citizen committees have been ex-tremely successful in designing goals and policy statements for a variety of cities throughout the country.

Community-wide housing and planning councils are found most often in large metropolitan areas. They are usually composed of civic leaders and profes-sionals and this combination of local importance and technical knowledge tends to give these councils a certain amount of nonofficial power. They function pri-marily to inform the public of government programs and policies. Often, they are instigators of civic improvement programs and are the force behind legisla-tive reform or specific projects.

A more limited type of citizen group is the special purpose planning group. These groups are formed by citizens who have special interests revolving around such issues as improving and rehabilitating neighborhoods, preserving business districts, and advancing industrial development. Occasionally, special purpose groups are organized on behalf of a particular group, as are the antipov-erty or urban design organizations.

Larger scale citizen based organizations include such intercommunity, re-gional, and national organizations as ACTION, a nonprofit public service orga-nization whose goal is the eradication of slums; and Urban America, Inc., a nonprofit educational organization. These groups draw members nationally and have many local chapters as well as having the support of other types of local citizens' groups. They are involved in research, education, public information, and discussion, and they frequently publish newsletters and other publications. Organizations such as Common Cause go a step further by maintaining a "people's lobby" in Washington, D.C., and by encouraging citizens to enter the political process directly.

Local planning organizations In addition to municipal field offices established by city hall, several planning jurisdictions have decentralized their district and long-range planning functions by establishing field planning offices in city neighborhoods. The field planning offices perform a number of important and useful functions. They can provide the central planning office with information on and interpretation of community problems, characteristics, and attitudes. They can improve relations with and attitudes toward the planning department by showing neighborhood residents that the city's planning office is actively concerned with their neighborhood.

Field planning offices can provide a familiar local channel for citizen input into the district planning and advance planning processes; this would include statements of neighborhood needs and goals. Field offices can also provide a steady flow of information to the neighborhoods regarding the ongoing district and local planning activities. Finally, they can provide planning advice, general planning education, and technical assistance to neighborhood groups and organizations involved in planning efforts. While field offices increase neighborhood contact with planning officials and provide means of communication and feedback, they do not provide for much neighborhood influence over the regulatory functions of urban planning.

The strength of neighborhoods The city planning programs discussed by the planners for Atlanta, Indianapolis, Portland, and St. Paul seem to place the highest priorities on planning for such [older] neighborhoods. . . . The typical approach appears to be one where the city planning agency plans to help organize the neighborhood and provide technical services. Many of the planners [have] stressed that the success of rejuvenation rests largely with the strength of such neighborhood organizations and their leadership. . . . Rather than attempting to provide services to all neighborhoods, there appears to be a stress on neighborhoods with the strongest prospect of making it. Even in the Cleveland program with its concern for groups with little existing strengths [it was made] clear that planners should deal with problems in neighborhoods where there was some likelihood of success.

Source: Excerpted from Anthony James Catanese, "Learning by Comparison: Lessons from Experiences," in *Personality, Politics, and Planning: How City Planners Work,* ed. Anthony James Catanese and W. Paul Farmer (Beverly Hills, Calif.: Sage Publications, 1978), pp. 193–94.

Many of the jurisdictions that are presently integrating citizen participation into their planning process have evolved citizen groups which can be categorized as citizen-involved, legally based planning and zoning organizations. Although their practices differ in many ways, they do have a number of common characteristics, such as: neighborhood boards or councils with a clearly defined amount of power; neighborhood planning and zoning functions which are part of a larger set of functions; a legal base for their neighborhood planning and zoning functions; and legally recognized power which is limited to advice only. The jurisdictions that have established these groups include: New York City; Dayton, Ohio; Birmingham, Alabama; Newton, Massachusetts; Portland, Oregon; Eugene, Oregon; and Simi Valley, California.

Two of the jurisdictions—New York and Dayton—assign the responsibility for their neighborhood planning and zoning functions to a network of neighborhood planning boards. The others assign the neighborhood planning and zoning functions to neighborhood councils with a set of responsibilities that includes a wide variety of city services. In Dayton the city is divided into six planning areas, each with a neighborhood planning board. These are called priority boards and are consulted on all planning and zoning matters related to their neighborhoods. In New York there are sixty-two planning districts, each with its community planning board. As in Dayton, the boards deal with all manner of planning and zoning issues relevant to their districts. The New York charter gives each local board the authority to consider all planning matters pertaining to its district and to be consulted on zoning questions. In both Dayton and New York, zoning matters referred to the boards for review and advice include zoning changes, zoning studies, variances, conditional use permit applications, and planned unit development (PUD) applications. In Dayton, subdivision applications are also referred to the boards for review and advice.

All the other jurisdictions assign a wide variety of functions to their neighborhood councils. Eugene has somewhat expanded the functions assigned to its neighborhood planning groups by giving them broad advisory power on such matters relating to the growth and development of their neighborhoods as land use, zoning, parks, open space and recreation, annexation, housing, community facilities, and transportation and traffic. In accordance with this provision, the city routinely notifies the neighborhood organizations of all proposed zonings, zoning changes, subdivisions, conditional use permits, and planned unit developments. The organizations then have a specified amount of time in which to review those matters pertaining to their neighborhoods and to submit their advice.

Portland goes one step further in enlarging the number of functions assigned to recognized neighborhood organizations. It adds human resource, social and recreational programs, and environmental quality to the areas in which the organizations give advice and recommendations and set priorities. The broadest advisory powers are assigned to neighborhood councils by Simi Valley, Newton, and Birmingham. The functions assigned include all the municipal services, including planning and zoning. All three jurisdictions refer all zoning matters, including zoning changes, appeals, use permits, and PUDs to the appropriate neighborhood councils for advice and recommendations. In all seven jurisdictions, neighborhood groups, in addition to having zoning changes referred to them, also have the power to initiate planning and zoning studies, to initiate plans, and to submit these plans as recommendations to either the planning commission or the city council.

In New York, planning boards may advise under their "own initiative . . . with respect to any matter relating to the welfare of the district or its residents."[10] In Portland, neighborhood associations are entitled to "recommend an action, a policy, or a comprehensive plan to the city . . . on any matter affecting the livability of the neighborhood including, but not limited to, land use, zoning [etc.]."[11] Although the power to initiate plans and proposals is given to all seven jurisdictions, most of the present practice involves comment and advice by neighborhood boards or councils on zoning changes, use permit applications, and PUDs submitted by others.

While most practices of neighborhood planning and zoning either have developed from earlier federal programs or have come into being by some legal act of the city concerned, an unusual experiment in grass roots neighborhood, voluntary, nonlegally based planning and zoning has been in progress over the past two years in the Lake View neighborhood on the North Side of Chicago. The local alderman, believing neighborhood residents should participate in decisions affecting their neighborhood, initiated the establishment of a voluntary community zoning board. The concept was approved and supported by the Forty-fourth Ward Assembly, a strong advisory body established earlier by the alderman and the Lake View residents. The experiment is unique both in its origin and in its status with the city's planning and zoning authorities: the Lake View experiment was created by a voluntary, cooperative act of a neighborhood and its representative. Although initially viewed with suspicion and recognized only as the alderman's advisers, the board has slowly gained respect and recognition in its own right, from both the Chicago planning commission and the city zoning board of appeals. As the Lake View zoning board became more knowledgeable and its positions became increasingly soundly based and persuasive, it gained in both status and stature. To date, in every case the zoning board of appeals has accepted the recommendations of the Lake View community zoning board. A proposal suggesting the creation of similar boards in all Chicago neighborhoods, but on a legal and fully recognized basis, has also been advanced. The members of this board are elected by the ward assembly, and the only finances available to it are the staff and office facilities of the alderman. The board deals only with zoning matters and to date has dealt only with minor zoning changes, appeals, and variances.

Within the context of Arnstein's Ladder of Citizen Participation, many of the present organizational forms of citizen participation in planning, at least technically, fall into the category of tokenism. The various citizen committees, even those which are legally based, are advisory and serve primarily to aid local officials in decision making. However, the citizen participation boards of Newton, Massachusetts, New York City, Simi Valley, California, and Eugene, Oregon (and of other places), although technically only advisory to their city councils, have in reality acquired a level of power which could quite properly place them in the category of citizen power.

Because of the high caliber of their advice, the widespread satisfaction with the programs among neighborhood residents, and their high degree of acceptance by city officials and institutions, the boards or councils often have a position of high status in the community and exercise a degree of positive influence very much beyond that envisioned in their original charter. Most boards and councils exercise a very real and dominant influence over the quality and direction of land development in their respective neighborhoods.

The special interest and national organizations are hard to place on Arnstein's Ladder because, while no actual power is delegated to them and they are not officially recognized partners in decision making, through their information systems and their organization of large groups of voters who elect the decision makers, their control appears to exceed tokenism. An additional category could be added under citizen power to include a frequently powerful form of citizen participation: that of the pressure group.

The planning process: a functional approach to participation

The previous section emphasized organizational approaches to citizen participation in local planning. However, a major problem in involving citizens in the planning process is that of defining the respective roles of the citizen, the planner, and the public official. Lack of definition of proper roles often causes unnecessary conflicts in situations that are already overly "adversary-oriented." It is equally essential to design a citizen participation process that clearly defines *when* and *at what stage* participation occurs. If this is to be accomplished, participation in the planning process must be looked at from a functional point of view consisting of a multi-stage planning process and a functional assignment of roles to citizens, professional planners, and public officials (see Figure 19–2). The following discussion is such a functional role definition for these three participants and also serves as a functionally based multi-stage planning model with suggested role assignments for each stage.

The citizen Within this approach to citizen participation, each of the participants brings particular insights, skills, and responsibilities to the process. Within such a framework the role of citizens involves all matters of values, goals, and objectives. Citizens should give direction to the plan since their city, their neighborhood, and, therefore, the quality of their lives that are affected. Thus, citizens should be the major decision makers in the delineation of values, goals, and objectives (Figure 19–2). They can further contribute to the planning process by participating in choosing among alternative designs, by participating in the approval and modification of the operational plans, and by contributing to the continuous feedback process. Through such additional participation citizens can ensure that the decisions made are consistent with the community's values and goals.

The planner   Professional planners bring their expertise to the process. Their role is primarily concerned with those aspects that require professional skills. However, because they work so closely with the citizens and are in fact a major factor in enabling the citizens to fulfill their own roles, professional planners must bring not only technical knowledge but also social skills in dealing with group meetings, discussions, conflict resolution, and the provision of information.

Figure 19–2
Participation in the
planning process.

Planning process steps	Participants		
	Citizens	Planners	Public officials
1. Assessing community values	X	O	
2. Determining goals and objectives	X	O	X
3. Data collection		X	
4. Design of criteria and standards		X	
5. Developing alternative plans		X	
6. Choosing an alternative	X	O	X
7. Detailed design of operational plan		X	
8. Modification/approval of operational plan	X	O	X
9. Implementation		X	X
10. Feedback	X	X	X

X = Major role
O = Facilitating or supporting role

Within this framework, then, the planner is the main contributor in the steps of gathering data relevant to the goals and objectives, designing alternatives, developing criteria for choice of alternatives, developing the operational plan, implementing the operational plan, and contributing to the feedback and modification process of the plan. The planner is also likely to be the person who presents the plan to the city council, although this is a role more successfully filled by a combination of planner and citizen.

In following this approach to citizen participation, the planner and the citizens also work together closely on several of the planning stages. Thus, while citizens are the main contributors in the delineation of values and goals, planners have an ancillary role in helping citizens state these values. For example, the content of the values surveys sent out to citizens by planners affects the values that will be chosen.

Planners also help to organize citizens' groups and their meetings while the values, goals, and objectives are being developed. In addition, planners work with the citizens at the stage of approval and modification by providing technical assistance and advice. Finally, planners and citizens work together on the final stages of implementation and feedback, with the planners providing the professional expertise and the citizens aiding them in this by ensuring that any changes are in accord with their goals.

The public official It is the responsibility of the public official to determine public goals and policies, to adopt plans, to adopt ordinances, and to spend funds to implement plans. The local government official makes final decisions in approving the goals, in choosing one of a number of alternative designs, in approving and modifying the operational plan, and in implementing the final plan. Local authorities quite properly have this power, since they are the elected officials responsible to the entire municipality and they can relate local goals, interests, and specific neighborhood plans to other city goals and constraints in choosing an appropriate alternative and a final operational plan. This power of final approval by the elected local officials often prevents particularly well-organized neighborhoods from dominating the city's time and budget, and equalizes opportunity for all neighborhoods and special interest groups within the city.

Applications of the functional approach Before the planning agency embarks on a participation program for a particular project or plan it should analyze the local situation and determine in advance the best times for participation by the three groups of actors (see Figure 19–2). The planning process is divided into a typical or common sequence of steps, with each step assigned to one or more of the three groups of actors. Depending on the particular community situation, it would be possible to complete Figure 19–2 by assigning weights or values for each step or each group of participants. This can be as simple as defining roles as *major, minor,* and *none*.

Once appropriate roles for citizen, planner, and public official are determined, it is necessary to determine the precise form or technique that will be used to facilitate participation. The specific form or technique that is chosen by a planning agency will depend on a number of factors: where in the planning process the participation is to occur; how much time or money is available for the participation; the skills of the planning staff in carrying out the participation process; the degree to which the area of the community is already organized into formal citizen groups; the types of issues that are involved; and the peculiarities of the local community.

The number and variety of citizen participation techniques that have been used at the local level are truly remarkable. Figure 19–3 provides a list and a thumbnail sketch of at least some of the more popular methods that are used. Some of these techniques can become "gimmicky" and if not used sincerely they can be defined as "games citizens play." However, if playing a game results in better mutual understanding among citizens, planners, and officials, then the game is worth playing.

The problems of participation

Citizen participation poses many problems for local officials, planners, and citizens. These problems can be grouped into three major issue areas: the costs and benefits of participation; power and control; and the planner's problems with his or her own professional role in citizen participation.

Costs and benefits

The costs and benefits of citizen participation are continually debated. One of the most frequently voiced arguments against citizen participation is that of economic waste. When decisions must wait for citizen feedback and, in some

Techniques appropriate for all steps
in the planning process

Charrette. An intensive, interactive problem-solving process with meetings convened around the development of specific plans.

Information and neighborhood meetings. Meetings sponsored by an official agency to inform citizens of potential programs and to obtain feedback.

Public hearings. The traditional, legally required meeting to take formal action on a proposal.

Public information programs. Long-term programs providing information by a wide range of methods.

Task force. An agency sponsored citizen committee with a specific task and charge relating usually to a single problem or subject.

Techniques appropriate for four steps
in the planning process[1]

Development of values, goals, and objectives

Citizen advisory committees. Citizen groups presumed to represent the ideas and attitudes of local groups; the purpose is to advise the planning agency.

Attitude surveys. If good sampling techniques are used and if questions are carefully constructed, this is a sound basis for allowing views to be expressed.

Neighborhood planning council. An organization formed by citizens which engages in a number of neighborhood programs, as well as advocacy and advice.

Citizen representation on public policymaking bodies. Appointing or electing citizens to serve on official city bodies.

Group dynamics. Group problem-solving techniques used to clarify goals, facilitate group interaction, and resolve conflicts within citizen groups.

Policy Delphi. The views of individuals and various interest groups, the local government, and the planning staff are presented in successive rounds of argument and counter-argument working toward a consensus.

Figure 19–3   Citizen participation techniques. Well recognized and defined techniques and formats for citizen participation are shown here. Use of any of the techniques depends on the issues involved, the resources available, the nature of the immediate neighborhood or other area, and other local factors. Techniques that may be appropriate for all steps in the planning process are shown first, followed by techniques that are grouped by values, goals, and objectives and other major steps in the planning process.

cases, approval, there is a greater expenditure of time and money. According to this view the increased costs of organization for items such as maintenance of additional offices, public meetings, printing of necessary information, and training of citizens for participation make citizen participation on any large scale a financially unsound proposition.

Another related argument against citizen participation is that of inefficiency in government. The creation of citizen boards, for example, introduces an additional group to be consulted with, listened to and accommodated in the decision-making process. In addition, increasing citizen participation increases the number of power struggles already plaguing government operations. Basic to this problem is the reluctance of local authorities to relinquish power. The complications caused by both these factors are seen as severely reducing the efficiency of government and thus the importance of citizen participation.

Still another argument against citizen participation, particularly those forms which grant anything more than limited advisory powers, is that it weakens our representative form of government. Proponents of this view argue that elected officials are clearly responsible to their constituents, and disagreement with their actions can be effectively dealt with at elections. In contrast, citizens' groups are not accountable in any legal sense for their decisions or actions. It is

Choosing alternatives

Citizen referendum. Citizens vote their approval or disapproval of a public measure by official ballots.

Community technical assistance. Professional assistance is given to citizens through either government or private funding in order to help them achieve their objectives.

Design-in. Citizens learn to work with some of the tools of community design, such as maps and photographs, which enable them to visualize proposed plans.

Fishbowl planning. Citizens address themselves to proposals through workshop formats.

Games and simulations. Citizens participate in formal games that simulate the planning–development process. Citizens take turns playing the roles of the various protagonists.

Media-based issue balloting. Citizens are informed about issues through local media and responses are returned by way of mailed "ballots." Can also include the use of telephone hotlines.

Goals–achievement matrix. A method of assessing project alternatives by weighting alternatives according to citizen group goals.

Plan implementation

Citizen employment. Employing citizens in official agencies working in neighborhoods.

Citizen training. Through the use of various educational techniques, citizens are given training in the planning process that enables them to more knowledgeably participate.

Feedback–modification

Drop-in centers. Centers with personnel who answer questions and provide literature on neighborhood projects.

Hotline. A telephone answering system staffed by planners or others who answer citizen questions and receive opinions.

---

1 The following references provide comprehensive discussions of the techniques summarized here: U.S., Department of Transportation, Federal Highway Administration, *Effective Citizen Participation in Transportation Planning*, vol. 2: *A Catalogue of Techniques* (Washington, D.C.: Government Printing Office, 1976); U.S., Department of the Army. Corps of Engineers, Institute for Water Resources, *Public Participation in Water Resources Planning*, IWR Report 70–7 (Springfield, Va.: Clearinghouse for Federal Scientific and Technical Information, 1970); Research Center for Urban Environmental Planning, *Planning and Design Workbook for Citizen Participation* (Princeton, N.J.: Princeton University Press, 1969); James Creighton, *Citizen Participation/Public Involvement Skills Workbook* (Los Gatos, Calif.: Synergy, 1973). Katherine P. Warner, *Public Participation in Water Resources Planning* (Arlington, Va.: National Water Commission, 1971).

Figure 19–3   (continued).

feared that citizens' groups can bypass institutions of representative government and behave arbitrarily within their communities.

A further objection to citizen participation is the fear of parochialism. Critics suggest that, given the opportunity, neighborhood citizen groups would make planning decisions only for the benefit of their own narrow interests, and the city would therefore become a disconnected array of separate communities.

A final argument against citizen participation is that some neighborhoods might use their decision-making power as an exclusionary device. For example, the various zoning and planning powers at the neighborhood level could be used to exclude potential residents along social or economic lines.

Thus, the arguments against citizen participation are primarily based on economic factors and a fear of misuse of power on the part of the new participants.

Regarding the benefits of participation, those favoring active citizen involvement believe that an important result of citizen participation is a better quality of political life. Active citizens' groups can ensure that elected officials are responsive to their constituents' needs and aware of their opinions. The political climate is further improved, according to this view, by the movement towards equalization of power that comes when officials must answer to active, involved citizens.

Another benefit of citizen participation is the resolution of social problems: citizen participation through neighborhood groups can be a major factor in integrating minorities into society. The creation of neighborhood institutions can restore a sense of community and increase community cohesion and unity, and services are often provided more quickly to neighborhoods with active citizen participation. Also, a service that is developed in cooperation with active citizen groups is more easily adapted to and integrated into the neighborhood it serves.

Another benefit of citizen participation is an increase in the quality of the administrative functioning of government agencies, officials, and planners. Responsiveness of central planning authorities to the needs of neighborhood residents is improved by increased communication and contact. The resulting programs and policies can be more effective because of the increase in neighborhood cooperation with the planning process. A reduction of the work loads of the central authorities is also possible when citizens are handling some planning matters in local boards or councils. Furthermore, authorities can receive corrective feedback on programs in progress and thus can improve their functioning. Residents of a neighborhood can also be a source of fresh ideas for solutions to local problems.

Power and control

The issue of control is basic to government, and the American tradition of popular control over government has undergone many changes. In addition to having the traditional citizen control mechanism of the public election, citizens now expect their officials to be responsive and accountable. Numerous federal programs of the 1950s and 1960s required strong support for citizen participation and control. One of the results was a power struggle between citizens' groups and local authorities and struggles within citizens' groups themselves for control of development resources and policy decisions.

In many instances these power struggles seriously impeded effective program development and implementation. For example, after only one year of the Model Cities programs neighborhood organizations to a great extent controlled the programs in five of the Model Cities communities.[12] In those communities they effectively controlled which programs were reviewed by the city council. This represented a challenge to government officials, who then began to view the citizens as competitors rather than partners. By 1969 the Model Cities administration was concerned about the extent of citizen control of the programs. Of particular concern to it were the following conditions that had arisen: program directors reporting to citizen policy groups and not to city government officials; citizens' groups being able to block a program; and the right to initiate a program lying entirely with the citizen group. U.S. Department of Housing and Urban Development (HUD) officials found it necessary to reassert the city's right to initiate plans in a memo in 1967.[13]

Residents' distrust of the local government has also added significantly to the problem of control. Programs such as Model Cities gave hope for legal involvement of citizens in neighborhood development, and this should have alleviated the distrust. However, many of the citizens who were most deeply involved in the Model Cities program and were receiving a great deal of help from the local authorities were often as disenchanted and discontented as were those receiving no help. One explanation for this is that as programs developed and were funded there were resources to fight over, and conflict developed. The scarcity of the allocated resources added to the competition, particularly because of the policy of awarding all the resources to one group—an approach in which sharing of resources was not possible.

Another explanation for this discontent, even with functioning programs, was the problem of rising levels of expectations. As long as problems seemed insoluble there was little activity, but when a solution seemed in sight the previously tolerated conditions became intolerable and a scramble for solutions ensued. Solutions under the best conditions take time, and the resulting frustration exacerbated long-standing distrust of local authorities.

Even at the level of token citizen participation there were problems of control. Citizens' committees would compete with local authorities for technical staff time and would thoroughly study an issue but would present only brief explanations to the actual decision makers in local government. Authorities, on the other hand, often ignored the recommendations of citizen committees. Furthermore, the citizen committees themselves were sometimes composed of special interest groups rather than of a cross section of a neighborhood.

Approaches to handling the problem of control have been proposed which attempt to satisfy citizens who wish to participate but which leave final decision making clearly in the hands of the local authorities. One rather cynical method proposed is the co-opting, by the authorities, of the leaders of the citizens' groups. Thus, by diverting the energies of the strongest members of the citizens' groups from public to private goals, or by deluding them with promises of being more effective in the pursuit of citizens' goals, the local government can reduce the effectiveness of citizen participation and keep it at what Arnstein calls the token level.

Another approach is a compromise which maximizes citizen input into program development but leaves final control with city officials. Proponents of this view argue that the stability of the community is maintained if control remains with elected authorities who can provide direction and coordination.

Neither of these proposed solutions would appear to be effective. The first, co-option, can only increase the distrust of local government and justify extra-legal means of citizen control. The second is only a statement of the problem itself: In whose hands does control remain?

Citizen participation and the planner's dilemma

Active citizen participation poses several problems for planners. There are philosophical difficulties such as defining the role of citizens in plan development. Planners assign various roles to citizens; these range from making use of citizens' ideas and opinions to viewing citizens' groups as their own power bases in support of their own plans. Citizen participation also poses human—and psychological—dilemmas for the planner. These include being in the middle of a conflict between local authorities and neighborhood residents; handling citizens' unrealistic beliefs about the planner's power to gain final approval of his or her plans; being asked to deal with neighborhood problems which are primarily social and outside of the planner's role; and being assigned to "communities" frequently too large and too diverse to be handled effectively. A third area of problems is the political arena; this includes the neighborhood, with its diverse citizens' groups competing for dominance, as well as the political relationships between the local authorities and the neighborhood groups.

Philosophical issues[14] A problem basic to the relationship of planning to citizen participation is that of professionalism versus popular decision making. Planning as a profession involves a complicated technical education, and some planners feel that their decisions are based on this knowledge and cannot be replaced by the decisions of lay persons. Citizens, on the other hand, feel that they should have control over decisions which influence their neighborhoods and their lives. In their attitudes towards citizen participation planners range from those who want no citizen control to those who willingly use citizen groups to advance their plans.

One group of planners views citizen participation as a form of public relations. These planners feel that citizens' groups should support the planner's proposals but should have no control over them. These planners view planning as too technical for direct citizen participation.

Another group of planners believes that, while citizens have the right to participate in developing plans for their neighborhoods, the planning process is a technical one and citizen participation should be limited. These planners attempt to balance citizen input with the planner's expertise.

Still other planners view citizen participation as a power base for securing the implementation of their own plans. Realizing that community pressure is necessary to implementation, these planners see citizens' groups as an essential component. To gain their support, these planners plan for those sections of the neighborhood which will provide the most active support in putting pressure on city hall.

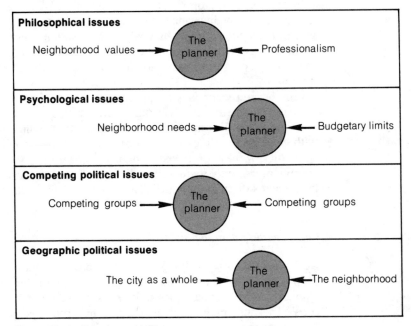

Figure 19–4 The planner's dilemma.

All of these attitudes are based on an erroneous concept of the planning process. Planning is not one activity; it is a complicated process with many components. Participation of citizens is relevant to some of these components; others are obviously the domain of planners. Still others are rightly decided on by local elected officials. The discussion earlier in this chapter and the listing in Figure 19–2 emphasize the need to analyze where and when each role is to be played.

Psychological issues Planners as individuals face certain problems in attempting to plan for a community. In their relations with residents they are often aware of specific neighborhood needs and are sympathetic to citizens' groups. At the same time, planners are well aware of the bureaucratic and budgetary restraints on community development and must try to explain political and economic realities to the residents. This frequently brings on the contempt of neighborhood residents, who see the planner as representing "the establishment." Also, when planners represent local government at public meetings, hostility and frustration can be vented at them.

Planners also face the responsibility, in the eyes of residents, for final acceptance of plans. Residents often believe—mistakenly—that planners have the final say in what is carried out and how funds are allocated. On the other hand, if planners convince residents that planners are not powerful, residents do not want to waste time working with them. It is hard to communicate a clear understanding of what, in fact, planners can and cannot do for neighborhood development.

The fact that planners do not choose the neighborhoods they are assigned to brings about two other problems of personal concern to the planner. One is that the community to which a planner is assigned is usually a fairly large area. Within a given "community" there may be many different populations; there may, at times, be "mini-neighborhoods," each with its own citizens' groups with conflicting interests pressing for the planner's attention. The other problem is that planners are assigned to areas not necessarily on the basis of need but rather on the basis of political decisions. On this latter basis, the planner may be assigned to a well-organized neighborhood with a few problems that can be speedily resolved to make the city government look effective, or to a neighborhood with problems that have already attracted attention by erupting into violence, while the quietly deteriorating neighborhood is overlooked. Thus, planners working with neighborhood groups often feel that they are either carrying out an unnecessary job or attempting an impossible job.

Political issues The city planner faces political problems within the community and also between the community and the local government. Within the neighborhood to which the planner is assigned there are usually several competing

Figure 19–5 Citizen protests and demonstrations take many forms. Shown here is a massive protest against nuclear power in Washington, D.C., in the spring of 1979.

groups, frequently divided along ethnic and income lines. It is often impossible for the planner to represent all of them, as they differ in needs as well as approaches. Planners faced with this problem usually either cease functioning completely or pick out and work with the group that they feel is most in need or most deserving. Either solution leaves groups within the community whose needs are not being served.

The size of the community can also limit the planner's community contacts. The same people frequently show up at meetings, and the result is that the planner is forced to work with the community representatives, who are frequently self-appointed and who often have special interests and, therefore, are not representative of the residents. A further complicating factor in working with a total community is the private citizen who advocates a particular group's view. In these situations the planner becomes enmeshed in local policies and is hampered in functioning professionally.

The planner can also be caught between the benefits of a particular project to the city as a whole and its harm to a particular neighborhood. Here, there is the problem of priorities. The planner's allegiance is to the city as a whole but his or her job is in the neighborhood in which he or she works.

A further political issue is that local government authorities can impair the planner's functioning when there are no set procedures for electing residents to citizens' groups and the city officials appoint citizens who share their own opinions and who do not represent the neighborhood.

Conclusion

The societal values underlying citizen participation are many. Among the most significant are: protecting citizens' rights; guarding the public interest; maintaining the stability of society; and reducing the alienation of individuals within a large technical society. There is a definite demand for citizen participation, and, when its benefits to the society are considered, it seems apparent that all efforts must be made to include citizen participation in the local planning process.

Although there are many arguments against citizen participation, including economic waste, government inefficiency, increased political conflict, weakening of representative government, parochialism, and exclusionary practice, these are primarily problems of appropriate administration, proper role assignment, and effective participatory techniques.

An important advance in achieving more stable forms of citizen participation would be achieved through a shift from reliance on federal guidelines to reliance on locally based guidelines and organizations. The federal government changes every four years; legislative approaches change in the amount and kind of support given to citizen participation. The type of citizen participation described and advocated here is a process that involves long-standing, continuous citizen participation. It can extend over many years, and, in fact, the development of the roles of citizens, planners, and local authorities within the process can itself take time. It would be detrimental to this local development if it were dependent on the vagaries of federal programs and policies. Local communities should themselves determine the level and kind of participation they want, and they should institute it at the grass roots level regardless of national political considerations.

Professional planners, because of their role in the planning process, their facilitator position vis-à-vis citizen participation, and their expertise vis-à-vis elected or appointed city officials, are in an advantageous position to encourage participation, choose the appropriate kind of participation for each part of the planning process, and help make such participation a successful contributor to the planning development and change process. To do so successfully planners should discard elitist notions regarding their role in the planning process, should learn to identify the rung on the ladder of participation appropriate for their community and their planning project, and, above all, should acquire a new set of communication, human relations, and problem-solving skills. Only thus will they be able to identify and successfully implement the participation methods appropriate to the task at hand and the people involved. In addition to their job as professional planner and their role as adviser to elected officials, planners are challenged to add a new, more difficult yet potentially most rewarding, dimension to their task—that of facilitating at the grass roots level a meaningful process of democratic involvement.

1   David J. Greenstone and Paul E. Peterson, *Race and Authority in Urban Politics: Community Participation and the War on Poverty* (New York: Russell Sage Foundation, 1973).
2   Robert K. Yin and Douglas Yates, *Street Level Government: Assessing Decentralization and Urban Services* (Santa Monica, Calif.: Rand Corporation, 1974), pp. 27–29.
3   A thorough discussion of Saul Alinsky's approach and analysis of specific cases is provided in: Robert Bailey, Jr., *Radicals in Urban Politics: The Alinsky Approach* (Chicago: University of Chicago Press, 1972).
4   Ibid., p. 56.
5   Paul Davidoff, "Advocacy and Pluralism in Planning," *Journal of the American Institute of Planners* 31 (November 1965): 331–38.
6   See: Martin L. Needleman and Carolyn Emerson Needleman, *Guerrillas in the Bureaucracy* (New York: John Wiley & Sons, Inc., 1974).
7   Sherry R. Arnstein, "A Ladder of Citizen Partici-

pation," *Journal of the American Institute of Planners* 35 (July 1969): 216–44.
8   George J. Washnis, *Implementing Decentralized City Services,* Management Information Service Reports, vol. 3 no. I–8 (Washington, D.C.: International City Management Association, August 1971).
9   Ibid., p. 10.
10 New York City Local Law 39.
11 Portland City Ordinance No. 137816.
12 Melvin B. Mogulof, *Citizen Participation: A Review and Commentary on Federal Policies and Practices* (Washington, D.C.: The Urban Institute, 1970), p. 70.
13 Ibid., p. 71.
14 Needleman and Needleman, *Guerrillas in the Bureaucracy;* much of the following discussion is based on this work, in which philosophical, psychological, and political problems are discussed extensively.

Economic development

Most economic historians believe that the 1930s was a time when the federal government made a fundamental shift in philosophy and policy concerning the relationship between the government and the economy. The shift was from the assumption that interfering in the economy was none of government's business to a policy of active involvement.

By the late 1970s it was apparent that a similar shift was taking place at the local government level. As one report noted:

Increasingly, cities are abandoning the notion that the role of government is to provide services while private sector market forces determine the mix of local industries, the expansion and movement of local firms, the number, location and mix of jobs. City governments are trying to find ways to consciously and purposefully influence their economies in order to provide jobs for urban residents, increase per capita income, and reduce the heavy and often inequitable bite of the local tax structure.[1]

The direct and indirect roles of local government have been described in 22 case studies that are summarized graphically in Figure 20–1.

Obviously, the federal government has played an important role in the evolution of increasing local responsibility in economic development planning. At the risk of oversimplification, it can be said that the Economic Development Administration of the U.S. Department of Commerce evolved from a rural-oriented agency in the mid-1960s to an urban-oriented agency by the late 1970s. In addition, the U.S. Department of Housing and Urban Development (HUD) was focusing its attention in the central and mature cities increasingly on economic development activities, particularly through its Urban Development Action Grants (UDAGs). (See Chapters 9 and 16 for a detailed discussion.)

As both federal and local experiences evolved, cities discovered that while they had provided a number of services in the past these services had not been provided within the context of an overall economic development strategy. Cities discovered that they were not particularly well organized for responding to private sector needs. They learned that urban planning techniques of the late 1960s and early 1970s did not provide adequate information or perspectives. They discovered that the multitude of federal programs related to economic matters did not necessarily fit together well at the local level. And they began to realize that they would have to change from a mode of regulating business to a mode of communicating and cooperating with business.[2]

The obstacles to effective urban economic development planning are formidable. Many cities are affected by national and state economic policies and decisions over which they have little or no control. Moreover, new federal program changes seem to come along every year. The interregional and intraregional migrations of population, business, and industry present still more obstacles. Both planners and economists wish that the analytical techniques available provided better answers. Nevertheless, elected officials cannot wait for theoretical best answers. Planners and public officials must do what they at least *think* is right; doing nothing is, indeed, unthinkable.

The purpose of this chapter is to provide an introductory discussion of urban economic development planning. The chapter begins with an overview of the economic problems of American cities, with particular attention given to the planning and analytical problems created by the existence of municipal boundaries. The next section describes some of the general approaches and strategies that cities follow in economic planning. Finally, the chapter reviews, in a general way, some techniques of local economic analysis, with emphasis on the elements of economic base studies, on forecasting methods, and on the evaluation of economic base studies.

A: Economic issues facing cities: the national perspective[3]

The focus of this chapter is central city economic development. The key issue in urban economics is the level of economic activity that takes place within the restricted municipal boundary lines of central cities. This issue is just beginning to be understood after three decades of the effects of various forces and counterforces on the central city. Even the basic statistics on the structure of the central city economy are not as yet readily available. The city economy cannot be "seen," and there have been few data with which to measure it.

The conventional wisdom talks about "urban economies" as the economic systems spreading across metropolitan regions. The art and science of urban economics prefers to deal with a metropolitan network of interrelationships. It pays almost no attention to the decisive importance of the invisible boundary line that separates the central city from other jurisdictions in the region.

Failure to understand the importance of the city limits—and hence the importance of thinking in terms of the "city economy" as a distinct part of the broader metropolitan economy—is at the heart of many of the nation's urban difficulties. It has seriously restricted the effectiveness of public policies in dealing with urban problems. It is the reason why *new* economic development strategies are called for in United States cities.

The evidence of the economic malaise within the invisible boundary lines of central cities is obvious and well known. The litany of problems—which can be more accurately classed as symptoms of problems—includes the following six items:

1. *Unemployment:* most of the nation's unemployed (and virtually all of the nation's so-called structural unemployment) are within central cities
2. *Deterioration:* most of the nation's deteriorated and deteriorating neighborhoods are central city neighborhoods
3. *Underproductivity:* within the central cities are incredibly large reservoirs of unused or underused economic resources—land, buildings, and people with limited productive output
4. *Disinvestment:* only a fraction of the total new private investment made each year in the nation's urban regions is flowing into the central city, and most of that goes into the highly specialized central business districts
5. *Decentralization:* even in the most prosperous metropolitan regions there is a continued outflow of jobs from central cities and a continued attrition in the number of business firms and establishments operating within the city limits
6. *Social burdens:* the cities have become the havens of the poor, the elderly, and the disadvantaged; they have the nation's highest rates of crime and delinquency; and they carry the heaviest loads of welfare and social services.

	CBD renewal		Community Devel. Block Grant program	Financing						Historic preservation	Industrial			Neighborhood economic development			Planning	Public development institutions			Public/private projects	Small business development
	Commercial	Residential		Air rights	Land banking	Special assessments	Tax abatements	Tax increment financing	Loan programs		Attraction	Retention	Manpower	Residential	Commercial	Industrial		Public	Private	Public/private		
Milwaukee: Department of City Development																		●				
Chicago: Mayor's Council of Mpwr. & Econ. Advisers																		●			●	
Portland: Office of Planning and Development																		●				
Chicago: Comprehensive Mpwr. & Econ. Planning											●	●	●				●					
Milwaukee: Menomonee Valley Redevelopment											●	●					●					
Dayton: Oregon Historic District			●						●	●				●	●						●	
Portland: St. Johns Business Dist Impvt. Prgm.			●												●							●
CDBG and Industrial Development			●									●										
New York: Bedford–Stuyvesant Restoration Corp.															●							
Kansas City, Mo.: Black Economic Union											●					●						
Providence Business Development Organization			●												●							●
Albuquerque CETA Program											●		●									
Rhode Island CETA Program											●		●									
Labor-Management Committees											●	●	●									
Philadelphia Industrial Development Corporation	●					●			●		●	●								●		
San Diego County: Economic Development Corporation						●					●	●				●				●		
Hartford Civic Center	●			●			●														●	
Minneapolis: Nicollet Mall	●					●													●		●	
Baltimore: Charles Center/Inner Harbor	●																		●	●	●	
Milwaukee: Neighborhood Preservation Program			●						●					●	●					●	●	●
Dayton Courthouse Square	●			●			●														●	
Minneapolis: Loring Park Redevelopment Project		●						●	●											●	●	

As the result of these trends and conditions, central cities have become increasingly dependent on outside (federal and state) resources to maintain their fiscal viability. Many cities are moving steadily toward a state of bankruptcy.

The urgency of local actions

Dealing with the causes of these problems becomes very much a matter of organizing the public and private resources within the central cities themselves. This caveat is coming to be understood increasingly. Positive interventions have to be made in the daily workings of the marketplace to provide incentives and supports to generate new private reinvestments within the city limits. Declines in the level of activity within the structures of city economies must be stemmed. The productivity of the economic resources within the central city must be strengthened and expanded.

The reasons for bold local initiatives are obvious. Most new private investments are made locally largely on the basis of alternative conditions both inside and outside the municipal boundary lines; so also are the private decisions made on whether to stay in business in the city or to move out. Many if not most of the factors that affect economic activity within the city are—or can be—decisively affected by local public policies. Regardless of the assistance that cities can receive from federal and state sources, the "push" factors that directly affect the private decisions to invest or reinvest in the city—congestion, obsolescence, public service delivery, security, taxes, capital, and operating costs—must be dealt with locally.

The most pressing problem in many cities is that the fiscal and organizational incapacities of the municipal corporations seriously limit the effectiveness of local efforts. These incapacities complete the vicious circle of adverse factors that causes further leakages from the city economy of jobs, enterprises, and investments.

The persistence of central area decline

The attrition of central city economies is taking place in face of continued overall growth in most metropolitan regions. Many of the older urban regions are not growing at their former rate, but most regions continue to expand as the result of the depth and diversity of their skills, resources, and institutional frameworks. Some regions, of course, have been affected by basic interregional shifts in economic activity. The important fact, however, is that in virtually every metropolitan region both jobs and investments are growing outside the central city boundaries and are declining inside. The same is true of the number of business establishments, of population, and of property values.

Although the decline of central city economies may be greatest in metropolitan regions with the slowest growth, there are, in fact, central city declines in virtually all metropolitan regions. In areas in which annexation makes it possible for central cities to expand their boundaries, primarily in the southeastern and southwestern states, the statistics would not show the same declines in

Figure 20–1 Examples of coordinated urban economic development. This matrix shows the wide variety of approaches to economic development that are being used by several large cities, quasi-public organizations, a state government, and private groups. The column head Manpower refers to programs in broad scale manpower planning, employment training (CETA), and labor–management committees. The column head Planning refers to broad scale manpower planning and to three inner city redevelopment projects. These approaches have been developed as twenty-two case studies that appear in *Coordinated Urban Economic Development: A Case Study Analysis*, published by the National Council for Urban Economic Development.

"city economies" as elsewhere. However, the same forces of inner area economic deterioration are in operation.

This is not to say that there are not immense problems in those parts of metropolitan areas that are outside the central city. Heavy growth and fiscal and environmental pressures are found in suburban jurisdictions. Many close-in suburbs are facing exactly the same kinds of economic pressures as the central city. However, the hard fact remains that the central city of most metropolitan regions is consistently losing its economic viability. This has profound implications not only for the cities themselves but for the metropolitan regions of which they are a part and for the nation as a whole.

Figure 20–2   The urban economist who is enamored of the metropolitan area may overlook the pressing economic problems within the city.

It is the persistence (as well as the existence) of adverse competitive forces that makes it difficult (and often impossible) for the private sector to invest, reinvest, or even operate profitably in the area embraced by the city limits. Although there are some favorable trends that might indicate better prospects for central city economies in the future, most basic forces are continuing to work toward further weakening of the private economic structure within the city limits.

Consumer markets continue to expand in the suburbs. New consumers attract a full range of service investments. Plants seek more land for expanded and efficient operations. Despite a new awareness of the rising fiscal and environmental costs of "horizontal sprawl," there are still vast suburban resources that will be used for continued expansion. Because of the larger, more immediate, and more certain investment returns on suburban enterprises under most existing competitive conditions, there has been a virtual dismantling of the private investment apparatus operating within many central cities (except within the central business districts). The costs, uncertainties, and insecurities of much central city development continue to restrict the attractiveness of central city investment.

The absence of more affluent market demands contributes to a downward spiral of support for housing maintenance as well as housing transfers in many central city neighborhoods. It is a paradoxical fact that large parts of most central cities are inadequately served by consumer facilities in spite of the continued availability of large amounts of consumer dollars. The deterioration of neighborhood commercial districts has become endemic. And, despite policy changes that now appear to be firming up, there are still distinct biases in the operation of federal spending and tax policies in favor of the continued flow of new private investments to the suburbs.

Figure 20–3   Boarded up store fronts and dingy strip commercial development are visible evidence of economic malaise in central and neighborhood business districts in all parts of the country.

Some mitigating factors   There is evidence of a forthcoming alleviation of some —even many—of the forces that adversely affect the central city economy. In and of themselves these changes will not turn the decline around, but they are potentially positive factors in a predominantly negative milieu. The heavy postwar migrations of low skilled and disadvantaged populations to central cities has been sharply reduced. Cities continue to play their historic role as staging areas for the upwardly mobile, but the pressures have lessened. There is a rising demand for central city housing on the part of middle income and upper income families, including some movement back from the suburbs into the central city. Increasing numbers of childless, "double breadwinner" households with large discretionary incomes are seeking convenient close-in living quarters rather than suburban housing, thereby adding strength to inner city markets.

Major physical improvements made in central cities as a result of strong civic and governmental efforts in recent years are beginning to pay off (for example, in new employment and jobs created by convention centers and other public facilities and by large scale downtown revitalization). Hundreds of neighborhood groups are supporting conservation and rehabilitation efforts that bring stability to many areas.

Some even longer-run trends also appear to be in the offing. Considerations of energy shortages, environmental protection, and quality of life are generating new forces in support of closer-in development and restrictions on sprawl patterns. The impact of high birthrates following World War II, which poured unprecedented levels of new entrants into the labor force and contributed heavily to teenage unemployment in central cities, is beginning to dissipate. And there is a new recognition at the national level that the problems of cities must be dealt with more effectively. There has even been the specific call to mobilize new efforts—national and local, public and private—to strengthen the economic base within the municipal boundary lines.

The problems of the city economy remain, however, and the task of dealing effectively with the complex forces involved has scarcely begun.

The need for competitiveness   From the standpoint of economic functions, the central city economic development problem is essentially one of inability to compete effectively enough for the private investment and entrepreneurial dollar. The following question is often raised: What are the functions of tightly bounded, built-up central city areas in face of the exploding pattern of metropolitan development since World War II? The answer is, of course, that the city offers and accommodates all of the same land uses that are found in the suburbs. However, for most of these uses there are vastly different market orientations.

The practical problem is how to attract the necessary private investments and reinvestments in response to these different markets within the city. This has to be done in face of both "pull" and "push" factors that have so adversely affected the competitiveness of the city economy in the past. Spurred by postwar affluence, America has built thousands of "new cities" in the metropolitan suburbs since World War II. Entirely new urban economic structures with a full depth and variety of activities have been formed outside the boundary lines of the "old" central city. The nature and the level of activities inside those boundary lines have been sharply affected.

Some city functions (such as those in the central business district) are both highly specialized and unique, and thus command strong investor interest even in the face of suburban competition. Most functions, however, find it difficult to compete with outward growth for the investment dollar. The markets for many central city uses reflect lower levels of consumer affluence. Because central cities are older and are substantially built, there are difficulties of land assembly and of higher costs of development. Obsolescence and deterioration produce negative environmental conditions in many cases, as do the problems of maintaining quality schools and security. Most of the city's development potential, therefore, requires major improvements and other types of public action before competitive investments are possible. As a result of these conditions, decisive public intervention is required to generate the legitimate investor interest that is necessary to maintain the economies of most cities.

Issues of geopolitics

Strong city action poses difficult political problems within the city, as action involves major outlays of public money. Action calls for a clear involvement of the municipal corporation—the city government itself—in the economic development process. It also calls for a new level of public–private cooperation in helping to create the conditions under which the private economy can flourish within the city.

The basic issues are essentially those of geopolitics. These issues clearly have both spatial (physical) and political implications. To reiterate what has been said before, the solution to most urban problems will depend on what happens—or does not happen—to the economies inside the political boundaries of the central city. The focus is on the structure of the *city economy*, about which far too little is known.

Figure 20–4   This engraving from the 1880s shows South Dearborn Street, Chicago, when it was the developing center for the printing industry. The building in the background with the clock tower is the Dearborn Street Railroad Station. By the 1970s almost all of the composition, printing, and binding companies had moved to the suburbs to exploit the technology that demanded horizontal plant layout and other changes described in this chapter and in Chapter 16.

For the short-run and intermediate futures, there are limited prospects of major changes taking place in city boundary lines (except through annexation, where annexation is possible), which would improve the capacities of the municipal corporation to deal more effectively with economic development problems. The central city must continue to operate within a restricted land area. Nor is there much short-term hope that new metropolitan arrangements will be made for sharing the problems of economic development on a regional basis. There is a possibility—but only a limited one—that some of the city's economic problems, particularly those of structural unemployment, might be partly alleviated by developments in the suburbs. For example, more unemployed or underemployed city residents might improve their opportunities by moving to the suburbs or commuting to suburban jobs. None of these metropolitan solutions appears to offer much immediate promise, however. Therefore, unless vigorous steps are taken to improve the productivity of the economy within the city limits, the deterioration of that economy is likely to continue.

The failure of past efforts

Unfortunately, past efforts to deal with urban economic problems through federal aid to the cities have been singularly ineffective. Billions of public dollars have been poured into central cities, but, as has been stated earlier, the outflow of private investment has continued and even accelerated. Except in specialized cases, the leverage of public dollars on private investments and reinvestments within the central cities has been limited. The dynamic factors of suburban growth and the massive inflow of lower income and disadvantaged populations into central cities have created forces that have eroded the viability of central city economies. In the face of these forces, most federal efforts to supplement local redevelopment programs have been primarily holding actions on behalf of those in need.

The three major federal programs to help cities with their redevelopment— slum clearance (housing), urban renewal, and Model Cities—had little fundamental effect on the basic economy of the city. The early slum clearance programs helped eliminate many of the most seriously deteriorated neighborhoods, replacing poor housing with better housing (mostly for low income populations). The program had little effect, however, on creating conditions more favorable to broad economic investment. Urban renewal had a much greater focus on economic development—the most successful projects were in and around central business districts, where spectacular results were achieved in many cities. However, although major new private investments were created they were largely limited in their geographic and demographic impacts. The Model Cities program reached much more deeply into the neighborhood structure of the central cities and involved widespread training and participatory processes. Again, however, the basic economic impact was minimal. The leverage on new private investment and reinvestment—both for the retention of existing economic activities and the creation of new ones—was not great.

During the years when these large scale categorical programs were operated by the federal government in central cities, the central city economies continued to deteriorate. The number of business enterprises in the city continued to decline. Industrial buildings became vacant. Former railroad and utility lands were taken out of active use. Spectacular new "cities" were built in the suburbs in the form of housing, shopping centers, industrial parks, and community facilities.

It is a shocking fact that the basic economies of most central cities are less viable today than before the operations of the massive programs of federal assistance designed to help them. The forces were so great that the programs had little effect on the city's competitiveness for the private dollar.

Two stages of policy changes

It would appear that the country has been going through a period of profound transition in its perceptions of the problems of cities. At the end of the 1970s there were two stages to this transition, one well under way and the other apparently in the offing.

The first stage: changes in federal grants   The first stage of this policy transition took place in the early 1970s when it became clear (on a bipartisan basis in Washington) that solutions to urban problems called for greatly increased initiatives at the local level. There was a massive shift in the nature of federal assistance. Most federal categorical grant programs were dismantled and replaced by systems of general and special revenue sharing. To many cynics, this shift appeared to be a callous federal indifference to the insoluble problems of cities. To others, however, it represented realistic recognition of the fact that the creation of conditions favorable to private investment activity in the cities had to be largely a local responsibility, aided and supported by federal funds. The major element in this first stage of federal policy transition was the establishment of the Community Development Block Grant program (CDBG), administered by the U.S. Department of Housing and Urban Development.

The CDBG approach has had profound implications for local government policymakers. In deploying block grants, local elected officials make difficult decisions involving consideration of the cost-effectiveness of the public expenditures. Basic questions of performance in generating jobs and investments are brought to the local political arena. By the end of the 1970s joint public–private collaboration in economic development enterprises had begun, and attention was being given to the leveraging of private investments with public dollars. There were moves toward incentives and supports, along with public expenditures, that might cause private dollars to flow back into the city.

Cities were reorganizing their staff structures to more effectively define community development and relate it to management, planning, budgeting, and programming. The CDBG process has generated extensive neighborhood and citizen participation activity. Out of this process, some new perceptions of economic development, among other goals, are emerging.

The second stage: economic rebuilding within city boundaries The first stage of policy change, discussed above, has been merely the prelude to a much more definitive set of efforts to reach the fundamental issue of central city economic development. It is true that the new institutional capacities are being built up at the local level to bring the public sector more directly behind private efforts in job creation and investment. What has not yet been done is to put these local efforts solidly behind the rebuilding of the economy within the city boundary lines per se. Until the necessity for doing this is fully recognized and the process is implemented, the leverage of public efforts on private activities and investments within the city will continue to be limited, even minimal.

This is the second stage of the policy transition, and it appears to be developing in the making of federal urban policy. This policy, still in the formative stage, is aimed at making the cities work as economically viable entities. The policy follows naturally and essentially from the earlier shift in emphasis toward local responsibility. This new perception recognizes the utter impossibility of dealing with urban problems outside the context of an economic base that can create jobs, investments, and tax base within the arbitrary boundary lines that separate the central city from the remainder of the metropolitan area.

The need for this second stage of policy transition has been brought into sharp focus by several obvious national realities. One is the persistence of structural unemployment, that hard core unemployment (affecting primarily the large teenage group and the older workers) which has substantially failed to respond to massively funded national programs. The great bulk of this structural unemployment is in the cities, and it is in the cities that it will be solved.

Another reality is the increasingly fragile fiscal position of major central cities throughout the country. The financial health of municipal corporations depends on the productivity of the economy, because the city governments depend on the economy for much of their tax support. Now the municipal corporations must help to sustain these economies. A third reality is the continued existence of poverty and the closely related problems of crime and insecurity. A fourth reality is the continued widespread shortage of decent housing for lower income city residents.

There has also been some current recognition of the fact that the chronic underproductivity of city economies is limiting the growth of the gross national product and possibly also contributing to the problem of "stagflation." The persistence of unemployment in the face of high levels of overall economic activity can be partly explained by the structural employment of the resident work force. Underuse of city land and buildings, as well as labor force, undoubtedly represents a less-than-optimal use of national resources. It puts a heavy drain on the public treasury, which must make up for the absence of revenues generated by production.

The city and urban economics

The emergence of these new perceptions of the role of the city economy in dealing with the nation's urban problems has not been accompanied by any widespread acceptance by either the practical policymakers (public or private) or the academic economics profession. The logic of revenue sharing and of more local responsibility for deploying public economic development funds has certainly been accepted; the failures of previous "top-down" efforts to stem the deterioration of the city's economic and fiscal base have been widely recognized. But the rationale for an aggressive program to stabilize the economy within the arbitrary city limits—to make this economy competitive with the rest of the metropolitan economy in the face of the seemingly overwhelming push and pull factors adversely affecting central city investments—has not been established. This is the major issue that must be addressed by both national and local policymakers.

The economy of cities has been generally perceived by both practitioners and academics as the urban economy, which, for all practical purposes, is metropolitan in scope. Highly sophisticated analyses of these "metroeconomies" have clearly established the intricate patterns of interrelationships among the functions of these operating systems. The workings, rises and falls, determinants, and policy processes involved in these metropolitan systems have been studied in great detail. The factors that affect their growth and development trends, their sensitivity to macroeconomic national policies, their responsiveness to secular and cyclical influences, and their vulnerability to shifting technological, political, and demographic forces have been repeatedly identified and evaluated, as have their structures of internal behavior—for example, the interfunctional linkages, the multiplier effects of one set of activities upon another, the export–import balances, and the institutional arrangements. A new art and science of metroeconomics has emerged that identifies a range of independent systemic forces affecting both the micro decisions of the industrial firms and the macro decisions of national fiscal and monetary policy.

The weakness of this practical and academic knowledge of how these urban metroeconomics work, however, is its incapacity to deal in any effective way with the corrupting effects of the central city boundary lines on overall metropolitan economic processes. The learned academic treatises have been almost oblivious to the fact that the mere existence of that boundary line introduces factors that completely disrupt the operations of the metroeconomy as a coherent and logically interrelated system. The facts are so obvious as to be startling. Failure to recognize these facts—on the part of the practical policymakers as well as the academicians—has been at the root of countless misdirected efforts to deal with the problems of cities.

The urban or metroeconomy can be easily and neatly described in terms of the sensitive interrelationships of conventional economics. Resources are allocated so as to obtain optimum returns. Advantage is taken of the external economies of conglomerate functions. Neat divisions of labor characterize the physical patterns of economic activity. "Basic" or export activities produce "nonbasic" or service activities according to formula. Import substitutions or replacements provide the dynamics of growth. The multiplier effect of strategic investments is felt throughout the economy. Creativity is achieved through specialized research and development inputs or as bright entrepreneurs take advantage of accumulated services, resources, markets, and other supports to set "incubator" industries into motion—and so on. As described, the metroeconomy represents the major part of the United States economy. Because of its intimate connections with the decentralized decision-making apparatus in the federal system it has a certain independence of its own. It is, indeed, not fully sensitive

---

New spatial patterns What can we say about the *process* of getting to a new spatial pattern? . . . Surely some neighborhoods *are* stronger than others. And the inexorable arithmetic is such that we can't hold them all. The total number is going down. . . .

If we cannot hold them all, I would much rather speed up the depopulation in some places and stop it dead in its tracks in others than to let it slowly gather momentum in both sets of places. It is too easy to set in motion a process of cumulative deterioration. . . . Are the suburbanites going to move back in? No, not for a long time. So we really need to transfer populations to round out the strategy. . . .

I favor user charges . . . to make people pay the costs they impose on society for the way they choose to live, the way they choose to move about the city, by bus or car. I think we need to discipline city residents, moving them away from self-indulgent and toward social-serving life-styles. . . . But, there also has to be a set of prices which says to people, in this new age of cities: Be responsible for the things you do that make life difficult for society. Reward citizens for economizing on society's resources by taking the bus, by being willing to cluster, by walking to work.

Source: Excerpted from Wilbur Thompson, untitled paper presented at the Conference on Managing Mature Cities, sponsored by the city of Cincinnati and the Charles F. Kettering Foundation, Cincinnati, Ohio, 9–10 June 1977.

---

to the macroeconomic policies of the federal government (the local power to thwart federal objectives on key economic and political issues, of course, is a well-known political phenomenon).

The fatal flaw What is missing in this definition of the theory and practice of urban economics is recognition of the fact that the central city segment does not function as a fully effective part of the overall system. The results of this are unemployment in the face of regional growth, poverty in the face of regional affluence, underuse of resources in the face of potential demand, underserved consumers in the face of massive distribution systems, municipal fiscal collapse in the face of rising regional wealth—in short, backwater economies separated out of massive urban complexes.

The difficulty is that the evidence of the above conditions—which is universally acknowledged—does not seem to be given any substantial credence in economic policy. The problems of the backwater economies are not seen as amenable to economic solutions: poverty, lack of training, obsolescence, high costs, insecurity, inadequate public services, congestion, pollution, and welfare dependence are not naturally dealt with by the free operation of market forces and hence they are ignored. The more they are ignored, the worse they get; the worse they get, the less capacity there is available to the city (that is, the municipal corporation) for removing the adverse factors and creating the conditions in which the private market might effectively operate.

It can be argued—and it is argued—that the complex of economic activities carried on within the physical limits of central cities does not constitute an economy. It does not have all of the interrelated, reciprocating mechanisms of the urban economy neatly put into metropolitan terms. It is not even a definable subeconomy with specialized functions and divisions of labor (except in the central business district and other limited sectors). From the standpoint of conventional definitions, the city is a no-man's-land with the following features:

1. Corridors of vacant commercial space
2. Rundown, inefficient neighborhood commercial districts
3. Acres of unused or underused "industrial" (for example utility or railroad) land
4. Unoccupied loft-type factories and warehouses
5. Inadequately maintained housing structures
6. Decaying docks and piers
7. Untrained, often unwilling, manpower
8. Abandoned property
9. Public acquisitions of tax delinquent properties.

The list can go on. To it can be added the problems that create the adverse conditions that produce the lack of private investment. These include the familiar litany: poor schools, mediocre public services, high taxes, restrictive codes, difficulties of land assembly, building costs, crime and insecurity, racial tension, air pollution, congestion, obsolescence. How can economists, either the practicing variety or the academicians, take such matters into account?

The economies of most cities are therefore in a shambles. This is true whether the metropolitan regions are growing or are not growing. At the city limit line there is a substantial breakdown of the intricate fabric of interrelationships that characterizes the functioning urban economy. Until and unless massive efforts are made in public and private channels and in the use of federal, state, and local resources to integrate central city economies effectively into the metroeconomic system, the central city economies will continue to deteriorate—as will the fiscal capacities of central city governments, to say nothing of the economic and social status of the city's residents.

The countercontention It is the contention of this chapter that such an integration—or rather reintegration—of the central city economy into the metropolitan economy is possible. So also was it apparently the contention of the national government during the late 1970s that singled out the viability of the central city economy as the key element in dealing with urban problems.

This contention carries with it no complacent or simplistic claim that the central city will—or "should"—regain its former status in the broader urban economy. There is no denying the validity of the pull factors in the operation of the free market in suburban expansion; there is also no denying the devastating effects of the negative push factors of central city disabilities, which make free market decisions to operate in behalf of central city investments and activities extremely difficult (if not impossible) to make. There are, however, immense resources that can be mobilized to stem the decline of—and provide stability for—the central city economic base.

The prospects that this second stage of national policy transition with respect to urban policies will succeed will depend largely on actions that are taken locally. The significant aspect of the changing attitude at the national level is the recognition that the spatial (the physical) aspects of the problem are important. It is what takes place within the central city limits that counts. Politically, it is a tremendously difficult and complex perception to implement. It depends, as noted above, on the kinds of responses that are forthcoming from the public and private leadership of the central cities themselves.

There have, of course, been some precedents in national policy over the past half century involving special efforts in behalf of particular geographic areas that were economically depressed. A number of programs in the 1930s dealt with sections of the country where the economies had become incapable of supporting the population. In more recent years there have been special programs targeted on depressed areas such as Appalachia and various other rural regions. Until fairly recent times, however, there has been no recognition that central cities—landlocked enclaves with heavy chronic burdens of unemployment, underproductivity, massive social dependency, and limited fiscal capacities—call for the same concentrated program targeting. The hope since the late 1940s has been that general prosperity, plus massive doses of federal funds flowing into local coffers, would be enough to bring the central economies along. It has not worked.

Some technical caveats

The foregoing description of central city economics obviously has elements of oversimplification and exaggeration. Both, perhaps, have been necessary to making key points forcefully. Many other relevant factors could obviously be brought under discussion. Two might be particularly noted.

First, one of the major factors in the overall economic slowdown in the larger metropolitan regions in the United States is the leveling off in the nation's manufacturing sector. There is a long-run flattening in the growth curve in manufacturing employment. For technological and other reasons there have also been substantial geographical shifts in the location of manufacturing establishments. As a result, manufacturing employment in the older metropolitan areas—the northeastern manufacturing belt, the Mid-Atlantic corridor, and the Midwest—has been declining. Within most of these metropolitan areas the heaviest declines have been within the central cities. In the suburban parts of some of the largest of the older metropolitan areas the overall level of factory employment has remained fairly stable and in some instances has shown some increases.

This fundamental change in the structure of the national economy has had a profound impact on the economies of many central cities. No programs of economic development could have done much to alter the trend of overall shrinkage in factory employment. It should be noted, however, that the vitality of manufacturing in the United States economic process is by no means undergoing a degree of deterioration represented by the overall slowdown in employment. Thousands of new manufacturing plants open each year, even as other thousands close. Manufacturing is still a very dynamic element in the economy, particularly in urban areas where innovations are most possible.

Second, another fundamental structural change in the United States economy is the increasing importance of service producing as against goods producing industries. This is, of course, also reflected in part in the manufacturing phenomenon noted above. A part of the new service employment expansion is, of course, related to local consumer populations. It has therefore been inevitable that the great bulk of the increases have taken place in the suburbs, where population has expanded.

Here, again, is a deep-seated structural factor which could not have been obviated by policies in behalf of the central city, but, along with the factory employment factor, it must be taken into account in evaluating the economic development prospects of the central city.

B: Economic development: the planning response

Economic development has become a planning and local government buzzword. To some cities it is an activity out of the blue—a planning fad that will pass with the next federal budget. To others it is recognition of an issue that only a few years ago was considered the province primarily of the Chamber of Commerce, with public involvement regarded as a questionable activity for local government. To small towns it is the boosterism and civic promotion of industrial development that preceded small town revival. To Sunbelt cities it is the growth outburst that resulted from their industrial development efforts and the interregional population shifts that characterized the 1970s. And to declining central cities, staggering under tax base decline and concentrated unemployment, it is a fiscal and political necessity.

Planning agencies are involved in such economic development efforts as gathering data, preparing economic analyses, coordinating local government departments, and integrating federal community development, economic development, and manpower funds. In growing communities with sound tax bases, population growth, and low unemployment among all population groups, environmental and development control issues may justly occupy the priority positions on the public agenda. Where unemployment, disinvestment, and declining population and tax bases are the problems of the day, economic revitalization and the encouragement of development must become the planning agency's top priority.

Federal interest in economic development is, of course, providing much impetus for local action. The Economic Development Administration (EDA) within the U.S. Department of Commerce has shifted to a more urban orientation after years of focusing on regional development. (Its rural and regional programs continue, however.) Figure 20–5 summarizes two major EDA programs with respect to planning requirements.

National urban policy increasingly emphasizes economic development. Joint and cooperative demonstration projects of EDA, the U.S. Department of Housing and Urban Development (HUD), and the U.S. Department of Labor have shown how federal resources can be closely coordinated with local government and private efforts. There is an increasing federal desire that Comprehensive Employment and Training Act (CETA) programs lead to permanent jobs in the private sector rather than to continued public employment. The 1977 amendments to the Housing and Community Development Act also broadened the eligibility of economic development projects for funding under the Community Development Block Grant program (CDBG), and the HUD Urban Development Action Grant program (UDAG) was instituted to provide additional aid to distressed cities.

In these federal programs the major goal is to increase both local job opportunities and the tax base in those communities suffering from high unemployment and declining or weakening private investment. In large measure this reflects an underlying premise that urban problems, housing problems, social and welfare case load problems, and fiscal problems all relate to the lack of jobs and resulting lack of income.

Taking local public action to increase economic activity within city boundaries is considered feasible and potentially effective. Energy costs for transportation of goods are considered by some observers to favor central city locations with better railroad facilities. Suburban land costs and tax rates are rising. Existing industrial areas that previously did not have space for expansion are now partly vacant. Industries that need to stay in Snowbelt cities and use natural gas can sometimes get it only by staying at their present sites, because of moratoria on new hookups. Retail and service sector growth, including hotels, retailing, banking, and insurance, still favor central locations, because of their interdependency and also to assure access to large regional markets and the labor pool. All of these factors now favor and make feasible governmental action to encourage economic development.

The objectives of local public action in economic development are to remove governmental impediments; to assist in providing and improving land and services and to provide public financial aid or incentives to make projects economically feasible and competitive; to market or promote the locality; and to improve the area's reputation, general climate, and receptivity to business. This portion of the chapter provides an introduction to economic development as a planning function.

Concepts of economic development planning

While economic development in the late 1970s and the 1980s resembles the industrial development and central business district (CBD) renewal of the 1960s, in certain ways there are very significant differences. Some activities reflect the experience and failures of past efforts: government has not, for the most part, become involved in expensive speculative ventures such as massive clearance projects without a firm commitment from the private sector. The emphasis has shifted from bricks and mortar to jobs, coordination, private sector roles, and the facilitating of private investment. The most important difference has been the explicit recognition that local government has an important, legitimate role in effecting its economic destiny.

With a new interest a new jargon has emerged. In a way, this jargon describes the style and the process of current economic development. The concepts are not new for the most part, but new words have replaced old terms such as intergovernmental coordination and cooperation, synergy, concentration of resources, and mobilization of resources just as surely as CDBG replaced Neighborhood Development Programs and Model Neighborhoods. Some of the more important of these terms and concepts are discussed below.

Leverage In economic development the principle of leverage is simply that public funds are used to encourage private investment of an equal or greater amount. The public sector exercises leverage when it invests a small amount of money, perhaps as an interest free or low interest loan, in a project that would otherwise not be undertaken. In a Wilmington, Delaware, hotel project that received a UDAG, for example, the city used these federal funds to take a $1.9 million second mortgage, with flexible pay-back provisions tied to the cash flow of the hotel. Private resources put up $7.3 million. The pay-back flexibility provided by public participation was important for financial feasibility. Nearly 200 jobs were created.

In housing rehabilitation financing, a program that provides interest subsidies through banks to encourage bank lending for rehabilitation would be considered "leveraged," since it facilitates private investment. An alternative often proposed for use of public funds is the revolving loan pool. This has the advantage that much of the initial capital (less any defaults) is eventually returned for reuse. Unless structured to be used in conjunction with significant private funds —such as in a second mortgage—it will not achieve significant leverage.

Typically, leveraging involves the use of public funds to reduce private risk or costs to a level that makes a project financially feasible. There are many types of costs that may be sensitive to portionately small infusions of public funds and will thus make a project feasible. For example, if the public pays for public improvements that would normally be paid for by a private investor in order to bring down site development or land costs for an in-city industrial plant expansion to a level competitive with the costs of land elsewhere or the costs of a move, the city will have leveraged its capital investment. In many of the early UDAG projects it was common for cities to request UDAG funds to defray public improvements such as street improvements, sewer and water improvements, and walk systems, to fulfill the public part of an improvement or development project.

Under the concept of leveraging, however, public investments are not made

Figure 20–5
Components of the
Overall Economic
Development Program
and the Comprehensive
Economic Development
Strategy.

To qualify for a variety of federal economic development aids, localities must prepare plans and reports according to federal regulations. Consequently, most local planning work frequently is conducted according to an outline of required components. By the late 1970s the Economic Development Administration (EDA) of the U.S. Department of Commerce required localities to prepare an Overall Economic Development Program (OEDP) and a Comprehensive Economic Development Strategy (CEDS).

The OEDP
The initial OEDP is a document that should provide a concise and accurate summary of a locality's geography, population, labor force, natural and man-made resources, and economic and social activities. The OEDP must examine development opportunities and problems, including the activities of agencies and organizations active in economic development activities, and provide a realistic development and work program that is aimed at: promoting the area's economic progress, improving community facilities and services, and providing for a continuing planning and development program. The OEDP must be updated annually with progress reports and, from time to time, with a completely revised OEDP.

The CEDS
By 1978 a more detailed planning process—the Comprehensive Economic Development Strategy—was required. Federal officials felt that the CEDS served as a bridge between two traditional functions—planning and implementation. The major segments of a CEDS document are as follows:

1.   A description and assessment of an area's economy must be set forth, including describing the export base, leading sectors of the economy, labor force characteristics, including minorities, and capital availability. In addition, data must be presented on out-migration, bankruptcy rates, substandard and vacant commercial and industrial properties, population loss, and unemployment and underemployment. Then the area's opportunities must be identified, including human, financial, institutional, natural, and infrastructure resources and capacities. An assessment of past actions in both private and public sectors must be made.

2.   Economic development goals must be identified and must be realistic, specific, and in priority order. It is necessary, for example, to identify target groups and specify employment characteristics, such as youth, minorities, and those displaced by technological change. Access to jobs must be considered. Goals concerning business retention, business expansion, and strengthening both the tax base and the community infrastructure must be identified.

3.   Local institutional resources, both existing and potential, must be identified. These include development agencies, incorporations, community organizations, and the private sector. Financial resources such as federal, state, local, and private funds must be specified. Finally, specific program tools—such as land banking and revolving loan funds—must be identified.

4.   Policy development for an investment strategy requires an analysis of past economic policies and a statement of current priorities.

5.   Policy priorities must be set. Policies could relate to such areas as industrial retention or expansion, community business revitalization, strip commercial revitalization, promotion of the central business district, and assistance to community development corporations.

6.   Program activities that will implement policy priorities must be identified. These might include industrial park development, tourism development, and minority business assistance programs. The criteria for evaluation also need to be developed to determine such measures as how much private investment may be generated by public investment, the number of jobs saved or created, and how the tax base may be increased.

7.   Specific projects should be identified. For each project there should be details as to timing, costs, source of funding, and justification.

8.   The document should also contain descriptions for administrative coordination and management. These include relationships between public and private sectors and how the various federal programs relate to each other within the particular area.

9. The locality must demonstrate a commitment to the development strategy by such measures as endorsement by the local legislative body, statements of commitment by elected officials and business organizations, local budgetary commitments, and submissions to other federal agencies for program funds to carry out the economic development plans.

Local government concern with economic development—particularly in Snowbelt cities coping with larger national forces of interregional shifts—has grown as these national policies have emerged. This concern is intimately related to cities' needs in three areas: (1) jurisdictional or governmental needs to protect the local tax base and fiscal resources in the face of continued fragmentation of the metropolitan tax base and continued demands to provide service to both low income and heavy daytime populations; (2) social needs that can be met only by more jobs and income for selected segments of the population (of greatest concern is minority youth with unemployment rates up to eight times national averages; there is growing worry that they may never recover occupationally or economically from their inability to obtain entry level opportunities as teenagers); (3) conservation needs to encourage reuse of the existing infrastructure and buildings in cities and to minimize transportation costs and energy use.

Figure 20–5 (continued).

speculatively. Firm commitments are desirable for significant public expenditures and in UDAGs they are required.

Linkage *Linkage* used to be called *intergovernmental* and *interagency coordination* and *cooperation*. Several federal agencies now play key roles in local economic development; these include Commerce, HUD, Labor, and, in some communities with community development corporations, the Community Services Administration of the U.S. Department of Health, Education, and Welfare. Virtually all states are involved in coordinated economic planning under EDA's 302 programs, and all states have some kind of business or economic development agency. Within local government and metropolitan agencies, the public works departments, transportation agencies, sewerage and water districts, port authorities, manpower programs, and capital budget processes may all be involved. In addition, state and federal environmental agencies' pollution control regulations may be critical limitations for some projects.

Linkage is coordinating the activities of all these actors to achieve a common goal. Everyone's resources are needed, and their various powers and energies need to be pointed in the same direction.

Packaging Packaging is a relatively familiar term whose meaning has not changed. It still refers to piecing together the financing, approvals, and other elements necessary to make a project viable and get it started. Someone must bring together the paperwork, agreements, and approvals for zoning, land, private equity, private loans, venture capital, public loans, loan guarantees, and public capital improvements so that a project can commence.

Partnership Partnership refers to putting together all the appropriate public sector and private sector people and organizations. A large part of the process of economic development really involves developing these public–private relationships. As with other ventures, it is necessary first to bring all of the appropriate people together: mayors, managers, planners, the Chamber of Commerce, major corporate heads, community leaders, and, especially, bankers.

The public–private partnership may be formal or informal. One type of partnership is the quasi-public local development corporation that is created to be a funnel for public funds. For example, the Philadelphia Industrial Development Corporation and its companion Citywide Economic Development Corporation (for neighborhoods) are bodies operating under contracts with the city that define the scope of their activities and their uses of public funds. Many cities will not need to develop formal vehicles for public–private cooperation. The specific attributes of local development activities and local powers should be fully explored before such a vehicle is established.

Targeting   Sufficient resources must be committed to one problem in one place to attain a critical mass. For example, if a city is trying to provide industrial lands to compete with lower land costs in the suburbs, it would not be wise to make sewer and street access improvements at twenty separate industrial locations around the city. Instead, the funds should be invested in a few locations to provide land assembly of vacant parcels, sewers, highway access, etc.

These concepts are not, of course, unique to economic development. The CDBG program requires the use of the same concepts and skills by local government. The purpose of such concepts is to coordinate the actions of a confusing array of actual and possible participants.

For planners, an additional concern is often to coordinate those actions into a coherent overall strategy that is based on sound analysis (about which more will be said). While this is a laudable objective, it can be carried too far. There are limits to economic analysis and what it can tell about constraints and potentials. At times it may be better to use an entrepreneurial approach and identify some possibilities on the basis of a general understanding of the local economy, evaluate their feasibility, and then proceed. Not all possible projects will be carried out in a short time frame. In many cases, what is needed most to get a comprehensive program off the ground is one successful and completed project.

One speaker at a planning conference in the late 1970s summarized the basic process of economic development as follows:

1. Identify who is involved in your community—the dozen people who have to be involved at both the policy level and the technical level: the mayor, the finance director, the city council, the utilities, the Chamber of Commerce, planning, zoning, etc.
2. Assess the economic development climate and issues emphasizing taxation, development regulations, and trends in the economy itself
3. Identify constraints and barriers, whether they are physical conditions, locational constraints, or important other community values that will not be compromised
4. Identify strong points such as location, rail facilities, water supply, etc.
5. Identify alternative program possibilities such as downtown projects, a new industrial park, helping existing firms expand, or other projects that are of interest to the key people
6. Set priorities, evaluate feasibility, and select a first project (and do not forget existing firms)
7. Do a demonstration project identifying federal and state funds and carry it through to implementation (as part of the planning process)
8. Keep the process ongoing, identifying new issues and prospects as they emerge and tackling new projects as the resources and time are available.[4]

The basic strategies of economic development planning

The basic strategies for local economic development action flow from the realities of business location decisions, the need to strengthen the local tax base, and the objective of increasing jobs for selected groups.

One basic strategy chosen by mature cities is the retention of existing industry, coupled with retail/convention/hotel projects for downtown and neighborhood commercial development. The objective is to retain income and tax base within the jurisdiction and provide entry level jobs in the private sector for the critical unemployed group—minority youth. Both the neighborhood commercial efforts and the hotels are believed to provide those entry level jobs.

Another strategy, the idea of promoting or attracting new industry from outside the city, has not been abandoned but has been given a much lower priority. On one hand, attraction is a form of piracy that may hurt other cities; on the other hand, the older central cities are the target of the attraction efforts of the suburbs, small towns, and Sunbelt cities. Experience suggests at this point that the most productive efforts may well be actions to retain existing firms and foster their expansion within the city. It is estimated that 80 percent to 90 percent of job growth, at least in the older cities, will come from retained expansion.

The third major strategy is to foster entrepreneurship. This has been largely the province of the Small Business Administration of the U.S. Department of Commerce (SBA) and the Community Services Administration of the U.S. Department of Health, Education, and Welfare, working with private business and with community development corporations. Small businesses are always high risk ventures, but this is still a fruitful, if difficult, option in some cases. In addition, small new ventures provide a good reuse for the kinds of vacant industrial structures found in many cities.

For most communities the principal option is to try to retain existing industry, attempt to discover which firms and industries have the greatest potential for expansion, and adapt public policies and efforts to help meet their needs.

Programs and techniques

Several programs and techniques used in local economic development efforts are discussed below. Most are geared to retaining business and industry.

Informal assistance City government can work with existing (or prospective) firms to ascertain their needs and to assist them in meeting these needs. These actions may involve such activities as clearing up immediate problems with governmental agencies and streamlining certain governmental procedures. This kind of effort is part of improving the business climate and the spirit of cooperation between business and government.

Land banking Land banking is a program intended to preserve and provide industrial space in the city. Typically, a program involves developing a fully served industrial park facility under city ownership.

Land banking can also involve simply acquiring and holding blocks of land until there is a development proposal, at which time services can be installed as appropriate.

Land banking sites can provide a range of types of industrial locations ranging from suburban type facilities to single buildings renovated and operated as "vertical industrial parks."

The city is likely to provide the land to business firms at less than market value or city cost in order to compete with the suburbs. The cost differential may be funded either by actual cash funding of the land banking/assembly program or by holding the land over time. When land is assembled and held, inflation in land values may permit an effective writedown without cash participation by the city. The city is attempting, through this type of program, to provide industrial land directly competitive with suburbs or other locations in cost and convenience. It is a jurisdictional strategy: the city is not as concerned with who is employed as with capturing the firm involved as tax base. Milwaukee and Philadelphia have well-developed and operating land banking programs.

Industrial redevelopment Industrial redevelopment programs, or rehabilitation programs, attempt to improve existing industrial areas. These areas have often lost their utility to industrial firms because of traffic congestion, changes in shipping practices (for example, from railroad to truck), lack of room for expansion owing to fragmented land and building ownership, and old and/or deteriorated sewers or other public infrastructure. Industrial redevelopment and rehabilitation programs use a combination of CDBG, EDA, and local funds to correct physical deficiencies, to help assemble land for expansion, and to solve various other problems. Milwaukee initiated an industrial redevelopment project for an older area adjacent to the central business district (CBD). Included in the project are access improvement from an adjacent freeway and a recycling facility for city solid waste.

CBD retail/hotel/office projects Central business district projects are seen by many as the "possible dream" in urban economic development. CBD office space and employment grew, even in many declining cities, in the 1970s, offsetting in part the loss of manufacturing jobs. At the same time, however, retail dominance of CBDs was severely eroded by suburban shopping centers. Many cities established downtown convention centers in an effort to attract convention business. In a number of cases convention centers were not supported by adequate hotel space.

CBD projects might contribute to city economic development in several ways. First, retaining retail sales within the city, as has been mentioned, is important to the tax base. Second, the hotel/convention centers, *if successful,* bring in extra income from outside the city and thus contribute to an overall increase in income to the city. Third, both retail and hotel/convention enterprises provide a source of entry level jobs for youth. It is hoped, of course, that these jobs do not become dead ends but instead provide basic job experience and so serve as a stepping-stone. In addition, continued office expansion offers a range of job opportunities, some at entry levels but many requiring more advanced skills. These skills can be provided through manpower programs.

Some neighborhood groups charge that CBD projects are undertaken at the expense of neighborhood improvements, particularly under UDAG. The argument is not without merit and echoes the sentiments of the latter years of urban renewal when pressure was brought to end CBD projects and use all funds in residential areas. CBD projects can be a windfall for elements of the business community. On the other hand, they provide job opportunities to a group with critical job needs and they contribute to fiscal health—a precondition to continuing to help the neighborhoods. CBD projects should be developed and evaluated against these criteria.

The public role may extend only to providing public improvements by usual means or it may involve use of public funds to defray costs of land assembly, street realignment, malls, landscaping, new sewers, or financial aid to private projects. These improvements are generally now made with private commitments to proceed, however, and not on the speculative basis of many past CBD renewal projects involving land acquisition and clearance. The resources available to communities, in addition to normal measures, include tax increment financing, local development corporations, CDBG funds, EDA funds, and UDAGs.

Neighborhood commercial programs Neighborhood commercial revitalization is of economic benefit in several ways. It is another retention type of strategy and is primarily oriented toward keeping retail sales and retail facilities within the jurisdiction. It also provides excellent entry level jobs for youth.

The city can provide: public improvements such as parking, streets, sidewalks, and landscaping; public financial aid to small businesses (local, Small

Business Administration, or both); and physical remodeling plans and financing to enhance attractiveness. Technical help with marketing and merchandising or other management problems may also be arranged using sources available under SBA assistance programs. Help in physical redesign of store fronts may also be offered through planning departments or design teams. In addition, in some locations buildings have important historic or architectural characteristics that can be restored and used in marketing and merchandising the area.[5]

Common to most of these programs is the concentrated application of financial and public improvement tools. Hence, capital improvements programming, capital funding sources from state and federal governments, and a complex litany of special local financing tools (such as tax increment financing, local development corporations that permit public resources to assist private projects, and other mechanisms) are important to the program. In addition, if state law permits, tax incentives in such forms as negotiated reduced assessments, gradual phase-in of property taxes, and fixed term tax abatements may all be used.

Issues in planning for economic development

Several important issues have emerged (or remain) as more and more urban local governments have become concerned with economic development. A number of these are briefly examined below.

Analysis of risk and potential Undertaking an economic development program can be a costly venture, both politically and financially. In the past, when economic development was more narrowly defined as attracting new industry, it could involve substantial public expenditures for promotion, land purchase, and infrastructure. Often, there was little consideration of whether there was much real potential to attract industry, or of what kinds of industry might be attracted.

While the retention orientation of current urban efforts reduces risk somewhat, there are still unresolved planning and analysis issues. Which firms or types of firms have the greatest growth potential and can be retained in the long run given the factors in their locational preferences is an important question. The use of such analytic techniques as shift-share analysis and other regional science tools can help identify those economic sectors with the greatest local potential. A few cities are attempting to develop more rigorous and systematic ways of identifying potential.

For most communities, however, there is limited formal analysis of potentials and limitations. Basically, descriptive data are collected on existing labor force, industrial structure, physical conditions, unemployment, and education. The EDA's Overall Economic Development Programs (OEDPs) require analysis of potentials, but in many cases OEDPs tend to be "wish lists" of local goals rather than strategies for economic development. A 1977 OEDP for an urban county in a relatively sophisticated eastern state with good university resources nearby had a one page discussion of potentials that sounded strikingly similar to the list of economic virtues that any local booster group might produce: x million people within y hundred miles, and so on.

By the late 1970s considerable effort was under way at the federal level to improve the quality of this analysis (see Figure 20–5). Nevertheless, the analytical foundation of some local efforts still concerns some officials and scholars.

Project analysis Despite the difficulty of developing a highly analytical development strategy, communities can analyze the potential benefits of particular projects. This is, of course, a problem primarily when some significant local aid is to be given, for example, a tax abatement, a sewer extension, industrial revenue bonds, or the creation of a tax increment finance district. The local government should be certain that the project is economically sensible and feasible (that a firm will not go out of business after a year, for example) and that the local benefits over a reasonable time outweigh the costs.

The techniques used for this kind of analysis are fairly well established; cost–benefit analysis is the fundamental tool. But it appears that relatively few local governments make routine use of cost–benefit analysis in any formal way. In large part this is because of the political nature of many local decisions: if a large enough constituency wants a bridge or a park or whatever, they get a bridge or a park or whatever they want. Some incentives or aid will continue to be granted without adequate analysis, but, whenever possible, economic development projects should be subject to cost–benefit and feasibility analysis.

As an additional aid, fiscal impact analysis can be incorporated into cost–benefit analysis. Fiscal impact analysis is in some measure used as a tool to get private development projects to pay their own way in a relatively narrow sense —that is, in terms of local costs and revenues. Any project for which a public subsidy is being considered is not likely to meet that limited test in the short run. It may help to clarify whether the locality is committing itself to ongoing costs over and above the initial assistance, however.

Environmental quality In efforts to protect and improve the environment the federal and state governments have adopted various measures affecting both the operations of businesses and industry and the processing and design of development projects. Increasingly, questions are asked about the relationship between economic development activities and air and water quality regulations. The conflict among various environmental, economic, and political interest groups is to be expected. The courts, the legislatures, and the Congress will be dealing with these issues for years to come.

Can local involvement really make a difference? Serious questions have been raised as to whether, in fact, any level of local government involvement can make a significant difference in levels of job opportunity and economic well-being. Incentives become less effective as everyone else adopts them in order to maintain a competitive position. In effect, the stakes are raised each time. Longer-term population shifts and energy availability appear to have significant interregional implications for the location of economic activity. The growing markets are the South, the Southwest, and the West. Market-oriented firms will tend to shift their locations—or at least their distribution functions—to reflect this over time. And there may perhaps be some inherent efficiency in allowing shifts to occur and not intervening.

To a local government faced with a declining tax base and rising unemployment, however, the implied rationality of letting things go is not politically acceptable. Hence, the government is forced to make an effort regardless of whether there is uniform agreement on the extent of potential. And there are many who believe it is possible for local efforts to make a difference.

The effects of past low taxation and poor services in southern and southwestern states are beginning to be reduced by growth in these states. As growth occurs, services are increased and some of the competitive edge is cut. Unions are making inroads—or, in some cases, companies are trying to fight off unionization by voluntarily raising wages. Hence the labor climate and labor cost advantages to firms are being slowly reduced as development occurs. Little is yet known about energy availability and the costs and implications in the long run. In the short run energy considerations seem to be creating more interest in central city sites and sites served by rail. Land costs in suburban areas have also been rising, thereby improving the competitiveness of central city land.

What is perhaps most important is that years of taking the city's economic base for granted have led many older communities to develop unnecessary barriers to the expansion and retention of firms and to ignore the investment potential of public funds in helping to maintain the physical environment of industrial districts. Clearly, local government can remove these barriers if nothing else, and can make public investments, particularly where they are matched by the willingness of firms to make commitments.

The burden of coordination Contemporary economic development efforts are characterized by attempts to coordinate federal, local, and state resources to provide jobs and economic growth, with specific kinds of benefits. The manpower training programs, Community Development programs, EDA programs in eligible areas, and similar programs must all be coordinated with local and state programs. Various local programs must be coordinated with each other and with the interests of various local groups and constituencies, all wanting public funds.

Figure 20–6   Conflict among environmental, economic, and political interest groups is to be expected.

The load this creates for local government planning and development agencies is substantial. The planner becomes the grand coordinator, the analyst, the unifier. In many ways this is an awesome challenge. With our federal system and governmental fragmentation at the local and metropolitan level, it is a burden that will have to be carried.

C: Economic base studies:
elements, forecasting, fiscal impact, evaluation

Urban economics is in its early stages of development, but it has deep historical roots. Economists, philosophers, geographers, sociologists, and political scientists have long been concerned with the phenomena controlling the economic life of cities.

The conceptual and theoretical roots of urban economics are deeply ingrained in and are similar to the aggregate analysis applied to national and regional economies. The logic inherent in such techniques as export base, input–output, or income–expenditure is applicable to any area regardless of its economic makeup, geographical dimensions, or political boundaries. From the practical point of view, however, the applications of these techniques become progressively more difficult as they are brought from the national level down to the level of a region and then to a subeconomic system[6]—a city or a suburban jurisdiction—of a metropolitan area economy. In addition, data are often not compiled below the regional level, which forces cities and counties to use extrapolations and other relatively crude techniques to refine their information.

The foundation of regional development theory is the larger body of knowledge relating to national development theory, often referred to as *development science*. However, regional development theory, beyond a general conceptual framework, is substantially different. While both aim at explaining long-term growth of an area (be it a nation or a region), there are vast differences in the operative premises underlying these two theories. These differences can be explained by two simple examples.

First, a nation enjoys considerable latitude and independence in its actions. The degree of independence that can be exercised by a region is quite limited. Second, an important foundation of regional development theory is the premise of interregional trade, while the national development theory deals with international trade. The interregional trade aspects of regional development are subject to different economic laws from those of international trade. Phenomena such as the economies of scale and external economies, for all practical purposes, can be ignored at the national level but they cannot be overlooked as critical elements in a theory dealing with regional development.

A framework of regional and urban change is a collection of one or more theories each attempting to establish through empirical investigations some causality or relationship between and among certain variables which permit articulation, orchestration, extrapolation, and analysis of growth, decline, stagnation, or stability of an urban region.

Regional economics and the development of base theory

The beginnings of regional economics can perhaps be dated by the writings of Alfred Weber, who provided the "classical" view of the emerging discipline in the early 1900s. His writings on the theory of industrial location give implicit recognition to the economic interdependence of regions in his *agglomeration analysis*.[7]

The more formal discipline of regional science developed after World War II. During the late 1940s and the 1950s, major theoretical contributions were made by Myrdal, Hirschman, Tiebout, North, Leontief, Isard, and others.[8] Myrdal and Hirschman advanced the concept of *comparative* advantage. In so doing, they created such terms as *spread, backwash, trickling down,* and *polarization*. Their work gave credence to the fact that all regions are not equal and that regional development will be governed by a particular sequence of events involving the region's stage of development and its resources. Their work provided the basic reasoning under which one region might dominate another in the growth cycle, or, given the sequence of events and stage of development, both regions might benefit in terms of development through interregional trade.

Other theories of regional development were set forth during the 1950s. Some of these stress the process of development within a region as resulting from the availability and exploitation of local resources. One such concept, for example, is based on the assumption that an area's development is a function of its exports, a concept of the economic base of a city. Tiebout, North, and Andrews furthered this theory after Hoyt and others had laid a foundation.[9]

Base theory essentially holds that the structure of the economy is made up of two broad classes of productive effort—the basic activities which produce and distribute goods and services for export to firms and individuals outside a defined localized economic area, and nonbasic activities whose goods and services are consumed at home within the boundaries of the local economic area. This distinction holds that the reason for the existence and growth of a particular region is its capacity to produce goods and services for "export" beyond local borders. These basic activities not only provide the means of payment for raw materials, food, and services which the region cannot produce itself but also support the nonbasic activities which are principally local in productive scope and market area.

Therefore, both sectors are related to exogenous or outside demand, the basic sector directly and the nonbasic sector indirectly. If exogenous demand for the exports of the region increases, the basic sector expands. This, in turn, generates an expansion in the supporting activities of the nonbasic sector. Since this theory holds that all economic activity can be classified as basic or nonbasic, it follows that changes in basic employment will induce changes in nonbasic employment.

Refinements in base theory   The foregoing concept provided a persuasive explanation for the development of regions that are well endowed with physical, human, locational, and organizational resources, but it did not convincingly explain the development process for the "poor" regions. Consequently, the authors of *Regions, Resources and Economic Growth*[10] attempted to fill the void by turning to a more general concept. This theory states that as incomes rise the demand for primary commodities falls; at the same time the demand for products and services produced by the secondary and tertiary sectors of an economy increases. This gives rise to further income gains, and so the cycle of growth continues. In effect, the theory establishes the thesis that a regional economy undergoes a sequence of stages in its development process.

The factors affecting the exports, the industrialization, and, consequently, the growth of a region are the basic foundations of the work of most contemporary theorists and practitioners of regional economic development. Isard,[11] with his emphasis on space economy analyses, has lent credence to the fundamental importance of linkage factors—interregional and interindustry linkages—in the study of a particular economy, whether national, regional, or local.

Some theoretical work by Leontief and some extensions of it by Isard[12] produced a theoretical construct and a technique popularly known as *input–output technique*. This technique provides static measures of interindustry relationships in a given geographical setting—localized, regional, or national. The technique is based on the premise that any given line of economic activity bears a specific measurable relationship to every other industry in the economy. It establishes a basic relationship between the volume of output produced by a given industry in any one nation, region, or locality and the volume of specific inputs required in the production process from all other industries located in the area of analysis or elsewhere.

Generally speaking, current regional economic theories attempt to explain the developmental process and growth of a defined region from two viewpoints—the "outside" and the "inside." The former emphasizes the processes of cause and effect in the transmission of growth between regions (the export base framework). The latter is concerned more with the forces of growth within the region itself (the resource base framework). Both external and internal perspectives are important in analyzing and explaining urban growth, decline, stability, or stagnation.

When a theoretical framework emphasizes external perspective, it does so not because of the irrelevance of internal factors and forces but because the simplification seems warranted that internal forces will respond in some definite way to external or export changes. Similarly, the emphasis on internal factors implicitly assumes that external markets will respond to the comparative advantage created by positive internal forces.

The recognition that both external and internal forces constantly interact means that the more persuasive theoretical and statistical frameworks are those that incorporate both perspectives. These so-called "mixed" perspective frameworks seek to incorporate both internal and external forces as underlying causes of urban change. They also attempt to incorporate interactions among local demand, local resources, local income, and local production and service capacities. Recent input–output approaches accomplish this by analyzing internally and externally generated final demand markets and their consequences for the production and purchase activities of local economic sectors.

It is clear that studies dealing with local economies must recognize and incorporate both external and internal perspectives. It is only by identifying the specific causal factors—be they resources, institutions, external demands, or linkages among them—that economic base studies can provide meaningful orientation for public policies.

Dual market theory   Augmenting the external–internal framework for analysis of regional and subeconomic systems are the effects of dual markets—that is, the division of significant economic elements into two subdivisions that may be complementary, competing, or parallel but are always of significantly different dimensions. The dual market theory can be set forth with the following postulates:

1.   Two different economic sectors/markets exist within all levels of the nation's economy
2.   The major distinguishing characteristic of dual economies is uneven development in the housing market, the labor market, the capital market, and other major sectors
3.   Overall, the two economic sectors are the primary, oligopolistic/monopolistic sector, and the secondary, traditional competitive sector.

Planners need to deal with the effects of these dualities, which can be quite local and specific. Two examples will help bring this theory into operational vision.

Capital markets   Planners, city and county managers, and elected officials are well aware of the uneven physical development that occurs at the regional level, and this has implications for economic subsystems such as cities. Regional status is manifested by the locational decisions of capital investors, the interregional migration of people, and the allocation of federal grants. These decisions influence and accelerate growth, stability, and decline, and the planner should know and take into account the effects of these influences. It provides a dynamic, rather than static, way of analyzing a problem or issue.

Labor markets   In our postindustrial age the labor market, in addition to its thousands of job classifications, can be analyzed as a two tier sector. The primary labor market comprises mostly highly trained and skilled professionals; the secondary labor market comprises mostly semiskilled and unskilled workers. This broad division is not new, but the importance of professionals in an increasingly service-dominated society is greater than ever before in our history. A highly visible effect of the two tier labor market can be seen in areas in which primary production is declining (often these are mature central cities, but it can apply to some smaller places as well), thus eroding the economic base.

Elements of economic base studies

A sound economic base study should be concerned with both short-term policy decisions and long-term development potentials. It should attempt to: (1) define within the broader regional context the development potential of a central city or other subregional economy in terms of the factors influencing private investment and the creation of employment opportunities; (2) articulate the specific public actions for stimulating and supporting these profit making and job creating enterprises in the central city or guiding the scale and nature of growth in the suburban jurisdictions; (3) evaluate the capacity of central city and suburban governments for undertaking and supporting the programs required; (4) project future levels of economic activity on the basis of reasonable assumptions with respect to private sector response to these public actions; and (5) measure the potential economic impact of indicated or desired developments so that the future demands for public services and facilities can be identified.

Areal and sectoral approaches[13]   Economic base analysis, like other aspects of planning, takes place within a geographic area, and different types of areas tend to develop different requirements for data and analyses. In many of the larger cities a threefold approach is used for economic planning: citywide, subcity, and sectoral.

For citywide purposes, the kinds of data and analyses are likely to include: (1) descriptive data, including such items as demographic and social indicators, governmental revenues and expenditures, and economic health indicators (unemployment, personal income, assessed property values, etc.); (2) economic base analysis; (3) forecasts and projections of major economic elements such as employment and large scale capital investment; and (4) correlation and modeling to check cause and effect interactions, including fiscal impact studies and simulations.

For subcity areas, the data and analyses are likely to include: (1) neighborhood classifications by demographic indicators, crime rates, building conditions, and other statistical measures; (2) transition data for monitoring trends, including school enrollments, building permits issued, and changes in assessed values; and (3) parcel-level information systems that are built on computer files for each parcel of land.

Cutting across citywide and subcity areas are many economic sectors. Among the most significant for sectoral analysis are: (1) the labor market, including profiles, demand/supply studies, and employment projections; (2) the manufacturing sector, including trend analyses, industrial attraction and retention programs, and studies for redevelopment of industrial areas; and (3) the commercial sector, including studies to define the local markets (buying power, consumer preferences, etc.), studies of the viability of local commercial strips, and a wide variety of central business district studies.

Common elements   Although the thrust and the depth of research and analysis vary, depending on the specific jurisdictional objectives (growth management and redirection of growth in the suburban jurisdiction or redevelopment of the economy in the central city), the following elements are common to the economic base study whether undertaken at the regional or the subregional (city) level.

1. *Analysis of past economic trends,* including such basic measures as population numbers and characteristics, labor force, employment by place of work and by place of residence, commuting patterns, income and poverty status of local residents, size and nature of specific types

of public and private enterprise, source of public revenues and expenditures, land values, and indicators of new economic activity such as new housing construction, value of new construction, and wage rates

2. Development of the *profile of the existing economy,* covering major strengths and weaknesses, comparison with other local economies, balance and diversity of economic activities, vulnerability to cyclical fluctuations, and economic specialization, if any

3. Analysis of the *linkage relationships* between the local economy and the larger regional, state, and national economies, including basic trends in industries and activities that are prominent locally and regionally and the shift in the locational patterns of activities within the region

4. Compilation of a comprehensive *inventory of local assets and liabilities,* including all types of resources—physical, human, locational, and organizational

5. Examination of *critical development factors and forces* that will affect the future of the local economy, both external and internal, including technological trends, markets, local attitudes toward growth, availability and cost of developable land, energy supply and cost of energy, and environmental constraints

6. Isolation of the *major growth potentials* in the local economy, taking into account the factors listed above, among others, and expressed in terms of specific types of economic activities and potential areas of their location within the local jurisdiction

7. Projections of realistic ranges of *future short- and long-term economic activity* in the area, expressed in terms of numbers and types of employment opportunities, population, housing requirements, and land requirements for specific uses

8. Evaluation of *specific public issues* to be faced if the area's economic potential is to be realized, including an evaluation of their direct bearing upon private investment and employment generators as well as redirection of growth and the fiscal and public service implications of indicated growth.

Preparatory steps   Clearly, a comprehensive economic base study that fully covers the above subjects is a rigorous research undertaking. As is true in any major piece of research, a number of preparatory steps must be taken prior to initiating the actual research. The major steps include the following:

1. Identification of study area boundaries
2. Development of a detailed work program
3. Development of an overall research framework, including individual staff assignments and task completion schedules
4. Identification of specific data needs and potential sources, both published and unpublished
5. Selection of agencies, individuals, and representatives of selected economic enterprises to be interviewed
6. Construction of pertinent survey forms and questionnaires.

A key step in an economic base study is the identification of specific data needs and data sources (item 4, above). Although the nature and the level of detail of required data vary, depending on the particular orientation of the study, a variety of common data are essential for understanding and analyzing the area's economic base.

Data sources   As noted earlier, the base studies entail compilation and analysis of a vast amount of data relating to numerous subject matters. While they are too numerous to describe in detail, the principal types of data and data sources typically used in a base study are listed below. These include materials published by federal, state, and local government agencies as well as data made available by numerous quasi-public institutions such as Chambers of Commerce, state university departments, and research bureaus of business and economics sources.

1. Population and housing data
   a) U.S. Censuses of Population and Housing (available on a decennial basis)
   b) *Current Population Reports,* Series P–25 and P–26, published annually by the Bureau of the Census
   c) Current population estimates prepared by many state planning agencies for counties, cities, and metropolitan areas
   d) Housing construction permit data by number of units authorized, by type of unit for permit-issuing place, published by the Bureau of the Census, C–40 reports
2. Employment data
   a) Resident employment data by industry sectors, published in decennial census reports
   b) U.S. Department of Labor, Bureau of Labor Statistics, *Employment and Earnings for States and Metropolitan Areas,* published monthly and annually with figures on nonagricultural wage and salary employment and average weekly earnings by industry groups
   c) State departments of employment security, at-place employment by industry for nonmetropolitan counties and labor market areas
   d) U.S censuses for retail trade, selected service industries, agriculture, mining, and manufacturing
   e) *County Business Patterns,* published by the U.S. Department of Commerce, presenting covered employment for states, metropolitan areas, counties, and independent cities
3. Income data
   a) U.S. Censuses of Population and Housing
   b) U.S. Department of Commerce, Bureau of Economic Analysis, estimates of total personal and per capita income for metropolitan areas and nonmetropolitan counties
   c) *Current Population Reports,* series P–26.
4. Other data sources
   a) New and expanded plants data typically available from state departments of commerce
   b) Special studies and research reports published by state and local colleges and universities
   c) Local operating departments and agencies of the city and county governments.

The data gathering task of the regional (as distinct from the local) planner is substantially simplified since most of the significant economic information is published in a regional format. The local planner is not so fortunate, however. The unavailability of relevant data for the subeconomic system (such as a city) of a metropolitan area (such as at-place employment and income figures) often makes it difficult for the local planner to define the economic base of his or her jurisdiction. The local planner frequently has to undertake painstaking data manipulation and estimating to put together a realistic profile of the economic base of the jurisdiction. There are methodological hazards in these activities, particularly with straight-line extrapolations, prorations, and other simplistic measures.

More often than not, the planner at the local level is called upon to create his or her own at-place employment estimates, which are essential for understanding the economic base. Among his or her sources are the journey-to-work tables and the various business censuses published by the U.S. Bureau of the Census, from which the planner can estimate the structural characteristics and magnitudes of the local employment represented in his or her jurisdiction. These sources, however, are crude (the data categories are very broad), and the time lag between compilation and publication may make them of limited usefulness.

Following the basic data collection, tabulation, and manipulation exercises, the planner (or his or her consultant) must analyze and go behind the numbers to understand and explain the workings of the local economic base. This includes assessing the economy's past performance; the forces affecting its growth, decline, stagnation, or stability; and the competitive position of the city or other subeconomic system in relation to other systems of a metroeconomy and to the metroeconomy as a whole. Subsequently, the planner must choose one of several techniques that are available to forecast or predict both short-term and long-term outlooks.

Economic forecasting techniques

The essential purpose of economic base studies is threefold: (1) to assess the strengths and weaknesses of available or latent resources and support systems; (2) to determine realistic levels of short- and long-term development potentials; and (3) to identify the barriers to their realization. On the basis of the findings of the studies, public policies can be devised to create the conditions and incentives—within the framework of overall public interest—which can generate an optimum private response for using an area's physical and human resources.

An essential product of the economic base study is the forecasting of future levels of economic activity in the area under study. The methods used in arriving at these projections and the credibility given to them as attainable goals, however, have been the subject of great intellectual debate. Forecasts based on the more sophisticated methodologies often take on the aura of gospel because of their impressive analytical techniques; the simplest and least sophisticated are often nothing more than straight-line projections. To have maximum value for the public decision maker, forecasts need to identify their specific assumptions relating to public policies and the effects that these policies might have on the types and levels of forecasted activities (via leverage on the private sector).

The following paragraphs will cover only the most commonly used techniques in the large inventory that is available. References to other techniques are provided in the Bibliography to this chapter.

There are several techniques or analytical frameworks (models) available to the local planner in projecting economic activity for his or her local jurisdiction. These techniques vary in degree of complexity from trend-line extrapolation to the complex and sophisticated methods involved in the input–output analysis. Each has an appropriate application in the overall economic base study depending on the desired products, the availability of funds and personnel, the time available for study, and the availability and quality of required data. Some of these techniques lend themselves to the detailed analysis of a subeconomic system and even the components of that system, but others are not that readily adaptable to such uses.

In the paragraphs which follow, four commonly known and used techniques are briefly evaluated: input–output, economic base multiplier, shift-share analysis, and structural component or sector analysis.

Input–output analysis   The theoretical underpinning of the input–output or interindustry linkage method has already been described, and only a brief description of the method and its pros and cons is presented here.

At the outset it must be pointed out that this method is usually very costly to employ. It usually requires the services of trained and experienced economists, econometricians, and statisticians over a considerable period of time. To be useful, it requires large and precise data inputs and computers to process data inputs. These practical restrictions have, to date, precluded the widespread use of this method for smaller metropolitan and submetropolitan areas. There have been some excellent examples of the application of this method for planning purposes at the larger metropolitan level, however.

Aside from its practical limitations, some of the theoretical limitations of the input–output approach are perhaps even more imposing. The method analyzes the economy at one point in time. The interindustry input–output flow tables are generally expressed in terms of gross dollar flows between the producing and the supplying sectors. The new industry-by-industry inputs of labor, materials, etc., that are required to produce the forecasted output totals are usually determined on the basis of factors prevailing at the time interindustry linkages were established—that is, the new inputs (supply side) examined to produce the new outputs (demand side) are based on the level of prices, the state of the technology, labor productivity, etc., prevailing at the time the industries were first analyzed.

While this shortcoming at the national level is not serious, since data inputs for such variables are constantly monitored, the technique's usefulness as an ongoing tool for small areas is reduced unless reliable new inputs for the area are constantly developed. The data for such variables are normally not available and must be empirically derived and updated.

With these caveats taken into account the input–output technique can be a valuable tool for analyzing the larger regional economies. Substantial empirical research has been conducted by several economists, however, that has made the technique more adaptable to small area analysis by aggregating various industry sectors and thereby reducing the time and costs involved in building essential inputs. For the planner who is more concerned with central business districts, neighborhood revitalization, and cost and benefit studies of new housing developments, the technique has little or no application.

Economic base multiplier   The premise underlying this analytical technique is that a local or a regional economy's growth depends on the expansion of its exports to other regions. The dollar flow and the income produced by the expansion of export trade with other regions generate expansion of demand for products and services produced and consumed by the local economy.

The economic base multiplier technique assumes that there is a fixed ratio between basic employment (export base employment) and nonbasic employment (local service producing sector employment). Having determined the base ratio (the multiplier), one can, by multiplying the change in the basic sector by the base multiplier, estimate the change in all other sectors (nonbasic employment). The same process can be used in forecasting changes in income, if there is a change in income generated through exports.

One of the most widely used approaches to estimating export-related or basic sector employment involves the use of *location quotients*. The assumption underlying the location quotient approach is that a local or a regional economy is a microcosm of the national economy. A location quotient *greater than one* indicates an activity in which a local economy is unusually specialized for its overall size. The higher the quotient is, the greater is the specialization in a given industry in the local area. A location quotient *below one* indicates the activity that is relatively underrepresented in a given local economy. In the context of economic base studies, an additional assumption is that specialized local activities with a location quotient above one are also basic economic activities, producing goods and services beyond local demands, exporting them to external markets, and generating income in the local area from outside.

Although this approach has been widely used in estimating export base activity and nonbasic activity, the method does not easily lend itself to forecasting future export base activity for a given local economy. The method relies on the current ratio to predict future changes in nonbasic activity on the basis of the change in basic activity. In reality, the relationship between basic and nonbasic activities is of a dynamic nature; the base constantly changes over time and thus the method's predictive capabilities are questioned. Moreover, the method deals only with forecasting nonbasic activities. The projection of export sector or basic activity must first be independently derived before the method can be employed in projecting changes in nonbasic activities.

Shift-share analysis The shift-share or step-down ratio method is a relatively simple and inexpensive technique for analyzing and projecting the structure of a local or regional economy, although it can vary considerably in the amount of details involved. Essentially, the method rests on the premise that the level of employment, income, or other measures in a small area (a region, county, city, or subarea of a jurisdiction) is functionally related to the level of that activity occurring within a larger area of which the smaller area is a part. Therefore, by analysis of historical data on the economic variables to be forecast, ratios are developed to express the functional relationship between the smaller economic unit and its larger economic unit. These ratios are then applied to reliable forecasts of economic variables for the larger geographical unit until, by a step-down process, numerical forecasts of the same variables are obtained for the smaller area.

The primary attributes of the shift-share method are the general availability of the data used, the straightforward methodology, and the reasonable results if assumptions and premises are sound in predicting future relationships and ratios between geographical units. The quality of results can suffer, however, from a lack of sensitivity to dynamic local, regional, or national factors which may cause a fundamental change in the long-term trends. Shift-share is one of the forecasting tools most commonly used by planners and economists because it can yield reasonable results when combined with sound analysis by knowledgeable researchers.

Component or sector analysis The component or sector technique is one of the simpler methods of economic analysis. Instead of analyzing and forecasting aggregate measures of economic activity such as total employment, income, or output, this method involves carrying out studies of the various components or sectors of the economy such as manufacturing, construction, and retail trade. Future trends are then predicted on a sector-by-sector basis.

An advantage of this method is that the in-depth sector analysis allows the researcher to go beyond the figures to identify causes of change taking place over time. This method also permits the analyst to make a direct sectoral comparison between his or her economy and those of other jurisdictions that make up the broader region, and any other larger area such as the state or the nation. The analyst can use this technique in conjunction with the shift-share technique and thus increase his or her ability to more accurately predict the sectoral changes over time into the future.

As is the case with the shift-share technique, however, the quality of results can suffer from a lack of sensitivity to dynamic local, regional, and national factors which may cause a fundamental change in any one given sector or its subcomponents over time. Application of this technique requires special knowledge of the individual sectors, including the factors affecting past and future change and the spatial or locational determinants of sectoral activity.

Other approaches In addition to the economic base techniques noted above, there are other methods that planners can use to understand and project the economic base of a community. Among them are trend-line projections and time-series and correlation analyses—all of them relatively simple techniques using data extrapolations or ratios.

There is no a priori basis for deciding whether more detailed analysis will yield more accurate forecasts. In theory, however, in-depth analysis should provide more finely tuned insights into the forces that influence change and thus should help the analyst in formulating well-founded premises, assumptions, and judgments for forecasting future changes. The importance of these premises, assumptions, and judgments is that they can provide a "handle" for public policy by identifying cause and effect relationships that might be amenable to the leverage of public actions.

Fiscal impact analysis

Although the primary focus of these remarks is on the economic base study, it might be well briefly to note another type of study which both planners and public administrators are being called upon to undertake or sponsor. This is the fiscal impact study. The growing interest of central city and suburban governments in pursuing growth management policies has generated a vast literature on the subject in recent years.

The primary use of fiscal impact studies is to assist city or county officials in determining whether a particular project or scale of development in the community will generate sufficient revenues to defray the necessary public service costs. Fiscal impact analyses are also used to evaluate the overall financial implications to local governments of alternative patterns and densities of land development. Although still in the formative stage, the state-of-the-art of fiscal analysis and planning has made significant strides. From being merely an accounting exercise in the past, fiscal impact analysis has developed into a technique that has given the planner new tools for evaluating alternative public policy options. It enables the planner to assess the fiscal effects of new land uses, redevelopment proposals, and alternative patterns of growth in both suburban and central city jurisdictions of a metroeconomy.

The techniques of fiscal impact analysis range from simple, one dimensional methods using generalized norms or standards to complex econometric models which simulate public costs and benefits applying to given types of development proposals, scales of development, or new patterns of development. A substantial amount of academic as well as empirical research is being carried out or sponsored by various institutions and governmental agencies to improve the reliability of various methods.

Inasmuch as residential uses account for the largest proportion of total land uses in a given community, most fiscal impact studies are concerned with costs and revenue implications by type, scale, and pattern of new residential development. Generally speaking, revenues associated with new residential developments can be relatively easily compiled using local property tax rates and value of new units data. A full-blown impact study may also estimate revenues that may be received through taxes on incomes of new households and retail sales taxes.

The assessment of public costs is more difficult than the estimation of revenues, however. It involves formulation of unit cost factors for the delivery of different types of public services (police, fire, water and sewer, transportation, etc.). Each community differs in the level of service that it provides or maintains. Consequently, cost factors or standards empirically or otherwise developed for one community are not necessarily applicable to any other community. The most successful approaches involve community specific revenue and cost estimates based on local government audits and other empirical surveys. Demographic data on population, households by type of housing, and income class of new households are correlated with unit cost data for various service categories to produce policy-oriented measurements—for example, the number of new policemen required to serve 100 new residents, or the number of new school-teachers and classrooms needed per 1,000 additional schoolchildren.

Although progress has been and is being made in refining approaches and techniques in estimating fiscal impacts of new residential developments,[14] little empirical work has been undertaken to assess costs and revenue implications of new industrial developments by type of industry, and of industrial redevelopment projects in the inner city. There are a number of other areas in which attention needs to be directed to an understanding and an assessment of their fiscal implications. These include the comparative cost and revenue analysis of households locating in rehabilitated structures in the central city versus their move into new units in the suburbs, and the costs and revenue implications of industry locating in the central city (through various public incentives) rather than moving to suburban locations. New approaches also need to be devised to assess situations in which the cost–benefit implications of both public and private participation are involved.

Evaluation of economic base analysis

Over the years the economic base study has been a mixed blessing to planners. It has been employed most successfully at the regional level in accordance with the caveats of the conventional wisdom relating to the definition of urban economics as a regional system. It has, in its way, provided the rationale for much of the public infrastructure on which the horizontal metropolis has been built.

It is fair to say, however, that historically most economic base studies have been ground out according to fairly prosaic formulas. Their main purpose has been to provide a framework for growth forecasts. Often, there has been too little concern about the validity of the basic premises; more important, there has been still less concern about the implications of the conclusions for the jurisdictions involved (particularly the central cities). There have been some outstanding exceptions—the comprehensive economic studies of the New York and Pittsburgh regions, for example, undertook detailed evaluations of local as well as regional economic structures. They included in-depth analyses of the forces determining the location of economic activities and the deployment of private investments, and they explored the implications of trends for public policy at all levels. Many if not most economic base studies, however, have been relatively routine products, even if—and often because—sophisticated forecasting techniques have been employed. They have provided minimal insights into the problems with which public policy must deal.

Deficiencies in economic base analysis   Three kinds of deficiencies have shown up in the general run of economic base studies. First, as implied above, many have been more concerned with the refinements of numbers than with the integrity of premises. Too often, the process of making economic base studies has involved "straining at gnats and swallowing camels." In planning schools and planning journals, professional advice to the planner on economic base analysis has often been overly preoccupied with the techniques of statistical manipulation, data classification, and definitions of economic activities for the purpose of forecasting. Instead of clearly identifying the key issues over which public policy might and should exercise its leverage, many have been disposed toward accumulating socioeconomic data (much of which material has been of dubious value to an understanding of problems).

Second, most economic base studies have had only a limited policy orientation. In part this has been due to their adaptation primarily to the metropolitan region through which few governmental actions are exercised. Even so, economic base studies have more often than not missed the mark in identifying either the actions necessary to achieve the indicated level of economic growth or the impact of the projected growth (or lack of growth) on the affected local governments. Planners have been given detailed instructions on how to assemble data from a variety of sources and to manipulate these data as a basis for forecasts. They have received less guidance on how to understand the workings of the metroeconomy, the processes involved in the interaction between public and private sectors, and the public leverages that might be employed to sustain or alter the course of economic development.

The third deficiency is the most serious and has been noted earlier—the shortcomings of planners in dealing with the economic subsystems of the larger regions. No one doubts that the parts must be evaluated in terms of the whole: certainly the metroeconomy has an overall unity derived from the interaction of free market and investment forces over and beyond the arbitrary boundary lines that separate governmental jurisdictions. However, it is precisely because the metroeconomy is a regional phenomenon that the component subsystems must be defined and articulated as a basis for public policy.

Generally speaking, the economic base study is failing to provide the analysis of structural economics at the jurisdictional (local government) level that can meet the planner's needs. It is falling short of defining the development or redevelopment potentials of the resources, both physical and human, within a jurisdictional boundary. To realize these potentials in a competitive regional market requires taking actions to remove restraints against the free flow of capital, and these actions must be taken within the framework of a responsible fiscal policy which must justify public outlays in terms of the viable activities that are generated.

The point must be stressed that many of the factors that create imbalances between the governmental jurisdictions in a region are created by the inability—or unwillingness—of the local governments to take the necessary steps to provide a favorable investment or reinvestment climate. The question is: How can local government policy be more than reactive to the forces of change in the free marketplace? Over what private economic decisions can it exercise a decisive leverage? The guidance given by economic base studies too often is only minimal.

Steps toward improvement The improvement of the economic base study to a point where it can answer such questions must await the maturing of the art of urban economics. As it stands now, urban economics is largely a collection of theories, many of which are only partially descriptive and only partially tested. Although new sophisticated approaches to regional forecasting have acquired vast appeal and credibility in recent times, it would be fair to say that the discipline as a whole is still struggling with how to explain what has already occurred. It is still too caught up in defining itself, differentiating between what is "urban" and what is "regional," and in modifying and refining tools to achieve a higher level of confidence in long-range predictive capability.

One should not interpret the foregoing comments as an across-the-board depreciation of urban economics and of the main tool it has provided for planners over the years. The deficiencies are as much the result of pressures of events as of academic shortsightedness. The horizontal redistribution of economic activities in response to new patterns of development has forced urban economic thinking to devise new understandings of the structure and workings of the broader metroeconomy.

Even with their too frequent preoccupation with definition and methodology, regional economic base studies have achieved a new level of understanding of the regional economic system and how it works. Certainly, the regional planner has made good use of economic base studies in his or her forecasting and overview activities. The local government planner has picked up some new tools for evaluating the regional interplay of economic forces. Moreover, the local government planner has gained broad insights through day-to-day dealings with the private sector in the processes of public–private interaction.

The entire broad area of economic base analysis calls for approaches that are targeted more precisely to the leverages of public policy. Until the viability of economic subsystems can be addressed more effectively, the fiscal viability of local jurisdictions will remain in a precarious situation. In addition, it should be kept in mind that some of our most important national domestic problems—particularly those of unemployment and underemployment, with the interrelated problems of underprivilege, crime, and disaffection—cannot be effectively dealt with solely through macroeconomic policies at the national level.

Conclusion

This chapter is organized into three major sections. The first has presented a national perspective of the economic issues affecting cities: the persistence of central area decline (and some factors offsetting this decline); the constraints of city boundaries; and certain policy changes that have taken place (in federal grants and in economic rebuilding, for example). There is also a discussion of the theory and practice of urban economics, followed by some technical caveats.

The second section of the chapter covers the concepts, strategies, programs, and methods of economic development planning. In addition, the risks and potentials in economic development are summarized, along with other issues such as environmental quality and the need for coordination.

The third section, on economic base studies, first covers regional economics and the development of base theory and then moves on to a discussion of the elements of economic base studies. A number of forecasting techniques are then described, including input–output analysis, economic base multiplier, and shift-share analysis. Fiscal impact analysis is also discussed. The chapter concludes with an evaluation of economic base studies and an assessment of the present state-of-the-art.

1   National Council for Urban Economic Development, *Coordinated Urban Economic Development: A Case Study Analysis* (Washington, D.C.: National Council for Urban Economic Development, 1978), p. vi.

2   Ibid.

3   The observations and conclusions in this section of the chapter evolved from earlier work conducted by Hammer, Siler, George Associates for the Community Development Agency of the city of St. Louis. The authors acknowledge the kind permission of that agency to use that work.

4   Richard Starr, "Small Town Planning: Economic and Industrial Development," paper presented at the National Planning Conference of the American Society of Planning Officials, Indianapolis, Ind., 29 April–4 May 1978.

5   See: Adrienne M. Levatino, *Neighborhood Commercial Rehabilitation* (Washington, D.C.: National Association of Housing and Redevelopment Officials, 1978).

6   For purposes of this chapter, the term *subeconomic system* refers to central cities, suburbs, and independent cities, and to counties as well. Thus, the subeconomic system, as contrasted with the region or *urban area,* has jurisdictional boundaries (the corporate limits, for example) and status as a

governmental jurisdiction (the municipal corporation, for example).

7   See: Alfred Weber, *Theory of the Location of Industries* (Chicago: University of Chicago Press, 1957).

8   See: Gunnar Myrdal, *Economic Theory and Under-Developed Regions* (London: Duckworth, 1957); Albert O. Hirschman, *The Strategy of Development* (New Haven, Conn.: Yale University Press, 1958); Albert O. Hirschman, *The Strategy of Economic Development* (New York: W. W. Norton & Company, Inc., 1978); Charles M. Tiebout, *The Community Economic Base Study* (New York: Committee for Economic Development, 1962); Charles M. Tiebout," Exports and Regional Economic Growth," *Journal of Political Economy* 64 (April 1956): 160–69; Douglas C. North, "Location Theory and Regional Economic Growth," *Journal of Political Economy* 63 (June 1955): 243–58; Douglas C. North and Roger L. Miller, *The Economics of Public Issues,* 4th ed. (New York: Harper & Row, Publishers, 1978); Richard B. Andrews, "Mechanics of Urban Economic Base: Historical Development of the Base Concept," *Land Economics* 29 (May 1953): 161–67; H. S. Perloff et al., *Regions, Resources and Economic Growth* (Lincoln: University of Nebraska Press,

1960); Wassily Leontief, *Input–Output Economics* (London: Oxford University Press, 1966); Walter Isard, *Methods of Regional Analysis* (New York: The Technology Press and John Wiley & Sons, Inc., 1960); Walter Isard and Thomas Langford, *Regional Input–Output Study: Recollections, Reflections and Diverse Notes on the Philadelphia Experience,* Regional Science Study Series 10 (Cambridge, Mass.: The M.I.T. Press, 1971); The Regional Plan Association, Inc., and Homer Hoyt, *The Economic Status of the New York Metropolitan Region in 1944* (New York: Regional Plan Association Inc., 1944); and Pittsburgh Regional Planning Association, gen. ed., *Economic Study of the Pittsburgh Region*, 3 vols. (Pittsburgh: University of Pittsburgh Press, 1964), vol. 3: *Region*

with a Future, ed. E. M. Hoover and B. Chinitz.

9   See note 8.
10 Perloff et al., *Regions, Resources and Economic Growth.*
11 See note 8.
12 See note 8.
13 This discussion of areal and sectoral data and analysis is abstracted from: National Council for Urban Economic Development, *Coordinated Urban Economic Development*, pp. 34–38.
14 Robert W. Burchell and David Listokin, *The Fiscal Impact Handbook: Estimating Local Costs and Revenues of Land Development* (New Brunswick, N.J.: Rutgers University, Center for Urban Policy Research, 1978).

21 Planning for urban housing

Housing is one of the most important elements in our lives and our communities —socially, physically, and economically. It is both shelter and a link to the neighborhood and the larger community. While housing begins as shelter, it is in today's parlance an environment. Inadequate, unsanitary, and unsafe housing can affect the physical health, mental health, privacy, and security of citizens. Slums, which are neighborhoods and areas of poor housing, have long been associated with crime, social disorders, and other social problems.[1] The crusades for better housing and for the elimination of slums were among the earliest moves toward city planning.[2] Poor housing was one of the factors that led to the adoption of zoning, subdivision controls, building and housing codes, sanitation ordinances, and other health and safety regulations that are now accepted as ordinary responsibilities of local government.

Beyond the physical condition of the house, the apartment building, and the neighborhood, the location of housing affects the quality of urban living. The quality of housing must be measured by access to community facilities, to public and private services, to shopping, to transportation, to fire and police protection, and, perhaps the most important consideration of all, to employment and public schools.

On the personal side, housing provides social contacts, friendships, a sense of social status, and a sense of belonging. Housing has an important economic impact. It represents a major portion of personal budgets, frequently 20 to 25 percent of income—and upward. Buying a home is the largest investment that most families make and is a principal form of savings.

Housing is a significant factor in the national economy. It represents about one-quarter of all capital assets. New housing construction represents about one-third of the value of all new construction undertaken annually in the United States. It exceeds in value the total of all new public construction, including public buildings, highways, and military facilities. In addition to expenditures for new housing, there are expenditures for additions, alterations, and repairs to housing. On top of this, tremendous infrastructure is required for housing— utilities, streets, and supportive community facilities such as schools, parks, and hospitals.

For local governments housing is a significant consideration. Residential development is usually the predominant user of urban land. Taxes on housing are a principal source of local government property taxes. Services to housing and services to the inhabitants of this housing comprise a major portion of local government expenditures.

At this point it is helpful to distinguish between publicly assisted housing and private sector housing. Publicly assisted housing is usually dated from the Housing Act of 1937, when the public housing program was initiated as federally assisted and publicly owned housing for low income citizens. Residency in such housing is limited to households meeting income eligibility requirements. There are other forms of publicly subsidized housing for both low and moderate income families and individuals. The government (usually federal) provides short- and long-term housing assistance payments (Section 8), below market rate interest mortgages or loans, and other guarantees and incentives. Such housing is usually owned by nonprofit, limited dividend, or cooperative organizations and, in some cases, by individual residents.

Despite the attention given publicly assisted housing, as of 1977 it comprised only about 3 percent of the housing stock in the United States.

The overwhelming majority of housing in the United States is provided by the private sector. It is constructed and owned or rented according to the principles of supply and demand. The building and real estate industries provide the housing. Planning has traditionally been involved in the zoning and subdivision controls and in the provision of community facilities for private housing. However, the government plays many other significant roles in the provision, support, and development of private housing, as will be shown in this chapter.

Public concern for housing began with attention to the slums and those living in them. Slums are an urban problem of long standing. In the past, attention to housing was most often sporadic and narrowly focused.[3] Since the late 1960s, however, concern for housing has accelerated. Housing emerged as a major source of discontent in the inner cities when the urban riots of 1967 and 1968 erupted. Beginning in 1968, federal housing programs expanded and housing planning became a mandated element in federal community planning. Some states require local housing plans as well. In the mid-1970s concern for housing reached beyond the poor to the middle class. The cost of housing began to increase at a more rapid rate than income, making adequate shelter at affordable prices a problem for countless families and individuals.[4]

Although the need for housing planning has grown, such planning is still limited. No national housing plan exists that is comparable, for example, with the interstate highway program. States, also, have not approached housing on an overall basis. When local government housing plans are prepared they are usually limited to one or more issues, such as building housing for low or moderate income households, overcoming exclusionary zoning, rehabilitating a neighborhood, redeveloping a community, resolving discrimination in marketing, or preparing a regional housing distribution plan. All of these plans are important but each is usually narrow in focus.

One of the major purposes of this chapter is to present housing in a broader framework. The components of the housing process are developed, including supply, demand, and financial and governmental roles. This is followed by coverage of housing goals, standards, and needs, and the issue of segregation. Attention is then given to developing a housing plan, including discussions of market analysis, comprehensive planning, and cost components. The chapter concludes with some suggested solutions to housing problems.

The components of housing

The complexity of the housing field can be seen in the range of elements involved in the provision, maintenance, and service of housing. This section presents the background of housing as seen in the principal components of supply, demand, finance, and government roles.

The housing supply component involves all existing housing stock; new construction; and the people, industries, and agencies involved in providing or maintaining the supply. The housing demand component refers to consumers of housing services, patterns of ownership, practices of marketing, characteristics of users, etc. Both supply and demand are greatly influenced by financial institutions and their operations. Finally, all levels of government play roles in the process. A principal concern of housing planning is identifying and implementing the roles of government in regulating, subsidizing, stimulating, servicing, and actually providing housing.

Figure 21–1   The American dream, and polls substantiate this, is to live in a single family detached house. An example is shown on the opposite page (top). Millions of unattached persons and families, however, live in other kinds of buildings—in high rises such as those shown immediately to the right, and in medium rise apartment buildings, row houses in many price ranges, and other types of dwelling units.

Housing supply

Characteristics of the housing supply   The basic unit of measurement for housing is the housing unit, whether it is a single family house, an apartment, or one of the units in a duplex. On this basis the United States had about 75 million housing units in 1977, not counting mobile homes, transient quarters such as hotel rooms, and group facilities.

It is said that the United States is a nation of homeowners. Data have shown that, as of 1974, 64 percent of all households owned the units they lived in. The ownership of rental property is also widely dispersed.

The 75 million housing units in the United States can be classified by tenure, housing type, size, cost, and other characteristics. Tenure refers to renter or owner occupancy. Type refers to building structure (single family, multifamily, attached, detached, garden apartment, town house, low rise, medium rise, or high rise). The most important measure of size is the number of bedrooms, which gives an indication of how many people can live in a unit. Floor area or number of square feet of space is also used. Cost is measured by rent or sales price. Gross rent, as contrasted with shelter rent, includes the cost of utilities. Other commonly referenced characteristics are condition of structure and availability of plumbing facilities.

Private sector housing accounts for most of the housing provided in this country, but government provides the backup that makes this housing possible. This is done in a variety of ways, as discussed later in this chapter.

Direct public participation in constructing or owning housing is minimal. With the exception of military housing, the federal government provides no housing directly. Local governments, with federal assistance, provide some publicly owned housing. This is in marked contrast to many other industrialized countries, with both capitalist and communist economies, where the government is the major producer of housing. In 1972 which, as of 1979, was the largest year for housing production in the United States, almost $45 billion in new housing was undertaken privately. In contrast, only $875 million (or less than 2 percent of the private new housing construction) was public construction for both housing and redevelopment.

Additions to the housing supply   Although new housing construction may receive much attention, it makes up a very small part of the housing stock at any one time. In any given year, new construction seldom accounts for more than 3 percent of the existing stock. In 1972, for example, there were 2.4 million housing starts (Table 21–1), which represented 3.3 percent of the existing stock (then about 71 million units).[5]

One concern about housing production is its fluctuation from year to year. It often rises or falls dramatically, causing unemployment in construction and financial problems for builders. Production was about 1.4 million units per year in the 1960s, varying somewhat from year to year. Then, in 1971, 1972, and 1973, it rose to more than 2 million units, only to fall drastically in the next few years.

Changing patterns in housing production   Starting in the 1960s (and spreading in the 1970s) several significant changes took place in housing production that reflected a combination of demographic changes, changes in consumer preferences, and inflation.

During the 1960s a significant amount of multifamily housing began to be produced.[6] In 1960, multifamily housing (two or more units per structure) represented about 21 percent of all housing starts. This percentage rose steadily, reaching about 45 percent by 1969, a level which was maintained until 1974, when housing production declined sharply.

Another change has been the growth of mobile homes. While not always in-

Table 21–1   New housing units started,
United States, 1960–77 (000).

| Year | Total | Private starts only | | | | | | Mobile home shipments |
| | | Total private starts | Single family | | Multifamily | | |
			No.	%	No.	%	
1960	1,296	1,252	995	79.5	257	20.5	
1961	1,365	1,313	975	74.3	338	25.7	90
1962	1,492	1,463	992	67.8	471	32.2	118
1963	1,642	1,610	1,021	63.4	589	36.6	151
1964	1,561	1,529	970	63.4	559	36.6	191
1965	1,510	1,473	964	65.4	509	34.6	216
1966	1,196	1,165	780	67.0	385	33.0	217
1967	1,322	1,292	845	65.4	447	34.6	240
1968	1,546	1,508	901	59.7	607	40.3	318
1969	1,500	1,467	811	55.3	656	44.7	413
1970	1,469	1,434	815	56.8	619	43.2	401
1971	2,085	2,052	1,153	56.2	899	43.8	497
1972	2,379	2,357	1,309	55.5	1,048	44.5	576
1973	2,057	2,045	1,132	55.4	913	44.6	567
1974	1,352	1,338	888	66.4	450	33.6	329
1975	1,171	1,160	892	76.9	268	23.1	213
1976	1,548	1,537	1,162	75.6	375	24.4	246
1977	1,900	1,987	1,451	73.0	536	27.0	277

Source: U.S., Department of Commerce, Bureau of the Census, *Construction Reports*, Series C–20. Data include farm housing.

cluded in housing starts, mobile home shipments have grown enormously. In 1961 about 90,000 mobile units were shipped. By 1973 this had reached a level of 567,000. Mobile homes have become a major source of new housing for lower and middle income families. With the rise in costs of single family homes, they represent the only resource for many families.

Mobile homes have not been accepted by many cities and counties. They depreciate rapidly, have to be financed by short-term loans at high interest rates, are regulated by different codes, and are taxed at different rates from houses on fixed foundations. Federal Housing Administration and Veterans Administration insurance is available for them, however.[7]

There has also been a change within the single family housing types. As of the late 1970s about 20 to 25 percent of such starts were attached housing—that is, town houses—largely resulting from the rise in suburban land prices.

One of the most significant aspects of housing has been the rising cost in relation to other costs and to income. This has priced the single family house out of the reach of many households. Between 1971 and 1976 the median price of a new single family home (across the nation) rose from $25,200 to $44,200, an increase of 75 percent in five years.

The development process   Housing development is a complex process. Before building, a developer must acquire land, secure zoning and other governmental permits, and prepare site plans, building plans, and specifications. Before a site is buildable, it must have access to community facilities such as roads, utilities, and water and sewer service. The entire process of housing development includes financing, planning, building, and marketing.

Figure 21–2 The origin, decline, and rehabilitation of a house.

1893–1930: Who built this house? The owner of the XYZ Hardware Company for himself, his wife, their four children, and two live-in servants.

1930–1979: Who lived in this house during its years of decline? Several large families, usually simultaneously, on an income spiral from moderate to low to poverty level.

1979 on: Who lives there now? Young affluent professionals. No children. Two incomes to finance rehabilitation.

The construction includes two phases: site preparation and building construction. The site preparation requires grading and building streets and extending water, sewerage, and other utilities to the building sites. The building construction is a combination of on-site and off-site work with various components of material and labor.[8]

Industrialized housing, or the factory production of housing, has frequently been proposed as a solution to high housing costs. The homebuilding industry has often been characterized as inefficient—composed of small, local builders who lack stability and continuity. Factory production is seen by its proponents as a way to increase production, reduce costs, provide efficiency, and stabilize employment in the construction industry. However, efforts at industrializing housing have not been successful. Most of these efforts have overlooked the fact that the provision of infrastructure and community facilities, local government approval, and significant land preparation are all very important parts of housing development. In addition, the homebuilding industry cannot be shown to be inefficient.[9]

As of the 1970s almost all new housing was built in the suburban portion of SMSAs (standard metropolitan statistical areas) where vacant land was available. In suburban areas the housing demand was conflicting increasingly with environmental concerns which advocated a no growth or limited growth philosophy. In 1950 about 41 percent of SMSA housing was in suburban areas and 59 percent in central cities. By 1974 this had changed: only 46 percent of SMSA housing was in central cities and 54 percent was in the suburbs. Some suburban areas, however, are now running out of prime housing locations.

Housing demand

Housing choice The basic housing consumption unit is the household. The demand of households in large measure determines where housing units will be located in relation to population. What households are willing and able to pay determines their housing choice, after location and surrounding environment have been considered. Households choose the location, amenities, and community as much as the specific housing type. The same house will bring different prices in different neighborhoods because households are also buying access to employment, transportation, environment, community facilities, educational opportunities, recreation, open space, and types of neighbors.

The wholesale exodus from the central cities in the 1950s and 1960s was not merely a move of whites from older to newer housing; it was also an exodus from the many problems of the city—from racial transition, poorer schools, increasing crime, and rising social problems. Households can seldom control their environment in immediate and individual ways but they can try to choose one that they feel is favorable.

Choice depends largely on income, because the bulk of the housing stock is supplied by the private sector. The poorer households have always had few selections to choose from. With rising housing costs, fewer households are able to occupy new housing; more must pay a greater share of their income for housing; and many more have fewer choices overall.

The demand for housing can be aggregated into a total housing market demand with many submarkets.[10] The major market is divided between renters and owners, and the majority of households own in this country. Government encourages ownership, believing that owners represent better managers of housing, contribute more taxes, make more of a contribution to the community, and have a bigger stake in the future. (Not all of the perceived advantages of ownership over renter housing are valid, but they are widely believed.)[11] Federal policies favoring homeowners are well established, including income tax deductions not available to renters.

The forms of ownership include cooperatives and condominiums, which provide most of the financial benefits of owning with some of the benefits of renting, such as more densely developed housing, common ownership of recreation facilities, and outside maintenance.

Other variations in demand, in addition to tenure, cost, and location, include size of units, type of structure, appliances, and age of building.

Consumers must often be matched with appropriate housing; this changes throughout a household's life cycle and varies by household type, which can include: single person households, large families, elderly households, households with school age children, "empty nesters" (couples whose children have left), female headed households, one parent households, and other categories—including an increasing number of disabled or handicapped persons living independently. An important part of housing analysis is studying the types of households and their income, age, family characteristics, size, race, ethnic background, and other socioeconomic factors to determine housing requirements.

Vacancy and filtering   Vacancy is a housing factor because it is the measure of choices available. There are many categories of vacancy. Some units are vacant because they are used seasonally or for migrant workers. The balance of vacancies are then considered *year-round*. Some of these are available for either sale or rent. The rest are not available, either because they are *held for occasional use* (as a second home), have already been sold or rented but are not yet occu-

Figure 21–3   Industrialization or factory production of housing has not been a major part of United States housing production (apart from mobile homes), but interest continues to be strong after more than a half century of efforts. Shown on this page is Habitat 67, a development of 158 dwelling units built for Expo 67 in Montreal. Top left: side forms and end panels, vertically hinged; top right: one piece precast units, each of identical exterior dimensions; bottom right: model of the complete project. In Miami, Florida, 373 modular units were built in the early 1970s on three sites by the Housing Corporation of America. At bottom left is one of the units being hoisted into place.

pied, or are held off the market for other reasons (for example, settling an estate). Vacation or recreation homes are usually considered a combination of seasonal and held for occasional use vacancies.

About 20 percent of households move every year, and about one in every seven moves is into a new unit. Ability to move depends on the availability of vacancies. Most moves are within the existing housing supply. Most moves are made within the same general region and are usually motivated by a change in the household's requirements. When a household moves, its former unit becomes available. This sets up a chain of additional moves, until eventually a household moves from a unit which is then removed from the housing supply, or a new household is formed which has occupied no other unit.

Filtering refers to the process created by the chain of moves, as housing passes through different household groups. Housing *trickles down* if it becomes available to a lower income family; it *trickles up* if it is occupied by a higher income family. Presumably, as better housing becomes available households will move from less desirable quarters. Therefore, new housing construction should help improve the total housing choice, because it sets up a chain of moves which will eventually allow the worst housing to be vacated and removed from supply. Therefore, filtering is sometimes proposed as a public policy whereby new upper and middle income housing improves the housing for the poor by making vacated units available.

While new construction is essential for maintaining and adding to the housing

Figure 21–3 (continued).   Views at top left, top right, and bottom left show, respectively, three stages for 56 town house modules assembled in the early 1970s in Corinth, Mississippi: (1) rail shipment from Stirling Homex Corporation in Avon, New York; (2) on-site assembly; and (3) completed units ready for occupancy. At bottom right is seen the most popular form of industrialized housing, the mobile home. Factory production is seen by its proponents as a means of increasing production, reducing costs, providing efficiency, and stabilizing employment in the construction industry. (See text discussion on page 621.)

supply and for helping in the elimination of the worst housing units, filtering alone is not sufficient for improving the housing of the poor. All housing requires maintenance. When poorer people move into better housing, the better quality may not be maintained because of insufficient income. Frequently, new household formations may absorb new housing construction, leaving little for filtering.[12]

A growing concern in filtering is *gentrification*. Substantial numbers of middle and upper income families have been moving into traditionally poorer urban neighborhoods, rehabilitating houses, and sometimes displacing the poor who live in the community. Most of these neighborhoods are inner city ones, convenient to jobs and city activities. The neighborhood is said to be *gentrified,* or occupied by gentry. The total impact of this is small to date, but it represents a trend that is good for city treasuries but often bad for longer-term residents who find rents and property tax assessments going up.[13]

Discrimination One very important consideration in housing demand is discrimination. Many people are excluded from portions of the housing market by deliberate marketing practices which prevent them from renting or owning. Blacks and other racial minorities have suffered most from such practices. However, women have also been discriminated against. People with children may be prevented from renting apartments, particularly when a seller's market prevails. Students, homosexuals, handicapped persons, welfare recipients, divorced persons, and some ethnic groups also meet with discrimination at times.

Patterns of segregation in housing result from discrimination and also from other causes. Being unwanted, many minorities do not attempt to move into some areas. Income disparities often prevent blacks and other minorities from securing access to much housing, particularly in newer suburban areas. The income disparity itself may be a result of discrimination—and certainly of long-term social inequities. In addition, studies tend to show that blacks generally pay more than whites for equivalent housing.[14]

The marketing of housing is dominated by the real estate industry, which sells and rents housing, and by the financial institutions which provide mortgage financing. Therefore, attempts to broaden housing choice frequently focus on the practices of these organizations.

The market area The housing market area is a term used to designate the region within which housing is generally competitive. People are tied to particular locations because of jobs, family, or other personal relationships, and they therefore seek housing in areas where they have reasons to live. They rarely move to a new region merely because of the availability of housing.

The housing market area is the physical area in which daily economic, geographic, and social interdependencies exist.

A housing market area is the physical area within which all dwelling units are linked together in a chain of substitution. . . . In a broad sense, every dwelling unit within a local housing market may be considered a substitute for every other unit. Hence, all dwelling units may be said to form a single market characterized by interactions of occupancy, prices and rents.[15]

The major factor in defining a housing market area is its interdependent economic and employment structure, but it will include shared institutions, transportation systems, educational and health facilities, wholesale and retail trade centers, and communication networks.

Financial aspects of housing

Mortgages and housing[16] Housing is extremely sensitive to conditions in the financial market. The cost and availability of money for mortgages influences whether households can purchase homes, whether investors will purchase rental properties, whether builders will produce new housing units, and whether families will move.

Housing, whether purchased by a resident owner or by an investor, is almost always a highly "leveraged" commodity. Few people will—or can—buy a residential property without a mortgage. The ratio of the loan (or mortgage granted) to the total value of the property is usually high, frequently from 80 to 90 percent of the value. This means that the owner's equity, or personal investment, is relatively low, hence, the owner "leverages" his or her money with a high ratio of borrowed money. This has a significant impact on the marketing of housing, and an even greater impact on the decision to build new housing.

The overall financing of housing includes: (1) short-term loans for constructing new housing; (2) long-term mortgages (in new housing this replaces construction financing); and (3) the secondary mortgage market, which buys existing mortgages and provides for liquidity for the original mortgage. Each of the phases of financing is an essential link in the complete process. If banks cannot place mortgages with an investor (in secondary mortgaging, for example) they will be unable or reluctant to make any additional commitments. Mortgage loans are generally long term, often for twenty-five to forty years.

The fluctuations in the construction of housing are largely attributed to housing's relationship to financial markets. Housing is said to be countercyclical. When the economy is booming, housing construction tends to decline; when the economy is in a state of decline, housing construction is likely to increase before other areas of economic activity do so. The factors behind this result from the patterns of financing housing.

Housing is financed from savings and loan associations, commercial banks, insurance companies, mutual savings banks, and other financial institutions. Savings and loan associations hold about 40 percent of all residential mortgage loans. When the economy is booming the demand for money increases, interest rates rise, and money flows from savings and loans into more profitable investments. Hence, less is likely to be available for home mortgages. When the economy is in a decline there is less demand for money, interest rates fall, other investment opportunities decline, and more money flows into savings and loans and banks. It is then available for mortgages.

Similarly, other financial institutions choose more profitable investments and put less money into housing when interest rates rise. The demand for money for housing must compete with other demands for money in our economy. The interest rate for housing loans and the amount of money available, then, are determined by factors outside of housing. However, because there is a large existing housing supply in relation to new housing, the costs of existing housing often do not rise fast enough to make new housing competitive. A rental investor cannot make a profit on new construction if his or her borrowing costs will be much higher than those for existing properties.

While the general economy plays an important role in the provision and availability of housing, the specific practices of financial institutions are also significant. As savings and loan associations, banks, and other institutions determine their own lending practices, they can decide who will get residential loans and which neighborhoods will be acceptable. Their practices have often discriminated against women and minorities, and against older urban neighborhoods. Frequently, banks and savings and loan associations will decide that certain areas or neighborhoods are not good risks for granting mortgages, because they fear transition or age is changing the area and lowering property values. They are then said to *redline* the area—that is, to designate an area in which they will grant no mortgages. Redlining then becomes a self-fulfilling prophecy; when mortgage money no longer is available and prospective buyers cannot get mortgages, the area becomes undesirable and properties decline in value. Redlining is under heavy pressure as an illegal practice as the result of federal regulations, local ordinances, and court decisions. Financial institutions—and insurance companies as well—are on the defensive when attempting to zone (that is, redline) any area for any financial or underwriting purpose.

Government involvement Government can regulate financial institutions and, through its regulations, can affect housing. For example, government determines which kinds of institutions can make what loans and frequently sets interest rates on loans. Many states have usury regulations which restrict the rates on home mortgages, but this serves to stop mortgage lending when the prevailing interest rates rise above the allowable mortgage rate. The federal government limits the amount of money that insurance companies can invest in residential mortgages. The President's Committee on Urban Housing in 1968 felt that one of the most important steps that public officials could take in housing was in fiscal and monetary matters, in avoiding policies that severly restrict the funds available to housing.[17]

Combating redlining Augmenting fair housing legislation adopted by the federal government, the Federal Home Loan Bank Board in 1978 issued regulations that prohibit discrimination solely because of property location (redlining). The regulations also cover several areas of potential discrimination for savings and loan associations and other federally insured lending institutions.

The major provisions now are the following: to prohibit member institutions from automatically refusing a loan because of the age or location of a dwelling; to require member institutions to maintain written loan underwriting standards which are available to the public upon request; to prohibit loan decisions that are based on appraisals that include discriminatory factors such as age or location; and to require member institu-

tions to tell potential borrowers that they have a right to file a written loan application, in order to discourage prescreening of potential loan applicants.

In addition, the regulations require member institutions to maintain a loan application register as a management tool to identify missed lending opportunities and as an enforcement tool to enable federal examiners to flag potential discriminatory loan decisions—as well as to cover Equal Credit Opportunity Act protected borrower characteristics including age, marital status, income from public assistance programs, and good faith exercise of rights under the Consumer Credit Protection Act.

Source: Abstracted from "Fact Sheet," Federal Home Loan Bank Board, Washington, D.C., 18 May 1978.

One of the most revolutionary actions in housing in this country was the establishment of the Federal Housing Administration (FHA) in 1934. The FHA changed the established practices of housing mortgages by creating mortgage insurance. The FHA did not actually lend money; it merely insured the mortgage. If a borrower defaulted on a mortgage, the FHA would assume the financial responsibility. This practice encouraged banks, which had been severely affected by mortgage default during the Depression in the early 1930s, to resume lending, since the federal government assumed the risk.

In fact, however, because FHA insured mortgages for longer periods of time and encouraged better loan-to-value ratios than had been the practice, home ownership became more widespread than ever before. After World War II the existence of FHA insured mortgage money contributed to the massive suburban subdivisions and the expansion of the 1950s and early 1960s. Similarly, the Veterans Administration (VA) guaranteed home mortgages for former military personnel. At one time, FHA and VA guaranteed the bulk of new homes. This is no longer true, as private insurance has replaced much FHA and VA activity.

The federal government has created secondary mortgage institutions such as the Federal National Mortgage Association and the Government National Mortgage Association to support its housing programs by buying certain authorized mortgages. The federal government also affects housing with its regulation of financial institutions. The Federal Reserve System regulates and provides credit to federally chartered member banks of its system. The Federal Home Loan Bank system provides credit and regulates federal savings and loan associations, which are the principal source of mortgage credit. It also provides deposit insurance and a secondary mortgage mechanism, the Federal Home Loan Mortgage Corporation.[18]

Governmental roles in housing

Federal government   Although governments in the United States provide little housing directly, their actions can have a significant impact.

While some federal actions are taken directly, more federal actions in fact affect housing indirectly. The federal government operates in several areas. It has been the major provider of financial assistance to low and moderate income groups through a variety of programs that began with the initiation of public housing in 1934, through a small scale and short-lived program of the Public Works Administration which ran until 1937. Housing assistance programs of all kinds, however, are almost always dated from the passage of the Housing Act of 1937. Its mortgage insurance programs, cited earlier, have affected the entire pattern of housing finance. It regulates credit through policies directing the Federal Reserve System and the Federal Home Loan Bank System. It has established major secondary mortgage markets to encourage lending for housing. Among its most important policies, however, may be federal income tax provisions. Homeowners can take deductions for mortgage interest and property taxes, and these together with an imputed rental value have been estimated to be worth more each year to homeowners than all expenditures for low and moderate income housing. Apartment owners have been permitted to take excess depreciation on their rental investments, and this has provided a tax shelter which has been a major factor in attracting investors to rental properties.[19]

The civil rights legislation of the federal government has, in part, been directed at providing equal housing opportunity. It prohibits discrimination in any federally assisted housing, bars discrimination in the sale, rental, or financing of most housing, and requires that federal agencies administer their programs with affirmative action. This is more than eliminating discrimination; it is actively promoting integration.[20]

State government   State governments have generally played a minor role in housing. Following World War II, several states initiated programs for home loans to verterans. New York pioneered in providing housing assistance, often developing the prototypes for later federal programs—but these were the exceptions. By the 1970s the majority of states had housing finance agencies which lent money to private developers or individual homeowners. The practice is to borrow through state bonds (which are tax exempt and therefore carry lower than market interest rates) and re-lend at lower interest rates to qualified builders and owners. These finance agencies often have additional powers to act as housing authorities. The extent of these activities has been small, but it is gradually accelerating, depending on a favorable financial climate for marketing state backed obligations.

In other areas states have basic powers which they have not often used. They can enact statewide housing codes and building standards. They are beginning to become interested in statewide development controls. They regulate state chartered financial institutions, and state civil rights laws can be effective in attacking discrimination.[21]

Local government It is the local government, however, that has the most direct impact on housing. Local governments can provide some housing assistance directly, usually in the form of tax abatements or rehabilitation loan programs. Many are active in the federal subsidy programs, particularly in public housing. But the major role of local governments is that they in effect control whatever is built in their jurisdictions. They also impose the great bulk of property taxes on residential services. They provide the basic services that urban communities require and, in so doing, are the major determinants of the quality of residential life. They provide the schools, the police and fire protection, and the streets, waste collection, water, recreation, and health and social services. They control the zoning regulations, subdivision regulations, and building codes, and all inspections of structures. They provide or authorize all the infrastructure for communities—streets, sewers, water, utilities. Nothing can be built without local approval.

Local development regulations and processing add substantially to the costs of new housing. In the late 1960s and the 1970s increased government regulation added significantly to escalating housing construction costs. Building standards have been raised; fees and impact taxes have grown; reviews and processing time have been extended; and growth controls have been added. Although controversy exists about the benefits of the greater regulation, little doubt exists about the impact of the added construction costs.[22] In support of increasing regulation of construction, however, are the costs of unplanned growth or sprawl, the long-term effects on governmental services, and the impact on the environment and on people.[23]

Housing depends on local government. Therefore, it is proper to focus housing planning at the local level. Most financial assistance is still federal, however, and local governments have tended to direct efforts at eliminating housing problems only toward those areas in which federal assistance is available. This has meant inadequate local attention to housing.

One major concern regarding government and housing is that many governmental decisions affect housing, although the housing implications of decisions are not considered at the time. This is true of financial regulations, highway decisions, and environmental policies, for example. The impact of government decisions on housing is not always made explicit.

Housing goals and standards

The Housing Act of 1937 was designed to provide federal assistance ''for the elimination of unsafe and unsanitary housing conditions, for the eradication of slums, for the provision of decent, safe and sanitary dwellings for families of low income and for the stimulation of business activity.''

It was our first major federal commitment to providing better housing for the poor. In 1949 Congress passed another landmark housing act introducing urban redevelopment, which later became urban renewal. This act called for ''the realization as soon as feasible of the goal of a decent home and a suitable living environment for every American family.''

Every housing act since then has reaffirmed that goal, but we have failed to eliminate the problems of inadequate housing in our society. Publicly stated housing goals have been more nearly platitudes than firm commitments to action.

This section describes the general meaning of governmental housing goals, sets forth seven housing standards, and then discusses briefly the magnitude of the housing problem and the question of housing and segregation. Because of differences in values, rising expectations, and constantly rising real costs of housing, it has been difficult to reach national consensus on very many housing goals except for broad platitudinous ones. This may account for the difficulty in measuring housing "inadequacy." If we cannot agree on definitions, how can we do any counting?

Despite these difficulties, students of housing point out that we are probably the best housed country in the world. The President's Committee on Urban Housing stated the following:

Despite the grim statistics . . . the United States is a world leader in the quality and relative quantity of housing . . . it is fair to conclude that the U.S. population, at least on the average, enjoys a combination of amenities and space per capita unequaled by any other country.[24]

Housing goals

Many goals affect housing policy and programs. As is the case in many other areas, goals can be conflicting. In general, housing goals fall into three general areas: community concerns; social and equity concerns; and production and stability concerns.

Community concerns   From the *community* perspective, the objective of housing policy is proper *public management* of housing and its environment.

Housing should be properly related to other community facilities, services to housing should be efficiently organized, the property valuation of housing should be safeguarded, and public safety must be protected.

For local governments housing is the major user of urban land; its occupants are the major consumers of services, and the revenue from its taxation is a major source of governmental income. Effective management of governmental affairs requires, then, that housing be coordinated with both capital and operating expenditures. New housing developments should be planned with community facilities and public services. Existing housing should be provided with adequate services. All should be protected from unnecessary hazards such as fire, faulty construction, and unsanitary conditions. And encouragement should be given to keep property upgraded sufficiently so that tax revenues are not lost.

Although these policies may not always be articulated, they are implicit in most local governments. Local governments have adopted programs of zoning, subdivision control, and building and housing codes which speak to the management aspects of housing and its development. So do the usual local practices of school siting, fire and police station location, park development, and location of other facilities. These must all be undertaken with housing in perspective.

Social and equity concerns   The *social* and *equity* goals have received more explicit definition, but, often, less attention. The major purpose of these goals is to extend housing adequacy (including the community goals just discussed) to everyone irrespective of income, race, national origin, family structure, or sex, and to eliminate constraints.

Safe, adequate housing, in proper environments, should be available to all households, at costs they can reasonably afford to pay. There should be no discrimination in the availability of housing or the opportunities associated with it. Housing should be provided for low and moderate income families, and communities should extend housing opportunities to all types of households.

While most local governments have some concern for the first set of goals, communities differ in their response to social and equity goals. Older urban communities are more likely to address them than are suburban governments. While every responsible local government will want safe housing, well-serviced communities, and sound housing stock, not every government assumes a responsibility to accept the poor, those disadvantaged in the housing market, and blacks and other minorities. Overt discrimination is one matter; simply not allowing housing that would serve the disadvantaged is another. A corollary to

Figure 21–4   Housing today needs to serve a wide variety of people
and ways of living—young singles, the elderly, families with children,
young affluent couples, and groups of many kinds.

ending discrimination is opening the suburbs by creating more housing opportunities. This would mean ending exclusionary zoning which precludes multi-family housing, mobile homes, or other housing for lower income groups. It would also mean encouraging housing development for lower income families. A major issue, one being argued in the courts, is whether every community has a responsibility to provide a share of housing for the poor, the disadvantaged, and those discriminated against.[25]

Production and stability concerns   Turning to housing from a national point of view, we find another set of goals concerned with *production* and *stability* in the housing industry from an overall economic standpoint. Housing construction is cyclical and seasonal, creating uncertainties in the industry, unemployment, and instability in financial investments in housing.

Housing production should be stabilized so that fluctuations in building construction are reduced, the country is ensured a steady supply of new units, investors are protected, and employment is safeguarded.

The stimulation of housing production is attempted from time to time, but, primarily, housing is affected by overall economic policies dealing with interest rates, credit reserves, discount rates, etc. This phase of housing policy is best addressed at the national level but is a major concern of many economists, builders, and construction workers.[26]

With the varied nature of housing goals, programs have often assumed multiple goals. Sometimes the expectations have been too great and the goals too many. It is not unusual to see a federal housing subsidy program that was designed to provide housing for the poor also being considered a production stimulus, required to overcome exclusionary suburban housing policies, and intended to introduce innovative housing types and imaginative site planning. This is far too much to expect from a modestly conceived financial incentive program. Housing policies can conflict, also, with each other and with other policies. Many suburban communities do not wish to allow housing for the poor because the poor require more services than do other residents. Efficiency—usually equated with low cost—in providing governmental services is in conflict with opening up the suburbs to the disadvantaged.

Similarly, environmental policies are often in conflict with the need for additional housing. Strict conservationists see additional development as a threat—particularly density housing development, which is seen as generating more traffic, storm water runoff, pollution, and waste, and less open space. Many communities are using environmental arguments to prohibit housing for low and moderate income households.[27] The goals of housing are by no means universally accepted.

Housing standards

It is necessary to distinguish between housing need and other concepts such as demand and supply. Need refers to a social or evaluative concept. Supply and demand are economic terms. Housing need refers to the gap between what exists and what should exist, or the amount of housing that would be required to provide adequate housing for every household without regard to its ability to pay.

Determining housing need requires the establishment of housing standards. Housing which does not then meet standards is inadequate. Standards of adequacy will vary in different cultures or according to societal values. What is acceptable in one circumstance may not be acceptable in another. Our worst slums may have better housing than the average housing in underdeveloped countries, but they would still be unacceptable in our society with its minimum standards and expectations.

This section suggests seven standards of adequacy which are traditionally accepted by housing specialists. However, many of them are very difficult to measure, many have little data available, and some perhaps cannot be quantified. Much of our available data come from census surveys, and we tend to limit our evaluations to such data, even though we know this is insufficient.[28]

The standards suggested are: cost, condition, crowding, choice, neighborhood, access, and control. The listing implies no order of importance.

Cost The cost of housing is relative to income. Households should be adequately housed without spending an excessive amount of their income. The standard for cost in housing is given as a rent–income or cost–income ratio. A ratio higher than 25 percent is generally a mark of housing need, although it is more severe for low and moderate income families who have to restrict purchases for food, clothing, health care, etc., if they spend too much on housing. With the general rise in rent–income burden, ratios higher than 25 percent are becoming more usual and acceptable for certain households.

Condition Housing units are a threat to health and safety if they are physically inadequate or structurally unsound, or if they contain hazards such as faulty wiring or heating, lead paint, etc. Condition refers to individual housing units or groups of units in the same structure and not to neighborhood-related problems. At one time the U.S. Bureau of the Census evaluated units as sound, deteriorating, or dilapidated, according to their physical condition. Some conditions are hazardous, some are threats to health, and others are threats to comfort. Units are considered substandard not only if they are physically in poor condition but also if they lack complete plumbing. In some areas units may be substandard if they lack central heating. In most cases the measure of condition is always given as a housing standard, although data may be difficult to obtain.

Crowding Housing size is usually defined by number of rooms. The usual measure of crowding in our society is number of people per room. Crowding is a health hazard, both physically and psychologically. An acceptable minimum is one person per room.

Choice It is important to allow people to choose those housing services which suit them best. One measure of choice is vacancy. A sufficient vacancy rate is necessary to allow people to find different housing as their needs change. This permits mobility. Too little vacancy inhibits moving; too much vacancy means deterioration in the entire housing market.

Choice is more than mere vacancy, however. It also encompasses the lack of discrimination so that every household can exercise housing choice without unreasonable constraints. Any practices of the market which limit housing opportunities beyond reasonable economic ones must be eliminated. While vacancy can be measured, discrimination is much harder to determine.

Neighborhood Adequate housing means an adequate environment, and this means an adequate neighborhood with adequate man-made and environmental features. Traditionally, little was done to measure neighborhood, although its importance was recognized. Since the late 1970s, however, the annual housing survey conducted by the Bureau of the Census for the U.S. Department of Housing and Urban Development has enumerated a wide range of neighborhood conditions and services. The neighborhood variable includes such features as lack of pollution (noise, traffic, air, and water), personal safety (freedom from hazards such as fire and crime), and adequate community health (protection from epidemics, unsafe water, rodents, and any other health threats). These are measures of the condition of the neighborhood and they extend beyond the individual housing unit. A unit may be safe, but the neighborhood may not be safe.

Access The issue of access is an extension of the neighborhood concept; it refers to the availability of community services and facilities. The most important are probably education and jobs, although other services such as shopping, health facilities, and recreation can be equally vital. Examples are public transportation and social services. Access encompasses the availability of opportunity and access to that opportunity. Sound housing where there are no jobs available is not adequate for the head of a household who must work. Housing for the elderly without public transportation may be like a prison. Again, it is a difficult standard to measure but its implications are obvious.

Control The final criterion is control. It is a matter of human dignity that each of us has some control over our environment. It is the essence of freedom. Control can be said to cover landlord–tenant relations, the ability to influence one's surroundings, and a sense of self-esteem. This is more than choice; it is the difference between being helpless and having a housing situation which belongs to one. Emphasis on home ownership is, in part, testimony to the belief that one should exercise some control over one's housing.

The magnitude of housing needs

Even with housing standards it is difficult to determine the magnitude of housing need. Some of the standards may be measured; some clearly cannot be. Many of the conditions overlap—for example, households paying too much for housing may also live in substandard units, in crowded conditions, and perhaps in poor neighborhoods.

Those with low incomes usually are the most disadvantaged in housing and usually gain access only to the poorest housing. In many cases it is possible to determine housing needs simply in terms of those with low and moderate incomes.

Certain groups of households are also usually the most disadvantaged in terms of housing. In addition to lower income households, these include black and other minority groups, the elderly, single person households, large families, and the handicapped.

Generally, when housing needs have been quantified they are overwhelming in relation to our ability to address them. The President's Committee on Urban Housing quantified housing needs and determined that there were 6.7 million occupied substandard housing units in 1966. If the nation were to eliminate them, they estimated that 8.7 million units would be needed to replace them within a decade (another 2 million substandard units would be added to the category in ten years). They also estimated that in 1968 there were 7.8 million households unable to buy decent housing.[29]

A more recent study estimated that there were 16.8 million households in the United States in 1973 with housing deprivation as measured by standards of condition, crowding, cost, and neighborhood. There were 6.3 million households in physically inadequate units, an additional 0.5 million in overcrowded units, another 6 million paying excessive rents, and 4 million living in unsatisfactory neighborhoods. In this estimate, overlap was systematically eliminated.[30] By this accounting of housing deprivation, almost one-fourth of all United States households in 1973 were inadequately housed.

What conclusions can be drawn from these gloomy statistics on the magnitude of housing needs in the United States? First, replacement of substandard housing remains a problem for many households even though impressive progress has been made since 1970 in reducing dilapidated housing and housing without plumbing facilities. Second, the excessive amount that many are paying for housing is a problem yet to be addressed. This is likely to get worse, as the costs of housing continue to escalate, making it a problem for the middle class as well as for the poor. The study just cited estimated that high housing production of 20 to 22 million units would be needed during the decade 1975–85 to meet replacement and household formation requirements. Even with this high level of production, housing deprivation will continue as a significant problem.[31] Compounding this problem is the prevalence of poor neighborhood environments and substandard services.

Housing and segregation

Almost any population or housing analysis shows the segregation that exists in metropolitan areas. Nonwhite households are not represented in the same proportions as white households in areas outside central cities. While they are slowly moving into suburban areas, they are not doing this nearly as rapidly as are whites. It is impossible to deal with housing without confronting the obvious disparities. Indeed, many suburban areas refuse to undertake *any* housing analysis or plan because it reveals the depth of this problem. Segregation is so deeply entrenched in housing that for many it is the primary housing problem. Indeed, segregation is one of the major forces underscoring the need for housing planning on metropolitan and regional bases.[32]

In 1970, for example, 79 percent of nonwhite households in metropolitan areas (SMSAs) lived in central cities. By contrast, only 46 percent of metropolitan area whites lived in central cities. By 1974 there was a slight change, and 77 percent of SMSA nonwhites were in central cities. In the four year period 89 percent of the growth of white households in SMSAs was outside central cities. For nonwhites the SMSA growth outside central cities was 33 percent. Although nonwhite households significantly improved their in-migration into suburban SMSAs, by 1974 they represented only 5.7 percent of suburban households; they constituted 11.7 percent of all United States households and 22.1 percent of all central city households.[33]

Most housing analyses show that there are more inadequately housed whites than nonwhites, but in proportion to the total population, there is a greater percentage of inadequately housed nonwhites. The issue is not purely income, however. It is segregation and discrimination.

Making a housing plan

This section concentrates on some planning approaches to housing and also covers the basic components of a housing market analysis, a structure for undertaking a comprehensive housing plan, and an analysis of housing costs.

Housing market analysis

The most common housing studies are market analyses which attempt to project either demand or need for housing. Such analyses can be simple demand studies or can be more detailed studies of need that build in assumptions about providing housing subsidies, replacing deficient housing, or providing housing for special groups. Primarily, they estimate the amount of housing that should be produced in a given period of time (usually short range) to meet the demand or need, however defined.

The housing market area   The first part of any housing analysis is determining the boundaries of the housing market area in which all housing units are competitive. This provides the basis for all data and statistical information.

As defined earlier, the market area is an economic, social, and geographic region or entity. All its parts are interdependent to a high degree. It can be described by commuting patterns to jobs, transportation facilities and patterns, and wholesale and retail trade areas. There are usually defined communication networks, such as newspaper circulation and radio and television coverage. It is an area which bounds the average person's daily life, if not in terms of individual travel then by supportive services. It is large enough to be relatively independent and small enough to encompass most daily travel. A major feature of the economic determinant is the employment structure: the market area is usually an interdependent employment area, sharing labor markets and employment centers.

In most cases the actual area defined is coterminous with political jurisdictions, or other already defined areas. Data are more easily obtained for such areas. An SMSA or a labor force area is a good basis for establishing a housing market area. Two or more SMSAs can be combined; several jurisdictions such as counties or townships can be joined. Coterminous urban areas as defined by census are possible. However defined, the region should be reasonable, should be a social and economic entity, and should be an area for which data are accessible.[34]

The components of change   Three factors usually determine future demand or need for housing units: change in the number and composition of households; replacement of existing units; and change in vacancy rate. Housing market analysis is the process of estimating these factors for a given time period in a given housing market area.

The change in households is derived from population change which in turn is usually influenced by economic factors such as employment growth. This analysis will usually include employment (or economic) trends and projections as well as population trends and projections. Once population is projected it is converted into household population. (Group population housed in institutions, hospitals, prisons, military barracks, etc., is excluded.) The household population is then divided by average household size to determine the future number of households, and the current number gives the change or first factor in demand. The important variables in determining this component of change are anticipated growth rate and change in household composition (size). The analyses must determine these.

The formation of households depends in part on the cost of housing and the ability of people to pay for housing. As housing costs rise the growth of households may decline as single people double up, children stay with their parents, and elderly persons stay with their families instead of establishing independent households. The incidence of household formation is a variable affected by both demographic and economic conditions.

The replacement of existing units is the second factor in the components of change. In any given time period existing housing units are removed from the housing supply. Some units are demolished because they have deteriorated beyond redemption. Others are removed for new development. Public actions such as highway construction, for example, can lead to removals. Some units are destroyed by natural causes or by disasters such as fire. In addition to removals there are conversions, both into and out of the housing supply. Housing units can be converted into other uses such as retail stores or office space. Some housing units can be added by subdivision of existing units.

It is necessary to make an estimate of how many units will be required to replace the net number of units removed from the existing housing supply during the study period. Occasionally, study will show that there was a net addition to supply resulting from conversions. This can happen particularly in second home areas, where seasonal units are converted to year-round occupancy. Obviously, public policy will influence this factor. A decision to eliminate substantial numbers of substandard units would add to the replacement needs of a community.

The final factor in determining future demand is alteration of the vacancy rate. A certain number of vacancies—usually 4 to 5 percent overall—are necessary to provide for reasonable mobility in any housing market. (This will vary between units available for rent and for sale.) The total housing supply by the end of the study period will have to include some vacant units. The change in vacancies between the beginning and the end of the study period becomes a factor in the demand.

An example of housing markets analysis   Table 21–2 provides a simple example of a housing market analysis (without deriving all of the assumptions on which the components of change are estimated).

A hypothetical housing market area is established for which the housing market demand between 1970 and 1980 is to be estimated. From census data, the 1970 population and households are determined. The population is projected to grow from 250,000 in 1970 to 325,000 by 1980. An estimate of 1980 group population is made and subtracted from the total 1980 population. The resulting household population is divided by the estimated 1980 average household size. By 1980 there will be 96,800 households, an increase of 29,100 over the 67,700 of 1970, following the assumptions in this model.

From census data, the 1970 vacancy rate (among year-round units) is found to be 3.3 percent. Obviously, more units will be required to increase the vacancy rate to 5 percent by 1980. A 5 percent vacancy rate by 1980 will necessitate that 2,800 units be added to the 2,300 vacant total in 1970.

After studying demolitions, conversions, projected public works which will remove units, and any other trends in losses, it is assumed that 5,000 units will be required to replace the units in the 1970 supply that will be removed by 1980.

The summation of these three estimates is given in Table 21–2. Adding the three factors together gives an estimated demand or need for 36,900 units between 1970 and 1980, or an average of about 3,700 per year. By 1980, if the total is met, the year-round housing supply will reach 101,900, with 96,800 occupied and 5,100 vacant. The total can be further analyzed to determine what kind of units should be built in terms of tenure, size, cost, structural type, etc.

This estimate becomes the basis for establishing housing policies. If there is not enough land zoned for the kinds of housing units in a project location, for example, this fact would have to be examined. If the housing industry should be unable to produce the volume, then stimulation or subsidy would have to be investigated.

Concepts of adequacy can be included in the analysis, and projected housing needs can be included in addition to market force determinations. These needs might increase the household formation, replacement, or vacancy rate. These additions will require public housing or public subsidies if these needs cannot be met by the private market. For example, a survey might show many elderly people living in rooming houses or in crowded family quarters who would occupy separate units if they were available. This number of additional households could be added to the household total as an additional need, to be met through direct public intervention.

Housing market analysis is a starting point in many housing studies but is not, in itself, the only or the major form of housing study. It is the format, however, for quantifying housing demand or need. The very numbers in such an analysis

Table 21–2   Example of housing market analysis for
hypothetical housing market area, 1970–80.

Component	1970 (census)	1980 (projection)
Population, housing market area		
Components of household change		
Population	250,000	325,000
Group population	20,000	25,000
Household population	230,000	300,000
Average household size	3.4	3.1
Households	67,700	96,800
Change in households, 1970–80		29,100
Replacement of existing units		
Lost through disasters		500
Demolitions, 1970–80		3,800
Loss through conversions		700
Replacements, 1970–80		5,000
Housing units		
Change in vacancy rate		
Total units	70,000	101,900[1]
Occupied	67,700	96,800
Vacant (no.)	2,300	5,100[1]
Vacant (%)	3.3	5.0
Change in vacant units, 1970–80		2,800
Total housing market, 1970–80		
Change in households		29,100
Replacements		5,000
Vacancy change to 5%		2,800
Total		36,900
Average annual no. of units		3,700

1 By definition, occupied units = households. In determining future vacancy, the number of households is the beginning point together with the percent of vacancies desired.

are matters for public policy determination. A housing study of condition might determine that 20 percent of the existing supply is deficient and should be replaced. Such a finding would alter the "replacement" factor in any equation which was committed to removing substandard housing.

All such analysis must start at the total housing market area level and then be divided into submarkets. The submarket applicable to a central city renewal project, for example, would have to compete with projects elsewhere in the total housing market area.

Comprehensive housing planning

The content of housing market analysis is well established. Beyond that, there is no model for comprehensive housing planning. Most "housing planning" is limited, usually focusing on available federal subsidies, categorical grants, or needs of low and moderate income families.[35]

Since housing is primarily supplied by the private sector, it is understandable that public planning has focused on areas in which the private market is unable to meet needs—that is, low and moderate income housing. However, the range of public action should be greater than providing housing subsidies (which in themselves have been grossly inadequate). This section, therefore, outlines a fuller set of elements to be included in a housing analysis and plan.

The three basic parts to any plan include undertaking research and analysis, setting goals and objectives, and developing programs for implementation. While they are not all-inclusive, the following paragraphs highlight the most important components.

Research and analysis   The first step is to delineate a housing market area, as defined earlier, with geographic and social subareas. The analysis and research should then address the components of the housing process for the market area and its submarkets.

Housing supply and market[36]   Existing housing stock, production, household characteristics, employment, income, and several housing projections are among the factors that go into the supply and market analyses outlined below.

1. *Supply.* The supply of housing must be examined in relation to the physical, social, and economic factors in its market area. Research on the supply should include information about *existing housing stock,* including its age, condition, type, tenure, value, cost, location, and vacancy rate; analysis of the *production of housing,* capacity of the industry, and additions to supply; evaluation of the *physical community,* including information about the adequacy of the man-made environment, facilities, and services such as schools, recreation, transportation, utilities, public services, and protection; analysis of the *natural environment* and conditions such as pollution and flooding; and data on the existing supply of *low and moderate income housing.*
2. *Market.* The market for housing concerns the people and households occupying housing, their characteristics, and the constraints they may face in securing housing. This will include information about *household characteristics* such as size, age, income, composition, employment, race, and other social and economic characteristics; *employment* and other opportunities in the local economy which influence the demand for housing; factors such as *discrimination* or distributive constraints existing in the market; and *management and marketing practices* in the private market, including real estate practices and tenant–landlord relationships.
3. *Identification of needs.* An analysis of the previous data should clarify the *housing deficiencies* which exist in any given market or submarket. In order to do this it is necessary to establish *standards* as indicated earlier.
4. *Projections.* Housing projections of supply and of population and household formations are important in determining future needs. This is the housing market analysis just referred to which estimates new household formation, replacements to supply, and vacancy requirements for the future. Economic projections of *employment* influence population growth; those of *income* help determine which households will need housing assistance.

Financial analysis   The availability and the distribution of financial resources by private lending institutions are vital to housing. Housing relies on construction financing, mortgage money, investment resources for rental properties, and improvement loans for maintenance. A housing study fully addressing these factors will consider credit policies and lending practices of local and regional financial institutions, interest rates, investment opportunities, and such issues as redlining and discrimination in lending. Although they may be beyond the authority of local or state governments, the regulation of financial institutions and the flow of money into them are critical and should be analyzed for their impact on the local situation.

Governmental structure   Each level of government has different functions, and the housing study must review the political structure in the market area and assess the impact of codes and land development powers, zoning, taxing powers and practices, resource availability of existing agencies, and laws and regulations affecting housing.

Goals and objectives   The second phase of the housing plan is establishing goals, priorities, and objectives. The goals must be realistic and should not assume some massive attention to housing that has never existed or some scale of subsidy that is impossible.[37] Beyond that, the goals have three considerations: who participates in formulating; what issues are addressed; and what time period is projected.

For participation, the planning process should involve the production industry, housing investors, the real estate industry, financial institutions, governmental agencies affected, and the most important consumer and civil rights groups, citizen groups, and community organizations.

The goals can include elimination of existing deficiencies; new construction, conservation, and preservation of existing housing; provision of community facilities and services; securing of governmental regulations affecting housing; creation of tax policies; financing of housing; allocation of resources to housing; and enlarging of housing choice.

Timing is especially important. The period planned for should be long enough to make change possible but short enough to allow for accuracy. Time periods set many years ahead tend to become unreal. It is best to plan in terms of five year goals, with some longer trend analysis or general goals up to ten years. These can be updated annually and broken into one year implementation targets.

Implementation   Analysis and goal setting must be combined with action. In the past this has often been limited to addressing only the needs as compatible with federal subsidy programs. The plan is, in fact, the way in which government (at whatever level) acts to facilitate, regulate, or supplement the private market. The areas in which the state or local government can act include: establishing development policies such as codes, zoning, permit processing, and subdivision controls; improving and providing community facilities and services through annual and capital budgeting; regulating private industry, including real estate and land development companies, financial institutions, and housing investors; allocating resources directly to housing by, for example, developing subsidies, rehabilitation loans, and subsidized mortgages; undertaking the development of housing; providing tax incentives; establishing housing-related agencies; assuring land availability; and directing governmental funds for schools, parks, and other facilities to areas complying with housing goals.

The components of housing cost[38]

The costs of housing are basic to many housing problems. Much attention is given to the needs of low and moderate income households and to the rising costs of housing in general. To improve the quantity or quality of supply it is usually necessary to address cost considerations for occupants, owners, and investors. There are also many misconceptions and myths about housing costs which frequently lead to erroneous public action.

The two major kinds of housing costs are initial development costs and occupancy costs. Reducing housing costs for occupants necessitates addressing both kinds.

Development costs are summarized in Table 21–3. They include land, construction, financing, and overhead costs (fees, profit, management, etc.). Land costs have escalated since the mid-1960s because of shortages of serviced land. Environmental restrictions or excessive local land use regulations are often responsible for increasing improvement costs of land. The construction costs include on-site labor and materials and equipment shipped to the site. Contrary to popular belief, on-site labor is not a major cost in housing. The industrialization of housing is not likely to achieve significant reductions in the cost of housing to consumers. Building materials, as shown in Table 21–3, are the largest single element in the cost of a house, and as of the mid-1970s were increasing sharply because of inflation. This cost element is extremely difficult to control except through materials innovations, which require building code revisions, and by basic changes in housing design and characteristics, which require changes in attitudes on the part of consumers.

Table 21–3 Housing development costs.

	% of total cost	
Cost component	Typical range	Single family example
Land	15–40	25
Acquisition	. . .	11
Improvement	. . .	14
Construction	40–65	47
Labor on site	. . .	15
Materials	. . .	32
Financing	10–15	11
Fees, overhead, profit	10–20	17

Source: Builder interviews by author.

Table 21–4 Housing occupancy costs.

	Typical % of total cost[1]	
Cost component	Renter	Owner
Mortgage payment (interest and principal)	45	55
Maintenance and repairs	15	10
Utilities	10	15
Taxes	15	20
Management	5	. . .
Vacancies, profit	10	. . .

1 Percentages subject to change; illustrative only.

Financing costs (the costs of construction or interim financing) are rising because of the overall demand for money. The final cost item, overhead, including profit, etc., is necessary for any private sector activity. The costs which have risen the most rapidly in recent years are land (particularly the improved cost) and financing. These are largely beyond the control of the housing industry.

The occupancy costs of housing vary for owner and renter occupied units (see Table 21–4). Both require mortgage payments (or some form of debt reduction which includes interest and principal). The mortgage payment reflects the initial development cost of the unit. Even a significant reduction in construction cost (were it possible) would have a much smaller effect on occupancy cost (actual cost to the consumer). The mortgage payment usually represents about one-half of total occupancy costs.

Maintenance and repairs usually require 10 to 15 percent of occupancy costs. This is the area that will be neglected when other housing costs rise beyond the consumer's capability to pay. It is omission of this expenditure which leads to decay and deterioration of housing.

Utilities are a major expense. With energy shortages and rapidly rising utility costs this item will assume a larger share of housing outlays in the 1980s.

Property taxes require a large share of the housing dollar. For renters, there are additional costs of management and owner profits.

When governments seek to subsidize housing costs they must address these components. Federal financing programs have largely concentrated on the mortgage payment, by reducing the interest cost or extending the term of the mortgage. The use of nonprofit sponsors eliminates the profit element. Other areas for housing relief center on tax abatements and grants or low interest loans for repairs and rehabilitation. Efforts at lowering initial construction costs are more limited. Land costs can be written down (as in urban renewal), or financing can be reduced by supplying low rate construction loans.

In any of these instances, however, the government merely assumes part of the real cost and does not really eliminate it. The problems with the cost of housing are likely to increase as costs continue to rise.

The local role in housing

Local agencies have a significant role in the improvement of housing, particularly when housing is viewed comprehensively—both private sector and public housing. In developing broad based goals and objectives for housing planning, it may help to look primarily at two areas: community concerns and equity concerns. The former have been of more direct, traditional interest to planning. Production stability concerns have fewer local applications.

Community concerns

Community concerns are traditionally involved in the planning process—in comprehensive planning, in growth management programs, in environmental regulations, and in capital budgeting. The point to be made is that housing should not be the sole concern of housing planners; it should be built into the process for planning and programs of all kinds.

When new housing developments of any size are proposed, development administration—including zoning, subdivision controls, and appropriate codes—is a significant part of the process. The timing of the development is important to ensure that housing costs are not inadvertently driven up. Excessive regulation can be a problem. Community development, in all of its ramifications, is important to housing. This may include urban renewal, rehabilitation, urban homesteading, and small business development programs. Planning can help put programs together to improve housing for all members of the community. Finally, building and housing code creation and enforcement are a significant part of local housing programs, in order to maintain housing quality.

Equity concerns

Providing adequate housing for low and moderate income households often requires some kind of housing assistance or subsidy. The federal government has been the major source of this assistance for many years.

Federal assistance to low and moderate income families has taken several forms: public housing, loans at below market interest rates, direct cash payments, and special mortgage insurance. Public housing was started in the mid–1930s for low income households. When the urban renewal program began to displace entire neighborhoods in the early 1950s, other moderate income households were found to need help, and interest rate programs were initiated which provided cheap mortgages. Since then, other programs have been started, including direct cash payments, which include rent supplements, housing allowances, and outright grants. Special mortgage insurance programs provide extremely favorable mortgage terms such as low down payments and extremely long-term loans to qualified owners.

It is possible to reduce housing costs in other ways at the local level—through property tax abatements, or circuit breaker limits, for example, as is frequently done for lower income, elderly homeowners.

Building codes provide structural and mechanical standards and specifications. Modernization of such codes is often proposed because they lack uniformity, vary from jurisdiction to jurisdiction, and are outdated. They are blamed for preventing experimentation in housing construction, restraining the use of new materials, adding to housing costs, and standing in the way of housing industrialization.

Housing codes are less widespread but regulate the facilities, maintenance, and occupancy of housing. They go beyond structural safety to regulating how many people may inhabit a unit, what plumbing must be available, etc. They have been difficult to enforce.

Code enforcement is a way of upgrading housing, but it can backfire on the residents it is designed to aid. It can drive people out of units or can result in an increase in occupancy costs.

Many other actions of an equity nature are available; some are quite narrow and intensely regulatory while others are broad based and areawide in nature.

From a planning point of view the most significant actions are those involving exclusionary zoning and growth management. These are the actions, usually involving suburban governments, that restrict housing to those who can afford it. Several court cases and other legal actions are changing this in a few jurisdictions.

Other measures that affect housing include rent controls, which help keep rents down for the poor (but may drive investors out or lead to neglected maintenance); affirmative action in real estate marketing practices; fair housing legislation to control steering and blockbusting; fair share housing plans to help open up housing in a wide area so that every community shares responsibility for housing the disadvantaged; elimination of redlining so that banks and savings and loan associations will not zone out areas where they issue mortgages; and establishment of tenant–landlord relations ordinances to improve conditions for renters.

Production and stability concerns are primarily addressed at the federal level through fiscal and monetary policy. However, state and locally imposed moratoria on construction, restrictive growth policies, and environmental controls do slow down new housing production.

Conclusion

This chapter has reviewed the elements of housing, including supply, demand, and financial and governmental roles in housing; housing goals and standards; and the development of a housing plan—including market analysis, comprehensive housing planning, and cost considerations.

Two national study groups in 1968 evaluated the nation's housing, and their reports are still the most comprehensive housing evaluations available. The President's Committee on Urban Housing (the Kaiser Committee)[39] and the National Commission on Urban Problems (the Douglas Commission)[40] established our first quantitative housing goals—26 million new or rehabilitated housing units in ten years (including 6 million units for low and moderate income families)—and recommended new federal subsidy programs that would help the nation work toward this goal. Congress adopted this goal in 1968, but the nation did not realize the goal for publicly assisted housing, achieving less than 50 percent of the 6 million units.[41]

Since that time, however, housing has begun to receive more attention at the federal, state, and local levels. More housing planning is now undertaken, largely through the local Housing Assistance Plan (HAP) that is required for receipt of federal community development assistance,[42] and housing is perceived in a wider framework.

The nature of housing problems has changed, too. An increasing number of households (not just the lower income ones) find that increasing housing costs are an excessive burden. With rising energy costs, the operating costs of housing are increasing. Changing family composition is changing the demand for housing both in type and in location. Governmental priorities are changing. Housing concerns are linked to many other government activities and programs. Housing must compete with other issues such as environmental issues and tax reduction.

In the past the private housing market has worked well for the vast majority of our households, and there was less public concern about housing, but this is not likely to be the case in the future. Governments at all levels will be taking a more active role in the provision, support, and regulation of housing. It is important for local officials to understand the complex nature of housing and its many relationships. This has been the focus of the present chapter.

1 Charles Abrams, *The Future of Housing* (New York: Harper & Brothers, Publishers, 1946), pp. 19–35.

2 Mel Scott, *American City Planning since 1890* (Berkeley: University of California Press, 1969), pp. 6–10, 127–33, 255–60.

3 American Institute of Planners, *Housing Planning* (Washington, D.C.: American Institute of Planners, 1971), pp. 5, 11–17.

4 For example, see: U.S., Department of Housing and Urban Development, *Final Report of the Task Force on Housing Costs* (Washington, D.C.: U.S. Department of Housing and Urban Development, 1978).

5 New stock is not a net addition to supply; a significant proportion replaces units that are lost. For example, from 1960 to 1970 about 14.4 million units were started, but they represented a net increase of only 10.4 million units.

6 See: Max Neutze, *The Suburban Apartment Boom* (Baltimore, Md.: The Johns Hopkins Press, 1968).

7 See: Margaret Drury, *Mobile Homes: The Unrecognized Revolution in American Housing* (New York: Praeger Publishers, 1970); and Constance B. Gibson, *Policy Alternatives for Mobile Homes* (New Brunswick, N.J.: Rutgers University, Center for Urban Policy Research, 1972).

8 For a description of the development process, see: J. Ross McKeever, ed., *The Community Builders Handbook* (Washington, D.C.: Urban Land Institute, 1968), pp. 1–120; and Marion Clawson, *Suburban Land Conversion in the United States* (Baltimore, Md.: The Johns Hopkins Press, 1971), pp. 58–110.

9 Leland S. Burns and Frank J. Mittleback, "Efficiency in the Housing Industry," in *The Report of the President's Committee on Urban Housing: Technical Studies,* vol. 2, ed. President's Committee on Urban Housing (Washington, D.C.: Government Printing Office, 1968), pp. 75–144.

10 William G. Grisby, *Housing Markets and Public Policy* (Philadelphia: University of Pennsylvania Press, 1963), pp. 47–76.

11 See, for example, the following references on the effects of housing development on municipal finances and services: New Jersey County and Municipal Government Study Commission, *Housing and Suburbs: Fiscal and Social Impact of Multi-Family Development* (Trenton: New Jersey County and Municipal Government Study Commission, 1974); and George Sternlieb et al., *Housing Development and Municipal Costs* (New Brunswick, N.J.: Rutgers University, Center for Urban Policy Research, 1973).

12 For discussions of filtering, see: Grisby, *Housing Markets and Public Policy,* pp. 84–110; Wallace F. Smith, *Filtering and Neighborhood Change* (Berkeley: University of California, Institute of Urban and Regional Development, Center for Real Estate and Urban Economics, 1964), pp. 17–33; and John B. Lansing, C. W. Clifton, and S. N. Morgan, *New Homes and Poor People* (Ann Arbor: University of Michigan, Institute for Social Research, Survey Research Center, 1969), pp. 36–55.

13 See: National Urban Coalition, *Displacement: City Neighborhoods in Transition* (Washington, D.C.: National Urban Coalition, 1978).

14 See: Chester Rapkin, "Price Discrimination against Negroes in the Rental Housing Market," in *Essays in Land Economics* (Los Angeles: Univer-

sity of California, Real Estate Research Program, 1966), pp. 337–45; and John F. Kain and John M. Quigley, *Housing Markets and Racial Discrimination: A Microeconomic Analysis* (New York: Columbia University Press, 1975), pp. 56–91.

15 Chester Rapkin, Louis Winnick, and David M. Blank, *Housing Market Analysis* (Washington, D.C.: U.S. Housing and Home Finance Agency, 1953), pp. 9–10.

16 For a complete survey of financial practices in housing, see: Sherman J. Maise, *Financing Real Estate* (New York: McGraw-Hill Book Company, 1965).

17 President's Committee on Urban Housing, *A Decent Home* (Washington, D.C.: Government Printing Office, 1968), p. 129.

18 For a summary of government involvement in financing, see: U.S., Department of Housing and Urban Development, National Housing Policy Review, *Housing in the Seventies* (Washington, D.C.: Government Printing Office, 1974), pp. 53–81.

19 Henry J. Aaron, *Shelter and Subsidies* (Washington, D.C.: Brookings Institution, 1972), pp. 53–73.

20 Civil Rights Act of 1964. Titles VI and VIII.

21 National Housing Policy Review, *Housing in the Seventies,* pp. 139–52.

22 See: U.S., Department of Housing and Urban Development, *Final Report of the Task Force on Housing Costs;* and National Association of Home Builders, *Fighting Excessive Government Regulations* (Washington, D.C.: National Association of Home Builders, 1976).

23 See: Real Estate Research Corporation, *The Costs of Sprawl: Environmental and Economic Costs of Alternative Residential Development Patterns at the Urban Fringe,* prepared for the U.S. Council on Environmental Quality, the U.S. Department of Housing and Urban Development, and the U.S. Environmental Protection Agency (Washington, D.C.: Government Printing Office, 1974).

24 President's Committee on Urban Housing, *A Decent Home,* p. 46.

25 Herbert M. Franklin, David Falk, and Arthur J. Leon, *In-Zoning: A Guide for Policy Makers on Inclusionary Land Use Programs* (Washington, D.C.: Potomac Institute, 1974), p. 30.

26 See: Federal Reserve Staff Study. *Ways To Moderate Fluctuations in Housing Construction* (Washington, D.C.: Board of Governors of the Federal Reserve System, 1972).

27 Mary E. Brooks, *Housing Equity and Environmental Protection: The Needless Conflict* (Washington, D.C.: American Institute of Planners, 1976), p. 2.

28 Jon Pynoos, Robert Schafer, and Chester W. Hartman, *Housing Urban America* (Chicago: Aldine Publishing Company, 1973), pp. 1–11.

29 President's Committee on Urban Housing, *A Decent Home,* pp. 40–45.

30 Bernard J. Frieden and Arthur P. Solomon, *The Nation's Housing: 1975 to 1985* (Cambridge, Mass.: Joint Center for Urban Studies of the Massachusetts Institute of Technology and Harvard University, 1977), pp. 80–98.

31 Ibid., pp. 131–41.

32 See: Mary K. Nenno, *Housing in Metropolitan Areas: Roles and Responsibilities of Five Key Actors* (Washington, D.C.: National Association of Housing and Redevelopment Officials, 1973). This report summarizes studies made for three areas: the state of Connecticut; Dade County (Miami), Florida; and the Minneapolis–St. Paul metropolitan area. The five key actors are the local government chief executive, the comprehensive planner, the community development administrator, the housing developer, and the housing consumer advocate.

33 U.S., Department of Commerce, Bureau of the Census, *Census of Housing: Annual Housing Survey* (Washington, D.C.: Government Printing Office, various dates).

34 See: U.S., Department of Housing and Urban Development, *Urban Housing Market Analysis* (Washington, D.C.: Government Printing Office, 1966), p. 506; and: U.S., Department of Housing and Urban Development, *FHA Techniques of Housing Market Analysis* (Washington, D.C.: Government Printing Office, 1970), pp. 11–16.

35 For an analysis of housing policy and planning studies, see: Harry J. Wexler and Richard Peck, *Housing and Local Governments: A Research Guide for Policy Makers and Planners* (Lexington, Mass.: Lexington Books, D. C. Heath and Company, 1975).

36 For a comprehensive presentation on the analysis of supply and demand data, see: Hammer, Greene, Siler Associates, *Regional Housing Planning: A Technical Guide,* prepared for the American Institute of Planners (Washington, D.C.: American Institute of Planners, 1972).

37 Anthony Downs, "Moving toward Realistic Housing Goals," in *Urban Problems and Prospects* (Chicago: Markham Publishing Company, 1970), pp. 115–55.

38 For detailed, if outdated, cost discussions, see: McGraw-Hill Information Systems Company, "A Study of Comparative Time and Cost for Building Five Selected Types of Low-Cost Housing," in *The Report of the President's Committee on Urban Housing: Technical Studies,* vol. 2, ed. President's Committee on Urban Housing, pp. 1–74; and: Elsie Eaves, *How the Many Costs of Housing Fit Together,* Research Report no. 16, National Commission on Urban Problems (Washington, D.C.: Government Printing Office, 1969).

39 President's Committee on Urban Housing, *A Decent Home.*

40 National Commission on Urban Problems, *Building the American City* (Washington, D.C.: Government Printing Office, 1968).

41 For a discussion of the pros and cons of continuing goals, see: Mary K. Nenno, "The 10-Year Housing Goals Show a Short Fall in Number of Units and a Need for Links to Fiscal Policy," *Journal of Housing* 35 (July 1978): 342–46.

42 For an authoritative guide, see: National Association of Housing and Redevelopment Officials, *A NAHRO Guide for Preparing a Local Housing Plan* (Washington, D.C.: National Association of Housing and Redevelopment Officials, 1976).

Bibliography and resource guide

This bibliography and resource guide is highly selective and represents informed judgments about basic and introductory references. Many additional books, periodical articles, and other references are cited in the endnotes to the individual chapters. Immediately below are listed eight professional associations and resource agencies that are of particular interest to planners and managers. Shown for each organization are name, address, and a condensed listing of services that bear on planning. Next is a listing of periodicals and other publications that are of value as continuing reference and information sources. Shown for each publication are name, frequency of issue, publisher, and annotation. The balance of this bibliography consists of additional references listed by chapters; this listing—mostly books—emphasizes general works that are deemed helpful for students and practitioners.

Associations and agencies

American Institute of Architects (AIA), 1735 New York Avenue, N.W., Washington, D.C. 20006. Urban design, environmental planning, professional policies and standards.

American Planning Association (APA), 1313 East 60th Street, Chicago, Illinois 60637. Organization for professional planners and appointed and elected officials in local government. Activities include research, professional standards and development, and a wide variety of planning publications.

Council of Planning Librarians, 1313 East 60th Street, Chicago, Illinois 60637. Issues bibliographies on a wide variety of city and regional planning subjects. More than 600 bibliographies available; complete list on request.

International City Management Association (ICMA), 1140 Connecticut Avenue, N.W., Washington, D.C. 20036. General management, planning and programming services, relationships of planning and budgeting, occasional reports on planning topics.

National Technical Information Service (NTIS), 425 13th Street, N.W., Washington, D.C.

20004. Clearinghouse for public sale of U.S. government publications, including those of the U.S. Department of Housing and Urban Development, the U.S. Department of Transportation, and the U.S. Department of Energy. Publishes weekly newsletter listing its acquisitions.

Urban Institute, 2100 M Street, N.W., Washington, D.C. 20037. Research, analysis, and publications on a wide range of topics in urban affairs, many directly related to planning.

Urban Land Institute, 1200 18th Street N.W., Washington, D.C. 20036. Research activities and publications on a range of topics in public policy, residential development, and land development.

Urban and Regional Information Systems Association (URISA), c/o Municipal Finance Officers Association, 180 North Michigan Avenue, Chicago Illinois 60601. Major interests are data sources, data usage, data management and reporting, and information systems; publishes a bi-monthly newsletter with developments in government information systems.

Periodicals

AIA Journal. Monthly. American Institute of Architects. Occasional articles deal with planning topics, especially urban design.

Architectural Record. Monthly. McGraw-Hill. Articles on building design; of particular interest are articles on large industrial structures.

Environmental Comment. Monthly. Urban Land Institute. Environmental law, land use regulation, and growth control.

Housing. Monthly. McGraw-Hill. Edited primarily for private sector; topics include residential development, small commercial development, and economics of the housing industry.

Journal of the American Planning Association. Quarterly. American Planning Association. Professional and scholarly coverage of planning and urban affairs through articles, commentary, and extensive book reviews.

Journal of Housing. Monthly. National Association of Housing and Redevelopment Officials. Articles, reports, and news stories on community development, housing, federal legislation, and related areas.

Land Economics. Quarterly. University of Wisconsin—Madison. Covers land economics, land and buildings as commodities, and assessment, taxation, and regulation on the value of land.

Land Use Law & Zoning Digest. Monthly. American Planning Association. Covers public regulation of zoning, subdivision regulation, and other aspects of land use, with abstracts of state and federal court cases, coverage of proposed and adopted legislation, brief articles on legal developments, and thorough documentation and indexing.

Landscape Architecture. Quarterly. American Society of Landscape Architects. Coverage includes open space and recreational development, urban parks, and water-related development.

Law reviews. These periodicals, mostly issued by law schools, include occasional articles on zoning, housing, real property taxation, and related planning topics.

The Municipal Year Book. Annual. International City Management Association. Occasional surveys and analyses of planning subjects as well as regular coverage of local government finance and other subjects of direct interest to planners.

Planning. Monthly. American Planning Association. Wide coverage of city and regional planning with articles, listing of job openings in planning, news reports and analyses, question-and-answer section, and book reviews and book notes.

Planning Advisory Service. Monthly. American Planning Association. Reports based on extensive research and analysis cover almost every conceivable subject in city and regional planning.

Urban Land. Monthly. Urban Land Institute. News and trends in land use and land development, particularly central business districts.

1 The Values of the City Planner

Bair, Frederick H., Jr., and Hedman, Richard. *And on the Eighth Day.* Chicago: American Society of Planning Officials, 1967.

Bolan, Richard S., and Nuttall, Ronald. *Urban Planning and Politics.* Lexington, Mass.: Lexington Books, D. C. Heath and Company, 1974.

Braybrooke, David, and Lindblom, Charles E. *A Strategy of Decision: Policy Evaluation as a Social Process.* Glencoe, Ill.: The Free Press, 1963.

Davidoff, Paul, and Reiner, Thomas A. "A Choice Theory of Planning." *Journal of the American Institute of Planners* 28 (May 1962): 103–15.

Harris, Britton. "The Limits of Science and Humanism in Planning." *Journal of the American Institute of Planners* 33 (September 1967): 324–35.

Hiltner, Seward. "Planning as a Profession." *Journal of the American Institute of Planners* 23 (Fall 1957): 162–67.

Marcuse, Peter. "Professional Ethics and Beyond: Values in Planning." *Journal of the American Institute of Planners* 42 (July 1976): 264–74.

Meyerson, Martin. "Building the Middle-Range Bridge for Comprehensive Planning." *Journal of the American Institute of Planners* 22 (Spring 1956): 58–64.

Rondinelli, Dennis. *Urban and Regional Development Planning.* Ithaca, N.Y.: Cornell University Press, 1975.

2 Historical Development of American City Planning

Berry, Brian. *The Human Consequences of Urbanization.* New York: St. Martin's Press, 1973.

Bridenbaugh, Carl. *Cities in Revolt: Urban Life in America, 1743–1776.* New York: Oxford University Press, 1970.

———. *Cities in the Wilderness: The First Century of Urban Life in America, 1625–1742.* New York: Oxford University Press, 1971.

Faltermayer, Edmund. *Redoing America.* New York: Harper & Row, Publishers, 1968.

Glaab, Charles N., and Brown, A. Theodore. *A History of Urban America.* 2nd ed. New York: The Macmillan Company, 1976.

Haar, Charles M. *Between the Idea and the Reality: A Study in the Origin, Fate, and Legacy of the Model Cities Program.* Boston: Little, Brown and Company, 1975.

Haworth, Lawrence. *The Good City.* Bloomington, Ind.: Indiana University Press, 1963.

Jacobs, Jane. *The Death and Life of Great American Cities.* New York: Random House, 1961.

McKelvey, Blake. *American Urbanization: A Comparative History.* Glenview, Ill.: Scott, Foresman and Company, 1973.

——. *The Emergence of Metropolitan America, 1915–1966.* New Brunswick, N.J.: Rutgers University Press, 1968.

——. *The Urbanization of America, 1860–1915.* New Brunswick, N.J.: Rutgers University Press, 1963.

Reps, John W. *The Making of Urban America: A History of City Planning in the United States.* Princeton, N.J.: Princeton University Press, 1965.

Schnore, Leo F., ed. *The New Urban History: Quantitative Explorations by American Historians.* Princeton, N.J.: Princeton University Press, 1974.

Scott, Mel. *American City Planning since 1890.* Berkeley: University of California Press, 1969.

Warner, Sam Bass, Jr. *The Urban Wilderness: A History of the American City.* New York: Harper & Row, Publishers, 1972.

Warner, Sam Bass, Jr., ed. *Planning for a Nation of Cities.* Cambridge, Mass.: The M.I.T. Press, 1967.

3 Planning Agency Management

Banovetz, James M., ed. *Managing the Modern City.* Washington, D.C.: International City Management Association, 1971.

Catanese, Anthony James. *Planners and Local Politics: Impossible Dreams.* Beverly Hills, Calif.: Sage Publications, 1974.

Finkler, Earl. *Dissent and Independent Initiative in Planning Offices.* Planning Advisory Service Report no. 269. Chicago: American Society of Planning Officials, 1971.

International City Management Association. *Effective Supervisory Practices: Better Results through Teamwork.* Washington, D.C.: International City Management Association, 1978.

Jacobs, Allan B. *Making City Planning Work.* Chicago: American Society of Planning Officials, 1978.

Kent, T. J., Jr. *The Urban General Plan.* San Francisco: Chandler Publishing Company, 1964.

Kraemer, Kenneth L. *Policy Analysis in Local Government: A Systems Approach to Decision Making.* Washington, D.C.: International City Management Association, 1973.

Powers, Stanley Piazza; Brown, F. Gerald; and Arnold, David S., eds. *Developing the Municipal Organization.* Washington, D.C.: International City Management Association, 1974.

Solnit, Albert. *The Job of the Planning Commissioner.* Rev. ed. Berkeley: University of California, University Extension Publications, 1977.

Walker, Robert A. *The Planning Function in Urban Government.* 2nd ed. Chicago: University of Chicago Press, 1950.

4 Information for Planning

Catanese, Anthony James. *Scientific Methods of Urban Analysis.* Urbana: University of Illinois Press, 1972.

Catanese, Anthony James, and Steiss, Alan Walter. *Systemic Planning: Theory and Application.* Lexington, Mass.: Lexington Books, D. C. Heath and Company, 1970.

Churchman, C. West. *The Systems Approach.* New York: Dell Publishing Company, 1969.

Croxton, Frederick E. *Elementary Statistics.* New York: Dover, 1953.

DeNeufville, Judith Innes. *Social Indicators and Public Policy.* New York: Elsevier, 1975.

Hatry, Harry P.; Blair, Louis H.; Fisk, Donald M.; Greiner, John H.; Hall, John R., Jr.; and Schaenman, Philip S. *How Effective Are Your Community Services? Procedures for Monitoring the Effectiveness of Municipal Services.* Washington, D.C.: The Urban Institute and International City Management Association, 1977.

Isard, Walter. *Introduction to Regional Science.* Englewood Cliffs, N.J.: Prentice-Hall, Inc., 1975.

Krueckeberg, Donald A., and Silvers, Arthur L. *Urban Planning Analysis: Methods and Models.* New York: John Wiley & Sons, Inc., 1974.

Webb, Kenneth, and Hatry, Harry P. *Obtaining Citizen Feedback: The Application of Citizen Surveys to Local Governments.* Washington, D.C.: The Urban Institute, 1973.

5 Finance and Budgeting

American Society of Planning Officials. *Local Capital Improvements and Development Management: Synthesis of the Literature.* Washington, D.C.: U.S. Department of Housing and Urban Development, 1978.

Aronson, J. Richard, and Schwartz, Eli, eds. *Management Policies in Local Government Finance.* Washington, D.C.: International City Management Association, 1975.

Burchell, Robert W., and Listokin, David. *The Fiscal Impact Handbook: Estimating Local Costs and Revenues of Land Development.* New Brunswick, N.J.: Rutgers University, Center for Urban Policy Research, 1978.

Golembiewski, Robert T., and Rabin, Jack, eds. *Public Budgeting and Finance: Readings in Theory and Practice.* 2nd ed. Itaska, Ill.: F. E. Peacock, Publishers, Inc., 1975.

Levy, Frank; Meltsner, Arnold J.; and Wildavsky, Aaron. *Urban Outcomes: Schools, Streets, and Libraries.* Berkeley: University of California Press, 1974.

Moak, Lennox L., and Hillhouse, Albert M. *Concepts and Practices in Local Government Finance.* Chicago: Municipal Finance Officers Association, 1975.

Snyder, James C. *Fiscal Management and Planning in Local Government.* Lexington, Mass.: Lexington Books, D. C. Heath and Company, 1977.

Steiss, Alan Walter. *Local Government Finance: Capital Facilities Planning and Debt Administration in Local Government.* Lexington, Mass.: Lexington Books, D. C. Heath and Company, 1975.

Wildavsky, Aaron. *Budgeting: A Comparative Theory of Budgetary Processes.* Boston: Little, Brown and Company, 1975.

———. *The Politics of the Budgetary Process.* 2nd ed. Boston: Little, Brown and Company, 1974.

6 City Development Plans

Altshuler, Alan. "The Goals of Comprehensive Planning." *Journal of the American Institute of Planners* 21 (August 1965): 186–95.

American Law Institute. *A Model Land Development Code.* Complete text, adopted by the American Law Institute, May 21, 1975, with Reporter's Commentary. Philadelphia: American Law Institute, 1976.

Chapin, F. Stuart, Jr., and Kaiser, Edward J. *Urban Land Use Planning.* 3rd ed. Champaign: University of Illinois Press, 1979.

Fishman, Richard P., ed. *Housing for All under the Law: New Directions in Housing, Land Use and Planning Law.* A Report of the American Bar Association Advisory Commission on Housing and Urban Growth. Cambridge, Mass.: Ballinger Publishing Company, 1978.

Jacobs, Allan B. *Making City Planning Work.* Chicago: American Society of Planning Officials, 1978.

Kent, T. J., Jr. *The Urban General Plan.* San Francisco: Chandler Publishing Company, 1964.

Rider, Robert W. "Transition from Land Use to Policy Planning." *Journal of the American Institute of Planners* 44 (January 1978): 25–26.

7 Utility Services

Binkley, Clark S., and others. *Interceptor Sewers and Urban Sprawl.* Lexington, Mass.: Lexington Books, D. C. Heath and Company, 1975.

Fair, G. M., and others. *Water and Wastewater Engineering.* 2 vols. New York: John Wiley & Sons, Inc., 1966, 1968.

Grant, Eugene L., and Reson, W. Grant. *Principles of Engineering Economy.* New York: The Ronald Press Company, 1974.

Greenberg, Michael R., and others. *Solid Waste Planning in Metropolitan Regions.* New Brunswick, N.J.: Rutgers University, Center for Urban Policy Research, 1976.

Hardenburgh, W. A., and Rodie, E. R. *Water Supply and Waste Disposal.* Scranton, Pa.: International Textbook Company, 1961.

Metcalf and Eddy, Inc., *Wastewater Engineering: Collection, Treatment, Disposal.* New York: McGraw-Hill Book Company, 1972.

Musgrave, Richard A., and Musgrave, Peggy B. *Public Finance in Theory and Practice.* 2nd ed. New York: McGraw-Hill Book Company, 1975.

Real Estate Research Corporation. *The Costs of Sprawl: Environmental and Economic Costs of Alternative Residential Development Patterns at the Urban Fringe.* Prepared for the U.S. Council on Environmental Quality, the U.S. Department of Housing and Urban Development, and the U.S. Environmental Protection Agency. Washington, D.C.: Government Printing Office, 1974.

Tabors, Richard D.; Shapiro, Michael H.; and Rogers, Peter P. *Land Use and the Pipe: Planning for Sewerage.* Lexington, Mass.: Lexington Books, D. C. Heath and Company, 1976.

U.S. Environmental Protection Agency, Office of Solid Waste Management Programs. *Decision-Makers Guide in Solid Waste Management.* 2nd ed. Washington, D.C.: Government Printing Office, 1976.

8 Urban Transportation

DeLeuw, Cather, and Company and the Urban Institute. *Characteristics of Urban Transportation Systems.* Prepared for the U.S. Department of Transportation. Washington, D.C.: Government Printing Office, 1974. Available from National Technical Information Service, Springfield, Virginia 22161.

Highway Research Board. *Highway Capacity Manual.* Highway Research Board Special Report 87. Washington, D.C.: Highway Research Board, 1965.

———. *Parking Principles.* Highway Research Board Special Report 125. Washington, D.C.: Highway Research Board, 1971.

Institute of Traffic Engineers. *Transportation and Traffic Engineering Handbook.* Englewood Cliffs, N.J.: Prentice-Hall, Inc., 1976.

Institute of Transportation Engineers. *Trip Generation: An Informational Report.* Arlington, Va.: Institute of Transportation Engineers, 1976.

Larwin, Thomas F., and Stuart, Darwin G. *Transportation Management Strategies: Prospects for Small Cities.* Washington, D.C.: U.S. Department of Transportation, Urban Mass Transportation Administration, 1975.

Transportation Research Board. *Better Use of Existing Transportation Facilities.* Highway Research Board Special Report 153. Washington, D.C.: Transportation Research Board, 1974.

Voorhees, Alan M., & Associates. *Short-Range Transit Planning.* Washington, D.C.: U.S. Department of Transportation, Urban Mass Transportation Administration, 1973.

9 Business and Industrial Development

Boykin, James H. *Industrial Potential of the Central City.* Research Report no. 21. Washington, D.C.: Urban Land Institute, 1973.

Gruen, Victor, and Smith, Larry. *Centers for the Urban Environment: Survival of the Cities.* New York: Van Nostrand Reinhold, 1973.

Hunker, Henry L. *Industrial Development: Concepts and Principles.* Lexington, Mass.: Lexington Books, D. C. Heath and Company, 1974.

Lion, Edgar. *Shopping Centers: Planning, Development and Administration.* New York: John Wiley & Sons, Inc., 1976.

Lochmoeller, Donald C.; Muncy, Dorothy A.; Thorne, Oakleigh J.; and Viets, Mark A. *Industrial Development Handbook.* Washington, D.C.: Urban Land Institute, 1975.

McKeever, J. Ross. *Business Parks, Office Parks, Plazas and Centers: A Study of Development Practices and Procedures.* Technical Bulletin 65. Washington, D.C.: Urban Land Institute, 1970.

McKeever, J. Ross, and Griffin, Nathaniel M. *Shopping Center Development Handbook.* Washington, D.C.: Urban Land Institute, 1977.

Nelson, Richard L. *The Selection of Retail Locations.* New York: McGraw-Hill Book Company, 1966.

Redstone, Louis G. *New Dimensions in Shopping Centers and Stores.* New York: McGraw-Hill Book Company, 1973.

———. *The New Downtowns: Rebuilding Business Districts.* New York: McGraw-Hill Book Company, 1976.

Salzenstein, Marvin A. *Industrial Performance Standards.* Planning Advisory Service Report no. 272. Chicago: American Society of Planning Officials, 1971.

U.S. Bureau of the Budget. *Standard Industrial Classification Manual.* Washington, D.C.: Government Printing Office, 1972.

10 Recreation Space, Services, and Facilities

Bannon, Joseph J. *Leisure Resources: Its Comprehensive Planning.* Englewood Cliffs, N.J.: Prentice-Hall, Inc., 1976.

Christiansen, Monty. *Application of a Recreation Experience Components Concept for Comprehensive Recreation Planning.* Harrisburg, Pa.: Department of Community Affairs, Bureau of Recreation and Conservation, 1975.

Clawson, Marion. *Methods of Measuring Demand for and Value of Outdoor Recreation.* Baltimore: The Johns Hopkins Press, for Resources for the Future, Inc., 1959.

Gold, Seymour M. *Recreation Planning and Design.* New York: McGraw-Hill Book Company, 1980.

———. *Urban Recreation Planning.* Philadelphia: Lea & Febiger, 1973.

Hatry, Harry P., and Dunn, Diana. *Measuring the Effectiveness of Local Government Services.* Washington, D.C.: The Urban Institute, 1971.

Lutzin, Sidney G., and Storey, Edward H., eds. *Managing Municipal Leisure Services.* Washington, D.C.: International City Management Association, 1973.

National Academy of Sciences. *Assessing Demand for Outdoor Recreation.* Washington, D.C.: Government Printing Office, 1975.

11 Education Services

American Association of School Administrators. *Open Space Schools.* Reprint of the AASA Commission on Open Space Schools. Washington, D.C.: American Association of School Administrators, 1971.

Carroll, Robert F., and others. *University Community Tension and Urban Campus Form.* Cincinnati: University of Cincinnati Press, 1972.

Educational Facilities Laboratories. *Surplus School Space: Options and Opportunities.* New York: Educational Facilities Laboratories, 1976.

Eismann, Donald; Burton, Nancy; and Woldt, Alice. *Schools and Neighborhoods Research Study.* Phase I: *Executive Summary;* Phase II: *Summary and Recommendations.* Seattle: City of Seattle and Seattle Public Schools, 1976.

Getzels, Judith N. *Recycling Public Buildings.* Planning Advisory Service Report no. 319. Chicago: American Society of Planning Officials, 1976.

Glazer, Nathan. *Affirmative Discrimination: Ethnic Inequality and Public Policy.* New York: Basic Books, Inc., 1975.

Hoppenfeld, Morton. "A Sketch of the Planning–Building Process for Columbia Maryland." *Journal of the American Institute of Planners* 33 (November 1967): 398–409.

Institute for Development of Educational Activities, Inc. *Shrinking Schools.* Dayton, Ohio: Institute for Development of Educational Activities, Inc., 1975.

Leggett, Staunton; Brubaker, William; Cohodes, Aaron; and Shapiro, Arthur S. *Planning Flexible Learning Places.* New York: McGraw-Hill Book Company, 1977.

Parsons, Kermit C., and Davis, Georgia K. "Universities and Community: Shopkeepers and Scholars in the University District." *Society for College and University Planning Journal* 1 and 2 (December 1970 and April 1971).

————. "The Urban University and its Urban Environment." *Minerva* 9 (July 1971): 361–85.

Taylor, Anne P., and Vlastos, George. *School Zone: Learning Environments for Children.* New York: Van Nostrand Reinhold, 1975.

Testa, Carlos. *New Educational Facilities.* Boulder, Colo.: Westview Press, 1975.

12 Planning for the Arts

American Council for the Arts. *Cities, Counties and the Arts.* New York: American Council for the Arts, 1977.

————. *Community Arts Agencies: A Handbook and Guide.* Edited by Ellen Stodolsky Daniels and Robert Porter. New York: American Council for the Arts, 1978.

Cwi, David, and Lyall, Katharine. *Economic Impacts of Arts and Cultural Institutions: A Model for Assessment and a Case Study in Baltimore.* National Endowment for the Arts Research Division Report no. 6. Baltimore: Johns Hopkins University Center for Metropolitan Planning and Research, 1977.

Hapgood, Karen E. *Planning and the Arts.* Planning Advisory Service Report no. 313. Chicago: American Society of Planning Officials, 1975.

National Research Center for the Arts. *Americans and the Arts: A Survey of Public Opinion.* New York: Associated Councils of the Arts, 1975.

Netzer, Dick. *The Subsidized Muse: Public Support for the Arts in the United States.* Prepared for the Twentieth Century Fund. New York: Cambridge University Press, 1978.

New York State Commission on Cultural Resources and New York State Council on the Arts. *Cultural Resource Development: Planning Survey and Analysis.* By Janet I. Harris. New York: Praeger Publishers, 1976.

O'Connor, Francis V., ed. *Art for the Millions: Essays from the 1930's by Artists and Administrators of the WPA Federal Art Project.* Boston: New York Graphic Society, Ltd., 1973.

Perloff, Harvey. *The Arts in the Economic Life of the City.* New York: American Council for the Arts, 1979.

13 Urban Design

Abrams, Charles. *The City Is the Frontier.* New York: Harper & Row, Publishers, 1965.

Appleyard, Donald. *The Environment as a Social Symbol: Within a Theory of Environmental Action and Perception.* Berkeley: University of California Press, 1979.

————. *Livable Streets: Protected Neighborhoods.* Berkeley: University of California Press, 1979.

Barnett, Jonathan. *Urban Design as Public Policy: Practical Methods for Improving Cities.* New York: Architectural Record Books, 1974.

Costonis, John J. *Space Adrift: Saving Urban Landmarks through the Chicago Plan.* Chicago: University of Illinois Press, 1974.

Cullen, Gordon. *The Concise Townscape.* New York: Van Nostrand Reinhold, 1961.

Gallion, Arthur B., and Eisner, Simon. *The Urban Pattern: City Planning and Design.* 3rd ed. New York: D. Van Nostrand Co., 1975.

Jacobs, Allan B. *Making City Planning Work.* Chicago: American Society of Planning Officials, 1978.

Kriken, John L., and Torrey, Irene Perlis. *Developing Urban Design Mechanisms.* Planning Advisory Service Report no. 296. Chicago: American Society of Planning Officials, 1973.

Lu, Weiming. *The Role of Urban Design in Local Government.* Washington, D.C.: National Science Foundation, 1976. Available from National Technical Information Service, Springfield, Virginia 22161.

Lynch, Kevin. *Site Planning.* 2nd ed. Cambridge, Mass.: The M.I.T. Press, 1971.

————. *What Time Is This Place?* Cambridge, Mass.: The M.I.T. Press, 1976.

Sitte, C. *City Planning According to Artistic Principles.* New York: Random House, 1965.

14 Subdivision Regulation and Land Conversion

American Law Institute. *A Model Land Development Code.* Complete text, adopted by the American Law Institute, May 21, 1975, with Reporter's Commentary. Philadelphia: American Law Institute, 1976.

Chapin, F. Stuart, Jr. *Urban Land Use Planning.* 3rd ed. Champaign: University of Illinois Press, 1979.

City of Boulder, Colorado. *Subdivision Regulations.* Chapter 32 of the Revised Code of the City of Boulder. Boulder, Colo.: City of Boulder, 1968.

Freilich, Robert H., and Levi, Peter S. *Model Subdivision Regulations: Text and Commentary.* Chicago: American Society of Planning Officials, 1975.

Institute of Rational Design. *Manual: Design and Control of Land Development in Suburban Communities.* New York: Institute of Rational Design, 1976.

Listokin, David, ed. *Land Use Controls: Present Problems and Future Reform.* New Brunswick, N.J.: Rutgers University, Center for Urban Policy Research, 1974.

Lynch, Kevin. *Site Planning.* 2nd ed. Cambridge, Mass.: The M.I.T. Press, 1971.

McHarg, Ian L. *Design with Nature.* Garden City, N.Y.: Doubleday Natural History Press, Doubleday and Company, 1971.

National Association of Home Builders. *Land Development Manual.* Washington, D.C.: National Association of Home Builders, 1977.

Reilly, William K., ed. *The Use of Land: A Citizens' Policy Guide to Urban Growth.* A Task Force Report Sponsored by the Rockefeller Brothers Fund. New York: Thomas Y. Crowell Company, 1973.

Scott, Randall W.; Brower, David J.; and Miner, Dallas D., eds. *Management & Control of Growth.* 3 vols. Washington, D.C.: Urban Land Institute, 1975.

State of Colorado, County of Boulder. *Subdivision Regulations.* Boulder, Colo.: County of Boulder, 1972. As amended.

U.S. Congress. House. *Report of the National Commission on Urban Problems to the Congress and to the President of the United States: Building the American City.* H. Doc. 91–34, 91st Cong., 1st sess., 1968.

Weimer, Arthur M., and Hoyt, Homer. *Principles of Real Estate.* 3rd ed. New York: The Ronald Press Company, 1954.

Yearwood, Richard M. *Land Subdivision Regulation: Policy and Legal Considerations for Urban Planning.* New York: Praeger Publishers, 1971.

15 Zoning

Anderson, Robert M. *American Law of Zoning.* 5 vols. Rochester, N.Y.: The Lawyers Co-operative Publishing Co., 1976.

Babcock, Richard F. *Billboards, Glass Houses and the Law: And Other Land Use Fables.* Colorado Springs, Colo.: Shepard's Inc., 1977.

————. *The Zoning Game.* Madison: University of Wisconsin Press, 1966.

Bair, Frederick H., Jr., and Bartley, Ernest R. *Text of a Model Zoning Ordinance: With Commentary.* 3rd ed. Chicago: American Society of Planning Officials, 1966.

Bosselman, Fred, and Callies, David. *The Quiet Revolution: Summary Report.* Prepared for the U.S. Council on Environmental Quality. Washington, D.C.: Government Printing Office, 1971.

Bosselman, Fred; Callies, David; and Banta, John. *The Taking Issue.* Prepared for the U.S. Council on Environmental Quality. Washington, D.C.: Government Printing Office, 1973.

Hagman, Donald G. *Urban Planning and Land Development Control Law.* St. Paul, Minn.: West Publishing Co., 1975.

Mandelker, Daniel R. *Environmental and Land Controls Legislation.* Indianapolis: The Bobbs-Merrill Co., Inc., 1977.

Rathkopf, Arden. *The Law of Zoning and Planning.* 3 vols. 3rd ed. New York: Clark Boardman Co., Ltd., 1974.

Toll, Seymour. *Zoned America.* New York: The Viking Press, 1969.

Williams, Norman, Jr. *American Land Planning Law.* 5 vols. Chicago: Callaghan & Company, 1974.

16 Maintenance and Renewal of Central Cities

Bollens, John C., and Schmandt, Henry J. *The Metropolis: Its People, Politics, and Economic Life.* 3rd ed. New York: Harper & Row, Publishers, 1975.

Catanese, Anthony James, and Farmer, W. Paul. *Personality, Politics and Planning: How City Planners Work.* Beverly Hills, Calif.: Sage Publications, 1978.

Frieden, Bernard J., and Kaplan, Marshall. *The Politics of Neglect: Urban Aid from Model Cities to Revenue Sharing.* Cambridge, Mass.: The M.I.T. Press, 1975.

Gorham, William, and Glazer, Nathan, eds. *The Urban Predicament.* Washington, D.C.: The Urban Institute, 1976.

Haar, Charles M. *Between the Idea and the Reality: A Study in the Origin, Fate, and Legacy of the Model Cities Program.* Boston: Little, Brown and Company, 1975.

Harrison, Bennett. *Urban Economic Development: Suburbanization, Minority Opportunity, and the Condition of the Central City.* Washington, D.C.: The Urban Institute, 1974.

Levin, Melvin R. *The Urban Prospect.* North Scituate, Mass.: Duxbury Press, 1977.

Sternlieb, George, and Hughes, James W., eds. *Post-Industrial America: Metropolitan Decline and Inter-Regional Job Shifts.* New Brunswick, N.J.: Rutgers University, Center for Urban Policy Research, 1975.

U.S. Congress. House. Committee on Banking, Finance, and Public Affairs. Subcommittee on the City. *How Cities Can Grow Old Gracefully.* Washington, D.C.: Government Printing Office, 1977.

17 Planning for Diverse Human Needs

Brooks, Michael P. *Social Planning and City Planning.* Planning Advisory Service Report no. 261. Chicago: American Society of Planning Officials, 1970.

Christensen, Kathleen. *Social Impacts of Land Development: An Initial Approach for Estimating Impacts on Neighborhood Usage and Perception.* Washington, D.C.: The Urban Institute, 1976.

Finsterbusch, Kurt, and Wolf, C. P. *Methodology of Social Impact Assessment.* Stroudsburg, Pa.: Dowden, Hutchinson, and Ross, 1977.

Kahn, Alfred J. *Studies in Social Policy and Planning.* New York: Russell Sage Foundation, 1979.

———. *Theory and Practice of Social Planning.* New York: Russell Sage Foundation, 1969.

Keeney, Ralph L., and Raiffa, Howard. *Decisions with Multiple Objectives: Preferences and Value Tradeoffs.* New York: John Wiley & Sons, Inc., 1976.

League of California Cities. *Social Element Planning in California.* Los Angeles: League of California Cities, 1977.

Moroney, Robert M. "Needs Assessment for Human Services." In *Managing Human Services.* Edited by Wayne F. Anderson, Bernard J. Frieden, and Michael J. Murphy. Washington, D.C.: International City Management Association, 1977, pp. 128–54.

Morris, Robert, and Binstock, Robert A. *Feasible Planning for Social Change.* New York: Columbia University Press, 1966.

18 Social Planning and Policy Development

Armentrout, Edmund H., and Horton, Gerald T. *Techniques for Needs Assessment in Social Services Planning: State Experiences and Suggested Approaches in Response to Title XX of the Social Security Act.* Atlanta, Ga.: The Research Group, Inc., 1976.

———. *Techniques for Resource Allocation in Social Service Planning: State Experiences and Suggested Approaches in Response to Title XX of the Social Security Act.* Atlanta, Ga.: The Research Group, Inc., 1976.

Erber, Ernest. *Urban Planning in Transition.* New York: Grossman Publishers, 1970.

Mayer, Robert R. *Social Planning and Social Change.* Englewood Cliffs, N.J.: Prentice-Hall, Inc., 1972.

Miller, Joan Hutchinson, and Horton, Gerald T. *Alternative Approaches to Human Services Planning: Nine Case Studies on Human Services Planning in State, Regional, and Local Organizations.* Arlington, Va.: Human Services Institute for Children and Families, Inc., 1974.

Puget Sound Governmental Conference. *Comprehensive Human Resource Planning Guide.* Seattle, Wash.: Puget Sound Governmental Conference, 1974.

———. *Guide to Human Resource Planning for Elected Officials.* Seattle, Wash.: Puget Sound Governmental Conference, 1974.

19 Citizen Participation in Planning

Arnstein, Sherry. "A Ladder of Citizen Participation." *Journal of the American Institute of Planners* 35 (July 1969): 216–44.

Davidoff, Paul. "Advocacy and Pluralism in Planning." *Journal of the American Institute of Planners* 31 (November 1965): 331–38.

Hallman, Howard. *Neighborhood Government in a Metropolitan Setting.* Beverly Hills, Calif.: Sage Publications, 1974.

Mogulof, Melvin B. *Citizen Participation: A Review and Commentary on Federal Policies and Practices.* Washington, D.C.: The Urban Institute, 1970.

Needleman, Martin L., and Needleman, Carolyn Emerson. *Guerrillas in the Bureaucracy.* New York: John Wiley & Sons, Inc., 1974.

Rodgers, Joseph Lee, Jr. *Citizen Committees: A Guide to Their Use in Local Government.* Cambridge, Mass.: Ballinger Publishing Company, 1977.

Rosenbaum, Nelson M. *Citizen Involvement in Land Use Governance: Issues and Methods.* Washington, D.C.: The Urban Institute, 1976.

Stewart, William H., Jr. *Citizen Participation in Public Administration.* Birmingham: University of Alabama Press, 1976.

Yin, Robert K., and Yates, Douglas. *Street Level Government: Assessing Decentralization and Urban Services.* Santa Monica, Calif.: Rand Corporation, 1974.

20 Economic Development

Chinitz, Benjamin. *Central City Economic Development.* Cambridge, Mass.: Abt Books, 1979.

Conroy, Michael E. *The Challenge of Urban Economic Development.* Lexington, Mass.: Lexington Books, D. C. Heath and Company, 1975.

Hirsch, Werner Z. *Urban Economic Analysis.* New York: McGraw-Hill Book Company, 1973.

Isard, Walter. *Methods of Regional Analysis.* New York: Technology Press and John Wiley & Sons, Inc., 1960.

Leigh, Roger. "The Use of Location Quotients in Urban Economic Base Studies," *Land Economics* 46 (May 1970): 202–5.

Muller, Thomas. *Fiscal Impacts of Land Development: A Critique of Methods and Review of Issues.* Washington, D.C.: The Urban Institute, 1976.

Myrdal, Gunnar. *Rich Lands and Poor.* New York: Harper & Row, Publishers, 1957.

National Council for Urban Economic Development. *Coordinated Urban Economic Development: A Case Study Analysis.* Washington, D.C.: National Council for Urban Economic Development, 1978.

Richardson, Harry W. *Regional Economics: Location Theory, Urban Structure and Regional Change.* New York: Praeger Publishers, 1969.

21 Planning for Urban Housing

Fishman, Richard P., ed. *Housing for All under the Law: New Directions in Housing, Land Use and Planning Law.* A Report of the American Bar Association Advisory Commission on Housing and Urban Growth. Cambridge, Mass.: Ballinger Publishing Company, 1978.

Hughes, James W. *Methods of Housing Analysis: Techniques and Case Studies.* New Brunswick, N.J.: Rutgers University, Center for Urban Policy Research, 1977.

Mandelker, Daniel R., and Montgomery, Roger. *Housing in America: Problems and Perspectives.* Indianapolis: The Bobbs-Merrill Company, Inc., 1973.

President's Committee on Urban Housing. *A Decent Home.* Washington, D.C.: Government Printing Office, 1968.

———. *Report of the President's Committee on Urban Housing: Technical Studies.* 2 vols. Washington, D.C.: Government Printing Office, 1968.

Pynoos, Jon; Schafer, Robert; and Hartman, Chester W. *Housing Urban America.* Chicago: Aldine Publishing Company, 1973.

Stegman, Michael. *Housing and Economics: The American Dilemma.* Cambridge, Mass.: The M.I.T. Press, 1970.

U.S., Department of Housing and Urban Development. *FHA Techniques of Housing Market Analysis.* Washington, D.C.: Government Printing Office, 1970.

———. National Housing Policy Review. *Housing in the Seventies.* Washington, D.C.: Government Printing Office, 1974.

Wexler, Harry J., and Peck, Richard. *Housing and Local Governments: A Research Guide for Policy Makers and Planners.* Lexington, Mass.: Lexington Books, D. C. Heath and Company, 1975.

List of
contributors

Persons who have contributed to this book are listed below with the editors first and the chapter authors following in alphabetical order. A brief review of experience and training is presented for each author. Since many of the contributors have published extensively, books, monographs, articles, and other publications are omitted.

Frank S. So (Editor, Introduction, and Chapter 5) is Deputy Executive Director of the American Planning Association (a consolidation of the American Institute of Planners and the American Society of Planning Officials). He has worked previously in local planning agencies. He holds a bachelor's degree in sociology from Youngstown State University and a master of city planning degree from the Ohio State University.

Israel Stollman (Editor, and Chapter 1) is Executive Director of the American Planning Association and Executive Secretary of its American Institute of Certified Planners. He was Executive Director of the American Society of Planning Officials prior to the consolidation with the American Institute of Planners, Chairman of City and Regional Planning at the Ohio State University, and Planning Director in Youngstown, Ohio. He holds a bachelor's degree from the City College of New York and a master's degree in city planning from the Massachusetts Institute of Technology.

Frank Beal (Editor, and Chapter 6) is Director of the Illinois Institute of Natural Resources, a state agency responsible for conducting research and providing information on the energy and environmental and natural resources of the state. He has served as Special Assistant to the Governor of Illinois on Energy and Environmental Affairs, and previously worked as Deputy Director of Research for the American Society of Planning Officials. Mr. Beal holds a bachelor's degree from Antioch College and a master's degree in urban planning from the University of Illinois.

David S. Arnold (Editor, and Introduction) is Director, Publications Center, Interna-

tional City Management Association. He has been with ICMA since 1949 with a variety of responsibilities in research, editing, writing, and publications production. From 1943 to 1949 he was on the field staff of Public Administration Service, Chicago. He holds a bachelor's degree from Lafayette College and a master's in public administration from the Maxwell School, Syracuse University.

Richard F. Babcock (Chapter 15) is a member of the law firm of Ross, Hardies, O'Keefe, Babcock & Parsons, Chicago. He is also an Adjunct Professor in the College of Urban Sciences at the University of Illinois, Chicago Circle, and a consultant in land use and housing to several public and private agencies. He was previously a governor's appointee to the Northeastern Illinois Planning Commission and was President of the American Society of Planning Officials in 1971–72. Mr. Babcock holds a bachelor's degree from Dartmouth College, and law and business degrees from the University of Chicago.

Richard S. Bolan (Chapter 18) is Professor of Community Organization and Social Planning at the Boston College Graduate School of Social Work. He has a B.E. from Yale University, an M.C.P. from the Massachusetts Institute of Technology, and a Ph.D. from New York University. Prior to his appointment at Boston College he was associated with the Joint Center for Urban Studies of M.I.T. and Harvard University, and served in various governmental planning posts. He was the Editor of the *Journal of the American Institute of Planners,* 1971–75.

Pastora San Juan Cafferty (Chapter 17) is Associate Professor at the School of Social Service Administration, University of Chicago. She holds a B.A. in English from St. Bernard College, and a master's and doctorate in American thought and civilization from George Washington University, Washington, D.C. She has served as an appointed official in federal and local government and has worked as a consultant to local, state, federal, private, and public agencies in housing, transportation, community and economic planning, and education.

Anthony James Catanese (Chapter 4) is Dean of the School of Architecture and Urban Planning at the University of Wisconsin—Milwaukee. He is Vice Chairman of the Milwaukee City Planning Commission. As President of A. J. Catanese and Associates, he has recently been involved in projects in Hawaii and Alaska. Mr. Catanese holds a doctorate from the University of Wisconsin.

Georgia K. Davis (Chapter 11) is Facilities Planner in the Howard County Public School System, Columbia, Maryland. She was formerly Director of Research at the American City Corporation, and a planner/programmer for the Rouse Company corporate headquarters building. Her work in development of school environments is an outgrowth of a series of papers prepared for the Carnegie Council on Children. She holds a bachelor's degree in interior design from the School of Architecture at Carnegie-Mellon University, and a master's degree in urban and regional planning from the Graduate School of Public and International Affairs, University of Pittsburgh.

Stephen B. Friedman (Chapter 20) is Principal Counselor with Real Estate Research Corporation in Chicago. He previously served as Senior Research Associate with the American Society of Planning Officials and as Planning Analyst with the Wisconsin State Planning Office. He holds a bachelor's from Goddard College and a master's in urban and regional planning from the University of Wisconsin at Madison. His work has included a range of development issues, including economic development strategies, public facilities policies, urban growth policies, and urban revitalization.

Laurence Conway Gerckens (Chapter 2) is Professor of City and Regional Planning at the Ohio State University. Formerly Chairman of the Planning Department and Director of the School of Architecture, he now travels extensively to lecture on American urban history. He holds a certificate in art from the Cooper Union, a bachelor's degree in architecture from the University of Cincinnati, and a master of regional planning from Cornell University.

Efraim Gil (Chapter 19) is Professor of Environmental Planning at Governors State University, Park Forest South, Illinois. He holds a bachelor's degree from San Jose State University and a master's degree from the University of Cincinnati. He was previously Senior Research Associate for the American Society of Planning Officials. He has served as a consultant to various private and governmental agencies; his research includes neighborhood planning, citizen participation, and energy planning.

A. Keith Gilbert (Chapter 8) is a principal in the firm of Alan M. Voorhees & Associates. Previously he worked for the city of San Diego, California, and is a recipient of the Past President's Award of the Institute of Transportation Engineers. He holds a bachelor's degree from the University of Mississippi.

Seymour M. Gold (Chapter 10) is Associate Professor of Environmental Planning, University of California, Davis. He has served as Principal Planner for Ann Arbor, Michigan; Recreation Planner for the state of Illinois; City Planner of the Detroit City Plan Commission; and Senior Planner with the planning consultant firm of Vilican-Leman & Associates. He has been a consultant to many state and national recreation agencies and conducts training institutes in leisure services and related areas. Professor Gold holds bachelor's and master's degrees in park administration from Michigan State University, a master's in urban planning from Wayne State University, and a doctorate in urban and regional planning from the University of Michigan.

Philip Hammer (Chapter 20) is founder and Chairman of the Board of Hammer, Siler, George Associates, economic consultants of Washington, Atlanta, and Denver. He has served as President of the American Society of Planning Officials and as Chairman of the National Capital Planning Commission in Washington, D.C. Mr. Hammer is an Honorary Member of the American Institute of Architects and is active on many boards of directors, including the Conservation Foundation, the Potomac Institute, the National Planning Association, and Planning and Development Collaborative International. He holds a bachelor's degree from the University of North Carolina, with two years of advanced study in economics and public administration at Harvard.

Walter G. Hansen (Chapter 8) is President of Alan M. Voorhees & Associates. He holds a bachelor's degree from the South Dakota School of Mines and Technology and a master's degree from the Massachusetts Institute of Technology. He worked previously for the U.S. Bureau of Public Roads, and managed the Boston Transportation Planning Review.

Janet I. Harris (Chapter 12) is Executive Director of the Indiana State Arts Commission. She has worked in state government and the arts since 1970, with the New York State Council on the Arts and the New York State Commission on Cultural Resources, and has served as cultural planning consultant in the arts and in community development. Ms. Harris holds a master's degree in fine arts and planning from the University of Cincinnati, and a bachelor's degree from Miami University. She was named Indiana Woman of the Year for 1979 by Women in Communications, and she has received the 1979 Sagamore of the Wabash Award for Leadership from the state of Indiana.

Elizabeth Hollander (Chapter 6) is Associate Director of the Task Force on the Future of Illinois, a public commission charged with developing a twenty year agenda, for the state. She formerly worked as Program Director for the Illinois–Indiana Bi-State Commission. She has served as a consultant to federal, state, and local governments in planning, urban development, and urban studies curricula for elementary school children. She holds a bachelor's degree from Bryn Mawr College.

John Lund Kriken (Chapter 13) is Director of Planning and Urban Design for the San Francisco and Los Angeles offices of Skidmore, Owings & Merrill. He is a member of the American Institute of Architects National Committee for Planning and Design, and is Secretary/Treasurer of the American Planning Association Committee on Urban Design. He has taught at the University of California, Berkeley; Washington University; and Rice University. He holds a master's degree in architecture/urban design from Harvard, and a bachelor's degree in architecture from the University of California, Berkeley.

William Lamont, Jr. (Chapter 14), is a member of the management consulting firm of Briscoe, Maphis, Murray & Lamont, Boulder, Colorado. He is currently serving as Project Director and Coordinator for a variety of planning projects. He was previously the Director of Community Development in Boulder, Director of the Graduate School of Urban and Regional Planning at the University of Colorado, a planning consultant with Bean, Lamont & Moberg, and a planner with the city and county of Denver.

Constance Lieder (Chapter 21) is Secretary of State Planning in Maryland. Prior to her appointment in 1979, she was a planning and housing consultant, and Executive Director of the Mayor's (Baltimore) Task Force on Population Migration. She was the first woman President of the American Institute of Planners, now consolidated with the American Society of Planning Officials as the American Planning Association. She has worked extensively throughout the country for private developers and governmental agencies, and has taught at the University of Maryland and Morgan State University. She is a graduate of Wellesley College, and holds graduate degrees from Harvard Graduate School of Design, University of Michigan, and Princeton University.

Lawrence Livingston, Jr. (Chapter 9), is the head of a San Francisco based city and regional planning firm. He has served as a consultant to some sixty cities and counties. He has prepared comprehensive plans, growth management studies, land use and transportation studies, central business district plans, urban renewal plans, and land use and development regulations. He is Lecturer in the Department of City and Regional Planning, University of California, Berkeley. He holds a bachelor's degree from Stanford University, a law degree from Yale University, and a master's degree in city planning from the Massachusetts Institute of Technology.

Enid Lucchesi (Chapter 19) is a planning and social research consultant. She holds a bachelor's degree from the University of Cincinnati and a master's degree in human relations services from Governors State University, where she is completing additional graduate studies in planning. She has worked in social services both in the United States and in Israel, and has conducted research in the areas of clinical psychology, population analysis, and planning.

Chester C. McGuire (Chapter 16) is head of a consulting firm specializing in housing economics. He was formerly Assistant Secretary for Fair Housing and Urban Development in the U.S. Department of Housing and Urban Development. Prior to that he was Lecturer in the Department of City and Regional Planning, University of California, Berkeley, and a principal in the firm Berkeley Planning Associates. He holds a bachelor's degree from Dartmouth College, and master's and doctor's degrees from the Graduate School of Business, University of Chicago.

Kermit C. Parsons (Chapter 11) is Professor of City and Regional Planning and Dean of the College of Architecture, Arts and Planning at Cornell University. He was a founding member and First President of the Society for College and University Planning and a consultant to the University of Ife, Nigeria, the New York State University Construction Fund, and the University of

Puerto Rico on campus planning. Recently, he has been an adviser on new campus site selection and campus planning to the Ministry of Education of the Republic of the Philippines. Dean Parsons holds a bachelor's degree from Miami University and a master's degree from Cornell University.

Louis B. Schlivek (Planning Portfolio) is a writer, photographer, and filmmaker who specializes in urban affairs. He is a graduate of Dartmouth College, where he majored in sociology. After four years with a Signal Corps motion picture unit in the South Pacific during World War II, he began his career with a series of thirty-six photo essays about New York and its suburbs for the *New York Times Magazine*. Over the past twenty years Mr. Schlivek has covered the New York urban region as Field Studies Consultant for the Regional Plan Association—the nation's oldest metropolitan planning organization. His projects for the association have taken him to many cities in other parts of the United States and Canada.

Praful B. Shah (Chapter 20) is President of Praful Shah & Associates, an economic and management consulting firm with offices in Columbia, Maryland. For the past fifteen years he has been consultant to local, state, and the federal governments in the areas of regional and urban economic development planning. He holds a master's degree from the University of Wisconsin at Madison and a bachelor's degree from the University of Bombay, India.

James A. Spencer (Chapter 3) is Associate Professor of Planning in the Graduate School of Planning at the University of Tennessee, Knoxville. He is also a consultant to the American Institute of Certified Planners. He holds a bachelor's degree from Union University and a master of city planning degree from the Ohio State University. Mr. Spencer has been active in the American Institute of Planners at the state and national levels, and has worked in city planning agencies in Ohio and Tennessee.

Richard D. Tabors (Chapter 7) is Manager of the Utility Systems Program at the Energy Laboratory and Lecturer on Urban Studies and Planning at the Massachusetts Institute of Technology. He holds a bachelor's degree from Dartmouth College and a doctorate from the Maxwell School, Syracuse University. He is a consultant in energy and environmental planning and is currently involved in utility regulation and management.

Alan M. Voorhees (Chapter 8) is Professor of Urban Sciences and Dean of the College of Architecture, Art, and Urban Sciences at the University of Illinois, Chicago Circle. He holds a bachelor's from Rensselaer Polytechnic Institute, a master's degree from the Massachusetts Institute of Technology, and a certificate from the Bureau of Highway Traffic, Yale University. He has served as Chairman of the Executive Committee of the Transportation Research Board of the National Academy of Sciences, and as President of the American Institute of Planners. He was the founder and President of Alan M. Voorhees & Associates, Inc.

Illustration credits

Chapter 1 Figure 1–1: David Macaulay, *City: A Story of Roman Planning and Construction* (Boston: Houghton Mifflin Company, 1974), p. 16; Figure 1–2 Drawn by David Povilaitis; Figure 1–3: Charles Thurow, William Toner, and Duncan Erley, *Performance Controls for Sensitive Lands: A Practical Guide for Local Administrators, Parts 1 and 2* Planning Advisory Service Reports nos. 307, 308 (Chicago: American Society of Planning Officials, July 1975), p. 73; Figure 1–4: Richard Hedman and Fred Bair, Jr., *And on the Eighth Day. . . .*, 2nd ed. (Chicago: American Society of Planning Officials, 1967).; Figure 1–5: Tri-County Regional Planning Commission, *M.E.T.R.O.* (Lansing, Mich.: Tri-County Regional Planning Commission, 1966). Reproduced with detailed description in Kenneth L. Kraemer, *Policy Analysis in Local Government: A Systems Approach to Decision Making* (Washington, D.C.: International City Management Association, 1973), pp. 123–26; Figure 1–6: Hedman and Bair, *And on the Eighth Day. . . .*

Chapter 2 Figure 2–1: Courtesy of the Library of Congress; Figure 2–3: Chicago Historical Society; Figure 2–5: National Association of Home Builders. Photo by Leon Trice.

Chapter 3 Figure 3–1: Drawn by David Povilaitis; Figure 3–4: International City Management Association, *Effective Supervisory Practices: Better Results through Teamwork* (Washington, D.C.: International City Management Association, 1978), p. 64. Drawn by David Povilaitis; Figure 3–5: Drawn by David Povilaitis.

Chapter 4 Figure 4–1: Drawn by David Povilaitis; Figure 4–6: Adapted from Albert Battersby, *Mathematics in Management* (Baltimore, Md.: Pelican Books, 1966), p. 53, reprinted by permission.

Chapter 5 Figures 5–1 and 5–2: City of Dayton, Ohio, Office of Management and Budget, *1977 Program Strategies,* February 1, 1977; Figure 5–3: Montgomery County (Maryland) Government, *Adopted Capital Improvements Program, Montgomery County Government Fiscal Years 1977–1982* (Rockville, Md.: Montgomery County Government, 1976), 2 vols., vol 1, p. 1156; Figure 5–4: City of Minneapolis; Figure 5–5: Philip B. Herr Associates, "Planning for Franklin (Mass.)" (Boston: Herr Associates, unpublished draft, July 1976), pp. 10–11.

Chapter 6 Figure 6–1: Verbonia (left), David Macaulay, *City: A Story of Roman Planning and Construction* (Boston: Houghton Mifflin Company, 1974), p. 12. Barrington area (right), "Barrington," *Planners Notebook,* vol. 3 no. 2 (April 1973), p. 3; Figure 6–2: Diagram (top), Harold M. Mayer and Richard C. Wade, *Chicago: Growth of a Metropolis* (Chicago: University of Chicago Press, 1969), pp. 276–77. Photo (below), Kee Chang, Chicago Association of Commerce and Industry; Figure 6–3: Daniel, Mann, Johnson, & Mendenhall, *Comprehensive General Plan—1990—for Alameda, California* (Los Angeles: Daniel, Mann, Johnson, & Mendenhall, 1968), p. 27.

Chapter 7 Figure 7–1: Richard D. Tabors, Michael H. Shapiro, and Peter P. Rogers, *Land Use and the Pipe: Planning for Sewerage* (Lexington, Mass.: Lexington Books, D. C. Heath & Co., 1976), p. 80; Figure 7–2: J. F. Kreissel, "Rural Wastewater Research," unpublished manuscript; Figure 7–3: G. M. Fair et al., *Water and Wastewater Engineering,* 2 vols. (New York: John Wiley & Sons, Inc., 1966, 1968), vol. 2, p. 24; Figure 7–4: Adapted from Metcalf and Eddy, Inc., *Wastewater Engineering: Collection, Treatment, Disposal* (New York: McGraw-Hill Book Company, 1972), p. 39; Figure 7–5: U.S. Environmental Protection Agency, Office of Solid Waste Management Programs, *Decision-Makers Guide in Solid Waste Management* (Washington, D.C.: Government Printing Office, 1976), p. ix; Figure 7–6: Rivkin Carson, Inc., "The Sewer Moratorium as a Technique of Growth Control and Environmental Protection," prepared for the U.S. Department of Housing and Urban Development, July 1973. Urban Systems Research and Engineering, Inc., "The Relationship between Housing and Water

Resources Planning and Management," prepared for the U.S. Department of the Interior, 1972.

Chapter 8   Figure 8–3: Chicago street photo from Chicago Historical Society; Woodfield Mall photo from "Case Studies" in *Shopping Center Development Handbook* (Washington, D.C.: ULI—The Urban Land Institute, 1977), p. 240; Figure 8–4: Minneapolis, City Planning Department, *Metro Center 1990* (Minneapolis: City Planning Department, 1979). Photo: Courtesy of Minneapolis City Planning Department; Figure 8–5: Alan M. Voorhees & Associates, Inc., in association with Cambridge Systematics, Inc., and Moore-Heder Architects, *Auto Restricted Zone/Multi-User Vehicle System Study* (Washington, D.C.: U.S. Department of Transportation, Urban Mass Transportation Administration, March 1977); Figure 8–6: National Association of Housing and Redevelopment Officials.

Chapter 9   Figure 9–1: Loebl Schlossman Dart & Hackl, Architects—Engineers; Figure 9–2: Homart Development Company; Figure 9–3: Faneuil Hall Marketplace, Inc.; Figure 9–4: Irvine Industrial Complex, from "Industrial Parks" in *Industrial Development Handbook* (Washington, D.C.: ULI—The Urban Land Institute, 1976), p. 6; Figure 9–5: Technology Park/Atlanta.

Chapter 10   Figure 10–1: Top photo, Chicago Historical Society. Bottom photo, Louis B. Schlivek, *Man in Metropolis: A Book about the People and Prospects of a Metropolitan Region* (Garden City, N.Y.: Doubleday & Company, Inc., 1965), p. 235.

Chapter 11   Figures 11–1 and 11–2: National Education Association; Figure 11–3: Madison-Morgan Cultural Center, Madison, Georgia. Photo: building exterior, Bob Moore. Photos: restored auditorium and classroom, Hiram Hanson; Figure 11–4: Columbia University; Figure 11–5: John Caffrey and Herbert H. Isaacs, *Estimating the Impact of a College or University on the Local Economy* (Washington, D.C.: American Council on Education, 1971), p. 7.

Chapter 12   Figure 12–2: Mount Royal Station (before), Baltimore & Ohio Railroad Company; Figure 12–3: Free Street Theater, Chicago; Figure 12–4: Karen E. Hapgood, *Planning and the Arts,* Planning Advisory Service Report no. 313 (Chicago: American Planning Association, 1975), p. 7; Figure 12–5: Hapgood, *Planning and the Arts,* p. 8.

Chapter 13   Figure 13–2: Weiming Lu, "Urban Design as Public Process,"

unpublished paper (Dallas, Tex.: City Planning Department, 1978), pp. 32–33.

Chapter 14   Figure 14–1: Drawn by David Povilaitis; Figure 14–2: Adapted from a chart prepared by the Arlington County (Virginia) Planning Division, in *Development Process: A General Description* (Arlington, Va.: Arlington County (Virginia) Planning Division, 1978); Figure 14–4: City Planning Board, Boulder, Colorado, 1968.

Chapter 15   Figure 15–1: Courtesy of the Library of Congress. Photo by Walker Evans; Figure 15–3: Levittown type houses, from "History of Residential Development," in *Residential Development Handbook* (Washington, D.C.: ULI—The Urban Land Institute, 1978), p. 2; Figure 15–5: San Francisco, Department of City Planning, *The Urban Design Plan* (San Francisco, Calif.: City of San Francisco, Department of City Planning, 1971), p. 82.

Planning Portfolio   All photos by Louis B. Schlivek, with the exception of the following: p. 454, top: The Rouse Company; p. 458, top: Minneapolis Chamber of Commerce; p. 464, entire page: Toronto Transportation Commission.

Chapter 16   Figure 16–1: U.S. Department of Housing and Urban Development; Figure 16–2: U.S. Bureau of the Census, *Construction Reports,* Series C-50; Figure 16–3: Drawn by David Povilaitis; Figure 16–5: City of Dayton, Ohio, Department of Planning.

Chapter 17   Figure 17–1: *Chicago Tribune;* Figure 17–2: Daley Plaza (top), C. F. Murphy & Associates, Architects. First National Bank Building Plaza (bottom), First National Bank; Figure 17–3: Chicago Historical Society; Figure 17–4: Chicago Housing Authority; Figure 17–5: Oscar Newman photograph; Figure 17–6: Duncan & Jones, Urban and Environmental Planning Consultants, in affiliation with Berkeley Planning Associates, *Methodology and Guidelines for Assessing Social Impacts of Development,* prepared for the Community Development and Environmental Protection Agency, County of Sacramento, California, July 1976, pp. 100–103, 105.

Chapter 18   Figure 18–2: Jay Galbraith, *Organization Design* (Reading, Mass.: Addison-Wesley Publishing Co., 1977), p. 31; Figure 18–3: Lensman/Simpson./Flint.

Chapter 19   Figure 19–1: Adapted from Sherry R. Arnstein, "Eight Rungs on the Ladder of Citizen Participation," in *Citizen*

Index

Page numbers in italics refer to illustrations.

Municipal Management Series

**The Practice of
Local Government
Planning**

Text type
Times Roman, Helvetica

Composition
Progressive Typographers, Inc.
York, Pennsylvania

Printing and binding
Alpine Press, Inc.
South Braintree, Massachusetts

Paper
Glatfelter offset

Design
Herbert Slobin